Basic Income

Basic Income

An Anthology of Contemporary Research

Edited by

Karl Widerquist, José A. Noguera,
Yannick Vanderborght, and Jurgen De Wispelaere

WILEY Blackwell

Blackwell Publishing was acquired by John Wiley & Sons in February 2007. Blackwell's publishing program has been merged with Wiley's global Scientific, Technical, and Medical business to form Wiley-Blackwell.

Registered Office
John Wiley & Sons, Ltd., The Atrium, Southern Gate, Chichester, West Sussex, PO19 8SQ, UK

Editorial Offices
350 Main Street, Malden, MA 02148-5020, USA
9600 Garsington Road, Oxford, OX4 2DQ, UK
The Atrium, Southern Gate, Chichester, West Sussex, PO19 8SQ, UK

For details of our global editorial offices, for customer services, and for information about how to apply for permission to reuse the copyright material in this book please see our website at www.wiley.com/wiley-blackwell.

Library of Congress Cataloging-in-Publication Data

Basic income : an anthology of contemporary research / edited by Karl Widerquist, José A. Noguera, Yannick Vanderborght, and Jurgen De Wispelaere.
pages cm
Includes bibliographical references and index.
ISBN 978-1-4051-5810-7 (cloth)
1. Guaranteed annual income. 2. Negative income tax. 3. Income. I. Widerquist, Karl.
HC79.I5B3416 2013
362.5'82–dc23

2013013473

A catalogue record for this book is available from the British Library.

Cover image: Workers on scaffolding around statue of Christ the Redeemer, Rio de Janeiro, Brazil.
Photo © Axel Gosseries.
Cover design by E&P Design.

Set in 10/12.5 pt Galliard by Toppan Best-set Premedia Limited

1 2013

MIX
Paper from responsible sources
FSC® C013604

Contents

About the Editors

Karl Widerquist is an Associate Professor of Philosophy at SFS-Qatar, Georgetown University. He holds a Doctorate in Political Theory from Oxford University (2006) and a Doctorate in Economics from the City University of New York (1996). He is the author of *Independence, Propertylessness, and Basic Income: A Theory of Freedom as the Power to Say No* (2013). He is co-author of *Economics for Social Workers* (2002) and co-editor of *Alaska's Permanent Fund Dividend: Examining its Suitability as a Model* (2012) and *Exporting the Alaska Model: Adapting the Permanent Fund Dividend for Reform Around the World* (2012).

José A. Noguera is an Associate Professor at the Department of Sociology of the Universitat Autònoma de Barcelona, Spain, and Director of the Analytical Sociology and Institutional Design Research Group (GSADI). He holds a PhD in Sociology from the Universitat Autònoma de Barcelona and has been a visiting researcher at the University of California, Berkeley and at the London School of Economics and Political Science. His research covers sociological theory, philosophy of social science, social policy, as well as normative social theory, and has been published in journals such as *Social Science Information*, *Basic Income Studies*, *South European Society & Politics*, *Travailler*, *Papers*, and *Revista Internacional de Sociología*. He is a member of the European Network of Analytical Sociologists, and serves on the International Advisory Board of the BIEN (Basic Income Earth Network). He is co-editor of *Papers, Revista de Sociologia*, and editorial board member of *Basic Income Studies*.

Yannick Vanderborght is Professor of Political Science at the Université Saint-Louis Brussels, where he currently directs the Research Centre in Political Science (CReSPo). He is also a member of the Hoover Chair (Louvain), of the Executive Committee of the Basic Income Earth Network (BIEN), and an associate editor of *Basic Income Studies*. He co-authored with Ph. Van Parijs *L'allocation universelle* (2005), and has published several articles on basic income and related issues. He is the co-editor (with Axel Gosseries) of *Arguing about justice: Essays for Philippe Van Parijs* (2011).

Jurgen De Wispelaere is a Postdoctoral Research Fellow at the Montreal Health Equity Research Consortium (MHERC), McGill University, Canada, and a Research Associate at the Analytical Sociology and Institutional Design Research Group (GSADI), Universitat Autònoma de Barcelona, Spain. Previously he taught at Trinity College Dublin and University College Dublin. His published work on basic income has appeared in *Analyse und Kritik*, *The Political Quarterly*, *Social Services Review*, *Policy and Politics*, *International Social Security Review*, *Politics and Political Studies*. He is a founding editor of the journal *Basic Income Studies* and co-editor of *The Ethics of Stakeholding* (2003) and *Recognition, Equality and Democracy* (2007). He is currently completing a book on *Republicanism*, co-authored by Simon Birnbaum and David Casassas.

Introduction: The Idea of an Unconditional Income for Everyone

Karl Widerquist, Yannick Vanderborght, José A. Noguera, and Jurgen De Wispelaere

The idea that has come to be known as Basic Income is, in an important sense, very simple. Bertrand Russell wrote in 1918, "A certain small income, sufficient for necessities, should be secured for all, whether they work or not" (Russell, 1918). According to Philippe Van Parijs, "A Basic Income is an income paid by a political community to all its members on an individual basis, without means test or work requirement" (Van Parijs, 2004).

In one form or another, under one name or another, this idea has been discussed for more than two centuries, but it is only in the last 50 years or so that it has become a major topic of academic research. Since about 1960, this literature has become extremely rich, covering such diverse topics as the philosophical justification of the idea; its economic and political feasibility; or its impact on freedom, social justice, economic activity, psychological wellbeing, and much more. At least some line of inquiry seems to exist on almost any aspect of the issue one could name, and more research on Basic Income is published each year.[1]

The need for a good anthology compiling some of the most influential research on Basic Income conducted in the last 50 years is obvious. Classics on the topic are scattered across numerous publications, ranging from obscure conference proceedings to the most prestigious scientific and philosophical journals. This book sets out to give a complete overview of these classics, with excerpts or full-length reprints of articles and book chapters discussing the central aspects of Basic Income.

This introduction sets the stage for that reading by providing a fuller definition and description of Basic Income, differentiating it from similar policies, discussing some of the controversies in the Basic Income debate, and previewing the literature presented in this volume.

What is a "Basic Income"?

Basic Income provides a stream of regular cash income to every citizen or resident in a given political community. Everyone receives the Basic Income in regular payments – monthly, weekly, or even daily. The payments could be made by check, by direct deposit, or by some other means.

Contrary to existing minimum income schemes, Basic Income is both ***universal*** and ***unconditional***. It is universal in the sense that it is paid to every citizen or every resident.

It is not a categorical benefit, which is only paid to certain individuals who fit specific criteria of eligibility. It is unconditional in the sense that recipients are not required to perform any duties in return for their benefit other than to maintain their membership in the political community. It is paid regardless of whether the recipient is working, willing to work, or has a work record. As a universal, unconditional benefit, it is paid regardless of whether the recipient has other sources of income and irrespective of disposable income. It is paid regardless of whether the recipient is young or old, able or disabled.

Most people who favor Basic Income do so because they believe that everyone should have unconditional access to the resources required to meet their basic needs, but there is no consensus in the literature whether that aspect is an essential part of the minimal definition. A Basic Income large enough to meet a person's basic needs is usually called a *full* Basic Income. A smaller, regular, unconditional payment is sometimes called a *small* Basic Income, or a *partial* Basic Income. Some authors in this volume use the term Basic Income or its equivalents to mean any nonzero unconditional income, while others use it only for an income sufficient to meet a person's basic needs.

Usually, Basic Income advocates argue that it should be paid on an *individual* basis. That is, to each woman, man, and child without any variation in the payment level according to family size. As a truly individual right, it is not dependent on the household size or type of family in which one lives. Payment on an individual basis also implies that separate payments will be made to each member of the family rather than one payment to the family as a whole or to a person designated as the "head" of household. Therefore, Basic Income avoids the possibility that one member of the family (usually the husband) controls all of the family's income and uses it to have control over his spouse. Of course, custodial parents will have to receive payments for young children.

Universal, unconditional, and individual: once properly understood these three key features make Basic Income a radical departure from traditional welfare-state policies. A great deal of the literature on the topic is therefore precisely focused on different ways of justifying this departure, and the important institutional and ideological changes it might generate. It is, therefore, important to understand exactly how Basic Income differs from most welfare policies.

Although welfare states differ greatly in specific policies and in their level of generosity, they all tend to involve a twofold strategy, combining policies designed to get those who can work into jobs with policies that provide direct benefits only for those who can't work for one reason or another. This strategy creates the need to categorize potential recipients. Policies to increase individuals' employability or to increase the number of jobs available are aimed at those deemed able to work. Unemployment compensation is aimed at those with the ability to work but who are unable to find a job. For those deemed unable to work, welfare systems typically need to further categorize recipients to fit one of many different means-tested programs. They might have one program for those too old to work, another for those too young, another for the long-term disabled, another for the short-term disabled, and so on. Welfare state programs are often conditional not only on fitting into one of these categories but also on having a past work record. This is often true of unemployment compensation, even if it is usually seen as an individual right.

Basic Income instead provides one small comprehensive benefit that protects everyone from destitution regardless of what might cause them to fall into destitution. Recipients do not have to work or to have a work record. They do not have to demonstrate that they are willing to work or that something makes them unable to work. Basic Income represents a major change in direction, even for the more generous welfare states.

How Does it Work?

This section explains how Basic Income works using a simplified example. Assume a Basic Income of $6,000[2] per year is in place and that a flat-rate income tax of 33.33% (one-third) finances all government spending including the Basic Income. The size of the Basic Income in this example is only for illustration; the Basic Income could be at any level. Most supporters prefer it at a level high enough to eliminate poverty, but many proposals suggest initially introducing it at a lower level. The flat income tax is only one of many possible ways to finance a Basic Income.[3] It is one of the most popular, partly because many Basic Income supporters believe that Basic Income should come along with an overall simplification of the tax-and-transfer system, and partly because it makes for simple examples.

Table 0.1 shows how a Basic Income scheme with these specifications affects selected levels of income. The first column shows income before taxes and transfers. We shall call this "market income," because it includes all income obtained in the market – wages, salary, and so on. The second and third columns show the Basic Income and the tax rate, both of which are the same at all levels of income under the assumptions above. The fourth column shows the taxes paid, which is simply one-third of market income. The fifth column shows income after all taxes and transfers, which is usually called "disposable income" by economists. It is simple market income plus transfers (which in this case is the Basic Income) minus taxes paid.

The first line shows that a person with no market income pays no taxes and has a disposable income equal to the Basic Income ($6,000). The third line shows that as someone begins to make some market income (say $6,000) one third of that ($2,000) is taken in taxes, but the individual still receive the full $6,000 Basic Income for a disposable income of $10,000. She is, therefore, a "net recipient" (of $4,000) in the sense that taxes she pays are $4,000 greater than the transfer she receives. Someone with a gross income of $18,000 is at "the break-even point." The $6,000 they pay in taxes exactly balance the $6,000 they receive in Basic Income. Everyone with an income above $18,000 is a "net contributor" in the sense that the taxes they pay exceed the amount they receive in Basic Income. For example, someone with an income of $30,000 pays $10,000 in taxes and receives a Basic Income of $6,000 for a final income of $26,000. The table also shows this relationship

Table 0.1 The effect on income of a Basic Income of $6,000 and a flat income tax of 33.33%.

1	*2*	*3*	*4*	*5*
Market income	*Basic Income*	*Tax rate*	*Taxes paid*	*Disposable income*
0	$6,000	33.33%	0	$6,000
$3,000	$6,000	33.33%	$1,000	$8,000
$6,000	$6,000	33.33%	$2,000	$10,000
$18,000	$6,000	33.33%	$6,000	$18,000
$30,000	$6,000	33.33%	$10,000	$26,000
$60,000	$6,000	33.33%	$20,000	$46,000
$180,000	$6,000	33.33%	$60,000	$126,000
$300,000	$6,000	33.33%	$100,000	$206,000
$600,000	$6,000	33.33%	$200,000	$406,000
$1,800,000	$6,000	33.33%	$600,000	$1,206,000

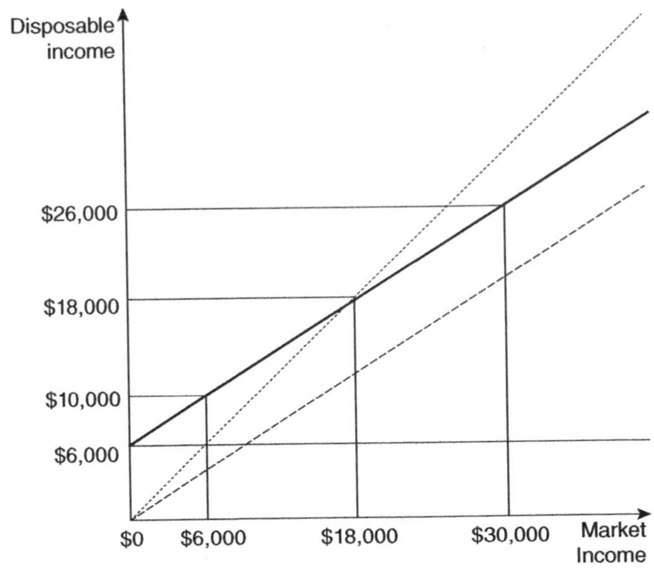

Figure 0.1 The effect on income of a Basic Income of $6,000 and a flat income tax of 33.33%.

between private and final income for several higher levels of income. Notice that the Basic Income gradually becomes less significant as income gets higher and that at high levels of income, final income is just slightly more than two-thirds of private income. For example, someone with a private income of $600,000 ends up with an income of $406,000 after taxes and transfers.

The same relationship is illustrated graphically in Figure 0.1. Market income is shown on the horizontal access, and disposable income is shown on the vertical access. If there were no taxes and no transfers, private and final income would be equal for all levels of income, and the relationship between them would be shown by the dotted 45-degree line. But, of course, all nation-states have taxes. The dashed line shows the effect of a one-third tax on income without any transfers, but we must add to that the effect of the Basic Income. The horizontal line at $6,000 shows that people at every level of income receive the Basic Income. The combined effect of taxes and Basic Income on final income is shown by the bold sloping line beginning at $6,000 on the vertical axis.

As this graph shows, a person with no private income has a final income of $6,000 (at the horizontal axis). Final income rises more slowly than private income but it always rises with income. Therefore, the bold line slops up but less steeply than the 45-degree line. At $6,000 of private income, final income rises to $10,000. The break-even point (where private and final income are equal) is the point at which the bold line crosses the 45-degree line. At $30,000 of private income, final income is $26,000.

The Basic Income system is structured to ensure that everyone who earns more market income has a higher disposable income than everyone who earns less, helping to preserve incentives to work more and/or to develop a professional career. A person will pay taxes on her additional income, but she does not have to give up her transfer income to start earning money privately. Most transfer programs in modern welfare states do not work this way. Recipients of social assistance, unemployment insurance, disability benefits, and many other transfer programs usually have to face the harsh tradeoff of having to sacrifice the whole of their transfer income if they take any job at all. This phenomenon is often called the "dependency trap" or the "poverty trap" by economists. Basic Income avoids this trap entirely.

This flat tax/Basic Income structure also gives everyone the same "marginal tax rate," meaning that the additional tax paid on any additional dollar of private income is the same for everyone. According to many Basic Income supporters, this feature should hopefully reduce disincentive and equity problems in the tax system. In most countries today individuals can face very different marginal tax rates depending on their current income, the source of their income, and whether they are receiving transfers. Many transfer recipients face extremely high effective marginal tax rates.

Of course, one can think of many adaptations of this simple example, and nothing in the definition of Basic Income ties it to any particular kind of financing. For instance, it is possible to replace the flat-rate taxation by a progressive (or even regressive) income tax. A Basic Income can also be financed through indirect taxation, such as a Value Added Tax, a sales tax, a wealth tax, or even state money creation. Since the early days of the Basic Income debate in the nineteenth century, the idea of land taxes, or taxes on the use of natural resources, have also been widely discussed. What is important here – what is central to every universal program – is that even though Basic Income is paid to all, rich and poor alike, it does not make the rich richer. In fact, under the Basic Income scheme exemplified above, the rich are likely to end up poorer than they would be without the Basic Income/flat tax system.

Variations on a Theme

All Basic Income schemes share the following features: the transfer is paid in cash; it is paid on an individual basis; it is paid regardless of other sources of income; and it does not require recipients to perform (or to have performed, or to show willingness to perform) any actions to maintain eligibility. Other features can vary without making the scheme something other than a Basic Income. Although the Basic Income is paid to everyone, not everyone necessarily receives the same amount every year of their life. For example, the elderly could receive a larger payment (perhaps in recognition that they have specific needs or that they have already worked enough and they are not expected to work) or they could receive a smaller payment (perhaps because they already benefit from some existing state pension system).

Children pose a particular problem for the design of a Basic Income scheme. The idea of a Basic Income is to individualize payments, possibly at a level high enough to meet everyone's basic needs. However, the basic needs of a family consisting of two parents and two children living together can be met much more cheaply than the basic needs of four single adults living separately. If the Basic Income is set at a level just enough to meet the basic needs of a single adult, the amount received by a family of four will be far more than enough to meet their basic needs. If it is set at a level just enough to meet the basic needs of a family of four, it will be far less than enough to meet the basic needs of single adults. For this reason some authors propose a smaller Basic Income for children, following the model of universal child benefits already in place in many developed welfare states.

Another question, answered differently by different Basic Income proposals, is what is exactly meant by "universal". By analogy with other universal schemes, such as basic pensions and child benefits, it usually means that the benefit is paid to all without means-test. But it might also mean, according to some, that in order to be truly universal a Basic Income should necessarily be paid at a uniform worldwide level, for instance under the form of global dividend. Most proposals, however, work within the confines of a nation state or even a smaller jurisdiction, such as a region or a province. Usually, then, Basic Income is considered to be a right of citizenship, but could also be extended to noncitizen residents.[4]

History and Related Proposals

Basic Income seems to have been invented independently by many different people in many different times and places. There is no one person who can be called the originator of the idea, and no one stream of thought from which all the different branches spring. For this reason, many different words for Basic Income are used by the authors in this volume, including Guaranteed Income, Guaranteed Annual Income, Unconditional Basic Income, Universal Basic Income, Citizen's Income, Social Dividend, Universal Grant, Demogrant, and many others. All of these terms are used more or less interchangeably. Since the 1980s, the expression "Basic Income" has been gradually taking over as the standard term in the English-speaking world, but terms such as Citizen's Income and Guaranteed Income remain common.

Several other terms used in the Basic Income literature are not interchangeable with Basic Income. The term, "Basic Income Guarantee," as it is most commonly used, is slightly broader than the term Basic Income. It should not be confused with the term Basic Income Grant, which *is* used interchangeably with Basic Income, especially in southern Africa.

The Basic Income Guarantee is a generic term for any unconditional policy ensuring that everyone will have an income large enough to meet their basic needs. Basic Income achieves this goal through the mechanism of a universal payment. Everyone receives the Basic Income and everyone pays taxes on their first dollar of market income. Another policy, known most commonly as the Negative Income Tax (NIT), instead pays only those who would be net recipients under the Basic Income system. Recipients pay no taxes on their first dollars of market income, but their Negative Income is gradually phased out. At the break-even point, once the Negative Income Tax reaches zero, individuals begin paying positive taxes on additional income.

Negative Income Tax and Basic Income can both achieve the same after-tax/after-transfer distribution of income. Negative Income Tax has the advantage that it does not involve people simultaneously paying taxes and receiving a Basic Income. Basic Income has the advantage that it provides its recipients with permanent economic security. People do not have to apply to receive it when their income goes down.

Other proposals are similar to Basic Income except that they are temporary. The Sabbatical Account, proposed by Claus Offe would allow recipients to live off the income guarantee for a limited amount of time over their life-course.[5] The idea of a Sabbatical Account is to allay the fear that people will try to live off the Basic Income for long periods of time. The Sabbatical Account would allow people to leave the workforce temporarily for any reason whether they were unemployed, couldn't find good enough work, wanted to take care of an infant or a sick relative, or even if they simply wanted to take some time off. But people would have to return to the labor force eventually.

The Stakeholder Grant, as proposed by Bruce Ackerman and Anne Alstott, is essentially a large one-time income grant given at the age of 18 or 21 (Ackerman and Alstott, 1999). Stakeholder Grants are similar to Basic Income, but at first sight they seem to have a very different goal. One of the clear goals of Basic Income is to alleviate or even eliminate poverty. One of the clear goals of Stakeholder Grants is to increase equality of opportunity by giving the young people resources to invest in capital or human capital at a time in their lives when many people are struggling to get by. However, this difference is not clear-cut. For various reasons, some young people might "blow their stake" immediately, thereby compromising their own future on a long-term basis. A regular payment, under the form of a smaller Basic Income, actually protects those who are more inclined to make such an unconsidered use of their stake. If this is true, a Basic Income can actually be expected to have a more reliable impact on equality of opportunity.[6]

The Participation Income, first proposed by British economist Anthony Atkinson, is also discussed in relation with Basic Income (Atkinson, 1996). In fact, it is sometimes presented as its most feasible version. In order to secure political support, Atkinson suggests that one should allow for soft conditionality: recipients would have to satisfy any one of several criteria for "participation", that is, socially useful contribution. Contrary to existing conditional schemes, this condition of participation would not only include having a paid job, or actively seeking for a job, but also taking care of an infant or a sick relative, doing suitable volunteer work, and so on.

A Brief History of the Basic Income Debate

The Basic Income idea has existed in one form or another for hundreds of years, but it has only become widely discussed in the last 50 years or so. It has attracted support from a very diverse set of groups and individuals, from the far left to the conservative right of the political spectrum.

Although prominent figures of their times, such as Hugo Grotius and Thomas Paine, discussed ideas along the lines of a Basic Income, the discussion of a true Basic Income in the nineteenth century was left largely to marginal figures and eccentric intellectuals, many of them within the European socialist tradition.[7] Gradually, however, it became a key component of the discussions about emerging welfare states. In the first half of the twentieth century, the idea became more respectable, partly thanks to the work of devoted intellectuals and activists.

For instance, in his *Proposed Roads to Freedom* (1918), Bertrand Russell offered a strong plea for a guaranteed income. In the same year, two members of the British Labour Party, Dennis Milner and his wife Mabel, published a *Scheme for a State Bonus* (1918), in which they proposed the introduction of a Basic Income for all citizens of the United Kingdom.' It was widely discussed during party conferences in the 1920s; for the first time, an important political movement focused directly on the idea.

In the 1960s and 1970s, Basic Income became a hot topic in many industrialized countries in Europe and North America. The political discussion was often connected with the work of academics, especially in economics. Among the major advocates of the idea were several Nobel laureates, such as James Meade, Jan Tinbergen, James Tobin, Gunnar Myrdal, Friedrich Hayek, and Milton Friedman.[8] Tobin managed to incorporate his *Demogrant* proposal into the platform of George McGovern, the Democratic Party's nominee for President of the United States in 1972.[9] Tinbergen was close to the Dutch

Labour Party and became involved in a Basic Income working group in the early 1980s. Among the most passionate supporters of Basic Income were also prominent figures such as John Kenneth Galbraith, Robert Theobald, and Robert J. Lampman.

In 1986 a group of academics and Basic Income activists gathered in Louvain-la-Neuve, Belgium, at a conference organized by Philippe Van Parijs. They decided to set up the *Basic Income European Network* (BIEN), which quickly became a platform for the exchange of information about Basic Income in Europe, and beyond. In September 2004, BIEN turned into a worldwide network and changed its name to the *Basic Income Earth Network*.[10] At national level, several networks have been created in the past three decades, and BIEN now has officially recognized 20 national affiliate organizations.[11]

Of course, because social policy largely remains under the authority of nation-states – even within the European Union – the Basic Income debate mostly remains a national (or even sub-national) issue. However, some common features emerge when one compares these national discussions. In particular, it is a striking fact that most left-liberal political parties are quite supportive of Basic Income. It is especially true of green parties in Europe and North America. Most of them have included some form of Basic Income into their political platform, and have been discussing it intensively as a worthwhile alternative to existing social assistance programs. By contrast, with a few exceptions, it also clearly appears that most trade unions and traditional social democratic parties are not enthusiastic about Basic Income (with some exceptions like Spain, where the Socialist Party incorporated it in its political program from 2001 to 2003, or the Netherlands, where a trade union strongly supported Basic Income during the 1980s). Some see it as a threat to the minimum wage legislation, while others view it as potentially justifying exploitation of workers by the voluntary unemployed, and still others see it as dangerous for the central role of paid employment as a mechanism of social integration.

Be that as it may, Basic Income has managed to get into the political agenda in many countries and terrains along the last decades. National governments and parliaments (for instance in Canada, Ireland, the Netherlands, the United Kingdom, and Spain) and some regional governments (like Catalonia and the Basque Country in Spain, or Quebec in Canada) have sponsored or analyzed reports on Basic Income. Basic Income has also often appeared in many electoral campaigns in countries such as Australia, Belgium, Canada, Germany, Ireland, Finland, the Netherlands, the United Kingdom, and the United States. In recent years, Basic Income activists managed to attract a lot of public attention in Germany, Italy, Japan, South Korea, and Spain.

In several developing countries (like Brazil, East Timor, Namibia, Nigeria, India, Iraq, Iran, or South Africa) the political interest in the proposal has also grown in recent years, giving rise to discussions, experiments, pilot projects, and social movements. Although none of these countries has yet introduced Basic Income, many have arguably moved in that direction by introducing "conditional cash transfers" (CCTs), need-based transfers with easily met conditions. Those that have been implemented have shown positive results. At least one CCT program was inspired by Basic Income: Brazil's *Bolsa Família* (Family Grant). In 2004, it was officially established as a first step toward phasing in a Basic Income, although no further steps have been laid out so far. Some consider CCTs, such as the *Bolsa Família*, as a necessary step toward Basic Income, because they tend to have far fewer conditions than the social welfare programs they replace (Suplicy, 2007). One contribution to this volume argues that such CCTs demonstrate the value of Basic Income because the benefits of CCTs are proving to be not from the conditions but from getting money in the hands of people who need it.[12]

The closest existing program to a Basic Income in the world today is probably Alaska's Permanent Fund Dividend. It meets the broad definition of Basic Income above, but it is sometimes called a resource dividend or a citizen's dividend instead of a Basic Income. The state of Alaska invests a portion of its oil revenue in a fund, and distributes a portion of the returns to that fund to each resident, each year. The Permanent Fund Dividend makes a regular, unconditional, in-cash payment to every U.S. citizen who lives in the state of Alaska for the full year. In that sense, it is a Basic Income. It is far less than enough to meet each individual's basic needs, and in that sense it is only a small or partial Basic Income.[13]

The amount of the Permanent Fund Dividend usually varies between \$1,000 and \$2,000 per person, per year, because of stock market fluctuations. This specific feature might potentially separate it from a Basic Income. Indeed, even if most proposed definitions of Basic Income do not specify that the payment must be the same amount every year, or every month, most proposals presume that the payment will be regular enough so that it provides recipients with some sort of permanent economic security. As a relatively small, variable payment that comes only once a year, recipients tend to see the Permanent Fund Dividend as a bonus to be used for discretionary spending rather than as something to (help) meet basic needs. Yet, it has proven to be effective and extremely popular. Many nations have discussed imitating it. Mongolia has promised to begin phasing in a resource dividend, and Iran now has already begun phasing in a program that very closely approximates a small Basic Income.

In the light of all these developments, even if Basic Income's political future remains uncertain, it is clear that it has now left the margins of the public debate.

A Glimpse of the Contents

This anthology is divided into nine sections, each covering an important area of the Basic Income debate.

The "Freedom" section examines the extent to which Basic Income can enhance individual liberty and the question of whether it promotes important freedoms that society should protect. This section includes Van Parijs's influential real-freedom-based argument for Basic Income, and others' freedom-based discussions of Basic Income, such as whether it promotes freedom as non-domination and whether unconditional freedom from poverty can enhance individuals' psychological wellbeing.

The "Justice" section looks at Basic Income from the standpoint of several important theories of justice and examines various justice-based arguments for and against Basic Income from these different schools of thought. These include left-libertarianism, right-libertarianism, Marxism, and communitarianism. This section also includes a discussion of whether Basic Income should be thought of as a right of citizenship. Should a citizen be unconditionally entitled to sufficient resources to meet their needs? Can Basic Income enhance democracy and lead to a more active citizenship?

The "Reciprocity and Exploitation" section examines one particular justice-based issue that has been especially important in the Basic Income debate: the question of whether recipients of Basic Income, or any other transfers, owe a reciprocal duty to contribute to society through work and whether the failure to fulfill this duty will lead them to exploit people who do contribute. Some critics see this criticism as a decisive objection to Basic

Income. Some supporters concede that Basic Income has a reciprocity problem but that it is on balance justified by other features of the policy. Other supporters argue that Basic Income does not involve a reciprocity problem and that a society without Basic Income is far more likely to have an exploitation problem.

The "Feminism" section examines whether Basic Income enhances gender equality. It shows how feminists are deeply divided on the issue. Some believe Basic Income will enhance women's ability to challenge the gendered division of labor. Others believe it will perpetuate traditional women's gender roles by making it easier for them to fall into household care work.

The "Economics" section examines Basic Income from the perspective of economic costs and benefits. What effect will it have on labor market productivity? How will it affect labor market participation? Is it sustainable in the long run? Basic Income received a great deal of attention from economists in the 1960s and 1970s. The U.S. and Canadian governments conducted a total of five social science experiments on the Negative Income Tax. This section discusses the economic debate and the evidence that has been revealed by the Negative Income Tax experiments and other sources.

The "Post-productivism" section discusses an economic issue that has been particularly important to the Basic Income debate: the question of whether the post-industrial economy has a greater need for non-work-based transfers. Authors debate the extent to which automation and environmental concerns are reducing the need for labor and whether Basic Income is a reasonable response to a post-productivist economy.

The "Implementation" section discusses issues of how a Basic Income could be put in place and administered, including how much it would cost, whether it could fit in with or replace existing programs, and what its administrative advantages and disadvantages may be. Some authors argue that Basic Income is actually easier to implement effectively than more familiar parts of the standard social welfare system. Other authors argue that once this seemingly simple idea is put into practice, it will need to become far more complex.

The section on "Institutions" discusses how Basic Income can be adapted to fit into the existing institutional setting. There are many modified versions of Basic Income and many closely related policies that don't quite fit under a strict definition of Basic Income. This section assesses the pros and cons of related proposals when compared with an "ideal" model of Basic Income. It considers whether one should focus on the differences between them or on their common features, and it considers whether they really foster the socio-political and economic feasibility of a Basic Income.

The book closes with the "Politics" section, which examines the political pre-conditions for building the coalition necessary to implement Basic Income in a democratic country. Although there is an impressive amount of evidence in favor of Basic Income, and it has crept into the mainstream policy debate in most industrial democracies, many authors argue that the implementation of a full Basic Income still faces a great deal of political obstacles and argue for a gradualist strategy of programs that move in the direction of Basic Income.

The Selection of the Texts

Our general aim for this book has been to reach an equilibrium between well-known, classic or pivotal contributions to the Basic Income debates and more specific texts that make interesting points but are relatively unknown or difficult to find. Similarly, we have tried to keep some balance between advocates and critics of Basic Income. Particularly, we have not included texts that deal with the historical aspects of the idea, or with very local or country-specific case studies or discussions (in part because the selection would have been too arbitrary, and in part because there are already some good monographs and anthologies available on those issues). Leaving aside these constraints, the main criteria for selection has been relevance for the Basic Income debates. We hope to offer a significant and representative (although obviously incomplete) sample of the contemporary work that is being developed on one of the most innovative and daring proposals for progressive welfare reform in the context of recurrent economic crisis and persistent inequality and poverty.

We did not have room to include nearly as many works as we would have liked to. The introduction of each section includes a list of further reading pointing the reader to some of the many more books and articles on all of these issues. The further reading list for this introductory chapter includes references on the history of Basic Income and introductions to the Basic Income debate. Because this is an English-language anthology, we decided to include only English-language references in our further reading section. For references in other languages, the Basic Income Earth Network's website (www.basicincome.org) has links to its national affiliates and to other Basic Income organizations around the world. Many of these websites have information, literature, and references to literature on Basic Income in a variety of other languages.

Notes

1. For a good overview of recent Basic Income research, see the Journal *Basic Income Studies*: http://www.degruyter.com/view/j/bis
2. Assume for this introduction that $ means United States Dollars, but the example could as well be in Euros, British Pounds, or any other currency.
3. See for instance Atkinson (1995).
4. This is especially true within the European Union, where member states have strong legal obligations regarding access to welfare benefits for residents from EU countries.
5. Offe and de Deken (1999), in this volume.
6. See for instance Van Parijs (2006).
7. See for instance Cunliffe and Erreygers (2001).
8. Note that more recently another Nobel, Herbert A. Simon, also expressed his support to the proposal. See Simon (2001).
9. For a good overview of the American debate in the 1960s–1970s, see Steensland (2008). According to Steensland, in the U.S., "guaranteed annual income plans were the welfare reform strategy of the late 1960s and 1970s" (p. ix).
10. See www.basicincome.org for further information.
11. Situation as of April 1, 2011. The latest national network to become an officially recognized BIEN affiliate is the Basic Income Korean Network (July 2010).
12. See Standing (this volume).
13. For further details on the Permanent Fund Dividend, see Widerquist and Howard (eds) (2012).

References

Ackerman, B. and Alstott, A. (1999). *The Stakeholder Society*. Yale University Press, New Haven.

Atkinson A.B. (1995). *Public Economics in Action: The Basic Income/Flat Tax Proposal*. Clarendon Press, Oxford.

Atkinson, A.B. (1996). The Case for a Participation Income. *The Political Quarterly*, 67 (1), 67–70.

Cunliffe, J. and Erreygers, G. (2001). The enigmatic legacy of Fourier: Joseph Charlier and basic income. *History of Political Economy*, 33 (3), 459–484.

Russell, B. (1918). Proposed Roads to Freedom. Blue Ribbon Books, *New York*, p. 110.

Simon, H.A. (2001). UBI and the Flat Tax. In P. Van Parijs (ed.) *What's Wrong with a Free Lunch?* Beacon Press, Boston.

Steensland, B.C. (2008). *The Failed Welfare Revolution. America's struggle over guaranteed income policy*. Princeton University Press, Princeton.

Suplicy, E.M. (2007). Basic Income and Employment in Brazil. *Basic Income Studies*, 2 (1), Article 10.

Van Parijs, P. (2004). Basic Income: A Simple and Powerful Idea for the Twenty-First Century. *Politics and Society*, 32 (1), 7–39.

Van Parijs, P. (2006). Basic Income versus Stakeholder Grants. In E.O. Wright (ed.), *Redesigning Distribution*. Verso, London.

Widerquist, K. and Howard, M. (eds) (2012). *Alaska's Permanent Fund Dividend: Examining its Suitability as a Model*. Palgrave Macmillan, New York.

Further Reading

Monographs

Atkinson, A.B. (1997). *Public Economics in Action: The Basic Income/Flat Tax Proposal*. Oxford University Press, Oxford.

Birnbaum, S. (2012). *Basic Income Reconsidered: Social Justice, Liberalism, and the Demands of Equality*. Palgrave Macmillan, New York.

Fitzpatrick, T. (1999). *Freedom and Security: An Introduction to the Basic Income Debate*. Palgrave Macmillan, Basingstoke.

Jordan, B. (1985). *The State: Authority and Autonomy*. Basil Blackwell, Oxford.

Jordan, B. (1987). *Rethinking Welfare*. Basil Blackwell, Oxford.

Jordan, B. (1989). *The Common Good*. Basil Blackwell, Oxford.

Meade, J.E. (1995). *Full Employment Regained? An Agathotopian Dream*. Cambridge University Press, Cambridge.

Milner, E.M. and Milner, D. (1918). *Scheme for a State Bonus*. Simpkin, Marshall & Co, Kent.

Moynihan, D.P. (1973). *The Politics of a Guaranteed Income*. Random House, New York.

Murray, C. (2006). *In Our Hands: A Plan To Replace The Welfare State*. American Enterprise Institute Press, Washington, DC.

Patterson, J.T. (2010). *Freedom is Not Enough: The Moynihan Report and America's Struggle Over Black Family Life: From LBJ to Obama*. Basic Books, New York.

Sheahen, A. (1983). *Guaranteed Income: The Right to Economic Security*. Gain Publications, Los Angeles.

Standing, G. (1999). *Global Labour Flexibility: Seeking Distributive Justice*. Palgrave Macmillan, Basingstoke.

Standing, G. (2002). *Beyond the New Paternalism: Basic Security as Equality*. Verso, London/New York.

Standing, G. (2009). *Work After Globalization: Building Occupational Citizenship*. Edward Elgar, Cheltenham.

Standing, G. (2011). *The Precariat: The New Dangerous Class*. Bloomsbury Academic, London/New York.

Steensland, B. (2008). *The Failed Welfare Revolution: America's Struggle over Guaranteed Income Policy*. Princeton University Press, Princeton, NJ.

Theobald, R. (1965). *The Guaranteed Income*. Doubleday & Company, New York.

Van Trier, W. (1995). *Every One a King. An Investigation into the Meaning and Significance of the Debate on Basic Incomes*. PhD. Dissertation. Katholieke Universiteit Leuven, Leuven.

Van Parijs, P. (1995). *Real Freedom for All: What (If Anything) Can Justify Capitalism?* Clarendon Press, Oxford.

Walter, T. (1988). *Basic Income: Freedom from Poverty, Freedom to Work*. Marion Boyars, London.

White, S. (2003). *The Civic Minimum: On the Rights and Obligations of Economic Citizenship*. Oxford University Press, Oxford.

Edited collections

Caputo, R. (ed.) (2012). *Basic Income Guarantee and Politics: International Experiences and Perspectives on the Viability of Income Guarantees*. Palgrave, New York.

Cohen, J. and Rogers, J. (eds) (2001). *What's Wrong with a Free Lunch?* Beacon Press, Boston.

Cunliffe, J. and Erreygers, G. (eds) (2004). *The Origins of Universal Grants*. Palgrave Macmillan, Basingstoke.

Dowding, K., De Wispelaere, J., and White S. (eds) (2003). *The Ethics of Stakeholding*. Palgrave Macmillan, Basingstoke.

Pateman, C. and Murray, M. (eds) (2012). *Horizons of Reform: Basic Income Around the World*. Palgrave Macmillan, New York.

Reeve, A. and Williams, A. (eds) (2003). *Real Libertarianism Assessed: Political Theory After Van Parijs*. Palgrave Macmillan, New York.

Samson, M. and Standing, G. (eds) (2003). *A Basic Income Grant for South Africa*. University of Cape Town Press, Cape Town.

Standing, G. (ed.) (2005). *Promoting Income Security as a Right: Europe and North America*. Anthem, London.

van der Veen, R. and Groot, L. (eds) (2000). *Basic Income on the Agenda: Policy Objectives and Political Changes*. Amsterdam University Press, Amsterdam.

Van Parijs, P. (ed.) (1992). *Arguing for Basic Income: Ethical Foundations for a Radical Reform*. Verso, London/New York.

Widerquist, K., Lewis, M.A., and Pressman, S. (eds) (2005). *The Ethics and Economics of the Basic Income Guarantee*. Ashgate, Aldershot.

Widerquist, K. and Howard, M.W. (eds) (2012). *Alaska's Permanent Fund Dividend: Examining its Suitability as a Model*. Palgrave Macmillan, New York.

Widerquist, K. and Howard, M.W. (eds) (2012). *Exporting the Alaska Model: Adapting the Permanent Fund Dividend*. Palgrave Macmillan, New York.

Wright, E.O. (ed.) (2006). *Redesigning Distribution: Basic Income and Stakeholder Grants as Cornerstones for an Egalitarian Capitalism*. Verso, London.

Academic journal special issues, debates, and symposia devoted to basic income

Aya, R. and Tromp, B. (eds) (1986). Symposium on "A Capitalist Road to Communism", *Theory and Society*, 15 (5).

Cohen, J. and Rogers, J. (eds) (2000). New Democracy Forum on "Delivering A Basic Income", *The Boston Review*, October/November.

De Wispelaere, J. and Fitzpatrick, T. (eds) (2011). Special issue on "Basic Income", *Policy and Politics*, 39 (1).

Harvey, P. (ed). (2005). Special issue of *Rutgers Journal of Law and Public Policy*, 2 (1).

Krebs, A. (ed.) (2000). "Basic Income? A Symposium on Van Parijs", *Analyse und Kritik*, 22 (2).

Political Quarterly, the (1996). Debate on "Citizen's Income", *The Political Quarterly*, 67 (1).

Widerquist, K. (ed.) (2005). Special issue on "The Basic Income Guarantee", *The Journal of Socio-Economics*, 34 (1).

Widerquist, K., Lewis, M.A., and Pressman, S. (eds) (2005). Symposium: "The Basic Income Guarantee and social Economics," *The Review of Social Economy*, 63 (4).

Wright, E.O. (ed.) (2004). Special issue of *Politics and Society*, 32 (1).

Journals

Basic Income Studies, http://www.degruyter.com/view/j/bis. (This is, so far, the only journal focusing specifically on Basic Income.)

Websites

The Basic Income Earth Network, www.basicincome.org. (This website has information about Basic Income and links to affiliate networks, which have multilingual bibliographical information about Basic Income.)

Basic Income News, www.BInews.org. (This website has recent news and commentary on Basic Income.)

The U.S. Basic Income Guarantee Network, www.usbig.net. (This website includes a discussion paper series on Basic Income.)

Part I
Freedom

Introduction
Freedom and Basic Income

Karl Widerquist

One of the most central concerns in the Basic Income debate is the issue of freedom. Does Basic Income enhance freedom by liberating the disadvantaged from the constraints society imposes on them or does it inhibit freedom by imposing unjustified duties on taxpayers? The answer depends to some extent on the definition of freedom. This section begins to address that question, by looking at several different freedom-based arguments for and against Basic Income from several different perspectives. The discussion is closely related to those in other parts of the book, most especially the "Justice" and "Reciprocity and Exploitation" sections.

In a chapter from Robert Theobald's edited book, *The Guaranteed Income* (1966), psychologist Erich Fromm (1966) discusses the effect that Basic Income will have of freeing individuals from "the threat of starvation against all who were unwilling to accept the conditions of work and social existence that were imposed on them." This change, Fromm argues, would shift individuals from the psychology of scarcity (which produces envy and egotism) to the psychology of abundance (which produces initiative, faith in life, and solidarity).

In "The Case for a Negative Income Tax: A View from the Right," economist Milton Friedman (1968) argues that a Negative Income Tax will free the poor from a cumbersome, paternalistic welfare system that puts them under constant supervision. He argues that it also has the potential to free business owners from regulations, such as the minimum wage, designed to support the poor.

Philippe Van Parijs (1991) makes the freedom-enhancing case for Basic Income, arguing that it enhances what he calls "real freedom," the freedom to do whatever one might want to do. At the same time he addresses the argument that Basic Income reduces the freedom of taxpayers using what he calls the Crazy-Lazy Challenge. Crazy and Lazy live on an island. Crazy prefers to work as much as he can. Lazy prefers to work only as much as he has to. If they were both restricted to working their half of the land, Crazy would have fewer resources than he would like to work, and Lazy would have more resource than he is willing to work. But if they trade, Crazy can work all of the land, paying Lazy a Basic

---

Basic Income: An Anthology of Contemporary Research, First Edition. Edited by Karl Widerquist, José A. Noguera, Yannick Vanderborght, and Jurgen De Wispelaere.

Income large enough that he can live without working, and giving both of them more real freedom. The full account of Van Parijs's real-freedom-based argument for Basic Income is in his book *Real Freedom for All: What (if anything) can justify capitalism?* (Van Parijs, 1995).

In, "Optional Freedoms," Elizabeth Anderson (2001) argues that Philippe Van Parijs's real libertarian justification of Basic Income has three important defects. First, it fails to properly prioritize freedom, equating the optional freedoms (such as the freedom to remain idle) with essential freedom (such as the freedom from disease). Second, it fails to recognize that some people have more difficulty converting income into freedom than others. Third, it promotes freedom without responsibility. Despite her skepticism she holds out the possibility that Basic Income might have some value as a part of a larger social welfare package.

Philip Pettit is one of the most prominent contemporary Civic Republican philosophers. According to Pettit (2007), Republicanism construes freedom, not as the absence of interference by others, but as the absence of dominating control. An individual is dominated to the extent that another agent's arbitrary power raises the probability of the individual acting according to the other agent's tastes. Pettit argues that Basic Income could free financially dependent wives or employees from dominating power that husbands or employers might have over them.

Karl Widerquist (2011) argues that the dominance of natural resources by any group of people (whether they be centralized governments or disorganized private owners) effectively forces the propertyless to labor for those who control resources, even if they would be able to provide for themselves in the absence of such interference. He argues that the freedom from forced service, defined as "effective control self-ownership," is central to what it means to be a free person. Comparing this concept to "real freedom," Widerquist argues that effective control self-ownership provides a stronger explanation why basic income must be unconditional and sufficient to meet an individual's basic needs and a more compelling defense against the reciprocity objection.

References

Theobald, R. (ed.) (1966). *The Guaranteed Income*. Doubleday, New York.

Van Parijs, P. (1995). *Real Freedom for All: What (if anything) can justify capitalism?* Oxford: Clarendon Press.

Further Reading

Barry, B. (1996). Real Freedom and Basic Income. *Journal of Political Philosophy*, 4 (3), 242–276.

Birnbaum, S. (2010). Radical liberalism, Rawls and the welfare state: justifying the politics of basic income. *Critical Review of International Social and Political Philosophy*, 13 (4), 495–516.

Birnbaum, S. (2011). Should surfers be ostracized? Basic income, liberal neutrality, and the work ethos. *Politics, Philosophy & Economics*, 10 (4) 396–419.

Birnbaum, S. (2012). *Basic Income Reconsidered: Social Justice, Liberalism, and the Demands of Equality*. Palgrave Macmillan, New York.

Casassas, D. (ed.) (2007). Debate: Basic Income and the Republican Legacy. *Basic Income Studies*, 2 (2), with contributions by D. Casassas, A. Domènech and D. Raventós, C. Pateman, P. Pettit, and S. White. http://www.degruyter.com/view/j/bis

Farrelly, C. (1999). Justice and a citizens' basic income. *Journal of Applied Philosophy*, 16 (3), 283–296.

Fitzpatrick, T. (2011). Social paternalism and basic income. *Policy and Politics*, 39 (1), 83–100.

Friedman, M. (1962). *Capitalism and Freedom*. University of Chicago Press, Chicago.

Friedman, M. and Friedman, R.D. (1980). *Free to Choose: a personal statement*. Harcourt Books, New York.

Hayek, F.A. (1994 [1944]). *The Road to Serfdom*. University of Chicago Press, Chicago.

Heath, J. and Panitch, V. (2010). Why cash violates neutrality. *Basic Income Studies*, 5 (1), Article 4. http://www.degruyter.com/view/j/bis

Lewis, M. (2005). Perhaps There Can Be Too Much Freedom. In K. Widerquist, M.A. Lewis, and S. Pressman (eds), *The Ethics and Economics of the Basic Income Guarantee*. Ashgate, Aldershot, pp. 13–54.

Mosley, D. (ed.) (2011). Should Libertarians endorse basic income? *Special issue of Basic Income Studies*, 6 (2), with contributions by P. Boettke and A. Martin, D. Moseley, M. Munger, B. Powell, P. Vallentyne, and M. Zwolinski. http://www.degruyter.com/view/j/bis

Murray, C. (2006). *In Our Hands: A Plan To Replace The Welfare State*. American Enterprise Institute Press, Washington, DC.

Reeve, A. and Williams, A. (eds) (2003). *Real Libertarianism Assessed: Political Theory After Van Parijs*. Palgrave Macmillan, New York.

Torisky, E.V. (1993). Van Parijs, Rawls, and unconditional basic income. *Analysis*, 53 (4), 289–297.

van der Veen, R.J. and Van Parijs P. (1986). A Capitalist road to Communism. *Theory and Society*, 15 (5), 635–655.

Van Donselaar, G. (1998). The freedom-based account of solidarity and basic income. *Ethical Theory and Moral Practice*, 1 (3), 313–333.

Van Parijs, P. (ed.) (1992). *Arguing for Basic Income: Ethical Foundations for a Radical Reform*. Verso, London/New York.

Widerquist, K. (2008). The physical basis of voluntary trade. *Human Rights Review*, 11 (1), 83–103.

Chapter 1

The Psychological Aspects of the Guaranteed Income

Erich Fromm

Originally published as The Psychological Aspects of the Guaranteed Income. In R. Theobald (ed.) (1966). *The Guaranteed Income.* Doubleday, New York.

This chapter focuses exclusively on the *psychological* aspects of the Guaranteed Income, its value, its risks, and the human problems it raises.

The most important reason for the acceptance of the concept is that it might drastically enhance the freedom of the individual.[1] Until now in human history, man has been limited in his freedom to act by two factors: the use of force on the part of the rulers (essentially their capacity to kill the dissenters); and, more importantly, the threat of starvation against all who were unwilling to accept the conditions of work and social existence that were imposed on them.

Whoever was not willing to accept these conditions, even if there was no other force used against him, was confronted with the threat of starvation. The principle prevailing throughout most of human history in the past and present (in capitalism as well as in the Soviet Union) is: "He who does not work shall not eat." This threat forced man not only to *act* in accordance with what was demanded of him, but also to *think* and to *feel* in such a way that he would not even be tempted to act differently.

The fact that past history is based on the principle of the threat of starvation has, in the last analysis, its source in the fact that, with the exception of certain primitive societies, man has lived on the level of scarcity, both economically and psychologically. There were never sufficient material goods to satisfy the needs of all; usually a small group of "directors" took for themselves all that their hearts desired, and the many who could not sit at the table were told that it was God's or Nature's law that this should be so. But it must be noted that the main factor in this is not the greed of the "directors," but the low level of material productivity.

A Guaranteed Income, which becomes possible in the era of economic abundance, could for the first time free man from the threat of starvation, and thus make him truly free and independent from any economic threat. Nobody would have to accept conditions of work merely because he otherwise would be afraid of starving; a talented or ambitious man or

Fromm, E. (1966). The Psychological Aspects of the Guaranteed Income. In R. Theobald (ed.) *The Guaranteed Income.* Doubleday, New York.

Basic Income: An Anthology of Contemporary Research, First Edition. Edited by Karl Widerquist, José A. Noguera, Yannick Vanderborght, and Jurgen De Wispelaere.

woman could learn new skills to prepare himself or herself for a different kind of occupation. A woman could leave her husband, an adolescent his family. People would learn to be no longer afraid, if they did not have to fear hunger. (This holds true, of course, only if there is also no political threat that inhibits man's free thought, speech, and action.)

Guaranteed Income would not only establish freedom as a reality rather than a slogan, it would also establish a principle deeply rooted in Western religious and humanist tradition: man has the right to live, regardless! This right to live, to have food, shelter, medical care, education, and so on, is an intrinsic human right that cannot be restricted by any condition, not even the one that he must be socially "useful."

The shift from a psychology of scarcity to that of abundance is one of the most important steps in human development. A psychology of scarcity produces anxiety, envy, egotism (to be seen most drastically in peasant cultures all over the world). A psychology of abundance produces initiative, faith in life, solidarity. The fact is that most men are still geared psychologically to the economic facts of scarcity, when the industrial world is in the process of entering a new era of economic abundance. But because of this psychological "lag" many people cannot even understand new ideas as presented in the concept of a Guaranteed Income, because traditional ideas are usually determined by feelings that originated in previous forms of social existence.

A further effect of a Guaranteed Income, coupled with greatly diminished working hours for all, would be that the spiritual and religious problems of human existence would become real and imperative. Until now man has been occupied with work (or has been too tired after work) to be too seriously concerned with such problems as "What is the meaning of life?" "What do I believe in?" "What are my values?" "Who am I?" and so on. If he ceases to be mainly occupied by work, he will either be free to confront these problems seriously, or he will become half mad from direct or compensated boredom.

From all this it would follow that economic abundance, liberation from fear of starvation, would mark the transition from a prehuman to a truly human society.

Balancing this picture, it is necessary to raise some objections against, or questions about, the concept of a Guaranteed Income. The most obvious question is whether a Guaranteed Income would not reduce the incentive for work.

Aside from the fact that there is already no work for an ever increasing sector of the population, and hence that the question of incentive for these people is irrelevant, the objection is nevertheless a serious one. I believe, however, that it can be demonstrated that material incentive is by no means the only incentive for work and effort. First of all there are other incentives: pride, social recognition, pleasure in work itself, and so on. Examples of this fact are not lacking. The most obvious one to quote is the work of scientists, artists, and so on, whose outstanding achievements were not motivated by the incentive of monetary profit, but by a mixture of various factors: most of all, interest in the work they were doing; also pride in their achievements, or the wish for fame. But obvious as this example may seem, it is not entirely convincing, because it can be said that these outstanding people could make extraordinary efforts precisely because they were extraordinarily gifted, and hence they are no example for the reactions of the average person. This objection does not seem to be valid, however, if we consider the incentives for the activities of people who do not share the outstanding qualities of the great creative persons. What efforts are made in the field of all sports, of many kinds of hobbies, where there are no material incentives of any kind! To what extent interest in the work process itself can be an incentive for working was clearly demonstrated for the first time by Professor Mayo in his classic study at the Chicago Hawthorne Works of the Western Electric Company (Mayo, 1946).

The very fact that unskilled women workers were drawn into the experiment of work productivity of which they were the subjects, the fact that they became interested and active participants in the experiment, resulted in increased productivity, and even their physical health improved.

The problem becomes even clearer when we consider older forms of societies. The efficiency and incorruptibility of the traditional Prussian civil service were famous, in spite of the fact that monetary rewards were very low; in this case such concepts as honor, loyalty, duty, were the determining motivations for efficient work. Still another factor appears when we consider preindustrial societies (like the medieval European society, or half-feudal societies in the beginning of the twentieth century in Latin America). In these societies the carpenter, for instance, wanted to earn enough to satisfy the needs of his traditional standard of living, and would refuse to work more in order to earn more than he needed.

Secondly, it is a fact that man, by nature, is not lazy, but on the contrary, suffers from the results of inactivity. People might prefer not to work for one or two months, but the vast majority would beg to work, even if they were not paid for it. The fields of child development and mental illness offer abundant data in this connection; what is needed is a systematic investigation in which the available data are organized and analyzed from the standpoint of "laziness as disease," and more data are collected in new and pertinent investigations.

However, if money is not to be the main incentive, then work in its technical or social aspects would have to be sufficiently attractive and interesting to outweigh the unpleasure of inactivity. Modern alienated man is deeply bored (usually unconsciously) and hence has a yearning for laziness, rather than for activity. This yearning itself is, however, a symptom of our "pathology of normalcy." Presumably misuse of the Guaranteed Income would disappear after a short time, just as people would not overeat on sweets after a few weeks, assuming they would not have to pay for them.

Another objection is the following: Will the disappearance of the fear of starvation really make man so much freer, considering that those who earn a comfortable living are probably just as afraid to lose a job that gives them, let us say, $15,000 a year, as are those who might go hungry if they were to lose their jobs? If this objection is valid, then the Guaranteed Income would increase the freedom of the large majority, but not that of the middle and upper classes.

In order to understand this objection fully we have to consider the spirit of contemporary industrial society. Man has transformed himself into a *homo consumens.* He is voracious, passive, and tries to compensate for his inner emptiness by continuous and ever increasing consumption (there are many clinical examples for this mechanism in cases of overeating, overbuying, overdrinking, as a reaction to depression and anxiety); he consumes cigarettes, liquor, sex, movies, travel, as well as education, books, lectures, and art. He *appears* to be active, "thrilled," yet deep down he is anxious, lonely, depressed, and bored (boredom can be defined as that type of chronic depression that can successfully be compensated by consumption). Twentieth-century industrialism has created this new psychological type, *homo consumens,* primarily for economic reasons, that is, the need for mass consumption, which is stimulated and manipulated by advertising. But the character type, once created, also influences the economy and makes the principles of ever-increasing satisfaction appear rational and realistic.[2]

Contemporary man has an unlimited hunger for more and more consumption. From this follow several consequences: if there is no limit to the greed for consumption, and since in the foreseeable future no economy can produce enough for unlimited consumption for everybody, there can never be true "abundance" (psychologically speaking) as long as the character structure of *homo consumens* remains dominant. For the greedy person there is always scarcity, since he never has enough, regardless of how much he has. Furthermore, he feels covetous and competitive with regard to everybody else; hence he is basically isolated and frightened. He cannot really enjoy art or other cultural stimulations, since he remains basically greedy. This means that those who lived on the Guaranteed-Income level would feel frustrated and worthless, and those who earned more would remain prisoners of circumstances, because they would be frightened and lose the possibility for maximum consumption. For these reasons I believe that Guaranteed Income without a change from the principle of maximal consumption would only take care of certain problems (economical and social) but would not have the radical effect it should.

What, then, must be done to implement the Guaranteed Income? Generally speaking, we must change our system from one of maximal to one of optimal consumption. This would mean a vast change in industry from the production of commodities for individual consumption to the production of commodities for public use: schools, theaters, libraries, parks, hospitals, public transportation, housing; in other words an emphasis on the production of those things that are the basis for the unfolding of the individual's inner productiveness and activity. It can be shown that the voraciousness of *homo consumens* refers mainly to the individual consumption of things he "eats" (incorporates), while the use of free public services, enabling the individual to enjoy life, do not evoke greed and voraciousness. Such a change from maximal to optimal consumption would require drastic changes in production patterns, and also a drastic reduction of the appetite-whetting, brainwashing techniques of advertising, and so on.[3] It would also have to be combined with a drastic cultural change: a renaissance of the humanistic values of life, productivity, individualism, and so on, as against the materialism of the "organization man" and manipulated ant heaps.

These considerations lead to other problems that need to be studied: Are there objectively valid criteria to distinguish between rational and irrational, between good and bad needs, or is any subjectively felt need of the same value? (Good is defined here as needs that enhance human aliveness, awakeness, productivity, sensitivity; bad, as those needs that weaken or paralyze these human potentials.) It must be remembered that in the case of drug addiction, overeating, alcoholism, we all make such a distinction. The study of these problems would lead to the following practical considerations: What are the minimum legitimate needs of an individual? (For instance: one room per person, so much clothing, so many calories, so many culturally valuable commodities such as a radio, books, etc.) In a relatively abundant society such as that of the United States today, it should be easy to figure out what the cost for a *decent* subsistence minimum is, and also what the limits for maximal consumption should be. Progressive taxation on consumption beyond a certain threshold could be considered. It seems important to me that slum conditions should be avoided. All this would mean the combination of the principles of a Guaranteed Income with the transformation of our society from maximal to optimal individual consumption, and a drastic shift from production for individual needs to production for public needs.

I believe it is important to add to the idea of a Guaranteed Income another one, which ought to be studied: the concept of *free* consumption of certain commodities. One example would be that of bread, then milk, and vegetables. Let us assume, for a moment, that everyone could go into any bakery and take as much bread as he liked (the state would pay the bakery for all bread produced). As already mentioned, the greedy would at first take more than they could use, but after a short time this "greed-consumption" would even itself out and people would take only what they really needed. Such free consumption would, in my opinion, create a new dimension in human life (unless we look at it as the repetition on a much higher level of the consumption pattern in certain primitive societies). Man would feel freed from the principle "He who does not work shall not eat." Even this beginning of free consumption might constitute a very novel experience of freedom. It is obvious even to the non-economist that the provision of free bread for all could be easily paid for by the state, which would cover this disbursement by a corresponding tax. However, we can go a step further. Assuming that not only all minimal needs for food were obtained free – bread, milk, vegetables, fruit – but the minimal needs for clothing (by some system everybody could obtain, without paying, say one suit, three shirts, six pairs of socks, etc., per year); that transportation was free, requiring, of course, vastly improved systems of public transportation, while private cars would become more expensive. Eventually one could imagine that housing could be solved in the same way, by big housing projects with sleeping halls for the young, one small room for older, or married couples, to be used without cost by anybody who chose. This leads me to the suggestion that another way of solving the Guaranteed-Income problem would be by free minimal consumption of all necessities, instead of through cash payments. The production of these minimum necessities, together with highly improved public services, would keep production going, just as Guaranteed-Income payments would.

It may be objected that this method is more radical, and hence less acceptable, than the one proposed by the other authors. This is probably true; but it must not be forgotten that, on the one hand, this method of free minimal services could theoretically be arranged within the present system while, on the other hand, the idea of a Guaranteed Income will not be acceptable to many, not because it is not feasible, but because of the psychological resistance against the abolishment of the principle "He who does not work shall not eat."

One other philosophical, political, and psychological problem has to be studied: that of freedom. The Western concept of freedom was to a large extent based on the freedom to own property, and to exploit it, as long as other legitimate interests were not threatened. This principle has actually been punctured in many ways in Western industrial societies by taxation, which is a form of expropriation, and by state intervention in agriculture, trade, and industry. At the same time, private property in the means of production is becoming increasingly replaced by the semipublic property typical of giant corporations. While the Guaranteed-Income concept would mean some additional state regulations, it must be remembered that today the concept of freedom for the average individual lies not so much in the freedom to own and exploit property (capital) as in the freedom to consume whatever he likes. Many people today consider it as an interference with their freedom if unlimited consumption is restricted, although only those on top are really free to choose what they want. The competition between different brands of the same commodities and different kinds of commodities creates the illusion of personal freedom, when in reality the individual wants what he is conditioned to want.[4] A new approach to the problem of freedom is necessary; only with the transformation of *homo consumens* into a productive, active person will man experience freedom in true independence and not in unlimited choice of commodities.

The full effect of the principle of the Guaranteed Income is to be expected only in conjunction with: i) a change in habits of consumption, the transformation of *homo consumens* into the productive, active man (in Spinoza's sense); ii) the creation of a new spiritual attitude, that of humanism (in theistic or nontheistic forms); and iii) a renaissance of truly democratic methods (for instance, a new Lower House by the integration and summation of decisions arrived at by hundreds of thousands of face-to-face groups, active participation of all members working in any kind of enterprise, in management, etc.). The danger that a state that nourishes all could become a mother goddess with dictatorial qualities can be overcome only by a simultaneous, drastic increase in democratic procedure in all spheres of social activities. (The fact is that even today the state is extremely powerful, without giving these benefits.)

In sum, together with economic research in the field of the Guaranteed Income, other research must be undertaken: psychological, philosophical, religious, educational. The great step of a Guaranteed Income will, in my opinion, succeed only if it is accompanied by changes in other spheres. It must not be forgotten that the Guaranteed Income can succeed only if we stop spending 10% of our total resources on economically useless and dangerous armaments; if we can halt the spread of senseless violence by systematic help to the underdeveloped countries, and if we find methods to arrest the population explosion. Without such changes, no plan for the future will succeed, because there will be no future.

Notes

1. Cf. my discussion of a "universal subsistence guarantee" in Fromm (1955).
2. The problem is all the more complicated by the fact that at least 20% of the American population live on a level of scarcity, that some parts of Europe, especially the socialist countries, have not yet attained a satisfactory standard of living, and that the majority of mankind, which dwells in Latin America, Asia, and Africa, is still living at hardly above starvation level. Any argument for less consumption meets with the argument that in most of the world *more* consumption is needed. This is perfectly true, but the danger exists that even in the countries that are now poor, the ideal of maximal consumption will guide their effort, form their spirit, and hence will continue to be effective even when the level of optimal (not maximal) consumption has been reached.
3. The need of restricting advertising and, even more, of changing production in the direction of greater production of public services are, in my opinion, hardly thinkable without a great deal of state intervention.
4. Here too, the totalitarian bureaucratization of consumption in the Soviet-bloc countries has made a bad case for any regulation of consumption.

References

Fromm, E. (1955). *The Sane Society.* Holt, Rinehart & Winston Inc., New York, pp. 335 ff.

Mayo, E. (1946). *The Human Problem of an Industrial Civilization*, 2nd edn. The Macmillan Company, New York.

Chapter 2

The Case for a Negative Income Tax: A View from the Right

Milton Friedman

Excerpts from Friedman, M. (1968). The Case for a Negative Income Tax: A View from the Right. In J.H. Bunzel (ed.) *Issues in American Public Policy*. Prentice-Hall, Englewood Cliffs, NJ, pp. 111–120.

All responsible students of the problem, whether on the left or the right, have come increasingly to recognize that present welfare programs have grave defects, and, in particular, that direct relief and aid to dependent children demean both the recipients and the administrators.

I was much impressed some years ago when Herbert Krosney talked to me about a study of New York welfare programs he was engaged on – and which has since been reported in a splendid book, *Beyond Welfare*.

In effect, he said to me, "You classical liberals are always talking about how big government interferes with personal freedom. The examples you give are always about things that matter to people like you and me – freedom of speech, of choosing an occupation, of traveling, and so on. Yet how often do you and I come into contact with government? When we pay our taxes or get a traffic ticket, perhaps. The people whose freedom is really being interfered with are the poor in Harlem, who are on relief. A government official tells them how much they may spend for food, rent, and clothing. They have to get permission from an official to rent a different apartment or to buy secondhand furniture. Mothers receiving aid for dependent children may have their male visitors checked on by government investigators at any hour of the day or night. They are the people who are deprived of personal liberty, freedom, and dignity."

And surely, he is right. No doubt, he who pays the piper calls the tune. No doubt, the taxpayer who pays the bill to support people on relief may feel that he has the moral as well as legal right to see to it that the money is spent for designated purposes. But whether he has the right is irrelevant. Even if he has, it seems to me neither prudent nor noble for him to exercise it. The major effect of doing so is to weaken the self-reliance of the recipients, diminish their humanity, and make them wise in the stratagems for evading the spirit of the restrictions imposed on them. And the effect on the administrators is no more salutary. Instead of welfare workers bringing counsel and assistance to the poor, they become

From Friedman, M. (1968). The Case for a Negative Income Tax: A View from the Right. In J.H. Bunzel (ed.) *Issues in American Public Policy*. Prentice-Hall, Englewood Cliffs, NJ, pp. 111–120. Reprinted with kind permission of Janet Martel.

Basic Income: An Anthology of Contemporary Research, First Edition. Edited by Karl Widerquist, José A. Noguera, Yannick Vanderborght, and Jurgen De Wispelaere.

policemen and detectives – enemies to be outwitted. That is a major reason why it is so hard for large cities to staff their welfare agencies and why they experience such high turnover.

It would be far better to give the indigent money and let them spend it according to their values. True, they may spend much of it in ways we disapprove of – but they do now, and not all the red tape in Washington will keep them from finding ways of doing so. If we spent the same amount on the poor in total, they would have more to spend – because of savings in administrative costs – and they would get more satisfaction per dollar spent – because they would waste less in circumventing the bureaucracy and would use the money for what they value most. In addition, at least some would grow in the course of making their own decisions, and would develop habits of independence and self-reliance. And surely, if social workers are hired on government funds, they should devote their energies to helping the indigent, and not spying on them.

This is the aspect of the Negative Income Tax that I believe has appealed most strongly to the left, and properly so. Here is one area where it has become patent how detailed government intervention affects the lives of its citizens; how it corrupts both the controller and the controlled. Having learned this lesson in one area, perhaps the well-meaning people on the left will be led to look at other areas in a new light.

The Hostility on the Right

The hostility toward the Negative Income Tax on the right is partly an automatic reflex to the enthusiasm for it on the left, partly, it is a valid reaction against fill-the-gap plans. But hostility arises also from two very different sources: first, the belief that a Guaranteed Minimum Income introduces a new principle into the relationship between the government and the people that would greatly weaken the incentives on the part of the poor to help themselves; second, the political judgment that it will not be possible to keep a Negative Income Tax within reasonable bounds.

The weakening of incentives

The first source of hostility confuses labels with substance. The elementary fact is that we now have a governmentally Guaranteed Minimum Income in substance though not in name. That is what our present grab-bag of relief and welfare measures is. In some states, it is even written into the law that anyone whose income is "inadequate" is entitled as a matter of right to have it supplemented and brought up to an "adequate" level, as judged of course by the welfare agencies. And whether explicitly specified in law or not, the same thing is true almost everywhere in the United States.

The most obvious component of the present *de facto* Guaranteed Minimum Income is direct relief and Aid to Dependent Children. Aside from the interference with personal freedom and dignity already referred to, these programs have the worst possible effects on incentives. If a person on relief earns a dollar, and obeys the law, his or her relief payment is reduced by a dollar. Since working generally involves costs – if only for better or different clothes – the effect is to penalize either industry or honesty or both. The program tends to produce poor people, and a permanent class of poor people living on welfare, rather than to help the unavoidably indigent. And it does so at high cost in waste and bureaucracy.

But this is only the tip of the iceberg. We have a maze of detailed governmental programs that have been justified on welfare grounds – though typically their product is "illfare": public housing, urban renewal, old-age and unemployment insurance, job training, the host of assorted programs under the mislabeled "war on poverty," farm price supports, and so on at incredible length.

Estimates of how much we are now spending on welfare programs vary widely depending on what specific programs are included. A modest estimate, which excludes entirely veterans' benefits and educational expenditures, is that federal, state, and local governments are spending roughly $50 billion a year. Much of this money is simply wasted – as in the agricultural programs. And most of it goes to people who cannot by any stretch of the imagination be classified as poor. Indeed, from this point of view the direct public assistance programs at least have the virtue that people who receive the payments clearly have a lower average income than the people who pay the taxes. There is not another welfare program for which this is unambiguously true. For some – for example, urban renewal and farm price supports – the people who are hurt almost certainly have a lower average income than the people who are helped. For social security, the situation is more complex but it may well be that on net it involves transferring funds from the poor to the not-so-poor rather than the other way.

The welfare iceberg includes also measures that impose restrictions on private transactions, and do not require direct government expenditures, except for enforcement. The most obvious is minimum wage rate legislation. Other items are the Walsh-Healy and Davis-Bacon Acts, and the whole range of legislation conferring special immunities on labor unions. The effect of most such legislation is to increase the number of indigent people. The minimum wage rate, for example, prices many unskilled workers out of the market and is the major explanation, in my judgment, for the tragically high unemployment rates among teenagers, especially Negro teenagers.[1] These measures involve a confusion between *wage rate* and *family income*. Persons who are capable of earning only low wage rates are for the most part youngsters or extra family members whose earnings supplement those of the main breadwinner. But even where the worker is the main breadwinner, it is surely better that he be free to earn what little he can than that he be unemployed, and better that, if government funds are to be used to aid him, they be used to supplement his earnings, not to replace them.

The Negative Income Tax would be vastly superior to this collection of welfare measures. It would concentrate public funds on supplementing the incomes of the poor – not distribute funds broadside in the hope that some will trickle down to the poor. It would help them because they were poor, not because they were old or disabled or unemployed or farmers or tenants of public housing. These characteristics are no doubt associated with poverty, but the association is very far from perfect.

Because the Negative Income Tax is directed specifically at poverty, it would both help the indigent more and cost far less than our present collection of progranms. One careful estimate, by Christopher Green, sets the cost of the 50% plan outlined above at $7 to $9 billion for 1964 (if public assistance payments are excluded from the income base used in calculating taxable income).[2] In that year, public assistance expenditures alone totaled $5.1 billion. Clearly, the elimination of public assistance plus only a modest reduction in other programs would be enough to finance that particular Negative Income Tax with no net cost.[3] And yet this 50% plan would provide more assistance to the bulk of the indigent than they are now receiving.[4]

Moreover, by substituting a fractional rate for the present 100% rate, the Negative Income Tax would give the indigent *more* incentive to add to their income by their own activity than they now have. Hence the above estimates overstate, and in my view significantly overstate, the net cost. Furthermore, these estimates make no allowance for a number of indirect benefits. Integrating the payment of assistance with the tax system would improve collection and reduce evasion under the income tax, reduce the concealment of income that takes place under our present relief programs, and permit elimination of most of the present bureaucracy administering the welfare programs.

Of course, the Negative Income Tax at any reasonable level would not meet the specific needs of every indigent family. Being general and impersonal, it cannot be adapted to cases of special hardship, and no doubt such cases would exist. However, by providing a basic minimum, it would reduce such cases to a manageable number, which could be taken care of by private charity. In my opinion, one of the great costs of the proliferation of governmental welfare programs is the elimination of a basic role for private charity, with its flexibility, diversity, and adaptability. An indirect virtue of the Negative Income Tax is that it would provide an important place for private charity to serve precisely that function which private agencies can serve best – handling the special case.

If we lived in a hypothetical world in which there were no governmental welfare programs at all and in which all assistance to the destitute was by private charity, the case for introducing a Negative Income Tax would be far weaker than the case for substituting it for present programs. In such a world, the negative income tax would indeed weaken incentives to work, For such a world, I do not know whether I would favor a negative income tax – that would depend on how effectively private charity was in fact providing for the destitute. But, whether desirable or not, that is not our world and there is not the remotest chance that it will be in the foreseeable future. Those, like myself, who would like to see the role of government reduced, only harm our own cause by evaluating a program by an unreal standard.

The political problem

A second major source of hostility from the right to the negative income tax is concern about its political effect. If we adopt an open-and-above-board program for supplementing the incomes of people below some specified level, will there not be continued political pressure for higher and higher break-even incomes, for higher and higher rates on negative income? Will the demagogue not have a field day appealing to the have-nots to legislate taxes on the haves for transfer to them? Will not the first sign of this process be the adoption of the negative income tax as an addition to all other programs rather than as a substitute?

These are all important questions. Clearly the dangers exist. But, like the incentive question, they must be evaluated in terms of the world as it is, not in terms of a dream world in which there are no governmental welfare measures. The relevant political question is whether the negative income tax is more susceptible or less susceptible to these dangers than alternative programs of the kind we now have or are likely to get. To this question. the answer seems to me clear: The negative income tax is less susceptible.

Why has the present grab-bag of programs been adopted? Because each appeals to a special interest that is willing to fight strongly for it, while few are willing to fight strongly against it; because the disinterested who seek to promote the general interest have been persuaded that every measure will contribute to helping a group that is disadvantaged; because, for many of the measures, there was no clear price tag, and the program could be voted without the simultaneous imposition of taxes to pay for it; because for still others, there are no direct costs at all – minimum wages are perhaps the clearest example; because, finally, no one who opposed the programs had an effective alternative to offer that would meet the real problems.

Politically, the right solution is to have a comprehensive program whose cost is open and clear. That is precisely what the negative income tax is. By linking it intimately with the general income tax structure, there is no way to raise the break-even incomes without raising the exemption for tax purposes, which clearly requires a higher rate on incomes above the exemption. The cost of the payments is in one lump sum that can be calculated and will be painfully visible to every taxpayer. It will be obvious that every rise in the rate applied to negative taxable income raises the cost. It may still be that the lower income groups will form a coalition to despoil the upper income groups for their benefit – but that danger will be less than now, when we are in the position of having the dog's tail cut off by inches, on the specious plea of benefiting the disadvantaged. Once the issue is open and clear, we must rely on the good sense and responsibility of the electorate. And I for one believe that experience has shown that we can rely on it; that in every Western country, the electorate has shown that it is proof – though clearly not 200 proof – against demagogic appeals simply to share the wealth.

The present problem is to halt the proliferation of the bad programs we now have and ultimately to dismantle them. But while these programs are on the whole bad, more or less incidentally they do help some people who are disadvantaged. Can we in good conscience mount a political attack on them unless we can provide an alternative way to achieve their good results? Can we be effective, unless we have a satisfactory answer to the inevitable charge that we are heartless and want to let the poor starve? And would we not deserve that charge, if we had no alternative? Most of these programs should never have been enacted. But they have been and they must be dismantled gradually, both for the sake of social stability and because the government has the moral responsibility to meet commitments it has entered into. The negative income tax is a way to replace existing programs gradually.

An additional enormous political advantage of a negative income tax compared with our present programs is that it does not generate a large bureaucracy to provide political patronage to the powers that be. It cannot be used as a political slush fund, as so many current programs – notably in the War on Poverty – can be and have been used.

There is no way whereby the bulk of us can tax ourselves to help the less fortunate that does not have political dangers. The negative income tax comes closer, in my opinion, to being politically consistent with a limited government and a free economy than any other method I have heard of.

Notes

1. See Brazen and Friedman (1966).
2. Green (1966). The lower estimate ($7.1 billion) assumes that double exemptions are not granted the aged in calculating taxable income; the higher estimate ($8.8 billion) assumes that they are.
3. Precise calculations require taking into account the fact that some part of other transfer funds go to persons with low incomes, so the reduction or elimination of such programs would increase the amount of negative income reported. There is not therefore a dollar-for-dollar saving. Because the above estimates exclude assistance payments from the tax base, this does not apply to the elimination of public assistance.

4. Green (*Transfer-by-Taxation*, pp. 163–165) compares present Aid to Families with Dependent Children (AFDC) with payments under this 50% plan, on the assumption that the Negative Income Tax payment would be the only income of the recipients. Even under this extreme assumption, he finds that only three states (New York, New Jersey, and Pennsylvania) are now paying under AFDC more than the recipients would get under the Negative Income Tax. For Old Age Assistance (OAA), the problem is more complicated because of the need to allow for OASDI benefits. Green estimates that under the 50% plan, "the elderly poor receiving public assistance would not receive as much income [. . .] as they are presently receiving through PA (public assistance) or a combination of PA and OASDI. However, the difference is not absolutely very great" (p. 165).

References

Brazen, Y. and Friedman, M. (1966). *The Minimum Wage Rate, Who Really Pays?* An interview with Yale Brazen and Milton Friedman. Free Society Association, Washington D.C.

Green, C. (1966). Transfer-by-Taxation: An Approach to Improved Income Maintenance. Background paper prepared for a conference at The Brookings Institution. The Brookings Institution, Washington D.C., p. 277.

Krosney, H, (1966). *Beyond Welfare.* Holt, Rinehart & Winston Inc., New York.

Chapter 3

Why Surfers Should Be Fed: The Crazy-Lazy Challenge

Philippe Van Parijs

Excerpts from Van Parijs, P. (1991). Why Surfers Should Be Fed. *Philosophy and Public Affairs*, 20 (2), 101–131.

In 1971, Hawaii established a one-year residency requirement for welfare entitlement. This measure was directed against so-called welfare hippies, who had been arriving in considerable numbers to take advantage of the beaches and of a comparatively generous assistance law. As Hawaii senator Wadsworth Yee eloquently put it: "There must be no parasites in paradise."[1] Senator Yee's confidence in his attitude would have been further boosted had he been able to read one of John Rawls's most recent articles. For what Rawls suggests is that one should add leisure time to his well-known list of social primary goods, precisely in order to be able to handle this sort of situation in a manner Senator Yee would have found congenial. The extra leisure enjoyed by those unwilling to work "would be stipulated as equivalent to the index of primary goods of the least advantaged. So those who surf all day off Malibu must find a way to support themselves and would not be entitled to public funds (Rawls, 1988)."

What I want to argue in this chapter is that Senator Yee was unfair to the welfare hippies, and that John Rawls is being unfair to the Malibu surfers. More precisely, I shall argue that a defensible *liberal* theory of justice, that is, one that is truly committed to an equal concern for all and to nondiscrimination among conceptions of the good life, does justify, under appropriate factual conditions, a substantial *Unconditional Basic Income.*

For the sake of this argument, I shall simply take it for granted that a defensible liberal conception of social justice, as characterized, needs to be *real-libertarian,* that is, must *maximin* – possibly subject to some constraints – people's *real freedom*, that is, the means they require for the pursuit of their conception of the good life, whatever that is. By "maximin" I mean that a strong priority is being given to the real freedom of those with the least amount of real freedom. This characterization is meant to be broad enough not to exclude the lexicographic variant of the maximin (or leximin), indeed, to accommodate a formula that would allow for significant increases in the real freedom of some of the better-off at the cost of a negligible decrease in the real freedom of the worst-off. But it does rule out a wide range of more egalitarian and more aggregative embodiments of the liberal

From Van Parijs, P. (1991). Why Surfers Should Be Fed. *Philosophy and Public Affairs*, 20 (2), 101–131. Reprinted with permission of John Wiley & Sons Ltd.

Basic Income: An Anthology of Contemporary Research, First Edition. Edited by Karl Widerquist, José A. Noguera, Yannick Vanderborght, and Jurgen De Wispelaere.

notion of equal concern. The characterization of "real freedom," on the other hand, is meant to leave open, at this stage, interpretations in terms of primary goods (qua background conditions and all-purpose means), capabilities, resources, opportunities, access to advantage, endowments, and so on. What it does rule out is welfarist accounts of the distribuendum a liberal should select. My claim is that the most sensible formulation of the real-libertarian conception of justice thus defined justifies, under appropriate factual conditions, the granting of a substantive Unconditional Income.

The best-known instance of such a conception is provided by John Rawls's Difference Principle in its original formulation, that is, the requirement that socioeconomic advantages (income and wealth, powers and prerogatives, the social bases of self-respect) should be maximinned, that is, distributed in such a way that the least advantaged end up with at least as many such advantages as the least advantaged would end up with under any alternative arrangement.

To understand the nature of this bias, consider Crazy and Lazy, two identically talented but rather differently disposed characters. Crazy is keen to earn a high income and works a lot for that purpose. Lazy is far less excited by the prospect of a high income and has decided to take it easy. With the Basic Income at the highest feasible level, as our interpretation of the "Rawlsian" criterion recommends, Crazy is rather miserable, because her net income falls far short of the income she would like to have. Lazy, however, is blissful. When added to the small income he earns, the grant he receives is more than sufficient to cover what he regards as his material needs. Does not the high grant justified by the "Rawlsian" criterion illegitimately discriminate against Crazy in favor of Lazy? Should one not, from a real-libertarian point of view, lower the grant to the point at which Crazy (who would pay less in tax) would be no less happy, no less successful in the pursuit of her conception of the good life, than Lazy (who would then be receiving a smaller grant)?

Underlying this phrasing of the objection, however, is the supposition that it is welfare, not some index of real freedom, that needs to be maximinned. But this is emphatically rejected by those committed to some form of real-libertarianism, usually on the ground that it would involve discrimination in favor of those with more expensive tastes.[2] The less happy Crazy is with the money she earns – which is already quite a bit more than what Lazy gets – the more money she should be allowed to have according to the criterion implicit in the objection. But if one assumes, as real-libertarians insist one must, that people can be held responsible for their tastes, letting Crazy get a higher income because she is less happy than others is illegitimate. It amounts to giving her more means than others have for the pursuit of her conception of the good life, *whatever this may be*, even though it does not make her better equipped for the pursuit of her conception of the good life *as it is* than others are for the pursuit of *their* conceptions of the good life. From a real-libertarian standpoint, Crazy can be left with more income than Lazy only if it helps increase the level of the grant, but not, as would here be the case, at the expense of a decrease in that level, and hence a worsening of the fate of the least advantaged. So far, the "Rawlsian" criterion is vindicated.

[However] Rawls's revised Difference Principle does not provide what we are looking for. It does not enable the real-libertarian approach to select a nonarbitrary "neutral" point which would not discriminate against either Crazy or Lazy. Should we give up? This would be premature. Ronald Dworkin's notion of equality of (external) resources provides us with exactly what we need. Let us see how, by returning once again to Lazy and Crazy.

In order to generate the level of income she wants to reach, it is safe to assume and crucial to notice, Crazy needs certain resources external to her talents, say a plot of land.

Endowing (identically talented) Crazy and Lazy with equal plots of land certainly constitutes one nondiscriminatory allocation of real freedom between them. But if this endowment is not tradable, if they are both stuck with it, this allocation cannot be optimal from a real-libertarian standpoint. For it will not give either Crazy or Lazy the highest attainable level of real freedom. Crazy may be desperate to use more than her plot of land, while Lazy would not mind being deprived of some or even all of his in exchange for part of what Crazy would produce with it. This directly yields the following suggestion. There is a nonarbitrary and generally positive legitimate level of Basic Income that is determined by the per capita value of society's external resources and must be entirely financed by those who appropriate these resources. If Lazy gives up the whole of his plot of land, he is entitled to an unconditional grant at a level that corresponds to the value of that plot. Crazy, on the other hand, can be viewed as receiving this same grant, but as owing twice its amount because of appropriating both Lazy's share of land and her own. Thus, in our society of Crazies and Lazies, the legitimate level of Basic Income is just the endogenously determined value of their equal tradable right to land.[3]

Would such a Basic Income be high? The total value of what gets officially bequeathed or donated in societies such as ours can be estimated at about 10 to 15% of national income. And the maximum sustainable Basic Income that can be financed on this basis will most probably fall far short of a per capita share of this value, owing to the adverse impact of taxation on the propensity to save, conserve, and so on.[4] Is there any way of expanding the legitimate tax base?

But suppose now that we are in a ***non-Walrasian economy***, that is, that for some reason, the labor market does not tend to clear. This may be because of obstacles to perfect competition, such as minimum wage legislation or union monopolies. But it may also be due to mechanisms that are consistent with perfect competition, such as those highlighted by the so-called insider-outsider and efficiency-wage theories of involuntary unemployment. Both sets of theories generate the conclusion that even in a competitive context, firms will pay their employees higher wages than those they could get away with by hiring equally skilled unemployed workers. According to the insider-outsider approach, even in the absence of collective organization, workers can durably claim a wage that significantly exceeds the market-clearing level because of the bargaining power they derive from the existence of hiring, training, and firing costs. According to the efficiency-wage approach, it is in the firm's interest to pay its workers more than the market-clearing wage because of a positive causal link between wages and labor productivity. In most variants, this rests on the assumption that workers shirk less if the cost to them of losing their job is higher. In other variants, it rests on the alternative assumption that workers will be motivated to perform better by the feeling that their employer is paying them more than would have been strictly necessary.[5] Thus, if any variant of either of these two approaches is correct, even a perfectly competitive economy would be non-Walrasian in the sense indicated.

Suppose further that in the context of such an economy, wealth has been distributed in impeccably equal fashion. It is then obviously impossible to say that the employed and the (identically skilled) unemployed enjoy equal access to the means required for the pursuit of their conception of the good life. In a non-Walrasian economy, in other words, people's endowment is not exhaustively described by their wealth (in the usual sense) and their skills: the holding of a job constitutes a third type of resource.[6] How can equality of resources be conceived in this modified context? One obvious suggestion is to proceed in exactly the same way as with external wealth. In the case of scarce land, we gave each member of the society concerned a tradable entitlement to an equal share of that land,

and the resource-equalizing level of the Basic Income was given by the per capita competitive value of the available land. Similarly, in the case of scarce jobs, let us give each member of the society concerned a tradable entitlement to an equal share of those jobs.[7] The resource-equalizing level of the (additional) Basic Income will then similarly be given by the per capita competitive value of the available jobs. If involuntary unemployment is high, the corresponding Basic Income will be high. If all unemployment is voluntary, no additional Basic Income is justified by this procedure.

If this is indeed the correct procedure, room is made for a sizable increase in the level of Basic Income that is warranted on real-libertarian grounds. For it amounts to sharing among all the *employment rents* otherwise monopolized by those in employment. These rents are given by the difference between the income (and other advantages) the employed derive from their jobs, and the (lower) income they would need to get if the market were to clear. In a situation of persistent massive unemployment, there is no doubt that the sum total of these rents would greatly swell the amount available for financing the grant.[8] And it is then no longer ludicrous to suggest that the nondiscriminatory concern with people's access to the means for the pursuit of their conceptions of the good life, the maximinning of real freedom, should demand that people be given an adequate Basic Income. Not, of course, under any circumstance, but *inter alia* under those circumstances – affluent societies with high rates of unemployment – in which a popular demand for Basic Income has been taking shape, under the pressure of a deep feeling of injustice. I say *inter alia* because, as soon as there are several types of jobs, the existence of employment rents no longer needs to be coextensive with involuntary unemployment: there may be huge employment rents even if everyone has a job, because many people with lousy jobs may be willing and able to do other existing jobs far more attractive (financially or intrinsically) than theirs at the going wage. What is crucial to my argument is the existence of large employment rents, as manifested by the presence of envy over job endowments, and not the fact that many people are without a job at all. The conclusion, therefore, fully applies to affluent countries, such as the United States, in which the rate of unemployment is comparatively low, just as much as to western Europe.

In practice, of course, it is impossible to organize an auction for each type of job in order to assess the rent associated with it, and capture as much of it as is worth capturing for the sake of maximizing the tax yield. The cruder method that simply consists in taxing jobs as a function of their wages is thus a handy second-best. The right of exit – the absence of involuntary *employment* – will guarantee that no job has a negative rent associated with it. And powerful mechanisms – collective bargaining, several variants of the efficiency-wage mechanism – will make sure that some rents keep reappearing, whatever the tax rate. Some people will of course lose out in the process: part of the rent they initially appropriated will be eroded or even disappear altogether as a result of their losing their job. But this is all right, as far as maximin real freedom is concerned, as long as the tax yield is being increased, and hence also the absolute share of the worst-off in the sum total of employment rents. We thus end up with a far higher Basic Income than seemed possible under the Dworkinian criterion. Indeed, for all practical purposes, we cannot be that far from what would follow from our initial "Rawlsian" criterion, which simply demanded that the absolute level of the Basic Income be maximized, without any restriction on the tax base.

Let me now return, by way of conclusion, to the welfare hippies and Malibu surfers with whom I started. Does justice require that they be fed? Somewhat more accurately, does liberal justice entitle them – no questions asked, no strings attached – to an income sufficient for them to feed themselves? If my argument is correct, it certainly does, at least in a society that is affluent enough to durably afford an Unconditional Income at that level.[9] For if liberal justice consists, as I have taken for granted it does, in maximinning the real freedom to pursue the realization of one's conception of the good life, those who take an unfair share of society's resources are not those who opt for such a low-production, low-consumption lifestyle. They are people like myself and most of my readers, who, thanks to the attractive job they were given, appropriate a huge employment rent.

Thus, it *is* just, contra John Rawls and Senator Yee, that Malibu surfers be fed, even though they will no doubt have to do their bit of productive work if they want to buy fancy surfboards or live in Malibu mansions. Moreover, [. . .] feeding them does not go against the widely held view that it is "unfair for able-bodied people to live off the labor of others." For this is a serious misdescription of what Malibu surfers are doing if all they live off is their share, or less than their share, of rents which would otherwise be monopolized by those who hold a rich society's productive jobs.

As often happens, the conclusions reached for the hard cases really matter only because of the a fortiori claims they warrant. While futile if it had no implication beyond Malibu surfers and their likes, the argument of this chapter, if correct, derives its practical importance from its direct relevance to the fate of an affluent society's unskilled workers, its excluded youth, its dependent housewives, its double-shift parents, its long-term unemployed. By challenging their resignation, by providing their revolt with intellectual backing, by immunizing their demands against a number of misguided or ill-intentioned objections, it may effectively help them to successfully stake their legitimate claims.

Notes

1. The story is told by Daniel P. Moynihan (1973).
2. See, e.g., Dworkin (1981a) and Rawls (1982) for typical critiques of welfarism on this ground.
3. Or, within the framework of Dworkin's parable, it is the expression, in income terms, of the value of the equal amount of clamshells each immigrant receives in order to bid for the resources found on the island. See Dworkin (1981b).
4. To get an idea of how universally far from 100% taxation tax systems have remained, just compare to the previous figure the observation that the total yield from inheritance and gift taxation is about 0.3% of GNP in Belgium, and that the total yield from these transfer taxes and annual wealth taxes is in no OECD country higher than in Norway, where it corresponds to 0.5% of GNP. See Sandford (1982), p. 205, on the basis of 1975 figures.
5. See Lindbeck and Snower (1985) and Akerlof and Yellen (1986) for useful surveys of microeconomic equilibrium unemployment theories in general, and efficiency-wage theories in particular, respectively. It is this sort of theory that I shall primarily have in mind in the remainder of this chapter. Insider-outsider and efficiency-wage models have the great advantage, in the present context, of contradicting the common claim that the resource inequality this section is concerned with would go away if, as those who make this claim usually recommend, the labor market were left to take care of itself.
6. I develop elsewhere (Van Parijs, 1987) the relevance of such job assets for a theory of social classes.
7. Such a job voucher system is suggested, independently of Dworkin's auction-based notion of equal resources, in two stimulating articles by Bert Hamminga (1983, 1988).
8. For relevant data about the empirical size of employment rents, see Schor and Bowles (1987).
9. And subject to a qualification relating to the treatment of handicaps and other inequalities of talents. See Van Parijs (1990).

References

Akerlof, G.A. and Yellen, J.L. (1986). Introduction to *Efficiency Wage Models of the Labor Market.* Cambridge University Press, Cambridge and New York, pp. 1–22.

Dworkin, R. (1981a). What Is Equality? Part I: Equality of Welfare. *Philosophy* & *Public Affairs*, 10 (3), 185–246, sec. 8.

Dworkin, R. (1981b). What Is Equality? Part 2: Equality of Resources. *Philosophy* & *Public Affairs*, 10 (4), 283–345.

Hamminga, B. (1983). Opstaan voor iemand misstaat niemand. *Maandschrift Economie*, 47, 395–410.

Hamminga, B. (1988). Arbeid en moraal in de spiegel van een utopie. In W. Goddijn (ed.) *Aftellen tot 2000.* Tilburg University Press, Tilburg, pp. 4–25.

Lindbeck, A. and Snower, D.J. (1985). Explanations of Unemployment. *Oxford Review of Economic Policy*, I, 34–59.

Moynihan, D.P. (1973). *The Politics of a Guaranteed Income: The Nixon Administration and the Family Assistance Plan.* Random House, New York, pp. 32–34.

Rawls, J. (1982). Social Unity and Primary Goods. In A. Sen and B. Williams (eds) *Utilitarianism and Beyond.* Cambridge University Press, Cambridge, pp. 159–186, sec. 4.

Rawls, J. (1988). The Priority of Right and Ideas of the Good. *Philosophy* & *Public Affairs*, 17 (4), 257 n.7.

Sandford, C.T. (1982). International Trends in the Taxation of Capital. In D. Kessler, A. Masson, and D. Strauss-Kahn (eds) *Accumulation et répartition des patrimonies.* Economica, Paris, p. 205.

Schor, J.B. and Bowles, S. (1987). Employment Rents and the Incidence of Strikes. *Review of Economics and Statistics*, 69, 584–592.

Van Parijs, P. (1987). A Revolution in Class Theory. *Politics and Society*, 15, 453–482.

Van Parijs, P. (1990). Equal Endowments as Undominated Diversity. *Alternatives to Welfarism*, special issue of *Recherches economiques de Louvain*, 56, 327–356.

Chapter 4
Optional Freedoms

Elizabeth Anderson

Excerpts from Anderson, E. (2001) Optional Freedoms. In P. Van Parijs (ed.) *What's Wrong with a Free Lunch?* Beacon Press, Boston, pp. 75–79.

Philippe Van Parijs advocates the provision of the maximum sustainable Unconditional Basic Income (UBI). His defense rests on a political philosophy that he calls "real libertarianism." I shall argue that Van Parijs's real libertarianism cannot justify a UBI, but that a UBI may have some promise as a supplementary part of a larger social welfare package that is justified on other grounds.

A policy to enact and maximize a UBI, conceived as a means to real libertarianism, suffers from three defects. First, it favors distributing income over direct in-kind provision of, or vouchers for, particular goods, such as health care or education. The preference for income rather than in-kind transfers reflects the commitment of real libertarianism to promoting freedom, conceived as a generic good; the real libertarian urges that we provide people with the resources they need to achieve their aims, whatever those aims are. Thus it gives no special priority to freedom from disease over the freedom to idle: freedom is freedom. As an account of what we owe to one another, that seems misguided. What we owe are not the means to generic freedom but the social conditions of the particular, concrete freedoms that are instrumental to life in relations of equality with others. We owe each other the rights, institutions, social norms, public goods, and private resources that people need to avoid oppression (social exclusion, violence, exploitation, and so forth) and to exercise the capabilities necessary for functioning as equal citizens in a democratic state.[1] From a social point of view, then, we should grant higher priority to securing certain goods, such as education, over others, such as surfing opportunities, even if some individuals prefer surfing to schooling. A maximal UBI risks overproviding optional freedoms at a substantial sacrifice – large enough to compromise social equality – to the particular freedoms we owe one another.

Second, in providing equal levels of income to all, the UBI does not adjust for the fact that, due to variations in internal traits, social roles, and other circumstances, some people are better able to convert income to freedoms than others.[2] Disabled people typically

Basic Income: An Anthology of Contemporary Research, First Edition. Edited by Karl Widerquist, José A. Noguera, Yannick Vanderborght, and Jurgen De Wispelaere.

require more resources to achieve equivalent freedoms – to move around, to get access to information, and so forth – than those who are not disabled. People who engage in unpaid dependent care work also require more resources to achieve equivalent freedoms to those who do not take care of dependents. (For example, to be free to participate in the realm of paid labor, they need access to alternative sources of care for their dependents while they work.) The UBI therefore best serves the interests of healthy adults who care for no one besides themselves. In taking income, rather than capabilities, to be the relevant space in which equality is to be pursued, the UBI assumes as the norm for human beings the perspective of the healthy, egoistic adult.

Third, in granting a Basic Income that is not conditioned on the willingness of the able to work, the UBI promotes freedom without responsibility, and thereby both offends and undermines the ideal of social obligation that undergirds the welfare state. A UBI would not only inspire a segment of the able population – largely young, healthy, unattached adults – to abjure work for a life of idle fun. It would also depress the willingness to produce and pay taxes of those who resent having to support them.

To deal with the first two problems, Van Parijs could argue that the UBI should be maximized only after the social provision of particularly important freedoms, such as public education and medical care, was secured, and that supplementary programs could give extra help to people with "special" needs. In the U.S. context, at least, this contrast between universal and "special" programs has typically led to underfinanced, stigmatizing support for those regarded as "special" (for example, contrast Medicare with Medicaid). But this contrast is simply an artifact of an accounting system that measures equality in terms of income rather than particular capabilities. From the standpoint of the particular capabilities people need to avoid oppression and stand as equals in society – things such as literacy, mobility, and health – everyone has the same needs.

The social insurance programs that form the foundation of modern welfare states constitute the terms of a great social contract. Like any insurance, they purchase a right to provision from others conditional on a willingness to provide for others, if one is able. Like any insurance, its recipients have an obligation to mitigate damages in recognition of the burdens they place on others. The social-democratic contract recognizes that over the course of a whole life, we are all dependent on caretaking by others for long periods in childhood, sickness, and old age, and some are dependent for their whole lives. This intergenerational contract is sustained and legitimated only by a recognition on the part of the able of an obligation to work and provide for the dependent and those who care for them. It is hard to see how such a contract can be sustained by a system that advertises as one of its virtues that it would free the able to live in idleness.

Suppose, however, we detached the UBI from its real-libertarian rationale. Could a UBI play a supplemental role in a welfare state founded on social insurance principles? Here we face a set of tradeoffs, with respect both to administrability and legitimacy. A UBI would not target expenditures to those who need them most, and would therefore both underprovide benefits and waste public expenditures on those who don't need them. Given high resistance to additional tax burdens, especially in North America, the risk is that such waste comes at the cost of other programs that could do more for the disadvantaged, the disabled, dependents, and those who care for them.

On the other hand, a UBI saves on the substantial administrative costs of targeting expenditures to these groups, and avoids the temptation to add demeaning and intrusive conditions to the receipt of public funds to ensure that the needy are "deserving." A UBI would have the advantage of being universal, and therefore undercut resentment of needy recipients, but the disadvantage of being unconditional, thereby inspiring resentment of undeserving recipients. It is telling that the only current example of a UBI is based on the distribution of Alaskan oil royalties: Americans, at least, don't resent unearned income, as long as it is attached to property ownership. This suggests that the legitimation problem in the United States could be solved by funding the UBI through revenues collected from the use of public property: the leasing of national forests and rangeland, oil and mining royalties, the periodic auction of temporary broadcasting licenses, and pollution taxes. Such a strategy would, however, ground the UBI on a principle of ownership rather than need, and also create public incentives to permit increased despoilment of public goods for the sake of private, if evenly distributed, gains. The main question is whether programs more carefully tailored to the needs of the disabled, the disadvantaged, dependents, and their caretakers – and to the particular freedoms we owe one another – would be more effective in delivering the promised goods, and win greater acceptance, than a UBI. I am not persuaded that the costs to the goals of social democracy would be worth the gains provided by a UBI, but I am open to empirical evidence to the contrary.

Notes

1. In defense of this thesis, see Anderson (1999).
2. Amartya Sen has consistently made this point in opposition to egalitarian views that regard resources as the relevant space of equality. See, for example, Sen (1992).

References

Anderson, E. (1999). What is the Point of Equality? *Ethics* 109 (2), 287–337.
Sen, A. (1992). *Inequality Reexamined.* Harvard University Press, Cambridge, MA.

Chapter 5
A Republican Right to Basic Income

Philip Pettit

Originally published as A Republican Right to Basic Income?
Basic Income Studies, 2 (2) (December 2007).

Introduction

The Basic Income proposal provides everyone in a society, as an unconditional right, with access to a certain level of income. Introducing such a right is bound to raise questions of institutional feasibility. Would it lead too many people to opt out of the workforce, for example? And even if it did not, could a constitution that allowed some members of the society to do this – at whatever relative cost – prove acceptable in a society of mutually reciprocal, equally positioned members? I assume in this short chapter, however, that none of these problems is insurmountable. I concentrate on the question of how far republicanism makes room for justifying something like a right to Basic Income, assuming that there are no problems of this kind with introducing and establishing such a right.

Any satisfactory argument for a Basic Income should satisfy two desiderata. First is that of ***adequacy***: the argument should establish a right to an intuitively adequate level of income.[1] Second is that of ***independence***: the argument should establish a claim to a non-nullifiable, nonstigmatizing Basic Income.

These desiderata should be relatively uncontroversial. The defenders of a Basic Income have all had an adequate income in mind, by some intuitive criterion of adequacy. And they have wanted to make such an income available as a right that is not subject to provisos about existing means, employment history, willingness to perform certain services, or anything of the kind (Van Parijs, 1995; 2001). The attraction of republican political theory is that it underwrites a Basic Income scheme argument that satisfies both of these desiderata better than do alternative schemes.

Utilitarian and Liberal Alternatives

Utilitarian theory makes a very good case for a financially adequate Basic Income, but it is not clear that it could satisfy the independence desideratum. If the government used the

Pettit, P. (2007). A Republican Right to Basic Income? *Basic Income Studies*, 2 (2) (December).

Basic Income: An Anthology of Contemporary Research, First Edition. Edited by Karl Widerquist, José A. Noguera, Yannick Vanderborght, and Jurgen De Wispelaere.

utilitarian criterion in making distributional decisions, it might turn out by happy accident that promoting utility would argue for giving each a Basic Income. But, that would not mean that people would enjoy Basic Income as a right; they would enjoy it only so long as this was for the utilitarian best.

A plausible liberal argument for a right to a Basic Income must offer a *liberal* reason – related to the cause of liberty rather than utility – for establishing a legal right to a Basic Income in every society. And that liberal reason ought to provide a more plausible ground than the utilitarian counterpart for establishing and maintaining such a regime.

First, let liberty be understood, in the spirit of contemporary liberalism, as the absence of interference by others. In particular, let it be understood as the absence of interference in the basic liberties: the absence of interference, roughly, in the harmless exercise of liberties of belief, expression, association, ownership, and the like. The cause of promoting the traditional basic liberties is unlikely to argue, in that case, for a regime in which everyone has a right to a Basic Income. Possessing those liberties will be maximized by inhibiting those who would interfere. And it is unclear what role a Basic Income policy would play in such a regime of inhibition.

Philippe Van Parijs (1995) directs us to a second, more promising way of arguing for a Basic Income right from within a broadly liberal vision. He argues that we should reject the distinction between the absence of maltreatment by others that allows us the possession of liberal liberties and the absence of natural or social obstacles that gives value to the possession of those liberties, enabling people to exercise them with greater ease or in a greater range of cases (Rawls, 1971). We should treat intentional obstruction and unintentional limitation on a par – we should see each as a variety of liberty-reducing interference. Since each reduces our choices, they are equally opposed, as Van Parijs says, to "real freedom." As we establish rights to legal protection against intentional interference, we should also establish legal rights against having to endure remediable limitations. And such rights might well include the right to a Basic Income.

But even this derivation of a Basic Income right is not fully satisfactory. For it is implausible to treat unintentional limitation as being as bad, in the ledger of liberty, as is intentional interference. If someone stands in my way, that's a different sort of challenge to my liberty than the challenge provided by the tree that has fallen in my path. If someone threatens me with harm if I take a particular action, that is a different sort of challenge than one which occurs when someone warns me that I will suffer harm, say from natural causes, should I take that action. It is entirely plausible to provide people with rights against intentionally imposed harm from others but not so plausible to provide them with rights against unhappy twists of fate, if the rights are supposed to be freedom-based.

We see that utilitarian premises do not provide an argument for a suitably entrenched right to a Basic Income. The premises invoked in this liberal approach might argue for such a right but are not suitably compelling. This approach is indifferent to the contrast, marked in traditional discussions of liberty, between the ill of being restricted by natural obstacles and the evil of being subject to the intentional constraints of others.

The Republican Turn

Republican political theory can make a firmer and more persuasive case for a right to Basic Income than any of these approaches.[2] In particular, it can satisfy not just the adequacy desideratum but also the independence desideratum – that is, the desideratum that utilitarianism would fail and that liberalism would satisfy only at the cost of rigging the requirements of freedom.

The basic distinction between republican and liberal political theory is that the former construes freedom, not as the absence of interference by others, but as the absence of a certain sort of dominating control. Let us say that others control me to the extent that their presence in my life raises the probability of my acting according to their tastes. And let us set aside the reasoned and nondominating variety of control exercised when others give me advice or information on a take-it-or-leave-it basis. Let us focus instead on *unreasoned* control.

Unreasoned control – henceforth, called "control" – may be exercised through interference, such as when others remove an option, replace it with a penalized alternative, or reduce my capacity to choose rationally, whether by exploiting a weakness or inducing false beliefs. But control may also manifest without such active interference. Suppose that others are in a position of being able to interfere in any of those ways that gets me to behave according to their tastes. And imagine that they decide to interfere only on a need-for-action basis. They leave me alone so long as I behave according to their taste, but they are ready to interfere if I begin to deviate from that pattern – or if their taste changes.

Such agents control what I do, whether or not I realize it, even when they find no reason to interfere actively. They exercise control by invigilating my behavior, monitoring it with a view to interfering when necessary – and only when necessary. If I manage to act as I choose, I am lucky; I happen to choose as they want me to choose. Whatever I do, then, I do by their implicit leave. In the words of the old republican complaint, I act only *cum permissu*: only with permission.

The view that unreasoned control takes away liberty and that it may assume a wholly invigilatory character is just the view, in more traditional terms, that liberty requires non-domination. I will escape domination only to the extent that I occupy a protected position and am empowered against such control on the part of others. My freedom will consist in that protected and empowered status.

Let liberty be restricted to the possession of the basic liberties: that is, let those liberties define the domain of freedom and let freedom require the mere possession of those liberties (Pettit, 2008). We can still argue for a right to a Basic Income, so long as the possession of those liberties is taken to require not just the absence of interference by others in the relevant areas of choice but also the absence of unreasoned control – the absence of domination (Pettit, 1997; Skinner, 1998; Viroli, 2002; Pettit, 2007c). The cause of promoting basic liberties in this republican sense does markedly better than the alternative justifications we have been considering.

The argument is straightforward. Others will control me, if only in the merely invigilatory fashion, only to the extent that the division of powers between us means that they can interfere with me at will – that is, without prevention – and at tolerable cost, that is, with a degree of impunity. If I am not assured a Basic Income, there will be many areas where the wealthier could interfere with me at tolerable cost, without their being confronted by legal prevention of that interference.

Suppose there are just a few employers and many available employees, and that times are hard. In those conditions I and those who like me will not be able to command a decent wage: a wage that will enable us to function properly in society. And in those conditions it will be equally true that we would be defenseless against our employers' petty abuse or their power to arbitrarily dismiss us. Other protections, such as those that strong trade unions might provide, are possible against such alien control. But the most effective of all protections, and one that should complement other measures available, would be one's ability to leave employment and fall back on a basic wage available unconditionally from the state.

Next suppose that you live in conditions where you, and perhaps your children, depend financially on your husband. In such conditions he is likely to control you, even though he never resorts to violence or other abuse. He may let you act as you please within certain limits, while being disposed to stop you – at the limit, by leaving you – if you breach those limits. You would live under your husband's control, almost certainly straining to keep within his restrictions, unless there is an effective, financially viable alternative such as that which a Basic Income would provide. Other protections may be available here as in the first case – for example, he may be legally required to provide maintenance should you separate – but these are unlikely to be equally effective and in any case they will be powerfully supplemented by a Basic Income.

Such examples show it to be entirely plausible that promoting the resilient, republican possession of basic liberties argues for establishing a legal right to a Basic Income. Such a right would mean that people had adequate income for functioning properly in society. And that income would mean that people would not have to beg the favor of the powerful, or even of the counter-clerk.

However, why give the Basic Income right to all, not to only those in need? A number of considerations might argue for this provision. A universal right of the sort imagined would resist electoral pressure for change better than would a needs-tested right, since it would benefit everyone in common, thus being a more entrenched and firmer bulwark against domination. A universal right would mean that those who rely on the Basic Income – distinct from the independently wealthy – will not have to assert their right on the grounds of being a class apart: people who depend on others' goodwill and are easier targets of control and domination. And a universal right symbolizes the fundamental equality of all in relation to the collective provisions of government; only some will depend on the Basic Income that all receive, but all can see that the income is there to depend on, should they themselves fall on hard times.

Would government itself exercise dominating control in establishing a Basic Income regime? Would it do so, for example, in relation to the wealthy who are the net creditors in the effected redistribution? As a matter of logic, the liberal government that interferes with people in order to reduce overall interference will have to take liberty-as-noninterference away from some in order to increase such liberty overall. But the government that interferes with people in order to reduce overall domination may not have to take liberty-as-nondomination away from any in order to increase such liberty overall. There is no similar necessity of logic here.

If I can stop a certain pattern of interference that you practice, or if I can make it too costly for you to continue it, then my allowing it does not mean that I am dominated. If I allow you to keep the liquor cabinet key or to hide my cigarettes, you still interfere with me when you act under that permission. But your interference will not be control or domination; the interference will be controlled or nonarbitrary.

Does the interference that government might practice in establishing a right to a Basic Income count as a controlling or dominating form of interference in the lives of those of us who are relative losers? Under appropriate conditions, it can be held to be controlled and nonarbitrary.

Let the activity of government in establishing a Basic Income right have to be supported by considerations that all of us explicitly or implicitly take to be relevant in public decision-making. And if it is not uniquely supported by considerations of that kind, let it be chosen from among acceptable candidates on the basis of some procedure – say, a parliamentary vote or even a referendum – that is supported by such considerations. To the extent that such conditions obtain, one can plausibly say that the measure introduced is an exercise of controlled interference, and so not dominating in itself (Pettit, 2007a; 2007b). The wealthy individuals who are relatively disadvantaged by the measure will not themselves exercise the required checking. But the co-governed people as a whole will exercise such checking; and if they do so by implementing a regime of common reasons or values, then they can be thought of as acting in a way that does not discriminate between wealthy and poor.

Conclusion

Utilitarianism fails to provide premises that would persuasively support a Basic Income right, because they would not argue for a suitably firm and universal right. Liberalism, even the left variety of liberalism, would not persuasively support a Basic Income right because the premises it has to invoke for the purpose, given a conception of freedom as noninterference, are not suitably compelling; they make freedom depend, not just on the possession of the basic liberties, but on the absence of natural obstacles to the exercise of those liberties.

Only republicanism serves well in the required role. The premises it invokes are inherently and independently persuasive, deriving from a well-established conception of freedom as nondomination. And, absent problems of feasibility, they give us plausible grounds for arguing in favor of a dispensation in which people enjoy a universal right to a Basic Income.

Notes

1. For an attractive way of identifying an adequate level, refer to Amartya Sen's notion of basic capabilities (Sen, 1985; Nussbaum, 1992).
2. For a congenial, republican case for Basic Income – which I had not known about when I wrote this piece – see Raventós (2007).

References

Nussbaum, M. (1992). Human Functioning and Social Justice. *Political Theory*, 20 (2), 202–246.

Pettit, P. (1997). *Republicanism: A Theory of Freedom and Government.* Oxford University Press, Oxford.

Pettit, P. (2007a). *Examen a Zapatero.* Temas de Hoy, Madrid.

Pettit, P. (2007b). Joining the Dots. In M. Smith, H.G. Brennan, R.E. Goodin and F.C. Jackson (eds) *Common Minds: Themes From the Philosophy of Philip Pettit.* Oxford University Press, Oxford.

Pettit, P. (2007c). Republican Liberty: Three Axioms, Four Theorems. In C. Laborde and J. Maynor (eds) *Republicanism and Political Theory.* Blackwell, Oxford.

Pettit, P. (2008). The Basic Liberties. In M. Kramer (ed.) *Essays on H.L.A. Hart*. Oxford University Press, Oxford.

Raventós, D. (2007). *Basic Income: The Material Conditions of Freedom*. Pluto Press, London.

Rawls, J. (1971). *A Theory of Justice*. Oxford University Press, Oxford.

Sen, A. (1985). *Commodities and Capabilities*. North-Holland, Amsterdam.

Skinner, Q. (1998). *Liberty Before Liberalism*. Cambridge University Press, Cambridge.

Van Parijs, P. (1995). *Real Freedom for All: What (If Anything) Can Justify Capitalism?* Clarendon Press, Oxford.

Van Parijs, P. (2001). A Basic Income for All. In J. Cohen and J. Rogers (eds) *What's Wrong With a Free Lunch?* Beacon Press, Boston.

Viroli, M. (2002). *Republicanism*. Hill and Wang, New York.

Chapter 6

Why We Demand a Basic Income

Karl Widerquist

Originally published as Why we demand an unconditional basic income: the ECSO freedom case. In A. Gosseries and Y. Vanderborght (eds) (2011). *Arguing about Justice: Essays for Philippe Van Parijs.*

Philippe Van Parijs's (1995) *Real Freedom for All: What (If Anything) Can Justify Capitalism?* makes a very thorough and challenging philosophical argument for Basic Income. But I believe that it has two important limitations that inhibit it from giving a compelling explanation why Basic Income supporters believe that support for the disadvantage must be not only universal but also *unconditional* and enough to meet an individual's basic needs. This chapter briefly discusses those limitations and then proposes an alternative argument for Basic Income that I believe relies on a more compelling concept of freedom, defined below as "freedom as effective control self-ownership" (ECSO freedom). This concept of freedom provides a stronger explanation why basic income must be universal, unconditional, and large enough to meet a person's basic needs.

Two Limitations to the Real Freedom Defense of Basic Income

Van Parijs's(1995) justification of Basic Income is founded on the notion of what he calls, "real freedom," the freedom to do whatever one might want to do. Van Parijs argues that the more resources people have available, the freer they are to do whatever they might want to do. The highest sustainable Unconditional Basic Income gets everyone access to as many resources as possible and leaves them free to do whatever they might want to do with those resources – even if what they want to do is to pursue leisure. One difficulty with this concept is that "the freedom to do whatever one might want to do" might not be the most compelling conception of freedom for society to promote and protect. But even as it is, the contention between the real-freedom-based argument and Basic Income has two important limitations.

The first limitation is that the concept of "real freedom" is so broad and hard to measure that it is unclear what kind of policy it supports (Barry, 2003). Everyone in a "real freedom"

From Widerquist, K. (2011). Why we demand an unconditional basic income: the ECSO freedom case. In A. Gosseries and Y. Vanderborght (eds) *Arguing about Justice: Essays for Philippe Van Parijs.* Presses Universitaires de Louvain, Louvain-la-Neuve, pp. 387–394. Reprinted with permission of Presses Universitaires de Louvain.

Basic Income: An Anthology of Contemporary Research, First Edition. Edited by Karl Widerquist, José A. Noguera, Yannick Vanderborght, and Jurgen De Wispelaere.

promoting society is entitled to something, but it is not clear whether that something is unconditional, basic, or an income. Van Parijs (1995: 35) specifically rules out any connection between Basic Income and basic needs, opting for the highest sustainable Basic Income, which can fall short or exceed the amount necessary to sustain a decent existence depending on various economic factors.

The highest sustainable Unconditional Basic Income makes people free to do some things that they might want to do but other kinds of government spending make people free to do other things they might want to do. A smaller income combined with other government services makes them free to do other things they might want to do. Devoting the highest sustainable level of taxation entirely to the provision of government services makes people free to do things they might want to do; a guaranteed job makes people free to do other things they might want to do; infrastructure makes people free to do other things they might want to do; conditional welfare programs make people free to do other things they might want to do.

It is difficult – and perhaps impossible – to measure which policy gives people the "most" real freedom (Barry, 2003). To give a definitive argument that the highest sustainable Basic Income provides the most real freedom, Van Parijs would need some theory of how to measure freedom and how to weigh one type of freedom against another. He would then need to give a definitive answer that the freedoms provided by the highest sustainable Basic Income add up to "more" than the freedoms provided by other government spending. I'm not convinced that it is possible to do so. If this can be done, it could turn out that real freedom justifies an Unconditional Basic Income, but it could also turn out that it justifies a very restrictive, conditional welfare state with strong funding of public infrastructure and services.

The second limitation of the real libertarian argument for Basic Income follows from the first. Because it does not give a compelling reason to show that individuals are unconditionally entitled to a cash income large enough to meet their basic needs, it does not provide a compelling reply to the reciprocity or exploitation objection to Basic Income. According to this objection, workers are needed to produce the income that will be distributed unconditionally. If recipients are not held to a reciprocal objection to help produce that income, they supposedly exploit the workers who do (White, 1997; van Donselaar, 2009). Although Van Parijs argues that Basic Income does not violate several definitions of exploitation, his central response to this objection relies on the concept of liberal neutrality. Basic Income gives people the opportunity to choose to work or not to work. These choices reflect two different notions of the good life, and a liberal government should be neutral between different individuals' notions of the good life.

This response is not sufficiently compelling because the reciprocity objection is not simply based on a desire to promote one version of the good life. It is based on a moral claim to resources. If one party has earned the right to use resources while another party refuses to do what is necessary to earn that right, neutrality is no reason to treat them both equally. Society should not be neutral between thieves and non-thieves. A more compelling argument for Basic Income has to explain why an Unconditional Basic Income does not violate – or why it is important enough to override – the reciprocity objection.

The following section explains a conception of freedom that I believe is intrinsically more compelling than real freedom. It shows how this conception of freedom can be used to make a clearer case that individuals are entitled to an income that is unconditional and sufficient to meet their basic needs. The final section shows how this argument for Basic Income provides a stronger reply to the reciprocity objection.

The ECSO Freedom Defense of Basic Income

My argument is based on a concept I call, "freedom as effective control self-ownership" (ECSO freedom). ECSO freedom is the effective power to accept or refuse active cooperation with other willing people (Widerquist, 2006). I believe that it is more compelling in itself than real freedom and that a case for Basic Income premised on ECSO freedom does not suffer from the two limitations in the real-freedom-based argument discussed above. ECSO freedom is defined in relation to self-ownership but it is a separate concept. It is narrower in some ways, and broader in other ways than self-ownership. It is narrower in that it concerns only the control aspects of self-ownership (as opposed to the income aspects). It is broader in that it involves the effective power (not merely the nominal right) to exercise "control self-ownership" (the control rights of self-ownership). I passively cooperate with other people if I simply stay out of their way. As long as any two people disagree about whether they're willing to get out of each other's way at any particular time, it is impossible for all passive cooperation to be voluntary. But it is possible for all active cooperation to be voluntary, if we each have the power to refuse interaction. It is not a certainty that some people must be forced to actively serve the interests of other people. If all people have an exit option, and the benefits to cooperation are sufficient, it is possible for all active human cooperation to be voluntary.

ECSO freedom is a theory of what I call "status freedom" as opposed to what I call "scalar freedom" or "freedom as a continuous variable." Although we do not have different words for these two meanings of freedom, the distinction is well understood in ordinary English. Scalar freedom is the absence of impediment, restriction, or interference. It treats freedom as a continuous variable, as a matter of degree as on a scale or a continuum. Status freedom captures another common definition of freedom: the absence of slavery, detention, or oppression. A conception of status freedom tries to capture the crucial distinction between whether an individual fits into the category of a free or an unfree person. Real freedom, along with freedom as noninterference, is a scalar freedom, under which a person can have more or less freedom, but it does not identify a cutoff between categories of free and unfree. A theory of status freedom is meant to identify the most important aspects of what it means to have the status of a free person. A theory of status freedom is not about counting the (possibly accountable) number of freedoms a person has, but identifying the most important freedoms, those that divide a free person from an unfree person such as a slave, a serf, or a subject of a totalitarian regime.

ECSO freedom has two components. A free person can interact with other willing people as they choose. A free person cannot be (directly or indirectly) forced to serve the interests of others. To have the first component a person must have the familiar civil rights of freedom of speech, movement, association, political participation, and so on.

To have the second component, the effective power to refuse unwanted cooperation, people need unconditional access to resources. Human beings are biological creatures who need a sufficient amount of food, water, and air to survive. They need shelter, a place to sleep, a place to stand, and a place to interact with other willing people. If someone can come between you and the minimum amount of resources you need to survive, not only do they directly interfere with your ability to live a decent and free life; they can also force you to do just about anything.

These basic needs are defined in an absolute and physical sense but they include the human need for interpersonal interaction and fulfilling them will require access to different goods at different times and places. See "The Physical Basis of Voluntary Trade" (Widerquist, 2010) for discussion of what level of Basic Income is required to meet basic needs. This argument also implies that society has a responsibility to make sure that a Basic Income high enough to meet basic needs is sustainable. See *Property and the Power to Say No* (Widerquist, 2006) for discussion of how to do that and what to do if it turns out to be impossible.

For millions of years, our ancestors had unconditional access to the resources they needed to survive. They were free to hunt and gather for themselves or with other willing people as they pleased, and no one would interfere with them. The Earth was their exit option.

The rules we live under today do not make most people free to refuse unwanted active cooperation with others. Land that was once free for all to use is now claimed by governments, businesses, and individuals. Most people reach adulthood with no direct access to the resources they need, they can only obtain resources by meeting conditions set by others – by employers or governments. They have the nominal right to refuse but they do not have the effective power to refuse; someone will interfere with anything they might do to support themselves (alone or in groups). They cannot work for themselves; they must work for a property owner or a government.

The preservation of this second component of ECSO freedom explains why individuals need an income that is unconditional and large enough to meet their basic needs. Such a policy is not simply desirable because taking leisure time to surf is something someone might want to do. It is needed because the power to refuse is essential to ensuring that *all of us* who work for others do so voluntarily.

People with an Unconditional Basic Income still have to buy things from property owners, but they are not forced to serve them. Government taxes property, distributes revenue to everyone, and presumably the propertyless use their money to purchase things from property owners. But this cannot be called a form of service *to* property owners. Suppose you agree to give me $50 and I agree to spend all of it in your store. Obviously, the whole of this transaction does not involve me serving you.

The power to refuse to work is important because working in a cash economy is very different from working for oneself directly with resources. With direct access to resources, a person works directly for her own goals. Without it a person must work for her employer's or her clients' goals all day to receive the cash to pursue her own goals when work is over. There is nothing wrong with working for cash as long as it is voluntary, but if the laws of the state put anyone in the position in which they have no direct access to resources, they give that person no choice but to work for someone who controls resources.

In a free society, with an economy built on truly voluntary trade between truly free individuals, it is unacceptable for any group of people to force others to serve them by taking control of all resources. That this force is indirect and systemic (rather than direct and individual) makes it no less powerful and threatening to freedom. It is not any particular employer's fault that the laws interfere with any independent use that propertyless people might make of resources. The government, which has the ultimate responsibility for making the rules of resource ownership, has the responsibility to make those rules in a way that respects the free status of each individual. That is, in a way that respects ECSO freedom. I argue elsewhere that although direct access to resources and in-kind benefits could conceivably provide the access to resources necessary to maintain this aspect of ECSO freedom, it is best protected in a modern market economy by an unconditional, in-cash Basic Income (Widerquist, 2010).

It is easy to see how this argument provides a much more compelling reason why benefits must be unconditional and at least enough to meet a person's basic needs. Basic Income is not about providing leisure for those who might want to pursue leisure. Basic Income provides an exit option that is an important component in protecting all people's standing as a free individual. It protects a worker from an unacceptable job. It protects a parent from a spouse who controls the family's access to resources. It protects a disabled person from an overly intrusive welfare state.

ECSO Freedom and Reciprocity

This argument for Basic Income is also better able to address the reciprocity objection. Rather than relying on a weak application of liberal neutrality, an argument based on ECSO freedom can show that the reciprocity objection is misplaced entirely. All able-bodied adults with the right knowledge can meet their own basic needs without working for property owners, if they are sufficiently free from interference. All an able-bodied individual needs from others to have ECSO freedom is a negative duty, a duty of forbearance. Others need only refrain from interfering with a sufficient amount of resources so that individuals can provide for themselves.

Our societies are badly failing in that duty. All the resources that a person might use to secure their own needs are claimed by property owners and governments. Basic Income, in this sense, is a replacement for the direct access to resources that our ancestors enjoyed. Basic Income is not "something for nothing:" individuals who receive it are held to the reciprocal obligation to respect other people's property claims.

Rather than relying on the neutrality principle to trump reciprocity, this argument employs the reciprocity principle *in defense* of Basic Income. Those who control resources are currently held to no reciprocal duty to compensate the propertyless for the loss of freedom created by the assignment of property rights over natural resources to some individuals and not others. Unless all property owners pay a rent sufficient to maintain an Unconditional Basic Income for everyone, they violate the reciprocity principle by indirectly forcing the propertyless to work for some member of the very group whose property claims interfere with their efforts to provide for themselves. To satisfy reciprocity the assumption of private property rights has to come with an obligation to contribute to an Unconditional Basic Income large enough to provide a reasonable exit option for everyone.

Conclusion

This chapter has argued four basic points. First, Van Parijs's real-freedom-based argument for Basic Income does not fully explain why Unconditional Basic Income must be unconditional, basic, or an income. Second, the real-freedom-based account doesn't present a compelling response to the reciprocity objection. Third, the ECSO-freedom-based argument provides a compelling reason why all individuals are entitled to an income that is unconditional and large enough to meet their basic needs. Fourth, the ECSO-freedom-based account provides a stronger response than the reciprocity objection.

References

Barry, B. (2003). Real Freedom and Basic Income. In A. Reeve and A. Williams (eds) *Real Libertarianism Assessed: Political Theory of Van Parijs.* Palgrave Macmillan, New York.

van Donselaar, G. (2009). *The Right to Exploit: Parasitism, Scarcity, Basic Income*. Oxford University Press, Oxford.

Van Parijs, P. (1995). *Real Freedom for All: What (If Anything) Can Justify Capitalism?* Oxford University Press, Oxford.

White, S. (1997). Liberal Equality, Exploitation, and the Case for an Unconditional Basic Income. *Political Studies*, 45 (2), 312–326.

Widerquist, K. (2006). *Property and the Power to Say No: A Freedom-Based Argument for Basic Income*. Doctoral thesis. The University of Oxford, Oxford.

Widerquist, K. (2010). The Physical Basis of Voluntary Trade. *Human Rights Review*, 11 (1), 83–103.

Part II
Justice

Introduction

Theories of Justice and Basic Income

Karl Widerquist

The "Freedom" section presented and discussed the most influential justification of Basic Income, that is, Van Parijs's "real libertarian" defense, which is heavily based on liberal-egalitarian values of individual rights, individual liberty, and equality. This section examines the justification of Basic Income more broadly. It presents articles looking at the role of Basic Income in promoting democratic citizenship and examining Basic Income from alternative traditions including left-libertarianism, libertarian-conservatism, Marxism, and communitarianism. As becomes clear when reading these essays, it is a curious feature of Basic Income that it can both unite people who subscribe to very different political theories, and divide people who subscribe otherwise to similar political theories.

Nicolaus Tideman and Peter Vallentyne (2001) discuss a left-libertarian justification for Basic Income in their article, "Left-Libertarianism and a Global Rent Payment." The main moral claims of left-libertarian theory are that all people have an equal right to natural resources and all people have a claim to self-ownership. Unlike Van Parijs's "real libertarianism," left-libertarianism focuses exclusively on natural resources for its redistributional base. Left-libertarians do not usually include things like labor market rents in the redistributional base as Van Parijs does. Tideman and Vallentyne discuss one way to put the right of equal access to natural resources into practice: charge private landholders rent for the privilege of holding land and redistribute that revenue as a universal Basic Income. Thus, each individual receives the monetary equivalent of one per capita share of the value of natural resources.

In "Guaranteed Income as a Replacement for the Welfare State," Charles Murray (2008) presents what he describes as a view of Basic Income from the libertarian right, but his article also reads like a conservative case for Basic Income. He argues that Basic Income will be more likely than the current social welfare system to lead people to embrace what he sees as a desirable version of the good life. He sees Basic Income as something that will make people stay in school longer, stay married, and seek to improve their lives through work.

In this brief excerpt from "A Capitalist Road to Communism," Robert van der Veen and Philippe Van Parijs (1986) argue that Basic Income (or "Guaranteed Income") can

---

Basic Income: An Anthology of Contemporary Research, First Edition. Edited by Karl Widerquist, José A. Noguera, Yannick Vanderborght, and Jurgen De Wispelaere.

establish the communist principle, "From each according to his abilities, to each according to his needs," in a capitalist economy without passing through state socialism. To the authors, this principle implies that the social product is distributed so that (i) everyone's needs are met and (ii) each individual's share of the social product is independent of his or her freely provided labor. No feature of his principle inherently requires collective ownership of the means of production. Basic Income obviously would not make every individual's share fully independent of her labor contribution, but it would move considerably in that direction.

Michael Howard (2006) uses Marxian theory to address seven objections to Basic Income in his article, "Why Marxists and Socialists Should Favor Basic Income." He addresses issues such as alienation and the possibility of a moral obligation. He concludes that the coercion to work is a core aspect of alienation and that a genuine socialist alternative should acknowledge the ambivalent moral significance of work.

The communitarian focus on shared common ends would seem to be at odds with the liberal individualistic justification of Basic Income. But Bill Jordan (1992) attempts to reconcile these two concerns in his article, "Basic Income and the Common Good." He argues for a concept of justice that gives rights to individuals and to minority groups but that also takes seriously common interests in a good quality of life. He then comes to a partially communitarian justification for Basic Income.

In "Associations and Basic Income," Bill Jordan (1989) argues that time spent out of the formal economy has been usually classified as "retirement," "illness," "unemployment," "leisure," or "household duties" – either an involuntary withdrawal or an earned withdrawal justified by previous contribution. But this view ignores how much contribution people make through voluntary organizations. Although voluntary associations are valuable and important to a just society, they are threatened by modern, advanced capitalist societies by the need to meet the commercial criteria of success and then from being taken over by commercial enterprise. Basic Income can relieve voluntary organizations from that threat and make possible a greater flourishing of voluntary organizations, working toward more active citizenship and more livable communities.

Further Reading

Ackerman, B., Alstott, A., and Van Parijs, P. (eds) (2005). *Redesigning Distribution: Basic Income and Stakeholder Grants as Cornerstones of a More Egalitarian Capitalism.* Verso, New York.

Anderson, E. (1999). What Is the Point of Equality? *Ethics*, 109 (2), 287–337.

Arneson, R. (1992). Is Socialism Dead? A Comment on Market Socialism and Basic Income Capitalism. *Ethics*, 102 (3), 485–511.

Carter, I. (2012). Left-libertarianism and the Resource Dividend. In K. Widerquist and M.W. Howard (eds) *Alaska's Permanent Fund Dividend: Examining its Suitability as a Model.* Palgrave Macmillan, New York.

Casassas, D. and De Wispelaere, J. (2012). The Alaska Model: A Republican Perspective. In Widerquist, K. and Howard M.W. (eds) *Alaska's Permanent Fund Dividend: Examining its Suitability as a Model.* Palgrave Macmillan, New York.

Dahms, H.F. (2005). Globalization as Hyper-Alienation: Critiques of Traditional Marxism as Arguments for Basic Income. *Current Perspectives in Social Theory* (vol. 23, Social Theory as Politics in Knowledge), pp. 205–276.

Fitzpatrick, T. (1996). Postmodernism, Welfare and Radical Politics. *Journal of Social Policy*, 25 (3), 303–320.

Fried, B. (2004). Left-Libertarianism: A Review Essay. *Philosophy and Public Affairs*, 32 (1), 66–92.

Jordan, B. (1989). *The Common Good*. Basil Blackwell, Oxford.

Jordan, B. (1996). *A Theory of Poverty and Social Exclusion*. Polity Press, Cambridge.

Kliemt, H. (1993). On Justifying a Minimum Welfare State. *Constitutional Political Economy*, 4 (2), 159–171.

Little, A. (1998). *Post-Industrial Socialism: Towards a New Politics of Welfare*. Routledge, London.

Mosely, D. (2011). Debate: Should Libertarians Endorse Basic Income? *Basic Income Studies*, 6 (2). http://www.degruyter.com/view/j/bis

Offe, Claus (2008). Basic Income and the Labor Contract. *Basic Income Studies*, 3 (1). http://www.degruyter.com/view/j/bis

Pateman, C. (2006). Democratizing Citizenship: Some advantages of a basic income. In E.O. Wright (ed.) *Redesigning Distribution: Basic Income and Stakeholder Grants as Cornerstones for an Egalitarian Capitalism*. Verso, London, pp.101–119.

Standing, G. (1999). *Global Labour Flexibility: Seeking Distributive Justice*. Palgrave Macmillan, Basingstoke.

Standing, G. (2002). *Beyond the New Paternalism: Basic Security as Equality*. Verso, London/New York.

van der Veen, R. (1999). The Adjudicating Citizen: On Equal Membership in Walzer's Theory of Justice. *British Journal of Political Science*, 29 (2), 225–258.

Van Parijs, P. (1992). Basic Income Capitalism. *Ethics*, 102 (3), 465–484.

Van Parijs, P. (ed) (1992). *Arguing for Basic Income: Ethical Foundations for a Radical Reform*. Verso, London.

White, S. (2003). *The Civic Minimum: On the Rights and Obligations of Economic Relationship*. Oxford University Press, Oxford.

Williams, A. (1999). Resource Egalitarianism and the Limits to Basic Income. *Economics and Philosophy*, 15 (1), 85–107.

Zelleke, A. (2005). Basic Income in the United States: Redefining Citizenship in the Liberal State. In K. Widerquist, M.A. Lewis, and S. Pressman (eds.) *The Ethics and Economics of the Basic Income Guarantee*. Ashgate, Aldershot, pp. 13–54.

Zelleke, A. (2011). The Capitalist Road to Communism: Are We There Yet? In A. Gosseries, and Y. Vanderborght (eds) *Arguing about Justice. Essays for Philippe Van Parijs*. Presses Universitaires de Louvain, Louvain-la-Neuve, pp. 415–422.

Chapter 7
Left-libertarianism and a Global Rent Payment

Nicolaus Tideman and Peter Vallentyne

Excerpts from Left-libertarianism and Global Justice. In B.M. Leiser and T.D. Campbell (eds) (2001). *Human Rights in Philosophy and Practice.* Dartmouth Publishing Co, Burlington, Vermont, pp. 453–457.

We defend a *left-libertarian* theory of justice, and discuss its implications for global justice. In our simplified world there are agents, natural resources, and artifacts. *Libertarian* theories of justice hold that *agents*, at least initially, own themselves, and thus owe no service to others, except through voluntary action. The most familiar libertarian theories (e.g., Nozick, 1974) are *right-libertarian* in that they hold that *natural resources* are initially unowned and, under a broad range of realistic circumstances, can be privately appropriated without the consent of, or any significant payment to, the other members of society. *Left-libertarian* theories, by contrast, hold that natural resources are owned by the members of society in some egalitarian manner, and may be appropriated only in ways that are compatible with the rights of all to natural resources. Left-libertarian theories have been propounded for over two centuries, but in recent years there has been a revival of interest in them. Theories roughly of this sort (but with some important qualifications noted below) have been explored (but not defended) by Gibbard (1976) and Kolm (1985, 1986), advocated by Grunebaum (1987), Steiner (1994), Van Parijs (1995), and Tideman (1991, 1994, 1997, 1998), and criticized by Cohen (1995).

Left-libertarianism has two central ideas: (i) Agents own themselves. (ii) The value of natural resources is owned in some egalitarian sense. Different left-libertarian theories have different conceptions either of self-ownership or of the relevant form of egalitarian ownership of natural resources (and indirectly of the ownership of artifacts). We start by explaining and motivating the thesis of self-ownership for agents. Then we discuss some different conceptions of egalitarian ownership of natural resources.

The core idea of self-ownership is that agents own themselves in much the same way that they can own inanimate objects. This ownership is typically taken to include, at a minimum (i) full *control rights* over (power to grant and deny permission for) the *use* of their persons (e.g., what things are done to them) and (ii) full *immunity from payment* for the possession and exercise of these rights (ensuring, for example, that the rights are not

From Tideman, N. and Vallentyne, P. (2001). Left-libertarianism and Global Justice. In B.M. Leiser and T.D. Campbell (eds) *Human Rights in Philosophy and Practice.* Dartmouth Publishing Co, Burlington, Vermont, pp. 453–457. Reprinted with the kind permission of the authors.

Basic Income: An Anthology of Contemporary Research, First Edition. Edited by Karl Widerquist, José A. Noguera, Yannick Vanderborght, and Jurgen De Wispelaere.

merely rented). One of us (Vallentyne) holds that self-ownership also includes (iii) full *rights to transfer* the rights they have to others (by sale, rental, gift, or loan), so that individuals are able to sell themselves into slavery. The other of us (Tideman) denies (iii), and holds that no one can rightly be compelled, on pain of physical punishment or loss of liberty, to fulfill a personal service commitment. On the other hand, this view does permit a person to pledge his/her accumulated physical wealth as security for a personal service commitment.

Self-ownership is one central ideal of left-libertarianism. The other is egalitarian ownership of the value of natural resources. There are many forms that this egalitarian ownership can take, and we defend one form.

One basic issue concerns the level of jurisdiction at which egalitarian ownership applies. One view is that the land occupied by each country is owned in some egalitarian manner by its citizens, but that non-citizens have no claim to the value of that land. This would be egalitarian internally, but viewed globally, this might involve an extremely inegalitarian distribution of rights over natural resources. Those who live in countries that control less valuable natural resources would thereby have less valuable ownership rights. Natural resources were not created by any (non-divine) agent, and no agent has any special entitlement to a greater share merely because he/she happened to be there first. Hence, any plausible view treats the egalitarian ownership of natural resources as holding at the global level (the entire world). This crucial claim is assumed in what follows.

1 According to one version of left-libertarianism, natural resources are *jointly owned* in the sense that authorization to use, or to appropriate, is given through some specified collective decision-making process (e.g., by majority or unanimous decision). One form of this approach – advocated (seemingly, at least) by Grunebaum (1987) – holds that collective approval is needed for any *use*, as well as appropriation, of natural resources. But as Fressola (1981) and Cohen (1986, 1995) have argued, this is implausible, since it holds that, for agents like us, no one has the right to *do anything* (e.g., stand in a given spot, eat an apple, or even breathe) without authorization from other members of society. For every action requires the use of some natural resources (e.g., occupying a spatial location), and thus no one is permitted to do anything without approval from others.
2 A more plausible form of joint ownership of natural resources – held perhaps by Grotius (1625) [. . .] and explored by Gibbard (1976) – holds that prior to any agreement agents are permitted to *use* natural resources in conformance with specified terms of *common use*, but they have no *exclusive* rights of use (no private ownership). Roughly, this means that they are permitted to use natural resources in various ways (occupy locations, breathe air, eat apples) as long as those resources are not then in use by others (and perhaps subject to certain conditions of sustainability), but they have no rights over any natural resources that they are not currently using. On this view, the initial rights over natural resources are like rights over public park benches. One has a right to use a resource (e.g., sit in one), but once one stops using it, one has no right to prevent others from using it.
3 Even this form of joint ownership of natural resources, however, is implausible. For it has the implication that no *appropriation* (i.e. acquisition of exclusive rights of use) could be just in the absence of actual collective agreement. It is most implausible to hold that the consent of others is required for just appropriation when communication with all relevant others is impossible, extremely difficult, or expensive (as it almost always is).

> And even when communication is relatively easy and costless, it is unclear why one needs the consent of others as long as one makes an appropriate compensatory payment for the natural resources appropriated.

A different sort of approach holds that agents may use, or appropriate, inappropriate natural resources without the permission of others, but if they do so, they acquire certain obligations. Below we suggest that some form of this approach is plausible. But first we must see that some forms clearly are not. An extreme form of this approach holds that anyone who *uses* natural resources (which is of course everyone) *forfeits all rights* of self-ownership (e.g., acquires an enforceable duty to do whatever maximally promotes equality). A slightly less extreme form allows agents to use natural resources subject to the rules of common use without any loss of self-ownership, but holds that anyone who *appropriates* (claims rights of exclusive use over) natural resources forfeits all rights of self-ownership. Both these views hold that agents are "initially" self-owners, and are thus "formally" versions of libertarianism. Neither is plausible because they allow self-ownership to be lost too easily.

A plausible conception of the ownership of natural resources must be compatible with reasonably *secure* (not easily lost) self-ownership. At a minimum it should allow inappropriate resources to be *used* by agents *without the permission of others* and *without any loss of the rights of self-ownership* – as long as it does not violate the property rights of others. Without some such condition of permissible use of natural resources, self-ownership has no real force, since it could be lost through the unavoidable use of natural resources. In addition, a plausible conception of the ownership of natural resources should be *unilateralist* in the sense of allowing agents to *appropriate* inappropriate natural resources without the consent of others – and with no loss of self-ownership – as long as they make an appropriate payment (to be discussed below).

In what follows, then, we consider some unilateralist conceptions of natural resource ownership (in conjunction with self-ownership). *Radical right libertarians* – such as Rothbard (1978, 1982) and Kirzner (1978) – hold that that there are no payment requirements for the appropriation of inappropriate resources. Agents are free to take ownership of whatever inappropriate natural resources they find (or mix their labor with). Obviously, this is a non-starter from a viewpoint that requires egalitarian ownership of resources. *Nozickean right libertarians* – such as Nozick (1974) – hold that the only payment requirements are those of a Nozickean proviso, which requires roughly that (taking account of the general benefits of a system of exclusive rights to natural resources), no individual be made worse off (in some appropriate sense) by the appropriation (compared with the situation before appropriation). It seems quite plausible that satisfaction of some form of a Nozickean proviso is a *necessary* condition for just unilateral appropriation. But Nozickean libertarians are mistaken in holding that it is *sufficient* for just appropriation. For a world without the possibility of appropriating exclusive rights to natural resources would leave people very poor. Little if any compensation is required by a Nozickean proviso. There is no excuse for those who first appropriate natural resources to insist that the whole gain in efficiency from institutions for exclusive appropriation of natural resources must be assigned to them, when there are alternative protocols for assigning the gain that would preserve most if not all of the efficiency gain. Those who wish to impose an institution and justify it on grounds of efficiency have, at most, a claim to the gain as compared to the next most efficient institution, not a claim to the gain as compared to no institution.

Georgist libertarians – such as eponymous George (1879, 1892), Steiner (1977, 1980, 1981, 1992, 1994), and Tideman (1991, 1994, 1997, 1998) – hold that agents may appropriate inappropriate natural resources as long as they pay the competitive value of the rights they claim. Because of potential problems with future generations (which we are here ignoring), the rights involved are usually understood as temporary in nature, and thus the competitive value is understood as the competitive *rent* owed for the rights claimed. For simplicity, we also make this assumption.

We believe that Georgist libertarianism is plausible. It allows agents to use and appropriate unowned natural resources as long as they pay the competitive value of the rights they claim. Furthermore, it holds that agents fully own the artifacts that they produce with their labor, as long as they pay the rent on the underlying natural resources they own and the owners of any other labor, natural resources, or artifacts involved in the production have consented (e.g., in return for a payment) to the use of these resources and have renounced any claim to the product. Thus, for example, if I produce some apples on some land that I have claimed, then I own the apples as long as I have paid any required rent for the land. If I hire someone to work for me, and rent some machinery from someone, then I own the apples as long as I have paid any required rent for the land, the wages to the hired hand, and the rent for the machinery.

We address below the question of how the rent payments are to be divided up. One of us suggests that they should be divided up equally, and one of us argues that they should be used to promote equality of effective opportunities for a good life (and thus divided up unequally). The point to note here is that, however they are divided up, the duty to make payments is limited to the competitive value of the rights over natural resources that one claims. There are no duties to contribute simply because someone is in need. Nor does the amount that agents are required to contribute depend on how fortunate they are with respect to their personal endowments (capacities, etc.) or their situational endowments (wealth, opportunities, etc.). The duty to make payments to others is based solely on the value of the natural resources one appropriates. If one appropriates none, one owes nothing.

There is, of course, a very wide range of possible answers to the question of how the rent payments should be distributed. One might hold, for example, that a utilitarian principle should be applied. We simply assume here that some sort of egalitarian principle should be applied. After all, natural resources are in some sense the common property of all.

One of us (Tideman) holds that the rent payments should be *divided equally* among all agents in the world. The net effect of this idea, in conjunction with the idea that competitive rent is owed for rights claimed over natural resources, is that agents and countries effectively owe rent payments only to the extent that they appropriate more than an equal per capita share of the value of natural resources. For if they appropriate just a per capita share, their share of the rent payments equals the rent they owe, and hence no net rent is due.

The other of us (Vallentyne) holds that the rent payments should be divided *so as to promote effective equality of opportunity for a good life*. There are, of course, many issues here that a full theory of equality promotion would have to address. What makes for a good life? How exactly are effective opportunities understood? On what basis are effective opportunities assessed? Are the requisite interpersonal comparisons possible? How is equality measured? These important issues are not addressed here, except to stipulate that the relevant equality promotion is to be done by making people's lives better, and not by leveling-down. For present purposes it suffices to contrast this view with the previous one. On Vallentyne's view, the rent payments are not normally divided up equally but rather divided up unequally so as to equalize effective opportunities for a good life (whatever exactly that requires). Someone who has advantageous unchosen personal capacities (e.g., a strong, beautiful, intelligent person with a happy disposition) gets less (and perhaps nothing) from the rent payments than a person with disadvantageous personal capacities (e.g., a weak, ugly, stupid person with a depressive disposition). (If our model had more than one generation, we might ask whether those who bring weak, ugly, stupid people with depressive dispositions into the world have an obligation to compensate those who thereby receive less rent.) The same point applies to those who have advantageous unchosen situations (e.g., those who come to start life in an especially desirable physical or social location). The most basic point on this view is simply that the division of the rent payments should compensate for unchosen inequalities in opportunities for a good life.

Because we both agree that the demands of equality are limited to how the rent payments should be spent, we both agree that agents and countries do not have a duty of justice to do whatever is necessary to promote equality. The economic duties of agents and countries are determined by the value of the natural resources that they appropriate, and do not depend on the needs or relative deprivations of others (except of course to the extent that this affects the competitive value of the rights claimed).

At issue is how the independently generated rent payments are to be divided. Tideman endorses the view that each agent has a right to an equal share of the value of natural resources. Vallentyne endorses the view that justice requires that the value of natural resources be used to promote effectively equality of opportunity for a good life. At issue between the two views is the question of whether disadvantages in unchosen characteristics entitles one to a greater share of the value of natural resources (the rent payments). This is a deep and controversial issue that we cannot develop here. Suffice it to say that the equal share view is a form of external resourcism – the view that justice is concerned only with the distribution of external (non-personal resources), and that the effectively equality of opportunity view is a form of welfarism – the view that justice is concerned with the distribution of all resources (personal and external) and with how they affect the opportunity for a good life.

References

Andelson, R.V. (ed.) (1991). *Commons Without Tragedy.* Shepheard-Walwyn, London.

Cohen, G.A. (1986). Self-Ownership, World Ownership, and Equality: Part II. *Social Philosophy and Policy,* 3, 77–96.

Cohen, G.A. (1995). *Self-Ownership, Freedom, and Equality.* Cambridge University Press, Cambridge.

Cunliffe, J. (1988). The Liberal Rationale of "Rational Socialism". *Political Studies,* 36, 653–662.

Cunliffe, J. (1990a). The Neglected Background of Radical Liberalism; P.E. Dove's Theory of Property. *History of Political Thought,* 11, 467–490.

Cunliffe, J. (1990b). Intergenerational Justice and Productive Resources; A Nineteenth Century Socialist Debate. *History of European Ideas,* 12, 227–238.

Cunliffe, J. (1998). The Liberal Case for a Socialist Property Regime; The Contribution of Francois Huet. *History of Political Thought* 9, 707–729.

Dove, P.E. (1850). The Theory of Human Progression and Natural Probability of a Reign of Justice. *The Science of Politics,* Part 1. Johnstone and Hunten, Edinburgh.

Dove, P.E. (1854). The Elements of Political Science, *The Science of Politics,* Part 2. Johnstone and Hunten, Edinburgh.

Fressola, A. (1981). Liberty and Property. *American Philosophical Quarterly*, 18, 315–322.

George, H. (1879). *Progress and Poverty*. Robert Schalkenbach Foundation, New York.

George, H. (1892). *A Perplexed Philosopher*. Robert Schalkenbach Foundation, New York.

Gibbard, A. (1976). Natural Property Rights. *Nous*, 10, 77–86.

Grotius, H. (1625). *The Rights of War and Peace*. A.C. Campbell (ed.). M. Walter Dunne, London, 1901; Hyperion Reprint Edition, 1979.

Grunebaum, J. (1987). *Private Ownership*. Routledge & Kegan Paul, New York.

Harrison, F., Hudson, M., Miller, G.J., and Feder, K. (1994). *A Philosophy for a Fair Society*. Shepheard-Walwyn, London.

Huet, F. (1853). *Le Regne Social du Christianisme*. Firmin Didol Frères, Paris.

Kirzner, I. (1978). Entrepreneurship, Entitlement, and Economic Justice. *Eastern Economic Journal*, 4, 9–25. Reprinted in J. Paul (ed.) *Reading Nozick*. Basil Blackwell, Oxford, 1981, pp. 383–401.

Kolm, S.C. (1985). *Le Contrat Social Libéral (Théorie et Pratique du Libéralisme)*. Presses Universitaires de France, Paris.

Kolm, S.C. (1986). L'Allocation des Ressources Naturelles et le Libéralisme. *Revue Economique*, 37, 207–241.

Nozick, R. (1974). *Anarchy, State, and Utopia*. Basic Books, New York.

Ogilvie, W. (1781). The Right of Property in Land. In M. Beer (ed.) *The Pioneers of Land Reform*. New York, Alfred Knopf, 1920.

Paine. T. (1795). Agrarian Justice. In M. Foot and I. Kramnick (eds) *The Thomas Paine Reader*. Penguin Books, Harmondsworth, 1987.

Rothbard, M. (1978). *For a New Liberty, The Libertarian Manifesto*, revised edition. Libertarian Review Foundation, New York.

Rothbard, M. (1982). *The Ethics of Liberty*. Humanities Press, Atlantic Highlands.

Spence, T. (1793). The Real Rights of Man. In M. Beer (ed.) *The Pioneers of Land Reform*. Alfred Knopf, New York, 1920.

Spencer, H. (1851). *Social Statics*. Augustus M. Kelley, New York.

Steiner, H. (1977). The Natural Right to the Means of Production. *Philosophical Quarterly*, 27, 41–49.

Steiner. H. (1980). Slavery, Socialism, and Private Property. *Nomos*, 22, 244–265.

Steiner, H. (1981). Liberty and Equality. *Political Studies*, 29, 555–569.

Steiner, H. (1992). Three Just Taxes. In P. Van Parijs (ed.) *Arguing for Basic Income*. Verso, New York, pp. 81–98.

Steiner, H. (1994). *An Essay on Rights*. Blackwell Publishers, Cambridge (Massachusetts).

Tideman, N. (1991). Commons and Commonwealths: A New Framework for the Justification of Territorial Claims. In R.V. Andelson (ed.) *Commons Without Tragedy*. Barnes and Noble, Savage, Maryland, pp. 109–129.

Tideman, N. (ed.) (1994). *Land and Taxation*. Shepheard-Walwyn, London.

Tideman, N. (1997) The Shape of a World Inspired by Henry George (unpublished manuscript). Department of Economics, Virginia Polytechnic and State University.

Tideman, N. (1998). Applications of Land Value Taxation to Problems of Environmental Protection, Congestion, Efficient Resource Use, Population, and Economic Growth. In D. Netzer (ed.) *Land Value Taxation: Can It and Will It Work Today?* Lincoln Institute of Land Policy, Cambridge (Massachusetts), pp. 263–276.

Van Parijs, P. (1995) *Real Freedom for All*. Oxford University Press, New York.

Chapter 8

Guaranteed Income as a Replacement for the Welfare State

Charles Murray

Excerpts from Murray, C. (2008). Guaranteed Income as a Replacement for the Welfare State. *Basic Income Studies*, 3 (2), Article 6.

While a Guaranteed Income (GI) is not on the current policy agenda of any goverment, it has unique potential in the years to come as the basis for a coalition of supporters from left and right. A GI is already attractive on ethical grounds for most people on the left. Those on the right of the political spectrum, including may on the libertarian right, are already reluctantly convinced that large-scale transfer payments are here to stay, and are consequently receptive to ways of spending the money that does not involve extensive bureaucracies and social engineering. In view of this convergence of views on GI, a grand compromise is potentially available: for the left, it represents larger government in that it constitutes a state-driven redistribution of wealth, while for rhe right, it offers smaller government in terms of the state's power to control people's lives.

Replacing or Augmenting the Welfare State?

From a practical standpoint, arguments for a GI in addition to the existing benefit system are moot. No matter how theoretically persuasive those arguments might be, no Western nation can afford to add a significant GI to its existing commitments. On the contrary, all Western nations need to restructure their existing benefit systems to avoid bankruptcy. If a GI is to be financially feasible, it must replace existing programs rather than augment them.

I regard this practical necessity as serendipitous. The real reason to scrap the advanced welfare state is that its apparatus is outmoded, ineffectual, and often counterproductive. Because this view is so central to the right's potential support for a GI, some explanation of it is in order.

The European and American welfare states evolved under the twin assumptions that resources were scarce and that government could allocate them effectively. The first

From Murray, C. (2008). Guaranteed Income as a Replacement for the Welfare State. *Basic Income Studies*, 3 (2), Article 6. Reprinted with kind permission of the author.

Basic Income: An Anthology of Contemporary Research, First Edition. Edited by Karl Widerquist, José A. Noguera, Yannick Vanderborght, and Jurgen De Wispelaere.

assumption was true during the first half of the twentieth century, in the sense that no country had ever been so rich that its wealth, divided evenly among everyone, would provide everyone with a comfortable living. After World War II, in a few countries, wealth increased so much that, for the first time, there was enough money to go around. It was technically possible for no one to be poor. Much of the energy behind the social turmoil of the 1960s was fueled by this revolutionary change.

Now let us consider the second of the assumptions: that governments could allocate resources effectively. During the early decades of the welfare state, it seemed simple. The indigent elderly depend on charity, so let the goverment provide everyone with a guaranteed pension. The unemployed husband and father cannot find a job, so let the government give him some useful work to do. Those who are sick cannot afford to go to a private physician, so let the government pay for health care.

It turned out not to be simple after all. The act of giving pensions increased the probability that people reached old age needing them. Governments struggled to find useful work for unemployed people and were ineffectual employers even when they did. The demand for medical care outstripped the supply. But despite the complications, these are the easy tasks. Scandinavia and the Netherlands – small, ethnically homogeneous societies, with traditions of work, thrift, neighbourliness, and social consensus – do them best.

Traditions decay when the reality facing the new generation changes. The habit of thrift decays if there is no penalty for not saving. The work ethic decays if there is no penalty for not working. Neighbourliness decays when neighbours are no longer needed. Social consensus decays with immigration. Even the easy tasks become hard as time goes on.

In the United States during the second half of the twentieth century, the welfare state confronted accelerating increases in the number of people who were not just poor, but who behaved in destructive ways that ensured they would remain poor, sometimes living off their fellow citizens, sometimes preying on them: the underclass. As the years passed, poor young men increasingly reached adulthood unprepared to work even when jobs were available. They were more disposed to commit crimes. Poor young women more often bore children without a husband. Poor children more often were born to parents who were incompetent to nurture them. When it came to solving these problems, it was obvious by the 1980s that government had failed. The growing evidence was that government had exacerbated the problems it was trying to solve. As the Americans were making these discoveries, an underclass also began to emerge in the British and Continental welfare states.

That the apparently straightforward tasks of the welfare state have become complex and underclasses are growing throughout the Western world are neither coincidences nor inevitable by-products of modernity. Over a process that takes decades to play out, the welfare state self-destructs. First it degrades the traditions of work, thrift, and neighbourliness that enabled the system to work at the outset; then it spawns social and economic problems that it is powerless to solve. Devising an effective replacement for the welfare state is not only a budgetary necessity but also a social imperative.

Long-term Effects

Among the peoples in the advanced welfare states of Western Europe – usually secular, often childless, often unmarried – it seems as if a new cultural consensus has been reached: that the purpose of life is to while away the time between birth and death as pleasantly as possible, and the purpose of government is to make the process as easy as possible. I disagree, holding that to live a satisfying human life requires being enmeshed in the stuff of life. By "stuff of life" I mean the elemental events of birth, death, growing up, raising children, comforting the bereaved, celebrating success, dealing with adversity, applauding the good, scorning the bad, making a marriage, making a living; in short, coping with life as it exists around us in all its richness, which in turn means coping with difficulties, challenges, and defeats. The chief defect of the welfare state from this perspective is not that it is inefficient in dealing with social needs (though it is), nor that it is ineffectual in dealing with them (though it is), nor even that it often exacerbates the very problems it is supposed to solve (as it does). The welfare state drains too much of the life from life. Specifically, it does so by stripping the institutions of family and community of many of their functions and responsibilities.

The GI returns those functions and responsibilities to family and community. In this sense, the importance of the GI on human relationships and the vitality of communities is not that each adult has US$10,000 a year, but that the government has withdrawn all the ways in which the apparatus of the withdrawal has made it easier for people to behave in ways that lead to satisfying lives.

Regarding marriage, the GI leaves everyone with the option of remaining single and moving in and out of short-term relationships. But most people want something deeper and more lasting than that, something that looks like marriage traditionally defined. Without the apparatus of the welfare state, marriage once again becomes the locus within which a man and woman can make a future together, laden with responsibilities and obligations that cannot be put aside.

Regarding the community, a GI that has replaced the welfare state makes the community once again the locus within which human needs must be met, and the effects could be profound. It is not necessary for everyone to become a volunteer social worker to find satisfaction in life, but it is important that human needs of those in trouble are dealt with in a way that is an integral part of everyone's life. In a society where the responsibility for dealing with human needs is consigned to bureaucracies, a disconnect develops between the recognition of suffering and the ordinary citizen's obligations to deal with it. That disconnect is reflected in everything from the way we teach (or fail to teach) virtue to our children, to the way we allocate our time among the competing needs of family, community, and personal pleasure. The GI removes that disconnect.

But the effects of the GI on communities are likely to go far beyond the human needs that the welfare state seeks to address. When the government assumes the core functions of community, it removes the means by which vital communities establish their value. It also cuts off nourishment to secondary and tertiary behaviors that have nothing to do with social work. According to the logic of the social engineer, there is no causal connection between such apparently disparate events as the establishment of a welfare bureaucracy and the erosion of community spirit. According to the logic I am using, there is a causal connection of great importance.

This has been the barest summary of my reasons for thinking that the effects of the GI on civic life will be transforming. At least with regard to the United States, history gives us good reason to think that those reasons are not grounded in wishful thinking, but in the way that families and communities actually behaved. Nothing stands in the way of the restoration of communities and families that behave appropriately and generously, and that actually solve human problems, except the will to put the responsibility for those problems back in their hands.

Chapter 9

A Capitalist Road to Communism

Robert van der Veen and Philippe Van Parijs

Excerpts from van der Veen, R. and Van Parijs, P. (1986). A Capitalist Road to Communism. *Theory and Society*, 15 (5), 635–655.

From a Marxian standpoint, "socialism" is not an end in itself. It is a means, indeed the best means or even the only means, to reach true communism. The term "socialism" here covers what Marx calls the lower stage of communism in the *Critique of the Gotha Programme*. It refers to a society in which workers collectively own the means of production – and in which therefore they collectively decide what these should be used for and how the resulting product should be distributed, namely according to the principle, "To each according to his labor." "Communisim," on the other hand, refers to the higher stage of communism, as characterized in the *Critique of the Gotha Programme*. It is defined by the distribution principle, "From each according to his abilities, to each according to his needs" – which implies at least that the social product is distributed in such a way (i) that everyone's basic needs are adequately met, and (ii) that each individual's share is entirely independent of his or her (freely provided) labor contribution.[1] Socialism, as defined, implies that "exploitation" is abolished – workers appropriate the whole of the social product – while communism, as defined, implies that "alienation" is abolished – productive activities need no longer be prompted by external rewards.

Capitalism as such does not imply that any part of the social product should be granted to anyone who contributes neither labor, nor capital, nor natural resources. But it does not exclude it either. It does not exclude the possibility of a "social income" whose recipients need not contribute anything to production at the time they receive it. It is of crucial importance, however, to distinguish between different formulas of "social income" in this sense.

Some of them are just indirect wages. They involve an indirect connection with labor contribution. For example, the right to a "social income" may be restricted to whose who are unable to work or unable to find work, as is roughly the case with unemployment benefits in advanced capitalist countries. Or it may be extended to people who freely choose not to work, but subject to the proviso that they have in the past performed some specified

From van der Veen, R. and Van Parijs, P. (1986). A Capitalist Road to Communism. *Theory and Society*, 15 (5), pp. 635–655. Reprinted with permission of Springer Science + Business Media.

Basic Income: An Anthology of Contemporary Research, First Edition. Edited by Karl Widerquist, José A. Noguera, Yannick Vanderborght, and Jurgen De Wispelaere.

amount of labor, as in Edward Bellamy's utopia recently revived, in a less rigid version, by Gunnar Adler-Karlsson (1979), André Gorz (1983; 1985), and Marie-Louise Duboin (1984). In all such cases, labor – or at least the willingness to work – remains the basis of the entitlement to a "social income," and increasing the size of the latter cannot be construed as a move toward distribution according to needs.

Other formulas, however, grant a genuine Guaranteed Income: the connection with labor contribution is completely severed. This is the case, for example, when any household whose income from other sources falls below some specified minimum is entitled to a transfer payment *making up for the difference* – which is roughly the way in which basic social security actually works in several advanced capitalist societies. And it is also the case when every individual, whatever his or her income from other sources, is entitled to an *Unconditional Grant*, the level of which depends only on such variables as age and degree of handicap (as rough proxies for basic needs) – an old idea advocated by Bertrand Russell (1981) that has recently become the focus of growing interest throughout Western Europe.[2]

In the case of these last two formulas, it makes sense to say that an increase in the level of the "social income" moves us closer (*ceteris paribus*) to communism, as defined by distribution according to needs. In both cases, it is possible to say that in any economy (defined by its technological level, its stock of labor power and capital, and the preference schedules of its members) some positive levels of a "Guaranteed Income" are sustainable, while others are not. And in both cases, it is therefore in principle possible to determine a maximum sustainable level of the "Guaranteed Income" (with given technology, stocks, and prefereences), which the pursuit of communism within capitalism should constantly aim for. Nonetheless, it is of paramount importance to see that the consequences associated with these two versions are by no means the same: whereas the former version would lock the trasition to communism in a dead end, the latter provides a promising way of effecting it.

Notes

1. Note that "communism," as defined, does not entail collective ownershiop of the means of production by the workers, i.e., "socialism" as defined above. But it does entail collective ownership of the social product by society as a whole: while the owners of means of production, labor power, and skills decide whether and how to put them to productive use, society appropriates all income flows in order to distribute them "according to needs" to all its members. This constitutes the etymological justification for our "thin" definition of "communism."
2. See, for example, Jordan (1973; 1985, Part 3); Cook (1979); Roberts (1982); Miller (1983); and Ashby (1984). For a survey of the discussion in various European countries, see Boulanger et al. (1985, Part 2).

References

Adler-Karlsson, G. (1979). Probleme des Wirtschaftswachstums und der Wirtschaftsgesinnung: Utopie eines besseren Lebens. *Mitteilungsdients der Verbraucherzentrale Nordrhein-Westphalen*, 23, 40–63.

Ashby, P. (1984). *Social Security after Beveridge: What Next?* National Council for Voluntary Organizations, London.

Boulanger, P-M., Defeyt, P., and Van Parijs, P. (eds) (1985). L'allocation universelle: Une idée pour vivre autrement. *La Revue Nouvelle*, 81 (special issue), 341–344.

Cook, S. (1979). Can a Social Wage Solve Unemployment? Working paper n. 165. University of Aston Management Centre, Birmingham.

Duboin, M-L. (1984). *Les affranchis de l'an 2000.* Syros, Paris.

Gorz, A. (1983). *Les chemins du paradis: L'agonie du capital.* Galilée, Paris.

Gorz, A. (1985). L'allocation universelle: version de droite et version de gauche. *La Revue Nouvelle*, 81, 419–428.

Jordan, B. (1973). *Paupers: The Making of the New Claiming Class.* Routledge and Kegan Paul, London.

Jordan, B. (1985). *The State: Authority and Autonomy.* Blackwell, Oxford.

Miller, A. (1983). *In Praise of Social Dividends. Working paper no 1.* Heriot-Watt University, Department of Economics, Edinburgh.

Roberts, K. (1982). *Automation, Unemployment and the Distribution of Income.* European Center for Work and Society, Maastricht.

Russell, B. (1981). *Roads to Freedom: Socialism, Anarchism and Syndicalism.* Allen and Unwin, London.

Chapter 10

Why Marxists and Socialists Should Favor Basic Income

Michael Howard

Excerpts from Howard, M. (2005). Basic Income, Liberal Neutrality, Socialism, and Work. In K. Widerquist, M.A. Lewis, and S. Pressman (eds) *The Ethics and Economics of the Basic Income Guarantee*. Ashgate, Aldershot.

[. . .] One might think that Marxists and socialists would all support Basic Income (BI), coming out of a tradition in which the ultimate principle of distribution in the "higher phase of communism" is to each "according to need."[1] However, in his classic formulation, Marx considered such a principle irrelevant for the "lower phase of communism," more commonly called socialism, that might conceivably replace capitalism, because in the latter there would still be substantial material scarcity, a division of mental and manual labor inherited from capitalism, and work that is mostly done out of necessity rather than as a form of self-realization. More appropriate for socialism is distribution "according to work" (Marx, 1977a). This amounts to a conditional reciprocity principle and, if the fruits of social labor are to be shared equitably, would seem to entail a right to work, but not an unconditional right to income.

These conceptions of socialist rights and distribution can be grounded in Marx's theory of alienation (Marx, 1977b). For Marx, to be a human being is to be fundamentally a social being, interdependent with others of the species. This interdependence can be conscious and positive, as in the love relations of a family, or the idealized bonds of citizens in the ancient Greek polis, or it can be unconscious, externalized, estranged, as in the universal system of needs embodied in the market economy. In the latter, it is typical for one to come to regard others as mere means for the satisfaction of one's own individual needs. Basic Income might be thought to further this sort of egoistic false consciousness, insofar as it is proclaimed to rest on a right to individual "real freedom" – freedom to opt out of the system of reciprocal exchange by taking one's Basic Income and refusing to work. Although real libertarianism shares with Marx an egalitarian critique of the inequality of wealth, income, and power in capitalist society, it aims to establish greater equality without challenging alienation from the species.[2]

From Howard, M. (2005). Basic Income, Liberal Neutrality, Socialism, and Work. In K. Widerquist, M.A. Lewis, and S. Pressman (eds) *The Ethics and Economics of the Basic Income Guarantee* (eds. Widerquist et al.) 2005; Ashgate, Aldershot, pp. 127–129, 129–132 and 133–134. Reprinted with permission of Ashgate, Gower & Lund Humphries publishing.

Basic Income: An Anthology of Contemporary Research, First Edition. Edited by Karl Widerquist, José A. Noguera, Yannick Vanderborght, and Jurgen De Wispelaere.

Alienation from the species, according to Marx's theory, is grounded in the alienation of labor. The worker alienates the product of labor when it is appropriated by the capitalist who has purchased the worker's labor power. The product, in the typical cycle of capitalist production, has the value added by the worker to the raw material; but the worker is paid only for the value of the labor power, not the value of the labor expended. The difference between these values is the source of capitalist profit and accumulation. Capital grows ever larger – and with this, the domination of the worker increases – as capital growth reduces other possibilities for access to the means of labor or the means of life. The worker is *forced* to labor to the degree that there is no alternative to starvation except working for wages. In the *Communist Manifesto*, Marx and Engels sum up the goal of the communist workers' movement as the abolition of private property, that is, of capital (Marx and Engels, 1977: 232). The point could be interpreted as putting an end to all "unearned income," that is, all income other than wages, such as that from interest, dividends, rent, and inheritance. This aversion to unearned income could be extended in a socialist society to Unconditional Basic Income, insofar as it too is unearned. As Jon Elster has put it (1986: 719), Basic Income goes

> against a widely accepted notion of justice [. . .] it is unfair for able-bodied people to live off the labor of others. Most workers would, correctly in my opinion, see the proposal as a recipe for exploitation of the industrious by the lazy.

David Schweickart (2000) goes further:

> we do not have a moral right to a BI. We do have a moral *obligation* to work. When we consume, we take from society. Justice requires that we give something back in return.

The overcoming of alienation, the first step of which is the abolition of private property, is more positively a democratization of the means of production. This involves, first, bringing the market economy under conscious collective control. This has often been understood to mean the replacement of the market economy by central planning, but it can also include more modest strategic planning and democratization of investment decisions, with space left for a market economy in goods and services. Second, democratization of the means of production includes the overcoming of the tyranny of the workplace through worker self-management. Alienation and domination give way to self-determination and self-realization through work. If everyone is to be so emancipated, there must be a right to employment for everyone who is able to work.

Let me first note that accepting the right (and obligation) to work does not entail rejecting BI. Pragmatic defenses of BI as a more effective way of eliminating the poverty trap than means-tested and work-linked alternatives are compatible with a view that there is no fundamental moral right to BI, and that there is in principle an obligation to *work* or at least to give back in some way. Proponents of *participation income* – a guaranteed income conditional on some form of social participation including not only paid work but also child care, elder care, volunteer activity, and so on – explicitly recognize this obligation, or at least its political salience, and make the BI at least loosely contingent on giving back (Atkinson, 1996). And one argument for BI is that it enables people to work by pricing themselves into a job, that is, "making jobs paying less than a living wage viable" (Barry, 1996: 243). That is, with a guaranteed income, individuals could augment their income through wages that otherwise would be insufficient for subsistence.

The objection that BI is exploitative has been answered sufficiently elsewhere (Howard, 2005a). I only add here that, to render this consistent with Marxism, we only need to think about *unearned income* in a different way. Traditionally, following the language of the *Manifesto*, private property, and with it unearned income, is to be "abolished," and following the model of the *Critique of the Gotha Program*, replaced with income proportional to labor. But an alternative is to socialize the property and share the unearned income equitably. John Roemer (1994) has proposed one way to do this, issuing citizens shares of socialized capital from which they would draw dividends, that is, a Basic Income. It is worth noting further that the *abolition* involved in the first path is only apparent – masking the unearned income tied to the control of land, capital, inherited technology, and jobs as assets (now controlled by collectives of workers rather than capitalists) in the form of payment proportional to labor. But those labor payments include unearned as well as earned income.

The most controversial part of unearned income is that deriving from employment rents on "jobs as assets" (Van Parijs, 1995). Without a tax on employment rents, the Basic Income yielded from other sources is likely to fall short of subsistence, and then many of the benefits associated with BI (such as the freedom to refuse work) diminish. Thus any substantial BI will probably require among its funding sources a tax on wages [. . .].

The objection that species interdependence, alienated by the market, will be further alienated by Basic Income is misplaced. Anyone who seeks more than the minimum will still need to work for it, and it will be immediately apparent that such work involves one in a web of connections with the rest of the species. Moreover, the failure to acknowledge unearned income by folding it all into wages would, itself, mask two equally important sorts of interdependence. First, wage workers often depend on others for the relatively high wages they enjoy, and this dependence is masked by too tight an allocation of income in proportion to work. For example, particularly in the United States in the 1950s and 1960s, the male wage earner implicitly was being paid for his own reproduction through the labor of a wife who was not remunerated, and who was economically dependent on the male in an invidious way. A Basic Income enabling homemakers to stay out of the wage labor market and to be less economically dependent upon a male wage earner is one way to acknowledge this unpaid labor and to call attention to a kind of interdependence that has been masked, without turning housework into wage labor (the household wage idea). Important here, also, is the dependence of the money economy and its agents on informal, household, and other economies that cannot easily survive transformation into commodity form. Becoming aware of this sort of interdependence is also a step beyond alienation. I'm a market socialist. But the only way the *socialist* in market socialism can be sustained against the alienating forces of the market is if the sphere of the market is clearly limited. The market should not dominate the household, the media, education, health care, or politics (Walzer, 1983). The second sort of interdependence is that between ourselves and nature, or more generally, the sources of unearned wealth and income. A BI tied to these is one way of socially acknowledging our shared dependence on natural resources, historical inheritances, and so on.

Most importantly, this objection overlooks the core aspect of alienation, which is the *coercion* to work. One is alienated from one's labor because one is forced to sell it to another and then to labor under the other's domination; under such conditions one feels estranged from one's labor and from the whole web of species interdependence with which it connects one. BI at a sustainable level is a step beyond alienation because it gives more workers the option to say no, and thus will exert some pressure on employers – whether capitalists or collectives of workers – to make the conditions of work more palatable. As work becomes more humane, the worker works more freely, and thus can become interdependent in a nonalienated way.

Closely related to the objection that BI masks our species interdependence is the criticism that it rests on an individualistic conception of freedom incompatible with socialist democracy, or with a movement in transition to socialist democracy. BI, it could be argued, promotes the idea that each person has a right to opt out of social participation; *real freedom* includes the right not to work or participate. Socialist freedom, on the other hand, is at least partly a freedom of groups – collectives of workers, communities, or whole societies – to determine their joint destiny collectively through democratic processes. Anyone excluded from such processes, by choice or by lack of available positions for participation, is deprived of an important freedom, analogous to being deprived of voting rights. Further, it might be added, the full overcoming of alienation involves self-realization through work.

The importance of self-realization through work can be understood in two different ways. First, it can be grounded in a philosophical ideal of human perfection. If this is what is meant, then it runs afoul of liberal neutrality. Some Marxists might say so much the worse for liberal neutrality, but in a pluralistic society the burden of proof will fall on them to show why everyone should embrace and be bound to this ideal. A less controversial understanding of the importance of work rests on empirical evidence that work is an important source of independence, achievement, advancement, family security, and self-esteem (Karst, 1997: 534, quoted in Harvey, 2003; Solow, 1998; Howard, 1984). But work is not the only source of these important values; even if it is one of the most important and if by work we mean paid employment, such strong linkage as there might be is in part due to the absence of other sources of independence, affirmation of one's worth, and opportunities for meaningful activity such as BI might afford.

This brings us to the question of what "work" should mean, and how it should be related to income and leisure in a socialist society. As Schweickart (2000) puts it,

> a genuine socialist alternative to capitalism should "abolish welfare as we know it," and undertake the difficult task redesigning our institutions so that every citizen can make a meaningful, productive contribution to the well-being of his or her fellow citizens. Not "real freedom for all," but rather, "real work for all" – "real work" that allows us to develop our individual abilities and to contribute meaningfully to our collective being.

A genuine socialist alternative should begin by acknowledging the ambivalent moral significance of work. On the one hand, it is one of the key ways we contribute to society, integrate ourselves into it, find our identity, exercise our capacities for creativity, and so on. On the other hand, it is necessary; and one way or another, human beings are constrained to labor in order to survive. The reality of work is that it shares in both of these aspects, some kinds of work more closely approximating the first, other kinds the second. The best summation I know of was made by Marx (1977c: 496–497):

> The actual wealth of society, and the possibility of constantly expanding its reproduction process, therefore, do not depend upon the duration of surplus labor, but upon its productivity and the more or less copious conditions of production under which it is performed. In fact, the realm of freedom actually begins only where labor which is determined by necessity and mundane considerations ceases; thus in the very nature of things it lies beyond the sphere of actual material production. Just as the savage must wrestle with Nature to satisfy his wants, to

> maintain and reproduce life, so must civilized man, and he must do so in all social formations and under all possible modes of production. With his development this realm of physical necessity expands as a result of his wants; but, at the same time, the forces of production which satisfy these wants also increase. Freedom in this field can only consist in socialized man, the associated producers, rationally regulating their interchange with Nature, bringing it under their common control, instead of being ruled by it as by the blind forces of Nature; and achieving this with the least expenditure of energy and under conditions most favorable to, and worthy of, their human nature. But it nonetheless still remains a realm of necessity. Beyond it begins that development of human energy which is an end in itself, the true realm of freedom, which, however, can blossom forth only with this realm of necessity as its basis. The shortening of the working-day is its basic prerequisite.

Economic Democracy (workplace democracy and democratic allocation of investment funds) addresses the rational regulation of our interchange with Nature "under conditions most favorable to, and worthy of" our human nature. Basic Income is a step toward the realm of freedom, constrained in its extent by the realm of necessity as its basis. Real work for all *and* real freedom for all, these should be the long-term goals of socialism [. . .].

There are different ways we might redesign our institutions so that everyone will have work, and I don't mean to suggest that employer subsidies are the only alternative to BI. But we must be careful not to be so tied to paid employment that we propose, even under socialism, something akin to employer subsidies – subsidies to cooperatives might have the same effect vis-à-vis an unemployed worker – and in the process perpetuate "work fetishism" (Van Parijs, 2001: 19). Of even greater practical importance, should we oppose a reform that is feasible under capitalism, and could be continued and expanded under socialism, and thereby indirectly strengthen the movement for employer subsidies as the default option in the effort to reduce unemployment?

There remains one further objection that makes reference both to the medium-term goal of democratic socialism and to the path toward this goal. If the goal is an egalitarian, democratic socialism of the sort described earlier, then – the ways Van Parijs (2001: 19) describes of how BI can support employment strategies notwithstanding – there is a legitimate worry that BI amounts to a resignation to, and way of compensating the losers for, a two-tiered economy consisting of a core of full-time, high-waged and highly skilled workers on the one hand, and a marginalized class of part-time, temporary, less-skilled and more lowly paid workers on the other. Andre Gorz (1992) calls this "Basic Income apartheid." By dividing the working class, progress toward a more egalitarian society, in which the work is shared and everyone has an equal opportunity to participate, is thwarted. A right to work, on the other hand, is partly constitutive of the goal of equal participation, and can guide social policies on the path from here to there. If capitalism is incompatible with full employment, socialism may be necessary to bring about real work for everyone; once people realize that, support for socialism can be expected to grow (Schweickart, 2002: 135–138).

The response to this criticism is not, as some BI advocates have done, to inveigh against work and a right to work, but rather to combine BI with labor market policies that ensure everyone a right to a decent job. These can include government funded work-creation schemes as well as statutory shortening of the work week. While it is important to acknowledge other forms of work besides paid employment and to facilitate them, it is important that these be choices for the unemployed, not poor alternatives to paid employment. So long as paid work remains a major source of self-expression, social advancement, and income – which we can expect in any capitalist or socialist society at the current level of technology – many who are excluded for lack of available jobs will be marginalized socially and financially.[3] This is not to say that labor market policy cannot include space for significant part-time and temporary work. But it is important that people taking such work do so because it enables them to undertake other meaningful activity such as care work and civic participation, or because they prefer the leisure, not because better paying and more fulfilling jobs are not available.

Notes

1. See van der Veen and Van Parijs (1986) for an argument for BI as a step toward this "communist" principle of justice.
2. I owe this objection and many of the other objections addressed in this section to David Schweickart's comments (Schweickart, 2000) [. . .].
3. For these and other important points in support of a right to work, see Harvey (2003). In a subsequent article I present a more critical view of a right to a job (Howard, 2005b).

References

Atkinson, A.B. (1996). The Case for a Participation Income. *The Political Quarterly*, 67 (1), 67–70.

Barry, B. (1996). Survey Article: Real Freedom and Basic Income. *Journal of Political Philosophy*, 4 (3), 242–276.

Elster, J. (1986). Comment on Van der Veen and Van Parijs. *Theory and Society*, 15 (5), 709–721.

Gorz, A. (1992). On the Difference Between Society and Community and Why Basic Income Cannot by Itself Confer Full Membership. In P. Van Parijs (ed.) *Arguing for Basic Income*. Verso, London.

Harvey, P. (2003). The Right to Work and Basic Income Guarantees: A Comparative Assessment. US Basic Income Guarantee Discussion Paper (February). http://www.usbig.net/

Howard, M.W. (1984). Worker Control, Self-Respect and Self-Esteem. *Philosophy Research Archives*, 10: 455–472.

Howard, M.W. (2005a). Basic Income, Liberal Neutrality, Socialism, and Work. *Review of Social Economy*, 62 (4) (December). Reprinted as Ch. 7 in K. Widerquist, M. Lewis, and S. Pressman (eds) *The Ethics and Economics of the Basic Income Guarantee*. Ashgate, Aldershot, pp. 122–137.

Howard, M.W. (2005b). Basic Income and Job Guarantees: Alternatives or Complements? Symposium: Basic Income Guarantees and the Right to Work. *Rutgers Journal of Law and Urban Policy*, 2 (1), 186–195.

Karst, K.L. (1997). The Coming Crisis of Work in Constitutional Perspective. *Cornell Law Review*, 82, 523–571.

Marx, K. (1977a). Critique of the Gotha Program. In D. McLellan (ed.) *Karl Marx: Selected Writings*. Oxford University Press, Oxford, pp. 564–570.

Marx, K. (1977b). Economic and Philosophic Manuscripts. In D. McLellan (ed.) *Karl Marx: Selected Writings*. Oxford University Press, Oxford, pp. 75–112.

Marx, K. (1977c). Capital. In D. McLellan (ed.) *Karl Marx: Selected Writings*. Oxford University Press, Oxford, pp. 415–528.

Marx. K. and Engels, F. (1977). The Communist Manifesto. In D. McLellan (ed.) *Karl Marx: Selected Writings*. Oxford University Press, Oxford, pp. 221–247.

Roemer, J. (1994). *A Future for Socialism*. Harvard University Press, Cambridge, MA.

Schweickart, D. (2000). Comment. Symposium on Michael W. Howard's *Self-management and the Crisis of Socialism: The Rose in the Fist of the Present.* Radical Philosophy Association Fourth National Conference, Loyola University, Chicago (unpublished).

Schweickart, D. (2002). *After Capitalism.* Rowman and Littlefield, Lanham, MD.

Solow, R. (1998). *Work and Welfare.* Princeton University Press, Princeton.

van der Veen, R.J. and Van Parijs, P. (1986). A Capitalist Road to Communism. *Theory and Society,* 15 (5), 635–655.

Van Parijs, P. (1995). *Real Freedom for All: What (If Anything) Can Justify Capitalism.* Clarendon Press, Oxford.

Van Parijs, P. (2001). A Basic Income for All. In *What's Wrong With a Free Lunch?* P. Van Parijs et al. Beacon Press, Boston.

Walzer, M. (1983). *Spheres of Justice: A Defense of Pluralism and Equality.* Basic Books, New York.

Chapter 11

Basic Income and the Common Good

Bill Jordan

Excerpts from Basic Income and the Common Good. In P. Van Parijs (ed.) (1992). *Arguing for Basic Income*, Verso, London.

Liberal Justice and Community

Liberal theories of justice have come under attack from communitarian critics, such as MacIntyre (1981) and Sandel (1982), who have in turn been fiercely rebutted, notably by Dworkin (1986) and Larmore (1987). The communitarians argue – very roughly – that individual identities cannot be separated from social purposes, and are constituted by community; and that shared common ends should have priority over abstract justice. The liberals retort that this leaves no way of settling disputes and allowing coexistence between rival conceptions of the good life, and that abstract but precise definitions of justice provide the only means of neutral arbitration between these. I want to try to have it both ways, by arguing for a concept of justice that gives clear rights to individuals and minority groups, but also takes seriously common interests in a good quality of life.

I must make it quite clear from the start that I am not about to try to locate the ethical foundations of the Basic Income in a virtuous traditional community of citizens, subscribing to a uniform moral code. What I do want to argue is that an adequate theory of distributive justice must include an analysis of democracy, membership and participation, and hence a theory of social relations which takes account of the ways in which people share their lives as a community. By this I mean that it will not suffice for a theory to say what individuals' basic rights should be, or what share of resources each should have. It must also be able to say how a community should govern itself, and what principles should inform the myriad coalitions, networks, clans, unions, neighborhoods, dependencies, associations, families, liaisons and friendships that make up its social relations. And these issues require a rather different form of analysis from the one adopted in liberal theories of justice.

Let me start from an impeccably liberal idea: that each individual's interests can be understood only by reference to his or her projects and commitments – that is to say, the

From Jordan, B. (1992). Basic Income and the Common Good. In P. Van Parijs (ed.) *Arguing for Basic Income*, Verso, London. Reprinted with permission of Verso.

Basic Income: An Anthology of Contemporary Research, First Edition. Edited by Karl Widerquist, José A. Noguera, Yannick Vanderborght, and Jurgen De Wispelaere.

purposes he or she pursues over time, and the patterns or consistencies in relationships which arise from forming or joining partnerships, networks, groups or associations of various kinds. I take it that some such idea of the individual as choosing his or her own purposes and relationships is indispensable to an ethical analysis of welfare or anything else, because it allows the individual a degree of moral autonomy, and a chance to express in action where his or her interests lie – by what is avoided as well as what is chosen. So it makes space for the variety of conceptions of a good life on which liberals rightly insist, and which MacIntyre-style communitarians seem to deny.

But we can also recognize immediately that there is really no such thing as an individual project, however we may strain to think of one. Poets need publishers and readerships, marathon runners need competitors and stewards, even hermits need people to get away from and pleasures to give up. And most projects directly involve other people for their fulfilment, not just as extras – timing the marathon, or marking out the route – but as co-participants. The most universal projects, like setting up a home and having a family, are explicitly shared with chosen others, and the relations they establish are integral to the projects themselves. It would be odd to set up home with someone, and then divide it up into exclusive territory with locked doors and fences. So projects and commitments are not distinct; most projects involve commitments to shared purposes, resources and values; indeed, sharing and associating constitute a large part of what the project is. Even though the requirements of an individual's projects may conflict with each other, and with his or her other commitments, they do not create interests which mark off one person's conception of the good life from others'; rather, they link individuals together in networks of association and co-operation, and create common interests in certain goods that they share and prize.

I would argue that every shared project needs three implicit or explicit mechanisms: one to sustain it (who does what and how), one to negotiate short-term problems (holidays, illnesses, running out of money), and one to settle serious disputes (I'm doing all the hard work, who do you think you're talking to, and it's my ball anyway). The first commits the participants to joint action, the second allows them to negotiate immediate snags, and the third lays down the rules under which the whole project can be fundamentally changed or wound up. Prudent projects also include a mechanism for reviewing progress and evaluation. So institutions which enable co-operation also allow for conflict, including ultimate conflict leading to divorce, dispersal or dissolution.

The Common Good

So far I have argued that autonomous individuals choose to share projects with others, and to bind themselves to relations which require joint decisions. The process of sharing and cooperation creates common interests and mutual obligations. It creates small communities, each with its characteristic social relations and decision-making procedures. These communities, constructed by the choices of those who form or join them, are exclusive in their membership. The rationale and procedure for selection varies between idiosyncratic mutual liking or attraction (as in friendships and marriages), planned search for complementary assets and skills (as in teams or enterprises) and ownership of similar resources (as in a landowners' association or chamber of commerce). Once formed, such groupings often have a common interest in excluding others from access to what they share.

But it is possible also to recognize certain aspects of life where sharing is inclusive rather than exclusive, and common interests exist independently of individual choices. Some goods are intrinsically shared, because they cannot be divided up and apportioned to individuals or groups, and because no one can be excluded from enjoying them – pure public goods. The example which springs to mind is the global environment. As human beings, we all depend on – yet take for granted – clean air and water, healthy vegetation and animal life and a balanced, sustainable ecological system. The environment represents a public good which is used by all and depends on the actions of all for its maintenance. We are now recognizing the threat to it from the greenhouse effect and the hole in the ozone layer, and that we all share a common interest in protecting an indivisible but finite resource.

Within the logic of potentially aggressive nation-states, defense is a public good for members of each political community. But ex-President Gorbachev has argued that, in a global context and in a nuclear age, peace is a public good (Gorbachev, 1988). Since all, including the would-be aggressors, share in the hazards of war's consequences, and in the benefits of peace, peace becomes an indivisible aspect of the world environment on which all depend equally for survival. In his United Nations speech he argued for co-operation, negotiation and dialogue towards a "universal human consensus" based on "universal human interests". This would be nonsense without a concept of a common good or humanity, based on such global common interests.

I want to extend this idea to include the notion of a quality of life which is enjoyed by members of a community, Once again, this quality of social relations is not divisible, and it depends on the actions of all members, In this sense it is like the "practices" described by Alasdair MacIntyre (1981) and William Connolly (1981: ch. 4) (voluntary submission to certain standards, promoting excellence which cannot be measured in terms of the amount of benefit gained by any individual participant), but it need not be confined to elitist academic, aesthetic and cultural activities of the kind they choose. It can include far more everyday and humdrum aspects of a society's civic culture, such as polite, convivial and tolerant relations between citizens in public places. In this sense, morality itself is a public good.

The features of these public goods to which I want to draw attention are:

(i) They are achieved (if at all) through active co-operation between individuals, which can be voluntary because it is for mutual benefit. Individuals recognize that they have an interest in the common good and that others as well as themselves will benefit from acting (or refraining from acting) in a certain way. Hence actions are neither self-interested (in the sense of referring only to the individual's own good) nor altruistic (in the sense of intending only the good of others), but tending towards the common good in what is perceived to be a variable-sum rather than a zero-sum game.

(ii) They are inclusive rather than exclusive goods. The fact that no one can be excluded from benefit is accepted as part of the nature of the goods, rather than seen as a problem (i.e. the free-rider problem, or the tragedy of the commons). Whereas in a self-interest analysis, the fact that individuals may try to cheat is seen as creating insuperable difficulties (unless compulsion is used to outlaw free-riding and ration common goods), in a common-interest analysis the fact that all are included motivates all to act together to create mutual benefits, or avoid mutual harm. In other words, the common good can be achieved only through recognition of common interests, leading to voluntary, concerted action.

(iii) Co-ordination between individuals is not by invisible hand mechanisms or compulsion, but by voluntary action, rational persuasion, debate, negotiation, bargaining and co-operation. People may, of course, choose to bind themselves to certain rules which then guide their conduct and their relations, and commit them to abiding by decisions made in the agreed way. But the mechanisms under which these rules are made include mechanisms for negotiating short-term problems and disagreements, and settling serious disputes between the participants, including issues concerning the rules themselves. In other words, individuals bind themselves to making the rules, abiding by them and changing them by agreed processes, which amount to ruling over themselves rather than submitting to the rule of some of them.

The really difficult issue for any communitarian theory of justice is the relationship between the processes of voluntary sharing between exclusive groups which choose each other and the processes by which people might come to co-operate as members of the human race, or as members of the same political society. Although there are similarities between the dynamics of both kinds of processes (sharing, trust, voluntarism, agreement), it is obvious that such exclusive common interest groups as households, associations, trade unions, economic classes and political coalitions have potentially competing or conflicting interests in relation to social goals and distributions which may outweigh their mutual interests in inclusive, co-operative social relations.

An adequate theory of distributive justice would have to address issues about the resources, talents and attributes individuals carry into their chosen shared projects, how they co-operate in these, and how they distribute what they produce; and it would also have to address issues about how all members of a society (or of the human species) can have access to a good quality of life, which includes shared projects. The institutional design of social relations derived from such a theory must somehow share out resources (and other divisible goods) in such a way as to allow all to share in the common good, which is the best possible quality of communal relationships. So I am looking for a theory which combines the liberal egalitarian's concern with distributions which allow equal autonomy, and the Aristotelian view of justice as "what tends to promote the common interest," because it allows "each to attain a share in the good life" (Aristotle, 1948: Bk III, ch. XII, s.i; ch. VI, s.3).

Equality and Quality

Here we immediately recognize a theme which has been with us since the eighteenth century but which, since Rousseau, has divided into two antagonistic camps. Those with a concern for equality (in the tradition of Tom Paine) want to share out rights and resources as fairly as possible, which means dividing things up. Those who value community and sharing in a good quality of life (in the tradition of Edmund Burke) want to keep things whole and emphasize their indivisibility. The former are cast as radicals, the latter as conservatives; and so it is in the modern debate between egalitarian liberals and communitarian conservatives. I want to argue the case for a radical communitarian egalitarianism – the only way, I would argue, of reconciling liberty, equality and ecology.

In the liberal analysis of justice, the fact that each individual has his or her own conception of the good life entails that each must have his or her fair share of welfare or resources so as to be able to pursue projects without undue interference from others. How this fair share is constituted, of course, varies considerably – between, for example, Rawls's "original position" contract, in which inequalities of shares are justified only if they do not make the poorest group worst off; and Dworkin's "clamshell auction," providing bundles of resources to each individual which are very different in composition, but equal in the sense that no one envies any one else's share (Dworkin, 1981).

Because liberals attach such importance to each individual's conception of the good life, they tend to see projects as individual activities. If social relations really consisted of myriads of such non-overlapping projects, it would make good sense for them to take the form of contractual exchanges of goods and services between individuals. If the basic units of society were individuals, each with separate and definable interests, related to their individual projects, then markets would be both the most efficient and the fairest way of co-ordinating all their activities. Each individual would behave in a self-interested way, with no reference to the interests of others, and their projects would be co-ordinated through the invisible hand. So long as each had a fair initial share, impersonal market mechanisms could be relied upon, until the next round of redistribution was due (either between transactions, or between generations).

But once we move from the counterfactual world of individuals with separate projects behind a veil of ignorance or on a desert island, these egalitarian redistributive principles lose a great deal of their force and coherence, for three main reasons:

(i) Other ethical claims on individuals arise directly from chosen commitments and shared projects. The most universally recognized and binding moral claims are those of family, friendship and loyalty to fellow members of exclusive clubs and associations, which arise from promises, from reciprocity and from sharing. The ethical principles derived from these – doing one's best for one's children, standing by one's friends, honouring commitments to associates – cut across the egalitarian distributive principles derived from the counterfactual worlds of individual projects, and weaken their claims.

(ii) The market exchanges which are endorsed as morally acceptable (in Dworkin already in the counterfactual situation, in Rawls subsequently) rely for their dynamic on self-interested motives and individual preferences. The logic of the market has its own ethical coherence, which is strongly linked to ideas of entitlement to property holdings, of fairness in process rather than outcome, and of desert through labor contributions (Acton, 1971; Hayek, 1960). If market exchange is acceptable, it is difficult to detach it from these strong principles, which assert freedom of exchange based on entitlement, ownership, labor and desert.

(iii) Individual holdings of resources which are morally validated as necessary for individual autonomy in liberal theory undermine the ethical claims of inclusive membership on which egalitarian redistribution must ultimately rest. The act of sharing out all resources by dividing them up (in the name of the individual claims of each person) actually destroys common interests in shared resources. In a world which has been subjected to repeated partition for the sake of egalitarian redistribution, inclusive membership based on shared public goods loses rather than gains moral force, because common interests are no longer visible.

These weaknesses in egalitarian liberal theories of justice are very effectively exploited by Nozick, whose examples constantly take advantage of the interplay between these three factors so as to loosen any moral grip their principles might gain (Nozick, 1974). His counterfactual world relies on the ethical endorsement of resource holdings, and its inhabitants are already endowed with real estate, automobiles, baseball bats and consumer-orientated preferences. He then proceeds to demonstrate the absence of binding moral claims for redistributive justice in a series of situations in which chosen ethical commitments and market exchange mechanisms provide more plausible (or less implausible) ways of settling competing claims on individuals.

These moves seem to me to expose a set of fundamental problems which this approach to distributive justice cannot overcome. This is why I would want to relocate the case for egalitarian redistribution in arguments for the common good, and for membership and sharing, rather than in partition for the sake of autonomy (Jordan, 1989). I would also want to seek an institutional structure for distributive justice which takes account of the distinctive ethical claims of shared projects and interest groups, and of the moral force of those principles which are associated with the market in the social relations that still rely for their dynamic on market mechanisms.

The first step in such an approach is to argue that the whole political association is a membership group, and hence that the state is a kind of club for the common good of the members of a political community. Like all other membership groups it is rather arbitrary in its composition, and potentially cuts across any attempt to identify and pursue the common good of humanity. Nevertheless, there are common interests which are shared by all citizens, and the state provides the means of identifying and pursuing these. Rather than trying to stipulate principles of distributive justice as a contractarian basis for the state, I would prefer trying to stipulate means by which these common interests can be sought (democracy).

To provide realistic and binding moral claims on members, the state must define and operationalize membership (citizenship) in terms that reconcile the obligations of the political community with the ethical claims of the various other communities to which citizens belong. This means identifying and upholding certain aspects of the life that citizens share as members of their society, and a quality of life that they prize. It relies on a large number of mechanisms for sharing, and on the provision of various shared resources and facilities which are chosen (democratically) as promoting the common good. Within this framework of analysis, the case for Basic Income must be made in terms of its potential for giving all members of the political community their due as citizens, and for promoting activities which improve the quality of social relations.

Second, however, if markets are to be justified as the means of permitting individuals or groups to exchange resources, then at least some of the moral notions associated with them must be institutionally endorsed. If the price mechanism is a fair as well as an efficient way of measuring comparative values in a process of allocation, and property holdings are justified for the sake of the autonomy individuals and groups need to pursue projects, then distributive justice must pay some heed to the principles associated with this system. Its outcomes must allow both some measure of differentiation in income according to effort, skill, luck, plausible advertising and all the other factors which go to make up the market system of comparative valuation; and it must allow the holders of certain assets some permanent title to a proportion of them as their due.

Empirical studies in the United States and West Germany of people's attitudes to their pay reveal that (even in these societies of relatively unequal rewards) individuals from all groups in society said that their earnings were proportionately fair, but claimed an additional £100 per month as their due (this was a constant across the whole range of earnings, and between the two countries) (Shepelak and Alwin, 1986; Wegener, 1987). This rather surprising finding seems to endorse the operation of the labor market and its relative rewards as just, with a mysteriously constant claim for an addition (the Basic Income?) which might be made in the name of some other principle of fairness (membership of society?). It appears to follow the expectations generated by equity theory (Homans, 1974; Adams, 1965), which regards contribution as the major differentiating factor in distributive justice, and to see the labor market as a fair system for evaluating contributions.

From a Marxist perspective, this endorsement of the labor market may be regarded as a product of false consciousness, and any willingness to validate its claims taken to be temporary and partial. But – as Philippe Van Parijs and Robert van der Veen have argued – there is a case for seeing a combination of a needs-based citizenship income and wage-based income as a transitional phase in a "Capitalist Road to Communism" (van der Veen and Van Parijs, 1986). And nowadays even advocates of a full Basic Income, enough to meet every citizen's living costs, recognize that it can be introduced only by stages, with earnings-related income still providing the major element in the short- and medium-term future.

The Case for Basic Income

The ethical evaluation of social relations in a community which claims to be a democracy should address the following questions:

(a) What interests do citizens have in common as members of their community, and what means do they have of participating in decisions about their social environment?
(b) Do those means allow the choice of decisions which are acceptable to all, or do the choices of a constant majority tend to reduce the participation in and control over decisions by a constant minority?
(c) If the latter, which particular institutions in society serve to divide the interests of the majority from those of the minority, and hence to exclude the minority from participation and control? (These institutions are likely to include distributive mechanisms which allocate assets, giving income advantages in economic relations as well as power advantages in political relations) (Roemer, 1982).
(d) Are these inequalities, exclusions and disadvantages temporary, and if so, how can their duration be minimized?
(e) If not, what institutional alternative might re-create common interests in inclusive membership and restore an anonymous shifting majority instead of a fixed and constant one?

Britain, at least, is not a society with a proper balance between fairness derived from market exchange and ownership and fairness based on communal sharing, such that democratic decision-making continues to be enlarged. As long ago as the early 1970s an identifiable minority was excluded from participation and control over collective decisions, and the economic and political status of a growing proportion of citizens has deteriorated still further in the past 10 years. The reasons for this seem to lie not only in the predominance of market-minded politicians, but also in the ineffectiveness of postwar welfare state institutions as means of creating common interests between citizens. They neither give this minority access to a share of marketed goods, nor create recognizable common interests in co-operation between citizens over issues of qualitative improvements in social relations.

This poses the question: which assets should be redistributed in order to provide more inclusive membership, and by what mechanisms?

In Britain, there is a constant advantaged majority of individuals who are members of households with at least one adult member in a full-time permanent job, which provides secure title to an income sufficent to meet basic needs plus housing expenses (or, in the case of elderly households, a pension drawn on such a job). The possession of such a job is the asset which gives the most relevant income advantages in British society (Jordan, 1989; ch. 6; Van Parijs, 1987), and usually provides the means to such other advantageous assets as owner-occupied housing and savings. Women and young people usually have a dependent and subordinate status in such households, but the institutional structure of society allows them modified incentives to participate (for example, in low-paid part-time employment) by virtue of this status. Their overall exclusive interests are thus defined by their membership of "job-rich" households, because of their share of the advantages gained by job-holding men with whom they live.

The case for Basic Income, in my view, rests on the perception that there is a substantial underclass who do not have access to jobs (in the sense defined above) or to pensions or other income derived from jobs, and who hence have no access to property of other kinds – jobs having become the property of minority. In Britain this underclass consists of:

(a) people with low earning power, whose actual or potential wages fall below their subsistence needs. Some of them are unemployed; others are in employment but receiving low wages plus means-tested supplements, which trap them in poverty (Parker, 1989);
(b) people with handicaps and those (mainly women) who care for them, who are excluded from the labor market either by the conditions attached to their income support, or by low earning power, or both;
(c) black people, who are excluded from jobs by a combination of discrimination and being trapped in deprived areas where their travel-to-work costs are high;
(d) people in depressed regions and deprived communities who face high travel-to-work costs, but cannot afford to move to more affluent and prosperous areas with better employment opportunities;
(e) women and young people living alone or as single parents, or sharing a household with a man who lacks a job, because the benefit system, confiscates almost the whole of anything they earn.

In other Western European countries, the underclass is differently constituted; for example, countries with higher benefits and decent minimum wages will have an underclass of households "headed" by males who are unemployed because they cannot earn the minimum wage and single parents, plus various groups in receipt of social assistance.

The injustice of these forms of exclusion from job assets, and hence from other forms of property, is reinforced by the generous tax allowances available to job-holders and members of their households both against their earnings and against borrowing, or against property. In Britain, the value of the tax allowances enjoyed by the better-off is equivalent to more than basic social security benefits; yet low-wage earners face tax at levels of earnings which are well below the point at which they cease to qualify for means-tested benefits, creating an extensive poverty trap (Parker, 1989). Because members of the underclass have little or no incentive to take employment, the British government is increasingly relying on compulsion or quasi-workfare schemes to harass them into low-paid work (Mead, 1986).

Basic income would share out social security benefits and income tax allowances in such a way as to allow access to employment for the whole adult population, and encourage job-sharing rather than job-reservation. Because it would be unconditional, its terms would allow people to take such employment as was available with security that their basic needs would be met. In an increasingly fragmented labor market, with more part-time and short-term employment contracts, it would give both men and women incentives to take such work. If Basic Income was introduced in a step-by-step way, with transitional payments of well below subsistence level, this would redistribute employment only at the lowest end of the labor market, and benefit the poor in marginal ways; but as its level rose, so it could effect employment at better wages, and the incentives of more earners.

If more generous allowances were paid to people with handicaps, their access to both employment and independence would be improved. Basic Income paid at equal rates to men and women would eventually give better incentives for sharing unpaid work in the household, and women would escape the role of full-time carers, in which the present benefit structure traps them. Basic Income could, of course, be used as a subsistence income by people wanting to do unpaid community work, or be pooled by those starting a co-operative – for example, a co-operative for people with disabilities, or carers. In general, it would allow a more rational division between paid and unpaid work, rather than encour aging the growth of service employment for its own sake.

The case for Basic Income as a response to the underclass phenomenon rests, therefore, on two features. By ameliorating (eventually eliminating) the poverty trap, it would give the excluded minority access to the market system of fairness by reward for effort, and hence to savings, property and other private goods. But also, by giving everyone a universal share of resources on the grounds of membership (citizenship), it would be a mechanism for including all in the common good.

In my view, Basic Income is the fairest way of sharing out rights, roles, obligations and access in our present situation, but it would not give rise to a just society without and equally determined policy commitment to communal resources for sharing in a good quality of national and local life. A revaluation of the public sphere would be an essential part of such policies, and would help to include the underclass in active citizenship roles. In other words, there should be a redistribution of value from private to public goods, as well as a new principle for the distribution of income.

Conclusions

Others [who argue for Basic Income] have looked for principles of justice – decision procedures that are strictly neutral between every kind of claim, and can apply to every situation – which will show that the distributions resulting from a certain kind or level of Basic Income are morally justified. My aim is a more modest one: to find the ethical principles that can best be applied to our present social relations in Western Europe, and to argue that Basic Income is a policy measure which – in combination with others – is most likely to allow the implementation of those principles.

My case for Basic Income is therefore only partially a communitarian one. Given that Basic Income involves giving individuals an equal measure of resources, aimed at increasing their autonomy, this is both inevitable and desirable. My argument is aimed at correcting the imbalance in liberal theory, by reasserting the claims of sharing, cooperation and democracy. Communities are groups of people who share in certain goods, some of which are indivisible. Principles of justice must take account of the way in which people share in common projects, and how they make choices about their shared environment.

References

Acton, H.B. (1971). *The Morals of Markets: An Ethical Exploration.* Longmans/Institute of Economic Affairs, London.

Adams, J.S. (1965). Inequality in Social Exchange. In L. Berkowitz (ed.) *Advances in Experimental Social Psychology*, vol. 2. Academic Press, New York.

Aristotle (1948). *Politics* (transl. E. Barker). Oxford University Press, Oxford.

Connolly, W. (1981). *Appearance and Reality in Politics.* Cambridge University Press, Cambridge.

Dworkin, R. (1981). What is Equality?: Part II: Equality of Resources. *Philosophy and Public Affairs*, 10, 283–345.

Dworkin, R. (1986). What Justice Isn't. In *A Matter of Principle.* Clarendon Press, Oxford.

Gorbachev, M. (1988). Speech to the United Nations. *The Guardian*, 8 December.

Hayek, F.A. (1960). *The Constitution of Liberty.* Routledge and Kegan Paul, London.

Homans, G.C. (1974). *Social Behaviour: Its Elementary Forms.* Harcourt, New York.

Jordan, B. (1989). *The Common Good: Citizenship, Morality and Self-Interest.* Blackwell, Oxford.

Larmore, C. (1987). *Patterns of Moral Complexity.* Cambridge University Press, Cambridge.

MacIntyre, A. (1981). *After Virtue: A Study in Moral Theory.* Duckworth, London.

Mead, L. (1986). *Beyond Entitlement: The Social Obligations of Citizenship.* Free Press, New York.

Norzick, R. (1974). *Anarchy, State and Utopia.* Blackwell. Oxford.

Parker, H. (1989). *Instead of the Dole.* Routledge, London.

Roemer, J.E. (1982). *A General Theory of Exploitation and Class.* Harvard University Press, Cambridge, MA.

Sandel, M. (1982). *Liberalism and the Limites of Justice.* Cambridge University Press, Cambridge.

Shepelak, N.J. and Alwin, D.F. (1986). Belief about Inequality and Perceptions of Distributive Justice. *American Sociological Review*, 51, 30–46.

van der Veen, R. and Van Parijs, P. (1986). A Capitalist Road to Communism. *Theory and Society*, 15, 635–655.

Van Parijs, P. (1987). A Revolution in Class Theory. *Politics and Society*, 15, 453–482.

Wegener, B. (1987). The Illusion of Distributive Justice. *European Sociologial Review*, 3, 1–13.

Chapter 12
Associations and Basic Income

Bill Jordan

Excerpts from Jordan, B. (1989). *The Common Good: Citizenship, Morality and Self-Interest.* John Wiley & Sons, Limited, Chichester.

The point about a Basic Income is that it is a citizenship share in the national product which is not paid in measure with people's contribution to the formal productive system. It therefore authorizes the release of everyone's time and energy from paid work in a new way and makes possible a new perception of, and use of, this "free time".

Up to now, time spent out of the formal economy has been classified as "retirement", "illness", "unemployment", "leisure" or "household duties". The first three have been framed as forms of involuntary withdrawal from the labor market, and incomes for them have been seen either as "earned" through previous work, or as conditional on willingness to continue work as soon as this is practicable. Leisure has been seen mainly as an opportunity for consumption, and household duties as the expression of moral obligations to kin.

Yet, in practice, as we have seen, association, self-help and community activity have tended to flourish precisely where some form of income has been provided for people, without corresponding work obligations being enforced. Where there has been long-term unemployment, where women have got an income in their own right, where people have had a retirement income yet remained fit and healthy, association and voluntary action have sprung up, and a significant minority of people have participated. The evidence is that this association and activity is valued for its own sake, and that it is one of the most important sources of a remaining sence of community in advanced capitalist societies.

This has occurred in spite of the overwhelming emphasis on production and consumption, and in spite of disruption and threat of attempts to turn part of it into a source of formal, state-organized paid work. It seems that, despite the obstacles, the discouragement and discincentives, people do recognize a value in association, and do create common interests through joining together. The very existence of "free time", even though it is defined in such a way as to inhibit purposeful association, allows this to happen, and it occurs spontaneously.

From Jordan, B. (1989). Consumption, Community and Social Relations. In B. Jordan, *The Common Good: Citizenship, Morality and Self-Interest.* John Wiley & Sons, Limited, Chichester. Reprinted with permission of John Wiley & Sons Ltd.

Basic Income: An Anthology of Contemporary Research, First Edition. Edited by Karl Widerquist, José A. Noguera, Yannick Vanderborght, and Jurgen De Wispelaere.

The Basic Income principle would greatly strengthen and endorse this tendency. For the first time, a Basic Income would create a "social wage" which corresponded to time and energy spent on association, in contrast with present income maintenance provision, all of which implies or enforces a form of exclusion, withdrawal, disengagement and isolation. The Basic Income principle would imply that there is a recognizable sphere in social life (which André Gorz (1982) has referred to as "the sphere of autonomy"), which is neither organized around formal production, nor around conventional consumption.

Part of the "social wage" would clearly correspond to the activities which are based on the household; one of the main advantages of a Basic Income is that it provides an income that recognizes unpaid domestic and caring work. But the Basic Income would certainly not increase the pressure towards the privatization of social life which is characteristic of the new orthodoxy. Instead, it would provide new opportunities for collective action, in which citizens would participate in their communities, and develop new social relations.

One objection to the Basic Income principle is that it seems to reward "leisure" or even "idleness", at the expense of industry, diligence and productivity.[1] Both the new orthodoxy and socialism claim to promote the common good by putting a premium on contributions to the output of formally produced goods. But experience of life in both advanced capitalist and existing socialist countries suggests that this devalues association, community and informal social relations to a dangerous extent, and creates interests in private consumption and in power which are a threat to the common good. By formalizing the social space for the associative element in human relations, the Basic Income principle allows the possibility of a republican notion of citizenship to re-assert itself.

Participation and Local Democracy

However, this slender opportunity could be greatly extended if local authorities were to give priority to promoting community groups and associations, and to encouraging participation in their own agencies and processes. Instead of being concerned almost exclusively with producing and delivering services, they might in addition (and, for some goods, instead) provide rooms, buildings, land, vehicles or other resources for people to act together in pursuit of their own mutual interests. This is an approach that has already been pioneered, to a limited extent, by some British local authorities, including (before its abolition) the Greater London Council (Blunkett, 1983).

One reason why these authorities have already tried this approach is a recognition of the limitations of the service-delivery model of local government. Local authorities were increasingly caught between resource restrictions by central government, the demands of rival client groups and those of trade unions representing their own workforces. They were faced with the fact that many consumers did not regard the services as "theirs", so that (if they were to resist pressure to cut back spending and to substitute commercial for public services) they had to encourage their electorates to feel a sense of involvement in and loyalty to local government agencies. Decentralization, consultation and community involvement, together with direct grants to self-help groups and cooperatives, were all attempts to find low-cost substitutes for services which were being criticized as remote, bureaucratic and paternalistic.

Criticisms of the new approach have focused on two main aspects. The first is the self-appointed and unrepresentative nature of the groups that have emerged through these initiatives. On the one hand, there is an unelected leadership which comes forward in previously disorganized or passive neighbourhoods; on the other, there are fringe groups, clustering around apparently marginal issues and minority interests. In this way, people who happen to put themselves forward achieve disproportionate influence in their communities, and eccentric or even deviant groups are able to gain resources out of measure with their distribution in the population at large. Well-publicized "loony left" causes seem to be subsidized out of the compulsory contributions of respectable ratepayers.

But it should not be surprising that previously excluded or disadvantaged people are among the first to take opportunities of this form of participation and activity. Denied access to mainstream economic and political participation, for them this presents an alternative chance to organize and have some influence. In particular, black groups who are marginalized in the economy and have little political leverage have most to gain by using any assistance available to organize for self-help and solidarity, for forging an identity and publicizing issues of concern.

This links with the second major criticism: that greater participation and association, especially by poor and minority groups, far from increasing social harmony and cooperation, actually leads to an escalation of conflict between rival interest groups. With the formation of new associations and new forums for disputing local issues, a greater consciousness of differences between groups, and of competition for resources, is created, with no satisfactory process for resolving conflicts. Alternatively (as with the Community Development Projects in the late 1960s), a greater number of groups presses harder on the local authority for increased provision of resources or services for their neighbourhood, ethnic or religious group, and for a greater share of power.

Yet these consequences of earlier attempts to increase participation and community activity are hardly surprising. In the past, these have usually been fostered either as a lower-cost alternative to traditional service delivery or as a harmless safety valve for sections of the population (blacks, poor people) who were being offered no real share of income or power. In the former case, those who were for the first time involved and consulted by local politicians and officials saw all too clearly that they were being invited to take part in an exercise of rationing, of dividing up a smaller cake. It did not escape their attention that, while the local government budgets were growing, they were not asked their opinion on how to spend them. In the latter case, it was obvious that the real power still remained in the mainstream institutions and agencies, and hence that little would change unless they could be pressured to concede some of this power. Groups which found their strength through community activism quickly focused on this mainstream political process; for example, black people gained political office, and influence on policy, in some local authorities.

What this history illustrates is that participation in associations and groups cannot be an alternative to a share in the economic and political spheres and a way of fobbing off those who are excluded from the mainstream. Conflicts over resources will indeed appear, and be impossible to resolve, if people see that all they are being invited to participate in is their own deprivation. A society which excludes and oppresses a large minority of its population certainly cannot afford to encourage association and community activity. This is why, for instance, Margaret Thatcher's government is so determined to limit the powers of local government, and to tackle the problems of inner cities through central government agencies and private enterprise rather than through the kind of local council that wants to promote participation and citizen involvement.

Any policy for revaluing and enabling association and active citizenship would have to go hand-in-hand with measures to include all members of society in the benefits of economic growth, and to share power more widely. This is why a Basic Income program seems a promising way out of the situation created by the new orthodoxy's approach to government. It would simultaneously enable a redistribution of employment in favor of previously excluded groups, and the greater involvement of all members of society in community activities.

At present, activists are most likely to come from the most deprived groups (who have no other legal way of meeting their needs) and (in larger numbers) from those with a secure income and spare time, mainly the recently retired. But the redistribution of free time which would be one of the main consequences of a Basic Income program would allow a far broader section of the population to be active in local affairs, and hence a far better balanced participation. In this way, the official democratic process could become more of a participatory democracy, and could integrate into it what is at present the unofficial politics of direct action, confrontation, anger and frustration. Those taking part in the process of decision-making would be far more representative of the community as a whole.

In this way, the republican ideal of self-rule by citizens would be combined with a much higher value being placed on association, as a source of selfinterested activity – for its own sake, as enjoyment and fulfilment of human potential, as well as for a share in what the political process delivers to its constituency.

Conclusions

The new orthodoxy's ideal citizens are private individuals, living in small households, in a suburban setting. Their needs are met by commercial suppliers. Their moral horizons stretch little further than their garden fence; they are concerned about each other, and wish their neighbors well, though not well enough to seek their well-being in any active way. They go to church to be reminded of their duties to look after themselves, and to be congratulated on their success in doing so. They subscribe discreetly to a charitable body which happens to have appealed to their sympathy.

For the new orthodoxy, association is part of what people consume during their leisure, from the proceeds of what they earn in the productive system. The purpose of association is pleasure, and all that is needed for its enjoyment can be supplied by market forces. Alternatively, if association is altruistically motivated, it is best organized through charitable voluntary bodies.

The republican tradition argues that association is a necessary part of the good society, and is the basis of, and the expression of, common interests in the common good. In a society which is organized around production and consumption of material goods, the associative basis of the common good becomes invisible, and retains only a shadowy existence, in the gaps between commercial activity and the processes of the state. It can only be revived, recognized and revalued by making a space for it, a sphere of its own, with its own income or "social wage". Within this sphere, people would associate for cooperative self-interest, mutual advantage.

Insofar as the Basic Income allows all citizens the chance to participate as autonomous equals in such a social sphere, it would enable far more extensive and diverse forms of association than exist in advanced capitalist or existing socialist societies. The range and significance of these would be further increased by the enabling role of local authorities. Unless there was a strong trend towards an egalitarian redistribution within the economic sphere, greater participation might initially focus on struggles for competitive advantage between rival groups; but this would tend to draw all interests within society into a more participative democratic process.

The type of active citizenship that this society would require would not be particularly restful. Harmony and cooperation would not be achieved by passive private consumerism, as in the new orthodoxy's ideal. People would argue, dispute and negotiate; groups would debate priorities and methods, means and goals. Machiavelli pointed out that republican Rome was often rowdy and quarrelsome, and that its more prosperous citizens complained that it was disorderly because there were so many disputes and protests among the people; but it was only by strenuous and active guardianship over liberty that good government was sustained. In rather the same way, an active, vigilant, energetic form of citizenship seems an important part of any alternative to the new orthodoxy's version of the good society.

This seems a logical development as technological progress makes more material production possible with less labor. Eventually, as numbers employed in industrial production fall, and the relative costs of services continue to rise, a mechanism is needed through which more time and energy can gradually be allocated to non-commercial activity. To call this "consumption" is to make it the mirror image of production, and to tie the right to enjoy it to the productive role. To call it "leisure" is to demean it unnecessarily, to deny its true significance. Association is a far more active concept, and implies an important alternative use of time and energy, and the creation of significant social relations.

Post-war Britain was not like this. The energy it invested in creating a better society was reflected in the civil life of the community (Ignatieff, 1988). The spirit of the welfare state informed the way people behaved in public, and lived their lives together. It is this active commitment to public goods, as much as the social services themselves, that needs to be recreated by an alternative program.

The Basic Income principle allows us to foresee the possibility of a gradual progression along the road from "full employment" to a society based on free association, the kind of society that Marx envisaged as the final stage in the transformation to communism. The point of this change would not be that it would involve more and more private consumption, and particularly consumption of commercial services, as in the new orthodoxy. In its model, it seems that many people will spend half their time working in out-of-town leisure and shopping complexes, and the other half consuming their products.

Instead, an increasing proportion of time and energy would be spent in association that is neither production nor consumption, but the active creation of good social relations. Whereas the new orthodoxy treats the public sphere of social life as a somewhat unfortunate necessity (which the rich spend money to minimize), the republican tradition sees it as the expression of common interests in what people share as members of society. As less time and energy is spent on formal production, so more time could be spent on the common good.

Public goods are not alternatives to marketed goods, just supplied to individuals in a different way. They focus on the life we live together, and the interests we share in this being of good quality. Even when public goods are provided by central or local government, they affirm these common interests. A good society recognizes the importance of the public domain, and invests energy and pride in creating a civil order which visibly and tangibly reflects good social relations.

The new orthodoxy's public face is ugly. It reflects the high priority that individuals give to private goods, and their fearful, hostile and exploitative relations. The sordid appearance of the environment, the deterioration of amenities and services, the tense atmosphere and high rates of crime, all portray a society in which social relations are discounted, and public goods have fallen into decay.

Note

1. See the criticisms of Robert van der Veen and Philippe Van Parijs's article by Jerry Cohen, Jon Elster and Hillel Steiner in *Theory and Society*, 15 (1987), pp. 631–758.

References

Blunkett, D. (1983). Towards a social policy: service "delivery" or community "participation"? In B. Jordan and N. Parton (eds) *The Political Dimensions of Social Work*. Blackwell, Oxford.

Gorz, A. (1982). *Farewell to the Working Class: An Essay in Post-Industrial Socialism*. Pluto, London.

Ignatieff, M. (1988). The tide will turn: private affluence will lose all savour amidst public squalor. *The Guardian*, 4 April.

Part III
Reciprocity and Exploitation

Introduction

Reciprocity and Exploitation

Karl Widerquist

Some supporters see Basic Income as the centerpiece of a socially just society. Other supporters see it as a pragmatic solution to poverty with important ethical drawbacks that are overcome on balance by the practical value of its effects on poverty. Some opponents see Basic Income as an outright threat to social justice. This section examines the most common justice-based objection to Basic Income, known with some variation by several different names: reciprocity, exploitation, parasitism, free-riding, or the Malibu surfer problem.

Because Basic Income is an unconditional payment, usually proposed at a level large enough to meet an individual's basic needs, it creates the possibility that individuals will stop working, live off the Basic Income, and spend their time pursuing frivolous leisure activities, such as surfing on Malibu beaches. Obviously, if a sufficient number of people did that, the program would become unaffordable, but the affordability issue is an *empirical* question about the economic feasibility of Basic Income, which is addressed in the "Economics" section. The question here has to do with the *ethical* implications of someone who receives a Basic Income without working or otherwise contributing to society.

Some opponents of Basic Income charge that any person who receives a payment from society owes a reciprocal obligation to contribute back to the society that generated that payment. Presumably someone has to work to generate that payment, and therefore, opponents argue that receiving that payment without making a reciprocal contribution exploits those who do work. Strictly speaking, "the reciprocity objection" refers to the act of receiving a payment without giving anything back, and "the exploitation objection" refers to the act of inflicting harm on someone by denying them a rightful share. Thus, the two are not identical, but they are closely related ideas and often discussed together.

Some Basic Income supporters admit that reciprocity and exploitation pose an ethical problem for Basic Income, but argue that the policy is justified overall because other effects of Basic Income – such as its effect on freedom, poverty, and equal opportunity – override the surfer problem. Other supporters argue that Basic Income does not violate the reciprocity and does not involve exploitation.

John Rawls (1988) does not mention any particular policy by name in this brief excerpt from his book, *Justice As Fairness: A Restatement*, but here he makes the clearest exposition

Basic Income: An Anthology of Contemporary Research, First Edition. Edited by Karl Widerquist, José A. Noguera, Yannick Vanderborght, and Jurgen De Wispelaere.

of his "Malibu surfer" objection to the principle underlying any policy that guarantees an income. While throughout his works, he argues that society should maximize the advantages of the least-advantaged individuals, he clarifies that those who refuse to contribute to the social product are not to be counted among the least advantaged. Under his theory of justice, those who surf all day off Malibu (instead of working) are assumed to be consuming eight hours of extra leisure per day and this added consumption is assumed to be equal to any benefit they would be entitled to under his redistribution scheme. They would have to find some way to support themselves and would not be entitled to public funds. Rawls's brief elusions to the Malibu surfer have become a symbol of this reciprocity objection.

Stuart White (1997) makes a reciprocity-based objection to Basic Income. He does not object to the right to an equal share of external wealth that underpins many arguments for it. But in his article, "Liberal Equality, Exploitation, and the Case for an Unconditional Basic Income," he argues that access to some external wealth should carry with it a corresponding obligation to make a productive contribution to the community in which that wealth is produced. Basic Income would allow individuals to avoid that obligation and thereby free ride off the efforts of others, while redistribution conditional on work effort would not.

In "Clamshell Rents? How Resource Equality Causes Exploitation," Gijs van Donselaar (2009) makes a strong exploitation-based criticism of Van Parijs's argument for Basic Income in general and of his Crazy-Lazy challenge (see the "Freedom" section) in particular. Van Donselaar argues that individuals who sell access to assets in which they have no interest are parasitic. Van Parijs's use of job assets or land as shared assets that form the tax base for Basic Income allows individuals who have no interest in those assets to benefit parasitically from their sale. Furthermore, he argues that it will allow such individuals to exploit workers in the sense that workers would be better off if the Basic Income recipients had never existed.

Brian Barry (2001) recognizes the importance of the exploitation objection to Basic Income, in his article, "Basic Income and the Work Ethic." He argues that the exploitation objection is a good reason not to endorse the highest sustainable Basic Income proposed by Philippe Van Parijs. But he argues that Basic Income has considerable benefits that are consistent with the work ethic, and that can successfully justify Basic Income on balance at the subsistence level.

In "Fairness to Idleness: Is There a Right Not to Work?," Andrew Levine (1995) responds to the reciprocity objection by assessing whether there is an equal right to idleness and assessing whether establishing a right not to work would create an unacceptable free rider problem. There is currently a very unequal right to idleness. It is available only to the wealthy. There is at least a prima facie case to equalize this right. Levine admits that equalizing this right would create a free rider problem, but argues that the free rider problem is extremely common in many areas other than Basic Income, and it does not necessarily outweigh the justification for the equalization of a right not to work.

In "Basic Income, Self-Respect, and Reciprocity," Catriona McKinnon (2003) addresses the reciprocity argument from a Rawlsian perspective. She argues that it is unclear whether the reciprocity argument can be successfully made by Rawlsians. She concludes, even if Rawlsians can make that argument, the reciprocity objection is not sufficient to overcome the commitment to Basic Income, given some practical considerations about the implementation of alternatives to Basic Income.

Karl Widerquist (1999) mounts a counter-attack to the reciprocity objection in his article, "Reciprocity and the Guaranteed Income." He argues that people who assert property rights over natural resources have forced obligations onto the propertyless without fulfilling a reciprocal obligation to compensate the propertyless for those obligations. Furthermore, putting individuals in the position in which they have no unconditional access to resources makes them vulnerable to exploitation from employers. Therefore, Widerquist argues, *only* an unconditional Basic Income can make a private property rights economy consistent with the value of reciprocity.

Robert van der Veen (1991) thoroughly addresses a version of the exploitation objection by Jon Elster in which workers are disgruntled by people who live without contributing to the system. Van der Veen argues that much of the potential for such resentment is based on the belief that if everyone did it, the system would not be sustainable. However, because the Basic Income is set at a sustainable level, living off the Basic Income is not terribly attractive and there is no realistic fear that everyone will do that. A much more realistic fear is that the economy will not be at a perfect equilibrium, and many people will live off Basic Income who would rather be working if the right job was available. The problem of an imperfect economy also means that the absence of a Basic Income will make it more likely for better-endowed individuals to partially live off the efforts of less-well-endowed individuals. Van der Veen doubts that this kind of exploitation is preferable to that which would exist under Basic Income.

Further Reading

Anderson, E. (1999). What is the point of equality? *Ethics*, 109 (2), 287–337. [Especially pages 298–299]

Arneson, R.J. (1992). Is socialism dead? A comment on market socialism and basic income capitalism. *Ethics*, 102 (3), 485–511.

Arneson, R.J. (2003). Should surfers be fed? In A. Reeve, and A. Williams (eds) *Real Libertarianism Assessed: Political Theory after Van Parijs*. Palgrave, New York.

Birnbaum, S. (2011). Should surfers be ostracized? Basic income, liberal neutrality, and the work ethos. *Politics, Philosophy & Economics*. First published online.

Bowles, S. and Gintis, H. (2000). Reciprocity, self-interest, and the welfare state. *Nordic Journal of Political Economy*, 26 (1), 33–53.

Couillard, P. (2002). A little water in a glass of wine or a glass of water with a little wine in it? Justice as reciprocity and the UBI: A possible reconciliation of two enemies? Chaire Hoover Working Paper (DOCH), 78, pp. 1–33.

De Wispelaere, J. (1999). Universal basic income: Reciprocity and the right to non-exclusion. Citizen's Income Trust Occasional Paper. Citizen's Income Trust, London, pp. 1–23.

De Wispelaere, J. (2000). Sharing job resources: Ethical reflections on the justification of basic income. *Analyse & Kritik*, 22 (2), 237–256.

Elster, J. (1987). "Comment on van der Veen and Van Parijs," *Theory and Society*, 15 (5), 709–721.

Farrelly, C. (1999). Justice and a citizens' basic income. *Journal of Applied Philosophy*, 16 (3), 283–296.

Galston, W.A. (2001). What about reciprocity? In J. Cohen and J. Rogers (eds) *What's Wrong with a Free Lunch?* Beacon Press, Boston, pp. 29–33.

McKinnon, C. (2003). BI, self-respect and reciprocity. *Journal of Applied Philosophy*, 20 (2), 143–158.

Meckled-Garcia, S. (2002). Why work harder? Equality, social duty and the market. *Political Studies*, 50 (4), 779–793.

Noguera, J.A. (2005). Citizens or workers? Basic income vs. welfare-to-work policies. *Journal of Law and Urban Studies*, 2 (1), 103–124.

Noguera, J.A. (2007). Why left reciprocity theories are inconsistent. *Basic Income Studies*, 2 (1), Article 5. http://www.degruyter.com/view/j/bis

Rawls, J. (1974). Reply to Alexander Musgrave. *Quarterly Journal of Economics*, 88 (4), 633–655.

Segall, S. (2005). Unconditional welfare benefits and the principle of reciprocity. *Politics, Philosophy and Economics*, 4 (3), 331–354.

Steiner, H. (1992). Three Just Taxes. *Arguing for Basic Income: Ethical Foundations for a Radical Reform*. Verso, London/New York.

van der Veen, R. (1998). Real freedom versus reciprocity: competing views on the justice of unconditional basic income. *Political Studies*, 46 (1), 140–163.

van der Veen, R. (2011). Why auntie's boring tea parties matter for the fair distribution of gifts. In A. Gosseries, and Y. Vanderborght (eds) *Arguing about Justice. Essays for Philippe Van Parijs*. Presses universitaires de Louvain, Louvain-la-Neuve, pp. 355–365.

Van Donselaar, G. (2003). The stake and exploitation. In K. Dowding, J. De Wispelaere, and S. White (eds) *The Ethics of Stakeholding*. Palgrave Macmillan, Basingstoke, pp. 94–113.

Van Donselaar, G. (2009). *The Right to Exploit: Parasitism, Scarcity, and Basic Income*. Oxford University Press, Oxford.

Van Parijs, P. (1995). *Real Freedom for All: What (If Anything) Can Justify Capitalism?* Clarendon Press, Oxford.

Van Parijs, P. (1997). Reciprocity and the justification of an unconditional Basic Income: Reply to Stuart White. *Political Studies*, 45 (2), 327–330.

White, S. (1997). Liberal Equality, Exploitation, and the Case for an Unconditional Basic Income. *Political Studies*, 45 (2), 312–326.

White, S. (1999). The egalitarian earnings subsidy scheme. *British Journal of Political Science*, 29 (3), 601–622.

White, S. (2000). Social rights and the social contract: political theory and the new welfare politics. *British Journal of Political Science*, 30 (3), 507–532.

White, S. (2003a). *The Civic Minimum: On the Rights and Obligations of Economic Citizenship*. Oxford University Press, Oxford.

White, S. (2003b). Fair reciprocity and basic income. In A. Reeve and A. Williams (eds) *Real Libertarianism Assessed: Political Theory after Van Parijs*. Palgrave, New York.

White, S. (2006). Reconsidering the exploitation objection to basic income. *Basic Income Studies* 1 (2), Article 4. http://www.degruyter.com/view/j/bis

Widerquist, K. (2005). *Does She Exploit or Doesn't She?* K. Widerquist, M.A. Lewis, and S. Pressman (eds) *The Ethics and Economics of the Basic Income Guarantee*. Ashgate, Aldershot.

Widerquist, K. (2006). Who exploits who? *Political Studies*, 54 (3), 444–464.

Wolff, J. (2004). Training, perfectionism and fairness. *Journal of Applied Philosophy*, 21 (3), 285–295.

Zelleke, A. (2005a). Basic income in the United States: redefining citizenship in the liberal state. *Review of Social Economy*, 63 (4), 633–648.

Zelleke, A. (2005b). Distributive justice and the argument for an unconditional basic income. *Journal of Socio-Economics*, 34 (1), 3–15.

Chapter 13
Brief Comments on Leisure Time

John Rawls[1]

Excerpts from Rawls, J. (2001). *Justice As Fairness: A Restatement.* The Belknap Press of Harvard University Press, Cambridge, MA.

In elaborating justice as fairness we assume that all citizens are normal and fully cooperating members of society over a complete life. We do this because for us the question of the fair terms of cooperation citizens so regarded is fundamental and to be examined first. Now this assumption implies that all are willing to work and to do their part in sharing the burdens of social life, provided of course the terms of cooperation are seen as fair.

But how is this assumption expressed in the difference principle? The index of primary goods, as discussed so far, makes no mention of work, and the least advantaged are those with the lowest index. Are the least advantaged, then, those who live on welfare and surf all day off Malibu?

This question can be handled in two ways: one is to assume that everyone works a standard working day; the other is to include in the index of primary goods a certain amount of leisure time, say 16 hours per day if the standard working day is eight hours. Those who do no work have eight extra hours of leisure and we count those eight extra hours as equivalent to the index of the least advantaged who do work a standard day. Surfers must somehow support themselves.[2]

Of course, if leisure time is included in the index, society must make sure that opportunities for fruitful work are generally available. We cannot discuss the complicated issues involved here. The point is that we can include leisure time in the index should this be workable and the best way to express the idea that all citizens are to do their part in society's cooperative work.

If necessary we can also include in the index realized native endowments and even states of consciousness like physical pain. However, for the sake of having an objective measure and relying on information that is readily available and easy to comprehend, it is much better not to include such goods in the index. But leisure time has a reasonably

Basic Income: An Anthology of Contemporary Research, First Edition. Edited by Karl Widerquist, José A. Noguera, Yannick Vanderborght, and Jurgen De Wispelaere.

objective measure and is open to view. It also meets the essential condition that primary goods must not presuppose any particular comprehensive doctrine.

Notes

1. Editor's note: Although this article does not mention Basic Income by any of its names, the author clearly takes a stand against unconditional benefits. It was from this essay that the "Malibu surfer" entered the Basic Income debate.
2. See Rawls (1988: 257, n.7). [Editor's note: In the cited article, Rawls takes this thought a little farther. He writes, "twenty-four hours less a standard working day might be included in the index as leisure. Those who are unwilling to work would have a standard working day of extra leisure, and this extra leisure itself would be stipulated as equivalent to the index of primary goods of the least advantaged. So those who surf all day off Malibu must find a way to support themselves and would not be entitled to public funds."]

Reference

Rawls, J. (1988). The Priority of Right and Ideas of the Good. *Philosophy & Public Affairs*, 17 (4), 251–276.

Chapter 14

Liberal Equality, Exploitation, and the Case for an Unconditional Basic Income

Stuart White

Excerpts from White, S. (1997). Liberal Equality, Exploitation, and the Case for an Unconditional Basic Income. *Political Studies*, 45 (2), 312–326.

Payment of a substantial Unconditional Basic Income (UBI), it is objected, will lead to the exploitation of productive, tax-paying citizens by those who, while capable of working, instead choose to live off their UBI. If a compelling case for the introduction of a substantial UBI is to be made, supporters of the proposal must attempt to defuse this "exploitation objection". Stating the challenge in more general terms, they must show how the proposal can be plausibly grounded in an attractive theory of distributive justice. In an important book, *Real Freedom for All: What (if Anything) Can Justify Capitalism?*, Philippe Van Parijs (1995) has risen to this challenge, attempting to show how a liberal egalitarian conception of justice directly supports the introduction of a substantial UBI. As a contribution to the emerging debate over the desirability of UBI I therefore propose in this chapter to examine the key arguments of Van Parijs's book and to consider whether these provide a successful response to the exploitation objection.

The External Assets Argument Stated

I begin with a reconstruction of Van Parijs's central "external assets argument" for the introduction of a substantial UBI. The argument has essentially five steps. The first step introduces a foundational moral principle, implicit in much recent liberal egalitarian thinking about social justice, which we may refer to as *the equal opportunity principle:*

P1 Each person should have equal opportunity to pursue a conception of the good life.

Now, individual opportunity and real freedom are centrally determined by personal endowments of external wealth and individuals' respective internal capacities (skills, handicaps, etc.). Exactly what counts as "external wealth" for present purposes will be

From White, S. (1997). Liberal Equality, Exploitation, and the Case for an Unconditional Basic Income. *Political Studies*, 45 (2), 312–326. Reprinted with permission of John Wiley & Sons Ltd.

Basic Income: An Anthology of Contemporary Research, First Edition. Edited by Karl Widerquist, José A. Noguera, Yannick Vanderborght, and Jurgen De Wispelaere.

clarified shortly. For the moment, let us simply note that if we make the simplifying assumption that individuals have identical internal capacities,[1] **P1** appears to imply that:

P2 Each person is entitled to an equal share of available external wealth.
And one way of interpreting **P2**, which I will explain in a moment, is:

P3 Each person is entitled to an Unconditional Income equal to the value of a per capita share of available external wealth.

To the proposition made in **P3**, Van Parijs then adds the following empirical claim:

P4 In the circumstances of at least some of the advanced capitalist countries today, an income equal to the value of a per capita share of external wealth will be a substantial income (i.e., one that is at, or close to, a level sufficient to cover a standard set of basic needs).[2]

From **P3** and **P4**, we then have:

P5 In at least some advanced capitalist countries today, each citizen is entitled to an Unconditional Basic Income set at or close to a level sufficient to cover a standard set of basic needs.

Where involuntary unemployment persists in competitive equilibrium, there will be a significant inequality in opportunity between those "insiders" fortunate enough to be in employment, and the involuntarily unemployed, the "outsiders", who are trapped, at least for some period of time, on the short-side of the labor market.

Now an important corollary of this equilibrium involuntary unemployment is the existence of substantial *employment rents* enjoyed by those fortunate enough to be in employment, which are given by the difference between the wage they receive and the hypothetical market-clearing wage. Van Parijs's innovative proposal is that we address the inequalities arising from job scarcity by including these employment rents in the tax base for financing a UBI. The underlying rationale for this proposal is essentially the same as the rationale for including the value of natural resources and transfers of other kinds of physical asset in the UBI tax base. In the same way we thought of May and June[3] as having rights to equal tradeable shares of land on their desert island, or equivalently, to an Unconditional Income equal to the value of a per capita share of this land, Van Parijs argues that we may regard the citizens of a non-Walrasian[4] society as having rights to equal tradeable shares of available jobs, or equivalently, to an (additional) Unconditional Income equal to the value of a per capita share of available jobs; and this amounts, Van Parijs tells us, to giving each person an equal share in the employment rents arising from job scarcity.[5] These rents will be particularly large when involuntary unemployment is high, but may still be considerable even if everybody has a job, because some of those with relatively poor jobs may want and be able to do more attractive jobs at, or slightly below, the relevant prevailing wage. Van Parijs argues that once the UBI tax base is accordingly expanded to include these employment rents, it becomes large enough to finance a substantial UBI.[6] Inclusion of "job assets" in the UBI tax base thus enables Van Parijs to make the empirical claim contained in **P4**, which together with **P3**, gives us the radical conclusion expressed in **P5**.

The Exploitation Objection Stated

To understand the exploitation objection we must first consider what principle of justice is allegedly violated by non-contributing, but productively able, recipients of a UBI. The relevant principle here is a *reciprocity principle*, according to which: those who willingly enjoy the economic benefits of social cooperation have a corresponding obligation to make a productive contribution, if they are so able, to the cooperative community which provides these benefits.

Theories of justice which make explicit appeal to the notion of reciprocity are often thought, however, to have anti-egalitarian implications. This is because reciprocity is usually conceived as requiring something like a strict proportionality between the value of the benefits an individual enjoys and the value of his/her productive contribution. Whether value is understood in market-based or Marxian terms, differences in the value of individuals' respective contributions will, to some controversial extent, reflect brute luck differences in personal characteristics, for example, in natural productive skill; a distribution of benefits in accordance with this conception of reciprocity will reflect these brute luck differences, and will therefore violate the equal opportunity principle. As Marx put it, a distributive rule of this kind "tacitly recognizes unequal individual endowment and thus the productive capacity of the worker as natural privileges" (Marx, 1976, 16).

However, the reciprocity principle need not be interpreted in this way; it can and (from a liberal egalitarian perspective) should be interpreted in a way that renders it consistent with the equal opportunity principle. Such a conception of reciprocity must: (i) link income entitlement to productive contribution (for the productively able), but without (ii) supporting income inequalities that reflect brute luck differences in productive ability, or (iii) prohibiting the income differentiation necessary to equalize opportunity amongst diverse individuals with brute luck differences in degrees of "neediness" (for example, in the amount of food needed to be well-nourished). In short, we need to formulate the reciprocity principle something as follows: Each person is entitled to a share of the economic benefits of social cooperation conferring equal opportunity (or real freedom) in return for the performance of an equal handicap-weighted[7] quantum of contributive activity (hours of socially useful work, let us say, weighted by labor intensity).

According to this egalitarian conception of reciprocity, entitlement to a given share of the economic benefits of social cooperation entails a corresponding obligation to make a productive contribution, but there is no presumption that one's contribution must be equal or directly proportional in value to the value of the benefits one receives. Intuitively, reciprocity is now conceived not as a matter of "putting in as much as one takes out", but of "doing one's bit".

The old slogan, "from each according to this ability, to each according to his need", arguably embodies exactly this egalitarian conception of reciprocity, though the underlying idea has potentially much wider application. Suppose, for example, that one rejected the thorough-going equalization of opportunity implied by this slogan (e.g., because one thought that any attempt to implement such a comprehensive egalitarianism would violate certain basic liberties), but that one accepted a more modest principle according to which each citizen has a right to an income sufficient to maintain a basic level of opportunity or real freedom. In this case, the egalitarian conception of reciprocity implies that in return for this decent minimum of income each citizen has a corresponding obligation to perform a decent minimum of contributive activity, the size of this minimum varying with degree of productive handicap. We may refer to this as *baseline reciprocity*.

The exploitation objection to a substantial UBI may then be stated more exactly as follows: Those who willingly enjoy a decent minimum of the economic benefits of social cooperation without satisfying their suitably adjusted reasonable work expectation violate the principle of baseline reciprocity, and thereby take unfair advantage of – that is, exploit – those citizens who do satisfy this expectation; payment of a substantial UBI is therefore unjust because, by completely detaching the receipt of a decent minimum of the economic benefits of social cooperation from the satisfaction of a suitably defined reasonable work expectation, it makes possible exploitation of this kind.

The External Assets Argument Stated

Does Van Parijs's external assets argument offer a rebuttal of the exploitation objection? In approaching this question, it will help if we distinguish three types of external wealth that, –according to **P2**, each individual has an equal right to: (i) pure natural resource;[8] (ii) transfers of non-natural wealth; and (iii) job assets. The UBI which Van Parijs seeks to defend can be seen as being built up in three "layers" from each of these sources, and we may evaluate the vulnerability of his argument to the exploitation objection by considering how – if at all – the objection applies to each respective layer.

As regards the first layer, derived from taxation of pure natural resource values, I think the exploitation objection has limited force. Why? Recall that the reciprocity principle on which the objection is based applies to the economic benefits of social cooperation. Pure natural resources, however, do not originate from the efforts of social cooperation; they are, so to speak, the pre-existing material on which social cooperators (or non-cooperating hermits) go to work. The distribution of these resources, or their monetized equivalent, thus appears to lie largely outside the scope of application of the reciprocity principle. By virtue of the "pre-social" status of these resources, we may say that each person is entitled to an equal share of them, or their value, simply qua person, and that this entitlement carries no (or only a very modest)[9] corresponding obligation to contribute productively to a given cooperative community.[10] Thus, at least some sort of UBI, financed from the taxation of pure natural resource values, is arguably resistant to the exploitation objection. However, such a UBI would not be sufficient to cover a standard set of basic needs (even before we take into account the way the UBI fund may be reduced by morally prior transfers to those with poor internal capacities).[11] To get a UBI closer to this level, one must add the value of the latter two types of external wealth – transfers of non-natural physical wealth and job assets – to the UBI tax base.

It is at this point, however, that the exploitation objection does appear to have force. Consider the nature of these assets. What I have termed "non-natural wealth" consists of a diverse range of resources, but they have in common that they are largely products of labor in a cooperative community and may thus be considered "economic benefits of social cooperation". Job assets are not economic benefits of social cooperation in quite the same sense; nevertheless, jobs can only constitute a type of asset in the context of a cooperative community – there are no jobs in the state of nature – and, as I noted above, a major reason for regarding jobs as assets is precisely that in societies like our own they are the primary means of gaining access, via a wage, to what Mill termed "the benefits of combined labor". In other words, it is sensible to see jobs as assets precisely because of the access they confer to the economic benefits of social cooperation. Consequently, when individuals claim a right to an equal share of transfers of non-natural wealth and/or of job assets, these claims may reasonably be interpreted as falling under the more general heading of a claim to a fair share of the economic benefits of social cooperation. But if this is so, then it would seem to follow that these claims also fall within the scope of application of the reciprocity principle. And if that is so, then it would seem inappropriate to distribute these assets, or the income derived from the taxation of their value, in the form of (additional) UBI. Why?

Because doing so would enable citizens to share in what are, in a direct or mediated sense, economic benefits of social cooperation, without demonstrating a willingness to make a corresponding productive contribution.

I must admit, however, of at least one qualification to this argument, concerning transfers of non-natural wealth. Imagine that five people suddenly find themselves on a desert island and begin economic cooperation. Ten years later they all simultaneously die, to be replaced by five new people. In addition to a stock of natural resources, these people find on the island a stock of machines produced by the previous generation. It seems reasonable to treat these assets in just the same way as pure natural resources, and thus, to enter them into the UBI tax base. Those who decline to engage in economic cooperation cannot be said to be free-riding on the cooperative efforts of co-existent individuals who do choose to engage in such cooperation if they appropriate an equal share of these assets for these assets exist, like pure natural resources, prior to/independently of present-day cooperative efforts. The implication is that where non-natural physical wealth is the product of members of past generations, who were not co-existent with contemporary prospective recipients of this non-natural wealth, the assets in question are properly treated in the same manner as pure natural resources, and transfers of this portion of the existing stock of non-natural wealth may therefore be taxed to finance a UBI. However, while this will boost the UBI justified by the external assets argument to some extent, it is unlikely, as Van Parijs would admit, to boost the relevant tax base sufficiently to support the introduction of a substantial UBI.[12]

Putting this qualification to one side, if the foregoing analysis is correct, then in order to prevent free-rider exploitation it would seem appropriate to make conditional the share out of employment rents and (some portion of) the value of transfers of non-natural wealth on willingness to make the minimum productive contribution required by the principle of baseline reciprocity. The external wealth fund should be redistributed in some form other than a UBI, in some manner that links participation in the fund with contributive activity.

Notes

1. Internal capacities include talents and handicaps.
2. Indeed, it could conceivably be even higher than this.
3. Editor's note: "May and June" refers to an example in which two people live on a desert island. White concludes that both have an equal and tradable right to a per capita share of the island's resources.
4. Editor's note: A Walrasian economy is one in which all markets are perfectly competitive and at equilibrium so that demand and supply are exactly equal at the prices prevailing for all commodities, and no one makes excessive profit by taking advantage of disequilibrium.
5. See Van Parijs (1995) pp. 106–109.
6. Once employment rents are included in the UBI tax base "it is then no longer ludicrous to suggest that the non-discriminatory concern with people's access to the means for the pursuit of their conceptions of the good life, the leximinning of real freedom, should demand that people be given an adequate basic income" (*Real Freedom*, p. 108).
7. Individuals may suffer "productive handicaps" which limit their ability to engage in production. Contributive activity is then properly weighted by degree of productive handicap so that these individuals need not perform the same number of "raw" hours of socially useful labor to be entitled to a given level of income as those who suffer no such handicap.

8. By "pure natural resources" I mean natural resources in their natural, unimproved state, and the "value" of pure natural resources is simply the value of natural resources in this state, e.g. the value a piece of land has in virtue of its natural fertility, deducting any value added by human improvements to its fertility.
9. Presumably there has to be some sort of state apparatus to enforce the right in question, in which case it can be argued that individuals owe some portion of their natural resource UBI back to society in return for the services this apparatus provides; equivalently, we may say that a portion of the UBI is paid as income in kind, in the form of these services, with the general cash payment being correspondingly reduced. I thank Amy Gutmann for raising this point.
10. A "cooperative community" is here conceived as an association of persons engaged in sustained economic cooperation on the basis of ground-rules that reflect a share, public conception of justice; in the case of a liberal egalitarian cooperative community, this concept of justice will incorporate the equal opportunity and reciprocity principles discussed above.
11. Van Parijs states this quite explicitly in an earlier paper, Competing Justifications of Basic Income in Van Parijs (ed.) (1992). It is also implied by his claim in Van Parijs (1995) p. 102, that the UBI financed only from our first two layers is likely to range from "the pathetically low to the frankly negligible."
12. See Van Parijs (1995) p. 102.

References

Marx. K. (1976). *Critique of the Gotha Program.* Foreign Languages Press, Peking, p. 16.

Van Parijs, P. (ed.) (1992). *Arguing for Basic Income.* Verso, London, p. 13.

Van Parijs, P. (1995). *Real Freedom for All: What (If Anything) Can Justify Capitalism?* Oxford University Press, Oxford.

Chapter 15

Clamshell Rents? How Resource Equality Causes Exploitation

Gijs Van Donselaar

Excerpts from Van Donselaar, G. (2009). *The Right to Exploit: Parasitism, Scarcity, and Basic Income.* Oxford University Press, Oxford.

My main interest in this chapter is to question the plausibility of Dworkin's distributive principle of external resources, the non-envy test, and the way this principle is put to use by Van Parijs in defense of Basic Income. We may or may not agree with Van Parijs when he argues that "If the wealth stocked on top of a cupboard is to be shared among all, it makes no sense to restrict it to those who are tall enough to reach it" (Van Parijs, 1995: 123). However, the main thrust of *Real Freedom for All* is that if the wealth stocked on top of a cupboard is to be shared among all, it also makes no sense to exclude those who are too indolent to reach for it – even if they are tall enough.

It is this implication that I want to question. Therefore, I shall make a radical abstraction here. In order to circumvent the special problems related to the unequal distribution of talents, handicaps, body length, and the like, I will simply consider the distributive problems of a population of which I assume that the members are equally talented.

So the question seems to be how will the right to sell or lease out resources, as part of the base line system of constraints and liberties, affect distributions of resources? I will try to work out this problem in more detail and see how it relates to the argument for a Basic Income. There are three questions that will especially concern me: given the presence or absence of the right to lease out resources in the base line system of constraints and liberties:

1. Which distribution(s) will be free of envy?
2. Which distributions will allow parasitic relations [. . .]?

And I will add one further consideration:

3. Which distributions will be Pareto optimal?

From Van Donselaar, G. (2009). *The Right to Exploit; Parasitism, Scarcity, and Basic Income.* Oxford University Press, Oxford, pp. 107–108, 112–123. Reprinted with permission of Oxford University Press.

Basic Income: An Anthology of Contemporary Research, First Edition. Edited by Karl Widerquist, José A. Noguera, Yannick Vanderborght, and Jurgen De Wispelaere.

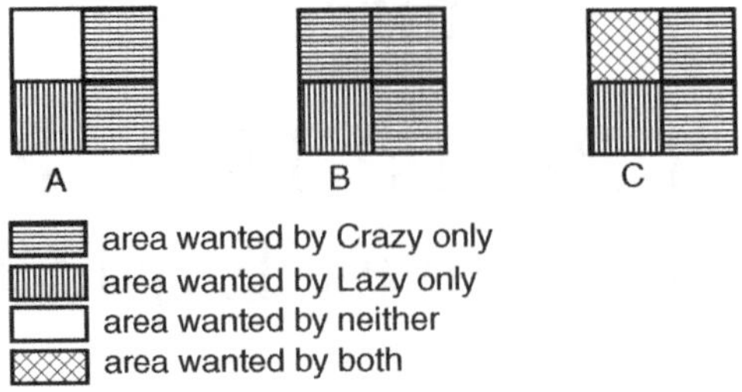

Figure 15.1 Resource-related preferences for work.

I shall confine myself to examples of very simple types of situations (which will prove to be complicated enough) involving only two persons and only one resource: let us think of land that can be used to produce a certain crop[1] (say: yams).

I believe there are three relevantly different situations when we ask how the respective interests of two persons may relate to the total amount of yam-specific fertile land that is available; all these situations answer to the idea that one of the two persons dislikes work more than the other. Following Van Parijs I shall call these two: Lazy and Crazy.[2] Moreover, as promised, I shall assume that their productive talents are identical, thereby circumventing (for argument's sake) the effects of the inequality of internal resources. Lazy dislikes work more than Crazy does, but if he works he will produce as many yams as Crazy does, in the same time, on an equally large plot of land. Now, imagine a piece of land consisting of four identical plots, all equally fertile and smooth to work on, and each of them requiring one day of equally strenuous farming labor (plowing, sowing, harvesting, etc.) in order to make it produce a certain amount of yams, no matter who does the work. The three situations are illustrated in Figure 15.1. I will call these three situations: constellations (of interest). In the following sections each of these constellations will be treated separately. In constellation A, Lazy's trade off between yams and leisure time is such that, in the absence of Crazy, he would want (and take) only one-quarter of the land to work upon, while Crazy's preferences are such that, in the absence of Lazy, she would want one-half of all the land to work on. Ergo: there is one-quarter of the land neither wants to work on. I will call these shares of land that they would want and take in the absence of the other their "independent interests."

Similarly, in constellation B, Lazy wants to work on just one-quarter of the land, while Crazy wants to occupy three-quarters. Between them they would divide the available land, if the distribution coincided with their independent interests. There would be no superfluous rest.

In constellation C, Lazy wants to work half the land and Crazy wants to work three-quarters of the land. Since they cannot both have their way, we must consider one-quarter of the land as contested between them. (See Figure 15.1) Now let us look at how the liberty or prohibition to lease out land, as part of the basic system, would affect the three questions about envy-freeness, freedom from parasitism. and Pareto optimality. The distributions in each case that I will consider are:

1. a mathematically equal distribution and
2. a distribution in which Lazy gets one-quarter of the land and Crazy three-quarters.

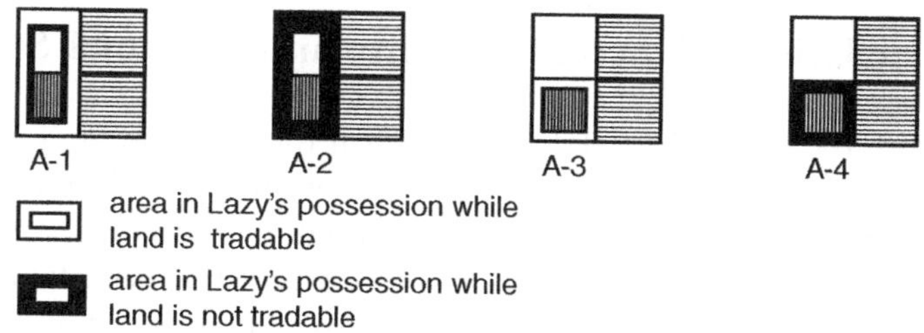

Figure 15.2 A-type constellations under four regimes (graphics to be read as before).

The reason for this latter selection will soon become clear.

So in all three constellations of interests we get four possible "regimes":

1. Lazy and Crazy both get half the land, and land is tradable.
2. Lazy and Crazy both get half the land, and land is not tradable.
3. Lazy gets one-quarter, Crazy gets three-quarters, and land is tradable.
4. Lazy gets one-quarter, Crazy gets three-quarters, and land is not tradable.

Of course, there are more possible regimes (Lazy gets nothing, Crazy gets all, etc.), but I shall ignore those because the four just mentioned will suffice to capture the general idea of how regimes work out in practice. Graphically, I will represent the four regimes as in Figure 15.2 (for the example of the A-type constellation of interests).

Some explanations: if Lazy's land is surrounded by a white border, it means that both he and Crazy are allowed (and technically able) to sell (shares of) their land. It means that if they would want to sell or lease out land there will be no external (practical or) legal impediments to doing so – provided, of course, that the other is interested. If, on the other hand, Lazy's land is surrounded by a black border, it means that neither he nor Crazy will be allowed to sell or lease out land even if they would both be interested in a transfer.

Picture it this way: if we (or the Auctioneer or Justice Personified) allow a person to be the rightful owner of a piece of tradable land, we (or He or She) will put that person on that land and then build a huge wall around it, which cannot be passed except through a gate of which the owner has the key. If he owns a non-tradable piece of land he will likewise be enclosed on his own property, but this time there will be no gate and no key. Ownership of non-tradable land simply means that others do not have access to that land and cannot be given access either. A certain regime allows parasitic relations if, given the constellation of independent interests, Crazy would be better off without Lazy, while Lazy would be worse off without Crazy (or vice versa).

A regime is Pareto inferior if, given the constellation of independent interests, both the positions of Lazy and Crazy can be improved by switching to another regime, or if the position of one of them can be improved without worsening that of the other by such a switch.

A certain regime satisfies the *non-envy test* if, given the constellation of independent interest, the situation is such that neither Lazy nor Crazy would prefer to have what the other has. So we check on the envy-freeness of a regime by letting the parties reverse their shares and then mapping their independent interests on those.

A-Type Constellations: Unconditionality and Maximal Sustainability

Let us proceed with the check. In A-1 Lazy owns half the land and he is allowed to trade (part of) it, but since Crazy possesses all the land she wants to work on, she will have no interest in any possession of Lazy at all. So Lazy, though permitted to, will not be able to extract any benefits from Crazy. And this is also true vice versa. Parasitic relations cannot emerge from A-1, since neither will be able to improve his or her position compared to the absence of the other.

Will the non-envy test be satisfied? It will. Since they both hold exactly the same parcels of land nothing would change in their situation if they switched shares. Could anybody's position be improved by switching from A-1 to one of the other three regimes? We can reduce Lazy's share and/or remove the liberty to sell land, and it will not affect the position of either. So A-1 is also Pareto optimal.

These conclusions also hold for A-2: there is no reason for Lazy and Crazy to envy one another if they hold exactly similar pieces of land, and there can be no parasitic transactions if trades are forbidden. Moreover a switch in regime would improve the position of neither.

But things change in A-3. In A-3 Lazy is allowed to trade his land but like before he will not be able to do so, since he owns nothing that Crazy finds interesting enough, so he will not be in a position to receive benefits at the cost of Crazy. There can be no parasitism. Nor would a switch of regimes improve anybody's position. But is the non-envy test satisfied? This time it is not. For if Lazy and Crazy would now reverse their shares, so that Lazy would have three-quarters and Crazy only one-quarter, then Lazy would be able to extract benefits from Crazy, given that he is allowed to lease out the part of his property he does not want to work on himself. Since Lazy owns more than he wants to work on himself while Crazy is interested in that surplus, he can trade with Crazy. That is Lazy's reason to envy Crazy in A-3.

Let us turn to A-4 type regimes. As before, Lazy owns only one-quarter of the land, which is precisely the amount he wants to work on, Crazy owns the rest which is one-quarter more than she wants to work on. But since neither is allowed to sell anything he or she owns, it does not matter to Lazy whether or not he possesses anything more than the plot he wants to work on himself. So he does not envy Crazy. Crazy, of course, prefers her own bundle to Lazy's bundle, since otherwise, [if the A-4 regime was exchanged], she would have less than she is independently interested in. A-4 also satisfies Pareto optimality: the other regimes would not be preferred by either of them.

Of the four regimes we searched in A-type constellations of independent interests only one fails one of the tests. That regime is A-3, which violates the non-envy test. A-1, A-2, and A-4 are all "normatively" equal distributions in Dworkin's sense, since they all satisfy the non-envy test, and they are all parasitism-proof and Pareto optimal on top of that.

Of course, we know that Van Parijs would opt for A-1 as the equal distribution, but it is interesting to note that although the distribution is mathematically equal, and although the parties are granted the right to lease out shares of their original property, and although Crazy is using a larger share of the resources than Lazy is, A-1 situations cannot provide us with an argument for an Unconditional Basic Income. Obviously, no yams-to-land exchanges would emerge from A-1, since although Lazy may be oversupplied, Crazy is not undersupplied and she will simply not be interested in the purchase of any additional land to her own. No market price will emerge and so there seems to be no justification for any system of taxation and redistribution that will result in a net transfer of yams from Crazy to Lazy.

And Van Parijs must be in agreement with this. He is. "Crazy wants a higher income and is therefore prepared to work more. If for this purpose she uses no more than an equal share of society's scarce resources – say, land – she should not he taxed one penny to help feed Lazy" (Van Parijs, 1995: 90). Yet, this simple observation must already be sobering to the basic income enthusiasts: the unconditionality of a right to a Basic Income has its limits and does not have the robustness it seemed to have in the beginning.

It may be offered as a rejoinder that there is some significance to the difference between having no right to a Basic Income and having a right to a Basic Income that is zero. Having an unconditional right to a Basic Income that is zero is still an unconditional right. Perhaps. But it is worthwhile to note that this distinction does not seem to do its work when Philippe Van Parijs argues against Senator Yee of Hawaii that he was being unfair to the Hawaiian "welfare hippies" (or to those who spend their day surfing off Malibu) when he wanted to deny them the right to a welfare grant (Van Parijs, 1991: 101). Perhaps Senator Yee never paused to ask whether or not there were still unoccupied fertile resources on Hawaii (did nor the hippies have a legal right to pick their own coconuts?), but, to my knowledge, neither did Philippe Van Parijs when he came to the rescue of the hippies' entitlement to full-time leisure. Yet, the unfairness or fairness of Yee's attitude vitally depends on that question even on Van Parijs's own terms. This is not even the only relevant question: he should also have asked whether there were still (perhaps well-paid) jobs available in "paradise."

But there is a more serious ambiguity in Van Parijs's argument. The justification for a Basic Income has in fact two aspects. There is the justification for having a Basic Income at all, which relies on the analysis of the market effect of equality of resources, and there is the justification for the highest sustainable Basic Income, which relies on the analysis of the incentive effects on the tax yield. From A-1 situations, we can learn that there is an inconsistency in these two arguments. For we find that there is no relation between market transfers from ideal equality and the highest sustainability of a Basic Income in reality. In A-1, the competitive value of the land is zero so that there is no case for a net transfer at all, but it does not follow that there is no tax scheme that would allow a stable net transfer of income from Crazy to Lazy. On the contrary, the odds are that there is a tax rate that would allow a stable Basic Income and a net transfer from Crazy to Lazy. There is no reason at all to assume that a taxation and redistribution that would result in a Basic Income of only one yam will eventually lower productivity in such a fashion that a Basic Income of only one yam cannot be sustained. In fact it may be much higher than that. In other words, a Basic Income that can be sustained is not in itself a Basic Income that can be justified. Or, more generally, the highest sustainable Basic Income can be much higher than the maximally justifiable Basic Income in "Dworkinian" terms. The maximally justifiable level of Basic Income is determined by the market value of resources that would emerge from equality. The highest sustainable level of Basic Income is determined by the incentive effects of taxation in actual fact. A-1 shows that there is no intrinsic relation between these two levels. And that in itself, I believe, suggests that there is something misleading in the idea of an unconditional right to a Basic Income that is as high as can be sustained. Whatever way we look at it, there can be no right of that kind, even if there may be some right to a Basic Income.

B-Type Constellations: Usurpation

Clearly B-1 might allow Lazy to make use of his share of land in a way that would be parasitic (see Figure 15.3 for B-type regimes). He owns a plot which is of no independent

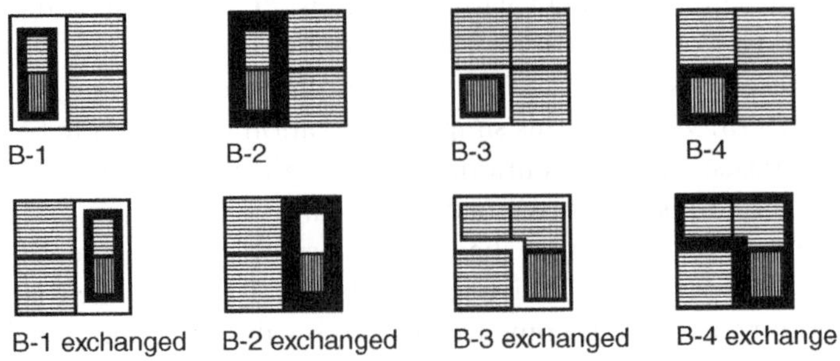

Figure 15.3 B-type regimes and their exchanges (graphics to be read as in previous figures).

interest at all to him, but which he can sell to Crazy because she has less in her possession than she wants to work on. Nevertheless, the non-envy test is passed, since exchanging their share would not alter the situation at all. Also, B-1 is Pareto optimal: we cannot change regimes without worsening the position of at least one of the parties.

In B-2, Lazy may not exploit Crazy in a similar way as in B-1, since now he is not allowed to sell the superfluous part of his property. The non-envy test is met because reversing shares does not change the situation. But B-2 is not Pareto optimal: both Lazy's and Crazy's position will be improved if we switch from B-2 to B-1. Crazy prefers being exploited, given that she controls a mathematically equal share. In this case introducing the right to have exchanges would be welcomed by both of them.

In B-3, Lazy is allowed to trade (part of) his share, but since Crazy is fully satisfied with her own three-quarters of the land, Lazy has nothing to trade with. However, the non-envy test is not passed, since if Lazy possessed three-quarters of the land and Crazy only one-quarter, he would have had something to trade with: two-thirds of his property, as will be apparent from a comparison with B-3 exchanged. B-3 is Pareto optimal nevertheless.

In B-4, no trades are possible so costs cannot be displaced, and the non-envy test will be passed, since the superfluous two-thirds of the land in the possession of Lazy in B-4 exchanged will then not be tradable either. B-4 is Pareto optimal; any change of regime would leave Crazy worse off or both unaffected.

So in B-type situations, there are two regimes that pass the non-envy test and prove to be free of parasitic opportunities. Those are B-2 and B-4, which happen to be the two regimes that do not allow land to be tradable. Only B-4, however, is Pareto optimal as well. So if envy-freeness, insensitivity to parasitism, and Pareto optimality were to be thought of as three independently desirable features of a distribution, then, in the B-type constellation of interests, a mathematically unequal distribution of non-tradable land would certainly stand out as superior to all other possibilities. We may also generalize this result over A- and B-types of constellations of interests. A-4 like B-4 satisfies all tests.

Unfortunately, Van Parijs does not share these desiderata that can be reconciled so neatly. It is clear that he believes, as before, that mathematical equality plus the liberty to sell is the relevantly equal distribution: B-1. But as we observed, B-1 blatantly violates the objection against parasitism. It would enable Lazy to take shares of land into his possession for which he has no independent interest whatsoever, not even a little, while Crazy would very much like to use that share in a productive way. Crazy is forced to work as a tenant for Lazy because Lazy has the right to own what he cannot use. As I will say: Lazy is allowed to be a usurper of land. Why should he be allowed to be that? Why should we believe that there is any distributive problem in B-types of situations? After all, if interests relate to land in the manner of A- and B-types, there is in fact no scarcity of land, so why do we not just allow Lazy and Crazy to use the shares they want to use? Why, in other words, would there be a case for distributing exclusive property rights to land? Why would it not suffice, in this case, to distribute access rights or rights of usufruct? Why bother issuing clamshells, having auctions, post-auction markets, and redistributive tax strategies? Just tell people not to rob each other of the fruits of their labor and each can do as he likes without being in the others' way.

Again, there seems to be a tricky ambiguity in Van Parijs's text. This time it concerns the definition of scarcity. Discussing how the value of land will be influenced by the ratio of supply and demand he says: "True, the fewer people are interested in some asset and the less keen they are to acquire it, the lower its value. In particular, if those interested in it are fully satiated with less than the total amount available, that is if there is no scarcity, the value of the asset would be zero" (Van Parijs, 1995: 105). But this is simply not true. In the B-type constellation of interests in land, Lazy and Crazy are fully satiated by the total amount available if we let each of them have just what he would also have taken without the other. There is no scarcity as long as we do not interfere with the shares that they would spontaneously have chosen to work on, each following their own trade-off between work and leisure. But it certainly does not follow that land will not acquire market value when, for some reason or other, we decide that each of them should have half of the resources available, and that superfluous shares may be sold. In fact we introduce scarcity of market supply by letting them share equally an asset that is not in scarce natural supply.

What seems to be happening here is that the rigid egalitarian concerns underlying Dworkin's (and Van Parijs's) distributive principle enforce an equal sharing of the land's commercial value, while that commercial value itself would not have existed in the first place without the egalitarianism. There is a suggestion of circularity: of course, Lazy will want an equal share once it is stipulated that he may sell what he cannot use – that is why B-3 fails the non-envy test. And, of course, both Lazy and Crazy will want to have the liberty to sell and buy, once it is stipulated that they shall have an equal share – that is why B-2 fails the Pareto optimality test. If the land is scarce, then both should have half; and if both have half, then the land is scarce. So is scarcity of natural supply a condition for a justifiable Basic Income or is it not?

It is not! In order to see why, we have to return to the foundations of Van Parijs's egalitarianism. What he wants is equality of real freedom, and having real freedom is having the freedom to do whatever one might want to do, not just the freedom to do what one happens to want to do. Resources are the carriers of real freedom. Equality of resources means equality of real freedom. We should not give Lazy fewer resources because he actually wants fewer. He might have wanted to work harder, and if we give him less than half of the land we have not given him an equal share of the freedom to work as hard as he might have wanted to. So here we have the true villain in the story that says that it is all right to exploit your fellow men: it is the concept of real freedom. It is the idea that you are entitled to the exclusive and unconditional control of options for which you have no actual use. Basic Income is justified by the market value of those options. Crazy is allowed to use Lazy's spare options, but Lazy will want yams in return. According to the doctrine of justice under scrutiny here, he shall have them. But that means that absence of scarcity in the natural supply of resources, and the tact of full satiation of all by what there is, cannot be a condition for a Basic Income. It implies that even the practice of pure speculation may be justified as a way of swelling the Basic Income: even if the natural supply of resources abundantly exceeds the amount that would satiate all, equality of real freedom

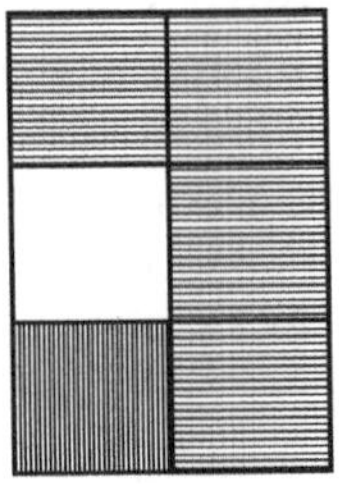

Figure 15.4 A variation of the B-type constellation.

will still allow (parasitic) transfers of the fruits of Crazy's labor to Lazy. Compare the variation in Figure 15.4 of the B-type constellation of interests and note that it will respond to the three tests in the same fashion as the original.

In order for Lazy to be able to make his parasitic profits out of the share in his possession that is wanted by Crazy, he must maintain a firm grasp on an area that is wanted by neither. He must not only usurp land that he does not want, he must also usurp land that nobody wants. There is land that nobody is using, but Crazy will have to be Lazy's tenant nevertheless.[3] And that is justified because Lazy is to be as real-free as Crazy is. There is no scarcity, indeed there is abundance, but that does not change the right of the parasite. It is hard to see how these observations relate to the statement quoted above.

Notes

1. Of course, simplifications like these may present special problems and ambiguities, but I do believe that they serve to bring out certain peculiarities that might have been lost in a more general treatment. Again, I feel confident in this approach, since Philippe Van Parijs also uses it in the explanation of the more qualitative aspects of his justification of Basic Income.
2. I follow Van Parijs in his choice of these two names, but we should take care to appreciate the irony. Monks in contemplative orders or people "who get engrossed in action painting" (Van Parijs, 1992: 126), or indeed surfers, may get up very early and go to bed late, quite exhausted from their activities; they are not lazy in the usual sense of the word. The point is that in order to be able to do only the things they want, they must benefit from (or are dependent on) the activities of others, while these others, by assumption, are not benefiting from the activities of monks, action painters, and surfers. The analysis in this chapter does not make a judgment on the inherent worth or desirability of the goals and purposes that "lazy" people set themselves, it only comments on how the realization of such goals and purposes relates to their claims on shares of resources.
3. Would this constitute a case of violating Lock's non-spoilage proviso, on top of his enough-and-as-good proviso?

References

Van Parijs, P. (1991).Why Surfers Should Be Fed: The Liberal Case for an Unconditional Basic Income. *Philosophy & Public Affairs*, 20, 101–131.

Van Parijs, P. (1992). Competing Justifications of Basic Income. In Van Parijs, P. (ed.) *Arguing for Basic Income: Ethical Foundations for a Radical Reform*. Verso, London, pp. 3–43.

Van Parijs, P. (1995). *Real Freedom for All: What (If Anything) Can Justify Capitalism?* Oxford University Press, Oxford.

Chapter 16

Basic Income and the Work Ethic

Brian Barry

Excerpts from Barry, B. (2001). UBI and the Work Ethic. In P. Van Parijs (ed.) *What's Wrong With a Free Lunch?* Beacon Press, Boston.

Asking about the pros and cons of Basic Income as such is rather like asking about the pros and cons of keeping a feline as a pet without distinguishing between a tiger and a tabby. Basic Income has very different characteristics at different levels. Many of the advantages that Van Parijs[1] claims for a Basic Income scheme would be realized only if it were pitched at subsistence level (or higher). Thus, for example, the uncertainty that inhibits people from moving from unemployment benefit (and, even more, disability benefit) would be allayed only if the unconditional alternative were enough to live on. Similarly, only a Basic Income at (or approaching) subsistence level would enable people to take time between jobs, get more training, or start a new business. Again, workers can refuse "desperation" jobs and women can leave abusive husbands only if the alternative income is adequate. The same goes for the possibility of engaging in full-time caring for children or for elderly or infirm relatives.

Despite this, the level of Basic Income actually plays no part in Van Parijs's arguments for it. He says at one point that he "favor[s] the highest sustainable such income," and adds that in the richer countries this level exceeds a reasonable definition of subsistence. But there is really no way of guessing what the highest level of basic income would be in any country after all the changes in employment and taxation had settled down into an equilibrium. If Van Parijs is right, though, we have to ask about the pros and cons of a Basic Income at a level higher than "a reasonable definition of subsistence." These are different from those of either a Basic Income below or one at subsistence level. In the end, I will defend a subsistence level Basic Income, in preference to Van Parijs's proposal.

Let me begin with the least demanding reform: introduction of a Basic Income at below subsistence level. If we are concerned about the "Malibu surfer" problem – the prospect of able-bodied people with employable skills choosing to live a life of self-indulgence, albeit at subsistence level – then maintaining the Basic Income below subsistence level solves it.

From Barry, B. (2001). UBI and the Work Ethic. In P. Van Parijs (ed.) *What's Wrong With a Free Lunch?* Beacon Press, Boston.

Basic Income: An Anthology of Contemporary Research, First Edition. Edited by Karl Widerquist, José A. Noguera, Yannick Vanderborght, and Jurgen De Wispelaere.

Unfortunately, however, it yields only in an attenuated form at best the advantages offered by a subsistence-level income that I quoted from Van Parijs. Moreover, the entire apparatus of welfare benefits would still have to remain in place, though benefits would, of course, be reduced by the amount of the Basic Income. Even here, however, the news is not all bad: in Britain, for example, the eminent economist Tony Atkinson has calculated that a Basic Income at a rate of half the standard state benefit would take millions of people off means-tested benefits, which are demoralizing, demeaning, and expensive to administer.

I have already listed a number of the advantages of a subsistence-level Basic Income. Moreover, its relation to the work ethic is not as one-sided as might appear at first blush. It is true that it reinstates the "Malibu surfer" problem. But at the same time it definitively abolishes the "poverty trap" that leads all traditional welfare systems down the path of coercion. The point of a Basic Income is that, in contrast to a conditional welfare benefit, it is not lost by taking a job. The result is that even very poorly paid work makes you better off than not working. Moreover, contingent benefits criminalize a large proportion of the population for working while drawing benefit, even though they could not live on what this work brings in. The middle class in Britain is engaged in mass collusion with the officially unemployed to get houses cleaned, gardens dug, and children minded. And neither party to the transaction normally feels the slightest guilt – nor should they. There is surely something crazy about the stipulation that those drawing unemployment benefit must be "available for work" at any moment, which rules out their using the time to improve their qualifications, engage in community work, or help a neighbor while earning a bit extra. This is, in my view, the knock-down argument for Basic Income at subsistence level.

From this point of view, the Malibu surfers are a drawback, but one worth putting up with for the advantages that are inseparable from the unconditionality of a Basic Income. A superficially attractive way of getting at the surfers while maintaining many of the advantages of a subsistence-level Basic Income is Atkinson's proposal of a "participation income." As one reviewer explains, "Atkinson defines participation to include: paid employment; self-employment; full-time education or training; intensive care work and approved forms of voluntary work."[2] But this opens up a nightmarish scenario of an enormous bureaucracy entrusted with arbitrary monitoring powers. My guess is that something like "participation income" might be necessary politically to get a Basic Income introduced, but that the expense and intrusiveness of administering it (as well as its lending itself so easily to fraud) would lead either to abandoning the whole experiment or moving to an unconditional Basic Income.

All this presupposes, of course, that surfers really are a drawback. For Van Parijs, they are from a practical point of view, since the more of them there are the lower the sustainable unconditional income will be. Clearly, his surmise that in wealthy countries the maximum sustainable Basic Income would be well above any reasonable definition of subsistence level presupposes that the proportion of the population who could contribute significantly to the economy and choose not to, would not be very large.

But what Van Parijs does not make altogether clear in his essay is that he rejects the idea that those who take a Basic Income (even one well above subsistence level) and do nothing for the community should be subject to reproach. As Van Parijs says at the start of his essay, he wishes to maintain that the highest possible Unconditional Basic Income is an entitlement derived from a theory of justice conceived in terms of "real freedom for all." In the essay, he only hints at the nature of this theory, laid out in his book *Real Freedom for All*.[3] and I cannot undertake to expound it in any detail here. I *can* say that by "real freedom" Van Parijs means (roughly) the ability to do what you want, and that his criterion of justice is that the freedom of those with the least real freedom is to be maximized. The means to real freedom so defined are resources, so (again, roughly) this means that the resources available to those with the least should be maximized. Those with the least are those who do nothing to generate any income for themselves by their own efforts. Hence, the size of the Unconditional Basic Income is what should be maximized.

Why is this just? Van Parijs has several answers to this question. One is that it is unfair if those who are congenitally lazy have a smaller chance to get what they want than those who are more inclined to work. But we do not believe that people with antisocial traits (strong dispositions towards, say, rape or pedophilia) should have as much chance to fulfill their desires as others, and if the wish to live at others' expense is an antisocial trait there is no reason for making special efforts to indulge it.

Another argument is that everybody living in a country is entitled to an equal share of "external assets," which underwrites a 100% rate of estate duty. Van Parijs then extends the notion of an "external asset" by calling on the theory of "efficiency wages," according to which it is profitable for employers to offer wages at above a market-clearing rate to induce employees to want to keep their jobs. As a result, there are always some people who could equally well do any given job and would be prepared to do it for less than those who hold the jobs are getting. On the basis of this, Van Parijs deduces that income tax rates should be set to produce the maximum possible yield: people who hold the well-paying jobs are beneficiaries of good fortune, and cannot object to having that good fortune taxed. Putting these two taxes together produces the revenue whose amplitude arouses such optimism in him.

The argument is unconvincing. It is hard to see why those who have no intention of engaging in paid employment should have any claim on the proceeds of a tax whose rationale is to offset the good fortune of those who have well-paid jobs at the expense of others who are just as qualified and would like to be doing them instead.

If I am right, then, the arguments that Van Parijs offers for the justice of maximizing the size of the Basic Income are defective. In their absence, I do not believe that there is any good case for pushing the demand for a Basic Income above the subsistence level. Of course, the notion of "subsistence" is still negotiable. It must be redefined for each society, so as to include the diet, amenities, and access to services that are widely thought to be necessary to "get along." It should also provide the material conditions for participating in the social and political life of the community. Something approaching a consensus has emerged in Western Europe that an income of half the median is, as a rule of thumb, what is needed to meet these criteria. Endorsing, then, the proposal for an Unconditional Basic Income at subsistence level, let me conclude by offering that interpretation of it.

Notes

1. Editor's note: See Van Parijs, P (2001) A Basic Income for All, in P. Van Parijs (ed) *What's Wrong with a Free Lunch?* Beacon Press, Boston.
2. White (2000). I can heartily recommend this article, incidentally, for a discussion of a number of the issues surrounding Basic Income and its rivals. For "participation income" see Atkinson (1996).
3. Editor's note: see Van Parijs (1995).

References

Atkinson, T. (1996). The Case for Participation Income. *Political Quarterly*, 67 (1), 67–70.

Van Parijs, P. (1995). *Real Freedom for All: What (If Anything) Can Justify Capitalism?* Clarendon Press, Oxford.

Van Parijs, P (2001) A Basic Income for All, in P. Van Parijs (ed) *What's Wrong with a Free Lunch?* Beacon Press, Boston.

White, S. (2000). Review Article: Social Rights and the Social Contract – Political Theory and the New Welfare Politics. *British Journal of Political Science*, 30 (3), 507–532.

Chapter 17

Fairness to Idleness: Is There a Right Not to Work?

Andrew Levine

Excerpts from Levine, A. (1995). Fairness to Idleness: Is There a Right Not to Work? *Economics and Philosophy*, 11 (2), 255–274.

To most people it seems obvious that able-bodied individuals in the prime of life who choose not to participate in the monetized economy cannot rightfully demand material support from public agencies. Hence the idea that it would be unjust to provide aid to the voluntarily idle.

I shall argue against this view. However, I shall not attempt a full-fledged defense of a right not to work. To mount such a defense, it would be necessary to address proposals for implementing this right institutionally, and to speculate on the consequences of one or another institutional implementation for such values as economic wellbeing, freedom and democracy. My aim is only to defend a right not to work insofar as considerations of justice pertain and, by doing so, to remove a potentially fatal obstacle in the way of such a right.

What follows assumes a liberal egalitarian understanding of justice that owes much to the work of John Rawls (1971) and philosophers influenced by Rawls. However it is not my intent to endorse liberal egalitarianism. My aim instead is to engage liberal egalitarians on their own terrain, and to push them to radicalize their own conceptions of what equality requires. Ultimately, I would want to argue that liberal egalitarianism is not egalitarian enough, not sufficiently disposed to equalize persons' conditions, though I will not attempt to defend this claim here. Before this suggestion can be constructively pursued, there is the prior task of ascertaining just how radical liberal egalitarianism is. To this end, I will argue that liberal egalitarianism decouples distribution from contribution to a greater extent than is commonly supposed, and that liberal egalitarians therefore commonly underestimate the radicalism of their own theoretical commitments.

Is Leisure Special?

Consider individuals who, in accord with their conceptions of the good, would be idle were they not also needy. Do they have alternatives to paid employment? Without public

Basic Income: An Anthology of Contemporary Research, First Edition. Edited by Karl Widerquist, José A. Noguera, Yannick Vanderborght, and Jurgen De Wispelaere.

or private provision, they can either work for a living, live on less than the minimal means of subsistence or support themselves illegally. The last possibility is a non-starter insofar as we are concerned with justice, and living on less than subsistence is, needless to say, not a viable alternative. Thus paid employment is the would-be idler's only genuine option. In this instance, entering the labor market is overwhelmingly determined by circumstances. The choice is, of course, voluntary but only in the formal sense that liberal egalitarians eschew. It is therefore fair to say that would-be idlers without independent means are involuntarily employed; that they are economically coerced into entering the labor market. To the degree that they are, withholding benefits from them would be objectionable in the way, though perhaps not to the degree, that conscripting them directly into the work force would be.

An obvious rejoinder is that liberals, committed to the idea that individuals ought to bear the costs and reap the benefits of their own free choices, have no cause to complain if leisure time (when it passes over into that part of the day ordinarily taken up by paid employment) is too expensive for most people to consume. To be sure, the wellbeing of those who do not want to work is diminished by the high cost of leisure; their desires are less satisfied and they are less happy than they would be were leisure cheaper. But the state's proper role cannot be to compensate for welfare deficits by satisfying expensive tastes. Seaside condominiums in posh resorts would also realize the desires and increase the happiness of many who cannot afford them. If the state is under no obligation to provide these amenities, neither is it under any obligation to subsidize the desires of individuals who attach an unusually high value to leisure.

This argument appears persuasive insofar as we are disposed to regard leisure as a consumption good among others, susceptible to being traded off for other things. It is commonplace, especially for economists, to suppose that everything is at least to some degree substitutable, and there can be little doubt that for many explanatory purposes it is useful to construe leisure this way. However, doing so is inappropriate when the aim is to ascertain what neutrality requires.

It is worth remarking that the commodification of leisure and even the distinction between work and leisure assumed throughout this discussion is to some degree specific to economic systems with labor markets,[1] and that even today those engaged in "meaningful" or "creative" employments cannot always clearly demarcate work-time from leisure-time. From a less historically particular vantage-point than the one economists typically assume, work and leisure are not always clearly distinguishable. But even when work and leisure are unproblematically distinct, as they are assumed to be throughout this discussion, it is plain that they coexist, as it were, on a dimension of such importance to human life – and to conceptions of the good that give lives their coherence and identity – that, from a normative point of view, they cannot properly be traded off against ordinary consumption goods.

Thus many of the considerations that can be marshalled in defense of a right to idleness can also be adduced in defense of a right to paid employment.[2] To make the case that the state ought to accord such a right – by promoting full employment policies and/or serving as an employer of last resort – one would have to show that, for some individuals, the benefits of employment are such that nothing can adequately substitute for them. Presumably, the relevant benefits would be non-pecuniary, since direct grants can always substitute for wages. Insofar as claims of this sort are based on the nature of work, they too are historically particular. Thus it is almost certainly relevant to any likely defense of a right to work that individuals generally cannot purchase jobs through markets; that employers buy employees' services while employees do not buy employers. It is also relevant that social norms are such that participation in the monetized economy is, for most people, a basis for self-respect and the respect of others.[3]

In much the same way, it is fair to view leisure as an intrinsic, non-substitutable component of particular conceptions of the good. The rationale is the same: like employment in the monetized economy, idleness can sometimes be so connected to individuals' self-understandings, to their relations with others and indeed to their very identities that trading off leisure for a wage can only be to the detriment of what matters fundamentally from a normative point of view. This is why, in some cases, leisure cannot rightfully be treated as just another expensive commodity. To view it as one among *n* axes in an individual's consumption space is to deny that it is special.

It is true, of course, that leisure can be purchased in a way that paid employment generally cannot.[4] But for all except the independently wealthy, leisure can only be purchased through income gained from paid employment; a prospect which defeats the idea of living in accord with a conception of the good for which idleness is mandatory and/or paid employment abhorrent. In contrast, ordinary consumption goods are paradigmatically substitutable. To be sure, seaside condominiums can figure in the realization of particular conceptions of the good. But they are not of such importance, even for individuals bent mainly on particular styles of consumption, that they cannot be replaced by other goods without loss in what matters intrinsically. On the other hand, if leisure is for some individuals what work is for others, no substitutions are available. Would-be idlers for whom leisure matters fundamentally will usually accept paid employment "voluntarily" inasmuch as they need food, clothing and shelter and are unable to obtain them so long as they remain idle. But the income that accrues from work is not a substitute for leisure in the sense that a house in the mountains might substitute for a seaside condominium. To be compelled by circumstances to take employment, in opposition to one's own conception of the good, is to be unable to do what matters fundamentally to oneself. Individuals who find themselves in this situation are effectively disabled by alterable social practices from pursuing their distinctive plans of life. Thus they are effectively denied equal treatment by prevailing institutional arrangements.

Proponents of neutrality are not committed to the idea that states are obligated to satisfy the expensive tastes of individuals whose desires exceed their budgetary constraints. But they are committed to according persons equal respect, and in order to do so they must ensure that resources are distributed in such a way that individuals have equal opportunities to obtain what matters fundamentally. What corresponds to the state's duty to support the voluntarily idle, therefore, is not a direct subsidy to individuals with expensive tastes, but a duty to ensure that whoever chooses to lead a life in which the consumption of expensive goods is fundamental has the opportunity to do so. Opportunities to obtain what matters fundamentally are means for pursuing projects that follow from conceptions of the good. Neutral states are obliged to treat such projects equally – to insure that there is equal opportunity for pursuing whatever falls within the acceptable range of particular conceptions.

This conclusion rests on a view of equal opportunity that is substantive, not merely formal, and on a distinction between what matters fundamentally and what does not. It would be worthwhile to elaborate upon these understandings. But for the present purpose I think we understand what is involved well enough. The prima facie case for a right not to work that appeals to liberal neutrality will almost certainly survive any plausible, substantive construal of equality of opportunity, and any defensible distinction between fundamental values and mere tastes.

Needless to say, states are under no obligation to ensure that individuals succeed in their various pursuits. Thus a person who undertakes to become a concert pianist cannot claim a right to be provided with concert halls and audiences. However, proponents of neutrality ought to accord this person a right to the means for cultivating the talents that warrant playing before audiences in concert halls, for pursuing the project of becoming a concert pianist under favorable conditions. Similar considerations obtain for those whose conceptions of the good entail abstinence from paid employment. There is no obligation on the part of the public to ensure that they succeed in their particular endeavors, whatever they may be. But states ought to allow them to pursue their objectives under conditions as favorable as those in which others – presumably the vast majority – pursue different, possibly incompatible, ends.

Of course, this conclusion can be countervailed by conflicting considerations – chief among them the expense of providing genuinely equal opportunities. If it costs more than a society at a given level of development can bear to provide equal opportunities for some fundamental plans of life, that is a reason, no doubt a compelling reason, for not doing so. I readily concede that it is fair to place the burden of establishing economic feasibility on those who would propose particular institutional implementations of a right not to work. But because I believe that most genuinely autonomous agents would find productive activity (pursued in or out of the monetized economy) an intrinsic part of their conceptions of the good, and because under real world conditions productive activity is generally attached to paying jobs, I am not worried that, in a genuinely free society, many people would choose unemployment or significant underemployment regardless of how a right not to work is implemented. I therefore doubt that a right not to work will prove unacceptably costly. But if we turn to the general issue and not the specific case, there is a lurking problem nevertheless: the problem of expensive fundamental values. How worrisome is this concern?

If ensuring equality of opportunity to pursue fundamental values imposes onerous costs on participants in the monetized economy, then perhaps it will be impossible to implement this liberal egalitarian requirement (or, at least, to implement it completely). However, partisans of neutrality need not fear this eventuality. Once we concede both that the state should ensure individuals' rights to work and not to work, what remains as a candidate for public support? Perhaps expensive "spiritual" pursuits. There are, of course, good liberal reasons why public authorities should distance themselves from religious affairs altogether. But even if we allow that conceptions of the good involving religious beliefs should be treated on a par with those that make work or leisure fundamental, there is still little cause for concern. We can, of course, imagine religions that require costly pilgrimages or lavish lifestyles. But real world religions, even those that encourage or require travel to distant places, make the fulfillment of these requirements individual responsibilities. There is no a priori reason why affordability problems cannot arise from this or any other quarter involving fundamental values. Problems generated by expensive fundamental values will always remain a theoretical possibility. However, they do not pose a practical problem for generally affluent communities committed to treating competing conceptions of the good fairly.

Of course, this empirical speculation could be wrong. But even if it is, the claim that a commitment to neutrality underwrites public efforts to ensure genuinely equal opportunities to pursue what matters fundamentally would not be embarrassed. We would only have to conclude that sometimes – though probably not in the case of a right not to work – what neutrality requires is swamped by countervailing considerations.

A Free-Rider Problem?

I would venture that the broad consensus against public support for the voluntarily idle rests, in part, on the conviction that reaping benefits without paying the costs incurred in their production, free-riding, is always wrong. However, it is a mistake to deduce opposition to a right not to work from a generalized opposition to free-riding. Contrary to what is widely (if unreflectively) assumed, free riding is frequently unavoidable and not always objectionable. Even so, the kind of free riding that a right not to work implies might always be unjust or, more plausibly, unjust in the context of relevant background conditions. If so, a right not to work would conflict with justice, notwithstanding the demands of neutrality. I will argue, however, that objections from this quarter do not succeed in undermining the liberal egalitarian case for a right not to work.

We should take care not to confound worries about the effects of free-riding on the production and reproduction of social practices with questions about its normative status. So-called free-riding problems typically arise in connection with the production of jointly produced and/or effectively non-excludable goods. It is claimed that these "public goods" would be under-produced or not produced at all in those (very common) instances in which individuals would prefer free-riding to contributing towards their production, and prefer least of all that other individuals free-ride on their own productive contributions. But since it has been assumed throughout this discussion that a right not to work will be implemented by states – that is, by institutional arrangements able to compel compliance – this worry is of no consequence in the present context. In any case, the concern here is with the justice of public support for those who choose not to work, not with difficulties in the way of organizing collective action or producing public goods.

There is a widespread belief, famously articulated by Hart (1955), according to which accepting a benefit creates a liability to contribute to its cost of (re)production. Presumably, those who fail to execute these obligations act wrongly because they violate a standard of reciprocity. In taking without giving back, they take unfair advantage of others. If free-riding, is understood as taking unfair advantage, and if the point of a theory of justice is to elaborate what fairness requires, then free-riding would of course be unjust, and the injustice of voluntary idleness would follow directly. But this conclusion is much too hasty.

I will not question the assumed connection between justice and fairness. Neither will I challenge the idea that free-riders, including voluntary idlers, take advantage of others. Nor will I deny that in doing so there is a sense in which they offend fairness. What I will question is the conclusion that the kind of unfair advantage idlers take is, on balance, objectionable from a normative point of view.

Perhaps the most direct way to see that opposition to a right not to work cannot be derived from a generalized opposition to free-riding is to realize that the general principle on which this argument rests would tarnish nearly all social interactions. The problem, in brief, is that in those situations in which it is necessary to coordinate individuals' behaviors in order to advance their interests – a range of conditions that includes but is not limited to so-called prisoners' dilemmas – there is no way to achieve coordination that is not substantially redistributive.[5] Individuals can cooperate by voluntarily deferring from doing what is individually best. Or they can concoct some "common power to hold them in awe," following the Hobbesian model (1651) that has become standard throughout modern political theory. But in neither case will the benefits that accrue to individuals generally correspond proportionally to the contributions they do or do not provide. The problem is not only that, for a wide range of human interactions, there is no uncontroversial way – and not always even a conceivable way – to determine real costs and benefits.[6] The deeper problem is that, even if we could agree on what it means to "get what we have paid for," hardly anyone ever would.

The most uncontroversially legitimate state function, acknowledged even by libertarian defenders of "minimal states,"[7] is the provision of public goods that markets are incapable of producing. But there are few if any public goods whose benefits, even as they spill over independently of contribution, do not affect individuals differentially. Almost without exception therefore, whenever a public good is supplied, some individuals are in varying degrees free-riding on the contributions of others. Outside the political arena too, it is seldom possible to engage in market transactions without free-riding to some degree – if only in consequence of the pervasive and unavoidable existence of externalities. More insidiously, each of us all the time free-rides on the culture, knowledge and techniques that are every living human being's inheritance from preceding generations. Thus we are bound sometimes to play the "sucker" and sometimes to benefit from the fact that others will be suckers for us. Free-riding and being, as it were, free-ridden upon is a fact of our existence as social beings. Unless we are prepared to condemn what is impossible to avoid, there can be no general proscription of free riding. Therefore, opposition to a right not to work cannot be deduced from the supposed normative reprehensibility of free-riding as such.

But since reciprocity and fair play are legitimate ideals, there is still at least a prima facie case against free-riding in this (and every other) case. Can opponents of a right not to work maintain that this prima facie case obtains after all relevant factors are taken into account? I have argued that the answer is "No" for anyone who attaches sufficient weight to the demands of neutrality. But it is worth reflecting on why this conclusion remains so counterintuitive. Part of the explanation may be that there is more force to the free-riding objection than has so far been acknowledged. But the larger part of the explanation is, I believe, a consequence of a way of thinking that was once reasonable, but that is rapidly becoming obsolete. It will be well to turn very briefly to this "historical" diagnosis before reflecting, again, on free-riding and its bearing on the case for a right not to work.

There can be little doubt that the virulent, material scarcities that have afflicted humankind throughout its history have profoundly conditioned intuitions about fairness that persist to this day. I would submit that the longstanding hostility to voluntary unemployment is an understandable functional adaptation to this (perceived) fact of human life. Why has this conviction survived the tremendous expansion of productive capacities of the past two centuries? The maldistribution of already existing affluence is certainly part of the explanation; because of it, significant scarcities persist almost everywhere. But these scarcities owe more to prevailing inequalities in the distribution of the world's resources than to a genuine inability to achieve a level of affluence sufficient to support the level of free-riding that we might expect in a world in which people are not economically coerced into working in order to subsist. Insofar as it is a functional adaptation to real world conditions, the conviction that militates against a right not to work is a residue of a historical moment that it is finally possible to supersede.

But even if our situation is no longer so dire as to warrant the intuition epitomized in the slogan "he who does not work shall not eat," are we justified in going to the other extreme by according public support to voluntary idlers? It is one thing, after all, to impugn the idea that it is unfair for able-bodied adults to live off the labor of others, and something else to establish a full-fledged right not to work. Now there is a sense in which the case presented here for a right not to work does indeed "free-ride" (metaphorically) on arguments that, strictly speaking, support less far-reaching conclusions. Thus I argued that those who abstain from paid employment have a claim for public support only if they are principled idlers, motivated by an appropriate conception of the good. Weak-willed or lazy idlers were then included only because there is no practical way to distinguish them from legitimate idlers. And in disputing the idea that free-riding as such is always and everywhere indefensible, I only argued that in many political, social and economic contexts, we cannot reasonably demand meaningful proportionality between contribution and benefit. The idea that we need not require beneficiaries of social cooperation to contribute anything at all is, at best, a special, limiting case of this result. Is this enough to defeat the demand for reciprocity in the case of those who choose not to work? Of course, most, if not all, voluntary idlers sometimes do contribute constructively to the wellbeing of working members of society, albeit not through the monetized economy. But there is no need to appeal to this understanding of productive contribution to defend a right not to work. My contention is not that voluntary idlers do not free-ride or that their free-riding is unobjectionable. My claim is that, at present levels of affluence, the fact that voluntary idlers free-ride is not a consideration of sufficient weight to counter the case for a right not to work.

The free-riding of voluntary idlers is of insufficient weight for just the reason that it is no longer a reasonable functional adaptation to real world conditions to demand that everyone do their "fair share" in the face of scarcity. Increasing affluence diminishes, without extinguishing, the moral urgency of reciprocity. At the same time, it enhances the importance of doing what is required to implement genuine neutrality. The rationale for both reciprocity and neutrality is a commitment to accord persons equal respect. Under some conditions, a way to achieve this end is to accede to the demands of reciprocity; in other (generally overlapping) conditions, genuine neutrality on the part of public institutions is instrumental for enhancing equal respect. In many cases, practices based on these strategies for insuring equal respect work in harmony. But they conflict when a right not to work is at issue. Then, I maintain, reciprocity, not neutrality, should give way. For the conditions under which reciprocity and neutrality are effective means for advancing equal respect are not quite the same. Roughly, the more scarcity there is, the more pertinent reciprocity becomes. With increasing affluence, its urgency recedes in neutrality's favor.

It has long been recognized that justice and therefore the kind of injustice that free-riding exemplifies matter less as the circumstances of justice – above all, scarcity itself – decrease in salience.[8] With diminishing scarcity, intuitions formed when free-riding mattered more lose their force, even as they linger on. But the imperative to treat persons equally remains intact. In these new circumstances, other means than those underwritten by a commitment to reciprocity come to the fore. For liberal egalitarians, the commitment to provide equal opportunities to individuals to pursue their own (appropriate) conceptions of the good comes into its own, swamping the free-rider worries raised by a right not to work.

Conclusion

Whether or not we are now at a point where the requirements of neutrality should take precedence over the principle of reciprocity is, of course, debatable. I have already registered the opinion that we are potentially at that stage now and would be there in fact if existing wealth were more equally distributed.[9] I shall not speculate further on this matter here, nor shall I venture an opinion on whether, taking all relevant factors into account, the world or some part of it ought now to accord a right not to work. My claim is only that justice – more precisely, liberal egalitarian justice with its commitment to fairness to competing conceptions of the good – supports its provision, at least in societies rich enough to entertain liberal egalitarian aspirations. Intuitions that suggest contrary positions are largely residues of historically superseded real world conditions, the views of Rawls and so many others notwithstanding. From a liberal egalitarian vantage-point, therefore, the claim that a right not to work ought not to be accorded because it is unjust fails. Indeed, the contrary is true. In conditions of relative affluence, in which genuine neutrality is possible and desirable, a right not to work is actually a requirement of justice. Fairness to goodness implies fairness even to idleness.

Notes

1. cf., among others, Sahlins (1972), Gorz (1989), Block (1990), Schor (1991).
2. cf., Arneson (1990), Elster (1988), and Moon (1988) argue against state provision of a right to work but in a way that supports the contention that work is special in the indicated sense. They each maintain that in existing circumstances employment of the involuntarily idle by the state cannot adequately realize the non-pecuniary benefits of paid labor. Elster argues, in addition, that implementation of a right to work by states would have detrimental macro-economic consequences.
3. It is worth remarking that the claim that work is special depends on these background considerations and on the intrinsic nature of work, but not on the underlying justificatory strategy proponents of a right to work endorse. I would venture that one could argue for the non-substitutability of paid employment on utilitarian or perfectionist grounds, by appeal to some notion of self-realization or indeed in any of the variety of ways that contemporary moral philosophers deploy. Whatever the underlying moral philosophical commitments of proponents of a right to work may be, the point is that, for at least some individuals some of the time, nothing can compensate satisfactorily for the lack of a (paying) job. For similar reasons, it is not necessary to endorse a particular justificatory strategy to defend a right not to work.
4. However, individuals with non-wage income (beneficiaries of direct state provision, for example) are able to purchase employment indirectly in the sense that they are able to assume positions they might not otherwise be able to "afford" to take.
5. cf. de Jasay (1989).
6. Market transactions are the one clear exception, but only insofar as conditions obtain such that market prices are efficiency prices.
7. cf., among others, Nozick (1974) and Baumol (1965).
8. See, among others, Hume (1739) and Rawls (1971).
9. cf. Van Parijs (1993, Ch. 10).

References

Arneson, R. (1990). Is work special? Justice and the distribution of employment and job satisfaction. *American Political Science Review*, 88, 1127–1147.

Baumol, W.J. (1965). *Welfare Economics and the Theory of the State*, 2nd edn. Harvard University Press, Cambridge, MA.

Block, F. (1990). *Post-Industrial Possibilities: A Critique of Economic Discourse.* University of California Press, Berkeley, CA.

De Jasay, A. (1989). *Social Contract, Free Ride.* Oxford University Press, Oxford.

Elster, J. (1988). Is there (or should there be) a right to work? In A. Gutman (ed.) *Democracy and the Welfare State.* Princeton University Press, Princeton.

Gorz, A. (1989). *Critique of Economic Reason.* Verso, London.

Hart, H.L.A. (1955). Are there any natural rights? *Philosophical Review*, 64, 175–191.

Hobbes, T. (1651). *Leviathan.*

Hume, D. (1739). *A Treatise of Human Nature.*

Moon, J.D. (1988). The moral basis of the democratic welfare state. In A. Gutman (ed.) *Democracy and the Welfare State.* Princeton University Press, Princeton.

Nozick, R. (1974). *Anarchy, State, Utopia.* Basic Books, New York.

Rawls, J. (1971). *A Theory of Justice.* Harvard University Press, Cambridge, MA.

Sahlins, M. (1972). *Stone Age Economics.* Aldine, Chicago.

Schor, J.B. (1991). *The Overworked American: The Unexpected Decline of Leisure.* Basic Books, New York.

Van Parijs, P. (1993). *Marxism Recycled.* Cambridge University Press, Cambridge.

Chapter 18

Basic Income, Self-respect, and Reciprocity

Catriona McKinnon

Excerpts from McKinnon, C. (2003). Basic Income, Self-Respect and Reciprocity. *Journal of Applied Philosophy*, 20 (2), 143–158.

Introduction

Rawls claims that "self-respect is perhaps the most important primary good,"[1] and includes the social bases of self-respect as one of the primary goods on a list which he takes to be the appropriate standard for interpersonal comparisons of advantage in the just society. The role of self-respect and a just distribution of its social bases has been well mapped (by Rawls and others) in relation to the question of what justice requires with respect to the distribution of individual rights and liberties.[2] However, the significance of Rawls's understanding of justice as partly defined in terms of the achievement of a just distribution of the social bases of self-respect for thinking about distributive justice, and policies fit to achieve it, has not been thoroughly explored. Self-respect is often wholly or partly defined in terms of a person's sense of her status, and this is true of Rawls's conception of self-respect. Focusing on the status-related component of self-respect naturally leads to thinking about its social conditions in terms of individual rights and liberties. However, when this focus is too exclusive, Rawlsians risk overlooking resources in Rawls's account of self-respect and its social bases which can be mined to radical effect with respect to questions of distributive justice in the liberal egalitarian tradition inspired by Rawls. This chapter aims to make good this deficit by mounting a self-respect-based argument for Unconditional Basic Income (UBI) as the policy best suited for realising Rawls's ideal of equality informed by his (and his followers') reflections on the nature and importance of the social bases of self-respect.

The idea behind Unconditional Basic Income is simple. Under a UBI scheme each person receives a grant fixed at the highest sustainable level regardless of their past, present or future work contribution, their willingness to work and their income from any other source. I shall do two things in this chapter. First, I shall argue that UBI maximins income and wealth understood as a social basis of self-respect.[3] Second, I shall examine the success of the most common objection to UBI: UBI violates reciprocity by allowing people to

From McKinnon, C. (2003). Basic Income, Self-Respect and Reciprocity. *Journal of Applied Philosophy*, 20 (2), 143–158. Reprinted with permission of John Wiley & Sons Ltd.

Basic Income: An Anthology of Contemporary Research, First Edition. Edited by Karl Widerquist, José A. Noguera, Yannick Vanderborght, and Jurgen De Wispelaere.

benefit from the fruits of social cooperation without contributing to that cooperation themselves. I shall argue that the only sense in which the reciprocity objection is available to Rawlsian liberals supports an alternative to UBI – "participation income" – that is almost indistinguishable from it in its distributive effects, and is less desirable than it for pragmatic reasons. The upshot of these arguments is that Rawls's conception of equality as maximin, combined with his commitment to the importance of the social bases of self-respect, commits Rawls, and those who share his conception of justice, to UBI.

Willingness to Work

One big difference between UBI and more traditional schemes of redistribution through welfare systems is that UBI does not incorporate a willingness to work as a condition on receipt of funds. If UBI has self-respect-related maximin advantages lacked by more traditional schemes, then the removal of a willingness-to-work condition from receipt of funds must make those worst off under this system better off in terms of their opportunities for self-respect than they would be under a system incorporating willingness-to-work conditions. I shall argue that this is the case. There are two sets of circumstances in which to make this argument: job abundance and job scarcity.

Job abundance

In conditions of job abundance – where there are more jobs than people – the imposition of a willingness-to-work condition means that everyone without independent means has no option but to work. Of course, some people will be lucky enough to find a job which coincides with their conception of the good and coheres with the plans which, if successfully executed, yield self-respect. But even when the nature of a person's job is tangential to her conception of the good, it may still afford her opportunity for self-respect by providing her with economic means and the time sufficient for participation in non-job related communities of shared interests. Alternatively, it may be that the person's self-respect depends on her sense of herself as an independent and contributing member of society, and her job – whatever it may involve – supports this.

People whose jobs contribute to their self-respect in any of these ways are among the best off with respect to income *qua* resource basis of self-respect. However, the perspective of maximin requires that we turn our attention to the worst off.

Focusing on the worst off, the question is whether *forcing* them to take a job in conditions of job abundance by imposing a willingness-to-work condition on receipt of funds makes them as well off as possible in terms of their opportunity for self-respect.[4] What disadvantages does such coercion impose on the worst off in conditions of job abundance? Imposition of a willingness-to-work condition in these conditions means that people worst off in terms of their opportunity for self-respect have no way of surviving without work. Given that the worst off do not find opportunity for self-respect in the workplace – and assuming, in non-utopian vein, that there will always be some people of whom this is true – this coercion conflicts with maximinning opportunity for self-respect by denying to the worst off the freedom-benefit of income. Furthermore, the income that the worst off receive in wages will often not make them as well off as they could be in terms of the leisure-quantity and leisure-quality benefits of income, because the worst off, *qua* worst off, will be forced into time-consuming and poorly paid work. So some of those already worst off in terms of the freedom-benefit of income will be made even worse off in terms of the other benefits of income, if the only source of income is wages, given job abundance and willingness-to-work conditions. Thus, if we are concerned to maximin opportunity for self-respect, we should remove willingness-to-work conditions from receipt of funds – at least in conditions of job abundance – thus securing for people for whom the workplace is not a site of opportunity for self-respect a source of income which carries freedom, leisure-quantity, and leisure-quality benefits, and thereby serves as a resource basis of self-respect.

It is no objection to the removal of a willingness-to-work condition that it makes the best off in terms of their opportunities for self-respect worse off than they would be were the condition to be retained: making the worst off as well off as possible in terms of any good might require this. But, in fact, there is no reason to think that such removal would worsen the position of those best off in terms of their opportunity for self-respect. How could it? Assuming job abundance, exempting all people from the necessity of taking a job does not detract from the opportunities for self-respect that lucky people find in their jobs. In fact, given that the values and ideals which inform a person's self-respect can change over time, even those for whom a willingness-to-work condition does not currently deplete opportunity for self-respect – because they find this in the workplace, or the leisure benefits work brings – would be unwise to assume that this will remain the case for the whole of their working lives. In which case, the freedom benefit of income distributed without willingness-to-work conditions increases the opportunity for self-respect of *all* people. So, removal of a willingness-to-work condition from receipt of funds not only maximins opportunity for self-respect – because it makes the worst off in terms of this good as well off as possible – it also improves the position of the best off with respect to their opportunity for self-respect.

Job scarcity

The case for removal of a willingness-to-work condition from the receipt of funds is even stronger once we drop the assumption of job abundance. If, as is likely, there are people for whom no job represents a set of opportunities for self-respect, a willingness-to-work condition forcing each of them into a job in conditions of job scarcity is likely to deprive others – whose opportunities for self-respect are job-related, and related to the very job that an unwilling person occupies – of a job. In that case, a scheme incorporating a willingness-to-work condition potentially makes *everyone* worse off in terms of opportunities for self-respect than they would be under a scheme lacking a willingness-to-work condition: not only are those who do not find opportunity for self-respect in the workplace forced into a job, but those who seek this site of opportunity are denied access to it.

The removal of a willingness-to-work condition on receipt of welfare in conditions of job abundance and job scarçity should be thought of as an acknowledgement that many jobs are menial, dangerous, degrading, exhausting, all-consuming, and exploitative, and that a society in which self-respect is acknowledged to be of fundamental importance to all people should be one in which its social conditions are secured for all; if not equally, then at least so that those with the least opportunity for self-respect can be assured that they would not have more of such opportunity under any alternative system of distribution.

The hope is that removal of a willingness-to-work condition and the freedom benefits it confers on income received by way of a UBI would place pressure on employers and governments to improve conditions for workers so as to increase the number of jobs providing opportunity for self-respect. This is not to say – in utopian vein – that UBI would create a world in which each person could hunt in the morning, fish in the afternoon, and be a critical critic after dinner. Rather, the pressure exerted on employers would be not only to improve the quality of work available, but also – with respect to jobs which are essentially and unavoidably dull, menial, and trivial – to increase the leisure-quantity and leisure-quality benefits of these jobs by improving conditions and increasing wages.

Means-Testing

UBI is not only not conditional on a willingness to work; it is also not means-tested. Arguments for the removal of means-testing are *prima facie* more difficult to construct than arguments for the removal of a willingness-to-work condition: there is force to the thought that money raised from taxes should be directed only at those who have least. Nevertheless, by reflecting on how *the way in which* funds are distributed can serve as a recognitional basis of self-respect, we can argue that the position of those worst off in terms of this basis of self-respect in means-tested systems is improved by the removal of means-testing from the procedure of redistribution. If this means that those who do not need public funds to live nevertheless receive them, so be it.[5]

First, means-testing requires a large amount of intrusion into the lives of applicants to ensure that they really do meet the conditions laid down. Interviews, forms requesting personal information on the applicant and her partner, bank statements, medical records, employment history, spot checks, follow-up procedures and so on, can all indicate that the applicant is being examined, assessed and judged from a standpoint of suspicion, if not outright hostility. *Prima facie*, the intrusion demanded by means-testing does not encourage a person to believe that others recognise and acknowledge her as capable and worthy of membership in a community of reason-exchanging beings. Rather, this intrusion is a sign that the person is not trusted by her fellow citizens. When a person is not trusted by her fellows there is always a justification available for excluding her from deliberation about important questions regarding the organisation of society. Such exclusion is not consistent with the person being acknowledged as a co-member of the community of reason-exchanging beings.[6] The availability of such a justification as an accompaniment to the lack of trust evinced by means-testing procedures shows these procedures to be damaging to the recognitional bases of self-respect.

Second, payments under a means-tested system can carry with them a social stigma. Wrong as it is, people surviving on benefits are often perceived as socially useless or personally inadequate (and sometimes these perceptions are actively encouraged by the organs of the state as a additional incentive for claimants to get off benefits). If conditional systems of welfare impose this stigma on claimants then the system damages the recognitional bases of self-respect for such people. It could be that removing means-testing from the administration of grants removes this stigma: if everyone gets UBI then receipt of UBI cannot be seen as singling out certain people as different from others.[7]

Prima facie, removing means-testing increases the recognitional bases of self-respect for those least advantaged with respect to this good. It prevents a system of redistribution becoming one in which "unfortunates breathe words of supplication and submit to the humiliating moral judgements of the state."[8] Combining these arguments with the arguments of the last section relating to the removal willingness-to-work conditions, maximin with respect to resource and recognitional bases of self-respect as realized by income translates as public policy into UBI.

However, some caution is called for with respect to the arguments related to means-testing just given. In relation to the first consideration above, it might be objected that the intrusion associated with means-testing could be managed so as to avoid communicating attitudes of hostility and mistrust on the part of those administering the welfare system qua representatives of the state. If there is no necessity that means-testing requires *hostile* intrusion then means-tested systems might be adjusted so as to avoid damage to the recognitional bases of self-respect for the worst off. With respect to the second consideration, it is possible that stigma would still attach to those who do not work under a UBI system, and who lack the outward signs of personal wealth and affluence. If the stigma that currently attaches to welfare claimants relates to their poverty rather than their status as claimants, then UBI cannot guarantee the disappearance of this stigma.

In sum, if institutional reform can render means-testing harmless with respect to the recognitional bases of self-respect for claimants, and if the sociology of stigma establishes that it is inevitable that the worst off in societies like ours will be ostracized and disapproved of, then the arguments just considered do not justify abandoning means-testing in the name of the self-respect of welfare claimants subject to the tests. Given that the arguments of the last section still stand, this would mean that maximin with respect to income *qua* social basis of self-respect would require that all people below a threshold of affluence ought to receive a grant irrespective of their past, present, or future work contributions, and irrespective of their willingness to seek and take up work. However, this is still a radical egalitarian policy proposal, as is evinced in the fact that most egalitarian objections to UBI relate to the removal of willingness-to-work conditions rather than means-testing. I address the source of these important objections in the next section.

The Reciprocity Objection

Reciprocity is a feature of the relations between people engaged in joint projects: it evokes the idea that each partner "puts in" or "gives" as much as every other partner. The reciprocity objection to UBI is that it allows people to benefit from the fruits of social cooperation without bearing any of the costs: UBI allows Rawls's Malibu surfers to free-ride on the efforts of others.[9] The reciprocity objection is not just that UBI permits non-contribution but, importantly, that it provides no justice-based grounds for criticism of those who fail to contribute. The reciprocity objection to UBI reflects the turn towards principles of personal responsibility in the egalitarian literature [. . .].[10] The thought behind the objection is that it is unjust that the costs of an able-bodied, competent person's choice not to work should be imposed on similarly endowed working people through taxation of their income and property to fund UBI: all else being equal, that such a person has chosen not to work means that she should be held responsible for bearing the costs of that choice.

In this section I shall map the key responses of liberal egalitarians to the reciprocity objection, and argue that even liberal egalitarians who accept the force of the objection cannot rule out UBI as the best way to maximin income qua social basis of self-respect. Camps of response can be mapped by the diagram in Figure 18.1.

(a) *UBI is a requirement of justice even though it violates reciprocity, because reciprocity is not a requirement of justice.* This is perhaps the most radical response to the reciprocity objection, and can be made in either a crude or a more nuanced form. The crude version is just a blanket denial that reciprocity has any role to play in making decisions about how

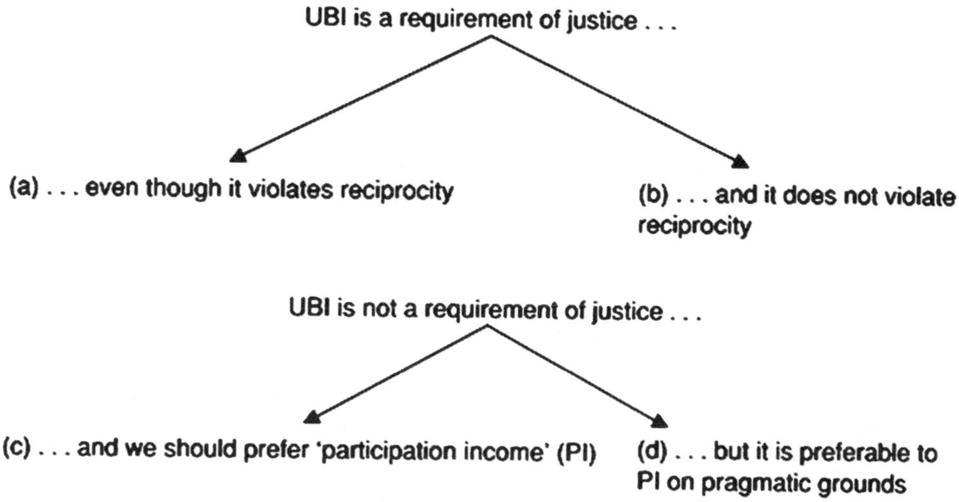

Figure 18.1

goods should be distributed: no thinker in the liberal egalitarian tradition makes this strong claim.

The nuanced version is that principles of distributive justice address the distribution both of entitlements and of privileges: reciprocity should not govern the distribution of entitlements (of which UBI is one) but should govern the distribution of privileges. This is Philippe Van Parijs's response to the reciprocity objection.[11] In essence, it amounts to claiming that the reciprocity objection begs the question against UBI by assuming that UBI claimants do something other than live off their own share of goods.

The main objection to this position is to insist that reciprocity ought to govern both the allocation of entitlements and the allocation of privileges. If we accept this objection, then it must be argued that UBI does not violate reciprocity.

(b) *UBI is a requirement of justice and does not violate reciprocity.* Here, the strategy is to claim that reciprocity should govern the allocation of both entitlements and privileges, but that Malibu surfers and their like contribute in a way that satisfies the principle of reciprocity and so are entitled to UBI. Again, there is a crude and a nuanced version of this response. The crude version is to claim that the surfers contribute to the cultural capital of their society by keeping alive a tradition of skills and a subculture. The problem here is the example can easily be changed to make the response counter-intuitive: what of the beer-guzzling couch potato? Or the dope-smoking Play Station addict? What skills and culture do they preserve?

The nuanced version of this response is this: the form of contribution which mandates return in the form of a UBI as an entitlement need not be activity-based, but ought also to be understood in terms of "gainful exchange" between parties affected by the redistribution either as beneficiaries or as tax payers. Reciprocity through work-contribution is sufficient, but not necessary, for gainful exchange. This response is suggested by Bill Jordan.[12] Combining this response with the self-respect-based arguments for UBI made earlier, we get the following position. In conditions in which jobs affording opportunity for self-respect are scarce, beer guzzlers can be seen as engaging in an exchange with those who seek sites of opportunity for self-respect in paid employment. By staying out of the job market, beer guzzlers relieve downward pressure on wages and decrease competition for self-respect-supporting jobs. However, for this exchange to be gainful to both parties, the beer guzzlers must not be denied opportunity for self-respect as a result of the exchange. If the arguments made earlier are correct, UBI is the best way to make this exchange gainful for guzzlers in terms of their opportunity for self-respect. Furthermore, given the nature of the exchange between the guzzlers and those seeking opportunity for self-respect in paid employment, imposing a willingness-to-work condition on the receipt of funds would defeat the purpose of the exchange.[13]

The most powerful objection to this position is that what is sufficient for gainful exchange is insufficient for reciprocity. Reciprocity requires some form of more active contribution to social cooperation: the claim that those who do nothing, while others are active, are contributing – furthermore, contributing in a way that generates entitlements – stretches credibility. If this objection is accepted, UBI appears to be defeated.

However, the success of this objection would be a Pyrrhic victory for anti-UBI Rawlsians. It would show that two values at the heart of the liberal conception of justice – reciprocity and a maximin distribution of the social bases of self-respect – are incompatible, *even in ideal theory*. If this is the case, then Rawlsians either have to give up one of these values, or accept that justice is, in principle, unachievable.

Setting this problem to one side, those who make this objection are nevertheless committed in principle to a radical scheme of economic redistribution which, I shall suggest, is either likely to manifest itself in a distribution of economic goods which is practically indistinguishable from UBI, or creates practical headaches that would lead any wise liberal egalitarian to prefer UBI.

(c) *UBI should be abandoned in favor of a "participation income"* (PI). This is the response favored by Stuart White. He offers the following interpretation of "baseline" reciprocity:

> Each person is entitled to a share of the economic benefits of social cooperation conferring equal opportunity (or real freedom) in return for the performance of an equal handicap-weighted quantum of contributive activity (hours of socially useful work, let us say, weighted by labour intensity).[14]

If baseline reciprocity is a requirement of justice then UBI ought to be abandoned in favor of PI. However, the participation necessary for receipt of public funds, given a Rawlsian liberal approach, cannot exclusively be defined in terms of paid employment. In *Political Liberalism* Rawls insists that any community of people to whom political justification is addressed must be conceived of as in conditions of permanent and reasonable pluralism,[15] which means that reasonable disagreement about moral, religious, and philosophical questions must be accommodated by political justifications. Given this, agreement between reasonable people with respect to White's principle of baseline reciprocity as a principle of justice must not be conceived of as agreement with respect to a narrow conception of what constitutes activity fit to satisfy the principle. If the principle is to be available to Rawlsian liberals as a ground for objecting to UBI, then the sense of "contributive activity" on which the principle hinges cannot be narrowly defined just in terms of paid work because, for example, carers, artists and poets without commissions, volunteer workers, and members of religious orders could reasonably object that they perform contributive activity fit to satisfy the principle of baseline reciprocity.

This means that, for Rawlsians, PI (like UBI) must not carry willingness-to-work conditions; unlike UBI, PI will carry a "willingness-to-participate" condition. And given the considerations above about reasonable disagreement, any PI scheme to which Rawlsians can commit must allow that very many activities which do not currently generate entitlements to public funds would become entitlement-generating: carers, homemakers, non-working artists, musicians and poets, and students would probably acquire an entitlement to PI under this proposal. Furthermore, in some cultures it might be that surfers would also acquire these entitlements: the tourist trade at Bondi beach has much to thank its surfers for. Under this proposal, only beer guzzlers and their like would be disqualified from receipt of public funds. Given that the number of such people is likely to be small, PI might differ very little from UBI in its distributive effects.

The most serious objection to PI is to the amount of bureaucracy involved in its administration, even in ideal conditions. Establishing each person's status as an on-going contributor (in the broad sense) to a scheme of social cooperation would require a bureaucratic apparatus that would dwarf current top-heavy welfare systems designed to check satisfaction of work-related conditions. For practically-minded people, and all those temperamentally suspicious of assigning these functions to the state, the following, and final, position might be the most attractive.

(d) *UBI is not a requirement of justice because it violates reciprocity but the practical difficulties of implementing a PI instead of UBI create unacceptable moral costs which make UBI preferable.* This is Brian Barry's view.[16] Some of the practical advantages often claimed for UBI are that it would massively streamline the existing benefits system, be hyper-efficient in terms of administration, and minimise the risks of big bureaucracy getting entitlements wrong and thereby damaging peoples' lives, perhaps irreparably. PI would involve an assessment of each person's level of contributive activity according to a standard which meets the reasonable disagreement test above. The potential for misclassification and legal challenges, combined with the likelihood of there being a large number of unclear cases in grey areas (is someone who paints one day a week, and recuperates from her artistic effort for the other six, a contributor?), and the likelihood that the number of genuine scroungers would be small, means that UBI is to be preferred over PI.

Notes

1. Rawls (1971), p. 440. See also pp. 92, 107, 443, 543–545, and Rawls (1993), pp. 106, 203, 318, 319.
2. See Rawls (1971), Ch. IX, §82, pp. 541–48. See also, for example, Feinberg (1970), The nature and value of rights, *Journal of Value Inquiry* 4, 243–260.
3. From here on in I shall abbreviate "income and wealth" to "income".
4. It might be objected that no one is literally forced to work by a willingness-to-work condition, for they are free not to work and not to receive benefits. This response trades on a Nozickean conception of freedom whereby a person is free if her actions are not constrained by the rights-violating actions of others. See Nozick (1974), pp. 26ff. The objection would be that as it has not yet been established that anyone has a right to UBI, it can't be claimed that denying them a UBI by imposing a willingness-to-work condition upon their receipt of a grant is a form of coercion. I reject the assumption hidden in this approach that we can determine the degree of

freedom of a person's state by examining the causal antecedents of that state. A person who gets trapped in a natural ravine through their own carelessness is not less unfree than a person who has been lured into a hidden man-trap by wily natives. In a similar vein, the freedom of a person who is starving because of her refusal to meet a willingness-to-work condition so as to qualify for a grant is just as compromised as that of a person who is starving because of a natural disaster.

5. Any UBI scheme could include a "voluntary renunciation" clause to allow unwilling recipients to refuse their UBI. Thomas Paine – an early advocate of a proto-UBI which he defended "in lieu of the natural inheritance, which, as a right, belongs to every man, over and above the property he may have created, or inherited from those who did" – also makes this suggestion when he states that, "Such persons as do not choose to receive [this grant] can throw it into the common fund" (Paine, 1987, p. 478).
6. Again, Thomas Paine was alive to the benefits of unconditionality in the distribution of public funds. In *Agrarian Justice* he recommends that, "the payments . . . be made to every person, rich or poor. It is best to make it so, to avoid invidious distinctions" (Paine, 1987, p. 478).
7. See Wolff (1998) Fairness, respect, and the egalitarian ethos. *Philosophy and Public Affairs*, 27, 99–122.
8. See Anderson (1999), p. 308.
9. See Rawls (1993), pp. 181–182, n. 9.
10. Editor's note: See the other chapters in the Reciprocity and Exploitation section of this anthology, especially Rawls, White, Van Donselaar, and Barry.
11. See Van Parijs (1991), esp. Ch. 4.
12. Jordan B. (2000) Justice and reciprocity. In Mckinnon and Hampsher-Monk (2000), pp. 51–70.
13. As an anonymous referee pointed out to me, this argument resonates with Bernard Mandeville's reflections that even criminals play a useful social role by keeping policemen, judges etc. busy, and by inducing plays, novels, newspaper stories etc. See Mandeville (1988).
14. White (1997), p. 318.
15. Rawls (1993), p. xvi.
16. Barry (1997) The attractions of basic income. In Franklin (1997).

References

Anderson, E. (1999). What is the point of equality? *Ethics*, 109: 287–337.

Barry, B. (1997). The attractons of Basic Income. In Franklin, J. (ed) *Equality*, London: Institute for Public Policy Research, pp. 157–171.

Feinberg, J. (1970). The nature and value of rights. *Journal of Value Inquiry*, 4, 243–260.

Franklin, J. (ed.) (1997). *Equality*. IPPR, London.

Jordan, B. (2000). Justic and reciprocity. In Mckinnon, C. and Hampsher-Monk, I. (eds). *The Demands of Citizenship*. Continuum Publishing, New York and London. pp. 51–70.

Mandeville, B. (1988). *The Fable of the Bees*. Liberty Classics, Indianapolis.

Nozick, R. (1974). *Anarchy, State and Utopia*. Blackwell, Oxford.

Paine, T. (1987). *Agrarian Justice*. Penguin Books, London.

Rawls, J. (1971). *A Theory of Justice*. Oxford University Press, Oxford.

Rawls, J. (1993). *Political Liberalism*. Columbia University Press, New York.

Van Parijs, P. (1991). Why surfers should be fed: the liberal case for an unconditional basic income. *Philosophy and Public Affairs*, 20 (4), 101–131.

White, S. (1997) Liberal equality, exploitation, and the case for an unconditional basic income. *Political Studies*, 45 (2), 312–326.

Wolff, J. (1998). Fairness, respect, and the egalitarian ethos, *Philosophy and Public Affairs*, 27, 99–122.

Chapter 19

Reciprocity and the Guaranteed Income

Karl Widerquist

Excerpts from Widerquist, K. (1999). Reciprocity and the Guaranteed Income. *Politics and Society*, 27 (3), 386–401.

If a man will not work, he shall not eat.
– Paul, Second Thessalonians, chapter 3, verse 10, c. 60 C.E.

He who does not work, will not eat.
– Captain John Smith, Jamestown, Virginia, 1608 C.E.

He who does not work, neither shall he eat.
– Article 18 of the Soviet Constitution, 1918 C.E.

A craftsman . . . has a work to do from which if he were forced to abstain life would not be worth living, but we do not say that a rich man has any such job to do.
– Socrates, as quoted in Plato's *Republic*, c. 399 B.C.E.

This chapter questions what could be the oldest principle in U.S. politics: "(s)he who does not work will not eat." In 1608, 12 years before the pilgrims arrived at Plymouth Rock, Captain John Smith established this principle for the first successful English-speaking settlement in what is now the United States. Captain Smith's principle has been endorsed by sources as diverse as the New Testament and the Soviet Constitution. Why take issue with such a widely held principle? Because as it is applied in modern industrial economies in which work is defined as employment, this principle conflicts with the principle of reciprocity (also known as "neutrality" or "equality before the law"). The principle of reciprocity states that government policy should not favor one group over another. To be consistent with reciprocity, this "work-or-starve" principle must be applied to all citizens. If the rules of a nation force some individuals to choose between work and starvation, a society must

From Widerquist, K. (1999). Reciprocity and the Guaranteed Income. First published in *Politics and Society*, 27 (3), 386–401. Reprinted with permission of SAGE.

Basic Income: An Anthology of Contemporary Research, First Edition. Edited by Karl Widerquist, José A. Noguera, Yannick Vanderborght, and Jurgen De Wispelaere.

force all individuals to face that choice. However, in most modern industrial societies, those who own a sufficient amount of land, natural resource rights, capital, and government bonds are exempt from the fear that they will not eat if they do not work, but those who do not possess such assets do face that fear.

A Guaranteed Income eliminates this violation of reciprocity by unconditionally ensuring that no one's income falls below the subsistence level. *Unconditionally* refers particularly to the absence of any work requirement. Under such a system, citizens work and participate in the economy by choice. The term *Guaranteed Income* is a generic term for any one of a number of plans, including the Citizen's Income, the Basic Income, the Negative Income Tax, and the Social Dividend. Proposals differ as to how the benefits are paid, how they are financed, whether they are to replace or exist alongside a pension system, how allowances are to be made for dependents, and other details. But all of these proposals share one crucial characteristic: they unconditionally guarantee that no one's income falls below the poverty level. For the intentions of this chapter, all of these plans can be considered equivalent and are used interchangeably.

The specifics of how a Guaranteed Income would work or the differences between them are not the subjects of this chapter. In simplest terms, under a Guaranteed Income system, a person who makes no private income, regardless of the reason, receives a fixed amount in the form of a cash transfer. As a person makes a small private income, some versions would reduce the transfer, and other versions would tax the additional earnings. In either case, a person with low private income will be a net recipient and will have a higher after-tax/after-transfer income than someone with no private income. As a person makes more private income, beyond some point, either the transfer is reduced to zero or the taxes become larger than the transfer, and that person becomes a net taxpayer. But for any two people, the one with the higher private income will always have the higher after-tax/after-transfer income. Thus, a Guaranteed Income preserves the incentive to earn more while ensuring that no one is completely destitute.

Stuart White and other critics of an Unconditional Guaranteed Income argue that it violates the reciprocity principle. White bases his criticism on Philippe Van Parijs's justification of a Basic Income presented in his book, *Real Freedom for All: What (if Anything) Can Justify Capitalism?* Van Parijs argues that the Basic Income is necessary to maximize what he calls "real freedom," the freedom to do whatever one might want to do. In other words, all people should have the maximum opportunity to pursue their own conception of the good life. He contends that existence of "brute luck" and "external assets" justifies redistribution in the form of an Unconditional Guaranteed Income. Brute luck is the result of risks one is compelled to take, such as an imperfectly fair labor market that people are forced to enter to obtain the means of survival. If people willingly play a game of chance, they have no legitimate reason to ask for a redress if they do not win, but if they are compelled to play a game of chance, they may have a legitimate reason to challenge the outcome. External assets include forms of wealth that no one (or no living person) produced, such as land, natural resources, and inherited wealth. It has long been recognized that the owner of a significant amount of assets can derive a permanent income from it without expending any personal effort either in the production or management of these assets. Van Parijs argues that all individuals are entitled to an unconditional income equal to the value of a per capita share of the total value of external assets because the return on these assets does not represent a reward for any individual's productive contribution but is a claim on the productive contribution of these assets themselves.

Van Parijs concedes that taxing land, natural resources, and inheritance will not provide enough revenue to support a Basic Income that would be sufficient to achieve real freedom for all. However, using an argument economists know as the "efficiency-wage theory," Van Parijs defines some jobs as a form of external assets. The efficiency-wage theory supposes that it is often profitable for firms to pay higher-than-market clearing wages to encourage loyalty and maximum effort from their employees, but this requires that not everyone who is willing and able to do a particular job is able to find one. Therefore, Van Parijs concludes that a job can be considered a type of external asset, and labor income can therefore be taxed to support a Guaranteed Income.

Stuart White uses the jobs-as-assets argument as the basis for his "exploitation objection" to an Unconditional Guaranteed Income. White acknowledges that an Unconditional Guaranteed Income supported by taxes on assets like natural resources and past wealth accumulation is reasonably invulnerable to the exploitation objection, but he claims that such assets cannot support an adequate Guaranteed Income. He concedes that to some extent, jobs can be considered external assets, but there is an important difference between job assets and other assets: one cannot receive any return on a job asset without work or at least some social cooperation. White, therefore, concludes that a Basic Income should be made conditional on what he calls baseline reciprocity: an income maintenance plan that redistributes the product of social cooperation should be conditional on some form of cooperation on the part of the recipient (i.e., a work requirement). As he puts it, "An unconditional basic income would allow non-working citizens to free-ride on the efforts of, and so exploit, working citizens" (White, 1997).

This chapter makes the case that an unconditional income is consistent with and required for reciprocity. Part l demonstrates that a Guaranteed Income is, in fact, a necessary requirement for reciprocity in a modern industrial society. Part 2 considers in detail White's exploitation objection and demonstrates that an Unconditional Guaranteed Income is consistent with reciprocity.

Part 1

This section demonstrates that an Unconditional Guaranteed Income is needed to reverse a violation of reciprocity that exists in modern market economies. In the absence of a modern society (in which land and natural resources are enclosed), people are free to work only for themselves. People are free to build their own homes and hunt, farm, or gather their own food, and they are free to cooperate with others who face the same choices. This may be work in a sense, but it is not work as defined as employment or labor. Working for oneself in nonmarket activity is considered leisure by the economic definition. In that sense, people in a society without privatized land and natural resources spend all of their days at leisure. They may be in a struggle for subsistence, but they are not forced to work for others.

In a modern industrial society without an Unconditional Guaranteed Income, a person who does not own a significant amount of external assets must work for others to survive. All the land and natural resources are privately owned, and one must work for the owners of these resources in order to earn the money to buy the things she needs to survive. Most people can earn much more working for others than they could possibly produce alone. For many people, probably the vast majority, the development of a market economy with privatized resources has been an enormous benefit that has allowed consumption well above subsistence; for the poorest people, however, this change has left them still struggling to survive. Their right to work solely for themselves was taken away generations ago, and they will be destitute if they are unwilling or unable to work for others. When work becomes synonymous with working for others, the idea that "(s)he who does not work, will not eat" is not a fact of nature but a consequence of how we organize our society.

The introduction of the work-or-starve principle is not necessarily a violation of reciprocity as long as it applies to everyone. However, some citizens of the United States know that even if they do not work, they will still eat. They are the owners of significant amounts of external assets, owners of capital and government bonds (which may or may not be external assets), and people, such as the disabled, who qualify for categorical transfers. The principle of reciprocity is violated when the principle of "(s)he who does not work, will not eat" is applied to some people but not others. One function of a Guaranteed Income is to eliminate this violation. A Guaranteed Income is compensation for giving up the right to work only for oneself, a right that would be available if society had not privatized natural resources.

Robert Nozick argues that private appropriation of land and natural resources is justifiable under criteria advanced by John Locke. According to Locke, a person obtains the right to appropriate these assets by mixing her labor with it, but there must be "as much and as good left for others in common." Today few – if any – external assets are left for others to appropriate. Nozick argues that in modern society, property rights to land are justifiable so long as no one is made worse off because of the appropriation, but he defines two ways in which being made worse off can be interpreted. The weaker interpretation is that those without assets should be able to live at least as well as they could have had no one appropriated any land. The more stringent interpretation is that those without assets should be compensated both for how well off they could have been had no one appropriated land and for the lost opportunities to appropriate land themselves (Nozick, 1974).

If the compensation proviso is to be followed, the least-advantaged people in an industrial society would have to be better off than they could possibly be in a society without appropriation of assets. Nozick argues that the opportunities for employment and entreprenuership that capitalism provides more than outweigh the potential loss so that no actual compensation is necessary (Nozick, 1974). This may be true for the many, but it is hard to make the case that it is true for everyone.

For example, a person with no home and no job prospects in Manhattan in the year 2000 is not even allowed to build a shanty or a fire, and some resort to eating out of garbage cans. A person with no home and no job prospects in Manhattan in 1500 could build a cabin, gather firewood, and fish in the Hudson River. In some areas, such as Hawaii, preindustrial residents were relatively free from toil as well as employment and could relax on the beach and surf all day if that's what they chose to do. Compensation, according to the weak interpretation, could be used to justify a subsistence-level Guaranteed Income without a work requirement, so that all individuals remain free to decide how to use their time. Compensation, according to the stringent interpretation, would require the "highest sustainable" Guaranteed Income. If a Guaranteed Income is considered to be compensation to those who would not otherwise benefit from the privatization of land, it is owed by all those who benefit from the current property relationship to all those who may not benefit.

The debate between White and Van Parijs about whether an Unconditional Guaranteed Income is consistent with reciprocity largely revolves around what qualifies as an external asset and whether taxing external assets can raise enough revenue to support an adequate Basic Income. However, this debate ignores one important fundamental point: the very existence of external assets is sufficient to justify an Unconditional Guaranteed Income on the grounds of reciprocity, regardless of the revenue that can be generated by taxing external assets alone. The relevant level for the Basic Income is not the amount that can be raised by taxing external assets but the amount that an individual should be compensated for lost access to unappropriated assets.

The owners of outside assets generate income partially or entirely because these goods are scarce and not everyone can own them. Therefore, it is not accurate to talk about market "distribution" and government "redistribution" of income because all market distribution of income depends on the prior assignment of land and natural resource ownership rights by the government. Only after the land and natural resource rights have been defined and initially assigned by governments (distribution) can market exchange begin (redistribution). The income that an owner derives from an outside asset is just as much government redistribution of income as if the government taxed workers and gave the money to landlords. The way we have chosen to define property rights has resulted in a situation in which one group has to work to survive and another does not and results in a violation of the principle of reciprocity.

White's argument assumes there are only two groups in the economy – "workers" and "recipients" – implicitly grouping external asset owners with workers. If groups are defined by the choices they have available to them, however, both workers and recipients belong to one group and external asset owners to another group. These are the group definitions that will be used in this chapter.

One could argue that workers can save their money and buy into the group of external asset owners. In a completely fair labor market, this would be possible for any one worker who has the ability, perseverance, and luck, but it is not true for all workers. One worker can buy external assets, but only by first working and then convincing the owners of external assets to part with them voluntarily. If all workers simultaneously set this as their goal and all have sufficient ability and perseverance, they will bid down the returns to labor and bid up the price of external assets. Their collective action would benefit those who already own external assets and hurt workers on average. Although some workers may be able to buy into the group of external asset owners, it would be impossible for all workers to do so, and therefore one cannot simply choose to be a worker or an external asset owner.

Without a Guaranteed Income, workers face the choice, "(s)he who does not work, will not eat," while owners of external assets do not face such a choice. Work is voluntary for external asset owners and mandatory for workers. This violation of reciprocity is a consequence of how a society decides to define rights to external assets. The position of workers is not envy-free relative to external asset owners because, given the choice, rational workers would rather derive income from external assets, even if they intend to work.

There are four ways society could rectify this violation of reciprocity. First, a society could seize all private holdings of external assets or tax away all the returns so that asset owners would have to work. This objective would be difficult to achieve while still allowing the market economy to operate with all of its benefits. Second, society could grant those who won't or can't participate in the labor market a plot of land on which they could maintain themselves. Great Britain seriously considered such a proposal in the early nineteenth century, and the United States once had such a plan in the form of the Homestead Act. Today, this type of plan would not be feasible because it is too expensive to obtain enough land, and it is unrealistic to expect the modem urban poor to adapt to subsistence farming. In a productive, industrialized society, it is less expensive for society to provide people money to buy food, shelter, and clothing than it is to provide them with land and natural resources to produce these things for themselves. Third, society could impose conditionality on the ownership of external assets in the form of a work requirement. For example, all people who own enough external assets to live on could be required to spend

40 hours a week in a community service job. This would apply a work-or-starve principle to all citizens and would not violate the principle of self-ownership because anyone could get out of this requirement simply by relinquishing ownership of external assets. However, this solution would probably strike most people as rather draconian. Fourth, a society could relieve workers from having to choose between work and starvation by introducing some form of Unconditional Guaranteed Income. If it is impractical to impose the work-or-starve principle on owners of external assets, reciprocity demands this principle not be imposed on anyone.

The level of Basic Income does not need to be based on the returns to external assets in a modern industrial society. Instead, it can be based on what an individual gives up to be part of an industrialized society: subsistence without employment. If the privatization of resources does not produce a return that allows the least advantaged person to be better off in that situation than in a society without privatized assets, it is not Pareto-superior and exploits those who would be better off in such a society. It should be noted that as long as external assets are privately held, a Guaranteed Income does not make society completely consistent with reciprocity. The Guaranteed Income removes the inconsistent application of the work-or-starve principle, and it is reciprocal in the sense that all people are free to chose whether or not to participate in the economic system. It cannot make the economic system completely fair, only voluntary. External asset owners will still live much better if they choose not to work than others will whether or not they choose to work.

Of course, many owners of significant amounts of external assets do work, but they are not forced to work by fear of starvation. The fact that so many assets owners work is evidence that it is not necessary to threaten people with starvation to give them an adequate incentive to work. The contribution to social product of those who own and manage resources is very large, and any plan to make their behavior conform to the reciprocity principle should be designed to leave the benefits of the market system in place.

Some authors define providing resources for others to use productively as a form of work or social cooperation, even if it involves no effort on the part of the resource owner (for example, see White, 1996). To address this, a distinction must be made between managing resources and owning them. By almost anyone's definition, someone who actively makes decisions about how resources are to be used is working. However, people who own large amounts of external assets can hire someone else to manage their assets and do nothing except receive payment. If work is defined so broadly that an absentee landlord is considered cooperating simply by allowing others to use the natural resources she controls, then a transfer recipient can also be considered cooperating because her claim to have all land and natural resource rights divided equally has been taken away. Thus, the rationale for a work requirement disappears.

Part 2

Part 1 demonstrates that an economy with privatized external assets but without an Unconditional Guaranteed Income violates reciprocity. However, a Guaranteed Income would be an insufficient solution if it creates another violation of reciprocity. Therefore, it is necessary to address White's critique in detail.

White argues that even if the external asset justification of an Unconditional Guaranteed Income stands, a Guaranteed Income exploits workers because at least some revenue will have to come from taxing workers, and some revenue will be transferred to people who do not work. Four propositions must be true for this conclusion to hold. First, taxation of external assets alone does not produce enough revenue to support an adequate Unconditional Guaranteed Income, so that at least some portion of the taxes must come from workers. Second, in the absence of baseline reciprocity, workers are entitled to the full value of their efforts. Third, wages in a market system without redistributive taxation directly reflect the full value of a worker's efforts. Fourth, after-tax wages in an economy with an Unconditional Guaranteed Income are less than they would be in its absence.

One can criticize White's conclusion that a Guaranteed Income exploits workers by challenging any of the four premises or by arguing that the existence of a Basic Income confers other benefits on workers that justifies taxing them. For example, one could challenge the first proposition that a Guaranteed Income cannot be financed solely by taxation of external assets. Michael Hudson estimates that in 1995, $2 trillion of the $5.9 trillion U.S. national income was made directly or indirectly from real estate, including rent, capital gains due to land appreciation, interest on loans for the purchase of land, and imputed rent to firms and households that both own and use land.[1] Block and Manza (1997) estimate that the net cost of a Negative Income Tax plan would be only $70 billion. Comparing Hudson's estimate of the revenue available to Block and Monza's estimate of the costs raises doubts about the claim that an adequate Guaranteed Income requires taxation of work.

Van Parijs, who accepts that an adequate Guaranteed Income requires taxation of labor income, challenges the connection between White's premises and his conclusion. He argues that even though some workers may be materially worse off with a Basic Income than without it, a Basic Income confers benefits on these workers that justify taxing them. One benefit is that it gives workers a greater choice. Workers have the option to sit out of the labor market, even if they choose not to exercise that option. Another benefit is income insurance. People buy private insurance against risks like automobile accidents, theft, fire, injury, and illness even though they hope the need never arises. The government can insure against income loss in the form of a Guaranteed Income. Everyone would benefit from the peace of mind that income insurance would bring them, even though not everyone would need it.

If one concedes that some workers will be materially worse off if an Unconditional Basic Income exists, it does not necessarily follow that reciprocity has been violated. The Guaranteed Income meets Foley's condition for equity: it is envy-free (Foley, 1967). Society would offer citizens two choices: do not work and receive a small unconditional income, or work and receive a higher income. Reciprocity exists in the sense that all people are equal before the law; the same rules apply to everyone.

According to White (1996), "To willingly enjoy such cooperative benefits without being willing to make such a reciprocal contribution is to claim access to these benefits on what are necessarily advantaged terms." In fact, most of those who live solely on the Guaranteed Income would be the least advantaged people in society. Because workers would have the option to stop working, we can conclude that if they do work, then they must find it preferable to not working. Recipients of a Guaranteed Income would not be taking advantage of a privilege that is unavailable to everyone else. Therefore, the position of a worker relative to a recipient is envy-free.

The same cannot be said for a recipient relative to a worker. Perhaps the recipient wants a job but can't find one or can't find one that pays above poverty wages, is not intelligent enough to hold a good job, has a sick relative to take care of, or is the victim of discrimination. There are any number of reasons why a jobless person living solely off a Guaranteed Income might be willing – but unable – to trade places with someone who works. Therefore, it is unclear that a nonworker's position is envy-free relative to a worker's position.

If one defines exploitation as one person taking advantage of privileges that are unavailable to another, one cannot say that the person who lives solely off a Basic Income exploits anyone. Therefore, based on the principle of reciprocity alone, a Guaranteed Income does not exploit workers to the benefit of nonworkers. In a capitalist system with a Guaranteed Income, work is purely voluntary, and one who accepts a job therefore accepts its terms.

Another problem with the exploitation objection is the assumption that workers' after-tax incomes will be lower with a Guaranteed Income than without one. It may seem obvious that a worker's after-tax income will be reduced if a worker pays taxes and a recipient receives a transfer derived from those taxes. However, people who opt not to work also do something that benefits workers: they reduce job competition, which drives up wages. It is not certain which effect will be greater, the taxation or the reduced job competition. The following example demonstrates that for low-wage workers, the effect of reduced competition is likely to be greater than the effect of an increased tax burden.

Assume there are two groups: owners of external assets who do most of the employing and workers. Assume there is no redistribution of income and a completely unregulated market, so that all workers must either work or not eat. Workers are effectively forced to accept a job, which means there is a large supply of labor, which in turn means there are lower wages, longer work hours, and poorer working conditions. Karl Marx described this as "exploitation," the same word White uses to describe recipients of unconditional transfers (see Tucker, 1978). Almost a century earlier and without using the word *exploitation*, Adam Smith recognized that workers would be paid less if they were desperate for jobs:

> It is not [. . .] difficult to foresee which of the two parties must, upon all ordinary occasions, have the advantage in the dispute, and force the other into compliance with their terms. [. . .] In all such disputes the masters can hold out much longer. A landlord, a farmer, a master manufacturer, or merchant, though they did not employ a single workman, could generally live a year or two upon the stocks which they have already acquired. Many workmen could not subsist a week, few could subsist a month, and scarce any a year without employment. In the long-run the workman may be as necessary to his master as his master is to him, but the necessity is not so immediate. (Smith, 1776)

Both Karl Marx and Adam Smith believed that worker desperation could create a situation in which workers would be paid less than they deserve or less than they are worth. However, both authors wrote before the inception of formal neoclassical supply-and-demand theory. In a supply-and-demand model, if workers become desperate for work, the supply of labor will increase along a given demand curve, driving down both wages and the marginal product of labor. Workers will still be paid in proportion to what they produce, but that would be true at any wage. Whether workers are paid less than their marginal product because they are desperate for work or whether their desperation for work drives down their marginal product to meet their wages is inconsequential for the argument here. In either case, if workers become desperate for employment, employers benefit because the cost of labor falls, and workers suffer because their real incomes decrease. There is nothing in the laws of supply and demand to ensure that the equilibrium wage will provide an above-poverty income. Regardless of whether workers are paid their marginal product, they are paid less if they must work to eat than they would be paid otherwise.

It is questionable whether trade can be considered voluntary if one party is desperate for survival and the other is not. For example, suppose Donald Trump falls off a pier. He asks me to throw him a rope. I respond, "How much?" We negotiate and decide that he will sign over to me ownership of all of his assets. If he values his life more than his money, this is a Pareto-improving transaction. I get my lawyer . . . we write up a contract . . . Trump signs . . . I throw him a rope . . . Trump lives. He pays me his entire fortune, which is equal to the marginal product of my labor as valued by the utility he receives by living the rest of his life. I have been paid my marginal product, but does this in any normative sense imply that I have been paid what I deserve? Any court in the United States would invalidate this contract because it was signed under duress.

Suppose, instead, that the manner in which a society has defined property rights causes members of one group constantly to face a state of duress. Workers must work or starve, while their employers do not experience this same duress. As in the above example on the pier, one person benefits from someone else's desperation even if the law of supply and demand holds, and an individual's pay reflects his (marginal) contribution to output. Trade is not truly voluntary if one side of the transaction is desperate and the other side is not, and the rates of return will be lower for the former than they will be for the latter.

Of course, not every supply-and-demand situation is imbalanced. If there is sufficient competition among employers, wages may not necessarily be unacceptably low. But how can we tell what is "unacceptably low" unless we allow workers the option to refuse to work? The current equilibrium situation is such that 10% of adults who work full-time year-round have incomes below the poverty line, and 8% of adults who work have incomes less than 50% above the poverty line (Kim, 1997). There does not appear to be enough demand for labor to create a market in which workers can command decent living standards.

The U.S. government recognizes the existence of this problem and has responded with minimum wage laws, labor regulations, public housing, rent control, and food stamps, in addition to many other programs – all designed to ensure that workers receive adequate wages, working conditions, housing, and food. These programs are necessary because workers do not have the right to refuse unacceptable employment, but they are inadequate in that all of them together have failed to eliminate poverty, even among full-time workers (Kim and Mergoupis, 1997).

An adequate Unconditional Guaranteed Income would solve this labor market problem. It would give all workers the ability to decline unacceptable employment, forcing employers to increase wages as a way of making employment more attractive. Whether the labor market is modeled using supply and demand, a bargaining game, or a monopsony, a decrease in workers' desperation for employment would allow them to command higher wages and better working conditions. Certainly workers who are net recipients would have higher after-tax/after-transfer wages. It is also possible that some workers who are net contributors to the program would have higher after-tax incomes because, although taxes will take a bigger portion of their income, their gross income will be higher due to increased wages. Therefore, one cannot say with certainty that even a net tax-payer's income would be harmed by a Guaranteed Income.

It is not a simple case of comparing a society without a Guaranteed Income that is perfectly consistent with the reciprocity principle to an exploitative Guaranteed Income scheme. White's (1996) conclusion – "An unconditional basic income would allow non-working citizens to free-ride on the efforts of, and so exploit, working citizens" – must be viewed in light of the possibility that the absence of an Unconditional Basic Income allows owners of external assets to exploit working citizens. If nonworking citizens allow workers to command higher wages by decreasing the supply of labor, it is hard to conclude that nonworkers exploit workers.

If the labor market effects are taken into account, the notion that harsh welfare reforms are a form of "tough love" does not hold up. Jason L. Saving (1997) asserts that reducing transfer payments will actually help most of the poor by forcing them into the labor market and freeing them from dependence on government transfer payments. However, such reforms would increase the supply of labor and drive down wages. With wages already below poverty level, these reforms are likely to increase the poverty of low-wage workers without eliminating poverty among former welfare recipients. These results are beginning to surface in studies of welfare reform (Levy, 1987). The more the welfare system is reformed to force every worker to accept any job that is available, the less able are workers to command salaries that provide a decent living.

The effect of an Unconditional Guaranteed Income on wages leads to the answer to a common question of any such plan – what if everyone does it? Critics of the Guaranteed Income have argued that if no one has to work, no one will work. Everyone will choose to live off the Guaranteed Income, and there will be no output to purchase. Supporters of an Unconditional Guaranteed Income usually respond by arguing that it is not characteristic of human nature for everyone to choose not to work, or that an Unconditional Income has more work incentives than does the current categorical transfer system. These are good arguments, but they overlook the fact that the market has a self-correcting mechanism to prevent everyone from dropping their jobs to collect an Unconditional Income.

Although an Unconditional Guaranteed Income would be granted to all people, it would not be granted to all factors of production. Of the three factors of production – land, labor, and capital – only labor would have a Guaranteed Income. Even if a real estate owner is happy to live solely off of a Guaranteed Income, the owner still wants a return on that real estate and therefore will require labor. If people leave the labor market, owners of external assets and capital will have a strong incentive to increase wages to entice workers back into the labor market. This will raise the living standards of workers relative to nonworkers, which in turn will increase the number of people who choose to work. The postulated problem that people will not work if they do not have to is, in fact, self-correcting.

The higher one goes in the wage spectrum, the less likely it is that after-tax wages will be higher with a Guaranteed Income than without one, and in that case, White's exploitation objection may hold true for at least some workers. However, because the distribution of income is skewed so that the majority of people have incomes closer to the lower end of the spectrum (Van Parijs, 1995), it is quite possible that a substantial portion of workers will see their after-tax income rise if an Unconditional Guaranteed Income is introduced. High-wage workers and entrepreneurs whose incomes do not come largely from external assets will likely see their after-tax incomes fall, but it is no longer a case of taxing all workers to help all nonworkers, as White implies. Many of the people who would benefit from the Guaranteed Income will be low-income workers, and many of the people who would pay the taxes will be people who are otherwise in a position to exploit workers.

If there is a component of exploitation in a Guaranteed Income, it is that a portion of the redistributed income comes from high-income workers, and a portion of it goes to people who do not work. It is by no means certain, however, that this will be a large portion of the redistribution or that there will be more exploitation with an Unconditional Guaranteed Income than without one. The workers who will be net contributors to a Guaranteed Income system will be higher paid workers who have more options available to them than those who benefit from the system, and they will have an exit option – the Guaranteed Income – if they do not like the result. In the absence of a Guaranteed Income, the lowest paid workers have the fewest options available to them and are invariably exploited. On balance, which is better? While high-wage workers may be exploited in a Guaranteed Income system by White's criteria (i.e., some of their income is redistributed to nonworkers), they are not exploited in the sense that they lack options available to recipients.

With an Unconditional Guaranteed Income, people with high earned income will at least be rewarded according to Van Parijs's weak effort principle: if higher private income reflects greater effort and a greater contribution, people who make greater contributions will still earn a greater income than people who make lesser contributions, although not as much as they would have if there were no Guaranteed Income. If wages do not perfectly reflect contributions, then the Guaranteed Income allows people to opt out if they don't think they are being fairly compensated. People with high earned income are also those most likely to obtain some of their income from outside assets and are among those who benefit from the way we have chosen to organize society. If one rationale for a Guaranteed Income is to compensate people who do not benefit from living in a society with privatized land and natural resources, it is justified that compensation come from those who benefit from this method of organization and not merely from the owners of outside assets.

Note

1. Michael Hudson, personal correspondence, 1997.

References

Block, F. and Manza, J. (1997). Could We End Poverty in a Post-Industrial Society? *Politics & Society*, 25, 4.

Foley, D.K. (1967). Resource Allocation and the Public Sector. *Yale Economic Essays*, 7, 45–198.

Kim, M. (1997). The Working Poor: Lousy Jobs or Lazy Workers? Jerome Levy Economics Institute Working Paper No. 194.

Kim, M. and Mergoupis, T. (1997). The Working Poor and Welfare Recipiency: Participation, Evidence, and Policy Directions. *Journal of Economic Issues*, 31, 3.

Levin-Waldman, O. (1996). *Reconceiving Liberalism: Dilemmas of Contemporary Public Policy.* University of Pittsburgh Press, Pittsburgh.

Levy, F. (1987). *Dollars and Dreams: The Changing American Income Distribution.* Russell Sage, New York.

Nozick, R. (1974). *Anarchy, State, and Utopia.* Basic Books, New York.

Saving, J.L. (1997). "Tough Love": Implications for Redistributive Policy. *Economic Review, Federal Reserve Bank of Dallas, Third Quarter.*

Smith, A. (1776). *An Inquiry into the Nature and Causes of the Wealth of Nations.* Random House, New York.

Tucker, R.C. (ed.) (1978). *The Marx-Engels Reader*, 2nd edn. Norton, New York.

Van Parijs, P. (1995). *Real Freedom for All: What (If Anything) Can Justify Capitalism?* Clarendon Press, Oxford.

White, S. (1997). Liberal Equality, Exploitation, and the Case for an Unconditional Basic Income. *Political Studies*, 45, 2.

Chapter 20

The Morality of the Universal Grant Versus the Ethics of Paid Work

Robert van der Veen

Excerpts from van der Veen, R. (1991). *Between Exploitation and Communism. Explorations in the Marxian theory of justice and freedom.* Wolters-Noordhoff, Groningen, ch. 6.

Even though the dominant ideology of the welfare state rejects the constitutional obligation to do "socially useful work" characteristic of existing socialisms, and the legal enforcement of that obligation, in some cases, through "parasite laws,"[1] it is firmly united on one general principle: that competent and able-bodied persons should be under economic compulsion to perform paid work, at least if they are not engaged in receiving education or doing household work in families supported by a (usually male) "breadwinner." This general principle is the core of the so-called "work ethic," which is perhaps better called the *ethic of paid work*.

Alongside views about the intrinsic value of paid work, however, the ethic of paid work includes a *direct* claim of justice, which asserts that compulsion of the able is right, quite independent of the intrinsic value of paid work. It is this claim which I shall seek to oppose at some length. For though that claim is rarely defended explicitly (a fact that only testifies to its wide currency), it is by far the most influential element of the paid work ethic.

Stated negatively, the justice claim says that it is inexcusably unjust for competent and able-bodied persons to *live off the fruits of others' paid work*, even if it were the case that the freedom of doing so could feasibly be extended to everyone (as it would be if the Universal Grant were sustainable at the subsistence level). And because this is inexcusably unjust, the institutional structure should disallow this particular freedom. In a discussion with van der Veen and Van Parijs (1986), Elster (1986, 1989) adduces the popularity of this claim as one of the major reasons why the proposal is bound to fail politically. And since Elster wholeheartedly endorses the claim himself, it is interesting to consider his argument in some detail.

From van der Veen, R. (1991). The Morality of the universal grant versus the ethics of paid work. In R. van der Veen, *Between Exploitation and Communism. Explorations in the Marxian theory of justice and freedom.* Wolters-Noordhoff, Groningen, ch. 6. Reprinted with kind permission of the author.

Basic Income: An Anthology of Contemporary Research, First Edition. Edited by Karl Widerquist, José A. Noguera, Yannick Vanderborght, and Jurgen De Wispelaere.

Elster formulates the claim in terms of *exploitation*:

> Most workers would, correctly in my opinion, see the [universal grant-, VdV] proposal as a recipe for the exploitation of the industrious by the lazy. (Elster, 1986: 719).

And again, more recently:

> [. . .] I shall simply argue that any such proposal [the universal grant, VdV] would fail because it would be perceived as unfair, indeed as exploitative. People who chose to work for an income rather than to live in a commune on the universal grant would have to pay higher taxes in order to support those who took the other option. They would think, correctly in my opinion, that they were being exploited by the other group. (Elster, 1989: 215).

Before proceeding further, a note on terminology is in order. I assume that Elster here uses "exploitation" in the everyday sense in which his commune members could be said to take unfair advantage of the workers. To prevent confusion with the Marxian notion of *class exploitation* as unfair advantage, I interpret Elster as saying that the commune members are *parasitic* upon the workers. This is another and perhaps more usual way to express the idea that the commune members are obtaining unjust advantages from the workers, because they decide to benefit from the grant without contributing to its maintenance, and without participating in the process of paid work, *both* of which, being able and competent, they could do if they wished. Duly qualified, this concept of parasitism is also more appropriate for describing the case at hand, as will be shown below. The question to be answered now is: why should one want to say that the non-working commune members *unjustly* benefit from the Universal Grant? One objection to Elster's view that this is a case of injustice is to deny that living off others' labor is unjust when everyone is given the same possibility:

> Facing this possibility, some will choose to do little or no paid work; while others will want to work a lot, whether for the additional money or for the fun of working, thereby financing everyone's universal grant. If the latter envy the former's idleness, why don't they follow suit? (van der Veen and Van Parijs. 1986: 726).

Elster calls this objection the "argument from freedom of choice." He (correctly) rephrases it as follows and then adds two brief replies:

> By assumption, everyone would be free to choose the universal grant. If some people chose not to do that, they could hardly complain if others did. Their preference for consumption over leisure would provide no reason for preventing others from acting on different preferences. To this I have two replies. First, some people might remain in the workforce simply because they believed someone had to be in the workforce. When contemplating the happy commune members, they might mutter angrily, 'What if everyone did that?'. Next, even if they in fact did prefer to work because they valued consumption, there would be no reason to tax them more heavily. They might well prefer the forty-hour week over the fifty-hour week they had to work because of the high taxes imposed on them by those who chose to live on the grant. Hence the argument from freedom of choice fails because the workers would be forced by the non-workers to work harder than they wished. (Elster, 1989: 215–216).

Since his discussion stops here, Elster apparently believes that these two replies defeat the "argument from freedom of choice," and thereby establish his claim about the injustice of the Universal Grant. But whether he believes this or not, both replies are unsuccessful in either respect. As to the first reply, it seems sufficient to observe that the rhetorical question "What if everyone did that?", by which the disgruntled workers criticize the happy commune members, is out of place. If no one worked, then there would be no grants to dispense, which here there plainly are. But this response takes the question too literally, and it may be more charitably interpreted, in a way tbat directly bears upon the issue of parasitism. The question "What if everyone did that?" may reflect the disgruntled workers' belief that the preference of quitting the workforce and living off the Universal Grant, which they themselves share with the happy commune members, is so widespread that if everyone who has this preference were to unrestrainedly act upon it, the work that needs to be done in society would no longer be forthcoming in sufficient amounts, so that not only the Universal Grant would break down, but also many needs would go unsatisfied. On this interpretation, the disgruntled workers' decisions to stay in the workforce, even though they would rather quit, is explained by the moral motivation of not wanting to be parasitic. These workers do not want, that is, to be people who benefit from a scheme to which all have access (the Universal Grant), without contributing to its upkeep (by performing sufficient taxable work) and who thereby also knowingly contribute to the ruin of an important good (the satisfaction of people's needs) by their openly unrestrained behavior, *given* that many others have the same tendency to act this way.

Now if this last-mentioned condition is indeed a necessary feature of genuine parasitism, as I think it is, it follows that Elster's disgruntled workers can consistently regard the happy commune members as parasites. And their rather inexplicit angry question then conveys a valid moral point, providing that their beliefs about the world are indeed correct.

However, in the case which is being discussed here, the scheme is not only being assumed to be *currently in force*, thereby enabling the happy commune members to live off the fruits of others' voluntarily supplied labor, at least for so long as people like the disgruntled workers decide to put up with them. The scheme is also being assumed to be *economically sustainable*. And this means that everyone who wishes to follow the example of the happy commune members is enabled to do so with impunity, without the nasty consequences feared by the disgruntled workers. For by definition, the sustainability of the Universal Grant (at the specified level) means that sufficient numbers of people will not want to follow the happy commune members, but will instead want to work for the income and the immaterial benefits which they can extract from their jobs. Indeed, if the subsistence level of the Universal Grant is sustainable in this sense, but also happens to be well below the *maximum* sustainable level, then it may even be the case that some workers would like to do more work than they were being offered, or would be unemployed altogether. Faced with that (admittedly unlikely) possibility, the "social" thing to do for Elster's disgruntled workers would then be to join the ranks of the happy commune members as soon as they could.[2] In any event, the disgruntled workers have no valid moral complaints against the behavior of their nonworking fellows under a genuinely sustainable Universal Grant. Hence their opinions can neither be cited as a valid reply to the "argument from freedom of choice," nor as a reason for denouncing the Universal Grant as an unjust proposal.

Yet I think that Elster's case of the disgruntled workers, while unsuccessful in both of these respects, may serve as an important warning to carefree supporters of the Universal Grant, because it shows how intimate the link is between beliefs about the feasibility and about the justice of Unconditional Incomes. Since most of the debate on the ethical desirability of Universal Grants is staged as an all-or-nothing contest between conditional and unconditional subsistence, with the sustainability of the latter being higly controversial, it is well to stress the importance of introducing Universal Grants step-wise [. . .].

Elster's second reply, in the passage above, deals with the fate of workers under the Universal Grant, who, unlike the disgruntled persons of his first reply, act unrestrainedly upon "industrious" preferences, but who would be better off acting upon those preferences under a regime without the Universal Grant, in which all able persons had to work (I am supposing "rentier idleness" to be excluded by this regime). When it comes to be decided which of these two regimes it is just to adopt, Elster unhesitatingly chooses the latter, because even though the Universal Grant-regime gives everybody the possibility of not working, it also imposes utility losses upon the "industrious," losses which they would not incur under the other regime, where no one had this possibility. Since the reverse holds for people with "lazy" preferences, who of course will lose out when everybody is made to work, Elster's choice of regime implies that the interests of people with "lazy" preferences should count for less. But he gives no reason as to why this is fair; no reason, that is, other than the one contained in his original "exploitation" claim. Elster's second reply therefore will not convince anyone who does not already share his view.

But what then, would be the just choice of regime here? If one bears in mind the proper terms of Elster's example, which are that everybody is able to either contribute to, or benefit from the scheme, in the net sense, no unemployment problems exist, and all have the same chances to develop their earning capacities, then it is hard to decide this issue. This is especially so when one leaves aside conceptions that condemn the very preferences of "lazy" persons as being unworthy of equal consideration in the calculus of justice. Intuitions may then differ on which of the two regimes (or which of the intermediate regimes with a more limited Universal Grant) is most obviously just. On Noziclk's entitlement theory of justice, as well as on the strict labor contribution principle, a Universal Grant would be flatly rejected. On an intermediate mix of the labor contribution and needs principles (with claims of need being independent of disability), any regime offering a positive Universal Grant up to the maximum sustainable level could be chosen. On a conception of "equality of external resources," the Universal Grant would be tied, as Van Parijs argues, to the estimated per capita value of nonhuman resources (Van Parijs, 1989, sec. 15). And on Rawls's difference principle, with an income-wealth index constituting the relevant primary good, the maximum sustainable Universal Grant would come out on top. In contrast to all these approaches, my criterion of leximin real freedom leaves the matter undecided. On this criterion, none of the regimes just mentioned is superior, for if we move from any one to any other, no one gains or loses in real freedom. As I shall discuss below, the background assumptions of Elster's example of "happy commune members versus workers" imply that all individuals considered by the example occupy economic positions. For such persons, the introduction of the Universal Grant may result in welfare losses or welfare gains, depending on whether they have "industrious" or "lazy" preferences, respectively, but none of them either gains or loses in real freedom.

Clearly, the above-mentioned problems of choosing between universal compulsion or universal freedom with respect to work, in the context of Elster's example, are due to the fact that this example deals with a very limited subset of the people who are actually affected by the social decision. When the others are brought in it soon appears that the force of the parasitism thesis, on which Elster's choice in favor of universal compulsion was seen to rest, is seriously diminished. Its force is diminished for two egalitarian reasons which are widely (though certainly not universally) shared in the welfare state: equality of access to paid work and the reduction of income differentials derived from "unearned" differentials in human capital.

If the Universal Grant is truly sustainable at subsistence level, then the effect of replacing it by a welfare state system of conditional grants is bound to create involuntary unemployment. This means that unless special policy measures are taken (rationing of labor-time, large-scale creation of subsidized jobs, or boosting economic growth which, it is hoped, will not be of the "jobless" variety), the preferred regime of universal compulsion to work will lead to far more unwanted idleness than will be present under the Universal Grant. And in any case, even if these special measures were successful, they would impose losses of various kinds upon many more than Elster's happy commune members. The fact that the Universal Grant is one possible way of dealing with structural unemployment, and with the inequalities of access to paid work thereby involved, does of course not make it uniquely just. But this fact does call attention to one point of relevance here: there is something radically wrong about the idea that it is *parasitic* not to contribute to the social product, or contribute less than one is able to, when the available opportunities to perform paid work depend on how many people want to seize them, for purely self-interested reasons which have nothing to do with the morality of working.

Next, Elster's example presupposes that we are looking at a group of people who are not only *able to work*, but all of whom are also sufficiently well-endowed with (effective) market earning power to be *able to contribute more taxes to the universal grant-scheme than the grant is worth*. This group was represented by economic position C, and it was distinguished from another group of able persons, represented by economic position B, whose limited market earning power renders them *unable* to pay more than the grant's worth of tax contributions.[3]

Group B obviously creates problems for the parasitism thesis. The most "industrious" of its members, who do everything to realize their highest earnings, can hardly be regarded as parasites. Yet, since they are net beneficiaries of the Universal Grant, they are undoubtedly living off the efforts of the hard-working net contributors in group C. Do we really want to abolish the Universal Grant, and redistribute from the lesser-endowed B's to the well-endowed C's, when both apply their talents to the same extent in paid work? Now consider the "lazy" members of group B, who either live off the grant, or perform part-time work in jobs of their own choosing. For all we know, many of the latter (and even some of the former) might apply their talents equally assidiously in non-lucrative activities. Are they to be blamed as parasitic for not choosing to minimize the net income benefit which they extract from the Universal Grant-scheme? If so, then how long should they perform paid work during their lives to be disculpated? Again, by posing tbese questions, I am not here asserting that people in the lesser-endowed group B have the moral right to live off the labor of people in the well-endowed group C. Nor am I here suggesting that if they do have this right, then the Universal Grant is the uniquely appropriate way of implementing it. My aim is the more limited one of undermining the easy confidence with which advocates of the paid work ethic, such as Elster, assert the thesis of parasitism to keep Universal Grant-proposals off the political agenda.[4]

As I have said at the beginning of this section, this purely defensive undertaking was motivated by the desire to show that the Universal Grant is capable of being defended against the parasitism thesis from widely shared ethical premises that are consistent with my theory of Marxian justice, but without invoking tbe theory's ruling principle of communism. In analyzing the parasitism thesis, I have now established that it is extremely difficult to sincerely maintain that thesis, in the face of the (present or future) sustainability of the Universal Grant, if one is committed to the following ethical views: (i) the preferences and lifestyles of "lazy" and "industrious" persons in society are equally worthy of being respected in the calculus of distributive justice, and (ii) in evaluating social reform-proposals which affect the relation between work and income, one must consider their potential for achieving equality in respect of people's chances to freely participate in paid and unpaid work, and their potential for reducing the inegalitarian consequences of unearned differentials in human endowments, without interfering with formal freedom. To be sure, these ethical views are certainly not universally shared, even in the most generous of contemporary welfare states. And as I have shown, neither do they constitute a conclusive moral case for adopting the Universal Grant. But these views are, I submit, sufficiently simple and sufficiently widely held to form the beginning of such a case, a case which may then be systematically elaborated along the lines of the Marxian theory of justice presented in this chapter.

Notes

1. For a useful overview of constitutional duties to perform socially useful work in various socialist (or ex-socialist) countries, and their enforcement by means of "parasite laws," see Becker (1980), pp. 36–38.
2. Observations like these raise the question of how sincere the opinions of people like Elster's "disgruntled workers" are, when these opinions are expressed as an objection to the proposal of Universal Grants, before that proposal has actually been carried through. In a particularly acute criticism of the existing conditional transfer system, Hamminga (1988–1989: 114) makes the point that under such a system, the sincerity of many workers' complaints about the "easy lives" of those who are "profiting from" social security benefits can not be tested, because these workers do not have the real option of following suit, due to the conditional nature of the transfers. If they did have the real option of quitting the workforce, then some of them would undoubtedly decide to keep on working for purely self-interested reasons, in which case they would not be able to sincerely maintain their complaints. With respect to the position held by the disgruntled workers, a similar point holds. As long as the choice of not working is institutionally closed, there may be many people who, when confronted with the Universal Grant-proposal, will voice the moral opinion that though they would rather stop working, they feel bound to continue *because someone has to work*. But once the Universal Grant-system actually exists, it is much more difficult to maintain that opinion, even though, as my discussion in the text shows, it is not logically ruled out when there are doubts about the system's permanent sustainability.
3. Editor's note: The terms "economic position B" and "economic position C" are so named because they refer to points on a diagram earlier in the book from which these excerpts are taken. The definition of B and C provided in the text here are all that is necessary for the argument at hand.
4. That Elster seems to be doing his utmost in doing just that may be judged not only from his specific endorsement of the parasitism thesis, but also from his more general remarks on the Universal Grant-proposal. Classifying that proposal together with Meade's proposal for a "property-owning democracy," Elster makes the following sweeping statements: I shall argue that [these] proposals are non-starters, because they do not rest on a simple conception of justice, rooted in equality, and capable of inspiring a mass movement. They are engineering blueprints for utopias – technocratic dreams or nightmares without the potential for animating a social movement. Attempts to implement them would meet with mass resistance because people would feel, correctly, that they were asked to participate in a large-scale experiment of no intrinsic value and highly uncertain extrinsic value (Elster, 1989: 214). I do not need to discuss these statements here, because this has already been done in van der Veen and Van Parijs, 1986: 725–729, with respect to an essentially similar general criticism in Elster, 1986.

References

Becker, L.C. (1980). The Obligation to Work. *Ethics*, 91 (October), 35–49.

Elster, J. (1986). Comment on van der Veen and Van Parijs. *Theory and Society*, 15, 709–722.

Elster, J. (1989). *Solomonic Judgements*. Cambridge University Press, Cambridge.

Hamminga, B. (1988–1989). De handel in het recht op arbeid. *Wijsgerig Perspectief*, 29 (4), 112–118.

van der Veen, R.J. and Van Parijs, P. (1986). Universal Grants Versus Socialism: Reply to Six Critics. *Theory and Society*, 15, 723–757.

Part IV
Feminism

Introduction
The Feminist Response to Basic Income

Yannick Vanderborght and Karl Widerquist

Feminists are deeply divided on the potential impact of Basic Income on gender equality. Part of the explanation lies in the very diversity of feminist political theory itself. But, as it clearly appears in the following selection of papers, this division might also be due to the uncertainty about the likely effects of Basic Income. In particular, whereas most authors in this selection agree on the importance of labor market participation as a source of economic independence for women, they have divergent views on the concrete contribution of Basic Income to that goal. Although some hope that it could help women gain the autonomy needed to challenge the gendered division of labor, others fear that it might also give them incentives to keep working in the domestic sphere instead. The most widely quoted reply to the latter objection is a freedom-based argument, which Philippe Van Parijs phrased as follows: "I've always found it crucial to distinguish between measures that modify women's choices by restricting their options and by expanding their options. Basic Income is unambiguously of the latter kind, and . . . I find that there is something insulting about considering women, in particular less-skilled women, to be less able than men to make a wise use of these expanded options."[1]

In a stimulating dialogue, Ann Withorn (1990) and Ann S. Orloff (1990) express deep disagreements about the impact of Basic Income on women. As such, it is very illustrative of the above-mentioned cleavage within feminism. Whereas Withorn argues that it can be seen as "especially favorable" to women, since it would offer income security and guarantee increased autonomy, Orloff maintains that feminists should beware of such measures that might provide women with good reasons to stay at home. Both articles are thus focused on the core of the feminist controversy, that is, the impact of Basic Income on the labor market participation of women.

Ingrid Robeyns (2000) helps to clarify the terms of this controversy, offering an excellent overview of the main arguments for and against Basic Income from a feminist perspective. Robeyns distinguishes between first and second order effects of Basic Income on women. First order effects refer to the impact on labor market participation of women, and their financial situation, while second order effects mainly refer to the impact on unpaid activities and the position of women within the household. Robeyns also deals with the

Basic Income: An Anthology of Contemporary Research, First Edition. Edited by Karl Widerquist, José A. Noguera, Yannick Vanderborght, and Jurgen De Wispelaere.

normative aspects of this discussion, questioning the degree to which Basic Income would enhance the real freedom of women.

In his own account of the feminist arguments for and against Basic Income, Tony Fitzpatrick (1999) stresses several of its potential advantages. For instance, by providing women with some form of permanent economic security, it would not only improve their capacity to exit from the labor market, but also from oppressive personal relationships. By "debureaucratizing" the welfare state, a Basic Income would also reduce the need for intrusive inquiries that are often likely to affect female claimants in the case of means-tested benefits. However, given the fact that it has nothing to say about gender as such, the introduction of a Basic Income could also lead to a renewed sexual division of labor, as it cannot by itself promote the diffusion of an egalitarian care ethic. Following the work of Nancy Fraser, Fitzpatrick also compares three feminist social policy packages, and examines the role played by a Basic Income in each of them.

By contrast, Carole Pateman (2004) states that by providing an ***individual*** right to economic security, Basic Income will advisedly put the unequal distribution of labor within households into question. Currently, wives do a "disproportionate share" of domestic work, allowing men to free ride by benefitting from their efforts without making any contribution in return. Basic Income, contrary to household based welfare programs, would help to solve this problem even if, Pateman argues, feminists should not see it as a "panacea."

In a similar vein, Ailsa McKay (2001) argues that by its focus on the effects of Basic Income on paid work and the labor market, a great deal of the literature has adopted some sort of "androcentric bias." To avoid that bias, advocates of Basic Income should drastically reconceptualize the notion of "work," in order to take fully into account the importance of unpaid domestic activities, which are currently undervalued within market-based economies, and massively performed by women.

Finally, Anne Alstott (2001) argues that Basic Income could help fill in gaps in U.S. social programs that leave women vulnerable. She shows how the link between social benefits and paid work in U.S. social programs put women at greater risk; partly because women spend more time in childcare, then earn less in the labor market and spend fewer years in the labor force. As a result, many single mothers live in poverty, and retired women have a much higher poverty rate than retired men. Basic Income will reduce this gender differential in income support by establishing the same income floor for everyone.

Note

1. Interview by Pascal Couillard, *USBIG Newsletter*, 3 (17) (August–September 2002).

Further Reading

Alstott, A. (2001). Good for women. In J. Cohen and J. Rogers (eds) *What's Wrong with a Free Lunch?* Beacon Press, Boston, pp. 75–79.

Bambrick, L. (2006). Wollstonecraft's dilemma: Is a citizen's income the answer? *Citizen's Income Newsletter*, 2, 3–12.

Fraser, N. (1997). After the family wage. A postindustrial thought experiment. In N. Fraser, *Justice Interruptus. Critical Reflections on the "Postsocialist" Condition*. Routledge, New York, pp. 41–66.

Funiciello, T. (1993). *Tyranny of Kindness. Dismantling the Welfare System to End Poverty in America.* The Atlantic Monthly Press, New York.

McKay, A. (2005). *The Future of Social Security Policy: Women, Work and a Citizen's Basic Income.* Routledge, London.

McKay, A. (2007). Why a citizens' basic income? A question of gender equality or gender bias. *Work, Employment & Society*, 21 (2) 337–348.

McKay, A. and J. Vanevery (2000). Gender, family, and income maintenance: A Feminist case for citizen's basic income. *Social Politics* 7 (2), 266–284.

Parker, H. (ed.) (1993). Citizen's income and women. BIRG discussion paper 2. Citizen's Income Trust (formerly BIRG), London, pp. 1–74.

Pateman, C. (2003). Freedom and democratization: Why basic income is to be preferred over basic capital. In K. Dowding, J. De Wispelaere, and S. White (eds) *The Ethics of Stakeholding.* Palgrave, Basingstoke, pp. 130–148.

Robeyns, I. (2001). Will a basic income do justice to women? *Analyse und Kritik*, 23 (1), 88, 105.

Robeyns, I. (ed.) (2008). Should Feminists endorse basic income? Special issue of *Basic Income Studies* 3 (3), with contributions by J. Baker, B.R. Bergmann, J.M. Elgarte, A. Gheaus, J. O'Reilly, I. Robeyns, and A. Zelleke. http://www.degruyter.com/view/j/bis

Van Parijs, P. (2001). Real Freedom, the Market and the Family: Reply to Seven Critics. *Analyse und Kritik*, 23 (1), 106, 131.

Young, M. (2010). Women's work and a guaranteed income. In S. Gavigan and D.E. Chunn (eds) *The Legal Tender of Gender: Welfare, Law and the Regulation of Women's Poverty.* Hart Publishing, Oxford, pp. 249–276.

Zelleke, A. (2011). Feminist political theory and the argument for an unconditional basic income. *Policy and Politics*, 39 (1), 27–42.

Chapter 21

Is One Man's Ceiling Another Woman's Floor?

Ann Withorn

Excerpts from Withorn, A. (1990). Is One Man's Ceiling Another Woman's Floor? Women and BIG. Paper presented at the conference Basic Income Guarantees: A New Welfare Strategy? University of Wisconsin-Madison, 6–8 April, 1990. Published as Women and Basic Income in the US: Is One Man's Ceiling Another Woman's Floor? *Journal of Progressive Human Services*, 4 (1), 29–43.

It seems that Basic Income Guarantee (BIG) proposals do offer a critical new opportunity: the chance to make the actuality of women's lives central to core social policy discussions. If presented effectively, I can see that BIG may afford a possibility to bring gendered "politics" back into the center of discourse about the state, in a way that has not been true for at least 70 years.[1]

At its theoretical best, BIG offers women the hope of a financial base separate from the sharing of men's wages, thereby allowing women to live more easily without men at any stage of their lives. It provides the economic base from which both women in couples and single mothers may be able to devise more flexible employment/nurturing/training arrangements. It begins to provide an economic way to recognize the work of caregiving. Reasonable child support payments become possible for noncustodial fathers with low wages. BIG would operate with less bureaucratic harassment and stigma than Aid to Families with Dependent Children (AFDC), or even Supplemental Security Income (SSI).[2] Finally, it may give women and men the power to refuse unsafe, or "dirty" jobs, along with the opportunity to accept rewarding, creative employment that may still pay lower wages (I'm not really sure that this achievement, especially, is possible under any form of capitalism, but I will leave this to the economists to consider). As a policy direction, BIG offers women more choice than even the most thoroughgoing "full employment" proposals, and is light-years ahead of the recent "welfare reform"-workfare proposals for poor women.

Obviously, such a list of potential benefits is imposing, and one would hope, striking enough to be developed more fully even by male advocates of BIG. My purpose here is

From Withorn, A. (1993). Women and Basic Income in the US: Is One Man's Ceiling Another Woman's Floor? *Journal of Progressive Human Services*, 4 (1), 29–43. Adaptation reprinted with permission of the author and Taylor & Francis Journals.

Basic Income: An Anthology of Contemporary Research, First Edition. Edited by Karl Widerquist, José A. Noguera, Yannick Vanderborght, and Jurgen De Wispelaere.

to encourage this process by identifying the issues currently raised by women about social policies that should be incoporated into BIG proposals.

The most general way in which feminist arguments should affect BIG proposals is to explain why a thorough "gendered analysis" is needed before the particular effects that BIG might have on women can be predicted. Much rich historical research has been done by feminists to show the complex pattern by which women's roles in the family became intertwined with state functions, in ways which usually served to control women, but did sometimes "protect" them from individual men and give them some basis to live without men – however penuriously. How will BIG alter these patterns? Feminists have viewed the most comprehensive and popular social programs within the welfare state (social security, unemployment) as serving male needs and male recipients, while programs for women have recieved both lower funding and lower status; how does BIG redress the imbalance?[3]

Feminists have shown that the welfare state is populated primarily by women – as recipients and workers – and how many of the functions of the welfare state have deeply gendered meaning. BIG proposals should show how single, married, or single parent women will fare as well as the impact on different types of women workers – from home and child care providers to social workers and bureaucrats. Answering these questions will both flesh out the model and provide more room to build political alliances.

In short, feminists now can argue from strong historical and social policy evidence that the welfare state is centrally concerned with women's lives and opportunities for development. Changes in it must be evaluated as much in relation to women's issues, as they are in relation to labor markets or concerns related to the development of the polity.

Basic Income can be seen as being especially favorable to women by offering: income independent from men; more automony in employment choices regarding both whether and how much they earn; more resources directly earmarked for children or elders for whom they care (Walter, 1989). By simply bringing the centrality of these issues to widespread attention, BIG proposals can make a positive contribution to policy discussions in this country. Unfortunately, however, little of the discussion in our "capitalist road to communism"[4] packet took up the specific impacts for women.

When we look at more particular areas of feminist concern, we can see similar positive arguments for BIG, should its proponents choose to make them. For years, feminists of many varieties have explored the meaning of the public-private split in women's lives. The public world has been the man's world of work and politics and the private world has been women's world of home and social reproduction. Although feminists have become increasingly complex in their analysis of these divisions, most of those who have looked at the welfare state have seen it as exerting negative "public" control over the private sphere – especially when there is no man in the home. AFDC and child welfare rules regulate much of poor women's parenting behavior – in the past, to keep her home even if she wanted both employment and some social assistance, and now to force her into certain jobs even if she feels that more time needs to be spent caring for her children. Depending on the level of individual and child benefits, BIG would probably do away with much of this control. Feminists, and welfare recipients, should welcome this freedom from state domination. Some, however, might still speculate about what other, non-income, collective obligations the society holds to the "private" world. BIG proposals must address what remains of the state after its installation. For example, what economic base would remain to allow the state to offer positive alternatives to "private" caregiving roles so that women do not remain responsible for them, albeit with more money to do so.[5] Would BIG help or hinder the development of increased community responsibility for those social obligations currently defined as "private?"

Essentially, BIG begs the central feminist (and socialist) question of whether the patriarchal capitalist welfare state can be transformed. It might well take away a critical negative operation of that state – the administration of a massive, "needs based" bureaucracy – and also eliminate gender-based discimination in tax and pension structures. But, BIG would not address all the other ways in which the state affects women, through its education, health, environmental and employment policies. To appeal to the many intellectuals and policy advocates influenced by feminism, BIG proposals must say more about the state, both about how supplying a Basic Income may give citizens more power in regard to it, and what programs should be eliminated, or changed, if the problems associated with destitution were dramatically reduced. (Of course, such discussions would consider the "big ticket" items like health care, housing, and child care, but I would also like to see discussion of "services" – like programs for teen parents, youths, seniors. Would these be considered market responsibilities once everyone had a Basic Income?)

If we think about other questions which feminists raise regarding the importance of process and participation, BIG proposals also may not be adequately developed. Can the "participation in the discourse of power and decision-making" that feminists like Kathy E. Ferguson[6] view as an essential base for combatting bureacracy be built into BIG? Many feminists have commented on how women's sense of security often depends on their ability to maintain relationships – with families and communities – does BIG's individualistic bias inhibit this? Nancy Fraser's argument that women have not been able to interpret, much less meet, their own social needs, would seem to be helped but not solved by a basic income. The arguments of Black feminists that white and black women often experience public programs in contrasting ways suggests that BIG be explored further in terms of its differential impact on white women and women of color. Stigma should be reduced by BIG, as should easy characterization of the receipt of social help as "dependence," but only if BIG is promoted in a certain way.[7]

Indeed, as I write this chapter, I am beginning to think that BIG will become a positive strategy to the degree that its proponents engage, and do not avoid, its feminist possibilities.

Conclusions: Is BIG Big Enough for Women?

Discussions like these are frustrating because what men present as a dramatic change, like BIG, often seems only a necessary but not sufficient beginning for the kind of change women really need. It is hard to never be satisfied.

The potential of BIG to be a "radical reform," to use Gorz's old phrase, clearly exists: it does offer recognition of the value of women's unpaid work and devalues the primacy of waged labor as the most legitimate form of human behavior. But I keep returning to the same qualifier: BIG alone is not big enough, it simply paves the way for broader discussions of the best ways, with Basic Income needs met, for society to provide more carefully for itself. Considering, then, the importance of all the questions and opportunities raised when we think about BIG and women, perhaps Van Parijs and company should proclaim BIG as not a capitalist road to communism, but a feminist one instead.

Notes

1. The argument that gendered politics was strongest in influencing the US state prior to the 1920s was made by Theda Skocpol in a talk on "Gender and the Welfare State" at Northeastern University (March 1, 1990). The analysis grows directly out of her earlier work in Weir, et al. (1988).
2. Editor's note: AFDC was a Federal social assistance program created during the New Deal. In 1996, the Clinton administration replaced it by a new program called Temporary Assistance for Needy Families (TANF).
3. See especially, Fraser (1987). Also see a series of historical papers being developed under the auspices of the Bunting Institute, Radcliffe College, Cambridge, MA and Pearce (1990).
4. Editor's note: The author refers to van der Veen, R. and Van Parijs, P. (1986) A Capitalist Road to Communism. *Theory and Society* 15 (5), 635–655. Excerpts from this paper are to be found in Part II of this anthology.
5. Walter (1989) cites H. Parker in summarizing this question. Also see Bonnar (1982).
6. Editor's note: See Ferguson (1984).
7. See Ferguson (1984) and Fraser (1987). For Black Feminist critiques of welfare see Omolade (1986; 1987), Carby (1982), plus several articles in the *Nation* Special Issue on Black Women. On the "dependency" point I cannot help wondering how BIG will address the issue, raised so aptly by Hilary Graham, that "for many women being dependent is synonymous, not with receiving care, but with giving it," cited in Hanmer and Statham (1988).

References

Bonnar, D. (1982). Caregivers Wages. In D. Dujon and A. Withorn (eds) *For Crying Out Loud: Women and Poverty in the United States.* Pilgrim Press, New York.

Carby, H. (1982). White Women Listen! In Centre for Contemporary Cultural Studies, *The Empire Strikes Back.*

Ferguson, K.E. (1984). *The Feminist Case Against Bureaucracy.* Temple University Press, Philadelphia.

Fraser, N. (1987). Women, Welfare and the Politics of Need Interpretation. *Hypatia*, vol. 2, no. 1.

Hanmer, J. and Statham, D. (1988). *Women and Social Work: Towards a Women Centered Practice.* Macmillan, London, p. 24.

Omolade, B. (1986). *It's a Family Affair: The Real Lives of Black Single Mothers.* Kitchen Table Press, New York.

Omolade, B. (1987). Black Motherhood: The Unbroken Circle, a Historical and Contemporary Perspective. *Wisconsin Women's Law Journal*, Fall.

Pearce, D.M. (1990). The Feminization of Poverty. *Journal of Peace and Justice Studies*, 2 (1), 1–20.

Walter, T. (1989). *Basic Income: Freedom from Poverty, Freedom to Work.* Marion Boyars Publishers, New York.

Weir, M. et al. (eds) (1988). *The Politics of Social Policy.* Princeton University Press, Princeton.

Chapter 22

Why Basic Income does not Promote Gender Equality

Ann S. Orloff

Excerpts from Orloff, A.S. (1990). Comment on Ann Withorn, Is One Man's Ceiling Another Woman's Floor? Previously unpublished paper, presented at the conference, *Basic Income Guarantees: A New Welfare Strategy?* University of Wisconsin, Madison.

Ann Withorn's chapter (see Chapter 21) asks if Basic Income Guarantee (BIG) could help advance the feminist political project, and examines several ways in which BIG proposals might be especially relevant for women. Withorn sees some merit in BIG, both from the point of view of progressive politics generally and for women specifically, but worries that making BIG our policy priority may undercut other necessary reforms. I am even less optimistic about the potential of BIG to advance a feminist or progressive political agenda.

Feminist analysts have noted that the welfare state affects two key aspects of women's unequal situation: their dependence on men for economic support and their responsibility for domestic labor. I was surprised that Withorn did not mention the latter – the domestic division of labor that is so crucial to the maintenance of women's disadvantaged position in society. BIG changes the *relative* resources available to men and women, and shifts somewhat the balance of power between men and women in marriage. Like Aid to Families with Dependent Children (AFDC), although on a higher level, a cash grant. reduces the costs of exiting marriage (or other relationships in which women are dependent on men). As Susan Okin (1989) (in offering a feminist reworking of Albert Hirschmann's work) has argued, such decreases in the costs of exit increase the power of women within relationships with men. Analysts of the family and household work have shown that it is the power differential within families that keeps women doing the vast bulk of domestic labor, even when they also participate in the paid labor force. Thus, BIG may contribute to some extent to women's ability to challenge the domestic division of labor – but I think we must ask whether this strategy is the most promising for challenging this linchpin of gender inequality. I would argue that, in fact, it is not. Overall, BIG may ease women's financial situation, leaving them "free to specialize in [. . .] activities" such as bearing and rearing children – perhaps living independently of men, but it does less to contest women's

Basic Income: An Anthology of Contemporary Research, First Edition. Edited by Karl Widerquist, José A. Noguera, Yannick Vanderborght, and Jurgen De Wispelaere.

near-exclusive responsibility for such domestic work than would a program of directly challenging the way work, paid and unpaid, is structured.

What of the potential for BIG to change the character of women's paid work? I found myself wondering over and over whether those who wrote of giving seemingly genderless people "freedom from toil" had considered anything but nasty wage-work, which I think they are right to assume might be upgraded or eliminated with the drying up of the pool of cheap labor. In this context, it does seem possible that a BIG would allow women in bad jobs in the service sector to "take those jobs and shove them," much as men in bad jobs might do. Yet there are some crucial differences between these female-dominated service-sector jobs and work in manufacturing and other sectors, as I am hardly the first to point out. Are there technological innovations which will change the character of the work of caring for people, including infants in diapers, sick toddlers, the incontinent elderly, and those ailing in hospitals? And if not – just who is going to do this dirty work? It is possible that the BIG would function to raise the pay for service sector jobs, but then who pays? The families who rely on this care? Or will women be "encouraged" to "specialize" in doing this work – unpaid, but with a BIG to cover their "basic" needs? Like many other feminists, I consider public provision of services to be more critical than simply offering subsistence-level remuneration for women to continue supplying the caregiving that traditionally has been their responsibility.

Generally, BIG seems to me to avoid directly challenging the persistent inefficiencies and injustices associated with the domestic division of labor and the various ways in which the workforce is kept intransigently hostile to those who want to combine wage work and nurturing (of children, parents, whomever). Rather, it offers "those who 'choose' to specialize" in nurturing a way out of fulltime commitment to paid labor. Like Withom, I am not so sure this is an unadulterated good for women. I would argue that jobs offer far more benefits than does unpaid labor in the home (even with a BIG): in addition to material resources, they provide networks of co-workers, self-esteem, an arena for demonstrating competence.[1] I don't doubt some women, and a few men, might opt for staying out of the labor force, especially given how difficult it is for anyone to combine nurturing and paid work, but let's not mistake this for challenging the roots of gender injustice.

Finally, I cannot speak about the ways BIG might fit into the politics of other countries, but it does seem worth considering where BIG fits into American political culture, and whether, given the content of that political culture, it offers the best policy strategy for women.

American progressives who want to influence policy have tended to be fairly unconcerned about the lessons of policy history, yet I think we can improve the chances of success for suggested reform by heeding them.[2] Our recent experience with the War on Poverty[3] and the political fallout from that interlude should make us very cautious about any policy that threatens to recapitulate the characteristics of those policy efforts. Basically, programs were proposed (and sometimes enacted) which pitted the non-working poor, primarily unemployed men and women of color and their children, against the tax-paying, working poor and the working class more generally (primarily white two-parent families), with disastrous consequences for the political strength of progressive forces. Proponents of BIG have stressed the importance of *universal* benefits, surely in response to the sad experiences with targeted and means-tested programs (which have not been limited to the United States). Indeed, in contrast to the War on Poverty, politically successful programs throughout U.S. history have offered universal benefits to broad groups of citizens, and avoided demeaning means tests. It has been possible to include some special help for the poor within these universalistic approaches. For example, within the rubric of Social Security, there is a degree of redistribution toward the poor (which certainly could be strengthened), and Irwin Garfinkel and others have proposed an assured benefit for the poor in the context of child support enforcement that will affect all divorcing couples. It seems quite likely that proponents of BIG may adopt more pragmatic policy proposals, given the political unlikelihood of an expensive, universal benefit. Indeed, many people have argued that a decent income for all is needed – but given the tremendous cost of such a universal grant, settle for a call for a targeted, but generous cash grant to the nonworking poor. I think that we should keep the universalism of the BIG approach, but look to programs that encourage work and ease the conditions of those combining work and nurturing rather than to permanent cash grants of any sort.

Quite simply, cash programs – when they involve able-bodied working-aged people, and exist as an alternative to, rather than as a supplement to work – have not been acceptable to the political public. (For example, David Ellwood [1988, p.37] cites a 1969 Gallup poll showing less than one-third support for a guaranteed minimum income – and this at the height of reformist fervor.) There is a far greater willingness to consider programs that provide the resources for people to live at a decent living standard – and note that popular opinion puts that *above* the poverty line – as long as they are trying to be personally responsible, which for Americans means working. BIG offers a benefit for *not* working. Although it is ostensibly a measure to help those displaced by structural unemployment, it does nothing to move them into jobs, and will depend on the taxes of those who do work to pay for it (even if they get the benefit, too). At the least, we need to worry about the potential for political backlash against "handouts." Programs which unite the interests of poor and non-poor workers, people of color and whites, would come more easily and, I would argue, on a more justifiable moral basis around jobs and family than around cash grants.

The demand that the poor be "working poor" to deserve help now means women, too. There is no longer much cultural or political support for women to stay home full-time, much less if this is done at public expense. I think this can be taken as an opportunity, in conjunction with the tight labor market, to contest women's second-class status in the workplace. There is clearly a challenge to enlighten people about the extent to which women continue to bear the burden of domestic labor, and to build support for programs to make the combination of work and nurturing possible for both men and women. But if we are successful, this will channel more resources to women, increasing their independence from men. This would also improve their *relative* standing vis-a-vis men far more than would a subsistence-level grant, allowing for a direct assault on one of the core components of women's inequality: the domestic division of labor. Programs that would ease the combination of work and nurturing and to provide jobs for those who need them tap into the strain of progressive thinking in American political culture that emphasizes the right to work and a decent living.[4] They would also provide direct support to women trying to balance child-rearing and wage-work, often on their own, and might well be combined with children's allowances to assist families when they are particularly in need of income, and earned income supplements for those for whom a job is not enough to provide a decent living. In the context of a focus on universalistic programs to support work and family life, temporary, decently-paid leaves of absence to care for newborns or ailing relatives would be important components of reform, but would be tied to labor-force participation. It would also be desireable to offer temporary training leaves for workers to upgrade their skills, and to offer temporary cash grants for people undergoing crises.[5] The potential support of the American public for such universal programs to underwrite family and personal responsibility has not been tapped fully since the New Deal – in part because some are bewitched by the idea that it's unfair to require people to work, while others are entranced by the simplicity of Negative Income Tax ideas. I believe we will get closer to utopia for women and men by changing the character of work, and the relationship between work and family, than through BIG.

Notes

1. I do not wish to imply here that unpaid nurturing work does not require competence. However, in our society, it is far more difficult to reap the rewards of demonstrated competence, both material and social, in the home than in the paid workplace.
2. I am here making a very abbreviated summary of arguments made in Weir, Orloff and Skocpol (1988).
3. Editor's note: The expression "War on Poverty" refers to anti-poverty legislation introduced by U.S. President Lyndon B. Johnson during the 1960s.
4. I would also ask, given the tremendous global disparities between North and South, if we should be devoting our energies to arguing for tax increases which offer to our citizens a Basic Income, rather than directing such resources to the areas of the world that surely need the resources as much if not more. The structural changes in the workforce and domestic division of labor, on the other hand, do not demand the same order of resources as BIG. Indeed, such innovations are apt to increase rather than decrease productivity, which makes financing domestic and international reform more possible.
5. Temporary cash programs are another matter. David Ellwood (1988) has recently argued for revamping welfare provision altogether, stressing universalistic services and a public jobs program, in conjunction with a more generous, but time-limited cash grant, to help people over crisis periods (divorce, job loss, etc.).

References

Ellwood, D. (1988). *Poor Support.* Basic Books, New York.

Okin, S.M. (1989). *Justice, Gender and the Family.* Basic Books, New York.

Weir, M., Orloff, A., and Skocpol, T. (eds) (1988). *The Politics of Social Policy in the United States.* Princeton University Press, Princeton.

Further Reading

Hirschman, A.O. (1970). *Exit, Voice, and Loyalty. Responses to Decline in Firms, Organizations, and States.* Harvard University Press, Cambridge, MA.

Chapter 23

A Gender Analysis of Basic Income[1]

Ingrid Robeyns

Excerpts from Robeyns, I. (2000). Hush Money or Emancipation Fee? A Gender Analysis of Basic Income. In R. van der Veen and L. Groot (eds) *Basic Income on the Agenda. Policy Objectives and Political Chances.* Amsterdam University Press, Amsterdam, pp. 121–136.

I want to address the question of whether a Basic Income is favorable for women and if so, under what conditions and to what extent. What are the gender-related effects of a Basic Income, and how will the introduction of a Basic Income interact with several gender-related aspects of society, such as gender roles? First, I provide a positive gender analysis of a Basic Income by distinguishing the first order effects and the second order effects. Second, some normative arguments are presented.

A Positive Analysis: First Order Effects

First order effects are the direct effects taking place in the short run. They are more visible, easier to recognize, and individuals are more aware of these effects than the second order effects, which only take place in the long run. There are three relevant first order effects: changes in labor market supply and participation, changes in income, and changes in direct wellbeing derived from (professional) activities as people have more possibilities to do the work they like most.[2]

Labor supply effects

If a Basic Income were introduced, what would be the expected labor supply reaction of men and women? Neoclassical economic analysis concludes it to be theoretically impossible to predict these labor supply effects (Atkinson, 1995; Nelissen and Polk, 1996). Do empirical studies perform better?

From Robeyns, I. (2000). Hush Money or Emancipation Fee? A Gender Analysis of Basic Income. In R. van der Veen and L. Groot (eds) *Basic Income on the Agenda. Policy Objectives and Political Chances.* Amsterdam University Press, Amsterdam, pp. 121–136. Reprinted with permission of Amsterdam University Press.

Basic Income: An Anthology of Contemporary Research, First Edition. Edited by Karl Widerquist, José A. Noguera, Yannick Vanderborght, and Jurgen De Wispelaere.

In general, most empirical research on labor supply and participation agrees that the labor market participation of women is positively influenced by the educational degree and the net wage, whereas the number of children, the age of women, the non-labor income of the household and the income of the husband all have a negative effect on women's labor market participation. Concerning the number of hours women work, a consensus only exists with regard to the negative effect of the number of children. Atkinson (1995) reviews the relevant literature and stresses the complexity of estimates on female labor supply. Empirical labor economists agree rather unanimously on the highly inelastic character of male labor supply. The change in female labor supply is much harder to predict, and depending on the estimation specifications, wage elasticities vary from close to zero to two.

As far as I know, there are only two studies estimating women's labor supply changes after the implementation of a Basic Income, both concluding women's labor supply will decrease. Késenne (1990) modelled the introduction of a Basic Income of 15,000 BF (about €360) on a small-scale representative Belgian sample, financed by a constant marginal tax rate of 42%. This change in the tax system would decrease the labor supply of women with about 20%, but Késenne argues that there would hardly be a decrease of the female participation rate. However, this is only possible if there is a large increase in part-time jobs.

Nelissen and Polk (1996) find on the basis of Dutch data a wage elasticity of the labor supply of 0.79 for women, compared to 0.10 for men. The elasticity of the non-labor income is –0.20 for women, while there is as good as no effect for men. The authors simulate a Basic Income amounting 900 Guilders (about €390). They simulate the situation in 1990 compared to 2015, and find an increase in the labor market participation of men from 77 to 84%, whereas for women it would decrease from 49 to 40%. An important finding is the large differentiation among women: for low skilled women, this decrease would be around 30%, compared to only 3% for female graduates.

Summarizing these labor market effects, we can expect that the labor supply of women will decrease, though probably not *en masse*. It is very difficult to give an idea of the magnitude of this effect. Microsimulations use information on the behavior of women actually in the work force, but a Basic Income could lead to such drastic cultural and socio-economic changes that we do not know how reliable this information is. Furthermore, the labor supply of men and women differs drastically over generations. Hence, information on the labor supply of the working-age women could be of limited predictive use for new generations. Social experiments might therefore be a better source of information on expected changes in the labor market. However, the current career interruption premia can serve as an approximation of such a real-life experiment, and it does show a strong gender effect.

We should also note that it is not clear whether predominantly low-educated or high-educated women will change their labor supply. A hypothesis might be that a small Basic Income has a negative effect on the labor supply of highly skilled women, whereas low skilled women will only redraw from the labor market when the Basic Income is high enough. A possible explanation could be that low skilled women are often more income insecure and poor, and therefore it would be impossible to withdraw from the labor market when there is only a small Basic Income.

Total income effects

It is very difficult, if not impossible, to predict the changes in total income for households, and for women's income expressed in absolute levels and expressed relative to their husband's income. Therefore, I give only some general remarks.

Those women who had no income from labor or unemployment benefits, will experience a pure income improvement. These are mainly housewives, women not eligible (yet or anymore) for unemployment benefits and students.

For married or cohabiting women, it is impossible to predict whether their income share relative to their partner will increase or not. To judge this effect, one has to take into account all the details of the Basic Income proposal that would be implemented, and of the particularities of the fiscal system of the country under consideration. For example, in a country with a progressive tax on labor earnings, a Basic Income proposal financed by a flat tax on wages will on average lead to a larger decrease in net wages for wives compared to husbands. This is because wives on average earn less then their husband, and therefore are less taxed under a progressive tax system. If then a Basic Income is introduced, and neither husband nor wife change their labor supply, the wife will have a greater labor income loss compared to her husband.

The amount of a Basic Income will be of crucial importance when we ask whether the Basic Income will compensate the labor income loss of those women previously working and who decrease their labor supply. It is obvious that a monthly basic income of, say, €500 will, in this respect, do a far better job than a Basic Income of €100.

For lone mothers, a Basic Income appears to be an improvement. If social security allowances are paid for the amount exceeding the basic income, as proposed in, for example, Gilain and Van Parijs (1996), single mothers can only improve their financial situation. The major positive effect will be a (partial) elimination of the poverty and the: unemployment trap. Jane Lewis (1998) claims that single mothers need incomes from all possible sources: fathers, the state, and labor. Single mothers experience great difficulties with decisions concerning paid labor, due to the responsibilities they bear both as primary care taker as well as breadwinner. Flexibility, therefore, has to be central when developing a social policy for single mothers. If a Basic Income is seen as a pedastal upon which other social policy rules can build, this will definitely be an improvement for single mothers.

Effects on the choice of labor and job

The last first order effect of a Basic Income is the higher subjective wellbeing that individuals can gain when they are able to choose the job they like better but which is worse paid, or when they can choose for unpaid care labor instead of wage labor. Many young mothers want to withdraw (temporarily) from the labor market to raise their children themselves. If these women have to choose between a badly paid job, or the possibility to stay at home. the second option is much more attractive to many of them.

Second Order Effects

In this section, I discuss the second order effects which appear the most important for judging the desirability of a Basic Income for women.

A revaluation of unpaid and care work

We can expect that a Basic Income will lead to some revaluation of unpaid work. In Western societies, there is a societal tendency to undervalue unpaid work, especially household work and care labor. European societies often value the job one has as the most important source of status and integration into society. A Basic Income will in an indirect way contribute to a financial revaluation of unpaid work, which might also help to increase the respect people show for this kind of work. However, it is not sure and even impossible to predict whether a Basic Income will lead to a *substantial* revaluation of unpaid work.

Gender-related effects of a Basic Income for children

An important gender-related effect will be the different effects a Basic Income for children will have on their father and mother. I see two direct ways in which a Basic Income for children has a beneficial effect for mothers.

First, the child's Basic Income can serve as a financial benefit or wage for the care taking parent, which is almost always the mother. Moreover, parents will receive the Basic Income for their children irrespective of whether they take care of the children themselves at home, or bring them to child care. It has been argued extensively, and shown by empirical studies (e.g. Ward, Dale and Joshi, 1996), that child care is of paramount importance for women in their decision to join the labor market or work at home. The Basic Income for children thus serves as a financial compensation for child care, independently of whether the mother or the father does this care, or whether they wish to pay a child minder to take care of their child. Second, female-headed households are over-represented among poor people. The poverty and unemployment trap many single mothers face will thus not only be weakened by their own Basic Income, but also by the Basic Income of their children.

Hence, the Basic Income for children has two positive effects for women. It is an (indirect) financial reward for people who are responsible for the day-to-day care of their children, independently of whether they look after their children themselves or whether they prefer to pay others to do so. And it is particularly helpful for single parents. This should be taken into account when the level of the Basic Income for children is fixed. Many Basic Income proposals entail lower levels of Basic Income for children, often 50% of the Basic Income of adults, or only provide a Basic Income from the age of 18 onwards. This choice is probably due to household economies of scale and the lower material needs of children. However, the immaterial needs of children, more precisely, their need for care, offer us a quite different perspective. To sum up, if we want a Basic Income to be beneficial for carers, we might need a Basic Income for children covering the cost of direct material needs plus the (opportunity) costs of child care. A Basic Income pitched at this level would allow carers the freedom to do the care themselves or to buy child care services on the market.

Psychological effects on housewives

One can expect a Basic Income, even when it is small, to be positively valued by housewives or househusbands. It gives them a feeling of contributing to the incomes of their families, and a feeling of getting more recognition for the care and household work that they do. Pahl (1989) notices that for British housewives the child allowances they receive are very important, even though they are very small.

Bargaining position and power in the household

Basic Income proposals often have an (implicit) concept of the household that is an idealization of how most households in Western Europe function in reality. Many social scientists recognize both conflicts and cooperation within households. As Sen (1990) argues, households can best be seen as "cooperative conflicts." In principle, all family members gain by the formation of a household, but how the gains from this cooperation are divided depends, among other things, on the bargaining position of the individuals.

It appears that the partner with the highest income is more dominant in decision-making, and women, with paid employment have on average more power than women working unpaid at home (Pahl, 1989). Ott (1995) shows with the help of game theory that specialization in unpaid labor weakens the bargaining position of housewives and that education and non-labor income increase the power of housewives in the household. Although these studies are limited in number and most of them are small-scale and thus difficult to generalize from, there is growing evidence that personal income increases power. This implies that the introduction of a Basic Income will increase the bargaining power of housewives. However, for women working on the labor market, everything depends on the first order effects of the labor supply and total net income change.

Non-pecuniary advantages of paid labor

Women who quit the labor market not only lose their labor income, but also some non-pecuniary advantages. For Orloff (1990) these advantages are the construction of a network of colleagues, a place where one can demonstrate one's competence, and a feeling of self-respect. Steil (1997) adds to this list increased self-esteem, affirmation, enhanced contacts and more independent children. Kildal (1998) argues that paid work structures everyday life, is a source of social relations and an escape from social isolation, a means to self-realization and an important source of self-respect. However, she also points out that these can also be attained through alternative activities, like voluntary work.

Decrease of human capital and expected income in the long run

Studies of the division of labor between partners do not always fully recognize the long-term effects of this specialization. Specialization can indeed be optimal in the short run, but it can lead to unwanted dependencies in the long run (Wunderink-Van Veen, 1997).

Human capital depreciates when it is not used. As a consequence, when re-entering after some years out of the labor market, the potential wage will have decreased (Joshi and Davies, 1993; Wunderink-Van Veen, 1997). The total expected income over the lifetime cycle will therefore decrease in three ways: the lack of income during the period that no paid labor is done, a decrease of the expected wage in case of an eventual return to the labor market and smaller personal pension rights. If the human capital of a woman erodes because she doesn't have a job for some years, the probability of financial distress in case of divorce or decease of the husband increases (Joshi and Davies, 1994).

Spillover effects on all women due to statistical discrimination

A last second order effect is the spillover effect on all women due to the changed labor market behavior of some women, through the process of statistical discrimination. Statistical discrimination is a form of indirect discrimination based on the fact that a person belongs to a group that fits certain characteristics. These characteristics are then used as proxies for the average productivity of that group.[3]

Women on average bear one or two children, take maternity leave, work fewer hours than men on the labor market, bear more responsibility for the household and care of the elderly and children, have more career interruptions and are more absent from the workplace. Employers have a possibly biased perception of this and conclude that women are on average less productive on the labor market than men. For an employer, it is rational to believe that an individual woman will share these (perceived) characteristics, because he has no information on her future behavior and commitments.

Thus, an employer will discriminate against a woman (by not hiring her or giving her a lower wage) because he has no exact information on her productivity and therefore looks at the average productivity of the group she belongs to, that is, women. In other words, their *perception* of the average productivity of the group counts. A woman who does not want children, who wants to pursue a career or has a husband who undertakes half of the household responsibilities, will thus have to bear the consequences of the fact that other women are "child and household oriented."[4]

This implies that if a Basic Income is introduced, and a group of women withdraws from the labor market, it will also *be expected* that other women will be less labor market attached and they will be statistically discriminated against. Hence, a Basic Income will probably worsen the statistical discrimination against women.[5]

Some Normative Arguments Pro and Contra

In this section, I will discuss four arguments which appear crucial in this normative evaluation, and indicate how they are used by proponents and opponents of a Basic Income.

Basic Income and economic independence

Economic independence is the key-concept of most second-wave Western feminists to their arguments against a Basic Income. However, dependency has many different meanings (Lister, 1990). Absolute economic independence is the degree to which a person can take care of herself and eventually dependent others, now as well as in the future. This is what counts if a woman or a man wants to leave an unhappy or violent marriage: without the potential of absolute economic independence, one has the choice of staying in the unhappy marriage, or moving into (deeper) poverty. Relative economic independence concerns the income of one spouse relative to the income of the other, for example, the income of one spouse should not be below 45% of total household income.

Ward, Dale and Joshi (1996) argue that paid employment is the only way for women to avoid economic dependence, either on their partner, or on the state. Absolute economic dependence on the husband can have negative consequences in the case of marital breakdown. This has been shown by Jarvis and Jenkins (1999), who studied the financial consequences of divorce or separation in the U.K. The mean net income of men after divorce increased with 2%, whereas for women and children it decreased dramatically (–14% and –18% respectively).

Can the opponents' claim that a Basic Income will worsen women's economic independence be supported? Whatever the level of the Basic Income, women (and men) who did not receive any income before would experience an improvement both in the level of their absolute as well as relative economic independence. The level of the Basic Income determines whether this improvement is limited to the psychological effects. If a Basic Income does not replace other social security allowances, but is made complementary to them, women on the bottom of the income and employment distribution will benefit from it.

Again, the problematic evaluation concerns, in particular, the women who decrease their labor supply. It is very difficult to judge how their incomes would change.

When one addresses the importance of the social security system for women's economic independence, child care appears to be of great importance. Joshi and Davies (1993) argue that child care provisions have to be seen as an investment in the human capital of women. They demonstrate for Britain that the resources generated are larger than the costs of child care, and that the revenue gain to the exchequer might even exceed the cost of a 100% subsidy. Ward, Dale and Joshi (1996) show that child care facilities are crucial in the decision for women to work full time.

Basic Income: more real freedom to choose – or less?

Parker (1993) claims that a Basic Income will give each individual more real choice between paid and unpaid work. Schokkaert, Van der Linden and Van Parijs (1997) also regard one of the advantages of a Basic Income as being that it would give everybody more opportunities for *temps choisi*, referring to the need to have more time for children or to interrupt paid work for other reasons.

Feminist critiques often question the concept of individual choice. This is not different in the Basic Income debate. ***From a household point of view, and in the short run***, it could be a rational choice of a husband and wife to introduce gender specific labor specialization. The moment they have to decide which one of the partners works less or withdraws from the labor market, the choice is often rather obvious, and the framework in which this choice is made may have a strong influence. In other words, gender related structures and constraints convert this choice from an individual autonomous choice under perfect information into a collective choice under socially constructed constraints with imperfect information and risks. This totally different nature of choice appears not to be fully acknowledged in most of the Basic Income literature.[6]

Advocates of a Basic Income want to extend the opportunity to choose to everybody, so that a *real choice* between paid and unpaid labor becomes possible (Van Parijs, 1995) However, this real choice, to be possible at all, needs more than only a Basic Income. First, spouses have to be aware of the expected consequences of a (temporary) withdrawal from the labor market, and women should not have the expectation that those they are taking care of now will necessarily take care of them later. The low percentage of women who get alimony for themselves and their children after divorce, together with the fact that not all fathers actually pay alimony, brings carers *de facto* into an insecure situation. Second, men and women should have equal opportunies, which requires the end of all kinds of gender discrimination. It might also require a labor market organized around the basic assumption that every breadwinner is also a homemaker. This again points to the importance of child care facilities, as has been stressed by Joshi and Davies (1993), Parker (1993), and Ward, Dale and Joshi (1996). The fact that these two conditions are not fulfilled yet, mean that these choices are not real choices, but choices taken under the existing constraints on the opportunity sets which are different for men and women.

Basic Income between unemployment benefits and housewife wages

In the strict sense, a housewife's wage is a wage or benefit for individuals working in the home, who are paid for their household and care labor. It could be made explicitly conditional upon taking care of small children. Organizations of housewives in Europe advocate such a housewife's allowance. They refer to the unjust situation occurring as some women who are now receiving unemployment benefit use it in an improper way (as they are *de facto* not available for the labor market). This also happens when working parents can apply for career interruption premia if they withdraw temporarily from the labor market, mostly to take care of small children. It is obvious that housewives are being treated unjustly as they perform the same care labor, but are not paid for it.

It is not certain, however, whether a housewife's wage would not create other injustices amongst women. It would have to be financed by general tax revenues. A working wife doing household chores after work and in weekends would hence have to pay taxes for women who do the same household chores in a paid fashion. With a housewife's wage, working women would face a triple disincentive: working outside the home increases their workburden, they are taxed extra to pay for the housewife's wage, and they do not receive any allowance for the household work they perform.

A Basic Income would resolve part of these problems. It is nondiscriminatory because housewives would get it, and would not feel treated unjustly especially with regard to career interruption premia and the improper use of unemployment benefits. For unemployed women, a Basic Income has the advantage that everyone receives it unconditionally, so that it cannot be denied for one reason or another. The fact that the unemployment benefits are conditional on the willingness to work and limited in duration, mean that women especially are denied benefits (Schokkaert, Van der Linden and Van Parijs, 1997). Further, contrary to the housewife's wage as defended by Krebs (1998), there is no need for a bureaucracy to handle the applications of carers with dependent children or parents.

The importance of the individual character of a Basic Income

The second wave women's movement in Europe wants individualization of social security entitlements. The women's movement is opposed to derived entitlements claiming that it increases the dependency of women on their husbands. It has also been argued that an independent benefit entitlement for women in the social security system is necessary for a full exercise of their social and political rights as citizens (Lister, 1990).

A Basic Income is an individual right *par excellence*. However, it is not at all obvious that individual social security rights will work to the financial advantage of women. If these rights are implemented in a society with persistent wage differences between men and women, partly because women bear more family responsibilities, and especially with a large part of women working part-time, a complete individualization of pension rights will in any case work to the disadvantage of women (Joshi and Davies, 1994). It has been argued that the individualization of entitlements may be part of a long-term strategy for gender equality, but in the short term it may worsen the social security position of women (MacDonald, 1998).

If a Basic Income is introduced, it might be better implemented together with a credit split system, where individual entitlements are determined based on the entitlements partners build up together during the period of marriage or cohabitation. In other words, all social security entitlements accumulated during the marriage would be divided if the spouses split up. A Basic Income appears perfectly complementary to such a credit split system, and it could soften the hard financial consequences of divorce for women who made choices under gender-specific constraints.

Notes

1. A related article on gender and Basic Income but focusing on the moral problems and related justice considerations, called "Will a basic income do justice to women?" is published in a special issue on Basic Income of *Analyse und Kritik*. I would like to thank Mieko Bond, Sarah Bracke, Loek Groot, Roland Pierik, Erik Schokkaert, Holly Sutherland, Guy Van Camp, Robert-Jan van der Veen and Walter Van Trier for comments on earlier versions of this text.
2. There are many more first and second order effects thinkable. I have tried to list all effects relevant for a gender analysis.
3. Productive is here used in a very narrow meaning, that is, the degree in which a person creates additive value in the market production process.
4. Goldin and Rouse (1997: 22) give some evidence of the (biased) perception of women's productivity and reliability in orchestras. While the difference between the average leave of a female musician and a male musician is very small and statistically insignificant, the alleged shorter tenure by women justifies a preference to hire males above females.
5. I have discussed some moral questions concerning statistical discrimination in Robeyns (2000).
6. I have given an explanation for this gender division of labor and why this is arguably *unjust* in Robeyns (2000).

References

Atkinson, A.B. (1995). *Public Economics in Action: The Basic Income/Flat Tax Proposal.* Clarendon Press, Oxford.

Gilain, B. and Van Parijs, P. (1995). L'allocation universelle: un scénario de court terme et de son impact distributif. *Revue belge de sécurité sociale*, 38 (1), 5–80.

Goldin, C. and Rouse, C. (1997). *Orchestrating Impartiality: The Impact of "Blind" Auditions on Female Musicians.* NBER Working Paper 5903.

Jarvis, S. and Jenkins, S. (1999). Marital Split and Income Change: Evidence for Britain. *Population Studies*, 53 (2), 237–254.

Joshi, H. and Davies, H. (1993). Mothers' Human Capital and Childcare in Britain, *National Institute Economic Review*, 146 (4), 50–63.

Joshi, H. and Davies, H. (1994). The Paid and Unpaid Roles of Women: How should Social Security Adapt? In S. Baldwin and J. Falkingham (eds.), *Social Security and Social Change. New Challenges to the Beveridge Model.* Harvester Wheatsheaf, London.

Késenne, S. (1990). Basic Income and Female Labour Supply: An Empirical Analysis. *Cahiers Economiques de Bruxelles*, 125, 81–92.

Kildal, N. (1998). The Social Basis of Self-respect: A Normative Discussion of Politics against Unemployment. *Thesis Eleven*, 54, 63–77.

Krebs, A. (1998). Love at Work. *Acta Analytica*, 20, 185–194.

Lewis, J. (1998). Work, Welfare and Lone Mothers. *The Political Quarterly*, 69 (1), 4–13.

Lister, R. (1990). Women, Economic Dependency and Citizenship. *Journal of Social Policy*, 19 (4), 445–467.

MacDonald, M. (1998). Gender and Social Security Policy: Pitfalls and Possibilities. *Feminist Economics*, 4 (1), 1–25.

Nelissen, J. and Polk, S. (1996). Basisinkomen: effecten op de arbeidsparticipatie en de inkomensverdeling. *Tijdschrift voor Politieke Ekonomie*, 18 (4), 64–82.

Orloff, A. (1990). *Comments on Ann Withorn: Is One Man's Ceiling Another Woman's Floor? Women and Big.* Paper presented at the 3rd International Conference on Basic Income, Florence.

Ott, N. (1995). Fertility and the Division of Work in the Family. In E. Kuiper and J. Sap (eds) *Out of the Margin. Feminist Perspectives on Economics.* Routledge, London.

Pahl, J. (1989). *Money and Marriage*. Macmillan, London, pp. 80–99.

Parker, H. (1993). *Citizen's Income and Women*. BIRG Discussion Paper 2, London.

Robeyns, I. (2000). Will a Basic Income do Justice to Women? *Analyse und Kritik*, 22 (2).

Schokkaert, E., Van der Linden, B., and Van Parijs, P. (1997). Repenser la solidarité entre les actifs. *La Revue Nouvelle*, 5/6, 106–121.

Sen, A. (1990). Gender and Co-operative Conflict. In I. Tinker (ed.) *Persistent Inequalities: Women and World Development*. Oxford University Press, New York, pp. 123–149.

Steil, J. (1997). *Marital Equality*. SAGE, Thousand Oaks.

Van Parijs, P. (1995). *Real Freedom for All. What (If Anything) Can Justify Capitalism?* Oxford University Press, Oxford.

Ward, C., Dale, A., and Joshi, H. (1996). Combining Employment with Childcare: An Escape from Dependence? *Journal of Social Policy*, 25 (2), 223–247.

Wunderink-Van Veen, S. (1997). New Home Economics: Children and Labour Market Participation of Women. In A.G. Dijkstra and J. Plantenga (eds) *Gender and Economics: A European Perspective*. Routledge, London, pp. 17–35.

Chapter 24

A Basic Income for Feminists?

Tony Fitzpatrick

Excerpts from Fitzpatrick, T. (1999). *Freedom and Security: An Introduction to the Basic Income Debate.* Macmillan, London.

Advantages and Disadvantages

We can identify four possible advantages which a Basic Income (BI) might hold for women, as well as three possible disadvantages.

One principal benefit concerns BI's capacity to enhance female independence because it would be paid to individuals rather than to households and on the basis of citizenship status rather than employment status. Put simply, because women have less financial independence than men under the current system, the individualized provision of a BI would mean that transfers modelled along these lines would give women more freedom and men proportionately less:

> Women do badly out of the existing social security system, and would do worse out of a residual welfare state – because in each case benefit entitlement depends on former labour market participation and earnings. Women would do better out of a Basic Income, because with BI work status becomes irrelevant. (Parker, 1993: 61)

A BI could empower workers by improving their ability to exit *from* the labor market, by providing them with a right of non-entry *to* the labor market and, consequently, by enhancing their voice *within* the market. By giving women an independent, unconditional income a BI could have similar effects in respect of the family (Purdy, 1988; Carlson, 1997: 23–25). Research suggests that many women remain trapped within violent relationships because they are unsure of what their economic circumstances (and those of their children) would be if they were to leave (Hooper, 1996). The guarantee of a BI whatever their personal circumstances would therefore improve the ability of all women, but especially the most vulnerable, to exit from such relationships. Furthermore, because with a BI women would know that they could rely upon some degree of financial security they might be less likely to regard marriage as a means to such security in the first place. Finally, a BI could be expected to help household income circulate more fairly than at present. Many studies have

From Fitzpatrick, T. (1999). A Basic Income for Feminists? In T. Fitzpatrick, *Freedom and Security: An Introduction to the Basic Income Debate.* Macmillan, London. Reprinted with permission of Palgrave Macmillan.

Basic Income: An Anthology of Contemporary Research, First Edition. Edited by Karl Widerquist, José A. Noguera, Yannick Vanderborght, and Jurgen De Wispelaere.

shown how resources continue to be controlled by the male partner, even where the day-to-day details of household expenditure are managed by the female partner (Pahl, 1989; Vogler, 1994; Vogler and Pahl, 1993, 1994). By being paid equally to both men and women a BI could therefore improve the influence, or the voice, that women wield over the household income especially if the child BI is paid to the mother and even where the male continues to be the main breadwinner (Pahl, 1986).

The second benefit which a BI could have is that it might reduce the sexual division of labor by raising the status of non-waged work, such as domestic and caring responsibilities, and by placing less emphasis upon the necessity of earning wages in order to provide a liveable income (Purdy, 1990: 201). The existing benefit system is heavily organized around male employment patterns. By being unconditional a BI widens the panorama of the transfer system: it does not pay in *return* for the performance of caring and domestic reproduction, but it does not exclude them as the current welfare system largely does. Some go so far as to insist that BI would actively strengthen family values and kinship networks on this basis (Clark and Kavanagh, 1996; Halsey, 1997). A BI would also make households less reliant upon wage-earning activity than at present, thus encouraging a reduction in male working hours and so providing the opportunity for men to increase their commitment to non-waged domestic responsibilities as their reliance upon waged work decreases:

> Basic Income paid at equal rates to men and women would eventually give better incentives for sharing unpaid work in the household, and women would escape the role of full-time carers, in which the present benefit structure traps them. [. . .] In general, it would allow a more rational division between paid and unpaid work [. . .] (Jordan, 1992: 172)

Walter makes a similar point:

> Men and women can therefore make choices about how they wish to live and work, based on their own values, commitments and desires without having to take into account financial incentives that all too often were cooked up in a previous generation when values, and certainly economic circumstances, were very different. (Walter, 1989: 118)

However, BI supporters are usually careful to stress that although BI could help to reduce the sexual division of labor it could not eliminate it entirely. Indeed, this qualification is used in order to take account of the kinds of arguments which insist that a BI, especially if unaccompanied by other reforms, could further entrench the sexual division of labor within society.

A third possible advantage follows on from this point and concerns labor market segregation. If the sexual division of labor impairs women's access to paid employment and if a BI would tackle the former then it could also be expected to address the latter. Under the present system, whether or not it is worth a woman working depends substantially upon the employment status of her partner, so that women's widespread (though by no means universal) confinement to the periphery of the labor market is due to this reliance. Where a husband or male cohabitee is unemployed then *his* entitlment to benefit is affected by the amount of income *she* brings into the household. This may make it unrewarding for such women to continue in employment so that many women in this situation give up work, losing their earnings and the degree of independence that they offer in the process (Millar, 1989). It is this disincentive effect which has contributed to the growing divide between two-earner and no-earner households in recent years. Under a BI system, by contrast, the man's BI entitlement is unaffected by the amount of money which is brought into the home by his female partner. It would therefore be worthwhile her continuing in employment even if he is unemployed: in short, it could make part-time work more financially worthwhile and so help to reduce the segregation between it and full-time work. Guy Standing brings these two advantages – regarding the sexual division of labor and job segregation – together by arguing that the

> provision of a basic income would help to achieve greater sexual equality in the labor market by improving women's bargaining position and by encouraging men to take part-time work, so allowing them to share more in domestic work. (Standing, 1992: 59)

The research of Parker (1993: 35–45) shows that a BI would: make part-time workers better off, especially those on low wages; reduce the poverty and unemployment traps and so make work more financially attractive; promote equal pay between the sexes since the lower earnings limit on contributions (which encourages the creation of low-paid jobs) would go. Furthermore, by not being based upon the male breadwinner model a BI pension would treat both sexes equally, substantially raising the retirement incomes of female pensioners (Parker, 1993: 47–60; Ginn, 1996). In general, it could reasonably be expected to redistribute income from men to women (Parker, 1993: 63).

The final advantage refers to the effects of a BI in 'debureaucratizing' the welfare state. It is female claimants who are more likely to experience intrusive enquiries by the state into their personal lives and sexual activities through the application of the cohabitation rule, because female dependency upon a male breadwinner is still taken to be the norm. Therefore the social control and the administrative surveillance which welfare systems give rise to have a significant gender dimension: female claimants are more likely to suffer from statist intrusion than male ones due to the perpetuation of sexist assumptions about female dependency. By paying an individualized income, regardless of whether those individuals are single, married or cohabiting, a BI "gets the state off people's backs," to coin a phrase; and if the state currently has a tendency to look over the shoulders of women more than of men then a BI reform would assist women disproportionately as a result (McKay and VanEvery, 1995).

However, there are several major objections which can be made against BI from a feminist point of view.

First, it is possible to accuse BI proponents of confusing decommodification and defamilialization. The former refers to a freedom, or relative freedom, from the market: the removal of the price tag which the market forces us to wear. Feminist theory – at least the left-leaning variety which we are considering here – tends to regard decommodification as a worthwhile objective; however, it is not by itself enough because many women are already decommodified, and already possess some degree of freedom from the market. Instead, women's social position might best be described as "familialized" (Lewis and Ostner, 1994; Lewis, 1992), that is, as household-dependent rather than market-dependent. A feminist social policy, therefore, should aim at a gendered form of decommodification: that is, at defamilialization; and it is this which BI advocates are accused of ignoring. In short, a BI would not address the sexual division of labor and, in fact, might actually entrench it further (Cass, 1991).

This criticism focuses upon the tendency of some BI supporters to regard the freedom from the market, which a BI might supply, as a freedom which men and women would share in equally. But if a BI were to be instituted on a Tuesday then the decisions which men and women would make about their lives on Wednesday would still be largely determined by the values and assumptions which they had possessed on the Monday (cf. Orloff, 1993). If those values and assumptions continued to be patriarchal in character then a BI might do no more than set them in stone:

> By removing obstacles to shorter hours of employment the BI expands men's job-free time, but it cannot ensure that men will spend their job-free time on domestic labor. (Carlson, 1997: 8)

Instead, if men could be said to free-ride on the domestic labor of women (Fraser, 1997; cf. Taylor-Gooby, 1991) then a BI might simply enable even more free-riding as men gain a greater freedom within the market – to take part-time work, for instance – but women continue to orbit around the private sphere and so continue to lack opportunities and voice within the public one. In short, BI potentially recognizes the value of unpaid work but says little about who is actually to perform it.

This objection is closely related to a second: that BI would either do nothing to undermine labor market segregation, or it would adversely promote such segregation (Cass, 1991). One of the stated benefits of a BI is that it would allow people to choose between paid and unpaid work: it might encourage some people to leave the labor market and others to take the places thus vacated, that is, those involuntarily unemployed at present.[1] However, some fear that this exodus from the labor market would consist predominantly of women, especially married women, whereas the trek into the market would consist mainly of men. In contrast to the job-friendly possibilities set out above a BI might introduce countervailing tendencies into the job market.

By reducing the gap between the incomes of those women with employment and those without it might induce many in the former group to join those in the latter. As of 1998, those earning less than £64 per week do not have to pay either tax or insurance contributions, but with a BI they would have to start paying tax on most of their earnings (once they started earning above a tax-free tranche). This combination of an unconditional BI and the requirement to pay tax on most earnings, even when wages were relatively low, might therefore encourage many low-waged workers to withdraw from the job market; and since most low-waged workers are women then such a withdrawal would obviously have gendered implications.[2] Furthermore, if BI's purpose is to assist in the deregulation and flexibilization of the labor market, providing little more than a cushion against market failure and job loss, then it could merely end up helping to create low-paid and poor quality junk jobs (Cass, 1991). When we add the above arguments together, therefore, we can see that a BI might reinforce the sexual division of labor (public/private divide) and labor market segregation (core/periphery divide):

> [. . .] just as women's current patterns of part-time labor force participation cannot be seen as a (real) choice, neither can their withdrawal from the labor force under BI be seen as the result of any '(genuine) freedom to specialize'. (Carlson, 1997: 23)

> In the worst case scenario the BI could become a minimum income for men (a floor on which they can build) and a maximum income for women (a ceiling above which they find it extremely difficult to rise). (Carlson, 1997: 9)

However, it was also pointed out above that BI supporters are not unaware of these possible adverse effects (e.g. Purdy, 1988; Offe et al., 1996). Walter (1989: 121–12), for instance, acknowledges that there is a pessimistic scenario but insists that this is an argument for combining BI with measures designed to avoid that scenario becoming a reality. Lister (1997: 189) also allows for the possibility of combining BI with policies aimed more directly at combating the sexual division of labor and labor market segregation, while Carlson (1997: 26) gives a qualified support for BI so long as it is included as part of a "policy package." We shall be examining this issue at further length, but, at the very least, this policy package would probably need to consist of: a minimum wage, extensive help with childcare, the reorganization of male and female working-time and various other measures across the fields of politics, public and social policy.

Before addressing this policy package there is a third and final reason why feminists might object to BI. It can be alleged that BI is too blunt a tool to successfully perform the job expected of it. For instance, by paying exactly the same to a woman on a low income as to the wife of a company director would not a BI be fortifying the class differences which exist between women of opposing income and occupational strata? Or to take another example, because the economic activity rates of Black, Indian, Pakistani and Bangladeshi women tend to be lower than those for White women (Walby, 1997: 61) would not a female-led exodus from the labor market also have a substantial racial dimension with women from ethnic minority communities being more likely to opt out of a labor market within which they experience more direct and indirect discrimination, and fewer job and career opportunities, than White women?[3] In short, BI is a universalistic policy which could neglect the particularistic differences between women.

In conclusion, BI offers neither unambiguous advantages nor unambiguous disadvantages to feminism. It reflects the equal status of women in that it would equalize the treatment of the sexes within the benefit system by individualizing the payment of transfers and by ending the bureaucratic surveillance of the present system. However, it has nothing to say in itself about sex and gender differences. It embodies a strong element of social rights by providing financial independence for women but although it *could* lead to the sharing out of caring responsibilities between men and women it might just as easily entrench the sexual division of labor by not actively promoting the care ethic. Similarly, a BI could open the doors between the public and the private, permitting women greater access to the former and men greater access to the latter, but if its labor market effects were adverse then those doors might just as easily slam shut and fortify existing labor market segregation.

Does this mean that BI is likely to remain on the margins of feminist debate? The answer to this question is heavily dependent upon what kind of gender equity we aim at. The significance and the efficacy of a BI alters depending upon which welfare model we choose to pursue, as the next section will make clear.

Three Policy Packages

If we are to design a policy package then how should this package be labeled? Is there a common denominator of reforms which all feminist commentators can agree upon? Or is it possible to distinguish between alternative versions of prescriptive reforms? In fact, both of these questions may be answered in the affirmative: there must be *some* common denominator in order for those prescriptions to be recognized as feminist in the first place; yet similar reforms proposals may have differing objectives and differing rationales.

To understand what this means we can draw upon the work of Nancy Fraser (1997). Fraser distinguishes between the following: the universal breadwinner model of welfare (which aims to foster gender equity by promoting women's employment); the care-giver parity model of welfare (which promotes gender equity by supporting informal care-work); the universal care-giver model of welfare (where caring responsibilities are shared more equitably between men and women). All of these models, or packages, may reasonably be described as feminist given the joint commitment to gender equity but they imply radically different approaches. We shall outline all three of these models in the subsections below and speculate as to the role which a BI could play in each of them.

Universal breadwinner

The aim here is to make women equal citizen-earners with men by upholding the employment ethic and the wage contract (Fraser, 1997: 51–55). To this end, women would require: employment-enabling services to free them from unpaid responsibilities; workplace reforms to promote equal opportunity; cultural reforms so that women identify themselves with the workplace (and so that men can accept this); macroeconomic policies to generate high levels of quality jobs; social insurance reforms to ensure that women's entitlements are equal to men's. Care-work would need to be shifted from the family to the market and the state, but the status of care-work *employment* should also be raised. Benefits would be strongly linked to employment status and record, but a residual means-tested safety-net would still be required.

This model therefore represents the attempt to make women more like men, at least when it comes to wage-earning activity: it means retaining the concept of the breadwinner but degendering it so that women compete on equal terms with men. It is the version of feminist social policy which is perhaps most compatible with existing social assumptions and institutions.

As such, BI would be unlikely to have much of a role to play if this model were put into operation. *If* BI has employment-friendly effects which do not result in a deregulated, downscaled labor market then it *might* have something to offer the proponents of this approach. However, the fact that BI is not conditional upon waged labor, implicitly recognizing the value of *unpaid* domestic care-work, means that it is unlikely to form a part of this policy package. The same considerations probably also apply to Participation Income[4] unless this were interpreted as a preferable alternative to traditional means-testing and selectivism. By and large, then, BI is as unsympathetic to this form of gender equity as it is to existing forms of sexual inequality. The adoption of a universal breadwinner package would more than likely imply the continuation of the insurance/assistance approach with any upheavals (substantial though they would be) being limited to the sectors of employment and macroeconomics.

Care-giver parity

The aim here is support for informal care-work as a means of promoting gender equity (Fraser, 1997: 55–59). Rather than shovelling people into the labor market this model proposes that women with caring responsibilities should be able to support themselves and their families either through care-work alone or through a combination of care-work and part-time employment. This approach is not about making women more like men but about raising the status of what most women do (care-work) to the status of what most men do (wage-earning), that is, a parity between the two. Many women would therefore alternate between (i) full-time employment, (ii) full-time care-work and (iii) part-time care-work plus part-time employment.

To this end women would require: care-giver allowances set at a level comparable to breadwinner wages; workplace reforms to facilitate the kind of life-pattern flexibility just mentioned; job search, retraining and flexitime; extensive social welfare programs. Here, then, most care-work would continue to remain in the home but would be supported with substantial public funds. Part-time jobs and care-work would have to generate as many entitlements to insurance benefits as full-time employment but, as before, a residual assistance tier would also be required.

A BI could begin to have relevance in this context, largely because it could make part-time work more financially worthwhile as a simple back-of-the-envelope calculation shows. A part-time worker making £60 per week pays neither tax nor insurance contributions on those earnings. If a BI of £50 per week were introduced, assuming that this could be funded out of a 35% tax rate and assuming that the first £25 of earnings were untaxed, then the earnings of the worker would be reduced to £47.75 (60 – 25 × 65% + 25). However, these earnings would then be added to the BI to yield a weekly income of £97.75. A BI might therefore assist in smoothing out the income of women as they move in and out of the labor market.[5]

However, many of the old problems remain. If a BI were to be paid to everyone, whatever their wage and/or care-giving status, then it would not embody the parity which this model requires. Therefore, even a full BI could not really substitute for the care-giving allowances that Fraser mentions. The appeal of a Participation Income, though, might well be considerable in that it would not be unconditional but would give a specific and substantial emphasis to the value of domestic labor and caring responsibilities. Indeed, if a large Participation Income could be afforded then this might simply be thought of as the very kind of care-giver allowance which Fraser recommends; and, given that it would not be means-tested, it could have the additional benefit of making part-time earnings attractive. Participation Income, therefore, seems to fit well with the care-giver parity approach.

Universal care-giver

Fraser (1997: 59–62) recognizes the virtues of the above models but is nevertheless critical of the former in its requirement that women adopt the habits and values of men (the burdens of "equal" citizenship), and of the latter for locking women into caring roles without requiring anything different from men (the burdens of "differential" citizenship). She therefore gives provisional support to a third, alternative model whereby men do their fair share of the primary care-work. Men must come to adopt female life-patterns rather than vice versa which basically means alternating between breadwinning and care-giving. At present, this combination of roles puts a considerable strain upon women as they try to juggle employment and domestic responsibilities. Fraser therefore anticipates that if both sexes came to regard these roles as valuable then the burdens which women presently carry would be shared out more equitably: would cease being "burdens" at all.

How might this model be made a reality? First, all jobs would have to be designed for people who are also part-time care-givers which means a working week shorter than that for full-time jobs and the support of employment-enabling services. Second, care-work activities would be distributed between the state, the household and civil society (Fraser talks of locally managed and democratically run care-work institutions). Finally, the most substantial change would be cultural, that is, a dismantling of the gendered assumptions which sustain the existing forms of social organization.

Would a BI have a role to play within this model? This would depend crucially upon whether guaranteeing a minimum income to everyone under the universal care-giver approach would involve entitlements based upon citizenship or entitlements based upon non-patriarchal conceptions of need and desert. Citizenship entitlements would obviously have a considerable role to play since Fraser is designing a post-industrial scenario where we would be less able to rely upon the formal market as the source of economic wealth and social identity. As the old forms of citizenship *practices* become redundant then organizing welfare provision around the inclusionary and universalistic status of citizenship becomes more and more crucial. But this is not to claim that a minimum income scheme has to be so organized nor that a BI automatically fits the bill. On a matter of principle we return to the problem mentioned above that a BI does not enforce unpaid work any more than it enforces paid work. For those, such as Fraser (1997: 62), who are worried about the free-riding of men on the care-work activities of women, a BI might not actually go far enough in tipping the balance in favor of care-work. Furthermore, and on the question of feasibility, it might simply be that a postindustrial labor market would not be able to finance anything more than a minimal BI.

As with the previous model, therefore, feminists who wished to go down this road might consider a Participation Income as the best alternative to a universalistic and unconditional BI. However, the problem with a Participation Income is in defining and monitoring the participative activities which are judged to be socially valuable. The problem is perhaps more acute for feminists than for welfare collectivists, for whereas the latter can remain closely wedded to employment-based forms of minimal income provision, the former have to make considerable room for non-employment activities. If we are to move closer to universalistic citizenship then the logic of paying a Participation Income to most but not all of the population might seem less just and less efficient than simply providing a BI: over the course of however many years it might seem more rational to transform the former into the latter.

A BI *could*, therefore, contribute to the formation of a universal care-giver approach but the extent of the contribution is uncertain. It might be that the introduction of a BI would have to follow the establishment of a range of other care-giver institutions and policies, although a Participation Income could be thought of as having more of a proactive role to play. This is not the place to design the details of the universal care-giver model; our task has merely been to speculate on the relevance of BI. However, this policy package would undoubtedly have to contain the kinds of reforms mentioned in the previous section:

- a minimum wage, to head off the possibility of a BI subsidizing bad employers;
- extensive child-care provision distributed across a range of welfare sectors;
- the reorganization of male and female working-time to make room for domestic commitments and to ensure that women do not lose out on job-based entitlements, for example occupational pensions;
- measures such as the strengthening of laws dealing with equal opportunities, equal pay and equal treatment.

Conclusion

We can reasonably conclude that BI is a proposal which feminists, especially those working in the field of social policy, should examine. At present, it is the universal breadwinner model which progressive governments, even if they do not put it in these terms, tend to support because it is that model which dovetails most neatly with the employment ethic, that is, the widely held assumption that paid work is the means to social stability and personal fulfilment. This is perhaps why the Scandinavian welfare states, the nations most advantageous to women at present, have gone for an employment-based strategy of promoting women's interests. If this interpretation of gender equity is the one which most politicians and policy-makers are likely to favor then, as suggested above, BI will probably have little role to play.[6] However, if such employment-based strategies are on the wane, whether due to post-industrialism or globalization, then the universal care-giver model may come to the fore and the attractions of a BI improve as a result.

Notes

1. Though the incentive effects are difficult to estimate in advance since they depend heavily upon the details of the BI scheme to be implemented.
2. Of course, all of this is to adopt a narrow economistic analysis where people work for money and for no other reason. But even putting to one side the fact that people work for a variety of non-economistic reasons as well (see McKay and VanEvery, 1995), is it really the case that a BI would cause women to reduce their working hours by the amount corresponding to BI's value, or would they not work the same amount of hours as before on the basis that a BI would boost their overall income and so make them better off?
3. We must qualify this by admitting that BI's labor market incentives are very difficult to estimate in advance.
4. Editor's note: Recipients of a Participation Income would have to satisfy any one of several criteria for "participation", i.e. socially useful contribution, in society. See the general introduction to this anthology, as well as Part VIII.
5. Returning us to the question as to whether part-timers would reduce their working hours in order to yield the same take-home pay as before, or work the same amount as before in order to boost their take-home pay.
6. The British Labour government seems to have adopted this kind of approach, albeit on a more modest scale than in Scandinavia.

References

Carlson, J. (1997). *Is a Basic Income Women Friendly? Assessment of the Problems and Prospects Associated with Basic Income Schemes.* Social Policy Paper no. 1, University of Hertfordshire.

Cass, B. (1991). Expanding the Concept of Social Justice: Implications for Social Security. In M. Adler, C. Bell, and A. Sinfield (eds) *The Sociology of Social Security.* Edinburgh University Press, Edinburgh.

Clark, C. and Kavanagh, C. (1996). Basic Income, Inequality and Unemployment. *Journal of Economic Issues,* 30 (2), 399–407.

Fraser, N. (1997). *Justice Interruptus.* Polity Press, Cambridge.

Ginn, J. (1996). Citizens' Pensions and Women. *Citizen's Income Bulletin*, 21, 10–12.
Halsey, A.H. (1997). Poverty and Wickedness. *Prospect*, April.
Hooper, C.A. (1996). Men's Violence and Relationship Breakdown: Can Violence be Dealt with as an Exception to the Rule? In Hallett, C. (ed.) *Women and Social Policy*. Harvester Wheatsheaf, Hemel Hempstead.
Jordan, B. (1992). Basic Income and the Common Good. In Van Parijs P. (ed.) *Arguing for Basic Income*. Verso, London.
Lewis, J. (1992). Gender and the Development of Welfare Regimes. *Journal of European Social Policy*, 2 (2), 159–174.
Lewis, J. and Ostner, I. (1994). *Gender and the Evolution of European Social Policies*. Working Paper 4/94, Centre for Social Policy Research, Bremen University.
Lister, R. (1997). *Citizenship: Feminist Perspectives*. Macmillan, London.
McKay, A. and VanEvery, J. (1995). *Thoughts on a Feminist Argument for Basic Income*. Department of Economics, Discussion Series no. 27. Caledonian University, Glasgow.
Millar, J. (1989). Social Security, Equality and Women in the UK. *Policy and Politics*, 17 (4), 311–319.
Offe, C., Mückenberger, U., and Ostner, I. (1996). A Basic Income Guarenteed by the State: A Need of the Moment in Social Policy. In C. Offe, *Modernity and the State: East, West*. Polity Press, Cambridge.
Orloff, A. (1993). Gender and the Social Rights of Citizenship: The Comparative Analysis of Gender Relations and the Welfare States. *American Sociological Review*, 58, 303–328.
Pahl, J. (1986). Social Security, Taxation and Family Financial Arrangements. *Basic Income Research Group Bulletin*, 5, 2–4.
Pahl, J. (1989). *Money and Marriage*. Macmillan, London.
Parker, H. (ed.) (1993). *Citizen's Income and Women. CISC*, London.
Purdy, D. (1988). *Social Policy and the Labour Market*. Macmillan, London.
Purdy, D. (1990). Incomes Policy, Citizenship and Basic Income. In P. Alcock et al. (eds) *The Social Economy and the Democratic State*. Lawrence & Wishart, London.
Standing, G. (1992). The Need for a New Social Consensus. In P. Van Parijs (ed.) *Arguing for Basic Income*. Verso, London.
Taylor-Gooby, P. (1991). *Social Change, Social Welfare and Social Science*. Harvester Wheatsheaf, Hemel Hempstead.
Vogler, C. (1994). Money in the Household. In M. Anderson, F. Beckhofer, and J. Gershuny (eds) *The Social and the Political Economy of the Household*. Oxford University Press, Oxford.
Vogler, C. and Pahl, J. (1993). Social and Economic Change and the Organisation of Money within Marriage. *Work, Employment and Society*, 7 (1), 71–95.
Vogler, C. and Pahl, J. (1994). Money, Power and Inequality within Marriage. *Sociological Review*, 42 (2), 263–288.
Walby, S. (1997). *Gender Transformations*. Routledge, London.
Walter, T. (1989). *Basic Income: Freedom from Poverty, Freedom to Work*. Marion Boyers, London.

Chapter 25

Free-riding and the Household

Carole Pateman

Excerpts from Pateman, C. (2004). Democratizing Citizenship: Some advantages of a Basic Income. In E.O. Wright (ed.) *Redesigning Distribution: Basic Income and Stakeholder Grants as Cornerstones for an Egalitarian Capitalism*. Verso, London, pp. 101–119.

The debates about Basic Income center on the figure of a man in – or avoiding – paid employment. This is very clear in one of the major criticisms of, and apprehensions about, the idea of a Basic Income; that is, that it would encourage free-riding and idleness. Free-riders breach the principle of reciprocity by obtaining the fruits of the efforts of others and contributing nothing themselves in return; a Basic Income, it is charged, would "inspire a segment of the able population [. . .] to abjure work for a life of idle fun" (Anderson, 2000: 16). But who is being seen as so prone to idleness and fun? The assumption guiding the discussion of Basic Income is that the problem is about men and employment.[1] A much greater problem about male free-riding to which a Basic Income is directly relevant, but about the household not employment, is therefore ignored.

Van Parijs appears to be an exception to the prevailing view of free-riding. Unlike most other participants in discussions of Basic Income he has noticed that free-riding exists "on a massive scale" in household interactions (1995: 143). But who are the free-riders in the household? Barry notes that full-time housewives can be seen as free-riders (1996: 245). But they can only be seen in that way if "work" is taken to mean paid employment.[2] As feminist scholars have emphasized for a very long time, housewives are working (unpaid) by undertaking the necessary caring work. Given the major contribution they already make for no monetary return at all, wives (women) are hardly likely to be the target of the objection that a Basic Income would lead to idleness and fun.

The majority of wives are now in some form of paid employment, but their labor force participation is usually different from that of men. This reflects the legacy of a wage system that enshrined the belief that husbands (men) not wives (women) are the "breadwinners."[3] Many more women than men work part-time and women earn less than men. The private and public sexual division of labor, that is to say, continues to be structured so that men monopolize full-time, higher paying and more prestigious paid employment, and wives do a disproportionate share of unpaid work in the home. Given the structure of institutions and social beliefs, this appears as a "rational" arrangement. The mutual

From Pateman, C. (2004). Democratizing Citizenship: Some advantages of a basic income. In E.O. Wright (ed.) *Redesigning Distribution: Basic Income and Stakeholder Grants as Cornerstones for an Egalitarian Capitalism*. Verso, London, pp. 101–119. Reprinted with permission of Verso.

Basic Income: An Anthology of Contemporary Research, First Edition. Edited by Karl Widerquist, José A. Noguera, Yannick Vanderborght, and Jurgen De Wispelaere.

reinforcement of marriage and employment explains why husbands can take advantage of the unpaid work of wives and avoid doing their fair share of the caring work. That is why there is massive free-riding in the household – by husbands.

Neither free-riding by husbands, nor its scale, is usually acknowledged in discussions of Basic Income and stakeholding.[4] This is because marriage and the household rarely enter the argument. The narrow parameters of discussion, and the influence of the assumptions of neo-classical economics, preclude attention to institutional structures and their interrelationships. Van Parijs is an exception in recognizing that a problem of free-riding exists in households, but his neo-classical theoretical apparatus leaves him unable to acknowledge that the problem is one of men (husbands) and the work of caring for household members. His argument is that free-riding arises merely because of differences in individual tastes or preferences. Free-riding, Van Parijs states, occurs when benefits enjoyed by both partners in a household are produced by only one of them, the partner who happens to care most about the particular benefit. His example is that the partner who most strongly values tidiness will make sure that the home is tidy.

"Tidiness" is part of the more general work of housekeeping, and there is abundant empirical evidence that shows that the female partner is most likely to do the housework, including tidying up. The empirical data do not show this pattern just by chance – female partners do not by some quirk happen to prefer tidiness more strongly than their male partners. The institution of marriage, and social beliefs about what it means to be a "wife" or "husband," have vanished in Van Parijs's analysis and there are merely two individuals, indistinguishable except for their different tastes for tidy surroundings. His theoretical approach in *Real Freedom for All* precludes analysis of the structure of relations between the sexes, and a crucial area of debate is, therefore, removed from discussion of Basic Income.

Indeed, some advocates of a Basic Income argue that it would make it easier for women to do "their" work in the home. Van Parijs remarks (2000: 7) that some women would probably use their Basic Income to "lighten the 'double shift' at certain periods of their lives." But, he continues, "who can sincerely believe that working subject to the dictates of a boss for forty hours a week is a path to liberation?" One can have grave doubts on the latter score – but also ask, first, whether working for a husband at home is the right path either, and, second, ask why *men* might not use their Basic Income to take on their fair share of the caring work.

Now is the time to ask the second question. The conditions under which the institution of employment: and the Anglo-American social insurance system was constructed have now crumbled. "Old economy" male breadwinner jobs are being swept away in global economic restructuring and "downsizing." New jobs have been created but many are low paid, lacking benefits and temporary, and economic insecurity is widespread. Views about femininity, masculinity and marriage are changing too, but since we are still in the midst of all these changes it is hard to know what the eventual outcome will be. Still, times of rapid change provide opportunities to investigate new ideas and look critically at old arrangements – including the moral hazard of institutions that give incentives to men to avoid their fair share of the unpaid work of caring for others. It has now become possible to rethink the connections between income and paid employment, between marriage, employment and citizenship, between the private and public division of labor, between caring work and other work, and reconsider the meaning of "work." But such rethinking requires a different approach from that taken by many participants in the debate about stakeholding and Basic Income. This is crucial if proper account is to be taken of women's freedom, which has received rather short shrift in discussions of a Basic Income.

As early as 1792, Mary Wollstonecraft argued in *A Vindication of the Rights of Woman* that rights, citizenship and full standing for women required economic independence, whether a woman was married or single. As Ackerman and Alstott (2006) emphasize, a capital grant would be a step in this direction, but a Basic Income would for the first time provide all women with life-long economic independence. Thus feminists might be expected strongly to support the introduction of a Basic Income.[5]

Yet this is not the case. Some feminists are critical of the idea because they fear a Basic Income would reinforce the existing sexual division of labor and women's lesser citizenship. They argue that the provision of an income without having to engage in paid employment would, in light of women's position in the labor market combined with lingering beliefs about the respective places and tasks of women and men, give women an even greater incentive to undertake more unpaid caring work in the household, and, conversely, men would have another incentive to free-ride. A Basic Income, that is, would reinforce existing limitations on women's freedom.[6]

This objection illustrates the importance of the reasons advanced for supporting a Basic Income. The probability of feminist fears being borne out is higher, for example, when the argument is made that to avoid weakening the "incentive to work" a Basic Income should be below subsistence level. This "incentive" is promoted with men and paid employment in mind. A Basic Income at this level provides no incentive for wives to "work" (i.e. enter paid employment); rather it would encourage them to do more unpaid caring work. Again, to support Basic Income on the grounds that it would improve the living standards of the poorest sectors of the population does not promote consideration of the structural connections between marriage, employment and citizenship, and the private and public sexual division of labor. Without the debates about Basic Income being informed by feminist arguments and a concern for democratization (and genuine democratization necessarily includes women's freedom and standing as citizens), the discussion will revolve around ways of tinkering with the existing system, rather than encouraging thinking about how it might be made more democratic.

Putting democratization at the center requires attention to institutional structures, especially the institutions of marriage and employment. For instance, Ackerman and Alstott remark in *The Stakeholder Society* that the "case for stakeholding does not ultimately rest on its effects on employment, marriage, or crime. It rests on each American's claim to respect as a free and equal citizen" (1999: 209). However (leaving crime aside), the respect accorded to women and men as free and equal citizens has a great deal to do the institutions of marriage and employment. It is not possible to understand women's lesser citizenship, as Ackerman and Alstott show in their discussion of social security, without understanding the relationship between their position as wives and men's position as workers.

Similarly, Van Parijs argues that while "a defensible long term vision" of an Unconditional Basic Income at the highest sustainable level is vital, nevertheless more limited and politically feasible proposals are also essential. He states that a household-based guaranteed minimum income "would definitely be a major change in the right direction" (2006: 16–17) – but the right direction according to which reasons? Household-based schemes disregard not only all the problems about the sexual division of labor, and the fact that women earn less than men, but also income distribution *within* households. Can it be confidently assumed that income would be distributed equally between husband and wife? A Basic Income is important for feminism and democratization precisely because it is paid not to households but to *individuals as citizens.*

A focus on individuals does not imply resort to the atomistic individualism of neo-classical economics. The problem of women's self-government and full standing as citizens is visible only when individuals are conceptualized within the context of social relations and institutions. A household-based Basic Income allows the problem of marriage, employment and citizenship to be avoided since wives (women) disappear into the category of the "family" or "household." To treat a Basic Income as a payment to households, rather than individuals, ignores the question of who performs the work of caring for household members. That is, it is tacitly assumed that reciprocity exists and that free-riding is only a problem about men avoiding employment.

This assumption is nicely illustrated by the picture of a male surfer on the cover of *Real Freedom for All.* In academic discussions, the surfer is used to represent non-contributors. But in the popular political imagination and the media other symbols of free-riding are present, such as the African-American "welfare queen," or, more recently, the "illegal immigrant" or the "asylum seeker."[7] The figure of the surfer not only obscures the problem for democratization of popular attitudes embodied in these other symbols, but also obliterates the systematic avoidance of one form of contribution – the vital caring work – by men who are *in employment.*

Nor do the numerous suggestions for conditions to be placed on payment of a Basic Income as a solution to free-riding – Atkinson's (1996) "participation income" is a well-known example[8] – get to grips with free-riding by men in the household. While the notion of a "contribution" may be broadened to include, for example, the work of caring for others, as in Atkinson's proposal, this is insufficient to focus attention on the structural problem of the connections between marriage, employment and free-riding by husbands. While payment of a Basic Income to a husband for his "contribution" through employment and to his wife for her "contribution" in the home is to recognize that she does indeed make a socially valuable contribution, this does little to calm the fears of some feminists that a Basic Income will merely reinforce women's lesser standing and the idleness of husbands in the household.

An adequate discussion of free-riding and reciprocity in debates about Basic Income is hampered by, on the one hand, the prevalence of an economistic or contractual sense of "reciprocity." In this interpretation of the term the recipient must make a contribution directly in return for every benefit received, a view that magnifies the problem of free-riding. On the other hand, by ignoring the household, participants in the debate tacitly presuppose that "reciprocity" in another sense, that is, mutual aid, characterizes domestic interactions.[9] To refocus the debate about Basic Income around its significance for democratization would mean replacing the preoccupation with one kind of free-riding with an examination of how to reinforce reciprocity in the sense of mutual aid across the social order. And that, in turn, would require widening the terms of debate, engaging with the large body of feminist analysis, moving away from the assumptions of neo-classical economics and developing a political argument.

Notes

1. The consequence for employment rates of a Basic Income is hard to determine in the abstract. On the one hand, it would act as a disincentive for individuals to be employed, since, *ex hypothesis*, they could live on the income. On the other hand, precisely because the income is paid whether or not individuals are employed, they could enjoy a better standard of life by taking a low paid job than by living on a Basic Income alone. It would thus act as an incentive to employment, and improve the flexibility of the labor market.
2. McKay and VanEvery (2000: 281) remark that critics of the free-rider objection argue in "masculinist terms which ignore the implicit relegation of family carers to this caregory."
3. For a discussion of support for this legacy in the Netherlands, see Plantenga, Schippers and Siegers (1999).

4. Editor's note: The Stakeholder Grant is essentially a large one-time income grant given at the age of 18 or 21. See the General Introduction to this anthology, and Part VIII.
5. For some examples of discussion of the importance of a Basic Income for women, see Walter (1989), Parker (1993), McKay and VanEvery (2000), McKay (2002), and on stakeholding Alstott (2000).
6. Like Robeyns (2001) I have frequently encountered this objection when I have talked about a Basic Income. It is less often seen in academic discussions.
7. My thanks to Harvey Goldman for his comments about the surfer at a talk I gave at UC San Diego in 2001.
8. For a conditional stake see Goodin (2003).
9. To apply "reciprocity" in the first sense to the household would have dire consequences, not least for infants. Political theorists in an earlier era saw reciprocity in my second sense as the primary law of nature. That is, they recognized that a social order *is* a system of generalized mutual aid and mutual forbearance. If reciprocity in this sense of the term breaks down, social order begins to disintegrate.

References

Ackerman, B. and Alstott, A.L. (1999). *The Stakeholder Society.* Yale University Press, New Haven, CT.

Ackerman, B. and Alstott, A.L. (2006). Why Stakeholding? In E.O. Wright (ed.) *Redesigning Distribution: Basic Income and Stakeholder Grants as Cornerstones for an Egalitarian Capitalism.* Verso, London, pp. 43–65.

Alstott, A.L. (2000). Good for Women. In Symposium: Delivering a Basic Income. *Boston Review*, Oct.–Nov.

Anderson, E. (2000). Optional Freedoms. In Symposium: Delivering a Basic Income. *Boston Review*, Oct.–Nov.

Atkinson, A. (1996). The Case for a Participation Income. *Political Quarterly*, 67, 67–70.

Barry, B. (1996). Real Freedom and Basic Income. *The Journal of Political Philosophy*, 4, 242–276.

Goodin, R. (2003). Sneaking Up on Stakeholding. In K. Dowding, J. De Wispelaere, and S. White (eds) *The Ethics of Stakeholding*, Palgrave, Basingstoke.

McKay, A. (2002). Arguing for a Citizen's Basic Income: A Feminist Perspective. Paper presented at the annual meeting of the American Political Science Association, Boston.

McKay, A. and VanEvery, J. (2000). Gender, Family, and Income Maintenance: A Feminist Case for Citizens Basic Income. Social Politics: *International Studies in Gender, State, and Society*, 7 (2), 266–284.

Parker, H. (1993). *Citizen's Income and Women.* BIRG Discussion Paper 2. Citizen's Income, London.

Plantenga, J, Schippers, J., and Siegers, J. (1999). Towards an Equal Division of Paid and Unpaid Work: The Case of The Netherlands. *Journal of European Social Policy*, 9 (2), 99–110.

Robeyns, I. (2001). Will a Basic Income Do Justice to Women? *Analyse and Kritik: Zeitschrift fur Sozialtheorie*, 1, 88–105.

Van Parijs, P. (1995). *Real Freedom for All: What (If Anything) Can Justify Capitalism?* Oxford University Press, New York.

Van Parijs, P. (2000). A Basic Income for All. *Boston Review*, Oct.–Nov., 4–8.

Van Parijs, P. (2006). Basic Income: A simple and powerful idea for the twenty-first century. In E.O. Wright (ed.) *Redesigning Distribution: Basic Income and Stakeholder Grants as Cornerstones for an Egalitarian Capitalism.* Verso, London, pp. 3–42.

Walter, T. (1989). *Basic Income: Freedom from Poverty, Freedom to Work.* Marion Boyers, London.

Wollstonecraft, M. (1993 [1792]). A Vindication of the Rights of Woman. In J. Todd (ed.) *Political Writings.* University of Toronto Press, Toronto.

Chapter 26

Promoting Gender Equity Through a Basic Income

Ailsa McKay

Excerpts from McKay, A. (2001). Rethinking Work and Income Maintenance Policy: Promoting Gender Equality through a Citizens Basic Income. *Feminist Economics*, 7 (1), 93–114.

Introduction

In recent decades, a Basic Income policy has emerged as a radical proposal for state welfare reform. Support for such a policy has been gaining ground throughout Western Europe in a wide variety of intellectual and political arenas.[1] Several models of the Basic Income proposal have been discussed, but no single model of the form such a policy would take has achieved universal accord. Debates among Basic Income advocates have addressed issues of gradual or full-scale implementation, levels of payment, methods of financing, and modes of delivery. However, there is a general consensus in the literature that a Basic Income proposal refers to the establishment of a universal Basic Income Grant, paid as a right to all citizens, without reference to any past, present, or future formal labor market participation. No account would be taken of existing, or alternative, sources of income and, in specifying the individual as the unit of assessment, a Basic Income policy safeguards against family forms influencing eligibility, either positively or negatively. Entitlement would be based on individual citizenship alone.

The concept of a Basic Income is not unique to the current "crisis in welfare" literature. Support for a state-sponsored and regulated scheme of income maintenance, which would guarantee the right of every individual in society to a minimum means of subsistence, can be traced back as far as the eighteenth century. Common to the various historical proposals are concerns for individual freedom and the inherent inefficiencies of traditional labor market processes in guaranteeing income security. Contemporary advocates share these concerns, albeit with differing emphases, but also draw attention to the inadequacies of current social security measures in the context of the socio-economic dynamics of modern capitalist structures.

Despite renewed interest and the existence of convincing theoretical and practical arguments justifying a Basic Income (see, for example, Van Parijs, 1992), to date no govern-

From McKay, A. (2001). Rethinking Work and Income Maintenance Policy: Promoting Gender Equality through a Citizens Basic Income. *Feminist Economics* 7 (1), 93–114. Reprinted with permission of Taylor & Francis Journals.

Basic Income: An Anthology of Contemporary Research, First Edition. Edited by Karl Widerquist, José A. Noguera, Yannick Vanderborght, and Jurgen De Wispelaere.

ment has adopted it. However, throughout the advanced capitalist world in recent decades all types of state-supported policies aimed at promoting income security have been criticized. Both the sustainability and the effectiveness of current schemes have been questioned. The debate focusing on the future direction of state welfare provision is therefore a topical one and the universal, unconditional, minimum-income guarantee option is an important element of that debate.

The purpose of this chapter is to emphasize the potential a Basic Income has for promoting gender-neutral social rights of citizenship. A central focus of the most prominent Basic Income theorists is the need to reassess the foundations of modern welfare capitalism in light of the apparent unsustainability of full employment. These theorists believe that existing social security measures are rendered ineffective by the explicit links made between traditional labor markets and methods of financing and patterns of delivery. They propose a Basic Income as a model of income maintenance policy, one which effectively dissolves the formal relationship between work and income. In their view, the model provides policymakers with a tool to support contemporary labor market structures as well as a means of fulfilling a necessary welfare function of the state. This crucial integration of economic and social policy is one of the main attractions of a Basic Income scheme, leading advocates to commend it as a means of promoting both social justice and economic efficiency.

From a feminist perspective, however, an androcentric bias is inherent within the current Basic Income debate. Social security mechanisms that are intrinsically linked to the labor market can be criticized for generating and sustaining gender inequalities. Although a Basic Income provides an opportunity to redefine work, the current focus remains centered on a productivist ethic. In the current literature, only a temporary, or partial, separation of work and income is envisaged. This separation will serve to promote the flexibility of labor on a micro level, which ultimately will improve the efficiency of modern labor market processes. Such an emphasis fails to recognize the social experiences of women. Identifying these experiences will draw attention to the potential a Basic Income scheme has for providing the foundations of a new gender-neutral conceptualization of social justice.

Women and Basic Income

Considering the potential a Basic Income has for promoting gender justice, the existing literature on it is disappointingly lacking in rigorous feminist analysis. Writers have tried to incorporate the situation of women into their competing arguments. However, since their objectives relate only to the operation of formal labor market processes, it is unclear how the resulting analyses can do anything but "add women and stir." In short, the current Basic Income debate is characteristic of an approach that simply includes "women as subjects without changing the tools of analysis" (Ferber and Nelson, 1993: 6).

Formal social security arrangements have traditionally served men more favorably than women. This is in part due to the direct relationship between insurance-based benefits and the labor market, but it is an indirect consequence of policies that fail to recognize the diverse roles of women as wives, mothers, workers, and caregivers. Women's historically limited access to the labor market and their lower earnings relative to those of men are well documented. Consequently, women are disadvantaged in terms of rights to benefits within a system based on contributions made while in paid employment. Legislation promoting the removal of discriminatory policies has enhanced women's formal position as claimants and established their rights to benefits. However, social and demographic factors, such as the increase in single-parent households (predominately headed by women), women's longer life expectancy, and the unpaid work undertaken primarily by women in providing welfare within the household, further contribute to gender bias in social security systems. Ignoring such factors when designing systems inevitably results in unequal outcomes. Social security programs that continue to emphasize the role of the worker, alongside the traditional male-breadwinner family model, implicitly promote male citizenship while simultaneously denying women's full inclusion as citizens by assuming their dependency on men.

References to women in the Basic Income literature have primarily focused on the advantages an unconditional income guarantee offers through promoting equal treatment between the sexes; recognizing the value of unpaid work; providing income security outside the traditional labor market, thereby strengthening family life; improving work incentives and incentives to invest in human capital; securing financial independence within families; and providing the basis for a more equal sharing of domestic responsibilities between men and women (see, for example, Jordan, 1988: 118–119; 1992: 171–172; Parker, 1993; Walter, 1989: 116–127). All of these perceived outcomes would apply in an analysis of the benefits a Citizens' Basic Income (CBI) would have for men.

Establishing a right to a Basic Income independent of work would have major consequences for women in determining their life choices and would provide the foundations for a rethinking of the relationships between men and women in families. However, the formal establishment of equal rights does not necessarily lead to equal outcomes. Although income security can exert a powerful influence on any individual's choices, it is not a unique factor in determining those choices. Therefore, although the advantages a CBI would have for women, listed above, may indeed be realized, they follow from generalized assumptions about patterns of men's behavior. I therefore believe that there is a major gap in the conventional case made for a CBI, which results from an androcentric preoccupation with paid work and the labor market at the expense of provisioning/caregiving work performed outside the labor market. More convincing arguments could be made for a CBI on the grounds of gender justice by providing insights into the range of structures that constrain women's choices.

Reconceptualizing Work and Income: A Feminist Perspective

Conceptually work is usually distinguished from leisure. The implication is that the cost of time spent engaging in activities clearly defined as work can be measured by the associated sacrifice of leisure time. This is not to say that all of those activities we deem enjoyable are categorized as "leisure" and activities involving pain, toil, or a sacrifice of enjoyment as "work." Work may be something we enjoy, but it is distinct from leisure in that it is not done solely for its own sake but must also be purposeful. Any activity that displays "the characteristic of using up time and energy for an extrinsic purpose" can be defined as work, in that desirable end results are created through a process that involves an opportunity cost of lost leisure time (Himmelweit, 1995: 3). These end results are not only produced for the enjoyment or satisfaction of the individual carrying out the activity, but also have a use-value that can be shared by others. It is therefore the productive, purposeful aspect of any activity that defines it as work.

For André Gorz (1994: 53), conceptualizing work in this way is a feature of modern industrial capitalism:

> So long as commodity production remained marginal and the great majority of needs were covered by domestic production and the village economy, the notion of "work" as such [. . .] could not take hold. People "produced", "constructed" and "prepared" things; they "laboured", "toiled", "drudged" and "attended to" a wide variety of specific "occupations" which had no common measure between them within the framework of the domestic community. And responsibility for the various activities was assumed by the husband, the wife, the children or the older members of the family according to an immutable division of labour. These activities were gendered [. . .] and thus there was no common denominator between them. They were not interchangeable, and could not be compared and evaluated in terms of a single yard-stick. The term "work" referred not to a creative or productive act but to the activity in so far as it entailed pain, annoyance and fatigue.

The dominance of commodity production and consumption over subsistence production brought about by the development of capitalist modes of production results in the depersonalization of work activities. This leads Gorz to assert that the modern notion of work refers to:

> the name of an activity fundamentally different from the activities of subsistence, reproduction, maintenance and care performed within the household. This is not so much because "work" is a paid activity, but because it is done in the public domain and appears there as a measurable, exchangeable and interchangeable performance; as a performance which possesses a use-value for others, not simply for the members of the household community carrying it out; for others in general, without distinction or restriction, not for a particular, private person. (Gorz, 1994: 53)

This socialization of productive activities means that the worker becomes separable from the resulting output. Producing goods and services for exchange in the public domain renders irrelevant the direct relationship between the person carrying out the task and their economic output. Activities are interchangeable between workers, and outputs become measurable in terms of their use-value to others. In modern terms the concept of work is associated with any impersonal activity that results in output that can be measured and presented as a commodity, or service, for sale or exchange in an impersonal public marketplace.

Many of the activities frequently performed by women are "invisible," in the sense that there is either no tangible output, or the actual nature, and therefore value, of the output is not transparent. Consequently these activities do not meet the conventional criteria that would allow them to be labeled "work." Although much progress has been made in valuing domestic work to illustrate the significance of women's productive contribution to the economy (see, for example, United Nations Development Programme, 1995) little has been done to quantify "provisioning" functions within the family. That is, the label "domestic work" is generally assigned to a range of "physical" tasks, considered essential ingredients in the efficient functioning of the household economy. Such tasks can either be undertaken by a person(s) employed for that specific purpose or can be performed by an individual member of the household who receives no formal remuneration for doing so. The latter I refer to as "internalized unpaid domestic work," which serves to draw the distinction between work done by the "hired help" and work done by wives and mothers themselves. As noted above, attempts at recognizing the value of internalized unpaid domestic work have at least got under way. However, in addition to internalized unpaid domestic work, many nonphysical exchanges or services performed in the household contribute positively to individual welfare, which prove even more difficult to quantify. Examples of "provisioning functions within the family" include the transfer of knowledge or skills, providing a safe and loving environment, expressing and acting from concern for the health and emotional needs of other family members, and organizing the distribution and allocation of resources within the family unit. Many of these activities are essential for human survival, particularly those concerned with the care of children (Nelson, 1993: 32). Nonmaterial sources of human satisfaction influence intra-family power structures and directly affect the economic position of women. That they remain in the periphery of the economics discipline is possibly because quantifying them would be a technically difficult thing to do. However, it more likely stems from the fact that such activities are not viewed as "important" simply because they are performed by women;

> Humans are born of women, nurtured and cared for as dependent children, socialized into family and community groups, and are perpetually dependent on nourishment and shelter to sustain their lives. These aspects of human life, whose neglect is often justified by the argument that they are unimportant or intellectually uninteresting or merely "natural", are, not just coincidentally, the areas of life thought of as "women's work". (Nelson, 1996: 31)

The "provisioning" aspects of human life that Nelson describes are fundamental in influencing the behavior of women. Furthermore, the more traditional dichotomy of work/nonwork has had detrimental effects on inequalities within households.

Market-based economies have an inherent tendency to value productive activities by the notion of opportunity cost. The increased participation of women in the formal labor market has resulted in attempts to measure production in the home in terms of the equivalent market wage and vice versa. The process of commodifying domestic work has resulted in the production of substitute goods that can be purchased in the marketplace. This can be achieved with relative ease when the producer and consumer are impersonal agents, performing their respective roles separately and autonomously. The same cannot be said about provisioning activities. This fact is further demonstrated when considering the needs that are satisfied by work/nonwork activities:

> As marketed substitutes become available for more and more of those domestic activities that count as "work," the apparent importance of the needs they satisfy increase relative to those remaining needs which are not perceived to be so readily met by the market. These tend to be the needs whose satisfaction requires activities which are inseparable from the person performing them, including caring and selffulfilling activities. These are the needs that remain invisible, of apparent marginal significance to the economy, and thus their importance to the actors within it easily ignored. (Himmelweit, 1995: 10)

The redistribution of work from the domestic realm to the market has indirectly resulted in the devaluing of the time and effort women spend fulfilling both their own and others' affiliation needs; that is, "the need of human beings to belong and to be loved" (Nelson, 1996: 73). Individual needs and desires are therefore socially constructed via the process of commodification. The principles of production and consumption dominate, and those activities that do not fit neatly into the economists' model of price theory become undervalued by society in general. Individuals who exhibit a preference for pursuing nonmarketable provisioning activities are labeled as nonworkers or "idlers," suffering from the negative connotations this implies. A witty but apt retort would draw upon the old adage, "relationships are hard work"!

As Nelson suggests in her above observations on the provisioning aspects of human life, it is clear that the undervaluing of "uncommodifiable" needs does not render them less important in terms of their contribution to individual welfare. However, in a male/work-dominated society, women continue to shoulder a disproportionate share of these "nonwork" activities, and their position has been undermined by the process of commodification. The choices that women make are influenced by this process and hence the preference is to perform "work" that is socially valued. This social construction of needs has obvious consequences in terms of the sharing of domestic responsibilities between men and women. Policies aimed at promoting equal sharing that ignore the social constraints imposed on choice will ultimately fail.

A CBI scheme that incorporates the recognition of equal rights of citizenship has the potential to reorient socially constructed preferences. But this potential will remain latent unless the model is accompanied by a reconceptualization of work and a better understanding of the sexual division of labor. Insights can be gained from the current work of feminists in the field of economics – a traditionally male-dominated and defined discipline – to incorporate theories of the social construction of gender:

> Feminist theory suggests that the definition focusing on choice, which looks at human decisions as radically separated from physical and social constraints, and the definition stressing material well-being, which ignores non-physical sources of satisfaction, are not the only alternatives. What is needed is a definition of economics that considers humans *in relation* to the world. (Nelson, 1993: 32)

By considering humans in relation to the world and not just within the world of work, we can identify gender-specific constraints that inform and influence choice. The tendency to polarize the analysis between work and "nonwork" results in a failure fully to understand and recognize the nature of the contributions women make to family life.

Nancy Folbre defines structures of constraint as the "assets, rules, norms, and preferences that delimit what people want and how they can go about getting what they want" (1994: 54). She further explains that distinctive sets of constraints can help shape collective identities and subsequent collective action. Women, a group defined by gender,

> have some similar assets (their reproductive and sexual endowments), are subject to similar rules (many rights and responsibilities are gender specific), are governed by similar norms (such as ideals of femininity), and express some similar preferences (such as enjoyment of caring relationships). (Folbre, 1994: 55)

This is not to say that all women share these similarities. The point Folbre makes is that socially constructed collective structures of constraint foster "group identity and create common group interests," which in turn provide natural allegiances conducive to powerful forms of collective action" (Folbre, 1994: 57–58). All four categories of constraint work together to form this group identity. Therefore, the removal of one would not necessarily eliminate the constraints imposed by the others on a particular group. Granting an equal Basic Income to men and women effectively removes basic economic constraints. However, to assume that the removal of asset constraints would result in equal outcomes ignores the influence of rules, norms, and preferences in the processes of cooperation and conflict between genders.

The emphasis on viewing a CBI as a tool for supporting more flexible forms of working implicitly encourages women to enter the realm of paid work. Constraints on choice in this area are effectively removed by providing independent income security. As women gain in terms of rights and increasingly enter the labor market, their jobs become an important source of identity. Furthermore, the continual process of substituting unpaid work normally performed by women in the home with goods and services that can now be purchased externally suggests that cultural identifications associated with family labor diminish in importance. The existence in the marketplace of relatively cheap substitute goods, produced and consumed impersonally, further devalues the work that women continue to do within the family. All of this assumes that women have suddenly switched from a preference for affiliation, that is, the need to be part of a collective loving family unit and to take on all of the rights and obligations that entails, to one for promoting their own self-interested autonomous needs, or as Nelson refers to "agency needs" (Nelson, 1996). This begs the question of who now should shoulder the responsibilities of caring for children and families?

> Much research [. . .] suggests the stylized fact that wives' increased agency has been permitted, not so much by husbands taking on affiliative work, but by decreases in wives' standards of living, particularly in regard to time for rest and recreation. (Nelson, 1996: 74)

If work is associated with productive outputs then surely affiliative work is productive, measurable by the positive contributions it makes to individual welfare. However, the personal nature of such activities renders them difficult, if not impossible, to measure. If such activities are continually devalued within market-based economies it is unrealistic to assume that by removing or altering one aspect of the social constraints imposed upon women, that is access to economic resources, the result will automatically be equal sharing between men and women of affiliative work. Individual preferences within market-based economies will be influenced directly by the value attached to activities producing identifiable and exchangeable output. Individuals may therefore demonstrate a preference for "valued work" that forms the basis for common cultural and social identities over "nonwork" activities. There is therefore no reason to assume men will alter their preferences, and while women may be influenced to pursue "socially valued" activities, there is no reason to assume they will do so at the expense of sacrificing their existing preference for affiliation. Men will continue to engage in "valued work" and women will now engage in both work and "nonwork" activities. The tendency to commodify all human activity results in unduly restrictive social citizenship rights, particularly those related to income security. Thus, policies aiming to achieve gender equality must take account of gender-based social structures of constraint and explicitly recognize the positive welfare contribution of "nonwork" activities.

Note

1. For example, the "Basic Income European Network" and "Citizens Income" in the U.K. exist to support and stimulate informed discussion concerning the Basic Income proposal.

References

Ferber, M.A. and Nelson, J.A. (1993). Introduction: The Social Construction of Economics and the Social Construction of Gender. In M.A. Ferber and J.A. Nelson (eds) *Beyond Economic Man: Feminist Theory and Economics.* University of Chicago Press, Chicago, IL, pp. 1–22.

Folbre, N. (1994). *Who Pays for the Kids? Gender and the Structures of Constraint.* Routledge, London and New York.

Gorz, A. (1994). *Capitalism, Socialism, Ecology.* (transl. C. Turner). Verso, London and New York.

Himmelweit, S. (1995). The Discovery of "Unpaid Work": The Social Consequences of the Expansion of "Work." *Feminist Economics,* 1 (2), 1–19.

Jordan, B. (1988). The Prospects for Basic Income. *Social Policy and Administration,* 22 (2), 115–123.

Jordan, B. (1992). Basic Income and the Common Good. In P. Van Parijs (ed.) *Arguing for Basic Income: Ethical Foundations for a Radical Reform.* Verso, London, pp. 155–177.

Nelson, J. (1993). The Study of Choice or the Study of Provisioning? Gender and the Definition of Economics. In M.A. Ferber and J.A. Nelson (eds) *Beyond Economic Man: Feminist Theory and Economics.* University of Chicago Press, Chicago and London, pp. 23–36.

Nelson, J. (1996). *Feminism, Objectivity and Economics.* Routledge, London and New York.

Parker, H. (ed.) (1993). *Citizens' Income and Women.* BIRG Discussion Paper No. 2. Citizens Income, London.

United Nations Development Programme (1995). *Human Development Report 1995.* New York-Oxford: Oxford University Press.

Van Parijs, P. (ed.) (1992). *Arguing for Basic Income: Ethical Foundations for a Radical Reform.* Verso, London and New York.

Walter, T. (1989). *Basic Income: Freedom from Poverty, Freedom to Work.* Marion Boyars, London and New York.

Chapter 27
Good for Women

Anne Alstott

From Alstott, A. (2001) Good for Women. In P. Van Parijs (ed.) *What's Wrong with a Free Lunch?* Beacon Press, Boston.

A Universal Basic Income (UBI) has much to offer, particularly to women. A UBI could help fill the gaps in U.S. social programs that leave women economically vulnerable. And the tax increase needed to fund the program poses no serious threat to the economy. The libertarian right will surely howl that "high taxes" dramatically reduce work and savings. But economic research challenges that prediction. Raising the right taxes, to fund the right programs, can render freedom and equality compatible with economic growth.

Refreshingly, Van Parijs[1] argues the case for the UBI in terms of freedom – a value too seldom invoked in American social welfare policy. For similar reasons, Bruce Ackerman and I have proposed stakeholding – a one-time, unconditional grant to young citizens. Although stakeholding and the UBI differ in important ways, I want to focus on their shared strengths: both proposals could enhance women's freedom and economic security by breaking the link between social welfare benefits and paid work.[2]

***

American women face two distinctive economic risks. First, they still take primary responsibility for child care and adjust their working lives to accommodate family needs. Second, and not coincidentally, women earn about 75% of what men earn. The combination of child care and low earnings translates into lifelong economic insecurity. Although women's rising rates of workforce participation have improved their economic prospects, the average woman's career remains shorter, more disrupted, and less remunerative than the average man's.

Despite these well-known facts, neither welfare nor Social Security[3] adequately addresses women's distinctive situation. Consider two examples. First are the single mothers. In 1998, one quarter of U.S. families with children were headed by women. Their median income was just $22,000, even though nearly 80% of single mothers were in the labor force. Almost 40% of single-mother families were poor in 1998. And welfare offers only

Basic Income: An Anthology of Contemporary Research, First Edition. Edited by Karl Widerquist, José A. Noguera, Yannick Vanderborght, and Jurgen De Wispelaere.

meager support. Welfare reforms in the mid-1990s adopted the faulty premise that poor single mothers just need to "get a job." In the typical state, welfare families now face a five-year lifetime time limit, and in the meantime collect benefits of just $700 per month. The booming economy and the phase-in of time limits have cushioned the transition to the new rules. But, at best, most welfare mothers will work in low-wage jobs that pay too little to support a family.

As a second example, consider the plight of older women. In 1998, 13% of elderly women were poor, compared to 7% of elderly men. The median income of elderly men is $18,000, compared to $10,000 for elderly women. The disparity reflects not only women's longer average life span, but also the residual effects of divorce, child-care responsibilities, and low earnings. The Social Security program has two serious flaws. First, benefits presume a lifelong work history, so women who interrupt paid work to rear children lose out. Second, although the program includes an extra benefit for wives, the rules work best for women in lifelong marriages with male breadwinners. The result is a notable gender gap. In 1998, women workers received less ($675 per month, on average) than male retirees ($877) – while women who claimed benefits as wives got just $400 per month. In contrast, a UBI offers benefits without a time limit, without a work test, and without a marriage test. Even a UBI below subsistence level could make a real difference in women's lives. In 1999, for example, the poverty line for one person was about $8,500. Consider a UBI of less than half, or $4,000. For the median single mother, that would mean an 18% increase in income – for the median elderly woman, a 40% increase.

And the UBI comes without strings, so women can choose for themselves how to spend the cash. For example, some single mothers would use the money to work harder. They might buy better food or housing, a car to get to work, or better day care. Others would trade money for time, by quitting a second job or taking a job with a shorter commute but lower pay. The UBI places that choice squarely where it belongs – with women.

The key virtue of the UBI is that it breaks the link between benefits and paid work. In contrast, fashionable reforms like the earned income tax credit (EITC)[4] and "privatized" Social Security take the wrong direction. The EITC is more humane than welfare, supplementing low wages without a time limit. But the EITC is paid only while one works – and in proportion to wages. Those who take time off, who work part-time, or who go back to school lose some or all their benefits. Social Security is more complex, because "privatization" connotes many different reforms. But the major plans would continue or strengthen the relationship between lifetime wages and retirement benefits. Indeed, some of the proposals would provide less protection for women than Social Security now does.[5] In contrast, a UBI would ensure that everyone can count on the same income floor, regardless of work history.

Notes

1. Editor's note: See Van Parijs (1995; 2001).
2. Bruce Ackerman and I (Ackerman and Alstott, 1999) propose that high-school dropouts should receive what is, in effect, a basic income. See pp. 37–39. We also propose a separate program of flat-rate citizens' pensions, which pay a Basic Income to the elderly. See pp. 129–154. We discuss why we favor stakeholding over a UBI at pp. 210–216.
3. Editor's note: The expression "Social Security" refers to the American old-age insurance program.

4. Editor's note: The EITC is a U.S. Federal tax expenditure aimed at providing extra income to the working poor.
5. For example, current Social Security provides for a spousal benefit and mandatory annuitization of benefits; both features tend to redistribute toward women. Some privatization plans would repeal both features.

References

Ackerman, B. and Alstott, A. (1999). *The Stakeholder Society.* Yale University Press, New Haven.

Van Parijs, P. (1995). *Real Freedom for All: What (If Anything) Can Justify Capitalism?* Oxford University Press, Oxford.

Van Parijs, P. (2001). A Basic Income for All. In J. Cohen, and J. Rogers (eds) *What's Wrong with a Free Lunch?* Beacon Press, Boston, pp. 3–26.

Part V
Economics

Introduction
The Economics of Basic Income

Karl Widerquist, José A. Noguera, and Yannick Vanderborght

Basic Income, and related policies such as the Negative Income Tax, received a great deal of attention from economists, especially in the United States in the 1960s and 1970s. As we mentioned in the general introduction to this anthology, several prominent economists endorsed the idea during the course of the twentieth century, including James Meade, James Tobin, Gunnar Myrdal, Milton Friedman, Friedrich A. Hayek, Herbert Simon, John Kenneth Galbraith, James Buchanan, Robert Theobald, and Anthony Atkinson. The main economic issues about Basic Income are its effects on efficiency, productivity, poverty, and labor market participation, as well as questions about the funding of such a scheme.

Many economists believe Basic Income can streamline the welfare system and make it more efficient at the same time. Some see it as a way to ensure labor market flexibility without an undue cost to precarious workers. Others worry that it will have a negative impact on labor market participation and productivity, making it ultimately unaffordable. This section presents several articles addressing these issues, although economic issues are also discussed in several other sections including "Implementation", "Institutions", and "Post-Productivism".

In a 1966 classic article entitled, "The Case for an Income Guarantee," Nobel Laureate James Tobin argues for Basic Income as part of a twofold strategy to treat the symptoms and causes of poverty. To a large extent, Tobin argues, Basic Income treats the *symptoms* rather than the causes of poverty. This might, after all, just be what is needed. But, he also stresses that, by getting rid of many of the perverse incentives that are inherent to a means-tested welfare system, it also treats some of the most important *causes* of poverty. Treating poverty might be a way to break the cycle of poverty. This is especially true if one considers that growing up in poverty is a cause of future poverty.

Nobel Laureate James Meade argues for the macroeconomic efficiency of Basic Income in "What Can We Learn from the Agathotopians?" taken from his 1990 publication, "Economic Democracy and Citizenship Income." Most of this article refers to Meade's fictional story of "Agathotopia," in his 1989 book, *Agathotopia: The Economics of Partnership*. Agathotopia is said to be near Utopia, but while Utopia has institutions ideally suited to the perfect people who live in it, Agathotopia has institutions ideally suited to the ordi-

---

Basic Income: An Anthology of Contemporary Research, First Edition. Edited by Karl Widerquist, José A. Noguera, Yannick Vanderborght, and Jurgen De Wispelaere.

nary, imperfect people who live there. According to Meade, because Basic Income ensures that workers are not wholly dependent on their wages for survival, they can accept a greater degree of labor market flexibility, which might reduce the incidence and severity of recessions. Pollution taxation can both improve efficiency and provide a great deal of revenue for Basic Income. Nationally held assets provide revenue for Basic Income and help maintain a stable level of investment.

Philippe Van Parijs (1990) discusses some of the economic issues in "Basic Income and Efficiency." He considers two possible negative effects of Basic Income on overall output. Individuals who are currently not eligible for benefits will become eligible, requiring additional taxes, discouraging output, and leisure will become more attractive relative to labor, potentially causing people to withdraw from the labor force. But he also considers several other factors that could more than make up for these negative effects on production levels. He argues that Basic Income is likely to make a massive contribution toward a more dynamic and less conflictual economy. Workers would be able to accept much greater flexibility in the labor market, and there will not be as great a need for conflicts over the distribution of market output.

In "Basic Income as a Basis for Small Business," Bart Nooteboom (1986) makes four arguments that Basic Income will stimulate small business. First, it will provide compensation for diseconomies of small-scale production. Second, it will allow more wage earners to become entrepreneurs. Third, it will be by far less complex and easier to deal with than the current "patchwork" of programs to support small business. Fourth, it will solve the problem of unfair competition that now exists between entrepreneurs who are and are not receiving some kind of social benefits.

In the 1960s and 1970s the U.S. and Canadian governments conducted five different Negative Income Tax experiments. The findings of these experiments could provide a great deal of evidence for the likely labor market effects of a basic income. Karl Widerquist (2005) critically reviews the findings of these experiments in his article, "What (If Anything) Can We Learn from the Negative Income Tax Experiments?" He shows that the researchers found that the decline in labor market participation attributable to the Negative Income Tax was within acceptable levels. It would not make the program unaffordable and it could have an unmeasured effect of increasing private sector wages which would further reduce poverty.

In "Efficiency and Participation: The Basic Income Approach" Bill Jordan (1994) discusses the labor market participation issue. He notes that there is no evidence of a strong correlation between efficiency and participation. Some nations had very high participation rates with low productivity, while other nations had combined high productivity with low participation rates. He also notes that there is little correlation between the number of people living on government benefits and overall efficiency.

Nobel Laureate Edmund Phelps (2001) argues forcefully against Basic Income in his chapter, "Subsidize Wages" According to Phelps, Basic Income and the taxes necessary to support it will both have unacceptable incentive effects, discouraging work and meaningful social participation. He argues that a better strategy to address poverty would be to subsidize wages in the low-wage labor market.

Nobel Laureate Herbert Simon (2001) argues just as forcefully for Basic Income in his article, "UBI and the Flat Tax." According to Simon, it is implausible to attribute all the poverty in the world to laziness on the part of the poor. It has to do with the resources available to people – resources to which people have a just claim of access. Comparing rich to poor countries, Simon argues that as much as 90% of national income is attributable to social resources, leaving a great deal of latitude for redistribution that is both efficient and justified.

Nobel Laureate James M. Buchanan (1997), one of the founders of the public choice school of economics, applies a public choice analysis to the welfare state and finds that the combination of a flax tax and a Basic Income is less likely to have rent-seeking problems than any other form of welfare state.

Koen Raes (1986) applies a Marxian class analysis to Basic Income and finds pessimistic conclusion that the class structure of capitalistic society would not support a Basic Income. The class interests that would oppose Basic Income would be much greater than the class interests that support it. Therefore, Basic Income would be politically unsustainable without a major change in the class structure of society – a change toward something like socialism.

Charles M.A. Clark (2005), in his article, "Cost Estimates for a Basic Income in the United States of America," addresses one of the most fundament questions about Basic Income: how much would it cost? He finds a very optimistic answer. According to Clark, the United States government could finance current government spending *and* a Basic Income large enough to eliminate poverty with a flat income tax rate of only 32%. His estimates rely on the assumption of poverty-level Basic Income and the elimination, only, of income support for people who would receive more under a Basic Income system than they are currently receiving.

Reference

Meade, J. (1989). *Agathotopia: The Economics of Partnership*. Aberdeen University Press, Aberdeen.

Further Reading

Atkinson, A.B. (1997). *Public Economics in Action: The Basic Income/Flat Tax Proposal*. Oxford University Press, Oxford.

Atkinson, A.B. (1999). The Distribution of Income: Evidence, Theories and Policy. *De Economist*, 144 (1), 1–21.

Bartlett, R., Davis, J., and Hoy, M. (2005). Can a Negative Income Tax System for the United Kingdom be Both Equitable and Affordable? In K. Widerquist, M.A. Lewis, and S. Pressman (eds) *The Ethics and Economics of the Basic Income Guarantee*. Ashgate, Aldershot, pp. 13–54.

Block, F. and Somers, M. (2005). In the Shadow of Speenhamland: Social Policy and the Old Poor Law. In K. Widerquist, M.A. Lewis, and S. Pressman (eds) *The Ethics and Economics of the Basic Income Guarantee*. Ashgate, Aldershot, pp. 13–54.

Bouquin, S. (2005). Social Minima in Europe: The Risk of Cumulating Income-Sources. In K. Widerquist, M.A. Lewis, and S. Pressman (eds) *The Ethics and Economics of the Basic Income Guarantee*. Ashgate, Aldershot, pp. 13–54.

Bryan, J.B. (2005). Have the 1996 Welfare Reforms and Expansion of the Earned Income Tax Credit Eliminated the Need for a Basic Income Guarantee in the United States? In K. Widerquist, M.A. Lewis, and S. Pressman (eds) *The Ethics and Economics of the Basic Income Guarantee*. Ashgate, Aldershot, pp. 13–54.

Bryan, J.B. and Lamarche Castillo, S. (2012). Politics, the Preservation of Natural Resource Wealth, and the Funding of a Basic Income Guarantee. In K. Widerquist and M.W. Howard (eds)

Alaska's Permanent Fund Dividend: Examining its Suitability as a Model. Palgrave Macmillan, New York.

Burtless, G. (1990). The economist's lament: Public assistance in America. *The Journal of Economic Perspectives*, 4 (1), 57–78.

Clark, C.M.A. and Kavanagh, C. (1996). Basic income, inequality, and unemployment: Rethinking the linkage between work and welfare. *Journal of Economic Issues*, 30 (2), 399–406.

Colombino, U., Locatelli, M., Narazani, E. et al. (2010). Alternative Basic Income Mechanisms: An Evaluation Exercise with a Microeconometric Model. *Basic Income Studies*, 5 (2), 1–31. http://www.degruyter.com/view/j/bis

Flomenhoft, G. (2012). Applying the Alaska Model in a Resource-Poor State: The Example of Vermont. In K. Widerquist and M.W. Howard (eds) *Exporting the Alaska Model: Adapting the Permanent Fund Dividend.* Palgrave Macmillan, New York.

Forget, E. (2011). The Town with No Poverty: The Health Effects of a Canadian Guaranteed Annual Income Field Experiment. *Canadian Public Policy*, 37 (3), 283–305.

Goldsmith, S. (2012). The Economic and Social Impacts of the Permanent Fund Dividend on Alaska. In K. Widerquist and M.W. Howard (eds) *Alaska's Permanent Fund Dividend: Examining its Suitability as a Model.* Palgrave Macmillan, New York.

Groot, L. (2004). *Basic Income, Unemployment and Compensatory Justice.* Kluwer Academic Publishers, Dordrecht.

Harvey, P.L. (2006). The relative cost of a universal basic income and a negative income tax. *Basic Income Studies*, 1 (2), Article 6. http://www.degruyter.com/view/j/bis

Hum, D. and Simpson, W. (2001). A guaranteed annual income? From Mincome to the Millenium. Policy Options Politiques, Jan–Feb, 78–82.

Hum, D. and Simpson, W. (2005). The Cost of Eliminating Poverty in Canada: Basic Income With an Income Test Twist. In K. Widerquist, M.A. Lewis, and S. Pressman (eds) *The Ethics and Economics of the Basic Income Guarantee.* Ashgate, Aldershot, pp. 13–54.

Jackson, W.A. (1999). Basic income and the right to work: A Keynesian approach. *The Journal of Post Keynesian Economics*, 21 (4), 639–662.

Jordan, B., Agulnik, P., Burbidge, D. et al. (2000). *Stumbling Towards Basic Income. The Prospects for Tax-Benefit Integration.* Citizens Income Study Centre, London.

Keeley, M.C., Robins, P.K., Spiegelman, R.G. et al. (1978). The labor-supply effects and costs of alternative negative income tax programs. *The Journal of Human Resources*, 13 (1), 3–36.

Labeaga, J.M., Oliver, X., and Spadaro, A. (2008). Discrete choice models of labour supply, behavioural microsimulation and the Spanish tax reforms. *Journal of Economic Inequality*, 6 (3), 247–273.

Lerner, S.C., Clark, M.A.C., and Needham, W.R. (1999). *Basic Income: Economic Security for All Canadians.* Between the Lines, Toronto.

Levine, R., Watts, H., Hollister, R. et al. (2005). A Retrospective on the Negative Income Tax Experiments: Looking Back at the Most Innovative Field Studies in Social Policy. In K. Widerquist, M.A. Lewis, and S. Pressman (eds) *The Ethics and Economics of the Basic Income Guarantee.* Ashgate, Aldershot, pp. 13–54.

Levy, H., Lietz, C., and Sutherland, H. (2006). A basic income for Europe's children? EUROMOD Working Paper, EM4/06, pp. 1–30.

Loek G. (ed.) (2005). Debate: Toward a Basic Income Experiment? Special Issue of *Basic Income Studies*, 1 (2). http://www.degruyter.com/view/j/bis (Contributions by L. Groot, J.A. Noguera and J. De Wispelaere, H. Peeters and A. Marx, I. Virjo, and K. Widerquist.)

Moffitt, R. (2003). The Negative Income Tax and the evolution of U.S. welfare policy. *The Journal of Economic Perspectives*, 17 (3), 119–140.

Munnell, A.H. (1986). *Lessons From the Income Maintenance Experiments.* Washington, DC: Brookings Institution.

Noguera, J.A. (2001). Some prospects for a basic income scheme in Spain. *South European Society and Politics*, 6 (3), pp. 83–102.

Pech, W.J. (2009). Behavioral economics and the basic income guarantee. *Basic Income Studies*, 5 (2), Article 3. http://www.degruyter.com/view/j/bis

Peter, H.R. and Lyall, K. (1978). *Reforming Public Welfare: A Critique of the Negative Income Tax Experiments*. Russell Sage Foundation, New York.

Phelps, E. (2001). Subsidizing Wages. In J. Cohen and J. Rogers (eds) *What's Wrong with a Free Lunch?* Beacon Press, Boston, pp. 51–59.

Pressman, S. (2005). Income guarantees and the equity-efficiency tradeoff. *Journal of Socio-Economics*, 34 (1), 83–100.

Robins, P.K. (1985). A comparison of the labor supply findings from the four Negative Income Tax experiments. *The Journal of Human Resources*, 20 (4), 567–582.

Standing, G. (1999). *Global Labour Flexibility: Seeking Distributive Justice*. Palgrave Macmillan, New York.

Standing, G. (2002). *Beyond the New Paternalism: Basic Security as Equality*. Verso, London/New York.

Standing, G. (2009). *Work After Globalization: Building Occupational Citizenship*. Edward Elgar, Cheltenham.

Standing, G., Unni, J., Jhabvala, R. et al. (2010). *Social Income and Insecurity: A Study in Gujarat*. Routledge, London.

Vandenbroucke, F. and Van Puyenbroeck, T. (2000). Activation and the burden of working: on instrument choice by a responsibility-sensitive egalitarian government. In R. van der Veen, and L. Groot (eds) *Basic Income on the Agenda: Policy Objectives and Political Choices*. Amsterdam University Press, Amsterdam, pp. 85–106.

Van der Linden, B. (2000). Fighting unemployment without worsening poverty: basic income versus reductions of social security contributions. In W. Salverda, C. Lucifora, and B. Nolan (eds) *Policy Measures for Low-Wage Employment in Europe*. Edward Elgar, Cheltenham, pp 93–120.

Van der Linden, B. (2002). Is basic income a cure for unemployment in unionized economies? A general equilibrium analysis. *Annales d'Économie et de Statistique*, 22, 81–105.

Van Parijs, P. and Genet, M. (1992). Eurogrant. *Basic Income Research Group (BIRG) Bulletin*, 15, 4–7.

Zeckhauser, R.J. (1971). Optimal mechanisms for income transfer. *American Economic Review*, 61 (3), 324–334.

Chapter 28
The Case for an Income Guarantee

James Tobin

Excerpts from Tobin, J. (1966). The Case for an Income Guarantee. *Public Interest*, 4 (Summer), 31–41.

In the national campaign to conquer poverty there are two basic strategies, which may be labelled concisely, if somewhat inaccurately, "structural" and "distributive." The structural strategy is to build up the capacities of the poorest fifth of the population to earn decent incomes. The distributive strategy is to assure every family a decent standard of living regardless of its earning capacity. In my opinion both strategies are essential; correctly designed, they are more complementary than competitive. To date the main emphasis of the Federal "war on poverty" has been the structural approach. I shall argue that the war will not be won without a new and imaginative distributive strategy as well.

General economic progress raises the earning capacities of the populations at large – even of the less educated, less skilled, less experienced, less motivated, and less healthy. Even without Federal programs (other than overall fiscal and monetary policies to keep the labor force fully employed and the economy growing), the incidence of poverty gradually declines. Measuring poverty by the government's official income standard ($3,130 a year for four-person nonfarm families, and amounts estimated to yield comparable standards of living for households of other sizes and circumstances), its incidence has fallen from 22% to 17% since 1959.

The "war on poverty" testifies that the decline has not been fast enough for the American conscience. But accelerating it by structural measures is bound to be a slow and expensive process. Adults must be trained or retrained; they must acquire work experience, good work habits, self-confidence, and motivation; they must be made medically fit for regular employment; they must be placed in jobs and often moved to new locations. What is required is almost a case-by-case approach. Leaving the aged aside, there are about 8 million poor households including 9.5 million persons of ages 22–54 and 3 million in ages 16–21. The task of upgrading the earning capacities of the present generation of adults is staggering, a fact which in no way diminishes the importance of the effort or the value of each individual success.

Basic Income: An Anthology of Contemporary Research, First Edition. Edited by Karl Widerquist, José A. Noguera, Yannick Vanderborght, and Jurgen De Wispelaere.

The earning capacities of the next generation may be successfully raised by general structural measures – radical improvements in the education, health, and residential environment of the 14 million children of the poor. Again, the urgent importance of these efforts is in no way dimmed by recognizing the great difficulties they confront.

But the structural strategy will take many years, probably more than a generation. Even then its success will be incomplete; there will remain a hard core of families with inadequate earning capacity because of ineradicable physical, psychological, or circumstantial disabilities. And in the interim many more families, with disabilities remediable but not remedied, will fail to earn a decent living.

Today's Symptoms, Tomorrow's Causes

A distributive strategy is necessary, too, and the sooner the better. Families must have a minimally decent standard of living, whether or not they now have the ability to earn it in the job market. This can be provided by public assistance, and to withhold it from poor families is neither just (since their disabilities are, if not irremediable, the consequences of past discriminations and deficiencies in public services) nor necessary (since the upper four-fifths of the nation can surely afford the 2% of Gross National Product which would bring the lowest fifth across the poverty line).

Sometimes income assistance is scorned as treating the symptoms of poverty, in contrast to the structural strategy, which treats the causes. This reproach is not justified. For one thing, there is nothing intrinsically wrong with treating symptoms, and sometimes it is the best the doctors can do. More seriously, the symptoms of today's poverty may be the causes of tomorrow's. The conditions of life in which many children now grow up may predestine them to low earning capacity as adults.

However, many of those who distrust the distributive strategy have a more sophisticated point in mind. They are afraid that more generous income assistance to the poor will actually retard improvements in their earning capacities. If a decent standard of living is guaranteed, why should anyone work to get it or to acquire the ability to earn it on his own? For centuries this cynicism about human nature has been the excuse by which the affluent have relieved their individual and collective consciences and pocketbooks of the burden of their less fortunate brethren.

We cannot dismiss the question just because it has a shabby history. "Human nature" is not a reason to withhold public subsidies from people with low-earning capacity. But it definitely is a reason to give the subsidies in a way that does not destroy but indeed reinforces the incentives of the recipients to work and to increase the economic value of their work. The war on poverty needs a distributive strategy, but one that is carefully designed to support and strengthen its structural strategy.

Unfortunately our present congeries of public assistance programs – Federal, state, and local – has just the opposite effect. The incentives built in to our present subsidy programs are perverse. Unless public assistance is reformed and rationalized, it will seriously handicap the structural weapons deployed in the campaign against poverty. An improved public assistance program will not be cheap. If it is designed to aid rather than retard the conquest of poverty, its cost will for some years be more than our present programs. But it offers the hope that the conditions giving rise to the need for public subsidies will gradually be remedied.

* * * *

What are the defects of public assistance today? First is its inadequacy. Our governments administer a bewildering variety of welfare and social insurance programs, from Federal Old Age, Survivors, and Disability Insurance (OASDI) to township relief. *Yet half of the poor benefit from none of these; and most of the public money spent to supplement personal incomes goes to families above the poverty line.*

These facts are shocking but not as surprising as they may at first appear. Eligibility to benefit from most government income supplements depends on circumstances quite remote from current economic need. For social insurance – OASDI and unemployment compensation – eligibility and size of benefits depend on past contributions by the individual or his employer. Many programs assist particular groups – veterans, farmers, retired railroad workers, the blind, and so on.

Even in the main noncontributory general assistance programs, economic need is a necessary condition for benefits but not a sufficient one. The most important of these is Aid for Dependent Children (AFDC), administered under Federal supervision by the states and localities, and financed almost wholly by Federal funds. AFDC payments are based on need, but the several states define need with widely varying degrees of realism and seldom attempt to meet fully even their own calculations of need. A 1961 study showed that the Middle Atlantic states met all the income requirements they estimated. The East South Central states – Kentucky, Tennessee, Mississippi, and Alabama – estimated need at 20% less, met on average only 61% (Mississippi 38%) of the need so estimated, and met full need in only 3% of their cases. Federal law permits payments only to families with children, and of these only to families without an employed male adult – where, in effect, the father has died or deserted, or is disabled or unemployed. Most states restrict eligibility more than the Federal law requires.

There are also Federally financed programs of assistance to the aged and disabled, which fill some of the gaps Social Security still leaves both in eligibility and in adequacy of benefits. For the indigent who qualify for nothing else there is old-fashioned local relief, but here the applicant may run afoul of local residence requirements and other defensive stratagems.

Incentives in Reverse

Second, public assistance is geared to need in a manner that provides perverse incentives to those dependent upon it. One major destructive incentive is the one which AFDC gives for the break-up or non-formation of families. *Too often a father can provide for his children only by leaving both them and their mother.* It is hard to imagine a social contrivance more surely designed to perpetuate dependence on "welfare" in one generation after the other. We know that the major problems of poor people of all colors are related, as both cause and effect, to unstable and chaotic family structures. We know that, for historical reasons, Negro families tend to be matriarchal. We know the crucial importance of home environment in education, and we know the dangers of depriving boys of male adult models. To accentuate all these difficulties by deliberate public policy is a piece of collective insanity which it would be hard to match.

The "means test" provides other disincentives – disincentives to work, to save, to gain skills. The "means test" seems innocent enough in appearance and intent. It says that the welfare payments shall be made only if, and only to the extent that, the family cannot meet its needs (as officially calculated) from its own resources. Thus if, in a given locality, the effective standard of need (which may be only a fraction of an estimated minimal budget) for a mother and four children is $2,500 a year, the family will receive $2,500 from the state if its members earn nothing on their own, $1,500 if they earn $1,000, $500 if they earn $2,000, and so on. This arrangement, under which your total take-home pay is the same no matter how much you earn, is obviously not designed to encourage work or training for future work. One way to describe it is to say that the marginal tax rate on earnings is (so long as earnings do not exceed $2,500 in the example) 100%. The accuracy of this description, so far as incentive effects are concerned, is not impaired by the fact that the "tax" on additional earnings is not a literal payment to the government but a reduction in the government payment to the family.

The means test also discourages thrift. Consider two self-supporting families, one of whom saves while the other incurs debts. When and if misfortunes occur, the welfare authorities will give full help to the second but will generally force the thrifty family to use up its savings. Similarly, a man who has over a lifetime of work acquired his own home may be required to surrender title to it if he can't get by without public assistance in his old age.

It is true that there remains the incentive to escape public assistance entirely, and, since the welfare standard of life is a meager one at best, this incentive may seem substantial. But to many welfare households, especially the broken homes, it is too big a jump to be a realistic aspiration. Unattainable goals may be demoralizing rather than motivating. Most welfare dependents cannot set their sights higher than part-time low-paid employment. Yet this may be extremely important, both to acquire work experience and rudimentary skill and to build up the family's morale and sense of achievement. The system is rigged against it; there is nothing in it for them.

The welfare system of the United States contains plenty of ironies. A nation which regards the integrity of the nuclear family as the very backbone of its social structure provides incentives for its dissolution. A society which views high marginal income tax rates as fatal to the incentives for effort and thrift essential to its economy imposes 100% rates on a large fraction of its population. The explanation of such bizarre behavior is probably that present welfare policies represent an uneasy compromise among several principles. Since the 1930s our society has acknowledged its responsibility to assure through government a minimal standard of living for all citizens. But the corollary charge on the public purse has been accepted grudgingly, and the fear that the "privilege" of welfare might be abused has dominated policy.

A by-product of this dominant fear is that much of the considerable administrative effort in public welfare reduces to detective work, to make sure there are no "cheaters" on the rolls, and to close surveillance of the clients' sources and uses of funds, to make sure that tax money is not wasted in riotous living. Everything confirms welfare families in the demoralizing belief that they cannot manage their own affairs. This tendency is reenforced by the propensity of legislators to give assistance in kind – surplus foods, subsidized housing, medical care for the indigent or "medically indigent." Eligibility for these specific benefits is usually defined by a maximum income limit, awkward to administer and perverse in incentive effects.

* * * *

An alternative approach, which commands the support of many economists of all political and ideological shades (Milton Friedman, Goldwater's chief economic advisor in 1964, was one of the first to suggest it) is a national system of income supplements graduated to income and to family size. For more fortunate citizens, personal income taxes likewise depend on income and family size; therefore the proposed income supplements can be called, not very felicitously, Negative Income Taxes. They may also be regarded as Federally Guaranteed Incomes, since they involve, among other things, Federal payment of a specified amount to every family with zero income.

Various proposals embodying one or more of these features have been set forth; and, as with all reform causes, the proponents differ widely in their reasons. Some – like Robert Theobald and W.H. Ferry of Robert Maynard Hutchins' Center for the Study of Democratic Institutions – are interested mainly in the Income Guarantee. They believe that automation is rendering work for pay obsolete, and that government handouts are the only way to give the public the means to buy the immense bounty produced by the automatons. They do not share, therefore, the concern of economists to provide incentives for work and for building up earning capacity. I disagree strongly with their diagnosis, but for other reasons I also advocate what amounts to an Income Guarantee.

The personal income tax would become a two-way street. At present, calculations of the tax form lead to two alternative outcomes: either the citizen owes something or he owes nothing. Under the proposal there would be a third possibility: the government owes him something. This would not carry the stigma of charity or relief; it would be a right of national citizenship symmetrical to the obligation to pay taxes. It would be uniform across the nation. A poor family would not suffer because of residence in a poor or unresponsive state or county, or because of migration. The government payment would not depend on the supposed causes of need (absence or disability of the husband, etc.) but simply on the fact of need as scaled to family income and size. Finally, the graduation of the "negative tax" to the family's income would, like that of the existing positive tax, give the family an incentive to earn more on its own.

In the design of an integrated allowance and tax schedule a compromise must be struck among three objectives: (i) providing a high basic allowance for families with little or no earnings, (ii) building in a strong incentive to earn more, and (iii) limiting the budgetary cost of the scheme, and in particular minimizing the payment of benefits to those who do not need them.

In discussing alternatives it is essential to keep in mind that some compromise is necessary, that there are inexorable conflicts among the three listed objectives.

From an overall economic point of view, there is no cost to the nation. This is a redistribution of income and consumption, not a governmental draft on productive resources such as is involved in building missiles or schools. But a burden nonetheless falls on those whose taxes are higher than they would be otherwise. It will doubtless be easier for them to accept the plan if the cost to them is a tax rate reduction foregone rather than an actual boost in rates.

An income allowance plan of this design in no way conflicts with the structural measures of the war on poverty. Indeed, people on welfare would have more, not less, incentive to enroll in training and apprenticeship programs. They will keep more of what they are paid while training, and more of what they subsequently earn. After financial detective work is turned over to the experts of the Internal Revenue Service, social workers can concentrate on their proper professional specialties, family guidance and rehabilitation. The crucial substantive needs in the public sector – for Headstart classes, community schools, clinics, hospitals, day care centers, and so on – must be attacked by other means. But a new distributive strategy can make its beneficiaries better able and better motivated to take advantage of improved public services.

Chapter 29

What Can We Learn from the Agathotopians?

James Meade

Excerpts from Meade, J. (1990). What Can We Learn from the Agathotopians? *Il Politico: rivista italiana di scienze politiche*, 55, 5–16.

The Agathotopians regard the successful introduction of institutions for achieving the necessary flexibility of rates of wages and of other forms of earnings as by far the most difficult economic problem that they have had to face.[1] They are quite clear that their introduction would have been impossibile if they had not been accompanied by effective measures to ensure that workers had, in addition to their earnings from work, a secure fixed income from some other source. They realized that such an alternative source of income would have an obvious equalizing effect on the distribution of income. It would greatly reduce the problem of risk-bearing by worker partners since it would constitute a completely risk-free component of income. Finally, by reducing the concentrated reliance of workers on their earnings for the finance of their needs it would greatly ease that acceptance of flexibility in rates of pay which was necessary for the attainment and maintenance of full employment.

There are in fact three main ways in which there can be assured to every citizen an income which is divorced from the level of, and the risks attached to, earned income:

- A first method is to design measures to attain and maintain a widespread ownership of capital wealth, so that every citizen has the benefit of some income from rent, interest, or dividends with the opportunity of reducing the risk of such incomes by spreading his or her ownership of property over a large number of independent sources. At the extreme, if the ownership of wealth were distributed among citizens in the same widespread manner as the ability to earn income, a shift of national income from pay for work to profits on capital would have no adverse distributive effects. What the citizen lost on the swings of pay he or she would gain on the roundabouts of profit.
- A second method is to replace existing social benefits which are paid to various categories of people (e.g. unemployment benefit, sickness benefit, etc.) by a single Basic

From Meade, J. (1990). What Can We Learn from the Agathotopians? Presented at the Third BIEN Congress. Published in English in an Italian journal: *Il Politico: rivista italiana di scienze politiche*, 55, 5–16; published by Front Cover Università di Pavia, Università di Pavia. Facoltà di scienze politiche, Università di Pavia. Istituto di scienze politiche, Istituto di scienze politiche di Pavia (Italy). Reprinted with permission of *Il Politico*.

Basic Income: An Anthology of Contemporary Research, First Edition. Edited by Karl Widerquist, José A. Noguera, Yannick Vanderborght, and Jurgen De Wispelaere.

Income payable to every citizen and financed simply out of the general tax revenues of the State.

- A third method is to arrange that, by one means or another, the State itself becomes the beneficial owner of a large part of the country's capital wealth so that it can use the rents, profits, or dividends received on that wealth for distribution in the form of an equal Social Dividend for each citizen.

The Agathotopians have made use of all of these three methods. They have taken steps to attain and then to maintain a more widespread and less unequal distribution of the ownership of capital in a way which is compatible with the greatest possible freedom of enterprise. They have exempted all savings from income tax and have combined this with a moderate annual rate of tax on large holidays of wealth and with heavy taxation on the transfers of wealth above a certain limit by gift *inter vivos* or by bequest at death. This enables citizens with little wealth to accumulate savings without any tax and allows individual entrepreneurs to use their wealth and plough back their savings into their business with little adverse tax effects. But the heavy taxation of transfers of wealth means that heavy concentrations of wealth in single ownership cannot be passed on.

The Agathotopians pay a Basic Income free of tax to all citizens. This payment has replaced expenditure on other social benefits which are no longer needed. It has also been combined with the elimination of all personal allowances under their savings-exempt income tax, all sources of income other than the Basic Income being subject to tax. For example, they include in the tax base an imputed rent on all owner-occupied homes or other real property. In Agathotopia tax evasion is considered as a very serious crime and they devote substantial resources to ensuring that such evasion is kept to a minimum. But the payment of a Basic Income on an adequate level they found to be a hideously expensive affair even after allowance was made for all these offsets. An intolerably high marginal rate of tax on savings-exempt income would have occurred if they had not had recourse to other sources.

The strain on the Agathotopian budget has recently been much relieved by improved political relations with their neighbours in the surrounding Topian Islands. This has enabled them to make substantial reductions in their expenditure on defence. This so-called peace dividend has been helpful to finance the raising of their Basic Income to a more adequate level.

Also, recently their tax revenue has been transformed by their concern to reduce the pollution of the environment which has resulted from modern methods of production. They set up a special Commission to survey the problem and to specify the cases in which the social environmental costs of certain activities were not being reflected in the private costs and prices at which such activities were being marketed. Such activities were the pollution of the atmosphere through the burning of fossil fuel; the congestion of road space through its free use for traffic and for the parking of vehicles; the disposal of wastes in rivers; the use of fertilisers which indirectly affected water supplies; and so on. The Agathotopians have consistently tackled these problems wherever possible by charging the polluter for the previously free use of the atmosphere or natural resources.

This they have done by the application of three rules: (i) to reduce the pollution by a tax or other charge rather than by direct regulation which raises no revenue; (ii) to tax the private car rather than to subsidise the public bus as a means of reducing road congestion; and (iii) in those cases in which quantitative regulation is necessary to raise revenue by auctioning the necessary pollution permits to the highest bidder rather than distributing the permits without charge on some other principle.

The yield of revenue raised in this way has been so great that it has transformed their budgetary problems. Not all this gross yield represents a net gain, since the pollution taxation of some activities has led to the reduction of the yield of other taxes on those activities. Moreover, in order to avoid the most undesirable distributional effects the level of Basic Income has had to be raised to offset the rise in price of such amounts of the newly taxed goods and services as were necessary to maintain an adequate minimum standard of living.

However, there remained a very substantial net revenue bonus even after allowing for these offsets. The reliance on a pollution tax (whose incentive effects are socially desirable) rather than on taxes, such as the income tax, (whose disincentive effects on work and enterprise are undesirable) enabled a given level of real Basic Income to be maintened at a markedly lower social cost.

Another form of tax employed by the Agathotopians to finance a really adequate Basic Income is the imposition of a special surcharge on the first slice of every citizen's income other than the Basic Income itself. This is a form of levy which in effect withdraws part of the Basic Income as a citizen's other income increases, a levy which is additional to the ordinary current rate of tax on income. This turned the Agathotopian Basic Income into something which is half way between a fully conditional social benefit and a fully unconditional social benefit. With a fully conditional benefit a citizen without other income is given a full-scale benefit, but this benefit is reduced pound for pound as the citizen's other income increases. This is the cheapest way to ensure that everyone has a minimum Guaranteed Income. Benefit is paid only so far as it is needed to bring income up to the minimum level. But it has the well-known effects of removing any incentive to earn any additional income, so long as any such income will be matched by an equivalent reduction in social benefit. A completely unconditional social benefit removes this disincentive effect, since the same tax-free social benefit is received regardless of the level of other income. But it is hideously expensive in that it hands out free of tax an adequate social benefit to every citizen however rich or poor. The Agathotopian Basic Income with a Surcharge on the first slice of other income falls between these two extremes. Every citizen, rich or poor, receives the same tax-free Basic Income but the Surcharge on the first slice of other income is the equivalent of a withdrawal of the Basic Income, not pound for pound but, say, one pound for every two pounds earned. The Surcharge may weaken but will not eliminate the incentive to earn more income; it can, however, enormously reduce the cost of the Basic Income.

Finally, there is a still more radical way in which the Agathotopians have raised finance for a Basic Income. The Agathotopian State does not possess a National Debt: it possesses instead a National Asset equal in value to some 50% of the total productive wealth in the country. The government does not manage the productive concerns which lie behind this wealth. It simply invests its wealth on the competitive Stock Exchange in the form of holdings in private competitive investment trusts and similar financial institutions. Thus the State's wealth is mingled with the savings of the private sector of the economy for investment in productive enterprises which are competitively managed as freeen-terprise undertakings.

This arrangement corresponds to what I have called Topsy Turvy Nationalisation. With the Nationalisation schemes undertaken, for example, by the Labour government in the UK after World War II the State took over the ownership and the centralised management of steel, railways, electricity, coal, and so on. But the State paid full compensation to the previous owners which meant that the State did not receive for its own free use the profits of such concerns, since this was offset by the payment of interest on the National Debt issued to raise the compensation cost of the nationalisation schemes. Thus the State became the owner-manager but without the benefit of an increased income. With Agathotopian Topsy Turvy Nationalisation the State obtains the beneficial ownership of the income earned on certain capital assets without undertaking any responsibility for the management of the business concerns, which is left to the private market.

The post-tax income so acquired by the Agathotopian State is used towards the finance of the Basic Income payable to all citizens. This source of revenue, once it had been established, has had no disadvantageous disincentive effects. The revenue accrues directly to the State and does not involve levying any rate of tax of anyone's earnings or expenditures; and since the transfer of capital assets to the beneficial ownership of the State has not been carried to excess, it is compatible with leaving the conduct of business to private competition. There are enough privately owned capital funds left to the operations of an effective free competitive capital market.

How did the Agathotopians ever reach this happy state of affairs in which the State came to own a National Asset in place of an existing National Debt?

There was one possibility which made a limited but nevertheless worthwhile contribution to the outcome. The State owned a number of business concerns which it managed itself and these enterprises were earning smaller profits than they would have made if they had been operated for maximum return by private competitive enterprise. Their privatisation was a help. They were sold to private entrepreneurs at the highest possible price which the State could achieve and the scale proceeds were used by the State to redeem National Debt on terms which led to a reduction in interest on the National Debt which exceeded the low profit previously being earned on these assets under State management. Of course, such privatisation was a help only because the revenue received from the sale of such assets was used by the State to reduce debt. It would not have helped if it had been used to finance current expenditures. In any case its contribution to the problem was strictly limited and the Agathotopians sought a further measure for raising the funds necessary for the accumulation of a National Asset.

For this purpose they drew a distinction between capital taxes (i.e. those which were likely to be paid largely out of the current savings or holding of wealth of the taxpayer), and current taxes (i.e. those which were likely to be paid largely at the expense of the taxpayer's current consumption). They realised that any such distinction was bound to be very rough and ready. But they made it by putting the yield of their Wealth Tax and Capital Transfer Tax into the capital-tax category, leaving all other tax revenue in the current-tax category.

They defined the current account surplus or deficit of the government's budget as excluding expenditures on capital assets and revenues from capital taxes; and they adopted the policy of ensuring that the government's budget should be managed in such a way as to show a surplus on current account to the extent to which, in the government's opinion, private savings needed supplementation in the national interest.

They instituted a National Asset Commission and arranged that any budgetary surplus on current account and the whole of the yield of their capital taxes were paid into the National Asset Commission. This commission used such funds to redeem the originally existing National Debt and to purchase National Assets, investing these funds through investments trusts and similar bodies on the Stock Exchange. The current dividends or other current receipts on such assets were then paid as revenue into the government's current-account budget.

By these means their capital taxes were in fact treated as a continuous, moderate, and acceptable form of capital leavy for the gradual building up of an endowment from which a Social Dividend might be earned to improve the level of Basic Income payable to all citizens. The process was continued until the National Asset Commission held some 50% of the nation's productive wealth, at which point the rates of capital taxation were reduced to the level which were required simply to maintain the National Asset at this 50% level of a growing total national wealth.

The process was a very prolonged one; but it proved to be a method to introducing a steady reliable and continuous improvement in the level of their Basic Income.

Note

1. Editor's note: This article was originally published in English in the Italian journal *Il Politico*. It refers heavily to the story of Agathotopia from Meade's 1989 book, *Agathotopia: The Economics of Partnership*. For background on Agathotopia, see the introduction to Section V of this volume.

Reference

Meade, J.E. (1989). *Agathotopia: The Economics of Partnership*. Aberdeen University Press, Aberdeen.

Chapter 30

Basic Income and Efficiency

Philippe Van Parijs

Excerpts from Van Parijs, P. (1990). The Second Marriage of Justice and Efficiency. *Journal of Social Policy*, 19(1) pp. 1–25.

Let us consider a measure that consists in replacing a simple minimum income system of the means-tested variety by a Basic Income that guarantees the same level of minimum income, or, more modestly, by one that introduces a lower, "partial" Basic Income and reduces all other replacement payments (pensions, unemployment benefits, student grants, etc.) by a corresponding amount. If the argument outlined above is correct, such measures could be defended by appealing to justice. But how could they be defended on grounds of efficiency? How could such measures be expected to have a positive impact on the national product? At first sight, the opposite is bound to be the case, for two reasons.

Firstly, such measures will involve granting a transfer to many people who currently get nothing. It follows that a greater tax yield will be required, and hence that marginal tax rates cannot but go up for significant categories of earners, thus generating a downward pressure on the national product. True, this implication must not be overstated. As long as we are speaking of a low Basic Income, much of it can be financed simply by a relabelling of the corresponding part of existing transfers (pensions, unemployment benefits, etc.) and by the abolition of a number of tax exemptions (for example, on the first slice of earned income) or tax rebates (for example, for dependent spouses) that no longer serve a purpose. Moreover, the increase in the tax yield required for the transfers themselves will be partly offset by a decrease in the administrative cost of the transfer system. In an era of computerized payments, the bulk of this cost is the cost of checking entitlements. Obviously, the less conditional the system, the lower the latter cost.[1] Finally, any net increase in the tax yield that may be required can be distributed in such a way as to minimize the effect on factor supply, for example by leaving reinvested profits untouched, or by taxing the *lowest* slice of all earned incomes at a higher rate.[2] There is no doubt, however, that the introduction of a significant Basic Income would involve some increase in marginal tax rates, and that this increase can be expected to exert a downward pressure on (declared, domestic) factor supply and hence on the (taxable) national product.

Basic Income: An Anthology of Contemporary Research, First Edition. Edited by Karl Widerquist, José A. Noguera, Yannick Vanderborght, and Jurgen De Wispelaere.

Things look even worse as soon as one reflects on the specific nature of the use that would be made of this increased taxation. What a Basic Income does is increase the feasibility or the attractiveness of escaping from the wage relationship in order to become self-employed, form a partnership, join a cooperative or simply stay at home. This increased bargaining power, this greater autonomy may be most desirable in itself. But, at least in a capitalist economy, it may have disastrous economic consequences. For even if capital income were not taxed at all in order to finance the Basic Income, the improvement of every worker's bargaining power would exert an upward pressure on wages and working conditions. The resulting negative effect on the rate of return to capital would foster capital flight, the substitution of consumption for saving, and perhaps even organized investment strikes.

The conclusion, it seems, is that introducing a Basic Income, even at a low level, while maintaining residual transfers, would lead to a significant fall in the expected national income. Indeed, this fall may be so significant that introducing a Basic Income at a level equal to the current level of means-tested benefits may simply constitute an unsustainable option. This pessimistic view is expressed in Figure 30.1. There it is being supposed that we have a means-tested guaranteed minimum income at level B, and that a Basic Income is introduced in this context, with the level of the means-tested benefit being cut by an amount equal to the Basic Income. t* now represents the share of Basic Income in expected disposable income, Y* the corresponding expected level of average disposable income, and G the corresponding expected level of Basic Income (G = T*.Y*). At low levels of t*, Y* is hardly affected, if at all, since the basic income is largely financed out of a reduction of existing benefits and tax allowances,[3] while giving no one a genuine possibility not to work. As t* grows, however, the expected average income starts being badly affected, both because of rising tax rates and because the Basic Income reaches levels at which it is no

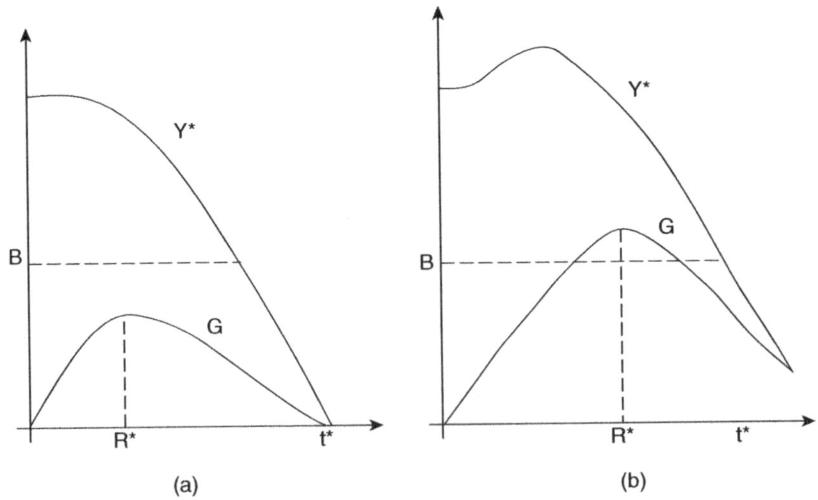

Figure 30.1 The economic value of Basic Income: two conjectures: (a) pessimistic; (b) optimistic.
t*, *Share of Basic Income in average disposable income*;
Y*, *expected average disposable income*;
G, *expected level of Basic Income*; B, *subsistence level of income*;
R*, *value of t* at which the expected level of Basic Income is maximised ("Rawlsian" position)*.

longer negligible as a source of bargaining power and hence of downward pressure on profits. The result is that even the highest feasible level of Basic Income (at $t^* = R^*$) falls short of basic needs (B).[4]

If this were the end of the story, the second marriage would have had it, for there would be no prospect whatever of the second partner ever turning up. Faced with arguments about the deadweight losses associated with higher marginal tax rates, economic advocates of Basic Income may quietly concede the point – just as Schumpeter could have agreed with all that has been said about the static inefficiency of monopoly capitalism. But just as Schumpeter argued that this was no more than petty accountancy, relative to the massive dynamic efficiency of the creative destruction associated with monopolistic firms, similarly contemporary economic advocates of Basic Income argue that quibbling about marginal tax rates is of little significance in regard to Basic Income's massive contribution to making our economy more dynamic, less cripplingly rigid, and less stiflingly conflictual than it would otherwise be. The argument has two main components.

The first and most developed component stresses the crucial role Basic Income would play, directly and indirectly, in fostering the flexibility of our economies. With a Basic Income, individuals can go through repeated and protracted periods in which their activities earn them less than a subsistence wage, for example as they retrain between two jobs, as they learn new skills on the job, as they keep old skills alive in a period of reduced professional activity and as they launch new businesses. As a result and without the (often opaque and costly) aid of special schemes, adjustments of all sorts are made easier and an entrepreneurial spirit is encouraged throughout society. This direct and individual impact on the flexibility of the economy is further reinforced by an indirect, collective impact. If each individual worker is protected by the availability of a significant unconditional income and the possibilities it opens up, there is less justification for a number of regulations which currently constrain the labor market, such as restrictions on patterns of working time or even minimum wage legislation. The sort of flexibility which modern technology increasingly requires could therefore acceptably be traded by the labor movement against the income security provided by a Basic Income (Variants of this argument can be found in Standing, 1986; 1989; Nooteboom, 1986; Meade, 1989.)

The second, more speculative component of the argument emphasises the costly conflicts increasingly generated in our economies, as a result of two major trends. The spread of significant environmental externalities and the increase in the share of wealth held in the form of information, rather than material goods, differ greatly in both substance and origin. But they have one feature in common: they greatly enhance the importance of property rights which are extremely difficult to define and enforce. Using Ouchi's (1980) typology, one can distinguish three types of social coordination. *Bureaucracies* are optimal when there are neither sharp conflicts of interests nor significant uncertainties about who is entitled to what. *Clans* are optimal when there are no conflicts but high uncertainties. *Markets* are optimal when there are conflicts but no uncertainties. When there are both sharp conflicts and high uncertainties, coordination breaks down and chaos sets in. This is what is increasingly threatening to happen in a market economy pervaded by the two trends mentioned above. Now, it seems safe to predict that these trends will persist, and hence that it will become increasingly difficult to make sure that whoever is responsible for wealth destruction/creation actually pays/is paid for the damage/benefit caused. Assuming that sharp conflicts of interest are with us forever, the only option open to forestall economically damaging chaos consists in reducing what is at stake in the market game, that is, in making an increasing part of people's material welfare depend on society's overall productivity, rather than on their individual contribution.[5] A Basic Income is the most natural way of institutionalising this solution.

For an economic advocate of Basic Income, it is wrong to be mesmerised – as are many economists who have only paid superficial attention to the Basic Income issue – by the threat of rising gross tax rates. For the tax-elasticity of factor supply, whether cheaply invoked or laboriously studied, is completely overshadowed by the considerations just outlined. If such an advocate is right, the effect of higher tax rates would be negligible in comparison. Indeed, the shift from the current system to a Basic Income system may involve no rise in overall tax rates at all, as the favorable impact on output growth would generate the required increase in the tax yield with unchanged rates. (One optimistic conjecture of this sort is represented in Figure 30.1b: even though the national product ends up falling with very high levels of Basic Income, it rises substantially as the level of Basic Income is being lifted towards the level of current means-tested benefits.) What about the second argument brought up by the economic critics of Basic Income, the argument that, whatever happens to tax rates, every worker's increasing freedom not to work (under any conditions) brought about by a growing Basic Income is bound to affect negatively the rate of return on capital, and hence the growth of output? An economic advocate of Basic Income is bound to give the same sort of answer as to the first argument: the advantages of a more flexible, less conflict-ridden economy will more than offset the disadvantages – in terms of profitability – of the workers' improved bargaining position. But the confidence with which this answer will be uttered is bound to be more fragile than in connection with the first argument. After all, we tinkered with tax rates on a massive scale during the last century, but in no society has more than a small minority of citizens ever been given the real option not to work.

My aim, in any case, has not been to establish that the introduction of a Basic Income would have "economic value" (that is, would boost average income), nor indeed that it would have "ethical value" (that is, would bring us closer to a just society). My aim has only been to indicate what form this two-fold case for Basic Income needs to take if it is to be successful. My own conviction is that, in advanced industrial societies, a strong claim of justice can be made, for a sizable Basic Income, and that sufficient confidence can be gained on the economic side for the proposal also to meet the second of our conditions in the near future. This confidence, however, is not independent of the first condition being met. For whether a Basic Income can boost flexibility (at least along the indirect, collective path delineated above), and whether it can significantly reduce the overall level of conflict, is very sensitive to whether a Basic Income is perceived as a fair way of distributing part of the social product. If organized workers, for example, see Basic Income as an outrageous racket on the fruit of their labor, the net effect on rigidity and conflict may well end up being negative.

This prompts a final methodological comment. If the initial conjecture of this chapter is correct, it is pointless to try to assess the political feasibility of a proposal such as this one through direct head counting, without looking first at the economic and ethical issues involved. But if the remarks of the previous paragraph are correct, it is also impossible to assess the key economic claims made about Basic Income independently of the ethical claims that are being made on its behalf. To put the matter more provocatively, the debate on Basic Income is one area in which there is nothing illegitimate about – duly circumscribed – wishful thinking. It is right that the conviction that a Basic Income is demonstrably just should influence the belief that introducing it would be efficient, and partly, therefore, the belief that it is politically feasible.

Notes

1. I here leave aside the important question of whether this would constitute an optimal enhancement of justice, as compared for example to redistribution towards poorer countries. The relevance of this question in the present context is limited by the following consideration: if I give an unfair advantage to one of my children over another, it is no excuse, and no justification of the status quo, if I point out that there exist other people even less advantaged than the less advantaged of my children.
2. In the least favorable case (from this angle), a "partial" Basic Income is introduced side by side with a residual means-tested benefit (that makes up the difference between the Basic Incomes of a household and the socially agreed minimum income for households without income from a further source). Even then, some reduction in administrative cost can be expected, as the reduction in the depth of the unemployment trap would reduce the number of people who would need to claim means-tested benefits.
3. As in James Meade's (1989: section III) proposal. Note that such regressive taxation *with a Basic Income* is more favorable to people with low potential earnings than progressive taxation with a means-tested benefit system that amounts to taxing low earnings at 100%.
4. Bear in mind that t^* is not the overall rate of taxation, nor the overall share of transfers, and that due to the partial replacement of existing benefits, a modest rise in t^* may be consistent with hardly any rise in the overall tax rate – indeed, for the reasons mentioned earlier on in this section, with a drop in this rate.
5. In this case, therefore, an adequate Basic Income is both economically unfeasible (because the maximum of G is below B) and politically unfeasible (because Y falls as G rises). But I could have drawn the curves in such a way that such an adequate Basic Income would be politically unfeasible (because economically damaging) but economically feasible.

References

Bowles, S. and Gintis, H. (1986). *Democracy and Capitalism.* Routledge and Kegan Paul, London.

Meade, J.E. (1989). *Agathotopia: The Economics of Partnership.* Aberdeen University Press, Aberdeen.

Nooteboom, B. (1986). Basic income as a basis for small business. *International Small Business Journal*, 5 (3), 10–18.

Ouchi, W.G. (1980). Markets, bureaucracies and clans. *Administrative Science Quarterly*, 25, 129–141.

Standing, G. (1986). Meshing labour flexibility with security: an answer to mass unemployment? *International Labour Review*, 125, 87–106.

Standing, G. (1989). *European Unemployment, Insecurity and Flexibility: A Social Dividend Solution.* International Labour Office, Geneva, January.

Chapter 31

Basic Income as a Basis for Small Business

Bart Nooteboom

Excerpts from Nooteboom, B. (1987). Basic Income as a Basis for Small Business. *International Small Business Journal*, 5 (3), 10–18.

The present chapter is limited to the effects of Basic Income (BI) on small and medium-sized enterprise (SME).[1] It does not treat the primarily social considerations for BI, from the point of view of unemployed or other social security recipients, the young, housewives, artists, and so on. It does not go deeply into the crucial problem of how to finance BI, or into considerations of the "work ethic," the relation to part-time labor or work sharing, and so on.

The effects of BI on SME form a relatively neglected topic, as small business generally tends to be neglected by economists, sociologists, policy-makers and media. Such neglect is difficult to justify, because SME is important for the economy, the labor market, general welfare and the political system.

The consequences of a BI for SME are not obvious, and require analysis. A fairly wide spread intuition among those who have not yet given careful thought to the idea of a BI, is that it is likely to sap energy and effort. That effect is indeed likely if the level of a BI were to be too high. In most proposals for a BI, the level is such that to a "standard family" of two adults and two children it would amount to something like the basic level of social security for such a household in countries with adequate social security systems. In most proposals, the BI for an adult varies from £100 to £150 per month. In most schemes, children below 16 or 18 receive less. In the present chapter I argue that a BI of that order of magnitude would stimulate and facilitate small business.

The more socially oriented arguments for SME reinforce other social arguments used by proponents of BI. More importantly, my thesis that BI stimulates and enhances small business yields an economic argument of growth, innovation and entrepreneurship.

This may serve as a counter-argument to economists who oppose BI on the ground that, although it may be viewed sympathetically from a social point of view, it is ultimately destructive socially, because it reduces growth and lowers the level of economic production and hence employment. My counter-argument is that in view of the positive effects on SME, BI generates more economic production and hence more employment, both of a higher quality.

From Nooteboom, B. (1987). Basic Income as a Basis for Small Business. *International Small Business Journal*, 5 (3), 10–18. Reprinted with permission of SAGE.

Basic Income: An Anthology of Contemporary Research, First Edition. Edited by Karl Widerquist, José A. Noguera, Yannick Vanderborght, and Jurgen De Wispelaere.

BI stimulates and facilitates SME in four ways:

- by providing a compensation for diseconomies of small-scale production, which are causing increase of scale, concentration and the ousting of smallness;
- as an incentive for wage earners to become entrepreneurs, thereby yielding their jobs to unemployed and generating new production with new employment opportunities;
- as an alternative to the present complicated patchwork of subsidies, fiscal allowances and other measures to support small business, which are often inefficient and by their complexity contribute to confusion, irritation, inequality of treatment and rigidity;
- as a solution to the problem of unfair competition presented by informal or formal entrepreneurship by recipients of social security. This is increasingly generating grudges among independent entrepreneurs, which is socially and politically undesirable, and is pulling many of them into the "black" economy.

The purpose of the present chapter is to explain and argue these points.

Compensation for Diseconomies of Small Scale

In some fairly fundamental econometric studies of productivity in retailing, which have meanwhile been published widely,[2] a systematic, significant and sizeable effect of scale in shop operations was found. This effect arises from a "threshold" in operating costs, or in other words costs that are incurred to operate a shop of any size, regardless of how much or little sales are actually achieved. This is illustrated in Figure 31.1. The cost curve in Figure 31.1 applies to shops that are reasonably similar with respect to type of products sold, service level and extent of physical production (bread baking, sausage production, packaging, repairs, etc.).

The threshold arises because throughout opening time of a shop, at least one person must be available to serve customers (behind a counter in case of a service shop; at a checkout point in case of self-service). According to this theory, annual threshold labor equals annual opening time. For example: if a shop is open for 50 hours per week for 50 weeks per annum, yielding a total opening time of 2,500 hours, at least one person must be available (at the counter or checkout) for every one of those 2,500 hours, yielding a "threshold labor" of 2,500 hours.

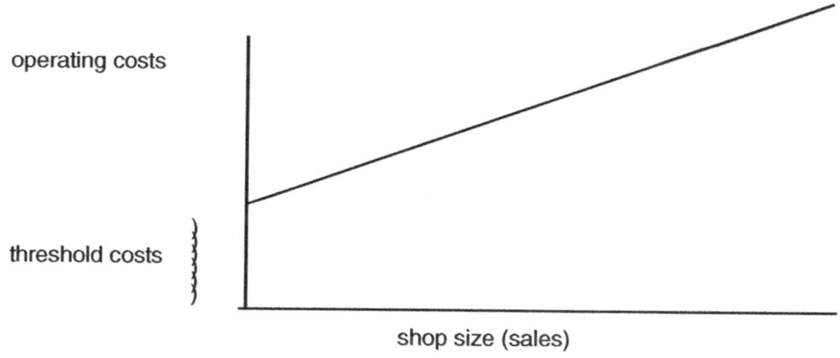

Figure 31.1

Figure 31.2

If a shop has multiple, independently staffed service areas or departments, the threshold must be multiplied accordingly. The reasoning behind the finding that the cost curve is straight is somewhat intricate and technical, and will not be discussed here.[3]

The point now is that the threshold yields a diseconomy of small scale: threshold costs weigh more heavily for small than for large shops of the same type. Figure 31.1 implies a relationship between labor productivity and sales size as illustrated in Figure 31.2. Towards the higher end of the scale, productivity does not vary much with size, but towards the lower end of the scale productivity drops sharply. Thus costs are higher, per unit of sales, for smaller shops.[4]

Due to the intensity of competition, prices (trade margins) cannot be higher at smaller shops. Hence, net profit per unit of sales is low for small shops. As a result, a small shop can often persist only because threshold labor is provided without reward by the shopkeeper or his family. In most Western European countries, this is increasingly considered unacceptable, and hence small shops disappear. A notable exception, in several countries, is the emergence of shops operated by ethnic minorities, for whom the unremunerated provision of threshold labor is (still) acceptable.

BI can serve as a reward for threshold labor. It would offset threshold costs. Thereby it would eliminate or reduce the main cause of diseconomies of small-scale, thereby providing a basis for small-scale retailing. The phenomenon discussed here applies not only to retailing, but also to hotels, cafés, restaurants and generally speaking all services where a service capacity is provided for consumers to visit and utilize. In other sectors (manufacturing of different kinds, construction, assembly, installation, transport) scale effects have not yet been studied in similar depth and detail. There is, however, persistent evidence of economies of scale there also, although its form is likely to be different (not so much a threshold cost, but a non-linear relation between costs and size, perhaps). As a result, a BI there also will reduce the effect of economies of scale, although it may not be such a perfect match to the problem as in the case of economy of scale in the form of threshold costs.

Incentive for Entrepreneurship

Entrepreneurship is risky in two respects: one may lose one's capital invested in the enterprise, and one may not earn sufficient income to live and support one's family, especially in the early years. Here I focus not on the risk of capital loss, but on the risk of insufficient income. In many countries there is a social security system which guarantees a minimum income if labor does not provide it. It is supplementary. First comes labor, and if that is impossible, or unavailable, or insufficient, then income is supplemented. It is a reward for old age, sickness, weakness on the labor market, maladjustment and failure. A failed entrepreneur can fall back on social security, but only after the failure has become manifest, and in such a position the receipt of social security benefits is generally considered a great shame. Present social security in general is associated with failure and shame.

My thesis is that many dissatisfied wage earners who are potential entrepreneurs with excellent or workable ideas and sufficient talent shrink back from taking the step to entrepreneurship, not primarily for lack of capital (for which they can go to a bank), but for lack of income to support the family during the formative years of the business, and for the shame of possible failure and the consequent need to live off the social security system.

BI would provide something one can always fall back on, in sickness and health, in failure and success, in a job and in self-employment. A minimum income comes first, and then labor. It would lower the threshold to entrepreneurship, while still not making it too easy.

A wage earner stepping out of a job to start up a firm would in the early years see his income drop, but he would have the BI for himself and his family to live on in those early years, and in the case of failure, without the shame of having to appeal to something that is awarded only in case of failure.

Alternative to Complicated Measures

In most countries there is a patchwork of regulations, fiscal measures and subsidies to provide opportunities for small business by compensation for economies of scale, lack of information or financial resources, unequal power in and access to markets, or to provide a form of social security for small entrepreneurs and their families.

Fiscal measures: deductions from VAT, income tax or rates, in relation to the level of sales, added value, profit income, investment, inventory or stocks, in order to facilitate small-scale operations or investment, or to make reservations for a pension or for insurance.

Subsidies: to facilitate investment (by subsidies for finance or by state guaranteed loans from banks), introduction of new technology, research and development, start-up of business, use of counselling/consultancy, the provision and use of information on markets and costs, energy saving, export, employment of unemployed, training outside or on the job, liquidation of unprofitable business, provision of infrastructural facilities, local shops in small neighbourhoods, appropriate location (by rent subsidies or the cheap provision of communal centers or services), promotional drives, and so on.

Other regulations: local planning, settlement restrictions, requirement of qualifications, price rules or guides, restrictions of unfair competition, monopoly rules, restriction of shopping hours, and so on.

In several countries the overall result is an intricate patchwork that is difficult for most entrepreneurs to grasp, penetrate and utilize effectively. It has become so complicated as to require specialised consultancy services or "subsidiologists". The many rules and regulations have to be administered and controlled; each with its own conditions, restrictions and interpretations. Many regulations are administered locally, by municipalities, where they are subject to varying interpretations.

The necessary procedures require an amount of time, effort, cost, irritation and delay ("transaction and agency costs" in economic parlance) that are often disproportionate to the size of the benefit involved. If all transaction and agency costs were included, they may exceed the benefit. Here also there is an economy of scale as a result of something like "threshold costs".

In the case of state guaranteed loans, for example, a bank will tend to be more interested in relatively large loans for larger firms, because small loans are not or hardly worth the effort involved.

It would be naive and simplistic to suppose that BI could replace all fiscal measures, subsidies and regulations. However, it might serve to replace all those measures that are intended, implicitly or explicitly, to:

- provide a compensation for diseconomies of small scale;
- improve cash flow, liquidity or financial reserves, for the sake of firm continuity or investment;
- provide a subsidiary income or social security for small entrepreneurs or their families;
- encourage the start-up of new business.

This would yield a substantial reduction of complexity, by a method that is simple and direct, does not operate via intermediary institutions, and thus reduces delays and transaction/agency costs.

Solution to the Problem of Unfair Competition from the Informal Economy

Present social security systems labor under the so-called "social security trap" (or "poverty trap"). In most cases, social security recipients must surrender those benefits to the extent that they start to perform paid labor (part- or full-time), or start up a business of their own. For each additional Guilder (Pound, Franc, Mark, Lira, etc.) they earn, they must refund 70% or more to the state (or that amount is deducted from their social security benefit). Under the present system, this must be the case, because otherwise social security plus wage or profit would quickly exceed the minimum wage for full-time labor, even if labor is only part-time.

The problem now is that for those who play the game according to the rules, the incentive to take any initiative for paid work is too slight. As a result, people either do not take any initiative (and are thus "trapped" in their social security) or they break the rules and enter the "informal" or "black" or "underground" economy by earning an additional income illegally, without reporting it to the authorities. Increasingly this informal activity is regarded as justifiable from a social point of view, or even from considerations of general welfare.

The argument is roughly as follows: "considering that there is so much unfulfilled demand for all kinds of services, and that social security recipients do not want to remain idle and want to feel useful, why not let them?". More and more people, including local authorities, find it increasingly difficult to consider and treat such activity as criminal or even unlawful. Some local authorities shut an eye to it, and others do not. Even central governmental authorities have begun to set up schemes that allow for "work with retention of benefits." In the Netherlands there even is a subsidy for starting up new business, that is awarded only to the unemployed. All this is understandable and defensible from a social point of view or even from considerations of general welfare. In any case, whatever one may think of it, it is a trend with a momentum of its own and cannot be stopped.

For small independent entrepreneurs, however, who hang on to marginal businesses by their teeth, so to speak, these developments are quite correctly seen as distorting competition, unjust, demoralizing and as an incitement to also bend the rules or to join the "black" economy. How would you feel if you operated a shop at a virtual loss, and a social security recipient would set up a shop in the same trade next door? It is part of the ethic of many small entrepreneurs to play a straight game, but those who persist are building up grudges and resentment. This may not be very visible, because it is again part of their ethic to mind their own business. But there is more here than meets the eye (or hits the media), and in the long run such resentment may yield political dangers.

BI would provide a solution to both the problem of the social security trap and the problem of unfair competition.

The social security trap would be eliminated since everyone receiving BI is free to obtain an additional income from employment or self-employment. One would, of course, have to pay tax on such additional income, but that would (have to) be less than the present refund percentage of 70 or more for social security recipients. (Preferably the total percentage of income tax plus any other social security contributions, and contributions to the financing of BI, should not exceed 50, and should preferably be no more that about one-third of gross earnings.)

The problem of unfair competition would be solved because *everyone* obtains the BI, including the self-employed. They would no longer have a cause for grudge.

Perhaps this is the most important argument for BI.

Notes

1. The boundaries between small, medium-sized and large enterprise are not the same in all countries. In the Netherlands small business has less than 10 persons engaged, medium-sized business between 10 and 100 persons engaged, and large business more than 100 persons engaged; outside of agriculture, which is treated as a separate category. Thus defined, SME encompasses 99% of all firms and almost 60% of all employment outside government and agriculture.
2. For a seminal publication, see Nooteboom (1982); for a survey of further publications, see Nooteboom (1987).
3. See Nooteboom (1982).
4. Mathematically, the formula of the cost curve in Figure 31.1 is: $h = d + e.q$, where: h = labor hours, d = threshold labor, q = sales size of the shop, e = some coefficient depending, among other things, on the type of trade.

   For labor productivity this yields: $p = \frac{q}{h} = \frac{q}{d + e.q}$ where p = labor productivity in terms of average sales per labor hour.

References

Nooteboom, B. (1982). A New Theory of Retailing Costs. *European Economic Review*, 17, 163–186.

Nooteboom, B. (1987). Threshold Costs in Service Industries. *Service Industries Journal*, 7, 65–76.

Chapter 32

What (If Anything) Can We Learn from the Negative Income Tax Experiments?

Karl Widerquist

Excerpts from Widerquist, K. (2005) A Failure to Communicate: What (If Anything) Can we Learn from the Negative Income Tax Experiments? *Journal of Socio-Economics*, 34 (1), 49–81.[1]

The Experiments

Between 1968 and 1980 five experiments were conducted in the United States and Canada that are known collectively as "the Income Maintenance experiments," "the Guaranteed Income experiments," or "the Negative Income Tax (NIT) experiments." They began at a time when the elimination of poverty was the stated goal of the presidential administration, when there was a growing movement for economic rights, and when many social scientists and policymakers believed that social policy reform was heading in the direction of a Guaranteed Income. But by the time all of the results were available the movement for eliminating poverty had dwindled and the idea of "welfare reform" was beginning to be associated with dismantling rather than rationalizing the welfare system.

The NIT experiments were the first large-scale social experiment to use the scientific method of randomly assigning human subjects into treatment and control groups just as medical researchers do when testing drugs. Some social scientists have called them, "experiments in how to conduct experiments," and it is arguable that they had larger influence on future social experiments than in the examination of the policy they were designed to test.

The primary aim of the NIT experiments was to test the side effects rather than the effects of a basic income guarantee. The central goal of an income support program is to raise the welfare of the destitute, and that it can do that is something that does not need to be tested. Although the effect on poverty of most social policies (AFDC, TANF, EITC, job training, education, etc.) requires testing, the conclusion that an NIT with a guarantee rate at the poverty line can eliminate poverty is true by definition.

The effects of the Negative Income Tax on health, homeownership, low birthweight, school performance, and other indicators of the wellbeing of recipients were tested and

From Widerquist, K. (2005) A Failure to Communicate: What (If Anything) Can We Learn from the Negative Income Tax Experiments? *Journal of Socio-Economics*, 34 (1), 49–81. Reprinted with permission of Elsevier.

Basic Income: An Anthology of Contemporary Research, First Edition. Edited by Karl Widerquist, José A. Noguera, Yannick Vanderborght, and Jurgen De Wispelaere.

reported in many studies (Avrin, 1980; Boumol, 1974, 1977; Bradbury, 1978, 1986; Cain, 1977; Elesh and Lefcowitz, 1977; Hanusheck, 1986; Kaluzny, 1979; Keeley, 1980c, 1980d; Kehrer and Wolin, 1979; Kerachsky, 1977; Knudsen et al., 1977a; Knudsen et al., 1977b; Ladinsky and Wells, 1977; Lefcowitz and Elesh, 1977; Mallar, 1977; Masters, 1978; Maynard, 1977; Metcalf, 1977; Michael, 1978; Middleton and Allen, 1977; Murnane et al., 1981; Nicholson, 1977; O'Connor et al., 1979; Ohls, 1980; Poirier, 1977a, Poirier, 1977b, Poirier, 1977c; Pozdena and Johnson, 1980; Rea, 1977; Robins, 1980b; Rossi, 1975; Thoits and Hannan, 1980; Weiss et al., 1980; Wooldridge, 1977). Most of these studies show positive effects, even for hard-to-change variables such as school performance and low birthweight, but discussion of these effects is beyond the scope of this chapter. For an overview of some of these effects see Levine et al. (2004).

Another side effect, the effect of the experiments on the divorce rate, inspired a large amount of controversy (Bishop, 1980; Cain, 1986; Galligan and Bahr, 1978; Ellwood, 1986; Groeneveld et al., 1980a,b, 1983; Hannan et al., 1977, 1978; Hum and Choudry, 1992; Tuma, 1986), but these findings are also beyond the scope of this chapter. See Hannan and Tuma (1990) and Cain and Wissoker (1990a,b) for two sides of this debate.

Table 32.1 summarizes the basic facts of the five NIT experiments. The first, the New Jersey Graduated Work Incentive Experiment (sometimes called the New Jersey-Pennsylvania Negative Income Tax Experiment or simply the New Jersey Experiment), was conducted from 1968 to 1972. The researchers originally planned to conduct the entire experiment in New Jersey, but they were unable to find enough poor whites there and had to open a second location in Wilkes-Barre, Pennsylvania to round out a racially representative sample. The treatment group originally consisted of 1,216 people and dwindled to 983 (due to drop-outs) by the conclusion of the experiment. The sample size consisted of black, white, and Latino, two-parent families with incomes below 150% of the poverty line, and with a male "head," who was not approaching retirement.[2] Treatment group recipients received a Guaranteed Income for three years.

The Rural Income Maintenance Experiment (RIME) was conducted in rural parts of Iowa and North Carolina from 1970 to 1972. It functioned largely as a rural supplement to the New Jersey Experiment, which focused on an urban population. RIME began with 809 experimental subjects and finished with 729. The treatment group received a Guaranteed Income for two years. Subjects met the same criteria as the New Jersey Experiment except that single-parent, female-headed households were also included. Few, if any, Latinos were included in the sample. Both RIME and the New Jersey Experiment began under the direction of the Office of Economic Opportunity (OEO) and were completed by the Department of Heath, Education, and Welfare when the OEO was abolished.

The largest NIT experiment was the Seattle/Denver Income Maintenance Experiment (SIME/DIME), which had an experimental group of about 4,800 people in the Seattle and Denver metropolitan areas. The sampled included black, white, and Latino, families with at least one dependant and incomes below $11,000 for single-parent families and below $13,000 for two-parent families. The experiment began in 1970 and was originally planned to be completed within six years. Later, researchers obtained approval to extend the experiment for 20 years for a small group of subjects. This would have extended the project into the early 1990s, but it was eventually cancelled in 1980, so that a few subjects had a Guaranteed Income for about nine years, during part of which time they were led to believe they would receive it for 20 years.

The Gary Income Maintenance Experiment (which is never abbreviated) was conducted between 1971 and 1974. Subjects were mostly black, single-parent families living in Gary,

Table 32.1 Summary of the Negative Income Tax experiments in the U.S. and Canada.

Name	*Location(s)*	*Data collection*	*Sample size: initial (final)*	*Sample characteristics*	G*	t**
The New Jersey Graduated Work Incentive Experiment (NJ)	New Jersey and Pennsylvania	1968–1972	1,216 (983)	Black, white, and Latino, two-parent families in urban areas with a male head aged 18–58 and income below 150% of the poverty line	0.5	0.3
					0.75	0.5
					1.00	0.7
					1.25	
The Rural Income-Maintenance Experiment (RIME)	Iowa and North Carolina	1970–1972	809 (729)	Both two-parent families and female-headed households in rural areas with income below 150% of poverty line	0.5	0.3
					0.75	0.5
					1.00	0.7
The Seattle/Denver Income-Maintenance Experiments (SIME/DIME)	Seattle and Denver	1970–1976 (some to 1980)	4,800	Black, white, and Latino families with at least one dependant and incomes below $1,100 for single parents, $13,000 for two parent families	0.75	0.5
					1.26	0.7
					1.48	0.7–0.025y
						0.8–0.025y
The Gary, Indiana Experiment (Gary)	Gary, Indiana	1971–1974	1,799 (967)	Black households, primarily female-headed, head 18–58, income below 240% of poverty line	0.75	0.4
					1.0	0.6
The Manitoba Basic Annual Income Experiment (Mincome)	Winnipeg and Dauphin, Manitoba	1975–1978	1,300	Families with head younger than 58 and income below $13,000 for a family of four	C$3,800	0.35
					C$4,800	0.5
					C$5,800	0.75

Sources: Robins et al. (1980a,b), Ferber and Hirsch (1978) and Hum and Simpson (1993).
*G = the guarantee level.
**t = the marginal tax rate.

Indiana. The experimental group received a Guaranteed Income for three years. It began with a sample size of 1,799 families, which (due to a large drop-out rate) fell to 967 by the end of the experiment.

The Canadian government initiated the Manitoba Basic Annual Income Experiment (Mincome) in 1975 after most of the U.S. experiments were winding down. The sample included 1,300 urban and rural families in Winnipeg and Dauphin, Manitoba with incomes below C$13,000 (Canadian) per year. By the time the data collection was completed in 1978, interest in the Guaranteed Income was seriously on the wane and the Canadian government cancelled the project before the data was analyzed. Fortunately, university-based researchers were eventually able to obtain and analyze the data, so that results are available today (Hum and Simpson, 1991, 1993).

Two parameters are central to the design of any Guaranteed Income. The first is the guarantee level or the minimum income level (*G* in Table 32.1), which is the amount the recipient receives if she has no private income. Theoretically, the guarantee level can be any number between zero and per capita GDP. If *G* is too low, the NIT will not significantly reduce poverty or increase income security, if it is too high, it will have such strong work disincentive effects that the program would be unaffordable. The experiments intended to find out whether a guarantee level sufficient to seriously reduce or even eliminate poverty was feasible. For that reason guarantee levels between 50% and 150% of the poverty line were tested.

The U.S. experiments all defined the guarantee level relative to the poverty line, testing nine different guarantee levels: 0.5 (50% of the poverty level) was tested in the New Jersey and Rural Income Maintenance Experiments; 0.75 was tested in all four of the U.S. experiments; 1.0 (just enough to eliminate official poverty) was tested in all of the U.S. experiments except SIME/DIME; 1.25 was tested only in the New Jersey Experiment, and 1.26 and 1.48 were tested only in SIME/DIME. Mincome, which defined its guarantee level in Canadian dollars rather than relative to the poverty level, tested guarantee levels of C$3,800, C$4,800, and C$5,800 per year. These levels were near the poverty line at the time.

The other central parameter of any Guaranteed Income system is the marginal tax rate (*t* in Table 32.1), also known as the "take-back rate:"[3] the rate at which benefits are reduced as the recipient makes private income.[4] In other words, the marginal tax rate is the effective income tax rate per dollar of private income for recipients of the Negative Income Tax. A higher marginal tax rate is associated with a lower overall tax-cost of program[5] but also with greater work-disincentives, and a greater potential "poverty trap." A lower marginal tax rate is associated with a greater redistribution of income towards people with incomes above the poverty line. Redistribution to this group might be desirable in terms of equity (as a reward for low-wage workers), but to do so would increase the cost of a program primarily conceived as an anti-poverty policy.[6] For these reasons, it is important to know what kinds of take-back rates are feasible and the work-disincentive effects of each. The experimenters tested nine different values of *t*: 0.3 (30%) was tested in the New Jersey and Rural Experiments; 0.35 was tested only in Mincome; 0.4 was tested only in Gary; 0.5 was tested in all of the experiments except Gary; 0.6 was tested only in Gary; 0.7 was tested in the New Jersey Experiment, RIME, and SIME/DIME; 0.75 was tested in Mincome. SIME/DIME tested two nonlinear income functions with marginal tax rates of 0.7 minus 0.025 times income and 0.8 minus 0.025 times income. The effect of these two nonlinear functions was to impose higher marginal tax rates on lower levels of income and lower marginal tax rates on higher levels of income.

The use of so many different rates of *G* and *t*, reduced the numbers of subjects receiving each type of treatment, and therefore reduced the statistical reliability of the results for each. Some of this tradeoff is worthwhile to allow for testing of a greater variety of potential parameters, but the experiments might have benefited from more coordinated effort to test a uniform group of widely spaced parameters.

Table 32.1 summarizes the configuration of the experiments.

The Work-Disincentive Results of the Experiments

Nearly half of the scholarly articles on the Negative Income Tax experiments deal in some way with empirical results for work incentive effects, and many of those present original estimates. Table 32.2 summarizes the findings of several of the studies on the work–effort response to the NIT experiments, giving the difference in hours worked by the experimental group relative to the control group in hours per year and in percentage terms. Results are reported for three categories of workers, husbands, wives, and "single female heads" (SFH).[7] Data was also collected for the work effort of youths, but is omitted from this table in the interest of brevity.[8] The five experiments found a range of work–effort reduction from –0.5% to –9% for husbands, which corresponds to a reduction of about 0.5–4 h per week, 20–130 h per year, or 1–4 fulltime weeks per year. The three studies averaging the results from the four U.S. experiments (Robins, 1985; Burtless, 1986; Keeley, 1981) found work reduction effects of 5%, 7% and 7.9%, respectively.

The response of wives and single mothers was somewhat larger in terms of hours, and substantially larger in percentage terms because they tended to work fewer hours to begin with. Wives reduced their work effort by 0–27% and single mothers reduced their work effort by 15–30%. These percentages correspond to reductions of about 0–166 h per year. The labor market response of wives had a much larger range than the other two groups, but this was usually attributed to the peculiarities of the labor markets in Gary and Winnipeg where particularly small responses were found.

Robins (1985), Robins and West (1980a,b), and Moffitt (1979a) all clearly present their findings as the difference between the labor supply of the treatment group and the control group, which should avoid any confusion with broader labor market findings to anyone who understands the difference, and one would expect everyone who reads technical articles is likely to understand. Others added a simple caveat (Keeley et al., 1978a; Moffitt, 1979b), but some were not as careful to avoid confusion. Orcutt and Orcutt (1968) claimed that the experiments could produce unbiased estimates of the disincentive effects and earnings effects of an NIT, when the lack of a demand response clearly makes this impossible (Browning, 1971). Ferber and Hirsch (1978, p. 1385) referring to the "labor supply response" as the "labor market response" despite explaining the difference later in the article. Kelly and Singer (1971) write, "No experiment paper should be complete without mention of possible response bias," but do not mention the experiment's inability to measure demand response as a source of bias. West (1980, p. 642) mentions three ways NIT can affect wages without mentioning the demand response. Most of these slips are small, but the omission of demand is more significant when researchers attempt to carry the results over to the cost of a national program.

Table 32.3 reports some of the labor market findings other than the simple difference between the hours worked by the treatment and control groups. Robins et al. (1980a) and Robins et al. (1980b) and Tuma and Robins (1980) found that the percentages are much larger if labor response is considered in terms of the increase in the length of spells out of work or the rate at which people who aren't working return to employment. These results

Table 32.2 Summary of Findings of Work Reduction Effect.

Study	*Data source*	*Work reduction* in hours per year** and percent*			*Comments and caveats*
		Husbands	*Wives*	*SFH*	
Robins (1985)	4 U.S.	−89	−117	−123	Study of studies that does not assess the methodology of the studies but simply combines their estimates. Finds large consistency throughout, and "In no case is there evidence of a massive withdrawal from the labor force." No assessment of whether the work response is large or small or its effect on cost. Estimates apply to a poverty-line guarantee rate with a marginal tax rate of 50%.
		−5%	−21.1%	−13.2%	
Burtlcss (1986)	4 U.S.	−119	−93	−79	Average of results of the four US experiments weighted by sample size, except for the SFH estimates, which are a weighted average of the SIME/DIME and Gary results only.
		−7%	−17%	−7%	
Keeley (1981)	4 U.S.	−7.9%			A simple average of the estimates of 16 studies of the four U.S. experiments.
Robins and West (1980a)	SIME/ DIME	−128.9	−165.9	−147.1	Estimates "labor supply effects." It goes without saying that this is different from "labor market effects."
		−7%	−25%	−15%	
Robins and West (1980b)	SIME/ DIME	−9%	−20%	−25%	Recipients take 2.4 years to fully adjust their behavior to the new program.
Cain et al. (1974)	NJ	–	−50	–	Includes caveats about the limited duration of the test and the representativeness of the sample. Notes that the evidence shows a smaller effect than nonexperimental studies.
			−20%		
Watts et al. (1974)	NJ	−1.4% to −6.6%	–	–	Depending on size of *G* and *t*.
Rees and Watts (1975)	NJ	−1.5 hpw**	−0.61%	–	Found anomalous positive effect on hours and earnings of blacks.
		−0.5%			

(*Continued*)

Table 32.2 (*Continued*)

Study	*Data source*	*Work reduction* in hours per year** and percent*			*Comments and caveats*
		Husbands	*Wives*	*SFH*	
Ashenfelter (1978)	RIME	–8%	–27%	–	"There must be serious doubt about the implications of the experimental results for the adoption of any permanent Negative Income Tax program."
Moffitt (1979a)	Gary	–3% to –6%	0%	–26% to –30%	No caveat about missing demand, but careful not to imply the results mean more than they do.
Hum and Simpson (1993)	Mincome	–17	–15	–133	Smaller response to the Canadian experiment was not surprising because of the make-up of the sample and the treatments offered.
		–1%	–3%	–17%	

*The negative signs indicate that the change in work effort is a reduction; **hours per year except where indicated "hpw," hours per week. NJ, New Jersey Graduated Work Incentive Experiment; SIME/DIME, Seattle/Denver Income Maintenance Experiment; Gary, Gary Income Maintenance Experiment; RIME, Rural Income Maintenance Experiment; Mincome, Manitoba Income Maintenance Experiment; SFH, single female "head of household".

largely reflect the fact that the reduction in labor hours was not primarily caused by workers reducing their hours of work each week but by remaining nonemployed longer if and when they became nonemployed. Increased periods of nonemployment might have an efficiency benefit if they lead to better matches between workers and firms.

Several studies estimating the additional tax cost caused by the work–effort response found widely divergent results. Rees and Watts (1975) estimated it would add 5–10% to the tax cost of the program. Ashenfelter (1978) estimated that the cost of the program without labor market effects would be 78% of cost with labor market effects, which is equivalent to saying that the reduction in work effort would increase the tax cost of the program by 28%. Keeley et al. (1978a) estimated that the labor supply response would account for 23–55% of total program costs (equivalent to an increase of 30–122%). Burtless (1986) estimated that work disincentive would nearly triple the tax cost of the program. All of these studies neglect the demand response, implicitly assuming that demand is completely elastic. Rees and Watts's conclusion is that the costs are small and so they apparently don't think it necessary to say that a demand response might make the costs even smaller. Only Keeley et al. (1978a,b) explicitly make the assumption of perfectly elastic demand. They admit that this reduces the accuracy of the results, and justify the assumption by speculating that employers could easily replace NIT recipients with workers who are not covered by the program.

Most of the studies that did include a demand response used data from the NIT experiments to examine particular changes in policy such as Carter's Program for Better Jobs

Table 32.3 Labor Market Findings Other than Simple Work Effort Reduction.

Study	*Data source*	*Findings*	*Comments and caveats*
Robins et al. (1980a,b)	SIME/DIME	Increase in length of spells out of employment: husbands: 9.4 weeks, 27%; wives: 50 weeks, 42%; single females: 56 weeks, 60%	The experimental group was somewhat more likely to leave employment and substantially more likely to remain nonemployed for longer spells than the control group.
Tuma and Robins (1980)	SIME/DIME	Change in rate of entering employment: husbands: −22.2, wives: −39.6, single female heads: −35.4	Conditional having become nonemployed. This reflects the fact that the labor-hours reductions were attributable more to longer spells of unemployment than to reductions in weekly hours of work.
Hall (1975)	NJ	Opt out rate: 125-50 plan: 13%; 100-50 plan: 25%; 50-50 plan: 94%	These are the percentages of participants in the study who received no benefits. But the results depend substantially on the participants, pre-experimental income.
Robins (1984)	SIME/DIME	Does not find evidence that 3-year and 5-year studies were biased relative to the response of the 20-year treatment group.	The available evidence is limited.
Cogan (1983)	NJ	Husbands reduce labor effort by −5 to −7 h per week, conditional on participation	This estimate was only for the sub-sample that actually received payments and so is not directly comparable to the estimates of labor response in Table 32.2.
Moffitt (1979b)	Gary	Eligible low income population: −4.5%	Simulation model, does not take demand into account, but warns, "Assuming the labor-supply curve is forward-sloping, which it probably is at low age rates, the experimental estimates over-state the final impact on employment (due to a demand response)."
		Total population: −1.6% The effect of an NIT on labor supply could be offset by unemployed workers if there is sufficient slack in the labor market.	

(*Continued*)

Table 32.3 (*Continued*)

Study	*Data source*	*Findings*	*Comments and caveats*
Keeley et al. (1978b)	SIME/DIME	Predicted labor supply response of a national program: husbands: –5.3%, wives: –22.0%, SFH: –11.2%	Applies the experimental parameters for labor supply functions to a national database to obtain estimates of the nationwide aggregate labor effect and so these findings are not directly comparable to those in Table 32.2. Finds that the results vary wide with the generosity of the program.
Greenberg (1983)	SIME/DIME	Response of the demand for labor had a small mitigating effect on hours.	Results depended on assumptions on the level of unemployment and the elasticities of demand and supply of labor and the substitutability and availability of workers making similar wages to those eligible for NIT.
Keeley et al. (1978a)	SIME/DIME	Labor Supply response accounts for 23–55% of programs with a positive net cost. That is, cost before labor supply response is 45–77% of total cost.	Range depends on the size of G and t. Justifies the assumption of perfectly elastic demand on employers' ability to substitute high-wage, high-skilled workers for workers who are likely to be affected by an NIT.
Robins (1980a)	SIME/DIME	Replacement of the 1974 welfare system with an NIT would have cost an additional \$2.2 billion to \$30 billion (\$55 to \$97 in 2004 dollars). The work–effort response would add \$0.2 to \$7.0 billion (\$0.6 to \$23 in 2004 dollars) to cost.	Range of responses depends on the size of G and t. Demand response not included.
Rees and Watts (1975)	NJ	Increase tax cost due to supply response: 5–10%	Demand response not included.
Ashenfelter (1978)	RIME	Estimates that the cost before the labor supply response would be only 78% of the cost after the labor supply response.	Demand response not included. Findings could be restated to say that the work–effort response adds 28% to the transfer cost.
Burtless (1986)	4 U.S.	\$3 in transfers raises the income of recipients by only \$1. Poverty among all families with children could be eliminated for an additional cost of \$61 billion (\$98 in 2004 dollars).	Demand response not included.
Maxfield (1980)	SIME/DIME	Labor supply response is highly correlated to the generosity of the NIT program.	Demand response not included.
Bishop (1979)	SIME/DIME	"Reduction in labor supply produced by these programs does tend to raise low-skill wages, and this improves transfer efficiency."	General equilibrium model focusing on efficiency effects, and so results are not directly comparable to those focusing on tax cost. Results are sensitive to assumptions.

and Income (Betson et al., 1980a,b; Betson and Greenberg, 1983), and so are not very useful for correcting cost estimates of an NIT for demand responses. Only Greenberg (1983) applied a microsimulation model with a demand effect to the cost of an NIT as examined in the experiments. He found that a wage response could slightly mitigate the effect on hours and costs but the general pattern remained in which a dollar spent on poverty reduction raises the incomes of the poor by less than a dollar,[9] but his results are tentative because they depended on assumptions about the elasticity of demand, the level of unemployment and the substitutability between NIT recipients and other workers (Greenberg, 1983). Bishop (1979) used a general equilibrium framework to examine the impact of several antipoverty programs including NIT on efficiency. The focus on efficiency rather than tax cost means that his results are not directly comparable to the others, but he finds that the NIT would produce a demand response that would increase wages and therefore it would reduce both the efficiency loss and the tax cost of the program. Unfortunately, there do not seem to be any articles employing a demand response in otherwise comparable models that generate comparable estimates of tax cost, hours worked, efficiency lost, and impact on inequality.

Notes

1. Editor's note: These excerpts were modified slightly from the original by the author.
2. Husbands were usually the primary income earners in a family, and researchers tended to describe this role with the status-implying term "head of household." Women could not be "heads" unless they lived with children and without a husband.
3. The practical working of the marginal tax rate is slightly different if the Guaranteed Income is administered as a Basic Income rather than as a Negative Income Tax.
4. Private income could include interest, dividends, capital gains, etc. But for the participants in these experiments it was overwhelmingly wage income.
5. Higher marginal tax rates could be associated with higher taxes costs if the supply of labor had a very high elasticity of substitution, but this was not expected and did not prove true in any of the experiments.
6. The Basic Income movement today puts less stress on the issue of poverty reduction and more stress on broader equity goals that make the issue of spending money on those already above the poverty line less important.
7. Meaning women with children and no husband.
8. Youths tended to have work-effort responses comparable in percentage terms to wives and single mothers. It was not correlated with an increase in school attendance, but was correlated with an improvement in school performance.
9. Personal correspondence.

References

Ashenfelter, O. (1978). The labor supply response of wage earners. In J.L. Palmer and J.A. Pechman (eds) *Welfare in Rural Areas*. Brookings Institution, Washington, DC.

Avrin, M.E. (1980). Utilization of subsidized housing. In P.K. Robins, R.G. Spiegelman, S. Weiner, and J.G. Bell (eds) *A Guaranteed Annual Income: Evidence from a Social Experiment*. Academic Press, New York.

Betson, D. and Greenberg, D. (1983). Uses of microsimulation in applied poverty research. In R. Goldstein and S.M. Sacks (eds) *Applied Policy Research*. Rowman and Allanheld, Totowa, NJ.

Betson, D., Greenburg, D., and Kasten, R. (1980a). A microsimulation model for analyzing alternative welfare reform proposals: an application to the program for better jobs and income. In R. Haveman and K. Hollenbeck (eds) *Microeonomic Simulation Models for Public Policy Analysis*, vol. 1. Academic Press, New York.

Betson, D., Greenburg, D., and Kasten, R. (1980b). Using labor supply results to simulate welfare reform alternatives. In P.K. Robins, R.G. Spiegelman, S. Weiner, and J.G. Bell (eds) *A Guaranteed Annual Income: Evidence from a Social Experiment*. Academic Press, New York.

Bishop, J.H. (1979). The general equilibrium impact of alternative antipoverty strategies. *Industrial and Labor Relations Review*, 32 (2), 205–223.

Bishop, J.H. (1980). Jobs, cash transfers, and marital instability: a review and synthesis of the evidence. *Journal of Human Resources*, 15 (3).

Boumol, W. (1974). An overview of the results on consumption, health, and social behavior. *Journal of Human Resources*, 9 (2), 253–264.

Boumol, W. (1977). An overview of the results. In H.W. Watts and A. Rees (eds) *The New Jersey Income-Maintenance Experiment, vol. III: The Impact on Expenditures, Health, and Social Behavior, and the Quality of the Evidence*. Academic Press, New York, pp. 1–14.

Bradbury, K.L. (1978). Income maintenance alternatives and family composition: an analysis of price effects. *Journal of Human Resources*, 13 (3), 305–331.

Bradbury, K.L. (1986). Discussion (of "Non-labor supply responses to the income maintenance experiments"). In A.H. Munnell (ed.) *Lessons from the Income Maintenance Experiments*. Federal Reserve Bank of Boston, Boston, pp. 122–125.

Browning, E.K. (1971). Incentive and disincentive experimentation for income maintenance policy purposes: note. *American Economic Review*, 61, 709–712.

Burtless, G. (1986). The work response to a guaranteed income. A survey of experimental evidence. In A.H. Munnell (ed.) *Lessons from the Income Maintenance Experiments*. Federal Reserve Bank of Boston, Boston.

Cain, G.C. (1977). Fertility behavior. In H.W. Watts and A. Rees (eds) *The New Jersey Income-Maintenance Experiment, vol. III: The Impact on Expenditures, Health, and Social Behavior, and the Quality of the Evidence*. Academic Press, New York, pp. 225–250.

Cain, G.C. (1986). The income maintenance experiments and the issues of marital stability and family composition and the income maintenance experiments. In A.H. Munnell (ed.) *Lessons from the Income Maintenance Experiments*. Federal Reserve Bank of Boston, Boston, pp. 60–93.

Cain, G.C., Nicholson, W., Mallar, C., and Wooldridge, J. (1974). The labor-supply response of married women, husbands present. *Journal of Human Resources*, 9 (2), 201–223.

Cain, G.C. and Wissoker, D. (1990a). A reanalysis of marital stability in SIME/DIME. *American Journal of Sociology*, 95 (5), 1235–1269.

Cain, G.C. and Wissoker, D. (1990b). Response to Hannan and Tuma. *American Journal of Sociology*, 95 (5), 1299–1314.

Cogan, J.F. (1983). Labor supply and negative income taxation: new evidence from the New Jersey-Pennsylvania experiment. *Economic Inquiry*, 21 (4), 465–484.

Elesh, D. and Lefcowitz, M.J. (1977). The effects of health on the supply of and returns to labor. In H.W. Watts and A. Rees (eds) *The New Jersey Income-Maintenance Experiment, vol. II: Labor-supply Responses*. Academic Press, New York, pp. 289–320.

Ellwood, D.T. (1986). Discussion (of "The issues of marital stability"). In A. Munnell (ed.) *Lessons from the Income Maintenance Experiments*. The Federal Reserve Bank of Boston, Boston, pp. 94–98.

Ferber, R. and Hirsch, W. (1978). Social experimentation and economic policy: a survey. *Journal of Economic Literature*, 16, 1379–1414.

Galligan, R.J. and Bahr, S.J. (1978). Economic well-being and marital stability: implications for income maintenance programs. *Journal of Marriage and the Family*, 283–290.

Greenberg, D.H. (1983). Some labor market effects of labor supply responses to transfer programs. *Social-Economic Planning Sciences*, 17 (4), 141–151.

Groeneveld, L., Tuma, N., and Hannan, M. (1980a). The effects of negative income tax programs on marital dissolution. *Journal of Human Resources*, 15, 654–674.

Groeneveld, L., Tuma, N., and Hannan, M. (1980b). Marital dissolution and remarriage. In P.K. Robins, R.G. Spiegelman, S. Weiner, and J.G. Bell (eds) *A Guaranteed Annual Income: Evidence from a Social Experiment*. Academic Press, New York.

Groeneveld, L., Tuma, N., and Hannan, M. (1983). Marital Stability. In D.L. Bawden and W.S. Harrar (eds) *Final Report of the Seattle–Denver Income Maintenance Experiment, vol. 1: Design and Results*. SRI International, Menlo Park, CA, pp. 257–387.

Hall, R. (1975). Effects of the experimental negative income tax on labor supply. In J.A. Pechman and P.M. Timpane (eds) *Work Incentives and Income Guarantees: The New Jersey Negative Income Tax Experiment*. Brookings Institution, Washington, DC, pp. 115–147.

Hannan, M. and Tuma, N. (1990). A reassessment of the effects of income maintenance on marital dissolution in the Seattle–Denver experiment. *American Journal of Sociology*, 95, 1270–1298.

Hannan, M., Tuma, N., and Groenveld, L. (1977). Income and marital events: evidence from an income-maintenance experiment. *American Journal of Sociology*, 82 (6), 1186–1211.

Hannan, M., Tuma, N., and Groenveld, L. (1978). Income and independence effects on marital dissolution: results from the Seattle and Denver income-maintenance experiments. *American Journal of Sociology*, 84 (3), 611– 633.

Hanusheck, E. (1986). Non-labor-supply response to the income maintenance experiments. In A. Munnell (ed.) *Lessons from the Income Maintenance Experiments*. The Federal Reserve Bank of Boston, Boston, pp. 106–121.

Hum, D. and Choudry, S. (1992). Income, work and marital dissolution: Canadian experimental evidence. *Journal of Comparative Family Studies*, 23 (2), 249–265.

Hum, D. and Simpson, W. (1991). *Income Maintenance, Work Effort, and the Canadian Experiment*. Economic Council of Canada, Ottawa.

Hum, D. and Simpson, W. (1993). Economic response to a guaranteed annual income: experience from Canada and the United States. *Journal of Labor Economics*, 11 (1 (part 2)), S263–S296.

Kaluzny, R.L. (1979). Changes in the consumption of housing services: the Gary Experiment. *Journal of Human Resources*, 14 (4), 496–506.

Keeley, M.C. (1980a). The effects of negative income tax on migration. *Journal of Human Resources*, 15, 695–706.

Keeley, M.C. (1980b). The effects of negative income tax programs on fertility. *Journal of Human Resources*, 15, 675–694.

Keeley, M.C. (1981). *Labor Supply and Public Policy: A Critical Review*. Academic Press, New York.

Keeley, M.C., Robins, P., Spiegelman, R. and West, R. (1978a). The labor supply effects and costs of alternative negative income tax programs. *Journal of Human Resources*, 13 (1), 3–36.

Keeley, M.C., Robins, P., Spiegelman, R. And West, R. (1978b). The estimation of labor supply models using experimental data. *American Economic Review*, 68, 873–887.

Kelly, T.F. and Singer, L. (1971). The Gary Income Maintenance Experiment: plans and progress. *American Economic Review*, 61, 30–42.

Knudsen, J.H., Mamer, J., Scott, R.A., and Shore, A.R. (1977a). Information levels and labor response. In H.W. Watts and A. Rees (eds) *The New Jersey Income-Maintenance Experiment, vol. II: Labor-supply Responses*. Academic Press, New York, pp. 347–368.

Knudsen, J.H., Scott, R.A., and Shore, A.R. (1977b). Household consumption. In H.W. Watts and A. Rees (eds) *The New Jersey Income-Maintenance Experiment, vol. III: The Impact on Expenditures, Health, and Social Behavior, and the Quality of the Evidence*. Academic Press, New York, pp. 251–276.

Ladinsky, J. and Wells, A. (1977). Social integration, leisure activity, media exposure, and lifestyle enhancement. In H.W. Watts and A. Rees (eds) *The New Jersey Income-Maintenance Experiment, vol. III: The Impact on Expenditures, Health, and Social Behavior, and the Quality of the Evidence*. Academic Press, New York, pp. 195–224.

Lefcowitz, M.J. and Elesh, D. (1977). Health and medical care utilization. In H.W. Watts and A. Rees (eds) *The New Jersey Income-Maintenance Experiment, vol. III: The Impact on Expenditures, Health, and Social Behavior, and the Quality of the Evidence.* Academic Press, New York, pp. 113–128.

Levine, R., Watts, H., Hollister, R. et al. (2004). Looking back at the negative income tax experiments from 30 years on. In M. Lewis, S. Pressman, and K. Widerquist (eds) *The Ethics and Economics of the Basic Income Guarantee.* Ashgate, New York.

Mallar, C.D. (1977). The educational and labor-supply responses of young adults in experimental families. In H.W. Watts and A. Rees (eds) *The New Jersey Income-Maintenance Experiment, vol. II: Labor-supply Responses.* Academic Press, New York, pp. 163–184.

Masters, S.H. (1978). Comments on Robert Michael: the consumption studies. In J. Palmer and J. Pechman (eds) *Welfare in Rural Areas: The North Carolina–Iowa Income Maintenance Experiment.* Brookings Institution, Washington, DC, pp. 171–173.

Maxfield Jr., M. (1980). Aspects of a negative income tax: program cost, adequacy of support, and induced labor supply reduction. In R. Haveman and K. Hollenbeck (eds) *Microsimulation Models for Public Policy Research.* Academic Press, New York.

Maynard, R. (1977). The effects of the Rural Income Maintenance Experiment on the school performance of children. *American Economic Review*, 67 (1), 370–375.

Metcalf, C. (1977). Sample design and the use of experimental data. In H.W. Watts and A. Rees (eds) *The New Jersey Income-Maintenance Experiment, vol. III: The Impact on Expenditures, Health, and Social Behavior, and the Quality of the Evidence.* Academic Press, New York, pp. 413–440.

Michael, R. (1978). The consumption studies. In J. Palmer and J. Pechman (eds) *Welfare in Rural Areas: The North Carolina–Iowa Income Maintenance Experiment.* Brookings Institution, Washington, DC, pp. 149–171.

Middleton, R. and Allen, V.L. (1977). Social psychological effects. In H.W. Watts and A. Rees (eds) *The New Jersey Income-Maintenance Experiment, vol. III: The Impact on Expenditures, Health, and Social Behavior, and the Quality of the Evidence.* Academic Press, New York, pp. 151–194.

Moffitt, R.A. (1979a). The labor supply response in the Gary Experiment. *Journal of Human Resources*, 14 (4), 477–487.

Moffitt, R.A. (1979b). The labor market replacement effect of a negative income tax. *Industrial and Labor Relations Review*, 33 (1), 85–94.

Murnane, R., Maynard, R., and Ohls, J. (1981). Home Resources and Children's Achievement. *The Review of Economics and Statistics*, 63 (3), 369–377.

Nicholson, W. (1977). Expenditure patterns: a descriptive survey. In H.W. Watts and A. Rees (eds) *The New Jersey Income-Maintenance Experiment, vol. III: The Impact on Expenditures, Health, and Social Behavior, and the Quality of the Evidence.* Academic Press, New York, pp. 15–44.

O'Connor, J., Madden, F., and Madden, J.P. (1979). The negative income tax and the quality of dietary intake. *Journal of Human Resources*, 14 (4), 507–517.

Ohls, J. (1980). The demand for housing under a negative income tax. In E. Stromsdorfer and G. Farkas (eds) *Evaluation Studies Review Annual*, vol. 5, p. 502.

Orcutt, G. and Orcutt, A. (1968). Incentive and disincentive experimentation for income maintenance policy purposes. *American Economic Review*, 58, 754–772.

Poirier, D.J. (1977a). Characteristics of attriters who took the attrition interview. In H.W. Watts and A. Rees (eds) *The New Jersey Income-Maintenance Experiment, vol. III: The Impact on Expenditures, Health, and Social Behavior, and the Quality of the Evidence.* Academic Press, New York, pp. 399–412.

Poirier, D.J. (1977b). Spline functions and their applications in regression analysis. In H.W. Watts and A. Rees (eds) *The New Jersey Income-Maintenance Experiment, vol. II: Labor-Supply Responses.* Academic Press, New York, pp. 369–382.

Poirier, D.J. (1977c). The determinants of home buying. In H.W. Watts and A. Rees (eds) *The New Jersey Income-Maintenance Experiment, vol. III: The Impact on Expenditures, Health, and Social Behavior, and the Quality of the Evidence*. Academic Press, New York.

Pozdena, R.J. and Johnson, T.R. (1980). Demand for assets. In P.K. Robins, R.G. Spiegelman, S. Weiner, and J.G. Bell (eds) *A Guaranteed Annual Income: Evidence from a Social Experiment*. Academic Press, New York.

Rea Jr., S.A. (1977). Investment in human capital under a negative income tax. *Canadian Journal of Economics*, 10 (4), 607–620.

Rees, A. and Watts, H.W. (1975). An overview of the labor supply results. In J.A. Pechman and P.M. Timpane (eds) *Work Incentives and Income Guarantees: The New Jersey Negative Income Tax Experiment*. Brookings Institution, Washington, DC.

Robins, P.K. (1980a). Labor supply response of family heads and implications for a national program. In P.K. Robins, R.G. Spiegelman, S. Weiner, and J.G. Bell (eds) *A Guaranteed Annual Income: Evidence from a Social Experiment*. Academic Press, New York.

Robins, P.K. (1980b). Job satisfaction. In P.K. Robins, R.G. Spiegelman, S. Weiner, and J.G. Bell (eds) *A Guaranteed Annual Income: Evidence from a Social Experiment*. Academic Press, New York.

Robins, P.K. (1984). The labor supply response of twenty-year families in the Denver Income Maintenance Experiment. *Review of Economics and Statistics*, 66 (3), 491–495.

Robins, P.K. (1985). A comparison of the labor supply findings from the four negative income tax experiments. *Journal of Human Resources*, 20 (4), 567–582.

Robins, P.K., Brandon, N., and Yeager, K.E. (1980a). Effects of SIME/DIME on changes in employment status. *The Journal of Human Resources*, 15 (4), 545–573.

Robins, P.K., Spiegelman, R.G., Weiner, S., and Bell, J.G. (eds) (1980b). *A Guaranteed Annual Income: Evidence from a Social Experiment*. Academic Press, New York.

Robins, P.K. and West, R. (1980a). Program participation and labor-supply response. *The Journal of Human Resources*, 15 (4), 499–523.

Robins, P.K. and West, R. (1980b). Labor-supply response over time. *The Journal of Human Resources*, 15 (4), 524–544.

Rossi, P.H. (1975). A critical review of the analysis of nonlabor force responses. In J.A. Pechman and P.M. Timpane (eds) *Work Incentives and Income Guarantees: The NewJersey Negative Income Tax Experiment*. Brookings Institution, Washington, DC.

Thoits, P. and Hannan, M.T. (1980). Income and psychological distress. In P.K. Robins, R.G. Spiegelman, S. Weiner, and J.G. Bell (eds) *A Guaranteed Annual Income: Evidence from a Social Experiment*. Academic Press, New York.

Tuma, N.B. (1986). Discussion (of "The issues of marital stability"). In A. Munnell (ed.) *Lessons from the Income Maintenance Experiments*. The Federal Reserve Bank of Boston, Boston, pp. 99–105.

Tuma, N.B. and Robins, P.K. (1980). A dynamic model of employment behavior: an application to the Seattle and Denver Income Maintenance Experiments. *Econometrica*, 48 (4), 1031–1052.

Watts, H.W., Avery, R., Elesh, D. et al. (1974). The labor-supply response of husbands. *Journal of Human Resources*, 9 (2), 181–200.

Weiss, Y., Hall, A., and Dong, F. (1980). The effect of price and income on investment in schooling. *Journal of Human Resources*, 15, 611–640.

West, R. (1980). Effects on wage rates: an interim analysis. *Journal of Human Resources*, 15, 641–653.

Wooldridge, J. (1977). Housing consumption. In H.W. Watts and A. Rees (eds) *The New Jersey Income-Maintenance Experiment, vol. III: The Impact on Expenditures, Health, and Social Behavior, and the Quality of the Evidence*. Academic Press, New York, pp. 45–72.

Chapter 33

Efficiency and Participation: The Basic Income Approach

Bill Jordan

Excerpts from Jordan, B. (1994). Efficiency, Justice and the Obligations of Citizenship. In J. Ferris and R. Page (eds) *Social Policy in Transition: Anglo-German Perspectives in the New European Community*. Avebury (Ashgate), Aldershot.

Efficiency and Participation

I want to take a critical look at the first part of the case against Unconditional Basic Incomes – that it would be inefficient, in purely economic terms, to allow employment to be elective. This argument rests on the notion that the universal provision of subsistence incomes would alter incentives in such a way as to make low-paid work – especially arduous, unpleasant, dangerous or monotonous work – less attractive than at present, and hence reduce the efficiency of the economy.

As it is stated, the argument usually focuses on low-productivity, low-wage work, rather than on the more efficient parts of production. This is not surprising, since employment in higher-paid work is – as Mead for one acknowledges (1986, p. 69) – already largely elective. Most high-status, high-productivity occupations offer generous early retirement schemes and voluntary redundancy terms to regular employees, and it is common for workers at the height of their powers to take advantage of these inducements. Furthermore, high-skill, high state training investment, or even indispensability for national prosperity are not seen as morally obliging their possessors to contribute to the national economy: nuclear physicists who take jobs abroad, resign to take up arts and crafts, or experience a monastic vocation are not criticized for turning their backs on their duties as citizens. Perversely it is those who have least to offer in terms of efficiency – whose participation is likely to lower rather than raise average labor productivity in the economy – who are the focus of concern over dependency and free-riding. Philosophers and politicians alike upbraid them for their hypothetical reluctance to serve in MacDonalds, or act as kissagram deliverers, house-plant watchers, or any of the burgeoning new menial occupations of the post-industrial economy.

There are several ironies in the rise of concern about conditionality and dependence. Insofar as the pioneers of the linkages between state benefits and citizenship obligations

From Jordan, B. (1994). Efficiency, Justice and the Obligations of Citizenship. In J. Ferris and R. Page (eds) *Social Policy in Transition: Anglo-German Perspectives in the New European Community*. Avebury (Ashgate), Aldershot, UK, pp. 109–113. Reprinted with permission of Ashgate, Gower and Lund Humphries Publishing.

Basic Income: An Anthology of Contemporary Research, First Edition. Edited by Karl Widerquist, José A. Noguera, Yannick Vanderborght, and Jurgen De Wispelaere.

are the same market-minded economists who during the 1980s favored the "shake-out" of inefficient unproductive workers from state-subsidized industries, it is ironic that they should now be happy to have the state pay bonuses to employers prepared to take an unwilling claimant from the dole queue for something called "employment training". It is doubly ironic that these problems over incentives arise most acutely in precisely the kind of economic environment favored by such market-minded enthusiasts (Minford with Ashton et al., 1985) – a fragmented, casualized labor market, free from restrictions such as minimum wages, with lots of temporary, sub-contract and part-time employment and self-employment, and a "targeted" benefits system, means-tested and with support being withdrawn as earnings increase. In such an environment, the "unemployment trap" operates strongly because of the insecurity as well as the inadequacy of earnings, and because of the delays and inefficiency associated with reclaiming (because of deterently complex procedures – Jordan et al., 1992); and the "poverty trap" operates strongly because of the simultaneous impact of income taxation and benefit withdrawal (Parker, 1989). This is the situation in Britain after the great experiment in market economics conducted by the Thatcher government; it is difficult to see how modest unconditional benefits could make it worse than it is now – at least in terms of the overall pattern. Clearly it would have to justify itself in terms of fairness at the micro-level.

The doubts over efficiency and unconditionality experienced in Germany, France and elsewhere in Western Europe have rather different origins. Benefit conditions and benefit levels are far more closely linked to employment and earnings than in Britain. In Germany and the Netherlands, for example, earnings-related unemployment benefits keep better-paid workers above the poverty line when they are unemployed, and the linkage between employment and the level of benefits is therefore quite explicit. Hence anxiety over unconditionality is tied in with anxiety over the adequacy of protection. A Basic Income might be better for lone parents and some low-paid workers, but not for those who get rather generous social insurance protection through contributions out of higher earnings. Break that link, and the whole structure of differentials, incentives and protection might crumble, along with efficiency and the high-earnings, high-productivity orientation of the workforce. The Netherlands and Belgium – and even France – seem willing to accept some structural unemployment as the price of this system.

However, to take a longer-term view of the social policy issues, it is important to assess what levels of participation are optimal for efficiency in the kinds of economy which will charactierize this decade and the next century. Throughout the 1970s and 1980s, the trends worldwide have been towards lower rates of participation among men of "working age," and higher among women; increased part-time and irregular (short-term) employment and self-employment; and – in the advanced capitalist countries – declining industrial and growing service employment (Standing, 1986). Beyond these generalizatsions, it is extremely difficult to perceive any reliable correlations between participation rates and economic efficiency. The economies with the highest participation rates for men and women have been the Soviet Union and the Eastern European countries: although they performed modestly well until the 1970s, they are now branded as monuments to inefficiency and low productivity. Two other economies with high participation rates, the United States and Britain, have also performed rather badly in this period, though Britain (not the United States) achieved very rapid productivity growth during the early 1980s, by reducing participation and creating high levels of unemployment (International Labour Office, 1990, pp. 27 and 42). Sweden and Denmark have high participation rates and are prosperous and efficient; but so is Norway, which has lower participation rates (International Labour Office, 1990, pp. 35, 40 and 42). The Netherlands has a very low rate of participation, and is a relatively successful economy: much the same is true of Canada (International Labour Office, 1990, pp. 21 and 39). The most successful economies of the 1970s and 1980s, Japan and West Germany, had participation rates around the average (International Labour Office, 1990, pp. 31 and 37) – similar to those of Austria, Australia and Hong Kong. In the rest of the world, some of the richest countries had low participation rates (Kuwait, Libya) and some of the poorest had high participation rates (Vietnam, Thailand, Mali).

As Gosta Esping-Andersen has pointed out, welfare state regimes have influenced the structure of labor markets and participation. In the Scandinavian countries, the social insurance system favors maximization of labor supply: older males stay in employment, and participation rates for women are very high (Esping-Andersen, 1990, p. 159). By contrast, welfare state regimes in Germany, the Netherlands, Italy and France encourage early exit from the labor market. In Germany particularly, social policies act against the growth of service employment, and favor high-productivity industrial employment (Esping-Andersen, 1990, p. 224). This leads to high rates of early retirement for male workers, and "a growing population of pensioners and non-actives" (Esping-Andersen, 1990, p. 224).

Hence there is no obvious reason why participation *per se* should be linked with efficiency, one way or the other. This is not very surprising, since economies are complex and varied. Germany's success has rested on sustaining high-wage, high-tech, high-value-added industrial employment (its proportion of manufacturing employment is far higher than any other advanced capitalist country's). Japan's has been achieved by the successful meshing of the two sectors in a dualized economy, with highly differentiated terms of employment and rates of productivity. But these are certainly not the only paths to success. Sweden has until recently succeeded in sustaining high-wage, high-productivity industrial employment and expanding high-wage public service employment. And pre-invasion Kuwait used its oil riches to offer every male Kuwaiti a civil service post, and used foreigners to do its industrial work and provide its services.

Similarly, there are no clear correlations between economic efficiency and "dependency rates" (i.e. numbers claiming from the state's benefits systems) or proportions of GNP spent on income maintenance. In general, the trend in the 1970s and 1980s has been for the numbers of claimants of unemployment benefit (or public assistance on account of unemployment) to rise; but there has also been a much less publicized and equally significant increase in numbers claiming by virtue of invalidity (Department of Social Security, 1989; Netherlands Scientific Council for Government Policy, 1985). Governments committed to reducing the unemployment statistics (such as Britain's in the late 1980s) have often been assiduous in driving up the numbers of invalids, or promoting early retirement (as in West Germany) – in effect reclassifying the unemployed so as to exclude them permanently from economic participation. Some successful economies – West Germany, Denmark – have spent high proportions of GNP on social protection, others – Japan, Hong Kong – have spent very low proportions. Where there is a strong case for caution in considering any radical proposal for changing an existing system of income maintenance (whether it is strongly employment- and earnings-related like Germany's, or income-tested and "targeted" like Britain's) is over possible sudden large alterations in incentives. It would be rash to introduce – at a stroke – a whole new scheme for flat-rate, universal, non-gender-specific, unconditional allowances, making some individuals much better off, others much worse off, and shifting the balance of advantage between "work" and "leisure" for a high proportion of the population in a dramatic way. But no serious advocate of Basic Income would propose such a move. Nowadays it is accepted that a step-by-step approach would be needed, taking account of existing structures; detailed schemes have recently been proposed for Britain and the Netherlands (Parker, 1989; Liberal Democrats, 1990; Netherlands Scientific Council for Government Policy, 1985). In the British schemes, "transitional" or "partial" Basic Incomes would gradually replace both income tax allowances and existing social insurance and social assistance benefits, but would not totally dispense with the latter. In the Dutch one, both national assistance and insurance-based systems would survive after the introduction of partial Basic Incomes. By these means, people at present facing economic exclusion through the massive disincentives of the poverty and unemployment traps would be given much better opportunities and incentives for participation, while those with satisfactory incentives would neither be suddenly faced with deterrent marginal tax rates, nor expansive inducements to give up their jobs. In this way, adjustments would be made at the margins: the biggest likely effects in Britain, for example, might be that some married women now doing part-time work for low wages would reduce their participation, while some men, women and young people now claiming would increase theirs.

By this gradualist approach, Basic Income advocates have made some sacrifices in terms of the magnificent simplicity and intuitive appeal to equity of their principle. However, at the same time they have destroyed the standard mindless dismissal of their schemes as "utopian" or dangerous; and in particular they should have undermined much of the case against unconditionality on grounds of inefficiency. Indeed there are strong grounds for arguing that a gradual move to unconditional partial Basic Incomes would increase economic efficiency (Standing, 1989; Parker, 1990). However, those who argue for Conditional Basic Incomes, tied in with an enforceable obligation to do paid work (either Gorz-style obligatory hours, or workfare-style work tests or public service), face a much more difficult task on issues of efficiency. If we know anything about forced labor schemes, it is that they are monstrously inefficient: this is as true of the Gulags as it is of the inter-war concentration camps, the make-work schemes that proliferated in Thatcher's Britain and prison labor. Enforcement costs – staff administering tests and conducting surveillance – are enormous, and work effort is abysmal. Of course, if the aim of such schemes is to reduce officially-recorded unemployment (as it often is) this is all to the good. In Britain in the 1980s, schemes like the community program created their own bureaucracies of pen-pushing MSC form fillers, supervisors and instructors: they deliberately packaged "employment" in part-time units, showering projects with untrained and unmotivated workers, often specifically instructed to take their time over what they were doing, and they intentionally gave them the most archaic, primitive tools to do their work (I have seen Community Program workers mowing playing fields with 18-inch mowers, and painting railway stations with 2-inch brushes). But if the claim of those advocating conditionality is that it is required for efficiency, these features of the schemes will not do at all. I have yet to hear of a single efficient, productive compulsory work program, and the motto of Eastern Europe – "you pretend to work, we pretend to pay" – stands as history's epitaph to the attempt to link guaranteed state incomes to guaranteed employment.

References

Department of Social Security (1989). *Social Security Statistics 1989.* HMSO, London.

Esping-Andersen, G. (1990). *The Three Worlds of Welfare Capitalism.* Polity, Cambridge.

International Labour Office (1990). *Yearbook of Labour Statistics*, 1989–1990. ILO, Geneva.

Jordan, B., James, S., Kay, H., and Redley, M. (1992). *Trapped in Poverty? Labour-Market Decisions in Low-Income Households.* Routledge, London.

Liberal Democrats (1990) *Common Benefit: Liberal Democrat Policies for the Reform of the Tax and Benefit Systems.* Federal Green Paper No.11, London.

Mead, L. (1986). *Beyond Entitlement: The Social Obligations of Citizenship.* Free Press, New York.

Minford, P. with Ashton, P. et al. (1985). *Unemployment: Causes and Cures,* 2nd. Edn. Basil Blackwell, Oxford.

Netherlands Scientific Council for Government Policy (1985). *Safeguarding Social Security.* WRR, The Hague.

Parker, H. (1989). *Instead of the Dole. An Enquiry into Integration of the Tax and Benefit Systems.* Routledge, London.

Parker, H. (ed.) (1990). *Basic Income and the Labour Markel.* Basic Income Research Group, London.

Standing, G. (1986). Meshing labour flexibility with security: an answer to British unemployment? *International Labour Review,* 125.

Standing, G. (1989). *European Unemployment, Insecurity and Flexibility: A Social Dividend Solution.* World Employment Research Project, International Labour Office, Geneva.

Chapter 34
Subsidize Wages

Edmund Phelps

In P. Van Parijs (ed.) (2001). *What's Wrong with a Free Lunch?* Beacon Press, Boston.

Several economists over the past couple of decades have been calling for a universal employment subsidy – a subsidy to firms for each low-wage person they employ without regard to parental or marital status. Self-support (vs. dependency), personal growth (vs. disengagement), integration (vs. marginalization) – these are our rallying cries. Now there come efforts to gain instead a reconsideration of a Universal Basic Income (UBI), or Demogrant – a periodic transfer payment to each resident with no conditions on working and earning. These two proposed innovations in social policy differ importantly, I will argue, in what they suppose a society is for. And they also rest on quite different assessments of the practical consequences they would have, if adopted.

In several ways I find the idea of a Demogrant attractive, as I did when, in the 1960s, I was a young economist just beginning to think about economic and social policy. A Demogrant would help to level the playing field by counteracting the ability of families – under market socialism and market capitalism – to bequeath their children advantages (such as individual freedom) over other children, their children's children, and so on. A Demogrant would permit low-wage workers to reject as inadequate the pay differentials offered by unsafe or unhealthy jobs. It would also bring an efficiency gain in giving people more of their total social benefit in the form of fungible cash to use as they prefer, and less in the form of free services whose amounts are chosen by the state. One can therefore understand the support that proposals for a Demogrant usually find.

The idea of a universal minimum income seems to enjoy especially wide appeal among the many Europeans who have an almost religious (and, in many cases, literally religious) sense of nation and community. To them it will appear to be further progress in the development of a society that feels the near-sacred value of each person's life and autonomy. Most of Western Europe, particularly the Continent, has already gone a long way toward providing universal – that is, unconditional – benefits to its citizens (and in most cases other residents): subsidized housing, free medical care and free education services, among other services.

Basic Income: An Anthology of Contemporary Research, First Edition. Edited by Karl Widerquist, José A. Noguera, Yannick Vanderborght, and Jurgen De Wispelaere.

Philippe Van Parijs[1] makes the strongest imaginable case for going the rest of the way by means of a UBI. But I remain opposed. For me, there are two sticking points. One of them, which I will take up later, has to do with consequences. The Demogrant device has no monopoly on the beneficial effects that make us like it, whatever the balance of its total benefits and total cost. The alternative to it – a subsidy to employers for every low-wage worker in their full-time employ – would have some of those effects and some other benefits as well. The subsidy, in pulling up paychecks and the number employed at the low-wage end of the labor market, would mitigate serious disadvantages of talent and background; it would expand the jobs that low earners could afford to reject; and it would widen low earners' latitude in meeting their needs.

The other sticking point is that the Demogrant idea seems in an important respect to go against the grain of the traditional American conception of a liberal republic. This conception, I will argue, would cause many Americans to hesitate to embrace a UBI while being willing, at least in principle, to contemplate low-wage employment subsidies.

Let's consider these two points, starting with the second.

1. Where can we look for the American conception of the liberal society? I suggest we need look no farther than John Rawls, widely regarded to be the leading moral philosopher of the twentieth century. His *A Theory of Justice*[2] is seen by many as the sourcebook of most of the new ideas of importance on how to think about matters of justice in economic and social policy, even if we don't always want to follow him to the letter. Since Rawls is an American writing against the background of American social history, the conception of society he expresses in that book is at least an important sample of American thinking.

The conception of liberal society there is in refreshing contrast to the more European one. It excludes religious states having a public purpose. It also excludes aggregations of persons engaged in solitary pursuits who might cooperate only for their mutual protection. For Rawls, a society (the sort of society he wants to consider, at any rate) is a cooperative enterprise in which individuals come together to participate in its interactive economy for the purpose of mutual private gain – largely, individual achievement and personal growth from career and family life. Accordingly, economic justice is about the distribution of those mutual gains among the individuals participating. It is wrongheaded to ask what this economic justice requires in the way of support for individuals who choose to opt out and live in isolation off the land, or sects that choose to break off from the larger society. Rawls's kind of justice is owed only to those who, being able and willing, participate and contribute at least something to the economy's pie.[3]

These views on the nature and function of society trace far back in American thought. Thomas Jefferson wrote that the early settlers came to the American continent for "the acquisition & free possession of property" – and for the "pursuit of happiness" in the process, as he was to say later. Calvin Coolidge encapsulated the cooperative-enterprise conception of society with his great apothegm, "the business of America is business." It came to be understood in the Progressive Era that the possibility of mutual gain, which Rawls built on, arose from the "social surplus" generated by the interaction of people's diverse talents and skills within society's central institution, the business economy. In his economics textbook, which was dominant for nearly the second half of the last century, Paul Samuelson never failed to bring up this social surplus, always citing the eloquent statement of the idea by the social theorist L. T. Hobhouse in his 1922 book *The Elements of Social Justice*. It is implicit, I think, that the social surplus is a flow of income that can be legitimately redistributed, since the way a free market would distribute it is morally arbitrary and a free market is an impossibility in any case.[4] It is also implicit in all these expressions, I believe, that the social surplus is to be made available for redistribution to the contributors, not to noncontributors. It would be incoherent to say that the contributors to society's enterprise, in generating a social surplus, have – as defenders of a UBI suggest – the obligation to share it with those who have not contributed. What do the latter have to do with it? If they can be shown somehow to have a claim, is there a claim of animals and other sentient creatures? If we earth people should discover Martians unwilling to trade or collaborate with us, do they nonetheless have a claim too?

2. The argument for UBI set out by Van Parijs appears to be substantially pragmatic. He appears to believe that, although it might go against the ideology of some to hand out the basic income *unconditionally*, the practical *effect* of doing so will be to encourage participation, hard work, self-support, achievement, and all the other desiderata dear to those with that perspective.

A UBI, Van Parijs writes, "makes it easier to take a break between two jobs, reduce working time, make room for more training, take up self-employment, or join a cooperative. And with a UBI, workers will only take a job if they find it suitably attractive, while employer subsidies make unattractive, low-productivity jobs more economically viable."

One can see that a UBI would open up some new job options to many people, just as inheriting a substantial sum of money would make it possible to try one's hand at composing music or writing a book. But financing it will entail lower after-tax wages and lower private saving until private wealth (defined to exclude the present discounted value of the expected stream of UBI) has reached a sufficiently reduced level; to a rough approximation, private wealth would fall by as much as social wealth (defined as the present value of the UBI stream) rose.

So there is no alchemy here by which a net increase of wealth is achieved and costlessly at that. At some point in middle age, the *average* worker-saver will have a lower *total* wealth, private plus social, than he or she would otherwise have had, since wealth per head (which I am taking to be unchanged) is an average of the wealth per head of the young, who now get their social wealth right off the bat, and the wealth per head of the old. The contention that there is a social gain from "moving up" people's wealth to the first year of adulthood, since the increased liquidity serves to increase freedom, depends on the assumption that the social benefit from the added liquidity is sufficiently large to overcome the social cost resulting from the reduction of after-tax rewards to working.

Of course, the main part of the argument is redistributive: the increased wealth would occur among those with little, the reduction of wealth would occur among those with much. But a low-wage employment subsidy scheme also would be redistributive in the same direction. So we must weigh the practical balance of benefits and costs posed by the UBI against the corresponding balance offered by low-wage employment subsidies. I see some serious drawbacks of a UBI; these drawbacks mirror the merits of low-wage employment subsidies.

I'll emphasize four drawbacks. First, the pay rates available to low-wage workers are already so low as to be demoralizing. A large UBI would seem towering to a low-wage worker, and would further depreciate his or her earning power; moreover, the UBI, in requiring higher taxation to finance it, would tend to reduce their net pay rates further. Worsened employee performance would follow and, since firms won't create jobs for workers who will quit or shirk or are absent at the drop of a hat, a large number of jobs held by low-wage workers in private business would become extinct.

Second, we are in dire straits to begin with in this regard. Work, career, and achievement are already threatened by a whole array of competitors – crime, unemployment, and the underground economy.[5] This is no time to launch a new scheme that would create further disincentives to work in the legitimate business economy. Marginalization must be *reduced*, not increased. Introducing a UBI would make that task harder.

Third, what matters to people is not just their total receipts; it is the self-support from *earning their own way*. No amount of UBI would substitute for the satisfaction of having earned one's way without help from parents, friends and the state – as valued as they are. I would note that, if the UBI were adopted in the United States, it would continue to rankle low-wage earners that their pay was less than half the median wage. The reason it would, I suggest, is that low-wage workers would view such low relative pay rates as bluntly showing that they cannot hope to earn their own way in the sense of gaining access to most of the median earners' way of life *through their own earning*; they can only gain access through the Demogrant, which they may see as demeaning.

Finally, what about Parijs's image of the workplace with its exhausted women and tyrannical bosses? I feel that many academics and others reared in relatively privileged circumstances cannot see how those working in a factory for 40 hours a week could value it as a means to mix and interact with others, to gain a sense of belonging in the community, and to have a sense of contributing something to the country's collective project, which is business. If I am right on these matters, we should feel sorry, not envious, about Van Parijs's surfer who feels lucky to be able to drop out of the world of work thanks to his UBI; he doesn't know what he is missing. And we shouldn't feel sorry about women "subjected to the dictates of a boss for 40 hours a week." They have the self-knowledge to know something that Van Parijs appears not to know about them: the sociability, the challenges, and the sense of contribution and belonging that those jobs provide are an important part of their lives, as they are of the lives of others.

The problem is that the low-end pay rates are much too low, so low that some low-end workers must take the least "liberating" jobs to make ends meet. The solution is not to endow workers with a UBI, so that they move to somewhat better jobs at a reduction in pay or else just drop out. That way lies dependency, unfulfillment, depression, and marginalization. The solution is to institute a low-wage employment subsidy, so that all pay rates facing low-wage workers would be pulled up to levels better reflecting the social productivity of their employment, their support of themselves, and their development. Then low-wage men and women could afford to avoid dangerous, unhealthy, or oppressive jobs and opt instead for more rewarding work. And many more people would be able to know the satisfactions of self-support, development, participation, and contribution.

Notes

1. Editor's note: Phelps refers here to Van Parijs, P (2001) A Basic Income for All, in P. Van Parijs (ed) *What's Wrong with a Free Lunch*? Beacon Press, Boston. and Van Parijs (1995).
2. Editor's note: Phelps refers here to Rawls (1971).
3. In conversation and correspondence I could never get him to endorse this interpretation. But he never protested it either. In a 1985 letter he commented that the presentation of his system

on pp. 144–149 of my textbook *Political Economy: An Introductory Text* (Phelps, 1985) accurately presented his position. That exposition makes explicit the premise that society is a cooperative enterprise for the contributors' mutual gain.

4. Some argue that this flow is the largest that can be legitimately redistributed. Aspects of the matter are taken up in Nozick (1974).
5. Europeans call the underground the "informal" economy and see it as a charming zone of idyllic exchange rather than a parasitic sector that lives off the legitimate economy through tax evasion and other covert practices that subvert respect for the law.

References

Hobhouse, L.T. (1922). *The Elements of Social Justice.* George Allen & Unwin.

Nozick, R. (1974). *Anarchy, State, Utopia.* Basic Books, New York.

Phelps, E. (1985). *Political Economy: An Introductory Text.* W.W. Norton & Company, New York.

Rawls, J. (1971). *A Theory of Justice.* Oxford University Press, Oxford.

Van Parijs, P. (1995). *Real Freedom for All: What (If Anything) Can Justify Capitalism?* Oxford University Press, Oxford.

Van Parijs, P (2001) A Basic Income for All, in P. Van Parijs (ed) *What's Wrong with a Free Lunch?* Beacon Press, Boston.

Chapter 35
Universal Basic Income and the Flat Tax

Herbert A. Simon

Excerpts from Simon, H.A. (2001). UBI and the Flat Tax. In P. Van Parijs (ed.) *What's Wrong with a Free Lunch?* Beacon Press, Boston.

I am in strong general agreement with Philippe Van Parijs's argument for a Universal Basic Income (UBI) or "patrimony" – a portion of the product of a society that should be shared by all of those who inhabit that society. To establish such a patrimony is equivalent to recognizing shared ownership of a significant fraction of the resources, physical and intellectual, that enable the society to produce what it produces. As the essay[1] makes a very strong case for the UBI and its feasibility, I will limit my comments to just two issues: (i) why a UBI (or patrimony) would be just; and (ii) some problems of incentives that such a system poses and that need to be handled effectively.

Justice

When we compare average incomes in rich nations with those in Third World countries, we find enormous differences that are surely not due simply to differences in motivations to earn. Laziness is not a principal cause of poverty. A more plausible explanation for the differences, in fact the explanation that is universally put forward, is that much greater resources per capita are available to some countries than to others. These differences are not simply a matter of acres of land or tons of coal or iron ore, but, more important, differences in social capital – principally, differences in stored knowledge (e.g., technology, and especially organizational and governmental skills).

Exactly the same claim can be made about the differences in incomes within any given society. In large part, these differences must be attributed to differences in capital ownership, of which the largest part is social capital: knowledge, and participation in kinship and other privileged social relations. In addressing the question of justice, therefore, we are assessing the justice of inheritance of such resources along bloodlines. This is a question of value, not of fact. I personally do not see any moral basis for an inalienable right to

From Simon, H.A. (2001). UBI and the Flat Tax. In P. Van Parijs (ed.) *What's Wrong with a Free Lunch?* Beacon Press, Boston, pp. 34–38.

Basic Income: An Anthology of Contemporary Research, First Edition. Edited by Karl Widerquist, José A. Noguera, Yannick Vanderborght, and Jurgen De Wispelaere.

inherit resources, or to retain all the resources that one has acquired by means of economic or other activities.

The usual argument for such a right is based on the assumption of perfectly competitive markets where factors of production are paid their marginal values and where there are no externalities. But this assumption does not hold to any reasonable degree of approximation in real societies. Access to the social capital – a major source of differences in income, between and within societies – is in large part the product of externalities: membership in a particular society, and interaction with other members of that society under practices that commonly give preferred access to particular members.

How large are these externalities, which must be regarded as owned jointly by members of the whole society? When we compare the poorest with the richest nations, it is hard to conclude that social capital can produce less than about 90% of income in wealthy societies like those of the United States or Northwestern Europe. On moral grounds, then, we could argue for a flat income tax of 90% to return that wealth to its real owners. In the United States, even a flat tax of 70% would support all governmental programs (about half the total tax) and allow payment, with the remainder, of a patrimony of about $8,000 per annum per inhabitant, or $25,000 for a family of three. This would generously leave with the original recipients of the income about three times what, according to my rough guess, they had earned.

Incentives

Economists are always quick to point out that people must be properly motivated to be productive. If average returns to effort were uniformly reduced by a factor of three, it is not clear why motivation to earn more would be reduced. The behavior of two-income families in the United States suggest that the desire for income is related much more to processes of social comparison than to the real wage rate after taxes or the relative desire for goods and leisure. Similar questions may be raised about savings and capital accumulation, but in discussing them, private savings should not be dissociated from social saving (either by government or by the processes of social exchange themselves), which commonly produces externalities that are not evaluated by the market and appear nowhere in the social accounts. In any event, the questions about incentives to work and save are empirical questions that should be settled by experimentation and observation and not by philosophical debate.

Note

1. Editor's note: Simon refers here to Van Parijs, P (2001) A Basic Income for All, in P. Van Parijs (ed) *What's Wrong with a Free Lunch?* Beacon Press, Boston.

Reference

Van Parijs, P (2001) A Basic Income for All, in P. Van Parijs (ed) *What's Wrong with a Free Lunch?* Beacon Press, Boston.

Chapter 36
Democracy and General Welfare

James M. Buchanan

Excerpts from Buchanan, J.M. (1997). Can Democracy Promote the General Welfare? *Social Philosophy and Policy*, 14 (2), 165–179.

My concern here is not particularly with how genuine constitutional choices are made, or should be made. My concern is more limited. Can constitutional constraints be designed that will allow legislative majorities to move beyond protective and productive state functions into the activities summarized under the "welfare-state" rubric, while, at the same time, holding in check the natural proclivity of majoritarian politics to promote particular rather than general interests? Is the welfare state in a democracy necessarily discriminatory in its operation?

Generality as a Constitutional Constraint

One means of subverting the predicted results of majority rule, and especially as aimed at producing more generality, is to change the rule itself. If majority rule were replaced with a more inclusive assent requirement, say, two-thirds, three-fourths, five-sixths, or in the limit, unanimity, outcomes of legislative choice processes would necessarily become less discriminatory in impact. I shall not examine this avenue for political reform in this chapter, since I have treated this subject matter in some detail elsewhere.[1] A further reason for shifting the focus away from this avenue is based on the recognition that the association between "democracy" as a political ideal and "majority rule" seems to be so well entrenched in public consciousness as to make serious challenge to the linkage futile.

For ordinary or in-period politics, therefore, I want to postulate majority-rule decision-making in legislative assemblies. In this setting, an explicit constitutional requirement that political action, as authorized by a legislative majority, must be general in its effects over all members of the body politic, offers what seems to be an attractive prospect. The question then reduces to: What actions that might be taken by legislative majorities would be constitutionally prohibited under enforcement of a generality rule?

From Buchanan, J.M. (1997). Can Democracy Promote the General Welfare? *Social Philosophy and Policy*, 14 (2), 165–179. Reprinted with permission of Cambridge University Press.

Basic Income: An Anthology of Contemporary Research, First Edition. Edited by Karl Widerquist, José A. Noguera, Yannick Vanderborght, and Jurgen De Wispelaere.

First of all, I should emphasize that existing constitutional understanding and interpretation does include elements of such a generality norm. Overt discrimination among persons and groups based on membership in majority coalitions would be considered unconstitutional in the United States and also in most modern democracies. The discussion here is directly informed by the U.S. political-legal environment, but the basic extension is applicable more generally to all liberal-democratic structures. Furthermore, elements of the generality norm go well beyond this strictly political limit. With some exceptions (e.g., affirmative action in the United States), legislative majorities cannot explicitly discriminate in the politically imposed treatment of persons based on criteria of race, religion, or gender. And such treatment, if attempted, would be declared unconstitutional by the understanding and traditional interpretation of equality before the law. By contrast, legislative majorities can discriminate among persons on criteria of geographical location, occupation, profession, industry or product category, economic status, age, family characteristics, productive capacity, and any number of other classificatory schemes. Extension of the generality principle to apply over all such categories of political activity would reduce the range of modern majoritarian politics dramatically, although it would not necessarily generate a reversion to government in its strictly night-watchman role.

As concerns political action in promoting welfare, however, which is the focus of this chapter would a generality rule eliminate the whole purpose of what is widely understood to be the welfare enterprise, described as the provision of income support to defined groups at the direct expense of other groups in the citizenry? Are welfare transfers compatible with any generality norm? In what follows, I suggest that it is possible to apply a generality norm to both the taxation and distribution sides of a system of social insurance.

A flat-rate tax

Any income transfer must be financed; the fiscal account has two sides, revenue and outlay. Consider, first, the application of the generality principle to taxation. An extreme libertarian (if he or she would acknowledge any taxation at all) might hold that only equal-per-head taxes would qualify and that any differentiation among persons would violate the generality norm. This argument incorporates an analogy between the private or market sector and the political sector. Persons face uniform prices in market transactions; the collective analogue is equal-per-head taxes. Such an argument must presume, however, that persons (families) can exist independently from collective association, that entry into and exit from each collective interaction is voluntary and attainable at relatively low cost and, further, that persons may purchase publicly supplied goods and services in quantities separately preferred. In a more comprehensive perspective, the political enterprise, inclusively considered, is scarcely voluntaristic in any market-analogue sense – entry and exit involve high threshold costs. There are elements of "publicness" that are necessarily present. Individuals cannot privately adjust desired quantities of politically supplied goods to tax prices. The generality principle would lose both meaning and its persuasive power if interpreted to imply equal-per-head taxation.

In the traditional public-finance literature, a tax is classified as general if it applies a uniform rate to a comprehensive base. The taxation of income at a proportional or flat rate meets the criterion of generality on almost any reckoning. The exemption, exclusion, or special treatment of any sort of income would represent violation of the generality norm. Also, and importantly, the taxation of some incomes at differentially higher rates or lower rates, including zero, would depart from generality. Only the taxation of all income, as received by all persons, and without exemption, deduction, or exclusion, at the same rate meets the standard here.[2]

Proposals advanced in the 1980s and 1990s aimed at modifying the U.S. federal tax structure through the introduction of some version of a flat rate of tax on income would, if enacted and treated as if they were constitutional, do much toward thwarting the majoritarian impulses toward discriminatory exploitation through the taxing process. However, most of these flat-rate tax schemes, as proposed, have failed to qualify as general because they have not eliminated all exemptions, such as income from investments as well as low-level incomes. Any exemption from the comprehensive tax must set up opportunities for majoritarian conflict which is, precisely, the primary result that the general tax should be aimed at avoiding. Generality, properly understood, would require that each and every dollar of income, by whomever received, be taxed at the same rate. With such a tax in place, members of prospective majority coalitions would operate in the knowledge that any change in the tax rate would impact on themselves in the same way that it impacts on others outside those coalitions. Membership, or the absence thereof, in the majority coalition, per se, would not affect tax liability, except indirectly through the composition of the tax base.

Demogrants

What is the outlay-side equivalent to the flat-rate tax on income in the context of the welfare enterprise? Justificatory argument in support of welfare transfers is beyond the scope of inquiry here. The discussion is limited to the question of possible reconciliation between welfare transfers and the generality norm. Here equal-per-head transfer payments, or Demogrants, meet the criterion for generality. All citizens would secure equal payments, as financed from the flat-rate tax on income. In net, the combined fiscal process would redistribute income from those persons who earn higher-than-mean incomes, pre-tax, to those who earn less-than-mean incomes, pre-tax. Politically, however, on neither the tax nor the transfer side of the fiscal account would particular groups be singled out for differentially favored or disfavored treatment. The natural proclivity for majority coalitions to use their decision-making authority to exploit members of minorities would be attenuated.

In characteristic patterns of pre-tax income distribution, the median income tends to fall below mean income, pre-tax. (High income earners raise the average [mean] income but may leave the median income earner unaffected.) In this situation, there would be positive redistribution predicted under the operation of majority rule because the median income recipients would also be the median voters whose preferences on the issue would tend to be controlling as well as consistent. In public-choice terms, the preferences would be single-peaked; hence, majority voting yields consistent results. Individual preferences as to the height of the rate of tax, and, residually, as to the size of the Demogrant, would vary inversely with pre-tax incomes. Those persons with below-mean incomes would prefer high rates of tax, while those with above-mean incomes, pre-tax, would prefer low rates. To this extent, distributional conflict would remain descriptive of majoritarian politics, even as constrained fiscally in the manner suggested here. The debates would be about the choice among positions "on the diagonal," however, and therefore would be categorically different from debates about alternatives that involve deliberate exploitation of any group.

Social insurance

I submit that a structure of equal-per-head transfer payments, or Demogrants, financed by a flat rate of tax on all incomes, if effectively constitutionalized and removed from the agenda of ordinary majoritarian politics, would allow an affirmative answer, of sorts, to the question "Can democracy promote the general welfare?" Legislative majorities would be empowered to set the rate of the flat tax and, with that, the size of the Demogrant, but specific actions aimed at discriminating favorably or unfavorably, on either the taxing or the transfer side of the account, would be out of bounds.

The rate of tax that would be predicted would depend on several factors: (i) the pattern of pre-tax income distribution; (ii) the predicted response behavior of persons as taxpayers and as transfer recipients; (iii) the predicted bureaucratic-administrative leakages in the fiscal process; (iv) the predicted mobility of persons among income classes; (v) the predicted lengths of periods between changes in rates of tax; and possibly others. Any rate of tax above zero would, of course, be predicted to impact negatively on the rate of economic growth. In effect, this impact might be considered to be the aggregate cost of the scheme of social insurance that the flat-tax/Demogrant system represents.

The positive political effects of this structure should not be overlooked. Majoritarian democratic process is preserved; it is not allowed to degenerate into the cross-group redistributive transfer absurdity that describes the "churning state" (de Jasay, 1985). The welfare state maintains legitimacy because it is seen to be basically nondiscriminatory in its operation. The structure would remain immune to some of the "end welfare as we know it" attitudes expressed by pundits, politicians, and philosophers in the 1990s.

Notes

1. See Buchanan and Tullock (1962). For the seminal analysis, see Wicksell (1896).
2. For extended discussion of the political efficiency of general taxation, see Buchanan (1994).

References

Buchanan, J.M. (1994). The Political Efficiency of General Taxation. *National Tax Journal*, 44 (4), 401–410.

Buchanan, J.M. and Tullock, G. (1962). *The Calculus of Consent: Logical Foundations of Constitutional Democracy.* University of Michigan Press, Ann Arbor.

de Jasay, A. (1985). *The State.* Basil Blackwell, Oxford.

Wicksell, K. (1986). *Finanztheoretische Untersuchungen.* Gustav Fischer, Jena.

Chapter 37
Basic Income and Social Power

Koen Raes

Excerpts from Raes, K. (1988). Basic Income and Social Power.
In A.G. Miller (ed.) *Proceedings of the First International Conference on Basic Income, Louvain-la-Neuve, Belgium, 4–6 September 1986.*
Basic Income European Network, Antwerp, pp. 106–122.[1]

Whilst Van Parijs (1985a) develops his "capitalist road to communism" on the basis of an uncoupling of income and work – considered to be a condition for establishing a society of free disposal over time – Gorz's (1986) "farewell to the proletariat" implies on the countrary, a fundamental redistribution of all heteronomous labor. Both recognize, however, in the growing mass of unemployed people the political basis to support their alternatives, and situate the interests of these unemployed people within the framework of an anti-productivist, ecological engagement.

We question in this chapter only the political feasibility of the "leftist version" of the Universal Grant, which really guarantees a decent standard of living to people who do not participate in production for the market, and is not an alms as is the case in many neo-liberal proposals, or Negative Income Tax schemes (see PVV–Jongeren, 1980; Raes, 1983: 199 a.f.) as well as its political tenability, once established under capitalist conditions. We will do so on the basis of some recent works on classes and class struggle and on exploitation. Though not having any "principled" objection against a society where no one is forced to work or to sell his labor power in order to earn a living (on the contrary!), and though indeed approaching (contra Nozick, 1974) the choice between exploitative labor conditions or starvation as one of the most degrading and unfree aspects of the capitalist mode of production (see Cohen, 1984), we think that the proposed road toward such a society is either unfeasible, or part of much more fundamental changes in social structure than is contended. We want to argue, that is, "why something like socialism is necessary for the transition to communism" (Wright, 1986).

There are, in the Western world, not many opportunities to decrease heteronomous labor(-time), necessary to maintain a certain level of economic development; we either evolve toward a society in which unemployment is a permanent situation for a certain part of the population, or toward a society in which wage-labor is for all members of the society only a (small) part of their social and personal activities. We either divide the population

From Raes, K. (1988). Basic Income and Social Power. In A.G. Miller (ed.) *Proceedings of the First International Conference on Basic Income, Louvain-la-Neuve, Belgium, 4–6 September 1986*. Basic Income European Network, Antwerp, pp. 106–122.

Basic Income: An Anthology of Contemporary Research, First Edition. Edited by Karl Widerquist, José A. Noguera, Yannick Vanderborght, and Jurgen De Wispelaere.

into workers and nonworkers or we redistribute the "available" and "necessary" labor, so that all persons participate in "working" and "nonworking" activities.

One alternative (which appears to be the main tendency in most Western countries today) will directly lead toward a dual society of unemployment, a society with on the one hand a quantity of qualified and corporatist wage-laborers that are very well paid and protected from intruders (we can refer here to what already exists in Belgium at the docks) and on the other a mass of unemployed or semi-unemployed people, working sporadically on the basis of precarious contracts. It will be a society with on the one hand a firm class of organized and conscious workers, and on the other hand a nonclass of nonorganized, dispersed nonworkers, a society in the process of what Gorz (1985: 99) calls *Suid Afrikanisering*, segregating one part of the population from another on a permanent basis. The marginal nonclass of nonworkers will, according to Gorz, no more find a job in central parts of the economy. The millions of jobs that were "created" in the United States during the last 10 years were not created in the industrial sector of the economy but in the sector of "personal services"; restaurants, guard – or custodian – services, cleaning, and so on. In activities, that is, for which no qualification is required and which are, so to say, in the service of the class of industrial workers.

The other alternative consists of a drastic redistribution of all necessary labor on the basis of a reduction of labor time, an alternative in which part-time work becomes the norm and in which all people work two or three days – or a quarter of a year – in the heteronomous sector and spend the rest of their time in productive or nonproductive autonomous activities. Here the society organizes the necessary labor so that the quantity as well as the quality are enough to guarantee a certain amount of wealth for all. It further provides access to the means people need to freely develop autonomous activities. In order to do so *all* people need at the same time to have access to jobs in the heteronomous sector and be liberated from prolonged labor times.

The ways by which labor time is to be reduced cannot be dictated in advance. Flexibility in ways of reducing and redistributing necessary labor time is as much in the interest of the workers as it is in the interest of capital owners. They can take a career (pensions), a year (holidays), a week (32-hour week or a three-day working week), or a day (six-hour working day) as a reference point. Today a "normal labor time" consists of 1,700 hours a year for normally employed people in Western Europe. If all socially necessary labor were to be distributed over the total population, this per capita labor time could drop to between 1,350 and 1,500 hours a year during the coming years and to 1,000 hours at the beginnings of the twenty-first century (including an unemployment percentage of 10–20%) (Gorz, 1986: 10).

One can even take a total career (of 25 years) as a reference point. Whilst actually people are normally working 40,000 hours in their lifetime, one can assume that in the twenty-first century people will have the possibility to decide when they will perform the 20,000 hours of labor they are socially required to perform; full time during 10 consecutive years, part time during 20 consecutive years, two months a year, 40 years with sabbatical breaks in between, and so on. However, it must be underlined that such proposals in which the available and necessary labor is redistributed over the totality of the active population and in which there remains an undissolveable tie between the right to an income and the right to work fundamentally differ from proposals in which the available and necessary labor is distributed over only a part of the population, the other part receiving a labor-independent Basic Income.

Sure, it is not the intention of proposals such as the Charles Fourier-proposal to create a dual society and a dualistic social division between workers and nonworkers. However, they cannot *guarantee* that such a division will not develop and neither can they ever guarantee that such a division will not develop and neither can they ever guarantee that a certain (high) Basic Income level will not drop to much lower levels. Not only for evident economic reasons, but for political (power) reasons as well.

Indeed, in the proposal of the Collectif Charles Fourier, two basic ideas are combined:

(i) deregulation of the labor power market and fiscalization of unemployment-insurances, and
(ii) institution of an unconditional fiscal basic right to a Basic Income (Collectif Charles Fourier, 1984: 9).

An important result will be a fundamental decline of the power of the unions in labor relations as well as in social security provisions. The provision of a Universal Grant becomes a task of the state machinery and the unions have no power or say over it. As the deregulation of the labor power market implies the abolishment of unemployment compensations, legal pensions, living minima, children allowances, minimum wages, and so on, the power of the unions – yes, their very existence as unions – will drastically shrink and be reduced to a corporative power that is limited to the plant in which it operates. Union activities will be focused on wage levels and working conditions and on nothing else, and if unions want to be strong, they will have to develop into corporations, defending only the job-related interests of those having work – even if against the interests of those not having work. (Admittedly, such a tendency *is* actually already present within the labor movement.) Under "Universal Grant" conditions, the unions are no longer defenders of the "class" of people who have to sell their labor power in order to earn a (decent) living – as it is possible to live decently without having to sell one's labor power – but only of the "group" of people who "freely" – or anyway much more freely than before – decided to work for a capital-owner.

Evidently, we do not criticize a Universal Grant for the sole reason that it weakens the power of the unions. But it would be an unforgiveable mistake, on the other hand, to underestimate the importance of the organized labor force in the defence of existing welfare allocations against recent attacks on it by capital-owners. Whatever the grounds for the critiques of union-functioning, it would be a "free rider" type of mistake to think that the working class would be better off without such strong unions. It may not be in the individual interest of one person to join a union – as long as there are enough others to join it. And it may even be that the existence of a union is against the interests of one specific individual worker. It does not follow, however, that unions are against the interests of all workers. (The so-called "fallacy of composition".) It remains an open question how it will it be possible to defend a Universal Grant allocation against inevitable attacks from capital-owners or other segments of the population, by lack of a strongly organized labor force.

On the other hand, it cannot be denied that a simplified and universalized Basic Income allocation can be considered as a means toward the "decommodification of labor power." It would further be in the immediate interest of all those people who cannot benefit – for one reason or another – from unemployment allowances. Sometimes – as in the United States – they consist of more than half of the unemployed people. The beneficiaries of unemployment benefits as a percentage of the unemployed are 87% in Canada (1982), 81% in Denmark (1982), 79% in Sweden (1983), 65% in Germany (1983), 55% in Japan (1979), 52% in France (1983), 43% in the United Kingdoom (1980) and 39% in the

United States (1983) (OECD-calculations, cited in Therborn, 1986). Further, it would drastically limit the power of a capital-owner over "his" workers as they become much more free to bargain about their working conditions and are no more structurally forced to sell their labor power. Capital owners will have to automatize all unattractive tasks or to attract laborers either on the basis of high wages or on the basis of interesting work conditions. The introduction of an Unconditional Universal Grant would:

(a) destigmatize nonwork and all nonworking people.
(b) eliminate the "unemployment trap" between conditional unemployment benefit and wages, and
(c) lead to an amelioration of the average qualities of work (as anyone really has the option not to work at all) (Van Parijs, 1985: p.144).

But is it plausible to suppose that this situation will last for a long time, without leading to fundamental changes in the social relations of power? Clearly, capital-owners, though having an interest in the social peace that will result from establishing a Universal Grant, will only be prepared to pay for it if a strong state apparatus can force them all to do so. Only a strong and steadfast state can force all those who are involved in productive activities in the market to finance the system of a Guaranteed Basic Income for all. We can indeed agree even with Milton Friedman that "there is no such thing as a free meal," and one part of the population is totally inactive in the sphere of economic production, whilst being consumers of its products (the Basic Income is intended to pay for something), this can mean only that another part of the population is

(a) prepared to be active in it and, more importantly
(b) prepared to pay taxes to the state so that the universal grant can be financed.

What will be taxed, as a consequence? Only the productive labor – of the workers or independent producers – and the profits of capital-owners. They will certainly not freely agree to pay, but will have to be forced. The power monopoly over the means of coercion – that is , the state – will have to be permanently present if permanently unemployed people are guaranteed a permanently Unconditional Basic Income.

One must, indeed, approach proposals to establish a Universal Grant not individualistically – in terms of individuals choosing either to participate in heteronomous labor or not – but socially – in terms of structural and organizational criteria and interdependencies. Socially one cannot, of course, "uncouple" income from labor. No society is, as a whole, able to provide its members a decent income without anyone working. There is no need for a labor theory of value in order to agree with this. If so, the so-called "uncoupling" of income and work only means that the group of (productive) workers is "uncoupled" from the group of (consuming) nonworkers – though the members of those social groups may vary over time – and that the state taxes the former group in order to guarantee the latter group a Basic Income. Those disposing of an unconditional income can only dispose of it because others are prepared to do the heterenomous labor, making possible the very existence of this income. That is to say that finally, one does not "uncouple" income from labor, one uncouples working from nonworking people.

It is exactly here that recent discussions within Marxism on class struggle and exploitation, as well as neo-liberal concepts of the "new class struggle" between so-called fiscal classes, are of fundamental importance. According to Van Dun (1983: 549, a. f.) the core of the state is the fiscal relation between those who are taxed and those who pay taxes. This relation is considered to be an aggressive assault on human rights, a relation of exploitation which can only exist because the state disposes of, and claims to have a right over, the monopoly over the means of coercion. There is an everlasting struggle between those holding positions of power in the state and their clients, on the one hand, and the productive economic agents on the other. The former have a tendency always to raise taxes, the latter to lower or abolish them. The new class struggle consists of nothing else than the struggle between the state bureaucracy and its clients who *consume* taxes, and all productive agents or savers in the economy who *produce* them. It results in a statist relation of exploitation, based on fundamentally antagonist interests. At different levels of society this antagonism can be recognized; the tension between the unemployed and those protected by minimum wages is part of it, as well as the conflicts between state managers and capital owners. (See also Lepage, 1978).

Though I reject neo-liberal (so-called "libertarian") class theories (see Raes, 1984) they contain an important truth; the income of those who do not participate at all in the heteronomous sphere is, one way or the other, derived from the labor of those who are productive in it and if this redistribution takes place by means of coercion there can be reasons to talk of *exploitation*, on the basis of class relations between workers and nonworkers. As a matter of fact, is the relation between productive income-producing workers and nonproductive, income-consuming non-workers not a standard type of a class relation, materialistically concerned with the distribution of material advantages? If we take Roemer's definition of exploitation, according to which a group is exploited (or an exploiter) if it could become better off (or would become worse off) if it withdrew from the economy according to certain rules – the so called "withdrawal concept of exploitation" – it can certainly be argued that the group of permanently unemployed people "exploits" the working class. Therefore, however, it must first be argued that they indeed are a social class.

Is the mass of permanently unemployed people to be viewed as a class apart from those who are selling their labor power, those who are hiring someone else's labor power and those who are self-employed? The importance of this question is not of purely academic interest, On the one hand, E.O. Wright questions whether socialism can be a potential objective of struggle for those people (Wright, 1978: 94), whilst P. Van Parijs argues that it is exactly this "social class" which consists of the fundamental political basis of the green movement (Van Parijs, 1986), and which will be the main interest group in the struggle to establish a univeral grant (Van Parijs, 1985: 146). Is Van Parijs, in doing so, not pleading to make explicit – "politicize" – a "new class struggle" within a duel society as well? In his analysis (1978), E.O, Wright defined the working class as those positions which

(a) occupy the working class position within the social relations of production . . . or
(b) are linked directly to the working class through immediate family or class trajectories, or
(c) occupy working class positions within political and ideological apparatuses [. . .] (Wright, 1978: 97)

Temporarily unemployed people are no conceptual problem for a class analysis of society as they are related to "trajectories" of class positions which define their basic class location (Wright, 1978:93). But the permanently unemployed need not be "members" of the working class. Politically and ideologically, they are a subordinated group of people, but they are not economically exploited, neither in terms of extorted surplus labor, nor in terms of extorted surplus value. Their interests may even be totally opposed to those of the proletariat, and in classical Marxist theory they would generally be identified as a "Lumpen-proletariat" and associated with rightist populist ideologies. As the capitalists they can have a stake in increasing the social rate of exploitation since this would make it easier for them to improve their own income (via an increase of the taxes levied on productive activity). It can always be argued that it is in their "fundamental" interest to struggle for socialism (one can argue that socialism is in the interest of capital owners as well) but at the level of immediate interests there exists an important gulf between working class interests and the interests of permanently unemployed (ie. *never* working) people.

Welfare payments come directly out of taxes and these taxes are levied on the laborers' work. An unemployment *insurance* guarantees the reproduction of wage laborers during periods when they cannot fine employment, but this is not the case for a Universal Grant. Wright does not adequately answer the question whether the permanently unemployed – being in a social position that is not directly determined by production relations – consist of a "contradictory location" (between proletariat and bourgeoisie) or a distinct class.

But recent developments in Marxist theories of exploitation (and in the first place his own book on classes) leave room for an interpretation, in which they can be considered a class. Indeed, in this most recent book, E.O, Wright (1985) argues (by referring to Roemer, 1982) in favor of a concept of class that is, and intrinsically, related to (capitalist) exploitation, in terms of a causal link between material advantages (income) and various categories of assets (control over productive forces). Classes and exploitation are defined in terms of income inequalities that are due to the unequal distribution of some asset (income, skill of organisational assets) – and not to choice or chance; there has to exist a positive causal link between a certain distribution of assets and a certain distribution of income. By this approach Wright avoids that the relation between permanently working and nonworking nonowning persons under capitalist relations within a Universal Grant setting, to be interpreted in terms of exploitation and/or class struggle (workers "choose" to work, nonworkers "choose" not to work). But one can raise the question whether there is in a dual society really room for a free chioce between working and nonworking and whether in due time the dual structure will not be reproduced as a class pattern, based on the unequal distribution of either wealth, skill or status, and protected by all sorts of institutional barriers.

One can hypothetically deduce the following class structure from the model of a capitalist society with a Basic Income:

(a) the productive labor force which is, on the one hand, exploited by the capitalist, and on the other taxed by the state;
(b) the unproductive permanently unemployed who are living from a Basic Income, guaranteed by the state and paid from taxes,
(c) capital owners who are living from (part of) their profits,
(d) state bureaucrats and repressive executives (the state) who are living off taxes. and provide the guarantee that (a) is "prepared" to work for (b), and pay for (c) as well as themselves.

This is an utterly improbable model of a society. What will prevent the permanently working class from organising itself in order to struggle aginst the exploitation, repression and taxing? What – and who – will prevent them – or the owners of capital – from associating with state bureaucrats and executives in order to abolish or diminish the Universal Grant? And what social power has the class of permanently unemployed at its disposal for defending its interst? The model of "Universal Grant capitalism" depends as a whole on the supposition that a permanent harmonious and solidary tie between (a), (b) and (c) is possible, or that (b) and (d) can from a coalition against (a) and (c). This is totally unlikely, as there is no material basis for such a solidarity, whilst (d) has no interest in associating with (b). A permanent association, on the other hand, between (a) and (c) can mean only that they do not have opposed interests and this implies that they are the same group; but then we have reached the stage of socialism – where the access to the means of production is socialized/democratized – exactly the stage (toward communism) which Van Parijs intended to avoid with his "Universal Grant capitalism".

However, it is much more likely that coalitions of (c) and (d), or of (a) and (d), will be formed, as the intersets of (d) do not inspire any economic or political reason for associating with (b). The permanently unemployed lack any (economic and therefore social) power. They are only a "begging party" which can neither withdraw its labor power, nor its capital as a means of pressure.

That is to say that even if the permanently unemployed have a clear insight into their collective interests, they lack the capaciti struggle for them. Here, as in Marxist discussions on the feasibility of socialism, it is the relation between interests and capacities which defines a scientific and nonutopian answer. As far as can be seen today, the permanently unemployed lack the structure as well as the organisational capacities to struggle collectively for their interests as they lack an economic power basis and live furthermore physically isolated from one another as well, so that the possibilities for self-organisation are scarce and purely accidental.

Social security schemes are, one way or the other, related to the sructural solidarity within a social class, a group of people similarly located within the relations of productions; the power of the other proletariat consists in its being a productive force within the production relations and its having, because of this, a power of the other means of prodution as well as the power to refuse its productive activities to the owners of capital. The proletariat has the power to *force* the capital-owners toward certain concessions.

The Universal Grant proposal lacks any such social power foundation. It puts the state in a (even more) central position by trasnsforming social security provisions into fiscal relations, and creates thus a (permanent) segment of the population that will be permanently dependent on the state and its repressive apparatus, as it lacks any social power itself. We think that it is utterly unlikely that, under present capitalist conditions, a Basic Income allocation can be more than a (neo-liberal) alms. As a consequence, it is of fundamental importance not to give up one's social power, needed to defend one's interests, and this power is situated within production, in heterogenous labor activities. The feminist movement has proven once again that only participation – for however short a period of time – within the sphere of production guarantees a say in other spheres of social life as well. This has nothing to do with "productivism" or "work ethics." It is based on the simple, though not simplistic, insight that in order to "guarantee" something one needs power, not moral arguments, and this power is situated in production, not in consumption.

Proposals to develop an alternative for classic Marxist schemes toward a communist society of free disposal over time and equal access to the means of production suggest that fundamental changes in the distributive relations of consumption can be realized without changing the capitalist relations of production. At first sight they thus have the attractive quality of avoiding references to the "violence" of class struggle.

It remains doubtful, however, whether they do not suppress the problem of social power (which Marxists exactly propose to solve by their concept of socialism) rather than having an alternative solution for it. It is between a Basic Income of 10,000 france and a Basic Income of 25,000 france that all the reality of class struggle is located. Within present-day socio-economical and political relations it is much more plausible that proposals to establish a Universal Grant end up in alms à la Milton Friedman instead of in abundancy à la Fourier, whilst instituionalising at the same time the "fiscal class struggle" which is so important in neo-liberal analysis (and ideology).

Criticising proposals to uncouple income and work does not mean at all that one embraces a work ethic, or that one is a victim of productivism. One is not a defender of capitalism because one claims a position within capitalist relations of production; there *are* no other production relations. Neither does it mean that one does not participate in the struggle against degrading, enslaving, sickness-creating or killing work conditions and the alienation and exploitation of laborers. On the contrary; it is only possible to organize the struggle from *within* the production process, from *within* the relations of production. One cannot fight productivism whilst giving up the power basis of the labor force.

As a consequence, only a drastic though flexible redistribution of the socially necessary, heteronomous labor can guarantee democratic and emancipatory replies to the problem of the falling quantity of socially necessary labor.

Note

1. Editor's note: This conference paper appeared unedited in a conference proceedings and was not revised for wider publication in the author's lifetime. It has several typos or missing references.

References

Collectif Charles Fourier (1984). De universale uitkering, Koning Boudewijnstichting. Arbeid-Morgen, Dialoog voor de Toekomst. Brussel, pp. 9–17.

Gorz, A. (1986). Wie niet werkt zal niettemin eten. Maakt het basisinkomen de robotmaatschappij leefbaar? *De Groene Amsterdammer*, 6, augustus, 9–11.

Lepage, H. (1978). *Demain Le Liberalisme*. Hachette, Paris.

Raes, K. (1983). Aan Hen de Keuze? Een kritisch essay over de ideologie van het neo-liberaal bezitsindividualisme. Masereelfonds, Gent.

Raes, K. (1984). Individualisme(n), Klassen en Sociale Conflicten, Een Kritiek op het Libertarisch Klassenbegrip. *Vlaams Marxistisch Tijdschrift*, 9–45.

Roemer, J. (1982). *A General Theory of Exploitation and Class*. Harvard University Press, Cambridge, MA.

Therborn, G. (1986). *Karl Marx Returning by the Welfare State* (mimeographed).

Van Dun, F. (1983). *Het Fundamenteel Rechtsbeginsel*. Kluwer-Rechtswetenschappen, Antwerpen.

Van Parijs, P. (1985a). Marx, L'ecologisme et la transition directe du capitalisme au communisme. In B. Chavance (ed.) *Marx en Perspective*. Ecole des Hautes Etudes en Sciences Sociales, Paris, pp. 135–155.

Van Parijs, P. (1985b). *A Revolution in Class Theory. Comment on Erik Wright's "general framework"* (mimeographed).

Van Parijs, P. (1986). L'avenir des ecologistes: deux interpretations. *La Revue Nouvelle*, 83, 37–45.

Wright E.O. (1978). *Class, Crisis and the State*, New Left Books, London.

Wright E.O. (1985). *Classes.* Verso, London.

Chapter 38

Cost Estimates for a Basic Income in the United States

Charles M.A. Clark

Excerpts from Clark, C.M.A. (2005). The Economics of Poverty in the United States of America. *Oikonomia: The Journal of Ethics and Social Sciences*, 4 (3), 6–19.

The following is a Basic Income (BI) proposal for the United States, based on the year 2002. The proposed Basic Income System here is a full one for children and adults, with a system of top-up payments for the elderly to bring all elderly above the poverty line. The Basic Income payments have been set at the official poverty threshold for an individual (and an estimate for a child) for the year 2002. The system of top-up payments for the poor elderly is designed to get them above the poverty threshold. Thus, if enacted, the Basic Income System would bring the official poverty rate in the United States to zero for all population groups. The Basic Income System would have payment levels – see Table 38.1.

This, in turn, would have the following costs – see Table 38.2.

The total costs of our Basic Income proposal would be just under 2 trillion dollars (Table 38.2). Add to this the cost of the other functions of the Federal Government, which in 2002 totaled $1,743 billion ($2,010,975 million minus the $267,322 million income security funds to be cut under a Basic Income proposal). Thus the total costs of the Federal Government would be $3,716.39 million.

Funding for the Basic Income System, as well as for the Federal Government in general, would be through a flat tax on all incomes, to replace the Federal Income Tax, as well as the other remaining sources of Federal Government Funding. However, this proposal produces a balance budget. The necessary flat tax to fund the Basic Income System and the rest of the Federal Government would be 35.2% (32.2% if we had allowed for the deficit that actually existed in 2002). There would be no income tax deductions. State and local tax and benefits systems in our example are left untouched, although obviously they would change dramatically (i.e., be reduced or eliminated, leading to reductions in local and state taxes).

From Clark, C.M.A. (2005). The Economics of Poverty in the United States of America. *Oikonomia: The Journal of Ethics and Social Sciences*, 4 (3), 6–19. Reprinted with permission of *Oikonomia*.

Basic Income: An Anthology of Contemporary Research, First Edition. Edited by Karl Widerquist, José A. Noguera, Yannick Vanderborght, and Jurgen De Wispelaere.

Table 38.1 Basic Income Payments, 2002.

Age	*Payment*
Under 18	$3,500
Adult	$9,359

Table 38.2 Cost of Basic Income System, 2002.

Age	*Payment*	*Population (millions)*	*Costs ($ millions)*
Under 18	$3,500	72.89	255,129
Adult	$9,359	179.87	1,683,422
Over 65			34,184
Total			1,972,735

Table 38.3 Federal Government Revenues (millions).

Flat Tax	2,722,000
Corporate Taxes	148,044
Social Insurance	700,760
Excise Taxes	66,989
Other	79,035
Total	3,716,828

Table 38.4 Income Distribution Effects of Basic Income System.

Income Quintile	*Without BI (2002)*	*With Basic Income (2002)*
Bottom	3.55	6.01
2nd	8.89	10.73
3rd	15.27	16.60
4th	24.09	25.75
Top	48.20	40.91

Source: Author's calculations. Totals may not equal 100% due to rounding.

Thus, under this proposal the total expenditures of the Federal Government would be $3,716.4 billion, while the total revenue would be $3,716.8 billion, leaving a small surplus of $400 million.

Distributional Impact

Using the 2002 consumer expenditure survey data, I have simulated how such a policy would affect the distribution of income in the United States. Table 38.4 presents the results

Table 38.5 Average Household Income by Quintile, 2002, Without and With Basic Income.

Income Quintile	*Without BI*	*With BI*	*Difference*
Bottom	8,323	14,109	5,786
2nd	20,859	25,189	4,330
3rd	35,817	38,946	3,129
4th	56,497	60,422	3,925
Top	113,044	96,005	–17,039

of this simulation. In Table 38.5 we see the average household income for each household quintile, and their gain or loss due to the Basic Income System.

Introducing a Basic Income System in the United States like the one proposed would have the dual effect of lifting everyone above the "official" poverty level, and of more than eliminating the rise in income inequality of the past three decades.

Part VI
Post-productivism

Introduction

Basic Income as a Post-productivist Policy

José A. Noguera and Karl Widerquist

The argument for the necessity of a "post-productivist" social policy has been an important part of the Basic Income debate at least since the 1964, when Robert Theobald, Gunnar Myrdal, Robert Heilbronner, and others signed an open letter (entitled *The Triple Revolution*) to the U.S. President arguing that the modern economy was in the process of breaking the traditional link between jobs and income. This particular economic issue has been so important to the Basic Income debate that it requires separate attention.

"Post-productivism" can have at least two meanings, although they are strongly related for some authors. First, post-productivism may refer to the necessity of taking into account ecological concerns when designing policy options; in this perspective, most Green parties and movements have been sympathetic to Basic Income proposals (or, at least, more sympathetic than other traditional ideological families). What is the relation of Basic Income to Green political programs? Would a Basic Income be a key part of a new ecological economy?

Secondly, post-productivism may also mean that work (especially paid work) is not or should not be a central pillar of society any more, and that full employment is an unattainable and/or undesirable political goal. Under this view (which may not only be compatible but also congenial to the first one), a post-productivist social policy would try to value unpaid activities and leisure time over formal employment, and would give citizens large opportunities to chose their life options outside of the conventional labor market. Would Basic Income be the logical consequence of implementing this kind of policy? What are the rationales for a post-productivist welfare state and how would Basic Income fit within it?

Two texts in this section deal with the first interpretation. Tony Fitzpatrick (1999), in "Ecologism and Basic Income," evaluates the pros and cons of a possible Green defense of Basic Income, and concludes that Basic Income may be an important ingredient of a

---

Basic Income: An Anthology of Contemporary Research, First Edition. Edited by Karl Widerquist, José A. Noguera, Yannick Vanderborght, and Jurgen De Wispelaere.

Green social model, but only if accompanied by a full ecological policy package. In "A Green Case for Basic Income?" (previously unpublished), Philippe Van Parijs, however, makes the case that the main ecological rationale for Basic Income lies not in its consequences for an ecological economy or for growth and employment, but in its radical option for a "free-time oriented preference structure;" hence, Van Parijs clearly favors the connection between Basic Income and the second understanding of "post-productivism."

On the side of this second interpretation Claus Offe (1992) offers a canonical explanation of the reasons to challenge the productivist welfare post-war consensus around full employment (the "productivist syndrome"), and to favor instead a Basic Income. These reasons include the crisis of the traditional models of family, of collective actors, and of social assistance programs as well as contributory ones. Offe explores the potential political responses that the main ideological families may give to this crisis, and concludes that only "the politics of Basic Income proposals" may face it successfully.

In an empirical and policy-oriented analysis, Robert Goodin (2002) brings the post-productivist discourse down to the research on existing welfare regimes, and identifies a specific "post-productivist" regime, with the Netherlands as its paradigmatic case and individual autonomy as its core guiding value. Since such a regime would try to make possible "welfare without (formal full-time) work," Basic Income is clearly in the "music" if not in the "lyrics" of its institutional architecture. However, Goodin explicitly observes a shift in the Netherlands from a "basic-income post-productivist regime" to a "participation-income" one.

In a similar fashion, Bert Hamminga (1995) proposes an original and provocative mental experiment: an hypothetical society (Eu) in which "Labor Rights" would be equally distributed among the population, so that citizens can buy and sell those rights in a free market, according to the value they attach to work and income. As Hamminga brilliantly argues, in such a situation it is to be expected that involuntary employment and involuntary unemployment would be eradicated, and those voluntarily unemployed would enjoy a Basic Income as a result of selling their Labor Rights. Hamminga's experiment was productively used by Van Parijs in his real-libertarian justification of Basic Income, and offers an imaginative way of designing the labor market in a post-productivist society with an out-of-work income guarantee, while avoiding reciprocity objections.

A well-known leading voice in the post-productivist intellectual movement from the 1980s has been André Gorz's. In "Beyond the Wage-based Society," Gorz (1997) abandons for the first time his initial opposition to Basic Income, and makes his support for the idea official. His position is a good example of a certain Green/New Left/post-socialist/humanist stream of thinking which has often sympathized with Basic Income (including authors like Fromm, Illich, Negri, Negt and others). This stream links the defense of Basic Income with the need for reducing working hours and raising leisure time and/or time for autonomous activities. The idea that knowledge has become the most important productive force is also an important rationale for Gorz's change of position. Gorz also refers to Marx and his praise in favor of leisure time, and argues for the "elimination of work" and its replacement by "personal activities."

Finally, in "The relevance of Basic Income for Post-industrial Economics," Fred Block (1990) argues that the technological and social requirements of post-industrial economies may generate the political conditions for a weakening of the work ethic and of the link between work and income; and that, he claims, may give rise to a new post-productivist coalition which abandons full employment as a political aim and endorses the idea of a Basic Income.

Further Reading

Arnsperger, C. and Johnson, W.A. (2011). The guaranteed income as an equal-opportunity tool in the transition toward sustainability. In A. Gosseries and Y. Vanderborght (eds) *Arguing about Justice. Essays for Philippe Van Parijs*. Presses universitaires de Louvain, Louvain-la-Neuve, pp. 61–69.

Beck, U. (2000). *The Brave New World of Work*. Cambridge University Press, Cambridge.

Birnbaum, S. (ed.) (2009). Debate: The Green Case for Basic Income. *Basic Income Studies*, 4 (2), with contributions by J.O. Andersson, S. Birnbaum, P.-M. Boulanger, G. Calder, T. Fitzpatrick, and P. Van Parijs. http://www.degruyter.com/view/j/bis

Gorz, A. (1992). On the difference between society and community, and why basic income cannot by itself confer full membership of either. In P. Van Parijs (ed.) *Arguing for Basic Income: Ethical Foundations for a Radical Reform*. Verso, London/New York, pp. 178–184.

Gorz, A. (1999). *Reclaiming Work*. Polity Press, Cambridge.

Haagh, L. (2011). Basic income, social democracy and control over time. *Policy and Politics*, 39 (1), 43–66.

Keane, J. and Owens, J. (1986). *After Full Employment*. Hutchinson, London.

Little, A. (1998). *Post-Industrial Socialism: Towards a New Politics of Welfare*. Routledge, London.

Meade, J.E. (1995). *Full Employment Regained? An Agathotopian Dream*. Cambridge University Press, Cambridge.

Offe, C. and Heinze, R. (1992). *Beyond Employment: Time, Work, and the Informal Economy*. Polity Press, Cambridge.

Perrucci, R., and Pilisuk, M. (eds) (1968). *The Triple Revolution: Social Problems in Depth*. Little Brown & Co, Boston.

Robertson, J. (1985). *Future Work: Jobs, self-employment and leisure after the industrial age*. Temple Smith/Gower, Aldershot; full text available online with a 2006 preface by the author: http://www.jamesrobertson.com/.

Robertson, J. (ed.) (1998). *Sharing Our Common Heritage: Resource Taxes and Green Dividends*. Proceedings of the International Conference of the Oxford Centre for the Environment, Ethics and Society, 14 May.

Theobald, R. (ed.) (1967). *The Guaranteed Income: Next Step in Economic Evolution?* Doubleday, Garden City, NY.

van der Veen, R. and Groot, L. (2006). Post-productivism and welfare states: A comparative analysis. *British Journal of Political Science*, 36 (4), 593–618.

Van Parijs, P. (1991). Basic income: A green strategy for the new Europe. In S. Parkin (ed.) *Green Light on Europe*. Heretic Books, London.

Van Parijs, P. (1992). Competing Justifications of Basic Income. In P. Van Parijs (ed.) *Arguing for Basic Income: Ethical Foundations for a Radical Reform*. Verso, London/New York, pp. 3–43.

Widerquist, K. (2006). John Maynard Keynes: Economic possibilities of our grandchidren. *Dissent Magazine*, Winter. http://www.dissentmagazine.org/author/karlwiderquist

Chapter 39
Ecologism and Basic Income

Tony Fitzpatrick

Excerpts from Fitzpatrick, T. (1999). Ecologism and Basic Income. In *Freedom and Security. An Introduction to the Basic Income Debate*. Macmillan, London, Ch. 9.

If I point out that ecologists are often the most vociferous supporters of Basic Income (BI) the reader may already be able to anticipate why. For an ecological perspective on welfare and benefit reform BI offers three main advantages. The first of these concerns BI's potential to assist in the dampening down of growth.

According to ecologists, the drive for ever higher levels of economic growth is fuelled by a number of factors: capital's need to accumulate, individual materialism and a productivist interpretation of redistribution (which says that the poor should be helped by increasing the nation's total stock of wealth rather than zero-sum redistribution from rich to poor). Whatever the motivation the common belief is that at a GDP of, say, £800 billion a country such as Britain is twice as well off as it was when GDP was £400 billion. What this economistic definition of welfare assumes, of course, is that the more "goods" there are then the higher the level of needs and desire fulfilment; but even putting aside the point made long ago by Fred Hirsch (1976), that material goods are "positional", that is, their utility diminishes in inverse proportion to their quantity, what this economism ignores is the fact that economic growth also generates "bads" which neutralize the positive effects of goods. To illustrate this using a simple example: the aspiration to acquire consumer goods, an aspiration which growth both requires and encourages, contradicts the no-wage/low-wage living standards which exist at the labor market's periphery, something which growth also requires and encourages. Indeed, Ulrich Beck (1992) insists that a post-industrial society is that which is characterized by its generation of bads. This contradiction between consumption (good) and the nonconsumption of the poorest (bad) leads to numerous social traumas such as crime, hopelessness and addiction, yet both sides of the equation derive from the simplistic link which is made between wellbeing and the unlimited expansion of material wealth.

According to ecologists, what we need is some way of breaking this link and of slowing the growth process down. A number of proposals have been put forward for changing accounting procedures so that indicators such as GDP are abandoned and ecologically

From Fitzpatrick, T. (1999). Ecologism and Basic Income. In *Freedom and Security. An Introduction to the Basic Income Debate*. Macmillan, London, Ch. 9. Reprinted with permission of Palgrave Macmillan.

Basic Income: An Anthology of Contemporary Research, First Edition. Edited by Karl Widerquist, José A. Noguera, Yannick Vanderborght, and Jurgen De Wispelaere.

sensitive indicators, which take account of both social and environmental bads, are introduced (Daly and Cobb, 1990; Anderson, 1991; Jackson and Marks, 1994). We would then have a better measuring-rod for assessing the true state of social welfare. But according to some a BI could also help to break this link (Johnson, 1973; van Parijs, 1985; Powell, 1989; Daly and Cobb, 1990; Hoogendijk, 1991; Lerner, 1994; Offe et al., 1996: 209–210). At present, most benefits are distributed to most individuals on the basis of the past, present or potential contributions which they have made, are making or could make to GDP growth. The insurance/assistance model is based upon this notion of productive contributions and when people defend the conditionality of benefit provision they do so on the basis that "the world doesn't owe anyone a living" or some such opinion. By being unconditional a BI breaks this link between making a contribution and receiving a benefit and so undermines the rationale of GDP growth. Or, to put it another way, by being paid irrespective of job record and status a BI undercuts the employment ethic and so challenges the productivist assumptions which legitimate that ethic.

Therefore, what other ideologies treat as a disadvantage ecologism tends to treat as a virtue (Mellor, 1992: 206). Welfare collectivists are worried about the possibility that a BI would permit people to opt out of the labor market altogether and a Participation Income is favored by some in order to avoid this possibility. For ecologists, meanwhile, people *should* be opting out of the labor market: the fewer people that are actually contributing to GDP growth then the more the brakes will be applied to such growth. In fact, we should aim at a full BI as soon as possible in order to provide people with the incentive to abandon wage-earning. In theory, the higher the BI then the slower the rate of GDP growth.

One objection to all of this, of course, is to point out that the full BI envisaged by ecologists is impossible: because as a full BI encourages a mass migration from the labor market then society's ability to fund that BI is correspondingly undermined (Irvine and Ponton, 1988: 73; Kemp and Wall, 1990: 78). However, putting aside the importance which ecologists attach to land and energy taxation as a source of BI funding, Green BI supporters usually defend an "optimal BI": one which slows growth down to an environmentally sustainable extent without the economy having to contract. This is illustrated in Figure 39.1.

As the level of BI increases so GDP growth begins to slow (line *X–O*). At point *OP* on the curve BI has reached its optimum level, so that any attempt to slow growth further

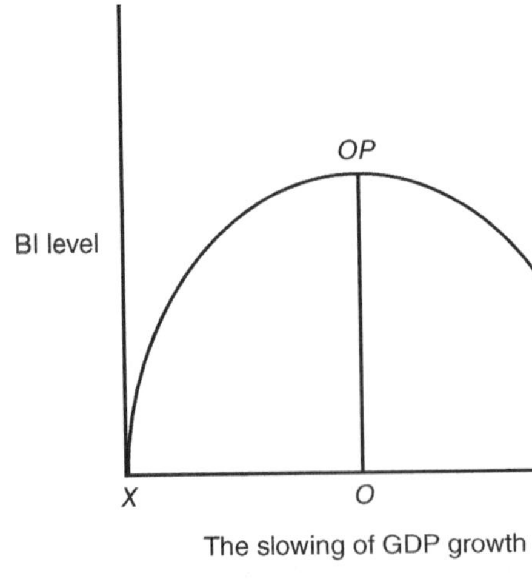

Figure 39.1 Basic Income and GDP Growth.

(line O–Y) would only lower the BI level by reducing the tax yield needed to fund it. This lower BI would then encourage people to reenter the labor market and so create more economic growth. In theory, then, using BI as an anti-growth measure means that GDP growth can only slow to point *O* on the horizontal axis because BI begins to decrease in value beyond point *OP* on the curve.

There are obviously important questions as to what level of income this optimal BI would imply. If it were still a relatively modest level then no great market exodus would occur and GDP growth would not slow down to any great extent after all, that is, GDP growth at point *O* in Figure 39.1 would not represent a significant change to that at point *X*; thus, a central Green justification of BI would be weakened. Green supporters, however, still insist that a BI is likely to produce the desired benefits even if an assessment of its full impact cannot be made until after it has been introduced.

The second major reason why ecologists support a BI deals not with its effects on the economy but with its embodiment of an ethic of common ownership. In Paine's early defence of something resembling a BI he argued that some form of compensation was needed for the way in which the economic system of private ownership (which Paine defended) has expropriated that which is, properly speaking, the common ownership of all. On this basis Paine justifies the setting up of a National Fund out of which a lump-sum grant and a citizen's pension should be paid.

Social wealth can be thought of as deriving from three sources: (a) natural assets, (b) economic and technological inheritance, and (c) the cooperative efforts of existing workers/contributors. Even if a BI cannot be justified with reference to (c) because it is received regardless of contributions to social wealth, it can be justified with reference to (a) and (b). This argument chimes with the insistence of Greens that the Earth's resources be thought of as held in common, so that being a global citizen means being a steward or a trustee whose duty it is to hand on the Earth to the next generation of common owners. This does not imply returning the Earth to a "state of nature" since resources, especially renewable ones, can be utilized; however, it also means that a certain proportion of the wealth which ultimately derives from this common ownership should be shared out unconditionally: common ownership implies a fundamental *equality* of ownership. Whereas the present transfer system provides most to those who contribute the most to environmentally damaging growth, a BI would express and embody a communal egalitarianism which is not captured by the insurance/assistance model. Obviously, a BI is not the only means of embodying this communal egalitarianism, but it is one which offers a realistic alternative to the present ways of distributing income by embodying an ethic of common ownership, our common interests and the common good (Jordan, 1992).

The final reason why many Greens support a BI is familiar to us by now and so can be mentioned briefly (Ekins, 1986; British Green Party, 1987, 1992, 1997; Irvine and Ponton, 1988: 70; Lambert, 1997: 60–61). Because a BI could reduce or eliminate the poverty and unemployment traps it would make part-time work and, depending upon its level, low-paid work more attractive and so could go some way to achieving the aim of redistributing available jobs by taking the emphasis away from the necessity of working full-time for several decades (Kemp and Wall, 1990: 77). As part-time employment became more financially worthwhile then many people might take up the option of working part-time and it is possible that an expansion in work-sharing activities could result, as well as an increase in people taking sabbaticals from employment. In short, and unlike insurance contributions, a BI: would provide a guaranteed minimum income for all, by repairing the holes in the benefit safety-net; would not be a tax on jobs; would improve the range of available alternatives (Nissen, 1992); would permit flexibility without being a charter for low-paid casualization.[1]

However, there are also three principal reasons why Greens might not wish to support a BI.

The first potential problem is that although a BI could have a role to play in a future ecological society its ability to carry us forward into that society is either limited or non-existent. Mary Mellor (1992: 206–207), for instance, is attracted to the principle of a BI but insists that its introduction is dependent upon a prior change in the ownership of productive property. Looking again at Figure 39.1, the allegation is that the difference between *X* and *O* is not that great: in other words, the optimum level of BI would not slow GDP growth down to any great extent. The achievement of a Green society and economy is going to require a massive change in public consciousness and institutional reorganization whereas a BI might do no more than consolidate existing values, assumptions and habits. Therefore, ecological critics echo those feminist critics who point out that the BI society existing on the Wednesday would be substantially the same as the pre-BI society which had existed on the Monday. According to Andrew Dobson, a BI

> [. . .] looks like a social-democratic measure grafted unsustainably onto the ailing post-industrial body politic, rather than a radically Green measure in the spirit of solutions to the problems of sustainability raised by the spectre of limits to growth. (Dobson, 1995: 111; cf. Frankel, 1987: 79–83; George and Wilding, 1994: 181)

Dobson therefore identifies what he takes to be a contradiction between the anti-materialism of Green thought and the fact that BI is dependent upon a high level of material wealth for its financing.

The second Green objection concerns, as so many times before, the unconditional nature of a BI. On one level it is true that a BI would enable people to opt out of the "employment society", with its ethos of competition and acquisition, and pursue other activities. The trouble is that there is no guarantee that these other activities will be environmentally friendly: perhaps they would merely be parasitic on the very productivism and materialism which Greens strenuously oppose. André Gorz (1992), for example, argues that although a guaranteed minimum income is a necessary condition for social participation it is not a sufficient condition and that the provision of a BI to an individual should be conditional upon the performance of a minimum amount of work during his/her lifetime. Alain Lipietz (1992: 93–99) agrees, arguing that an unconditional income scheme is not only unfair on those who finance it, but is morally debilitating for those who cannot find employment and so become dependent upon it:

> [. . .] a universal allowance of around two thirds of minimum wage would be acceptable only if it meant that those who received it were *prepared* to show their solidarity with society. [. . .] A permanent state of affairs where some people are helped to do nothing is not only provocative to people in work, it is also psychologically painful for those being helped. (Lipietz, 1992: 99)

In response to these kinds of objections, Jan Otto Andersson (1996a, 1996b), has argued that raising the level of an unconditional income in the hope of achieving a full BI is unlikely to encourage those activities and lifestyles which are most conducive to an ecological society (cf. Dobell, 1996). As an alternative, he believes that a small but unconditional BI for all (which can still be supported due to its promotion of personal autonomy) be combined with a Citizen's Wage which, not being a million miles away from a Participation Income, would be provided to those who engage in activity outside the labor market which is judged to be socially useful and environmentally friendly. The objective here is to promote the expansion of the Third Sector, that is, that which is organized around neither the state nor the market, a goal which Andersson shares with Jeremy Rifkin (1995: 256–267) who has also argued in favor of tying the guaranteed income into service in the communal activities of a "social economy".

The final objection states that there is a contradiction between the decentralization which Greens desire and the fact that a BI would have to be administered centrally, for example, to facilitate redistribution from rich areas to poor ones (Frankel, 1987). This objection, though, depends upon a vision of a Green society as being as decentralized as administratively possible, perhaps along the lines suggested by Bookchin (1972) or Sale (1985). However, if we were not to favor this type of anarchistic approach, and if we envisage a continuing role for central government, which seems necessary since a global economy does not cease being environmentally destructive just because a group of people form themselves into a "bioregion," then the contradiction vanishes: BI can be a form of central administration whose function, in a Green society, could be to facilitate the decentralized self-management of Andersson's Third Sector (cf. Dobson, 1995: 210).

As with previous ideologies, then, we find that Greens too have various reasons both to support and to oppose a BI. It embodies a social right not to engage in productivist, wage-earning activity (while making it easier to take part-time work) but says little about the obligations which we owe to nonhumans and to future generations. It perhaps takes into account the environmental consequences of growth but the effects which its introduction would have in slowing GDP growth down are uncertain. It guarantees a minimum income for all and challenges the employment ethic, but it also seems to depend upon the very ecologically damaging activities to which Greens object. The question, then, is whether a BI could be made to work in such a way that the above objections to it can be discarded. As with feminism, there is no specific Green BI, but there is a policy package to which a BI could belong.

Conclusion

Drawing upon the work of pro-BI supporters such as Robertson, Gorz and Offe we can see that a Green policy package should include not only BI but also land and energy taxes, working-time reductions and the expansion of informal exchanges in the third sector. On one level, therefore, this means that a BI would constitute one of the four ingredients of the ecological package. However, given that Robertson, Gorz and Offe all identify BI as having an essential role to play, perhaps we should regard it as something of a common denominator: as a means of establishing links between the advocates of land/energy taxes, working hour reductions and informal economies. Viewed in this way a BI would not so much be another ingredient of the Green policy package as an instrument by which that package is constructed in the first place.

Note

1. Although Greens do seem more willing than most to contemplate abolishing minimum wage legislation (British Green Party, 1995a; 1995b).

References

Anderson, V. (1991). *Alternative Economic Indicators.* Routledge, London.

Andersson, J.O. (1996a). Fundamental Values for a Third Left. *New Left Review*, 216, 66–78.

Andersson, J.O. (1996b). *Why a Citizen's Income Should be Combined with a Citizen's Wage.* Paper presented to the Sixth International Congress of the *Basic Income European Network*, Vienna International Centre, Vienna, 12–14 September 1996.

Beck, U. (1992). *Risk Society.* Sage, London.

Bookchin, M. (1980). *Towards all Ecological Society.* Black Rose, Montreal.

British Green Party (1987). *General Election Campaign Manifesto.* Green Party, London.

British Green Party (1992). *General Election Campaign Manifesto.* Green Party, London.

British Green Party (1995a). *Minimum Wages or Basic Income – or Both.* Green Party, London.

British Green Party (1995b). *A Guide to the Green Party's Basic Income Scheme.* Green Party, London.

British Green Party (1997). *General Election Campaign Manifesto.* Green Party, London.

Daly, H. and Cobb, J. (1990). *For the Common Good.* Green Print, London.

Dobell, R. (1996). The Dance of the Deficit and the Real World of Wealth. *Family Security in Insecure Times.* National Forum on Family Security, Ottawa.

Dobson, A. (1995). *Green Political Thought: An Introduction*, 2nd edn. Routledge, London.

Ekins, P. (ed.) (1986). *The Living Economy.* Routledge, London.

Frankel, B. (1987). *The Post-Industrial Utopians.* Polity Press, Cambridge.

George, V. and Wilding, P. (1994). *Welfare and Ideology.* Harvester Wheatsheaf, Hemel Hempstead.

Gorz, A. (1992). On the Difference Between Society and Community, and Why Basic Income Cannot by Itself Confer Full Membership of Either. In Van Parijs, P. (ed.) *Arguing for Basic Income.* Verso, London.

Hirsch, F. (1976). *The Social Limits to Growth.* Harvard University Press, Cambridge, MA.

Hoogendijk, W. (1991). *The Economic Revolution.* Merlin Press, London.

Irvine, S. and Ponton, A. (1988). *A Green Manifesto.* Macdonald Optima, London.

Jackson, T. and Marks, N. (1994). *Index of Sustainable Economic Welfare.* Stockholm Environment Institute in cooperation with the New Economics Foundation, Stockholm.

Johnson, W. (1973). The Guaranteed Income as an Environmental Measure. In H. Daly (ed.) *Toward a Steady-State Economy.* W.H. Freeman, San Francisco.

Jordan, B. (1992). Basic Income and the Common Good. In P. Van Parijs (ed.) *Arguing for Basic Income.* Verso, London.

Kemp, P. and Wall, D. (1990). *A Green Manifesto for the 1990s.* Penguin, Harmondsworth.

Lambert, J. (1997). *No Change? No Chance!* Jon Carpenter, London.

Lerner, S. (1994). The Future of Work in North America: Good Jobs, Bad Jobs, Beyond Jobs. *Futures*, 26 (2), 185–196.

Lipietz, A. (1992). *Towards a New Economic Order.* Polity Press, Cambridge.

Mellor, M. (1992). *Breaking the Boundaries.* Virago, London.

Nissen, S. (1992). The Jobs Dilemma: Ecological Versus Economic Issues. *Basic Income Research Group Bulletin*, 14, 9–11.

Offe, C., Mückenberger, U., and Ostner, I. (1996). A Basic Income Guaranteed by the State: A Need of the Moment in Social Policy. In C. Offe, *Modernity and the State: East, West.* Polity Press, Cambridge.

Powell, R. (1989). Towards Ecological Security. *Social Alternatives*, 9 (1), 15–16.

Rifkin, J. (1995). *The End of Work.* G.P. Putnam's Sons, New York.

Sale, K. (1985). *Dwellers in the Land.* Sierra Club, San Francisco.

Van Parijs, P. (1985). Marx, l'écologisme et la transition directe du capitalisme au communisme. In B. Chavance (ed.) *Marx en Perspective.* Editions de l'Ecole des Hautes Etudes, Paris.

Chapter 40

A Green Case for Basic Income?

Philippe Van Parijs

Excerpts from Van Parijs, P. (1987) *Basic Income in a Green Economy: Why Not and Why?* Paper presented at the Second European Green Congress (Stockholm, 28-20 August). Previously unpublished.

Whether Astrid and Gunnar are old or young, rich or poor, whether or not they work, whether or not they are able to work, whether or not they are available for work, whether they live on their own or with one another, give them each, out of State funds, an income sufficient to cover their basic needs. This is, in a nutshell, what Basic Income consists in.

In the last few years, this old idea has become, throughout Europe, the focus of sustained attention and intense discussion as it has never been before.[1] From the far Left to the far Right, all political groupings have, to various extents, been touched by this revival of interest. But none as much as the Greens. In all countries where there is both a debate on Basic Income and a Green Party, those who join the former most enthusiastically tend to be members of the latter or, if not, close to it. Moreover, many European Green Parties have made Basic Income a central component of their socio-economic policy, and those which have not are actively discussing the matter. Finally, some Greens argue that the introduction of a Basic Income constitutes the very core of a Green conception of the economy, and the only thing that sets it off sharply from both liberal and socialist blueprints.[2]

But why is this? Why do Greens tend to be more favorable than others to the idea of a Basic Income? And why must they be? What is the exact nature of this strong link which seems to exist between wanting the world to be green and wanting people to get a Basic Income? Indeed, does such a link really exist? Is it not based on sheer confusion? These are the questions I want to address.

The First Reply

Ecological limits to growth and structural unemployment

A first explanation of why Greens find (and should find) Basic Income so congenial goes about like this. Greens are highly concerned with the depletion of our natural resources

From Van Parijs, P. (1987) *Basic Income in a Green Economy: Why Not and Why?* Paper presented at the Second European Green Congress (Stockholm, 28-20 August). Previously unpublished. Printed with kind permission of the author.

Basic Income: An Anthology of Contemporary Research, First Edition. Edited by Karl Widerquist, José A. Noguera, Yannick Vanderborght, and Jurgen De Wispelaere.

and the destruction of our environment. In order to keep these processes under check, they want to stop economic growth, or at the very least to slow it down in the most advanced industrial countries. Low rates of output growth, however, are most likely to fall short of the rate at which labor productivity increases, due to technological progress. As a consequence, we need less and less labor to achieve the level of production we think is desirable, and unemployment is bound to expand. There is nothing like massive unemployment to generate a broad social consensus around pro-growth policies. As a consequence, whether or not they are bothered by the unemployment problem as such, Greens who mean business must find a way of tackling the unemployment problem through means other than the fostering of economic growth.

And this is where Basic Income comes in. For Basic Income consists precisely in giving everyone an unconditional income whether or not (s)he makes any contribution to the gross national product – that is, to the magnitude whose increase is, by definition, growth. It therefore reduces people's incentive to make such contribution, that is, to work or invest in the formal sphere. And it increases instead the part of their lives which they will be able and keen to spend either producing nothing at all or, possibly, engaging in informal production – which is on average far more labor-intensive and less natural-resource-intensive than formal production is.[3]

Suppose that ecological concerns do give rise to substantial unemployment. Does Basic Income constitute a solution, or even *the* solution to it? What do we mean exactly when we say that there is (involuntary) unemployment? That some people who would like to work cannot find an employer (whether public or private) who finds their work worth the going wage he would have to pay for it. Barring growth, there are two extreme ways of fighting unemployment in this sense. One consists in subsidizing less productive jobs out of the product of more productive ones, in such a way that the services of most of the currently unemployed become worth hiring for some employer. The other consists in reducing the maximum amount of time people who have a job are allowed to work for (whether in a week or in a lifetime) up to the point where most of those currently unemployed can be employed to do some of the work the others are no longer allowed to do. Qua systematic solutions to the unemployment problem in an economy with slow growth and faster productivity growth, the first strategy consists in attempting to bring down the rate of productivity increase to the level of the rate of growth, so that all can remain employed as much as they want to produce the same level of output as before; while the second strategy consists in using the gap between productivity increase and output increase to reduce everyone's working time, thanks to some rationing system.

Basic Income shares features of both. Along with compulsory working time reduction, it will induce those currently employed to give up part of their current work, whether to do nothing or to do work they find intrinsically more attractive. It will do so, however, not by threatening with a penalty those who are caught working more than some stipulated maximum, but by making paid activities less attractive (due to higher marginal rates of tax for those earning a lot) and unpaid activities more attractive (due to the unconditional nature of the income it consists in) than they would be in its absence. Along with employment subsidies, on the other hand, Basic Income makes it possible to cut the cost of labor to the employers while maintaining the employees' incomes, and thus makes economically viable a number of jobs which were not productive enough for them to pay a decent wage in the absence of transfers from more productive activities. But it does so by subsidizing not the employers but the (potential) employees, and therefore gives the latter a freedom completely foreign to employment subsidy policies: the freedom to choose between using the subsidy to work at a low cost for one's employer, to supports one's self-employment or simply to consume.

I do not want to go here into any detail on the question of whether any of these strategies could realistically be expected to get rid of chronic unemployment. I happen to believe, for reasons I have partly sketched elsewhere, that this is definitely not true for compulsory working time reduction, whereas it is for both the Basic Income and employment subsidy strategies.[4] But whether or not my pessimistic assessment of the first of these strategies is correct, it is no doubt the case that ecological constraints do not in themselves unequivocally recommend Basic Income as the adequate cure. Assuming ecological limits to growth do indeed generate endemic unemployment [. . .], Greens need independent reasons for justifying their preference for Basic Income, at least over employment subsidies, and also over working time reduction for those who do not want to rule out the latter on grounds of feasibility. Even if we had successfully tackled all the difficulties we found on our way [. . .], therefore, we would still lack an explanation (short of mental confusion) for why Greens tend to be in favor of a Basic Income, and even more a justification for why they ought to be.

The Second Reply

An explanation: cognitive dissonance

It is therefore worth turning to a second possible reply. It is, I think, a valid generalization, that on average those joining Green movements attach comparatively little importance to income and the acquisition of goods, and comparatively great importance to the disposal of free time and the intrinsic value of their work. But why is this the case? Why is there a correlation between having this kind of preference (roughly, a high ranking of leisure relative to income) and advocating limits to growth? We have just seen that this cannot be because ecological concern with growth mandates a shift to more free time, which Basic Income would make possible. The causal link, I conjecture, rather runs in the opposite direction and has less to do with moral conscience than with what social psychologists call "cognitive dissonance." People to whom getting a higher income is comparatively unimportant are far more likely to put up with – and a fortiori to greet with glee – the prospect of a slowdown or even a standstill of our aggregate income, than people for whom the ability to buy ever growing amounts of material goods and services is of paramount importance. At the same time, given the comparatively high value they attach to being able to use their time as they wish, they obviously have an interest in a Basic Income, indeed in as high a level of Basic Income as is economically feasible. In other words, being "green" and supporting Basic Income have a common cause: a free-time oriented preference structure. Self-interest turns people with such a preference structure into Basic Income supporters, and the tendency to avoid cognitive dissonance explains why people with this preference structure are overrepresented in the Green movement.

A justification: maximum real freedom for all

This may do as an explanation of Green support for Basic Income, but hardly as a justification for it. When asked why a Basic Income should be introduced, we cannot just reply that it is in our interest – even though its being in the interest of a sufficiently large number of people is no doubt a necessary condition for its having a fighting chance of ever being introduced. Justification requires an appeal to values, not just to factional interests. And justification is essential to the public debate of a democratic society. Had the argument scrutinized in the first part of this chapter turned out to be defensible, it would have provided us with a justification as well as an explanation: concern with the welfare of our followers (or even of our own later selves!), fairness to them would have made the introduction of a Basic Income, if not imperative, at least commendable. Unfortunately, the argument did not stand up to the close inspection we subjected it to. Hence our search for an alternative justification, which matches the explanation just given.

Such justification – which is, I believe, the only sound justification for the sort of level of Basic Income we want – must appeal to the value of freedom. More precisely, it must justify Basic Income (at as high a level as is sustainable) as the way of giving everyone as much real freedom as possible. Real freedom contrasts with sheer formal freedom: unless they are detained in a prison or in a mental hospital, adult members of our societies generally have the permission to run their lives as they please, that is, to consume whatever they want, to work a lot or not to work at all. But they seldom have the means of doing so. Basic Income, it hardly needs saying, does not give everyone the means of consuming or doing whatever (s)he fancies. But providing its level is maximized, it gives each as much of them as one possibly can.

Note that what is at issue here is not just the real freedom to consume, as approximated, in a market economy, by people's purchasing power. If that were the case, any variety of minimum income guarantee would do.[5] And the freedom to live the life one wishes to live would fallaciously be reduced to the freedom to buy the goods one wants to buy. There is more to life than consumption, and more to real freedom, therefore, than what can be granted by any old form of minimum guaranteed income. To provide in addition a real freedom to work, that is, to perform paid work, it is essential that the guaranteed income should be given in a form which makes it an employment (including self-employment) subsidy. This implies that it must take the form of a transfer whose benefit is not withdrawn as people start earning. For if the least "productive" among the unemployed have to experience a loss of income if they are to find a job at a wage which makes it worth it for the employer (whether public or private) to hire her/him, it is fair to say that they cannot "afford" to work, that they do not have the real freedom to perform paid work. Finally, it is of even greater importance for our purposes to note that there is also more to life than work and consumption and more, therefore, to real freedom, than what can be granted by a minimum guaranteed income linked to a work requirement – as when it takes the form of a right to work backed by employment subsidies or of an allowance restricted to those, among the able-bodied unemployed, who make themselves available for (waged) work. The sort of life one would like to live may consist primarily in mountain climbing, in bringing up one's kids, in non-mercenary love-making, in practicing transcendental meditation, or in reading poetry to a flock of geese. It may consist, that is, in activities which common usage does not recognize as work. The real freedom not to work, therefore, is just as worthy of our attention as is the real freedom to consume or the real freedom to work. And if we are concerned with the real freedom to run one's life in the comprehensive sense thus suggested, what we need is admittedly a guaranteed income (to guarantee the freedom to "consume"), but one which takes the form of a grant paid to every individual, whether or not (s)he earns further income (to guarantee the freedom to "work"), whether or not (s)he is looking for employment (to guarantee the freedom not to "work"). What we need, in other words, is Basic Income.[6]

This second attempt at justifying Basic Income from a "green" perspective is obviously more successful than the previous one. Not only does the fight against unemployment appear as a direct consequence of the central value judgment adopted – rather than a more or less ad hoc accretion to it. But the preference for Basic Income over employment subsidies as the key weapon in that fight is, as pointed out above, another consequence of it. And so is, indeed, the preference of Basic Income over compulsory working time reduction. For taking freedom at heart demands, surely, that one should not prevent one person from doing a job he enjoys and does well for as long as he wishes, while simultaneously forcing another to do part of that same job less well and less keenly, just in order to subsist.

Conclusion

Let me rehearse very schematically the conclusions of my (perhaps too intricate) argument. We here are all "Greens" – and rightly so. We also are on average far more favorable to Basic Income than any other group on the political scene – and rightly so again. But we are not in favor of Basic Income, and should not be, because we are "Greens" (i.e. concerned with the environment and the depletion of natural resources). It is not just that qua "Greens", we have no special reason to be concerned with unemployment, but also that there is nothing specifically "green" (in this sense) about Basic Income as a solution to unemployment.

Rather, we are "Greens" – again as a rough generalization – because we give the growth of our income, our ability to command more material goods, a comparatively low priority. And this is also the reason why we are – on average – in favor of Basic Income. To defend it, therefore, we must not argue that it is called for by ecological concerns. It is not. To defend it, we must rather argue that introducing it constitutes the only way to give everyone, as much as is currently possible, the actual means of living the sort of life (s)he wants to live – including a sort of life which escapes the rat race, which does not fit the pattern the market rewards. No one would have her/his liberty reduced in the process, nor her/his legitimate rights violated.

This is, I believe, the correct way of understanding the indirect, but fundamental link between ecological concerns and Basic Income. It is indirect, and it is fundamental to our movement, just as the link between socialism, that is, the collective ownership of the means of production, and universal suffrage has been both indirect and fundamental to the socialist movement. As a culmination of a long series of liberal fights for democratic rights, the great and irreversible achievement of the socialist movement in our societies has been the introduction of universal suffrage. Similarly, as a culmination of a long series of socialist fights for rights of social security, the great and irreversible achievement of the Green movement may well turn out to be the introduction of a Basic Income or, as I prefer to call it, of a universal grant.

Notes

1. The oldest unambiguous formulation of it (to my knowledge) is contained in a memorandum submitted in 1796 by the Anglo-American revolutionary Thomas Paine to the French Directoire under the title "Agrarian Justice" (Paine, 1796): Thomas Paine argues that each individual person is owed this sum (at her/his 21st birthday and as from the age of 50 by way of compensation for the private appropriation of the commonly owned Earth. For an overview of the

current state of discussion in Europe, see the newsletter of the Basic Income European Network (c/o Chaire Hoover, Place Montesquieu 3, 1348 Louvain-la-Neuve).

2. I examine and defend such a view in Van Parijs (1986).
3. More or less explicit versions of this argument linking ecological concerns and Basic Income are put forward, for example, by Johnson (1973), Stoleru (1974: 306–308), Cook (1983: 6), Albeda (1984: 100), Van Parijs (1985: last section), Meyer (1986: 2), Mückenberger, Offe, and Ostner (1987: 11).
4. This argument is developed in Van Parijs (1991).
5. Not, however, a system of social insurance, whose benefits are restricted to those who have worked (enough) in the past and thus paid adequate premiums.
6. This real-freedom justification of Basic Income is now elaborated in Van Parijs (1995).

References

Albeda, W. (1984). *De Crisis van de werkloosheid en de verzorgingstaat.* Kok, Kampen (NL).

Cook, S. (1983). *Can a social wage solve unemployment?* Working Paper 165, University of Aston Management Center, Birmingham.

Johnson, W. (1973). The guaranteed income as an environmental measure. In H.E. Daly (ed.) *Toward a steady-state economy.* Freeman, San Francisco, pp. 175–189.

Meyer, N. (1986). An alternative budget for Denmark including a basic income. Paper presented at the First European Conference on Basic Income, Louvain-la-Neuve, September 1986, p. 2.

Mückenberger, U., Offe, C., and Ostner, I. (1987). Das staatlich garantierte Grundeinkommen: ein sozialpolitisches Gebot der Stunde. Bielefeld.

Paine, T. (1974). Agrarian Justice. In P.S. Foner (ed.) *The Life and Major Writings of Thomas Paine.* Citadel Press, Secaucus, NJ, pp. 605–624.

Stoleru, L. (1974). *Vaincre la pauvreté dans les pays riches.* Flammarion, Paris.

Van Parijs, P. (1986). L'avenir des écologistes: deux interprétations. *La Revue Nouvelle* (Bruxelles) 83, 37–47.

Van Parijs, P. (1991). Basic income: a green strategy for the new Europe. In S. Parkin (ed.) *Green Light on Europe.* Heretic Books, London.

Van Parijs, P. (1995). *Real Freedom for All: What (if Anything) Can Justify Capitalism?* Oxford University Press, Oxford.

Chapter 41

A Non-productivist Design for Social Policies

Claus Offe

Excerpts from Offe, C. (1992). A Non-productivist Design for Social Policies. In P. Van Parijs (ed.) *Arguing for Basic Income. Ethical Foundations for a Radical Reform*. Verso, London.

A set of factual – if not outright "ontological" – assumptions, all of which are actually challenged by the experience of advanced industrial societies in the 1970s and 1980s, belong to what one could term the "productivist syndrome." Below I discuss the five most important of these empirical assumptions which have been rendered questionable by recent trends of social and economic change. I refer to them as "productivist" assumptions because they are centered on the notion that production and productivity are both individually and collectively desirable, and hence on the morally self-evident criterion of material reward.

1. Most people live in *families* and derive their means of subsistence from an income in which all members of the family share; family households thus provide – and can legitimately be required to provide – a precondition for productive activities or (future) productive activities of its members as well as a "micro" social security network for the benefit of family household members; at the same time, the family contributes to the viability of the "macro" social security system (in particular old-age pensions) and to the maintenance of a demographic balance through the procreation and primary socialization of children.

2. Most families, unless they belong to the small sector of the self-employed, have at least one permanently *employed breadwinner;* this presupposes as the "normal case" both a prevailing (subjective) orientation towards employed labor and the (objective) availability of employment. The income that is generated through employment helps to accumulate individually as well as collectively the funds out of which the "social wage" and other welfare state expenditures are to be paid. At the same time, the fact that people are "normally" employed and derive a family wage from their employment limits the extent to which claims against the funds for the social wage will be made. That is to say, most people can rely on their own income (rather than transfers) for most of their needs for most of the time.

From Offe, C. (1992). A Non-productivist Design for Social Policies. In P. Van Parijs (ed.) *Arguing for Basic Income. Ethical Foundations for a Radical Reform*. Verso, London. Reprinted with permission of Verso.

Basic Income: An Anthology of Contemporary Research, First Edition. Edited by Karl Widerquist, José A. Noguera, Yannick Vanderborght, and Jurgen De Wispelaere.

3. A societal system of *collective actors*, representing labor, employers, self-employed people, agriculture, the professions and public-sector employees, performs the function of aggregating, mediating, legitimating and negotiating distributional conflicts, the continuous outcomes of which constitute a "meso" social security network for those broad social categories represented by them. They also serve to define and consolidate broad social categories within which socio-economic fates are relatively homogeneous.

4. The welfare state, in both its social security and its social assistance branches, is a supplementary "macro" social security mechanism which takes care of all those "residual" needs and deficiencies in social security that are not covered by either the micro or the meso system. It will be able to do so, via a growth dividend extracted by the welfare state, to an ever wider extent the more the productive potential of a national economy increases.

5. One of the main modes of operation of the welfare state – namely, its reliance upon mandatory contributory schemes covering (at least) old-age and health expenditures – is in fact supported by citizens largely out of considerations of economic prudence alone, and is hence morally undemanding, politically relatively uncontroversial, and supported by a broad and stable consensus. This consensus derives partly from interest-rational considerations of the broad majority of the population and partly from the certainty that cases of risk and need that the welfare state covers are not "behavior-contingent" – that is, not attributable to deliberate (and morally objectionable) acts by those who are entitled to those benefits.

All these five "productivist" assumptions have become much harder to accept as valid and reliable representations of the social and economic reality of advanced industrial societies. The family as an institution, the labor market, the intermediary system of negotiations between representative collective actors, the effectiveness of social security and social assistance in covering all social and substantive categories of need and risk – as well as, finally, the consensus supporting this set of institutional arrangements – are undergoing symptoms of stress and widely perceived insecurity.

Political Responses to the Perceived Insecurity of Security-generating Mechanisms

There are basically four strategic options that one would adopt in response to the uncertainties and insecurities concerning the premisses of the welfare state. I want to specify them briefly and then explore the case for one of them, the Basic Income proposal.

First, *economic liberals* propose that since the empirical premises of the welfare state as itemized above are partly and progressively fading away, what remains to be done is to bid farewell to overly generous standards and promises of security, and let the market decide. This strategic option involves in part the outright abolition of transfers and services, in part a more narrow targeting and means-testing of the clientele of the welfare state. It also involves a lesser role for collective actors, particularly unions, in negotiating wage and other agreements. Fewer regulations and less protection will in the long run, according to the liberal philosophy, be rewarded by increases in productivity, competitiveness, employment and, eventually, *per capita* income, which in turn will and should rightly be the main resource from which individuals buy security in the market.

Second, the *conservative* strategy recommends the selective punishing and rewarding of people's attitudes towards work, education, health, the legal order and the family. Instead of favoring a lesser role for organized labor as well as fiscal austerity, conservatives set out to strengthen society's "moral fibre" and emphasize the line that demarcates "deserving" from "undeserving" and illegitimate categories of claims and claimants.

Third, the *social democratic* version of strategic responses, even to the extent that it is prepared reluctantly to recognize the fragility of the assumptions underlying the welfare state, still denies the need for a basic reorientation and insists instead upon the need and feasibility of defending and even further expanding the welfare state and its productivist premises. All that is needed for such defense is political determination and its potential for activating solidaristic and universalistic moral and political commitments among employees and voters.

Finally, there is a poorly defined and clearly undertheorized bundle of strategic proposals that come from what I would like to term the "post-industrial Left" and can be described as *left-libertarian* in their ideological orientation. These proposals emphasize the values of security *and* autonomy, and envisage the possibility of reconciling the alleged antagonism prevailing between the two in relying upon the idea of *citizenship* and the positive rights and entitlements, such as the entitlement to a Basic Income associated with it.

The case for citizenship-based entitlements to a Basic Income differs from some or all of the preceding options in that:

(a) not class, occupational status, earnings or employment record but *citizenship* is the basis for entitlement to transfers and services;
(b) not paid labor but "useful activities," including activities performed *outside employment and the labor market* and hence escaping formal measurement and accounting, constitute the moral justification of the claim to benefits, to the receipt of which no behavioral preconditions are to be attached;
(c) not the protection of (relative) status or the rewarding of desert but coverage of *basic needs* is the criterion of justice; and
(d) not (absolute) security but a *sustainable* level of risk and the maintenance of *autonomous options* concerning the citizen's responsible conduct of his or her life is the key value.

In contrast to this set of moral intuitions, the social democratic project of defending (on the European Continent) a contributory and incomes-graduated system of transfers is based upon not citizens', but employees' rights and duties. Mandatory contributions to the systems of old-age pensions, health insurance and unemployment insurance are (within upper and lower limits) tied to the legal status of being an employee, and benefits are allocated (with the limited exception of the case of health services) in accordance with the duration of employment and the income earned during that employment. What reasons are there to question the moral validity (as well as the fiscal viability) of this "employment-centered" model of the welfare state that social democrats are so eager to defend in most West European countries?

(a) The maintenance of expensive universalist social security systems, even the mainly contributory ones, requires, owing to labor-market and demographic imbalances, an increasing amount of fiscal subsidies. Under the premises of an open economy, these subsidies can be financed only by a steady process of economic growth and the growth dividend it generates for the state budget in general and for social policy programs in particular. Economic growth, in its turn, whether or (more likely) not it is accompanied by the attainment of full employment, has in all its currently visible varieties and paths an unequivocally disruptive impact upon the natural environment. The continued dependency of social security upon economic growth conditions the immediate interests of employees in ways which will favor growth even at the expense of environmentally and ecologically sound policies. The productivist link that ties social security to economic growth and budgetary growth dividends operates as an effective brake upon more stringent varieties of policies aiming at environmental protection, as the clients of this type of welfare state will naturally be inclined to prefer economic growth over the preservation of natural resources.

(b) The employment-centered arrangements of social security and social welfare reserve the rights and entitlements of full welfare state citizenship to those enjoying stable employment and their dependants. As the functional link between economic growth and employment has become more uncertain, and as the link between the gainfully employed earning a "family wage" and the family as an institution serving as a micro social security network has also become more tenuous, the dispersion of wealth through employment and family relations has become more restricted – for example, to the majority of what is often referred to as the "two-thirds society." At the same time, the emphasis that the welfare state and the arrangements for social security place upon formal employment makes it counter-intuitively attractive for many to enter the labor market in spite – or even because – of the relatively shrinking demand for labor. The influx of those who have no other claim to the means of subsistence (and no other hope for the recognition of their social "worthiness") than through labor-market participation, marginal and unstable employment in an increasingly "deregulated" labor market, and unemployment and other benefits that are contingent upon their "preparedness to accept formal employment" moves the system ever further away from anything approaching a "labor-market equilibrium." Moreover, wage- and payroll-related modes of financing social security have the obvious effect of burdening the market prospects of labor with the costs of its own "security", thus generating a rational incentive for employers to restrict their demand for labor still further. Taken together, these two effects of the employment-centered social security system – making the status of being employed relatively more attractive as compared to other life forms outside employment *and* making it more costly to employ labor – are likely to contribute positively to a permanent labor-market imbalance.

(c) Fiscal, labor-market demographic strains will give rise to a politics of welfare state retrenchment and consolidation which, while protecting the interests of those *in* stable employment, deprives everyone else of welfare rights – the unemployed, the poor, many woman, adolescents, the disabled and chronically ill, war survivors and, to an extent, even pensioners. The alleged universalism of employment-centered social policies thus turns under conditions or retrenchment into its opposite: into a particularism favoring the productivist core of employed members of society.

(d) The historical roots of the postwar welfare state accord are to be found in the appreciation by the political forces representing the middle class (including the privileged sectors of the working class: skilled male workers) that they stood to gain significantly from the arrangement. It is probably only a slight simplification to argue that social security universalism based upon employment status was a means of "bribing" the middle class to support the welfare state, or to buy its political consent (or at least its political acquiescence, as suggested by the "hush-money" metaphor that some commentators have employed). Gains for the middle class became the necessary precondition for making social security for the "underclass" (including the less privileged segments of the working class) politically feasible. Had such gains not been provided for, the predictable political response of the middle class would have been a very effective appeal for stringency and austerity in welfare spending. To the extent that this interpretation is valid, it highlights a noteworthy contradiction between the economic and the political rationalities of the welfare state. From the point of view of economic efficiency, any nonselective or nontargeted social policy arrangement – and certainly a fully universalistic one – is vastly inefficient, in that it spreads limited resources to "all" where only "some" actually need it, thereby depriving the system of its capacity to provide the latter with even their minimum requirements. But from the point of view of politics, this blatantly inefficient use of resources makes perfect sense, as the practice of spreading entitlements to benefits to "all" is the inescapable political precondition that must first be met in order to make the arrangement sufficiently popular with the middle class. Thus the consent-buying portion of total expenditures can be looked upon as a "political investment" the yield of which is the benefit that is eventually channelled to the "truly" needy target group which depends upon the welfare state's support.

Does that allow us to conclude that a return to strictly selective principles of social welfare, based on large-scale needs tests and means tests, is called for – as is advocated by the proponents of the neo-liberal welfare backlash? I do not think so. Instead, I believe that a universal and adequate Basic Income could be designed to become a synthesis of the more desirable features of universalism and selectivity. Such a synthesis would have to consist of several components:

(i) The most important component is an unconditional, subsistence-level, tax-financed right to income based upon citzenship rather than labor-market participation.

(ii) The extreme universalism embodied in such a Basic Income would have to be complemented by a tax structure that ensured that all those who participate in gainful employment and thus do not really depend upon the Basic Income will contribute – through direct and indirect taxation and in distributively progressive ways – to its financing.

(iii) As it would not be surprising to find a massive middle-class opposition mobilizing against such a scheme – which does, in fact, involve considerable downward redistribution of income and income security – the arrangement would have to be based upon legislation that provides for something like the following procedural rule: revisions of the scheme that would restrict access to the Basic Income and/or its (GNP-indexed) level could not be passed except by a majority equal to, say, 90% of the net contributors. For instance, if at a given point 20% of the adult population actually claimed the Basic Income, a downward revision of levels or eligibility criteria would become effective only if it were supported by a majority of at least 72% of the legislative body. Such procedural protection of structural minorities would decline in strength as the minority increased: the more it approached parity, the closer we would come to the standard simple majority rule.

(iv) Extensive cooperative and other institutional forms of non wage labor outside formal employment must be experimentally developed in order to expose the near-monopoly that the institutional arrangement of formal employment holds over the universe of useful human activities in competition with alternative modes of "getting things done." While emancipating society from the dictatorial imperatives of economic growth (as conventionally measured), such a scheme would not only provide individuals with the option of "opting out," temporarily or permanently, of formal employment (albeit on a probably very moderate level of state-provided subsistence), but would also free them to develop their skills and their potential for useful activities, alone and in cooperation with others, that are normally underutilized in employment in general and in unemployment in particular (cf. Offe and Heinze, 1990).

The Politics of Basic Income Proposals

1. The Basic Income cannot and should not be presented as a panacea to open the road to a "good society." First, because, should the proposal eventually turn out to be a strategy to that end (which I believe it is), it will be only one element in a *policy package* within which other elements are equally important. Second, because we cannot claim to know enough about the short-term and long-term effects of the proposal once it is implemented, unpleasant surprises cannot be excluded – or rather, they must be excluded in practice through thoughtful experimentation and the cautious exploration of the many questions, problems and potential side-effects about which we simply do not yet know enough. Third, rather than being a formula for the foundation of a new social order, it might be more realistic and honest to argue for Basic Income in terms of a defensive measure to preserve and expand notions of social justice against a welfare backlash that has already started and must be expected to continue in view of the above structural changes.

2. The political implementation of Basic Income schemes involves two steps. The first – and by far the more uncertain – step concerns the problem of how a sufficiently broad alliance of social and political forces can be built to win support for such a proposal of tying the right to sufficient (subsistence) income to citizenship rather than employment (or the preparedness to accept employment). This problem cannot be dealt with fully here (cf. Mückenberger et al., 1989). The second problem concerns the question how, *after* the scheme has been instituted, its proponents and direct beneficiaries might be able to withstand the foreseeable pressure to revise it in negative ways – by outright abolition, or by gradual restrictions of eligibility or transfer levels.

3. The obvious question to which proponents and direct beneficiaries of Basic Income will be most vulnerable is this: If "you" are not engaged in gainful employment, and not even prepared to find and accept such employment once it is made available to you, why should "we" be forced to subsidize your *voluntary* unemployment? To resist the tempting consequences of this Victorian logic, which are by no means a speciality of conservative and economic liberal political authors (cf. Elster, 1986), it will probably not be enough to point to the limited capacities of the labor market, the family and the system of corporate actors effectively to spread an adequate portion of society's wealth to each and every citizen. In addition, it will be necessary to be able to demonstrate that (i) the voluntary unemployed are actually – at least in the typical and quantitatively relevant case – involved in "useful" activities, although the usefulness of these activities is not measured by the institutional procedures of

the employment contract and paid work; and (ii) the labor invested in the self-development of human resources (such as health, training and other components of "human capital") deserves to be remunerated as much as the actual utilization of human capital in paid labor itself. If one wishes to be able to make this point as compellingly as it will need to be made, one will have to provide for institutional alternatives to employed work as well as for meaningful arrangements for manpower development, rehabilitation and training.

4. Even if the "Victorian" unwillingness to reward "work-shyness" could be successfully overcome by this argument on social justice, the question remains why people should actually *prefer* the general idea of citizenship-based rights to income over the conventional full-employment alternative. Even if the idea could be shown to be acceptable in terms of *social justice*, why should it also be desirable in terms of individual and collective interests? Even if the majority granted the right, would the minority of those who directly benefit at any given point in time be willing to use it without feeling marginalized by it? What kind of consideration should make a life outside formal employment desirable for relevant proportions of the citizenship? To answer this question, individual as well as collective gains may be cited, not only the definitive "infeasibility" of the supposedly most-preferred alternative of full employment. Individual gains consist in the options that a Basic Income scheme would create. These options consist in the possibility to choose any combination of employed work and the income that goes with it, on the one hand, and other activities that a person wishes to pursue, on the other. This option, which amounts to the availability of a *choice concerning the individually most appropriate free time/income mix*, is normally precluded in a society where full social and economic membership status is tied to full-time and lifelong employment, and any deviation from this (male) standard is considered deficient (cf. Gorz, 1988). My intuition is that the taste-forming impact of this choice, once it becomes available, will be strong enough not only to offset the losses in income from employment on the part of (potential) employees, but also partly to neutralize employers' obvious and opposite interest in making the most extensive possible use of any individual employee and the human capital embodied in him/her. To the extent that this intuition turns out to be valid, the option of discontinuous participation in employment would cease to be considered second best (due to the unavailability of "full" employment) and would instead be seen as the most-preferred alternative – even under conditions where full employment was thought to be feasible.

5. As to the *collective* benefits of the optionality of labor-market participation created by the Basic Income, three points appear to be relevant. First, while the right to income as an unconditional citizen right would certainly not by itself alleviate the environment and ecological risks and dangers involved in industrial growth and the "full" employment that is contingent upon such growth, it would probably contribute in indirect ways. For it removes some of the "productivist" pressures and anxieties and thus paves the political road towards targeted and selective environmental policies, some of which are bound to entail the termination of certain lines of production and production processes. The Basic Income makes an ecological critique of industrialism politically more affordable. Second, a major impact may be expected upon the level of overall social integration: as people who are – temporarily or permanently – outside employment lose their stigma of deficiency and failure, and are instead looked upon as legitimate citizens involved in respectable activities other than paid work, many of the symptoms and social pathologies of marginalization would probably disappear. Third, the temporary escape from employed work that a Basic

Income would make feasible – and, indeed, attractive – would contribute an ongoing process of the creative regeneration of skill, health and training, thus helping to maintain and enhance the productivity of human capital.

6. The Basic Income would also induce conditions which amount to an indirect strategy of work humanization. Employees would find it affordable to refuse many of the least attractive and poorly paid jobs, as the alternative of claiming a Basic Income without being employed on such jobs becomes an attractive one. As a consequence, the recruitment of labor for such jobs would become significantly more expensive to employers; this in turn would induce efforts on their part to eliminate such jobs through technical or organizational innovation.

7. Finally, the extent to which people would actually claim the Basic Income and for what portion of their lifetime, is an open question. Many alarmed responses to Basic Income proposals seem to be based upon the implicit fear that a wholesale defection from employed work would be the inevitable consequence. This is by no means a plausible conjecture. First, under all realistic calculations the level of the Basic Income, while being (by definition) sufficient for subsistence, would remain so moderate as to maintain much of the relative preferability of employment, wherever it is in fact available at decent wages and in decent working conditions. Thus the disincentive effect would remain limited. Second, the overall incentive effect of the Basic Income might well turn out to follow a logic of what could be called, in view of the mass exodus of East German refugees during the summer of 1989, the "GDR paradox." The paradox is this: had the government of the GDR granted its citizens the right to leave, many of them would have stayed. The failure to grant this right was one of the immediate causes of the decision of many to leave illegally. Applying this logic to the labor market and the effects of the Basic Income scheme, one might arrive at the anticipation that "the right to leave" would certainly (as intended) cause many persons to withdraw their labor-power from formal employment, which they could afford to do, given the unconditional safety net of the Basic Income and the consequent effective optionality of employment. Those marginal employees who have stayed in the labor market mainly for fear that leaving would involve the definitive decision never to come back would certainly use this option. But this "right to leave" would also – to an unknown but hardly negligible extent – be used in order to acquire new social and technical skills to generate energies and preferences that would eventually facilitate the return into voluntary gainful employment. Thus the net effect would be a more flexible and optional life pattern, on the one hand, and a requalification of the workforce, on the other – both of which might well add up to a new condition of full employment on the basis of a significantly reduced share of lifetime in employed work for the average person.

References

Elster, J. (1986). Comment on Van Der Veen and Van Parijs. *Theory and Society*, 15, 709–722.

Gorz, A. (1988). *Critique of Economic Reason*. Verso, London.

Mückenberger, U., Offe, C., and Ostner, I. (1989). Das staatlich garantierte Grundeinkommen – ein sozialpolitisches Gebot der Stunde. In H.L. Kramer and C. Leggewie (eds) *Wege ins Reich der Freiheit. Festschrift für André Gorz zum 65. Geburtstag*. Rotbuch, Berlin, pp. 247–278.

Offe, C. and Heinze, R.G. (1990). *Organisierte Eigenarbeit. Das Modell Kooperationsring*. Campus, Frankfurt am Main/New York.

Chapter 42
A Post-productivist Welfare Regime

Robert E. Goodin

Excerpts from Goodin, R.E. (2001). Work and Welfare: Towards a Post-productivist Welfare Regime. *British Journal of Political Science*, 31 (1), 13–39.

Different welfare regimes differ in many important respects. One which has come to recent prominence, among welfare theorists and practitioners alike, is the way in which they articulate the demands of work and welfare (OECD, 1997; Esping-Andersen, 1996: 66–87; 1999). Liberals rally to the slogan, "Work, *not* welfare." Under a liberal welfare regime, people are supposed to earn their living on the labor market, and public welfare programs are supposed to serve only as a residual fall-back (Polanyi, 1944; Titmuss, 1974: 30). The corporatist slogan is, "Welfare *through* work." This is Titmuss's "industrial achievement" model, wherein a family's welfare entitlements are based on workplace contributions that the (typically male) breadwinner and his employer have made to the social insurance scheme throughout his working life (Titmuss, 1974: 31; Land, 1980: 55–77; Lewis, 1992: 159–171; Fraser, 1994: 591–618; Sainsbury, 1996). The social democratic slogan is, "Welfare *and* work." Under a social democratic regime, welfare benefits are treated as citizens' rights; but citizens have a corresponding responsibility to make productive contributions whenever they reasonably can, and social democratic governments adopt "active labor market policies" to help them do so.[1]

Importantly different though all of those approaches are, equally important is what they all have in common. They are all essentially "productivist."[2] They are all centrally concerned to ensure a smooth supply of labor to the productive sectors of the formal economy, and they are all anxious that the welfare state not get too badly in the way of that. In terms of an aphorism standardly presented as a plain truth of *a priori* logic, "Without work there can be no welfare." If no one produces anything, there will be nothing for government to redistribute to anyone. It would be simply self-defeating for government, in pursuit of social welfare objectives, to undermine the productive sector of the economy too badly.

Of course, no welfare regime – not even the liberal one – accords absolute priority to economic productivity in the "equity–efficiency tradeoff." Still, all the standard models of

From Goodin, R.E. (2001). Work and Welfare: Towards a Post-productivist Welfare Regime. *British Journal of Political Science*, 31 (1), 13–39. Reprinted with permission of Cambridge University Press.

Basic Income: An Anthology of Contemporary Research, First Edition. Edited by Karl Widerquist, José A. Noguera, Yannick Vanderborght, and Jurgen De Wispelaere.

the welfare state see economic productivity as a great constraint to be reckoned with. They are all sensitive to the "productivist problematic" in that sense. They all must, in one way or another, reassure themselves that productivity will not be too badly undermined by their social welfare policies.

Another broad class of "post-productivist" models would take a fundamentally different attitude towards work and welfare.[3] Their slogan (in hyperbolic form, as slogans inevitably are) might be, "Welfare without work." Under a post-productivist welfare regime, as under a social democratic one, people's welfare entitlements would be strictly independent of their participation in paid labor.[4] But unlike social democrats, post-productivists would make no extraordinary efforts to get people into work alongside that.

Post-productivists would take a relatively relaxed attitude to relatively large numbers of people drawing welfare checks rather than pay checks for relatively protracted periods. Of course, not everyone could do so. Like everyone else, post-productivists need enough people to work in the productive sectors of the economy to finance public transfers to those not. Post-productivists are not anti-productivists. Their point is simply that economic productivity can be sustained at moderately high levels on the basis of far less than full employment, full-time for absolutely everyone of working age.

Post-productivists mostly see this as a matter of social choice, collectively opting for a more relaxed life. Some of them say it is also a matter of economic necessity, supposing that there is and will remain a serious oversupply of labor in advanced capitalist economies. That further claim may or may not be true: unprecedentedly high employment rates such as have been experienced in the United States in recent years might seem to belie that claim. But even if advanced capitalist economies can (at least in some periods) use all the labor they can get, the central post-productivist claim is simply that they need not. Economic productivity can be sustained perfectly well without trying to put everyone into full-time work.

The "post-productivist problematic," thus construed, is very different from the productivist one. On the "work" side of the ledger, the problem is presented more as one of rationing jobs than of filling them.[5] On the "welfare" side of the ledger, the problem is presented as one of decoupling income from paid labor, securing a decent level of income for those who (by choice or necessity) fail to secure one for themselves in the ordinary labor market.[6]

Different welfare regimes are characterized by their differing priorities and core value commitments. Liberals focus on values of efficiency, corporatists on stability and social democrats on equality. The core post-productivist value commitment is to *autonomy*.[7]

Even if we cannot specify with any precision what exactly is required for autonomy, we can specify certain things that preclude people from being self-legislating agents with "the capacity to reflect upon their lives and shape them" (Dworkin, 1988: 31). Dire economic necessity is clearly one among them. It is a boringly analytical truth that "necessity is the enemy of choice," and hence of autonomy. So too is interpersonal domination, in its various forms. No one can be self-legislating who is utterly subject to the will of another.

Post-productivists build on such partial analyses of autonomy in framing their central policy concerns. They strive to secure people's autonomy by ensuring that people receive an *income adequate to their needs*, on terms which *impinge minimally on their freedom of action*. That latter condition implies that their income must not be made "conditional" on anything else: people must have an adequate income in their own right, independently of household attachments, of labor force participation, or of jumping through any bureaucratic hoops.[8]

"Impinging minimally on their freedom of action" also implies that people's income should come to them in such a way that leaves them with sufficient "discretionary time" in which actually to make use of it. Time is the ultimately scarce good; and time is a crucial component in the fully-specified production function for any other good. People can be, and often are, "time poor" as well as "money poor." Controlling how people spend their time is an important element of social control and a significant barrier to their full autonomy. Post-productivists are acutely sensitive to all these issues.

These, then, are the three principal policy priorities which follow from post-productivists' concern with autonomy. First, they want *income adequacy*. Second, they want *temporal adequacy*. And third, they want both to be provided in a way which involves *minimal conditionality*.

Such post-productivist priorities have never been fully and formally embraced by social policy makers anywhere in the world. Still, intimations can be found. I shall suggest that – on the work–welfare side of the social equation – the Netherlands in the late 1980s and early 1990s provided a fair indication of what post-productivism might look like in practice. Those who suppose that the post-productivist ideal is impossibly Utopian should look to the Netherlands in that period and think again.

Looking at the performance of that unique exemplar of the post-productivist regime, it seems to have proven unusually successful at promoting "autonomy" along all the dimensions of concern to post-productivists, ensuring both income adequacy and temporal adequacy in ways which are minimally conditional and hence autonomy-respecting. This chapter proceeds to a brief discussion of how that came about in the Netherlands and what has happened there since (which might best be seen as a shift from a "Basic Income post-productivist regime" to a "Participation-Income post-productivist regime"). It ends by recalling, however, that interesting though the case of the Netherlands may be, it is the larger work-and-welfare and associated time-and-money way of looking at welfare states – post-productivist potentially among them – that is of central concern.

Other countries might equal the Netherlands in terms of their low political pressure to work (low active labor market program participation rates); and other countries might better it in terms of the disposable income that they provide to no-earner households. But no country matches or betters the Netherlands in terms of both criteria taken together. No country provides, at one and the same time, both more money to nonearning households and less pressure to participate in active labor market programs.

The Dutch Experiment: How Did It Happen? Can It Last?

Talk as we may for comparative analytical purposes about ideal "regime types," no actual welfare state is characterized by a single unified animating idea. The Netherlands – like all countries – came to its welfare regime largely by accident, through a combination of historical accretions, socio-economic exigencies, political cross-currents and so on.[9]

Certainly, no politician in power ever intended to make the Netherlands post-productivist. Some, in more recent years, have come to advocate some such model rather more explicitly.[10] But at the outset, generous provision for people outside the workforce was motivated in the Netherlands more by a neo-corporatist concern to signal social recognition of the value of unpaid labor, particularly in child-rearing and community work.

For the most part, Dutch politicians seeing the Netherlands heading in a post-productivist direction have tried to reverse that trend. They complained bitterly about the way in which sickness and disability benefits were being used to buy out surplus labor by facilitating the early exit of workers from the workforce; and they instituted a swag of welfare reforms from 1987 onwards to try to reduce welfare dependency and to increase employment rates.

Dutch labor-force participation has indeed increased dramatically over the past decade. But significantly from the perspective of the post-productivist model, most of that growth has come in the form of part-time female labor-force participation. "Among couples the modern work pattern in the Netherlands is one of 'one-and-a-half jobs,' the man working (nearly) full time, the woman part time." By 1996, fully one in five employees in the Netherlands had a job politely characterized as "flexible" (very part-time, temporary, on-call, or such like).

The prime minister's battle cry may be, "Work, work, work," and an explicit "activation obligation" was written into the 1996 revision of the Social Assistance Act.[11] But both the Christian Democratic party and the Labor party continue to emphasize the value of unpaid "voluntary work, the upbringing of children and neighbourhood care" as all being valuable forms of labor; and public opinion clearly supports them in that.[12] Those are all classically corporatist concerns, in a way. But they are also ones which, in the right circumstances, can feed powerfully into a broadly post-productivist vision.

Perhaps the best way to characterize the changing Dutch work–welfare arrangements over the past couple of decades is to distinguish two distinct styles of post-productivist regime, one organized around unconditional "Basic Income" and the other organized around "Participation Income" conditional on socially-useful labor. Fifteen years ago, Dutch work–welfare arrangements effectively (albeit unintentionally) approximated the former; today they more nearly (and perhaps only slightly more intentionally) approximate the latter. Everyone is being pressed to do some work, but not necessarily very much.

As I said at the outset, "welfare without work" understood literally is an impossible ideal. If no one were producing, there would be nothing to distribute, much less redistribute. But it is perfectly possible, within those constraints, to valorize a broader range of things as socially useful "work" and to allow individuals more autonomy in arranging their working time (paid and unpaid) as they will.

Economists tell us there are twin tradeoffs to be faced in these realms. One is between work and leisure; another is between equity and efficiency.

The Dutch in the 1980s and early 1990s would seem to have opted in a relatively dramatic way for the "less productive" fork in both dimensions, sustaining simultaneously low working hours and high public welfare benefits. Economists insist that they have to pay an economic price for those choices, and it was precisely such fears that led Dutch political leaders to back away from the bolder form of post-productivism in recent years.

But consider the economic facts. Despite leisurely working hours and generous social welfare policies at its post-productivist peak, the Netherlands none the less managed to turn in a very strong economic performance. Over the period 1989–1994, the average year-to-year increase in Dutch GDP was 2.3%. That makes Dutch GDP growth the fourth highest among the 18 countries of the old OECD, substantially higher than the average growth of 1.6% over that period experienced by those 18 countries taken as a whole. Of course, no one knows how much the Dutch economy would have grown had its work and welfare policies been different. Still, at the very least we can say that even a bold post-productivist option proved economically eminently affordable, for the one country that has come closest to implementing it.

Notes

1. Sweden, Esping-Andersen says, practises "productivist social justice," wherein the "welfare state invests in optimizing peoples capacity to be productive citizens" (Esping-Andersen, 1994: 711–732 at p. 722); see further Esping-Andersen (1999: ch. 4). It should come as no surprise that "laborist" ideology animates social democratic welfare regimes, given their political roots in labor movements (Korpi (1983); Esping-Andersen (1985); Castles (1978)).
2. A term Esping-Andersen (1994: 713) uses in a rather more specific way to characterize the Swedish model, in particular. Note that they all adopt a fairly narrow understanding of what might count as a "productive" contribution, defining it in terms of paid but not unpaid labor (which is possibly equally productive, in some broader sense).
3. The term is adapted from Offe (1992: 61–80). My "post-productivist" phrasing seems to get their emphasis more nearly right: post-productivists are not opposed, or even indifferent, to economic output (as the "non-productivist" formulation might seem to imply); they have simply "gotten over" being utterly fixated on it, as productivists have been (something the "post-productivist" phrasing seems better at capturing).
4. "Decommodified," in Esping-Andersen's famous phrase (Esping-Andersen, 1990).
5. Hence post-productivist proposals of "shorter hours" strategies aimed at spreading employment around See also proposals for "sabbatical accounts" (Offe, 1997; Hamminga, 1995: 23–35).
6. Hence post-productivist proposals for "Basic Income." See Meade (1984: 129–146) and Van Parijs (1992; 1995). A variation on "Basic Income" is "Participation Income," paid conditionally on participation in some socially-useful activity; see Atkinson (1996: 67–70).
7. One of the things we might, and on any sensible description of the good life should, autonomously choose to do is to render ourselves vulnerable to certain others in certain ways. To argue for autonomy is not to enshrine autarky but rather mutually-chosen interdependencies (Goodin, 1985, ch. 7).
8. Thus, post-productivists would share the social democratic impetus towards "decommodification," making people's income streams independent of labor market participation; Esping-Andersen (1990: 21–22). They would also insist that those social benefits should come in the form of welfare rights, rather than discretionary payments; Reich (1964: 733–787) and Goodin (1988: ch. 7). They would also be anxious that women should have an independent claim in their own right; see Lewis (1992) and Sainsbury (1996).
9. As nicely captured in Van Kersbergen and Becker (1988).
10. "The post-productivist Left in the Netherlands" within the Labour Party (PvdA) is now explicitly calling for a "relaxed organization of labour"; van der Veen (1999: 351–381, at pp. 367–373).
11. Van Oorschot and Engerlfriet (1999). The "activation obligation" is an "availability for work" requirement applying to anyone in receipt of income support, except for single parents of children under five and unemployed persons over 57.5 years of age; Visser and Hemerijck (1997: 148).
12. Van der Veen (1999: 366–373). Whereas some 93% of respondents say that the obligation to find paid employment should be applied "strictly" to young unemployed persons, only 34% think it should be applied strictly to the "unemployed who are active in voluntary associations or community," only 16% think it should be applied strictly to "single parents with children aged 6–12, and less than half that many think it should be applied strictly to children younger than that (Van Oorschot and Engerlfriet, 1999: 19).

References

Atkinson, A.B. (1996). The Case for a Participation Income. *Political Quarterly*, 67, 67–70.
Castles, F.G. (1978). *The Social Democratic Image of Society*. Routledge & Kegan Paul, London.

Dworkin, G. (1988). *Theory and Practice of Autonomy.* Cambridge University Press, Cambridge, p. 31.

Esping-Andersen, G. (1985). *Politics Against Markets.* Princeton University Press, Princeton, NJ.

Esping-Andersen, G. (1990). *The Three Worlds of Welfare Capitalism.* Polity, Oxford.

Esping-Andersen, G. (1994). Welfare States and the Economy. In N.J. Smelser and R. Swedberg (eds) *The Handbook of Economic Sociology.* Princeton University Press, Princeton, NJ, pp. 711–732.

Esping-Andersen, G. (1996). Welfare States Without Work: The Impasse of Labour Shedding and Familialism in Continental European Social Policy. In G. Esping-Andersen (ed.) *Welfare States in Transition.* Sage, London, pp. 66–87.

Esping-Andersen, G. (1999). *Social Foundations of Post-industrial Economics.* Oxford University Press, Oxford.

Fraser, N. (1994). After the Family Wage: Gender Equity and the Welfare State. *Political Theory*, 22, 591–618.

Goodin, R.E. (1985). *Protecting the Vulnerable.* University of Chicago Press, Chicago.

Goodin, R.E. (1988). *Reasons for Welfare.* Princeton University Press, Princeton, NJ.

Hamminga, B. (1995). Demoralizing the Labor Market. *Journal of Political Philosophy*, 3, 23–35.

Korpi, W. (1983). *The Democratic Class Struggle.* Routledge & Kegan Paul, London.

Land, H. (1980). The Family Wage. *Feminist Review*, 6, 55–77.

Lewis, J. (1992). Gender and Welfare Regimes. *Journal of European Social Policy*, 2, 159–171.

Meade, J.E. (1984). Full Employment, New Technology and the Distribution of Income. *Journal of Social Policy*, 13, 129–146.

Offe, C. (1992). A Non-productivist Design for Social Policies. In P. Van Parijs (ed.) *Arguing for Basic Income.* Verso, London.

Offe, C. (1997). Towards a New Equilibrium of Citizens' Rights and Economic Resources. In OECD, *Social Cohesion and the Globalizing Economy.* OECD, Paris, pp. 81–108.

Organisation for Economic Co-operation and Development (1997). *Making Work Pay: Taxation, Benefits, Employment and Unemployment.* OECD, Paris.

Polanyi, K. (1944). *The Great Transformation.* Rinehart, New York.

Reich, C.A. (1964). The New Property. *Yale Law Journal*, 73, 733–787.

Sainsbury, D. (1996). *Gender, Equality and Welfare States.* Cambridge University Press, Cambridge.

Titmuss, R.M. (1974). *Social Policy.* Allen & Unwin, London.

van der Veen, R.J. (1999). Participate or Sink: Threshold Equality Behind the Dykes. *Acta Politica*, 34, 351–381.

Van Kersbergen, K. and Becker, U. (1988). The Netherlands: A Passive Social Democratic Welfare State in a Christian Democratic Ruled Society. *Journal of Social Policy*, 17, 477–499.

Van Oorschot, W. and Engerlfriet, R. (1999). Work, Work, Work: Labour Market Participation Policies in the Netherlands, 1970–2000. Paper presented to Research Committee 19, International Sociological Association, Prague, September 1999.

Van Parijs, P. (1992). *Arguing for Basic Income.* Verso, London.

Van Parijs, P. (1995). *Real Freedom for All.* Clarendon Press, Oxford.

Visser, J. and Hemerijck, A. (1997). *A Dutch Miracle: Job Growth, Welfare Reform and Corporatism in the Netherlands.* Amsterdam University Press, Amsterdam.

Chapter 43

Demoralizing the Labor Market: Could Jobs be Like Cars and Concerts?

Bert Hamminga

Excerpts from Hamminga, B. (1995). Demoralizing the Labour Market: Could Jobs be like Cars and Concerts? *Journal of Political Philosophy*, 3 (1), 23–35.

In Eu, a country with 5 million able-bodied adult citizens, there are only 4 million jobs.[1] For 20% of those fit for jobs there is no work, and they have to live with an income paid by those who work. Yet no one is dissatisfied, at least not in the sense of knowing someone else with whom an exchange of position would be preferred. The reason for this surprising satisfaction is the way in which the transfer incomes arise: at the beginning of every year a "Labor Bank" issues 20 million "Labor Rights" distributing them freely and equally over all able-bodied adult citizens (so each gets four Labor Rights). The Labor Bank also has the power to determine how many Labor Rights you need to have the right to occupy a job: in circumstances described above, it decides on five.

With only four Labor Rights, you have no full right to occupy a job. (For simplicity, let us assume Eu has only full-time jobs.) If, however, you could find someone willing to transfer one of his or her four Labor Rights to you you would have just such a full right. The price you would be willing to offer for such an additionnal Labor Right depends on your expected wage (out of which you pay for it, after all), and on the value you attach to *working*. If you regard the price of buying a Labor Right as high, you can consider the alternative of selling your own four Labor Rights and living from their yield this year (you just said the price was high!) without a job.

If you lived in Eu, you would have to reconsider these alternatives every year. In other respects Eu is quite a normal country: all the people differ, and they all change their minds over time. There are those who had a job last year and want to keep it: they just buy (again) the additional Labor Right needed.[2] There are those who opted for unemployment last year and wish to do so again: they sell their Labor Rights again. The same is done by those who wish to stop working. Those who wish to join the workforce must apply for jobs that are left over and, if hired, buy their full right to it by buying an additional Labor Right.

It makes no sense to own Labor Rights in amounts other than five (if you want to work) or zero (if you do not). So in early January in Eu – shortly after the Labor Rights are

From Hamminga, B. (1995). Demoralizing the Labour Market: Could Jobs be like Cars and Concerts? *Journal of Political Philosophy*, 3 (1), 23–35. Reprinted with permission of John Wiley & Sons Ltd.

Basic Income: An Anthology of Contemporary Research, First Edition. Edited by Karl Widerquist, José A. Noguera, Yannick Vanderborght, and Jurgen De Wispelaere.

submitted to the law of supply and demand on a free market – we find them in the hands of 4 million able-bodied adult citizens occupying the 4 million jobs available in Eu. The other 1 million Eunians must have been satisfied by the Labor Right price that arose on the free market and have decided freely to accept an income for the coming year of four times the Labor Right price.(At least they must have preferred this to occupying a job and enjoying its wage after deduction of the cost of buying one Labor Right.) They realize it will be legally *forbidden* for them to occupy a job this year (unless, sometimes in the year, they can buy, for some residual value, five Labor Rights from other who want a rest). They do not like that aspect of their situation, but they accept it at the prevailing rate of the Labor Right price. They have been "bought out" for a year, freely deciding to take the price.

The other 4 million able-bodied adult citizens will work, but they have no reason to feel mistreated or jealous because 1 million others have income without needing to work. They too could, if they wished, opt for "unemployment" by selling their Labor Rights. They would thereby be handing over their right to occupy a job to someone who attaches more value to it, while themselves apparently considering unemployment preferable at the prevailing Labor Right price arising out of the market equilibrium. Quite a sensible exchange!

The economist's habit of analysing price formation on the free market works quite well in Eu. There are two main factors that determine whether you will be on the supply or demand side of this market. The most obvious one, from customary perspectives on Labor economics, is the ratio between your annual income (after deduction of the cost of the addtional Labor Right you need) if you opt for work and your annual income resulting from selling your four Labor Rights. Let us call this the "wage/unemployment benefit ratio" in Eu. A higher Labor Right price implies a lower wage/unemployment benefit ratio: if that price settles at such a lower equilibrium, the employed are apparently satisfied with a relatively lower income.

The second factor determining whether you will be on the supply side or the demand side of this market is at least as important. That is just the value you attach to *working*.[3] How deeply do you desire to occupy a wage-earning job, *irrespective* of its income? If very deeply, then you will be ready to pay a high price for the additional Labor Right you need; and you will then be among the hard core of the demand side. If not so much, then you will be ready to sell your Labor Rights even at a relatively low equilibrium market price and you will be at the supply side, among those dragging down the price.

On the free market for Labor Rights one single price will be formed, because all Labor Rights are exactly the same. The *equilibrium price* will be determined by the average labor preference, that is the average value that 5 million able-bodied adult citizens attach to work as supplied in jobs offered in Eu. The Labor Right price fixes the wage/unemployment benefit ratio and, reflecting upon that ratio, you will deicide whether or not to work this year.

Supposing Eunians' individual labor preferences are very diverse (that is, have a high standard deviation), there will be both a lot of people with high labor preference willing to pay a high price for the Labor Rights and also a lot of people with low labor preferences willing to take a low price for their Labor Rights. The equilibrium Labor Right price will be somewhere in the broad range between the critical values set by supply siders and demand siders, and for both parties the equilibrium price is much more than they were ready to accept.[4]

If Eunians are more conformist in their labor preferences, small changes in the Labor Right price can pull lots of them over the border separating those opting for jobs and those opting for unemployment. It yields high price elasticity for Labor Rights, resulting in many people watching EuTV every night to see where the rates are going. But nothing can prevent the formation of an equilibrium market price for the Labor Right: if the price is too high, there will be suppliers of four Labor Rights on the market (potentially unemployed) unable to find buyers. As long as they do not find any, they will have neither income nor work. And the same holds for the hesitating potential buyers. The price will go down quickly. If the Labor Right price is too low, candidates for jobs are waiting for Labor Right-sellers that do not appear. They can be called up only by bidding higher, so the Labor Right price goes quickly.

The beneficial effects of large *differences* between the individual Eunian's labor preferencs may be somewhat surprising, but the role of the average Labor preference id quite familiar to us. Many of us tend to think that man is lazy by nature, and see in social security a means for too many to realize their preferred state. Many others tend to think labor is Man's Essence, and argue in favor of state guaranteed employment. (Arneson, 1990). These two visions are both reflected in Eu's market laws: if the average labor preference is low, many people are ready to sell Labor Rights at a low price. Those willing to work will have to pay little and be relatively rich. If the average labor preference is high, people are willing to pay a high price for the additional Labor Right they need. The unemployed will be relatively rich, and all Eunians consider this to be fair, because in this case also the unemployed have a high labor preference, and it is a big sacrifice for them to refrain from working this year. Money is only a small consolation, and if it is to serve as compensation, it must be a lot. In Eu, "people's endowment is not exhaustively described by their wealth and their skills: the holding of a job constitutes a third type of resource" (Van Parijs, 1989: 56).

What Makes Eu So Strange to Us

We are not at all used to seeing unemployment benefits as one side of an exchange, in which the unemployed offer their right to work. We want them desperately to apply for jobs and find one as soon as possible. A Eunian who has opted for unemployment is free to apply for a job, but if selected is not allowed to enter that job before having bought the required Labor Rights. Without Labor Rights, jobs are *forbidden* to you. They are occupied by owners of Labor Rights, who have paid the prevailing market equilibrium price for them. In Eu, there's no discussion for whether people ought to work. It is not a matter of morals or politics or ethics. Jobs are like cars and concerts. Opting for employment is a matter of taste and your own preferred way of enjoying life.

Of course, as a Eunian, I would be delighted if my preferences were not shared by many. If I like to work, I will tell everybody how nice it is to be unemployed. (This is because I sell leisure, and I am interested in getting a good price.) If I am lazy, I sell work. Accordingly, I would stress the educational value of work, along with all other pro-work arguments I have picked up in bars and streets. Whatever I want and say, I am not likely to start moralizing.[5]

In Eu, unemployment benefits are the compensation for the sacrifice of Labor Rights. Everybody is free to supply or demand Labor Rights. Because of that, an equilibrium price arises which is such that exactly 4 million able-bodied adult citizens opt for a job, and exactly 1 million opt for living without a job for the coming year. All parties agree, and no Eunian has the dignity problems familiar from our own society (Arneson, 1990: 1140–1144).

In our own world, we have four types of able-bodied adult citizens shown in Table 43.1 below. In case A, you have a job, and you are satisfied with it in the sense that you would not want to exchange your situation for that of some unemployed person. In case B, you have a job, but you actually would prefer to be member of group D. In case C, people are

Table 43.1 A Typology of Employment.

	voluntary	*involuntary*
employed	A	B
unemployed	D	C

unemployed and dissatisfied: in C, you dream of being in A. In case D, you are unemployed, but that is all right with you: you would not want to exchange your situation for that of any employed person.

In Eu's free market, all these preferences would be reflected in prices for which Labor Rights are bought and sold. In our world, it is otherwise. We moralize, making it a matter of politics and collective compromise. We concoct complicated criteria for deciding which inactive able-bodied adult citizens may receive a benefit, for determining the rate of the benefit, for deciding who is going to pay for it and how much. To Eunians, we look like communists deliberately. organizing market failures for the sake of nineteenth-century morals.

Eunians would nod their heads hearing our discussions on Man's Labor Needs and Duties and associate them with our attempt to allocate a scarce good (jobs) not by market economic means, but by central *dirigiste* regulations. What we settle by our political compromises between the various visions on labor of liberals, social democrats, Christians and what have you is, in Eu, settled by the free market, as we are ourselves accustomed to doing with all other scarce goods.

Social Security and Minimum Subsistence

In our worlds, social security acts as a political *correction* to the labor market. That latter mechanism determines the level of wages and the demand for labor; and since demand runs chronically short of supply in many segments, this means chronic unemployment. Because we do not allow the income of the unemployed to fall below subsistence, we make a correction politically: we oblige the employed to pay some tax or premium, and use it to finance unemployment benefits. This is the origin of our discussions of the limits to be set to this correction: we equate this to the limits we set to political *distortion* of the free labor market process. It would take us a lot of effort to explain to a Eunian what we mean by "distortion" in this context.

Eunians have "social security," though, for it is impossible for people with a high labor preference to buy Labor Rights from those with a low labor preference at a price that would set the latter below subsistence. The potentially unemployed would simply not sell their Labor Rights at such a price, and prefer to buy an additional Labor Right and occupy a job. At such a Labor Right price, everybody would be on the demand side, so the Labor Right price will rise.

But the same social security applies to the potentially employed. The price of Labor Rights can never rise so high as to put them below subsistence. Such a price would pull them all to the supply side, and the market would bring the Labor Right price down.

Insofar as the term "social security" is applicable to Eu, it is so in the sense that no one need fear sinking below subsistence. In our own world, this is felt as a one-sided warrant to the unemployed, but in Eu it is a perfectly symmetrical guarantee. How then can we explain to a Eunian what we mean by limits to social security?

Eunians do not come to a political determination of what constitutes "minimum subsistence." Everybody has his or her own ideas as regards his or her own minimum subsistence (though of course you cannot set your limit so luxuriously high that it cannot be reached either by working nor by selling your Labor Rights and remaining unemployed). In a sense, therefore, Eunians have a Basic Income. But unemployed Eunians do not have the feeling they "do nothing for it." They have chosen to sell their right to work, a right they have in the exact proportion of 80%, as determined by the decree of the Labor Bank. Abstinence from labor is, in Eu, regarded as a sacrifice.

Who Suffers? Who is Good?

In our world, we all seem to suffer. If you are in group A or B, you need to pay taxes and premiums to unemployed people who do nothing in return. If you are in B you are even worse off, because you would like to be such an unemployed person but you are not allowed to be (unless you are lucky enough to be fired). If you are in C, you are not given the opportunity to work and hence do something in exchange for your income, and you do not like that. If you are in D, you cannot even say so openly, because you are likely thereby to violate the conditions under which you receive your unemployent benefit.

What preference *should* we have, if we listen to what people tell us? We tend to consider "full employment" (a job for each and every able-bodied adult citizen) as the ideal situation, though most of us realize this cannot be achieved. It is clear that nobody needs to be ashamed to be in A (voluntarily employed). What about B? Morals apart, it seems a little embarrassing to be continuously in a situation you do not prefer without doing anything about it. But in case B (the case of involuntary employment) there is a big consolation: you do your *duty*. The origins of this moral gratification are old and deep. These very ideas frame our *dirigiste* quasi-communist regulation of the labor market: labor is *sacrifice*, income is *mercy*. (Face it: also socialists and liberals usually have a labor ethic that is essentially Christian.)

If you acquire an income without labor – case D – you are better off, in the sense of being on a higher utility plane. But you are better off in a way shared by thieves, burglars and other parasites who evade their duties. The satisfaction, if you are in B, is moral. In Eu, people in B have a ready remedy – they would immediately sell their Labor Rights. In our own society, people in B (that is, people whose labor preference is so low as to offset even this moral compensation) need to take immoral actions. They have to negotiate an involuntary dismissal with their employer, and then go to the social security authorities and declare solemnly they will swiftly apply for vacant jobs and enter one as soon as possible – but they do not mean a word of it. In our culture, it may not be forbidden to have such *preferences* (how, after all, can you forbid preferences?) but you are supposed not to translate your preference into *actions*. A morally sound able-bodied adult citizen who does not like to work is supposed to stay in B and be happy about this, proud to do something for his or her income. Nonetheless, we all believe there are some people in D. Your estimation of their number depends on your political preferences. But most of us judge them uniformly negatively.

Who is *good*? Our rules are such that the unemployed are forced to be willing to enter a job, and though nobody asks about preferences directly unemployed persons clearly can make a decent impression if they assume a C profile. We generally consider membership of B to be preferable to membership of C: the involuntary employed do their duty, which unfortunately cannot be said of those in C (or D). With a C-profile, you may be able to claim pity and solidarity. Not so with a D-profile! This explains that the four groups have a decreasing order in social "visibility:" A > B > C > D. This order also gives our moral ranking.[6]

Notice that categories A and C have traditionally been disqualified as objects of economic inquiry.[7] The reason is simply that it is relatively easy to know whether someone is employed (A, B) or unemployed (C, D). But it is much harder to distinguish members of A from those of B or members of C from those of D. Even for yourself, if you work, it is difficult to know whether you are a member of A or B. When you negotiate your wage with your employer, you certainly assume a B profile: you want good compensation for your labor. But in your leisure time you may score better with an A-profile: you love your work, you could not do without it. We have no point at which the personal, internal choice of an A or B profile has market consequences for ourselves. The structure of the world we live in thereby creates loss of self-knowledge and hence self-confidence. It is this kind of self-confidence that Eunians are trained to have.

Unemployed persons have, in our world, the same problem of never really knowing within themselves whether they are in C or D. In their contacts with social security authorities, they will certainly assume a C profile. But somewhere else you may hear them deriving esteem from claiming that unemployment is no problem to them or is even preferred to a working life. Which is the truth of the matter? This is hard to know, even for yourself, because you have no occasion to confront the choice in any practically meaningful way. Eunians have to make the choice year in and year out. For us, it is harder to acquire the relevant self-knowledge.

This is caused by the prevailing ideology of labor. It stipulates an ideal of a world with no one in C or D: a world with no ***unemployment***. Eunians have another ideal: a world with no ***involuntariness***. And they have realized it: at the moment Labor Rights were first issued, members of B exchanged with members of C. The former C members thus went to A: the involuntarily unemployed became voluntarily employed. We tend to like that. But, in our world, this is impossible because these jobs are occupied by B-members, whom we moralistically do not want to deprive of the opportunity to do their duty. In Eu this obligation is cancelled, so jobs of B members go unfilled, and B members become D members.

In Eu, B and C are empty sets. Cancelling the moral obligation to work would not lead to any vacancies. As long as there are vacancies, less than 4 million able-bodied adult citizens prefer work at the prevailing wage and Labor Right price levels. That, however, also means that some are still trying to sell Labor Rights, while at that moment receiving neither a wage nor a yield from selling Labor Rights. The Labor Right price will go down and the wage/unemployment benefit ratio go up until exactly 4 million prefer to enter a job, and prefer ***working*** to enjoying a yield from selling Labor Rights with no job. Thus it is guaranteed that, in Eu, Group A contains 4 million and D contains 1 million able-bodied adult citizens. B and C being empty, nobody suffers the fate of being involuntarily in a dispreferred state.

If the number of available jobs drops in such a way that structural unemployment in Eu rises to 40%, all able-bodied adult citizens get three Labor Rights and will be told that they need five to enter a job. This reduces A to 3 million able-bodied adult citizens and increases D to 2 million. B and C still remain empty.

If, later on, the number of available jobs rises in such a way that structural unemployment in Eu drops to 4%, all able-bodied adult citizens get 24 Labor Rights and will need 25 to enter a job. Maybe some Eunians regret such a development, because people's labor preferences might have fallen in the period of high unemployment. Maybe, on the contrary, they thank their Gods (certainly different from ours) for this rise of employment. Anyhow, exactly 4,800,000 will immediately opt for working, and the remaining 200,000 will immediately opt for being unemployed.

Non-needy Bohemians

The contrast between Eu and our own world reaches its peak in the moral judgment of able-bodied adult citizens with a D profile. Here, they are often distrusted, and we tend to feel no "responsibility" for them: we do not want to feed them out of "our" income for which we have the decency to work.[8] D members are also a very useful symbol and instrument for demagogues who argue in favor of reducing unemployment benefits. If, in our world, you are a D member, you will be wary of letting other people know.

In Eu, their presence is highly appreciated. They are the hard core of the supply side of the market in Labor Rights: they help keep down the price, thereby keeping up the wage/ unemployment-benefit ratio. In their turn, these "non-needy Bohemians" appreciate A members.[9] Members of A are willing to pay a high price for their Labor Rights. This diversity in labor preference relaxes the tensions in their society. No Eunian feels the need to discuss the general validity of some system of Labor Ethics; on the contrary, they would consider such a general Ethics to be highly dangerous for the stability of the labor market and thus for their society.

We tend to look upon an unemployed able-bodied adult citizen who receives a benefit "without giving anything in return" as a defect, and we look for "causes" of this defect. Either this able-bodied adult citizen falls personally short of what he or she should be, or something is wrong with his or her environment which fails to create enough jobs.

This is why we insist on using the term "unemployed" for a special type of inactive able-bodied adult citizen: those who desire a job, but cannot find one. Our bureaucrats are anxious to keep this group distinct from other inactives, such as schoolchildren, students, artists, and those who enjoy an old-age pension. The difference is sought in the ***motives*** each has, or ought to have, in claiming nonwage income. We need to give separate moral and economic rationale for each group's receiving a nonwage income: schoolchildren and students will serve our country in the future, artists do this even now, both really "work" in a sense and "do something" for their nonwage income. Older people did so in the past. But "real" unemployed people would like to do so and are unable to, due to defects in themselves or in our economy. Every "real" unemployed person is, therefore, one too many.

In Eu, the pathological interest in all these fine distinctions is relaxed. You decide for yourself whether you want to quit work and why. Education may be a motive. But it does not matter whether you do this because you want to become wiser, abler, capable of more interesting work (which, mind you, is not better paid in Eu), or to help needy people, express yourself artistically, enjoy art, sports or just lazy leisure. We distinguish anxiously between these and many other motives, because we need strict rules for claiming benefits in our complex bureaucracy. In Eu, however, civil authorities can save themselves the trouble.

Eunians may read Arendt (1958), Canivet (1991) and Gorz (1988) with great interest. They do so not because they want a solution for the ***social*** problems that prompt these authors to ponder the meaning of "labor," "work," "action," "paid action," "labor in itself" and "autonomous action;" the "social" problems have been solved, or at least are shared by all Eunians in egalitarian fashion. Their interest is to make a good choice, in harmony with their age, situation, character, desires in life and financial needs. Thinking about what a job would mean to them, and what unemployment would mean to them, is a necessary prerequisite for making decisions you will not later regret, and thus for their optimal self-realization.

Notes

1. "Able-bodied adult citizens" is here used in the sense of Arneson (1990: 1128).
2. Their employer must agree to their being kept on, of course.
3. That is how much you yourself value working: there is, remember, no moralistic component here.
4. There will be "employment rent" in the sense of Van Parijs (1991: 124; forthcoming, para. 5ff).
5. Unless I find myself trying to agree on a Labor Right transaction with someone sensitive to moralizing, which presumably few Eunians are.
6. There may, however, be some dispute as to the relative praiseworthiness of A and D. Both groups do their duty, but with an A profile you claim this is no sacrifice to you. With a B profile, you do your duty though you would prefer to be in D. Now, some of us have moral convictions that rank a service that is felt as a sacrifice higher than a service that is not.
7. "Political Economy makes entire abstraction of every other human passion or motive: except those which may be regarded as perpetually antagonizing principles to the desire of wealth, namely aversion to labor, and desire of the present enjoyment of costly indulgences" (Mill, 1836: 312).
8. See, for instance, the quotations in the indispensable paper by Philippe van Parijs (1991): "There must be no parasites in paradise" (Senator Yee, Hawaii); "those who surf all day off Malibu must find a way to support themselves and would not be entitled to public funds" (John Rawls); "it is unfair for able-bodied people to live off the labor of others" (Jon Elster).
9. The term comes from Arneson (1990: 1127).

References

Arendt, H. (1958). *The Human Condition.* University of Chicago Press, Chicago.

Arneson, R.J. (1990). Is work special? *American Political Science Review*, 84, 1127–1147.

Canivet, M. (1991). Le travail selon André Gorz: présentation et commentaire. *Le droit on travail*, 13, 47–63. Institut des science du travail, Paris.

Gorz, A. (1988). *Métamorphoses du travail. Quête de sens: Critique de la raison économique.* Galilee, Paris.

Mill, J.S. (1836). On the definition of political economy. In J.M. Robson (ed.) *Essays on Economy and Society* (vol. 4 of Mill's Collected Works). University of Toronto Press, Toronto.

Van Parijs, P. (1989). Maximin real freedom in a non-Walrasian world. In Van Parijs, *What (If Anything) Is Wrong with Capitalism?* Mimeograph. Chaire Hoover d'éthique économique et sociale, Université Catholique de Louvain, Louvain-la-Neuve, Belgium.

Van Parijs, P. (1991). Why surfers should be fed: the liberal case for an unconditional basic income. *Philosophy and Public Affairs*, 20, 101–131.

Van Parijs, P. (forthcoming). Free riding versus rent sharing: should Gauthier support a basic income? In F. Farina, H. Hahn, and S. Vanucci (eds) *Ethics, Economics and Rationality.* Oxford University Press, Oxford.

Chapter 44
Beyond the Wage-based Society

André Gorz

Excerpts from Gorz, A. (1997). Sortir de la société salariale. In *Misères du présent. Richesse du possible.* Galilée, Paris. (English translation: *Reclaiming Work: Beyond the Wage-based Society.* Polity Press & Blackwell, Cambridge, 1999.)

Security of income is the first precondition for a society based on multi-activity. Unconditionally guaranteeing everyone an income for life will, however, have a fundamentally different meaning and function depending on whether that income is (1) insufficient or (2) sufficient for protecting him/her from poverty.

(1) The guarantee of a Basic Income at less than subsistence level, which its advocates hope to see substituted for most forms of income redistribution (family allowance, housing, unemployment and sickness benefits, basic state pension, etc.), functions to force the unemployed to accept dirty, low-status jobs on the cheap. This is the position of the "Friedmannite" neo-liberals of the Chicago School, and also of German liberals like Mitschke and of the British conservatives. In their view, unemployment is explained by the fact that many potential jobs with low skill levels and low productivity are unprofitable at normal rates of pay. These jobs have, consequently, to be subsidized by allowing the worker to combine an insufficient Basic Social Income with an equally insufficient income from work. In this way, a kind of "secondary labor market" is created, protected from competition from low-wage countries but "protected" also from the provisions of labor legislation, which is destined to disappear. The lower the Basic Income, the greater will be the "encouragement" to take any work at all, and the more new "slavers" will be able to specialize in employing a cheap workforce in fly-by-night operations providing service work on a contract and sub-contract basis.

American workfare, which received President Clinton's imprimatur in late July 1996, links the right to a very small welfare allowance with the obligation to perform unpaid – or very low-paid – work of "social utility" for a municipal authority or approved association. Workfare has many advocates in France and Britain – and in Germany, where municipal authorities have begun to threaten the long-term unemployed with the withdrawal of their benefits if they do not perform work of "public utility" (cleaning, earth-moving, clearance

From Gorz, A. (1997). Sortir de la société salariale. In *Misères du présent. Richesse du possible.* Galilée, Paris. (There is an English translation: *Reclaiming Work: Beyond the Wage-based Society.* Polity Press & Blackwell, Cambridge, 1999.) Reprinted with permission of Polity Press.

Basic Income: An Anthology of Contemporary Research, First Edition. Edited by Karl Widerquist, José A. Noguera, Yannick Vanderborght, and Jurgen De Wispelaere.

work, etc.), for which they are paid an hourly rate of 2 DM, which is intended to cover their travel and clothing expenses.

All forms of workfare stigmatize the unemployed as incompetents and scroungers, whom society is entitled to force to work – for their own good. In this way, it reassures itself as to the cause of unemployment: that cause is the unemployed themselves. They do not have, it is said, the social skills and requisite will-power to get a job, and they will consequently be put to the most menial tasks. In reality, the high rate of unemployment among the unskilled is due not to their lack of professional skills, but to the fact that (both in France and in Germany) one-third of skilled or highly skilled people are in unskilled occupations (for want of being able to find anything better) and have thus elbowed out those who ought normally to be able to fill those jobs. Instead of subsidizing unskilled jobs by way of a Basic Income, it is the redistribution of skilled jobs that ought to be subsidized by considerably lowering the hours of work in those occupations.

The ultra-conservative conception of workfare does, however, coexist with a post-Fordist conception, defended by Yoland Bresson among others. Bresson advocates a universal, unconditional "subsistence income" (*revenu d'existence*) of 1,800 French francs (c.£180) per month which would perform the function both of a total or partial unemployment benefit and of an incentive to accept casual part-time jobs with variable wages and hours. "The future is one of discontinuous employment, and we have to give everyone the means to fit themselves into the new system [. . .] In this context, the subsistence income is a means, not an end in itself" (Bresson, 1995).

According to this conception, the "subsistence income" is to *enable* employment to become intermittent, and may even *encourage* such intermittent employment. But who is to benefit from it? That is the question. A very low "subsistence income" is in fact a subsidy for employers. It allows them to find labor while paying less than subsistence-level wages. But while it is enabling for the employers, it is an imposition upon the workers. Since they are not guaranteed a sufficient Basic Income, they have to look continually for some kind of casual work or temporary job and are, therefore, incapable of living their lives on a multi-activity basis. In this case, the "subsistence income" gives a sizeable boost to deregulating the wage relation, to making employment more insecure and "flexible," and to replacing it with a commercial contract. We see here the traps inherent in demanding continuous income for discontinuous work. Unless, of course, *the breaks in work, its discontinuity, reflect not capital's discretionary power over labor, but the individual and collective right of those performing work to control how they manage their own time.* We shall return to this below.

(2) Granting each citizen a *sufficient* social income follows an opposite logic: the aim is not to force the recipients to accept any kind of work on any terms whatsoever, but to free them from the constraints of the labor market. The Basic Social Income must enable them to refuse work and reject "inhuman" working conditions. And it must be part of *a social environment which enables all citizens to decide on an ongoing basis between the use-value of their time and its exchange-value*: that is to say between the "utilities" they can acquire by selling their working time and those they can "selfprovide" by using that time themselves.

Such a Universal Grant of a sufficient income (I shall return to this at greater length below) must not be understood as a form of assistance, nor even of social protection, leaving individuals dependent upon the welfare state. It must be understood, rather, as a prime example of what Anthony Giddens calls a "generative policy" (Giddens, 1994). That is to say, it must give individuals and groups increased resources for taking charge of their own lives, further power over their way of life and living conditions. The aim is not to enable people not to work at all, but rather to give genuine effect to the right to work: not the right to that work you are "employed" to do, but to the concrete work you do without having to be paid for it, without its profitability or exchange-value coming into the equation.

The granting of a sufficient Basic Income to all citizens must, therefore, be inseparable from developing and making accessible the resources which enable and encourage self-activity to take place, the resources with which individuals and groups can satisfy by their own unshackled efforts part of the needs and desires they have themselves defined. This is why discussions of the precise amount of a sufficient income have no great meaning in themselves: they distract from the essence of the question which the current social changes really raise by situating those changes within the framework of wage-based society and seeking to finance the Universal Grant by fiscal redistribution. Now, the prospect which lies before us and which should be the backdrop to our thinking is a future with less employment and less selling of labor and services, but with a growth in collective facilities and services, in nonmonetary exchange and self-providing. According to Frithjof Bergmann, high-tech self-providing could easily cover 70% of needs and desires on two days' work a week.

The schemes which are currently being debated could move us closer to that ultimate goal or further from it; they could open up this potential future or close it off; they could show up the need for a break with the present system or by-pass that need. It is on this basis that they have to be judged.

It was, indeed, in this spirit that the Universal Grant of a sufficient social income was advocated by libertarian communists and socialists, whose aim was not to redistribute or "share" employment, but to abolish wage-labor and the compulsion to work, to sweep away capitalist business and the state. These included Bellamy and Popper-Lynkeus at the dawn of the twentieth century, the French "distributists who followed Jacques Duboin's theories; the Proudhonite "Ordre Nouveau" intellectual movement of Robert Aron, Arnaud Dandieu and Alexandre Marc in the 1930s; Paul Goodman in the USA in the 1950s; and at least some of the German "Greens" who, in the 1980s, rediscovered this tradition and adapted some of its ideas to present conditions.

For many years I rejected the idea of a social income which would allow people to "live without working." This I did for reasons quite contrary to the disciples of Rawls, who see "work" as "a good" which must, in the name of justice, be distributed equitably. But "work" is not "a good." It is a necessary activity, carried out in the modern period according to norms defined by society, at the demand of society, imparting a sense that one is capable of doing what society needs. It gives recognition, socializes and confers rights because it is itself required as an obligation. In this way, "work" draws people out of their private solitude; it is an aspect of citizenship. And it represents, more fundamentally (as work one does) – beyond its particular social determination – a mastery of self and of the surrounding world which is necessary for the development of human capacities.

As the need for work diminishes, fairness requires that it should also diminish in everyone's life and that the burden of work should be equitably distributed. This is why, in previous works, I wanted the guarantee of a full income for all to be linked to all citizens performing the quantity of work required for the production of the wealth to which their income entitled them. This could take the form, for example, of 20,000 hours which individuals could spread over their working lives in as many "tranches" as they wished, on condition that the gap between two working periods did not exceed a certain interval.

This formula, which I advocated from 1983 onwards, was consistent with the prospect of wage-labor and the "law of value" disappearing: the Guaranteed Social Income was no longer a wage (cf. Gorz, 1985: 40–4) It was consistent with taking back, and gaining control of, time. But it was not consistent with the perspectives opened up, and the changes brought about, by post-Fordism. I am therefore abandoning it for the following four reasons.

In Defense of Unconditionality

(1) When intelligence and imagination ("general intellect") become the main productive force, working time ceases to be the measure of labor; indeed, it ceases to be measurable. The use-value produced may bear no relation to the time taken to produce it. It may vary greatly from person to person, or depending on the material or immaterial nature of the work. Lastly, stable employment paid according to the number of working hours per week is in rapid decline. It is becoming increasingly difficult to define an irreducible *quantity* of work to be performed by each person over a determinate period. It is impossible to measure the working hours of the self-employed or of craftworkers or the providers of intangible services. Only the granting of a Basic Social Income can encourage these people – in most cases it is the only thing that can allow them – to reduce their professional activity in order to lead a multi-active life. Only the payment of a Basic Income will absolve them of the need to fight, in a crowded labor market, for the few crumbs from the ever smaller sums employers distribute to pay for labor. The *universal, unconditional* grant of a Basic Income is, therefore (in a context which I shall specify in detail below), the best instrument for redistributing both paid work and unpaid activities as widely as possible.

(2) The *unconditional* right to a sufficient Basic Income will doubtless bring some immediate objections. How can we avoid a growing mass of scroungers living off the work of others? Won't those others refuse to carry the burden and demand the prohibition of such idling? Won't they call for work to be made compulsory in the form of workfare or obligatory community service?

Many advocates of a Universal Grant, both liberal and socialist, make these objections. But they then run up against the following difficulty: what is to be the content of the compulsory work to be demanded in return for the basic living allowance? How is that work to be defined, measured and distributed when the importance of work in the economy is declining? And how are they to avoid compulsory work competing with, and even destroying, an increasing proportion of normally paid public activities and jobs?

Claus Offe and Jeremy Rifkin respond, with others, by situating this compulsory work in the third Sector of activities which meet needs that cannot be paid for, or profitably carried on, within the market economy. It is to be "voluntary care work or educational activities, community work with approved associations". In this way, the universal allowance would serve to create "a post-industrial domestic sector" (Offe, 1995). It would become the payment for voluntary work performed for recognized non-profit-making bodies. It would make "voluntary" work compulsory.

Diane Elson makes a similar proposal: "Alongside the right to a grant should be the duty, on the part of able-bodied adults, of undertaking some unpaid household work of caring and providing for those who are unable to take care of themselves. Persons already undertaking care of a young or old or sick or handicapped person would be exempt" (Elson, 1998: 29).

So, in the one case (Offe), the concern to have a *quid pro quo* in terms of work which does not compete with normal employment produces the nonsensical prospect of compulsory voluntary work. The perverse effects of this provision are clear for all to see: real volunteers would have alongside them "pressed" volunteers, and there is every likelihood these latter would be treated as second-class workers and given the least rewarding work, since they would be doing the same things as the real volunteers were doing from conviction and for free, but would appear to be doing it (or would be suspected of doing it) simply in order to draw their allowance. Compulsory voluntary work then becomes a trap: it devalues the work of the volunteers who are pressed into doing it.

In the other case (Elson), the obligation on the recipients of a Basic Income to perform domestic work (intentionally) blurs the distinction between productive and reproductive labor. The latter is equated with the former and regarded as interchangeable with it. In this way, the private character of domestic activities is denied. Parents' obligations to their children, adults' obligations to their elderly parents would all be set up as social obligations and placed under public control. Spontaneous behavior between persons – where spontaneity is, in fact, crucial to the emotional value – would be administratively monitored and standardized.[1]

In each case, the grant of a Basic Income is conceived as a payment for family activities which are thus irresistibly drawn into the field of those activities whereby one is called on to "earn one's living." Entitlement to the Basic Income requires either having children of one's own, or looking after other people's children and households, or working in the "voluntary" sector. Activities whose normal meaning lies in an absence of self-interest become a means for acquiring an income. There is then no reason why the list of activities "which may be regarded as work" should not extend to the artistic, cultural, religious or sporting fields.[2] If these kinds of activity themselves became a means to qualify for the Basic Income, they would in their turn be drawn within the ambit of instrumental reason and administrative standardization.

It is important that we grasp precisely what is at issue here. If we want the Universal Grant of a Basic Income to be linked to the performance of equivalent work as its justification, two conditions have to be met. First, that work has to be work within the public sphere which is of benefit to everyone, and, second, that work *must be able to have payment* (in this case, of the Basic Income) *as its aim, without the fact of payment corrupting its meaning*. If it is not possible to meet this latter condition, and if the Universal Grant is intended to promote voluntary, artistic, cultural, family and mutual-aid activities, then the Universal Grant has to be guaranteed to everyone unconditionally. For only if it is unconditional will it be possible to protect the unconditional nature of those activities which are only fully meaningful when done for their own sake. After arguing against it for many years, I have therefore come round to the position of those who advocate a *sufficient* (not a minimal) Basic Income which is "strictly unconditional," as Alain Caille and Ahmet Insel put it (Caillé and Insel, 1996: 13). I see this as the only way to preserve the voluntary sector and to protect from socialization and economicization – while at the same time making them accessible to all – those activities "which derive their value from being done for their own sake."

(3) The Universal Grant of a Basic Income is the most appropriate arrangement for a situation in which the "general state of science" is coming to be the main force of production (Marx, 1973: 704). and in which direct working time is becoming negligible by comparison with the time required for the production, reproduction and extended reproduction of the capacities and skills of the workforce in the so-called "immaterial economy." It would be interesting to calculate the number of weeks or years spent on basic and continuing training, in the training of trainers, and so on, for each hour, week or year of direct work performed in the economy. And training itself is a small matter by comparison with all that it takes to provide for the development of the capacities of imagination, interpretation, analysis, synthesis and communication integral to the post-Fordist workforce. In the "immaterial" economy, "the worker is both the labor power and the one who directs that labor power." It can no longer be detached from his/her person:

> Worker, work and labour power tend to merge in self-producing persons. And that production takes place not just in the workplace, but in schools, cafés, stadiums, neighbourhoods and discussion groups, on trips, at theatres and concerts, through newspapers and books etc. In short, it takes place wherever individuals come together and produce the world of social relations. (Gorz, 1967: 117)

In progressive firms, continuing training is already part of work (and working hours) and is paid for as such. But this extension of the employment contract to include training is not without its disadvantages, since it subordinates the right to training, and the nature of that training, to company interests. It develops a merely functional, limited autonomy in individuals, of a kind which can be controlled and subjected. By contrast, it is one of the functions of an Unconditional Basic Income to make the right to develop *one's* capacities an unconditional right to an autonomy which transcends its productive function; an autonomy experienced and valued for its own sake on a variety of planes: moral (autonomy of value-judgement), political (autonomy of decision-making regarding the common good), cultural (invention of life-styles, consumption models and arts of living) and existential (the capacity to take care of oneself, rather than leave the experts and authorities to decide what is good for us).

Beyond the "Labor Theory of Value"

(4) There is a further argument in favor of an Unconditional Social Income. It is the arrangement best suited to the economy that is beginning to emerge on the other side of the impasse into which current trends are leading. An increasing volume of wealth is produced with a decreasing volume of capital and labor. As a result, production distributes a decreasing amount of pay and wages to a decreasing number of workers. The purchasing power of a growing proportion of the population is falling. Unemployment, poverty and absolute destitution are spreading. The rapidly growing productivity of labor and capital produces a surplus of labor power and capital. And the latter now attempts to expand either without passing through the mediation of productive work at all (simply by transactions on the financial or currency markets) or by investing in low-wage countries. The contraction in the volume of wages – ***and also the tax breaks which states accord capital to prevent its flight*** – lead to a situation in which those activities and investments which do not bring short-term returns (research, education, public services and amenities, environ-

mental protection, etc.) can no longer be financed.[3] As the privatization of public services continues and social expenditure and benefits keep on falling, the question usually directed at the advocates of a Basic Social Income comes to encapsulate the problem of the system as a whole: "Where are you going to get the money from?" Although working time is no longer the measure of created wealth, it still remains the basis for the distribution of incomes and, for the most part, for the sums expended and redistributed by the state. ***The trend within the economy is thus for the amounts that are to be levied and redistributed to cover individual and collective needs ultimately to exceed the amounts distributed by and for production.*** It is not merely the Universal Grant of a Basic Income which cannot be funded on this basis. It is the whole of the state and the society which are coming apart at the seams (something which is very visible in Great Britain and the USA). Wassily Leontief summed up the situation in the following metaphor: "What would happen if we suddenly found ourselves in [Paradise]? With all goods and services provided without work, no one would be gainfully employed. Being unemployed means receiving no wages. As a result, until appropriate new income policies were formulated to fit the changed technological conditions everyone would starve in Paradise" (Leontief, 1982: 155).

Leontief didn't say precisely what new income policy he had in mind, but Jacques Duboin indicated the "exit" as early as 1931 and Marx did so in 1857 (in the *Grundrisse*, which Duboin could not have known):[4] ***the distribution of means of payment must correspond to the volume of wealth socially produced and not to the volume of work performed.***

As René Passet so succinctly puts it, "What we regard today as secondary distribution will become primary distribution." Because it is the product of integrated, "man-machine-organization" systems in which "the contribution specific to each person is no longer measurable," "the national product becomes genuinely collective property [. . .] The question of distribution is no longer one of commutative, but distributive justice." (Passet, 1996).

The distribution of means of payment will no longer take the form of a wage, but of what, even in his day, Duboin called a "social income." This no longer reflects the "value" of the labor done (that is to say, of the products necessary to reproduce the labor power expended), but the needs, desires and aspirations society chooses to meet. It requires the creation of another sort of money, which cannot be hoarded and which Passet, following Duboin, calls "consumption money."[5]

This is where present developments are heading. They are rendering the "law of value" obsolete. They require, in fact, a quite different economy in which prices are no longer a reflection of the cost of direct labor contained in the products and the means of labor, a cost which is becoming increasingly marginal, and the price system no longer reflects the exchange-value of products. Prices will necessarily be political prices and the price system will reflect society's choice of a model of consumption and civilization, its choice of a way of life.[6]

When fully thought through, the Universal Grant of a Basic Income can be seen as equivalent to a pooling of socially produced wealth. It is a pooling, not a "sharing out" (the sharing out comes afterwards: you can only share out between everyone what belongs to everyone, what is, at the outset, no one's). René Passet expresses this clearly when he writes of the national product as "genuinely collective property" produced by collective labor in which it is impossible to assess each person's contribution. As a consequence, the "from each according to his labor" becomes obsolete. The "collective worker" is tending to be supplanted by a fundamentally different virtual subject as the direct work of shaping matter is replaced as the main productive force by the "general state of science [. . .] or the application of this science to production," that is to say, by the capacity of "social individuals" to make use of techno-science through their own self-organized cooperation and exchange. It is then "the free development of individualities" (I am continuing to paraphrase the *Grundrisse* here) by "the reduction of necessary labor to a minimum," and the production of use-values according to needs, which become the objectives.

The call for a sufficient, universal, Unconditional Basic Income fits in to such a vision. It cannot be achieved immediately, but we must begin to conceptualize it and prepare the way for it as of now. *It has heuristic value: it reflects the most basic and advanced meaning of present developments.* Conversely, it shows up the nonsensical nature of a system which makes unprecedented savings of working time, but turns that time into a disaster for those who save it, because the system can neither share it out, nor share out the produced or producible wealth, nor recognize the intrinsic value of "leisure and time for higher activities" (Marx, 1973). It reveals the way this disposable time is individually and collectively appropriated as a major issue. And it shows the capacity for autonomy – the individual and social ability to make meaningful use of one's disposable time and enjoy it – as a cardinal virtue. It points forward to that other society which can be seen emerging out of present trends.

It is no mere intellectual pastime or self-indulgence to clarify the perspective to which these trends point. It is on such clarification that the capacity to give the most advanced meaning to the changes which are taking place depends. And the capacity also to develop actions, arenas of conflict, and practices which keep that meaning responsive to the latest developments by seeking to take control of those changes. The ultimate goal to which the Unconditional Grant of a Basic Income points is that of a society in which the necessity of work is no longer experienced *as such* because each person, from childhood onwards, will be involved in, and feel the attraction of, a general proliferation of artistic, sporting, techno-scientific, artisanal, political, philosophical, ecosophic,[7] relational and cooperative activities all around him/her; a society in which means of production and facilities for self-providing are accessible to everyone at any time of day, just as databanks and teleworking resources already are; in which exchanges are principally exchanges of knowledge, not of commodities, and do not therefore need to be mediated by money; in which the immateriality of the main form of productive work corresponds to the immateriality of the main form of fixed capital. *Once it has been eliminated as a separate, autonomized power*, productive work will consist mainly in the capacity to take advantage of the accumulated knowledge, to enrich and exchange it, *without the valorization of that knowledge imposing itself on individuals as an alien demand*, without it dictating to them the nature, intensity, duration and hours of their work.

It is in this sense that we must understand Marx's remark that "free time, i.e. time for the full development of the individual [. . .] from the standpoint of the direct production process [. . .] can be regarded as the production of fixed capital, this fixed capital being man himself" (Marx, 1973: 711–712). In other words, free time enables individuals to develop capacities (of invention, creation, conception and intellection) which give them a virtually unlimited productivity, and this development of their productive capacity, which can be equated with the production of a fixed capital, *is not work*, though it produces the same outcome as work "from the standpoint of the direct production process." It is not work, because it was made possible by "the general reduction of the necessary labor of a society to a minimum" (Marx, 1973: 706). It is this "time freed up for their own development" which makes it possible for them to take as their goal "the free development of individualities," their "artistic, scientific etc. development" (Marx, 1973: 706). And it is this free development of individualities which reappears in production as the capacity to create an unlimited variety of wealth with a very small expenditure of time and energy.

In other words, the increase in the productive capacities of individuals is *the consequence, not the goal* of their full development. The goal is not to maximize production for production's sake or power for power's sake – this is the difference between "man" and "fixed capital" – but to save on the working time and expenditure of energy *necessary* for achieving a fulfilled life.

"Truly wealthy a nation, when the working day is 6 rather than 12 hours," wrote an anonymous Ricardian, whom Marx quotes repeatedly, in 1821 (Marx, 1973: 706). It is impossible to state more clearly that *the full development of the productive forces makes the full employment of the productive forces* (in particular, labor power) *unnecessary* and makes it possible for production to become an activity of secondary importance. The "massive" productivity which techno-science bestows on human labor means that *the maximization of free time, not the maximization of production, becomes the immanent destination and purpose of economic reason.* "Real Economy – saving – consists of the saving of labor time" (Marx, 1973: 711). "Real economy" leads to the elimination of work as the dominant form of activity. It is this elimination of work and its replacement by personal activity which we must now make our political goal; it is a goal we can make tangible by achieving changes which are practically attainable as of now.

Notes

1. The state of Singapore recently passed a law making it compulsory for children of elderly parents to take care of them. This led the children concerned to request attestations from their parents to the effect that they did provide care. The concern of those who spontaneously took care of their parents was thereby contaminated by an obligation to the state. As for those who do not take care of their parents, they don't have much difficulty getting their parents to sign bogus declarations.
2. In fact, at a symposium of 500 private and public decision-makers organized by the Gorbachev Foundation in September 1995, the guarantee of a minimum subsistence income was regarded as indispensable in the long run by a large majority of the participants. In their view, the employment rate was going to fall to 20% and the unemployment rate was going to rise to 80%. "Social integration will have to be achieved by charitable work in the third sector, by neighbourhood mutual aid schemes, by engaging in sport or all kinds of voluntary activity. 'These activities could be given new status by the payment of a small remuneration,' argues Professor Roy" (quoted by Martin and Schumann, 1996: 12–13).
3. Between 1979 and 1994, German company profits rose by 90%, while wages increased by 6%. However, company taxation as a percentage of tax revenue fell from 35% in 1960 to 25% in 1980 and 13% in 1994. In the same period, taxes on wages and salaries as a percentage of total tax revenue rose from 16% in 1960 to 30% in 1980 and 36% in 1994. If company taxes had remained at 1980 levels, Germany's tax revenue would have increased by 86,000,000,000 DM instead of falling by 9%. From Eisel and Erb (1996: 351).
4. The *Grundrisse* was not published until 1939 (as *Rohentwurf* – rough outline) by the Marx–Engels–Lenin Institute in Moscow. The first edition available to the public was published by Dietz (Berlin) in 1953.
5. René Passet and Jacques Robin's vision in *Transversales* is of a "plural economy *with* a market" and various types of money: one type would be capitalizable and would be of unlimited validity and convertibility; another would be "consumption money" with a time limit on its validity and no possibility of hoarding it; there would also be local currencies which would be restricted in

their circulation and convertibility and whose life-span would be short. It was already Jacques Duboin's conception that this consumption money should be cancelled by the act of purchase it permitted. This is because it is not coming out of taxes on primary income. In an economy in which production barely distributes wages any more, it cannot be. The money by which demand is funded can only be a social money, which is issued in quantities determined by political considerations.

6. All modern states practise political pricing already. All products and services are either subsidized or taxed at very different rates (ranging from tenths of 1% to multiples of 100%). This does not prevent us from still having markets, knowledge of costs, and price competition.
7. The term "ecosophic" was coined by Félix Guattari in *The Three Ecologies* (1989: 131–147), and its meaning was developed extensively in *Chaosmose* (Galilée, 1992). A condensed definition of the term is given in Guattari's article "Vers une 'Ecosophie.'" It reads: "An 'ecosophy,' that is to say a perspective including ethical dimensions, and articulating together the entire range of scientific, political, environmental, social and mental ecologies, is perhaps destined to be substituted for the old ideologies which improperly sectorized the social, the private and the civil, and which were incapable of establishing connections between the political, ethical and aesthetic domains" (Guattari, 1990: 2–3).

References

Bresson, Y. (1995). Le partage du temps et des revenus. *Economica*, (February–March).

Caillé, A. and Insel, A. (1996). Vers un revenu minimum inconditionnel? *La Revue de Mauss*, 7, 1st semester.

Eisel, D. and Erb, G. (1996). Vom Elend des kapitalistischen "Sozialstaates." *Neue Gesellschaft/Frankfurter Hefte.*

Elson, D. (1988). Market Socialism or Socialization of the Market? *New Left Review*, 172, Nov–Dec.

Giddens, A. (1994). *Beyond Left and Right. The Future of Radical Politics.* Polity Press, Cambridge.

Gorz, A. (1967). *Strategy for Labour: A Radical Proposal.* Beacon Press, Boston, p. 117.

Gorz, A. (1985). *Paths to Paradise: On the Liberation from Work.* M. Imrie (transl.). Pluto Press, London.

Guattari, F. (1989) The Three Ecologies. *New Formations*, 8, Summer, pp. 131–147.

Guattari, F. (1992) *Chaosmose.* Galilée, Paris.

Guattari, F. (1990) Vers une "Ecosophie." *Transversales Science/Culture*, 2, March–April.

Leontief, W.W. (1982). The Distribution of Work and Income. *Scientific American*, 247 (3).

Martin, H-P. and Schumann, H. (1996). *Die Globalisierungsfalle.* Rowohlt, Hamburg.

Marx, K. (1973). *Grundrisse.* Penguin Books, Harmondsworth.

Offe, C. (1995). Freiwillig auf die Anteilnahme am Arbeitsmarkt verzichten. *Frankfurter Rundschau*, 19 July.

Passet, R. (1996). La Sécu entre deux chaises. *Transversales*, 37, Jan–Feb.

Chapter 45

The Relevance of Basic Income for Post-industrial Economies

Fred Block

Excerpts from Block, F. (1990). Reflections on the Political Economy of Basic Income Grants in the U.S. Paper presented at the Conference on "Basic Income Guarantees: A New Welfare Strategy?" Madison, Wisconsin, April 6–8. Previously unpublished.

In my view, the United States is currently experiencing a transition from an industrial to a postindustrial economy.[1] This transition makes obsolete much of the Conventional Wisdom about how the economy works, since that wisdom was rooted in nineteenth-century industrial capitalism. Yet in the 1980s and 1990s in the United States, free market economic ideas have more prestige and legitimacy than at any time since the 1920s. This is not an entirely unfamiliar pattern; people often seek to deny the reality of a major historical transition by ritually reinvoking long-established beliefs; this can be an effective defense against facing the new situation. The consequence, however, is that any serious discussion of actual economic and social problems requires considerable effort to clear away these layers and layers of intellectual cobwebs.

The conventional argument against Basic Income grants is that they interfere with the proper functioning of the labor market. On the one hand, they provide individuals with an attractive alternative to taking low-wage work. This has the effect of forcing employers who want to fill such jobs to raise the wages to a level higher than the marginal productivity of the people hired. On the other hand, the existence of an Income Guarantee can also diminish the authority of employers by making the threat of job loss less frightening. This loss of managerial authority is assumed to reduce productivity both through increased shirking and a more general decline of employee compliance with managerial wishes.

These arguments rest ultimately on the assumption that both labor market and managerial coercion are necessary for a market economy to operate effectively. However, this assumption is problematic. Under conditions of high worker skill, traditional forms of employer coercion become problematic. This is particularly clear in contemporary work settings that have been reshaped by computer-based automation.[2] When worker tasks are complex, it becomes inordinately expensive to monitor employee performance closely, since the monitors must have a complete understanding of the tasks. Moreover, with complex tasks, it is often the case that management simply does not know the most efficient way

Basic Income: An Anthology of Contemporary Research, First Edition. Edited by Karl Widerquist, José A. Noguera, Yannick Vanderborght, and Jurgen De Wispelaere.

of organizing the labor process. Furthermore, workers are unlikely to look favorably on the continuous introduction of new technologies in these settings as long as they fear that their jobs might be jeopardized by technological advances. Finally, in these automated settings, the main contributions of workers are often their attention and their capacity for problem-solving. Neither of these characteristics is easily increased through coercion.

In fact, throughout the history of capitalism, there have been islands of labor-management cooperation that have functioned well in the sea of managerial coercion. These islands have been described by Sabel and Zeitlin in their effort to reconstruct the importance of high skilled craft production in the development of capitalism (Sabel and Zeitlin, 1985: 133–176). In the settings they describe, highly skilled workers were largely insulated from both labor market and employer coercion. According to economic theory, these craft industries were doomed to failure because without effective management coercion, workers would shirk or demand wages that eroded profit levels. However, in some instances, these high-skilled craft industries survived for one hundred years or more. This experience suggests that labor-management cooperation can serve as a functional substitute for coercion. In the context of cooperative relations, workers were able to collectively monitor their own work levels and to negotiate wage bargains that were reasonable from the employer's perspective.

The dysfunctionality of managerial coercion with high skills and these historical experiences of cooperation suggest the distinct possibility that today an effective market economy requires generalizing these cooperative patterns. It is striking that the two nations that have been most successful in high-tech manufacturing – Japan and West Germany – have evolved complex institutional mechanisms for creating high levels of worker-management cooperation. These countries have understood something which is rarely grasped in the United States – that in the contemporary world economy, nations do not get richer by putting more people to work in sweatshops sewing shirts, but by raising the proportion of the labor force in high-value-added activities.

In a word, the standard economic arguments against Basic Income grants can be stood on their head. Under current conditions, the phasing in of a Guaranteed Income can be a key factor in generalizing the kinds of cooperative employment relations that are indispensable for the effective utilization of advanced technologies. Since employers in the U.S. have a clear preference for coercion over cooperation, there is a need for social policies that persuade employers of the futility of coercive strategies. A Guaranteed Income could begin to do that by shifting the balance of power in the labor market, so that employers would have little choice but to experiment with cooperative employment relations.[3]

In low-wage sectors of the economy, the Income Guarantee would place strong pressure on employers to cut labor costs through automation. This is a desirable consequence because it would push up productivity levels in sectors that have relied on labor-intensive production.[4] At the same time, the Income Guarantees would provide. a much more adequate safety net for employees displaced from low-wage employment. To be sure, the system of Income Guarantees would have to be linked to an extensive system of adult education and retraining to assure that many people would use their time outside of work to raise their skill levels. It would be essential, of course, that this system of education and retraining be universal, so that the present stigma associated with "employment training" would disappear, and the combination of Guaranteed Income and retraining opportunities would serve both groups that are currently marginal to the economy and core sector workers who lose their jobs as a consequence of economic restructuring and the decline of defense production.

One of the most important features of the income grant in this context is the opportunity it provides individuals to engage in entrepreneurial activities, particularly in the service sector of the economy. By pooling their allowances, groups of individuals would have the opportunity to create their own jobs by starting a community newspaper, an environmental watchdog group, a childcare center, or a home repair business. These initiatives would serve both as a mechanism to take up slack in the labor market and to strengthen that vital part of the economy between the corporate sector and the public sector.

Political Coalitions

Implementing a Basic Income would require building a powerful political coalition that linked together trade unionists, minorities, environmentalists, feminists, and peace activists. The demand could help to bring together this coalition because Basic Income provides benefits to all of these constituencies. For one thing, they address a core feminist concern by providing women with a dependable income that reduces their economic dependence on men. For another, the demand can be advanced in a way that emphasizes both inclusion and transformation. The institutionalization of Basic Income grants can simultaneously address the quantitative issue of poverty and the qualitative issue of alternatives to the paid employment provided by the corporate economy. For example, feminist and environmental groups can use the Basic Income grants as a means to increase significantly the options for people to work at providing childcare services or environmental monitoring. Such alternative forms of employment can be a powerful tool for social movement organizing.

In this respect, the contrast with the full employment demand could not be more striking. The demand for full employment contains an implicit stage theory – first we get everybody a decent job and then, we can begin to worry whether those jobs make sense given our views on the arms race and the protection of the Earth. Because of this implicit stage theory, advocates of full employment always have difficulty reaching beyond economic interest groups. One other difference between Basic Income grants and the full employment demand is also important to note. The idea of full employment through Federal legislation that makes the government the employer of last resort instantly unifies all employers in opposition. If employers are not attracted to the anti-full employment coalition by their fears of a tighter labor market that gives employees greater bargaining power, they can still be attracted to the coalition by two other fears. The first is the fear of higher taxes since the costs of job creation are considerable. The second is the fear that the resulting expansion of public sector employment will begin to substitute for privately provided goods and services.

Certainly such fears are exaggerated; the Swedish case provides ample evidence that a serious full employment policy can work to serve the interests of employers over the long term. However, it is also the case that the institutionalization of full employment in Sweden was a concession to a highly organized and class conscious labor movement; full employment was a lesser evil compared to socialism. It is unlikely that U.S. employers will face that same kind of choice.

In contrast, the demand for Basic Income grants need not so effectively unify employers in opposition. For one thing, the proposal is far more amenable to compromise. In the case of full employment, compromise means passing a Federal commitment to full employment without providing the resources for implementation. This does very little for those wishing to address problems of poverty. In the case of Basic Income grants, the obvious compromise is to phase in the program with a relatively stingy level of grants that would be perceived as not having too much impact on the labor market. Then, following the model of Social Security, it should be possible to gradually raise the level of the basic grant over a period of years.

Such a strategy would be likely to defuse a portion of the business opposition. Moreover, some large employers with relatively skilled employees could very well be persuaded to support the initiative. On the one hand, it would have little adverse immediate effect on their labor market situation, since their employees would still suffer a substantial income loss if they were forced on to the Basic Income grant. On the other hand, they could come to perceive the income grant system as beneficial to them in the long term because the elimination of poverty and related ills would ultimately expand the pool of employees who could be trained for skilled work.

To be sure, there would still be intense business opposition to Basic Income grants, especially if the idea were placed on the political agenda by the kind of coalition that I have discussed. In particular, large employers, such as the fast food chains, who depend heavily on low wage employees, would see such legislation as a major threat to their profitability. The point is only that such resistance can be surmounted if two conditions pertain. The first is that there exist some significant divisions that prevent the business community from showing a united front. The second is that the hypothetical coalition be strong enough to exert considerable force both in the electoral arena and through popular mobilization. While it is impossible to say how much force is enough, I have in mind mobilization on the scale of the civil rights and anti-war movements of the 1960s.

Notes

1. This position is elaborated in Block (1987; 1990).
2. It is my assumption that the dominant tendency is for computer-based technologies to raise employee skill levels. This position is argued at length in Block (1990: ch. 4).
3. Needless to say, such a change would not occur immediately. A Basic Income grant would place pressure for more cooperative employment relations at the lower ends of the labor market. At the higher ends, other policy initiatives would be necessary to persuade employers to abandon coercion.
4. This is similar to the benign consequences of the solidaristic wage policy in Sweden which has forced low wage sectors of the economy to invest heavily in new technologies.

References

Block, F. (1987). Rethinking the Political Economy of the Welfare State. In F. Block, R.A. Cloward, B. Ehrenreich, and F. Fox Piven, *The Mean Season: The Attack on the Welfare State*. Pantheon, New York.

Block, F. (1990). *Postindustrial Possibilities: A Critique of Economic Discourse*. University of California, Berkeley.

Sabel, C.F. and Zeitlin, J. (1985). Historical Alternatives to Mass Production: Politics, Markets and Technology in Nineteenth-Century Industrialization. *Past and Present*, 108 (August 1985): 133–176.

Part VII
Implementation

Introduction

The Implementation of Basic Income

Karl Widerquist, José A. Noguera, Yannick Vanderborght, and Jurgen De Wispelaere

This section discusses problems and challenges that will arise if and when a society decides to begin the actual implementation of Basic Income. This issue is extremely contentious in the Basic Income debate because the introduction of a full Basic Income would be an incredibly large change, even to the most progressive existing social policy regimes. Thus, many questions arise. Should it be introduced gradually or all at once? What are its likely effects on present welfare state designs? How would existing institutions be affected? Which challenges would have to be faced by policy-makers in charge of executing a Basic Income program?

Fred Block and Margaret Somers (2005) address one of the oldest arguments in the implementation debate. Would Basic Income (or similar policies) allow employers to reduce the wages of the poor – knowing that low-wage workers will receive an income floor from the government? Block and Somers trace this argument to an observation about the Speenhamland system of poor relief that was in place in England in the late eighteenth and early nineteenth centuries. They show how impressions about Speenhamland have affected the social policy debate, and reexamine the evidence to show that Speenhamland did not cause a decline in wages.

In his previously unpublished paper "The Stability of Basic Income," Jos de Beus (1992) shows that, contrary to what most of its supporters argue, the implementation of a Basic Income in the real world is not as simple as it appears at first sight. In fact, he writes, "a stable Basic Income scheme must be complex." It should, in particular, include several mechanisms that will provide incentives to maintain and improve solidarity, or even "communitarian commitment and togetherness."

In "Basic Income and the Welfare State" (1995), Samuel Brittan shows how the implementation challenges faced by a Basic Income will most likely force some to make strong compromises. However, he claims that it is possible to get existing welfare systems closer to Basic Income in an incremental way, and that the implementation of a Basic Income should be conceived as an ongoing process rather than as an "all or nothing" issue. Following this line, he explores a set of partial reforms of the present welfare benefits which would incorporate some of the features of Basic Income, and he discusses different payment methods that

Basic Income: An Anthology of Contemporary Research, First Edition. Edited by Karl Widerquist, José A. Noguera, Yannick Vanderborght, and Jurgen De Wispelaere.

would improve the administrative feasibility of the idea; Brittan's general (and original) idea is to "deconstruct" or "unpack" Basic Income into its constituent components in order to introduce independent progresses in each of them.

In a similar fashion to Brittan, José A. Noguera, in "Basic Income and Contributory Pensions" (2001), explores how to make a Basic Income program fit the existing architecture of one of the pivotal programs in contemporary welfare states: contributory "pay-as-you-go" pension systems which exist in most European countries. He analyzes the different normative principles underlying contributory benefits and Basic Income, as well as the problems of institutional adjustment between them, and concludes by proposing a possible solution for those problems through a public funded pension system which would top up Basic Income for the elderly, without raising equity problems.

Although Basic Income would face some implementation problems, it would also offer some solutions for achieving some of the goals of present welfare systems. The two following chapters give some illustrations about these advantages associated with the implementation of a Basic Income. In "Basic Income as a Minimally Presumptuous Social Welfare Policy," Robert Goodin (1992) argues not that Basic Income reflects a more thorough understanding of social reality, but that it simply relies on fewer assumptions about social reality. In more discriminating social welfare policies, it is essential to properly identify what category each applicant belongs in, creating opportunities for errors. Basic Income avoids this and similar errors because it simply does not divide recipients into categories.

Similarly, in "The Basic Income Guarantee as an Exit Option", Joel Handler and Amanda Sheely Babcock (2006) argue that Basic Income would be much easier to implement than present conditional and workfarist programs, which lead to a nightmare of monitoring compliance and sanctioning noncompliance by their clients. According to Handler and Babcock, workfarist policies fail to achieve the current welfare system's goal of getting all recipients into paid jobs with wages sufficient to support their families. Given the realities of the labor market, caseworkers concentrate on the most promising cases, and the people in need of the most help are left out. With Basic Income in place, and less pressure to get recipients into the labor market, caseworkers could concentrate on meeting their needs, so the implementation of social services would be clearly improved and the balance of power between clients and caseworkers would be redistributed.

By contrast, Jurgen De Wispelaere and Lindsay Stirton, in "Practical Bottlenecks in the Implementation of a Universal Basic Income," maintain that Basic Income poses particular implementation challenges of its own. Many of these challenges arise because of the unique scale of a policy that affects literally every citizen in a polity. Achieving the comprehensive target efficiency to which Basic Income advocates are committed implies resolving a number of administrative bottlenecks that not all welfare administrations are equipped to deal with. In particular, the lack of effective oversight mechanisms may prevent each eligible individual from effectively receiving their Basic Income. While these challenges do not invalidate the case for Basic Income, advocates do well to take these matters seriously when moving their proposal to the stage of policy implementation.

Further Reading

Blais, F. (2002). *Ending Poverty: A Basic Income for All Canadians.* Lorimer Paperback, Halifax, Nova Scotia.

Block, F. (2005). From poverty to perversity: Ideas, markets, and institutions over 200 years of welfare debate. *American Sociological Review*, 70 (2), 260–287.

Clark, C.M.A., and Kavanagh, C. (1996). Basic income, inequality, and unemployment: Rethinking the linkage between work and welfare. *Journal of Economic Issues*, 30 (2), 399–406.

De Wispelaere, J. and Stirton, L. (2004). The many faces of universal basic income. *The Political Quarterly*, 75 (3), 266–274.

De Wispelaere, J. and Stirton, L. (2007). The public administration case against participation income. *Social Service Review*, 81 (3), 523–549.

De Wispelaere, J. and Stirton, L. (2011). The administrative efficiency of basic income. *Policy and Politics*, 39 (1), 115–132.

Fitzpatrick, T. (1999). *Freedom and Security: An Introduction to the Basic Income Debate.* Palgrave Macmillan, New York.

Goodin, R.E. (2003). Sneaking Up on Stakeholding. In K. Dowding, J. De Wispelaere, and S. White (eds) *The Ethics of Stakeholding*, Palgrave Macmillan, Basingstoke, pp. 65–78.

Groot, L. (2004). *Basic Income, Unemployment and Compensatory Justice.* Springer, New York.

Haarman, C., Haarmann, D., Jauch, H. et al. (2008). Towards a Basic Income Grant for All. Basic Income Grant Pilot Project, Assessment Report. Basic Income Grant Coalition, Namibia, Windhoek.

Jordan, B. (2011). The perils of basic income: ambiguous opportunities for the implementation of a utopian proposal. *Policy and Politics*, 39 (1), 101–114.

Offe, C. (2005). Wasteful welfare transactions: Why basic income security is fundamental. In G. Standing (ed.) *Promoting Income Security as a Right: Europe and North America.* Anthem, London, pp. 69–82.

Offe, C. (2008). Basic income and the Labor Contract. *Basic Income Studies*, 3 (1), Article 4. http://www.degruyter.com/view/j/bis

Standing, G., and Samson, M. (2003). *A Basic Income Grant for South Africa.* University of Cape Town Press, Cape Town.

Vanderborght, Y. (2005). The basic income guarantee in Europe: The Belgian and Dutch back door strategies. In K. Widerquist, M. Lewis, and S. Pressman (eds) *The Ethics and Economics of the Basic Income Guarantee.* Ashgate, Aldershot, pp. 257–281.

van der Veen, R. (2004). Basic income versus wage subsidies: Competing instruments in an optimal tax model with a maximin objective. *Economics and Philosophy*, 20 (1), 147–183.

Van Parijs, P. (1996). Basic income and the two dilemmas of the welfare state. *The Political Quarterly*, 67 (1), 63–66.

Widerquist, K. and Howard, M.W. (eds) (2012a). *Alaska's Permanent Fund Dividend: Examining its Suitability as a Model.* Palgrave Macmillan, New York.

Widerquist, K. and Howard, M.W. (eds) (2012b). *Exporting the Alaska Model: Adapting the Permanent Fund Dividend.* Palgrave Macmillan, New York.

Chapter 46
The Shadow of Speenhamland

Fred Block and Margaret Somers

Excerpts from Block, F. and Somers, M. (2003). In the Shadow of Speenhamland: Social Policy and the Old Poor Law. *Politics & Society*, 31 (2), 283–323.

In 1996, the U.S. Congress passed the Personal Responsibility and Work Opportunities Reconciliation Act that ended the entitlement of poor families to government assistance. The debate leading up to that transformation in welfare policy occurred in the shadow of Speenhamland – an episode in English Poor Law history. This chapter revisits the Speenhamland episode to unravel its tangled history. Drawing on four decades of recent scholarship, the authors show that Speenhamland policies could not have had the consequences that have been attributed to them. The chapter ends with an alternative narrative that seeks to explain how the Speenhamland story became so deeply entrenched.

"Speenhamland" is not a well-known term. Those who know the reference are most likely to have read about it in Karl Polanyi's classic work, *The Great Transformation* (Polanyi, 2001 [1944]; ch. 6–7). But even most of those who are familiar with the reference would be astonished to learn that Speenhamland has had a very real impact on social policy debates in England and the United States for two full centuries. In the twentieth century, this impact has generally occurred under the radar of explicit political debate and publicity.

One such incident occurred in the United States during the Nixon Administration when Daniel Patrick Moynihan developed his Family Assistance Plan. As Moynihan recalled,

> In mid-April Martin Anderson, of [Arthur] Burns's staff, prepared "A Short History of a 'Family Security System'" in the form of excerpts on the history of the Speenhamland system, the late eighteenth-century British scheme of poor relief taken from Karl Polanyi's *The Great Transformation.* (Moynihan, 1973: 179)

The gist of Anderson's memo was that in that earlier historical case, the intended floor under the income of poor families actually operated as a ceiling on earned income with the consequence that the poor were further immiserated. Anderson worried that Moynihan's income

From Block, F. and Somers, M. (2003). In the Shadow of Speenhamland: Social Policy and the Old Poor Law. *Politics & Society*, 31 (2), 283–323. Reprinted with permission of SAGE.

Basic Income: An Anthology of Contemporary Research, First Edition. Edited by Karl Widerquist, José A. Noguera, Yannick Vanderborght, and Jurgen De Wispelaere.

floor might inadvertently produce the same unintended consequence. Anderson's memo was sufficiently powerful that Nixon asked Moynihan to investigate the accuracy of Polanyi's historical analysis. Moynihan's staff were sent scurrying off to investigate the views of contemporary historians on this question. The Family Assistance Plan was ultimately defeated in the U.S. Senate but only after Richard Nixon had a conversation about the work of Karl Polanyi (Moynihan, 1973: 179–180).

Canada had a similar episode more recently. In December 2000, newly reelected Prime Minister Jean Chretien floated as a trial balloon the idea of a comprehensive antipoverty program based on a Guaranteed Annual Income for all Canadians. A flurry of press reports followed including an article in the *National Post* that explicitly referred to the Speenhamland enactment of a Guaranteed Income scheme in 1795. The article insisted that in this earlier episode, employers had paid below-subsistence wages, and some workers chose the collection of benefits over work:

> The first enactment of a guaranteed annual income may have been in 1795 in England, where the Speenhamland system extended subsidies for the infirm to include able-bodied workers. [. . .] The system revealed the challenge inherent in designing such a policy; the supplement served as a subsidy that allowed employers to hire workers at below-subsistence wages, and allowed landlords to raise rents. Meanwhile, some workers found themselves better off collecting benefits than working. (Chwialkowska, 2000)

In both of these cases, the Speenhamland story in which an income floor was inadvertently transformed into an income ceiling served as a chilling cautionary tale against governmental initiatives to establish a Guaranteed Annual Income.

The same argument has been repeated by progressive thinkers in current debates over the desirability of establishing a Universal Basic Income for all citizens.[1] Analysts who favor using state action to improve the situation of the poor question whether a well-intentioned minimum income would follow the Speenhamland precedent and become a maximum income (Bluestone and Ghilarducci, 1996; Howell, 1997; Clement, 1997). They fear that employers would use the increased income received by the poor as an excuse to lower the wages that they pay these employees.

We propose to rethink and retell the story of Speenhamland. This means, fundamentally, showing how the findings of recent studies in social and economic history undermine the Speenhamland stories that have been deployed in social policy debates. But this involves more than simply reporting other scholars' results; we are offering our own analyses of some of the important remaining puzzles in this literature. We are also making a contribution to the history of social theory. While we are critical of Karl Polanyi's history of the Speenhamland episode, we are in fundamental agreement with one of his core theoretical arguments. Polanyi insisted that classical political economy was deeply shaped by the effort to explain the persistence of poverty in the Speenhamland epoch (Polanyi, 2001 [1944]: ch. 10; Procacci, 1991: 151–168). Specifically, Malthus and Ricardo relied on arguments about biological drives to explain human behavior, and the resulting "naturalism" became an important part of mainstream economics. We hope to build on that insight by unraveling the naturalizing logic that critics of public assistance continue to invoke. Moreover, we will offer our own alternative narrative that both makes sense of recent historical findings and helps to explain the centrality of the Speenhamland story to classical political economy.

The Speenhamland Stories

Speenhamland refers to a town in Berkshire County, England, where the county squires decreed in May 1795 that the poor should be entitled to a specific quantity of assistance depending upon the price of bread and the size of the family. This form of provision is often called aid-in-wages because when the gap between wages and the price of bread widened, the parish used poor relief funds to supplement the wages of workers and their families (Polanyi, 2001 [1944]: ch. 7; Webb and Webb, 1927: 168–189). As the program spread (although it is a subject of debate as to how widely it was practiced) among England's parishes, it generated controversy. It was perceived by critics that all precedent had been violated by providing relief not just to the infirm, the aged, or the dependent but also to the "able-bodied." These criticisms were further fueled by the dramatic increase in local poor rates (taxes) and by the findings of a series of Parliamentary reports that played a considerable role in shaping public opinion.[2] The most important of these was the Royal Commission Report of 1834 that issued a devastating indictment of Speenhamland and created irresistible pressure for the New Poor Law passed later in the same year. Based on what we now know to be a nonsystematic and ideologically driven method of collecting answers to a survey questionnaire, the published report confirmed what the commission had set out to document in the first place (Blaug, 1963; 1964; Marshall, 1985; Finer, 1972: 11–32; Cowherd, 1977: ch. ix–x; Henriques, 1979: ch. 2). The main evidence mobilized in the report was hundreds of stories from local parish officials – mostly clergy – confirming the immorality and degradation of the rural poor. The report concluded that Speenhamland and the Old Poor Law more generally were wrong-headed intrusions of state power into self-regulating labor markets. Poor relief created new and perverse incentives that led to increasing pauperization. Exponential increases in childbirth and illegitimacy, declining wages and productivity, assaults on public morality and personal responsibility, and the development of a culture of indolence were only some of the effects attributed to Speenhamland.

The Royal Commission Report was widely distributed, and it influenced a broad range of scholars up through the middle of the next century. In fact, until quite recently, the report was treated as one of the important moments in the rise of the social sciences – one of the first times that a government body relied on systematic collection and analysis of data to analyze an important social problem. But a number of recent scholars have persuasively shown that the Commissioners did very little data analysis and simply used an elaborate structure of appendices to give more weight to their "findings."[3] Moreover, there was little in the commission's arguments that was original; their narrative drew heavily on arguments that had been elaborated by Joseph Townsend and T. R. Malthus in the last part of the eighteenth century.

Polanyi's Contribution

When Karl Polanyi began to explore the Speenhamland episode in the 1930s virtually all of the historical sources available to him affirmed that the Speenhamland episode had degraded the rural poor. Nevertheless, Polanyi was determined to challenge the use that market liberals – especially the Austrians von Mises and Hayek – had made of Speenhamland.[4] They had argued that Speenhamland precisely prefigured the disastrous consequences of state interventionism in the late nineteenth and early twentieth centuries. They claimed that all efforts to use government to improve the life chances of the poor would end up undermining the economy's vitality and would ultimately hurt the people that the policies had been intended to help. As a supporter of the achievements of municipal socialism in Vienna, Polanyi was determined to demonstrate the flaws in the historical parallel that these free market theorists had developed.[5]

Polanyi's strategy was to bring a greater degree of institutional specificity to the historical comparison. Instead of just discussing markets and state action in the abstract, he sought to unpack the Speenhamland episode by looking more closely at the actual workings of institutions. His central argument was that the Speenhamland incident could not be generalized to later cases of state action because it occurred before the working class was capable of mobilizing to defend its own interests. This was exemplified by the existence of the Anti-Combination Laws that prohibited all trade union activity. Polanyi is explicit that had it not been for these laws, Speenhamland aid-in-wages might well have "had the effect of raising wages instead of depressing them as it actually did" (Polanyi, 2001 [1944]: 85). But even more fundamental than the legal obstacles to trade union activity was the fact that the complicated payment system that Speenhamland initiated prevented rural workers from understanding their actual social position.

> [Speenhamland] prevented laborers from developing into an economic class and thus deprived them of the only means of staving off the fate to which they were doomed in the economic mill. (Polanyi, 2001 [1944]: 103).

In sum, the difference between Speenhamland and Vienna is that in the former workers had not organized themselves as a class, so there was no mechanism to block state action from producing perverse consequences.

Reconstructing the Reality of Speenhamland

The empirical complexities and causal gaps are enough to make us suspicious about both of the Speenhamland stories, but a close examination of the historical evidence is even more devastating. First, the very Speenhamland system that allegedly produced significant-work disincentive effects turns out to have been far less common than earlier believed. When properly defined as strictly limited to a bread scale that provided different levels of support depending on family size, it becomes apparent that Speenhamland could not have produced the effects that have been attributed to it. Second, there is strong evidence against the decline in rural productivity that both stories have claimed to have been one of the effects of Speenhamland. Finally, when we look more closely at what happened to the rural standard of living across the period from 1790 to 1834, it is very difficult to resist the conclusion that rising poor law outlays were a response to the loss of established forms of family income rather than a cause.

The limited pervasiveness and episodic nature of the bread scale

Speenhamland is itself a contested term. Some have used it to cover the full range of relief policies in which able-bodied individuals and their families received assistance, while others have used it more narrowly to refer to the specific use of a bread scale in allocating assistance. We will define Speenhamland strictly as the use of a bread scale to determine assistance by the size of the family and the cost of wheat.[6] While the Royal Commission Report takes pains to condemn all forms of assistance to the able-bodied, its initial focus is on the allowance system, and it differentiates between parishes that occasionally provide allowances and others where such assistance has been routinized:

> In others it is considered that a certain weekly sum, or more frequently the value of a certain quantity of flour or bread, is to be received by each member of a family. The latter practice has sometimes been matured into a system, forming the law of a whole district, sanctioned and enforced by the magistrates, and promulgated in the form of local statutes, under the name of *Scales*. (Her Majesty's Royal Commissioners, *Report*, 21)

This is immediately followed by the printing of a number of representative examples of such scales, including one particularly impressive table from a parish in Essex that provides precise allowances for more than 20 different wheat prices ranging from one to seven shillings per peck. Much of the report's subsequent fury is then directed against this "allowance system."

Yet few of the indictments of Speenhamland hold up against the evidence. The claim that the use of the bread scale starting in 1795 was unprecedented is simply wrong. Wage-price indexing for the able bodied goes back to the 1349–1351 Ordinance and Statute of Labourers and was most elaborately spelled out in the famous 1563 Tudor Statute of Artificers (5 Eliz c 4) (Tawney and Power, 1924: 338–350; Tawney, 1972: 37–92; Lipson, 1943: 253; Somers, 1994a; 1994b: 1301–1350). Moreover, bread scales were used in years of high wheat prices at other times in the second half of the eighteenth century (Henriques, 1979; Neuman, 1982).

Another misperception is the belief in Speenhamland as a continuous 40-year policy with territorial and temporal uniformity. Mark Blaug first called this into question with path-breaking research that challenged the geographical uniformity of its application (Blaug, 1963; 1964). Blaug showed that the use of the bread scale was not geographically universal even in wheat-growing areas. Neuman in a sample of sixteen parishes in Berkshire County itself found none that used the Speenhamland scale in the whole period up to 1834 (Neuman, 1982: 160). Poynter, Baugh, Huzel, Lees, and King also stress the limited use of the bread scale (Poynter, 1969: 79–85; Baugh, 1975; Huzel, 1989; Lees, 1998; King, 2000). Baugh suggests that it was much more common for parishes to respond to years of very high grain prices by using poor relief funds to purchase grain that was then redistributed to households. In others, the farmers sold wheat to their employees at below-market prices or, as had happened in earlier famine years, extracharitable efforts by the rich provided some of the poor with food (Baugh, 1975: 59).

Even so, it is useful to think of the bread scales in certain parishes in 1795 and subsequent famine years as the first Speenhamland episode. In 1795, in 1802–1803, and still again in 1812, a confluence of several factors created the kind of calamity that forced many parishes to take action. In each case, two bad harvests in a row coincided with wartime limitations on agricultural imports from the Continent. The dramatic and severe upward spike in the price of wheat that followed placed this dietary staple well beyond the reach of most agricultural, rural-industrial, and even urban working people. Moreover, as the poor shifted their demand to coarser but cheaper grains, their prices spiraled upwards as well. The consequence was severe distress and the outbreak of food riots in which protesters seized grain from middlemen and bakers.[7] In 1795, these riots occurred against the backdrop of revolutionary events on the other side of the English Channel, so that local elites had strong incentives to respond to the threat of famine and revolutionary disorder.

The claims of Speenhamland's critics notwithstanding, the use of the bread scale as a response to famine was a very logical method to respond to these immediate crises without permanently altering wage rates or long-term relief patterns. (It is consistent with Sen's argument that famines are rooted not in absolute shortage but in problems of entitlement to food (Sen, 1982).) As soon as the price spike passed, most households would no longer be eligible for assistance because the standard wage would purchase a sufficient amount of bread.

There are two striking features of this initial Speenhamland episode. First, there is very little difference in the trend of poor law outlays between those parishes that adopted the bread scale and those that used other means to distribute food to the hungry. Baugh analyzed data from more than 700 parishes in Essex, Kent, and Sussex and showed that poor relief outlays very closely tracked the fluctuations in the price of wheat (Baugh, 1975). Sokoll extensively analyzed Ardleigh, a parish in Essex that did not adopt the bread scale in this early period, and he shows that its outlays also rose and fell in parallel with the other agricultural parishes in Essex that Baugh examined (Sokoll, 1993). Second, as Sokoll emphasizes, these patterns undermine one of the core claims of the Royal Commission Report – that allowances have a kind of addictive and self-expanding effect (Sokoll, 1993: 142). The Commissioners claimed,

> Profuse allowances excite the most extravagant expectations on the parts of the claimants, who conceive that an inexhausible fund is devoted to their use, and that they are wronged to the extent of whatever falls short of their claims. (Her Majesty's Royal Commissioners, *Report*, 49)

But in this episode, whether parishes used the formal mechanism of the bread scale or other methods of distributing relief, what is so striking is that outlays fell virtually immediately as the price of wheat fell.

The second discrete Speenhamland episode occurred in the years after the end of the Napoleonic Wars and was not related to famine conditions.[8] With the end of the war, there was a period of severe economic contraction marked by a dramatic decline in wheat prices. There was some downward adjustment of wage rates in this period, but this adjustment was much smaller than the sharp fall in prices. As a consequence, some farms simply went out of business and other agricultural employers sharply reduced their employment levels both during the growing season and particularly during the winter months. Assisted by the introduction of threshing machines – the proximate trigger of the famous 1830 Captain Swing riots – that further reduced the demand for labor in the critical months after the harvest, all these processes significantly increased rural unemployment and distress and accounted for the sharp rise in poor relief outlays after 1813.[9]

There is strong consensus in the recent literature that the post-1813 renewal of Speenhamland measures was catalyzed by a shift from inflation to structural transformation in employment opportunities, leading primarily to radically new patterns of seasonal unemployment.[10] The period was also marked by the decline of women's farm labor income and an accelerated decline of rural crafts that had provided employment for women (Berg, 1994; Valenze, 1995).

But while the bread scale returned, its meaning nonetheless shifted in an important way. In the earlier period, employed farm workers would receive an income supplement, contingent on family size and the wheat price, to help them get through the period of high food prices. In the later period, the bread scale was used primarily to determine the amount of relief that seasonally unemployed farm workers were entitled to, given the size of their families.[11] The importance of this seasonal dimension of poor relief is amply supported by data showing that poor relief outlays were often two or three times higher in the winter months than in the spring or summer (Emmison, 1933: 3–98; Snell, 1985; Boyer, 1990; Reay, 1996). As Boyer has argued extensively, there were strong reasons for parish authorities to provide relief in the winter for unemployed farm workers. Employers were constantly worried by the threat of out-migration, which would mean labor shortages during the summer months and severe shortages at harvest time (Boyer, 1990: 31–43). Without such relief, levels of out-migration whether to the north or to urban areas would have been much higher.

This second phase of Speenhamland is exemplified by events in Ardleigh – the Essex parish that has been closely studied by Sokoll. The parish had no earlier history of the use of the bread scale, but a formal bread scale was instituted in September of 1823 followed in 1831 by another Speenhamland statute (Sokoll, 1993: 140). This late adoption of the bread scale by parish officials is especially notable because it occurs after decades in which Speenhamland had been denounced for its horrible consequences. This suggests that there was widespread skepticism at the time with the anti-Speenhamland rhetoric and that local officials were undeterred by the rhetoric because they were simply trying to find the best practical way to deal with the crisis presented by high levels of unemployment.

Trends in productivity and wages

The standard Speenhamland stories insist that rural productivity collapsed in the face of the corrosive impact of the Poor Law. The available data provide no support for this claim. Total wheat production increased substantially between 1790 and 1834; Fairlie's estimate shows that wheat production fluctuated sharply between 1791 and 1811 and then more than doubled by 1834.[12] This increase was facilitated by an expansion in acreage; Holderness estimates that acreage increased from about 2.45 million acres in 1801 to 3.4 million in 1836 – an increase of almost 39% (Holderness, 1989: 84–189). But it wasn't only increased acreage; Holderness suggests that yields per acre might have risen by 33% between 1790 and 1830 (Holderness, 1989: 140); Overton suggests that the increase was 15% between 1801 and 1831.[13]

The official decennial census of population did not begin until 1801. Even then, the early censuses did not ask about employment, so estimates of the size of the agricultural labor force between 1801 and 1831 in the southeastern counties are little more than guesswork. Nonetheless, the labor force seems to have grown substantially more slowly than either wheat output or acreage. Wrigley estimates that for the whole country, the number of adult males employed in agriculture increased from 910,000 in 1811 to 981,000 in 1831 – growth of only about 8% (Wrigley, 1986: 295–336). Since the wheat-growing counties were home to a large portion of English farm workers, it is unlikely that labor force growth in these counties was substantially faster than national growth. Given the doubling of wheat output between 1811 and 1834, there can be little doubt that output per worker rose in this period. Overton suggests quite substantial increases in labor productivity in agriculture across the whole period from 1800 to 1850 (Overton, 1996: 1–20). Moreover, even Clark, who has been most outspoken in criticizing the idea of a productivity-increasing "agricultural revolution" in the first three decades of the nineteenth century, acknowledges that labor productivity was either constant or increasing slightly in this period (Clark, 1991; 1999).

Since the available data on productivity in the wheat-growing regions are sketchy at best, a number of analysts have supported the Speenhamland thesis by arguing that agricultural wages fell sharply in this period and that it is reasonable to see wages as a reliable proxy for productivity. Influential historians writing in the first half of the century such as Hammond and Hammond, Webb and Webb, and Mantoux have insisted that wage levels fell dramatically during the Speenhamland period (Hammond and Hammond, 1966 [1911]: ch. 7; Webb and Webb, 1927: 422–423; Mantoux, 1962 [1928]: 431–439). However, most of the available data series that we have that trace rural wages in this period reveal the same basic pattern. Rural weekly wages for men rise from 1790 through to the end of the Napoleonic Wars, there is then a sharp decline during the agricultural depression, followed by a recovery and a slightly rising trend from the early 1820s through to 1834. The first systematic series on agricultural wages was developed by Bowley at the end of the nineteenth century, and it rises from 53 in 1790 to 105 in 1812, then falls to 72 in 1824 before rising to 79 in 1834.[14] Eccleston found a similar pattern in five Midland counties, and Richardson reports a parallel pattern in wages on a large farm in Essex (Eccleston, 1986: 143–156; Richardson, 1991: 70–90). More recently, Clark has developed a series for weekly winter wages in the southeastern counties based on various surviving estate records, including those used by Richardson, and he finds the same basic pattern (Clark, 2001). The respected historian K.D.M. Snell calculated trends in annual wages for farm servants in a number of southern counties from a unique data set drawn from settlement examinations. For most counties or groups of counties, Snell's findings move in the same pattern as weekly wages cited elsewhere in the literature, but in some counties he did find that wages fall steadily from the 1820s onward (Snell, 1985: 412–417).

Interpreting these patterns of nominal wages has been extremely difficult because of the dramatic price changes that occur across this period. There is no question that in the famine years, such as 1795, 1802-1703, and 1812, the price spike in grains led to dramatic, albeit temporary, declines in the real wage. Nevertheless, the view advanced by Prothero that wage levels during the Napoleon Wars doubled while prices actually tripled is no longer accepted (Prothero, 1912). When one brackets the famine years, real agricultural wages clearly rose between 1790 and 1815. Since the post-Napoleonic period was one of steadily falling price levels,the small recovery in nominal wages between 1824 and 1834 reported by Bowley understates the gain in real wages in this period.

In the end, we come to the conclusion that the question that has preoccupied so many analysts – Were agricultural real wages higher or lower in 1834 than they were in 1795? – is the wrong question. There are three different reasons. First, the reality was that real wages – with the critical exceptions of the famine years – first rose, then fell, and then rose. Second, when rural workers are compared to the inhabitants of urban England who had greatly expanded access to a wide variety of manufactured goods between 1790 and 1834, there can be no doubt that their relative standard of living declined sharply during this period of industrial transformation. Finally, translating weekly wages into a standard of living depends critically on the number of weeks of employment available per year, and we know that seasonal unemployment rose dramatically in the countryside after the Napoleonic Wars (Snell, 1985; Boyer, 1990).

Instead of focusing on the wrong question, then, it is the Royal Commissioners' claim that Speenhamland policies damaged rural productivity that must be scrutinized. The argument is already undermined by evidence that the bread scale was not pervasive or continuous. It is further weakened by both the data on agricultural output and the trends in weekly wages that provide no support for a claimed collapse of rural productivity.

Household Income and the Poor Law

It is precisely because of the variety and variability of the income sources on which families relied that it is extremely difficult to identify any clear trends in average family income across this period. The best estimates that we have come from surviving family budget data that have been compiled by Horrell and Humphries (Horrell and Humphries, 1995). They indicate that for the low-wage agricultural sector – that tends to overlap with the southeastern counties – there was a small upward trend in real household income between 1790 and 1834. But this average figure conceals much variation, and poor relief outlays represented a rising component of family income, rising from a negligible level in the early period to 8% of family income for the 1821–1840 period. In this context, poor relief can best be understood as a mechanism to sustain family income in a context in which it had become increasingly difficult for the rural poor – through no fault of their own – to piece together an adequate income.

The increasing importance of poor relief can be seen as compensating for three broad trends. First, rural craft industries suffered a dramatic decline in the southeastern counties in the period after 1790 (Snell, 1985; Allen, 1992: 38–42). Some of this decline had been going on for centuries, but the pace of decline was clearly accelerated by the rapid rise of industrial production in the northern part of the country (Hudson, 1986; 1989; 1992; Kriedte et al., 1981). This meant that opportunities for family members, especially women, to supplement income with labor on rural craft production simply disappeared in many places. Second, enclosures and consolidations of holdings meant that many rural laboring families lost the capacity to earn additional income by keeping farm animals or maintaining a vegetable garden. In fact, during the Speenhamland period, a major alternative to the poor law that was widely debated was to provide laboring families with allotments – small pieces of land – that would make self-provisioning a real alternative to poor relief in hard times (Barnett, 1967: 162–183). But while the idea was widely discussed, it was never implemented beyond a few localities. Third, particularly after 1813, the demand for farm labor diminishes, so that there are reduced earning opportunities for wives and children while men experienced longer periods of unemployment in the winter and early spring months.[15] Reay, for example, finds that in one Kent parish, 60% of farm laborers and small farmers required poor relief during the winter months in the 1830s (Reay, 1996: 129; see also Emmison, 1933).

In short, the family budget data provide a different angle of vision that further undermines the conventional Speenhamland stories. Instead of bread scales undermining work effort, we get a picture of a rural population facing broad structural forces that undermine their capacities for self-support. In this context it is difficult to see increasing poor relief as anything but a partial remedy to problems outside the control of the rural poor.

A Revisionist Narrative

It seems useful, therefore, to suggest an alternative narrative that would place these new historical findings into a framework that social policy analysts might find compelling. This alternative narrative centers on the problems of legitimating the new science of political economy that emerged out of the fundamental contributions of Malthus and Ricardo. Malthus and Ricardo famously disagreed on some key theoretical and policy issues, and later thinkers, such as Marx and Keynes, explicitly embraced one while denigrating the other.[16] But there was also much agreement between the two figures, and ultimately it was Malthus's critique of the Poor Law that helped divert attention from the negative consequences of Ricardo's first great policy success – the decision at the end of the Napoleonic Wars to restore the pound's parity to its prewar level. In short, the construction of the Speenhamland story was intimately connected to Britain's embrace of the gold standard.

The return to gold

This restoration, however, occurred against the backdrop of a severe rural crisis that had begun right at the end of the Napoleonic Wars. The fall in wheat prices in 1813 and 1814 produced a massive collapse of rural banks that had failed to hold on to any reserves. Between 1814 and 1816, 240 rural banks stopped payments leading to a destruction of wealth and a disappearance of credit (McCulloch, 1938 [1845]; Fussell and Compton, 1939). The result was a dramatic increase in unemployment as both farmers and other employers were forced to cut back both investment and the size of their labor force. But as the deflation took hold, there was an ironic consequence – the value of the pound started to rise so that the goal of restoring the prewar parity appeared substantially closer. The response of the authorities in 1816 and 1817, therefore, was to prepare for the resumption of gold payments at the old parity, and in May of 1819, Parliament passed legislation to restore gold payments within two years (Viner, 1965 [1937]). While there is intense controversy over the specific policies that the government and Bank followed in restoring gold, there is widespread consensus that the sustained effort to return to the prewar parity had a profoundly deflationary impact. On the one side, the government was precluded from pursuing the kind of countercyclical policies that could have revived the rural economy. On the other, the sustained tight money policies greatly restricted the availability of the credit that farmers desperately needed.

Moreover, the deflationary pressures did not end with the success of restoration; the gold standard simply made the pressures on the rural economy permanent. Wheat prices continued to fall until 1829, and after that, prices were stabilized at a very low level. The failure of rural banks was also continuous across the whole period from 1815 to 1830 (Fussell and Compton, 1939: 186–189). This context of falling prices and limited credit forced farmers to reduce labor costs and that, in turn, produced chronic rural unemployment and increased use of poor relief. The ongoing pressure of low wheat prices forced the more successful farmers to put increasing resources into labor-saving technology such as the threshing machine. Since hand threshing of wheat could represent as much as one-quarter of the whole year's quantity of farm work, mechanization had a huge impact on the rural demand for labor in the winter months (Gash, 1935). Triggered by these high rates of unemployment, the machine smashing in the Captain Swing riots of 1830 exploded (Hobsbawm and Rude, 1968: 315–321). This outbreak of rural disorder played a key role in undermining elite support for the Old Poor Law (Dunkley, 1982; Mandler, 1987).

Absent Ricardo's eloquent pleas for a restoration of the prewar parity, policymakers might well have chosen a less deflationary set of policies. Had the rural economy not suffered the additional shock of the deflationary pressures of gold, the wheat-growing areas might have experienced a recovery and an earlier rebound of wheat prices. Without the ideological commitment to laissez-faire policies, moreover, the government might have embraced policies that helped to cushion the economy in periods of contracting demand, including provisions for a steady flow of credit to farmers (Hilton, 1977; Gordon, 1976:

71–79). Under any set of policies, there would ultimately have been a problem of a rural labor surplus that could only be solved by more rapid rates of out-migration. But the Ricardian policies dramatically intensified the problem – so that this massive readjustment had to be handled over 20 years rather than 40. As Polanyi eloquently argues, government policies can help protect ordinary people simply by slowing the rate of change, but the Ricardian policies did exactly the opposite; they vastly accelerated the problem of rural surplus population (Polanyi, 2001 [1944]: 39).

The road to the new poor law

The Captain Swing riots in 1830 gave new urgency to Poor Law debates. Yet the parliamentary stalemate was not broken until the Whigs came to power and passed the Reform Act of 1832 that expanded the suffrage and gave the middle class effective representation (Poynter, 1969: ch. 9; Brundage, 1978; Dunkley, 1982). While the Reform Act was still pending, the Whig government appointed the Royal Commission to investigate the Poor Laws. While all of the Commissioners had been deeply influenced by Malthus's arguments, they rejected his abolitionist policy solution. Their critical rhetorical move was to adopt the language of reform and to argue that "reformed parishes" – those that replaced outdoor relief with workhouses for the poor – had effectively eliminated all of the negative consequences of Speenhamland. In short, by narrowing Malthus's critique of the Poor Law to focus on the "allowance system" and by proposing concrete reforms rather than abolition, the Royal Commission was able to generate a strong parliamentary consensus that led to passage of the New Poor Law.[17]

What the Royal Commissioners succeeded in doing was to mobilize and modify Malthus's arguments to rescue political economy from its responsibility for the plight of the rural poor. By effectively blaming the victims for the macroeconomic policy mistakes that had intensified rural poverty, they turned a potential disaster into a policy triumph. In doing this, they made an enormous contribution to the legitimation of political economy. The severity of the agricultural downturn might well have undermined the whole belief in laissez-faire and self-regulating markets. Classical political economy was in its infancy in this period, and its ultimate maturation and worldwide influence were hardly a foregone conclusion.[18] While it is difficult to think through such a radical counterfactual, an alternative and more pragmatic strand of economic thinking might have become institutionalized in the place of the Ricardo tradition. Instead, the ultimate policy triumph of the New Poor Law diverted attention from the new science's first major policy failure and solidified the electorate's faith in market self-regulation.

In sum, the Speenhamland myth was created in the years of agricultural downturn to divert blame for a deep agricultural crisis away from government policy and toward the rural poor who were the major victims of the economic downturn. Since the decision taken by the government on Ricardo's advice to restore the prewar parity of the pound intensified the rural depression, the mythology worked to cover up the first major policy failure of the new science of political economy. The importance of this myth becomes apparent in thinking about the diffusion of economic liberalism during the course of the nineteenth century. England's ability to persuade other countries to adopt free trade, the gold standard, and the belief in market self-regulation depended on its ability to present itself as a great economic success story (Semmel, 1970; Kindleberger, 1975). Were other societies aware that the price that England had paid for economic liberalism was severe economic hardship in the countryside in the 1820s, 1830s, and 1840s, both the English model and its policy ideas would have been considerably tarnished. By shifting the blame for the problems on to Speenhamland and all its pernicious evils, the economic liberals successfully reframed the agricultural downturn into a problem of individual morality and an enduring parable of the dangers of government "interference" with the market.

Conclusion

Our review of the historical evidence suggests two conclusions. First, the perversity story lacks empirical support. The experience of the Speenhamland period is that poor relief did not hurt the poor; it helped to protect them from structural changes in the economy that had made it far more difficult for people to earn a living. Second, the doubts that have hung over Guaranteed Income proposals since Speenhamland lack historical foundation. While it is theoretically possible that a floor under incomes would be transformed into a ceiling, this certainly did not happen during the Speenhamland period, and there is little evidence that it has ever happened. In fact, there are good reasons this theoretical possibility is rarely likely to occur in practice. In contrast to Speenhamland, most contemporary Income Guarantee proposals, including variants on the Negative Income Tax, do not require that recipients work. Hence, when employees are faced with an employer who is progressively lowering wages to take advantage of the Income Guarantee program, they are likely to quit and look for alternative employment since they know that they will be protected by the Income Guarantee from economic hardship during their period of unemployment. Moreover, under most circumstances, employers avoid unilateral reductions in wages precisely out of the fear that they would drive away existing employees and make it harder to fill vacancies. It seems only logical that if an Income Guarantee were in place, employers would become even more cautious about imposing wage cuts.

Welfare and income maintenance policies need to be debated free of the mythologies that were created 200 years ago. Above all, we need to move beyond the naturalized Malthusian accounts that see the behavior of the poor as always determined by their biological drives. Discarding the naturalizing blinders and examining the actual situation of the rural poor during the Speenhamland period, we are forced to recognize the central role of larger economic processes such as the severe agricultural deflation and the shift of industry to the North in explaining mounting rural poverty. Relief payments actually provided some protection against these structural pressures. The contemporary lesson is obvious; it is time to reject the ideological claim that the best way to fight poverty is by imposing increasingly stringent conditions on ever shrinking transfer payments to poor households.

Notes

1. Recent writings in favor of the Basic Income idea include Van Parijs (1992); Block and Manza (1997: 473–511); and some of the pieces included in Cohen and Rogers (2001).
2. Among the most important reports were Parliamentary Papers, *Report from the Select Committee on the Poor Laws* (1817), *Report from the Committee on the Poor Laws* (1819), and *Report from the Select Committee on Labourers Wages* (1824). The Royal Commission Report was published as *Report from His Majesty's Commissioners for Inquiring into the Administration and Practical Operation of the Poor Laws* (B. Fellowes, London, 1834).

3. In addition to Blaug (1963; 1964); Marshall (1985); Finer (1972: 11–32); Cowherd (1977: ch. ix–x); Henriques (1979: ch. 2), see Brundage (1978: 60–65).
4. Polanyi (2001 [1944]: 298–299). On Polanyi in Vienna, see Polanyi-Levitt and Mendell (1987), and Congdon (1990: 78–84).
5. For more on Polanyi's analysis of Speenhamland, see Block (forthcoming).
6. Our definition of Speenhamland also excludes child allowances. The justification is simply practical – to make the story more manageable. Child allowances represented only a small proportion of poor law outlays and played little role in arguments about work disincentives. Moreover, this chapter will not address the issue of child allowances as a possible encouragement to excess fertility.
7. The best account of these famine years is Wells (1988); see also Tilly (1995: 228–232).
8. Napoleon abdicated for the first time in early April 1814 and then returned from Elba for three more months of war in 1815. Hence, in annual series, 1813 generally marks the peak of the wartime boom since it was the last full year of war.
9. On the threshing machine, see Fox (1978: 26–28). On Swing, see Hobsbawm and Rude (1968). On the rise in unemployment, see Gash (1935: 90–93); Snell (1985); Boyer, (1990).
10. Note, for example, that Snell (1985) and Boyer (1990) agree on this point.
11. With this change in meaning, there was also a change in generosity. The post-1813 scales, even holding the price of wheat constant, were considerably less generous than those used in famine years. But the famine payments established a floor for full-time ***employed*** workers, while the post-1813 payments were going to households of ***unemployed*** workers. For a somewhat misleading comparison of the scales, see Hammond and Hammond (1966 [1911]).
12. These estimates are cited in John (1989: 1054–1155).
13. Overton (1989: 9–21). Eric Jones estimated that yields per acre rose 16% between 1815 and 1819 and between 1832 and 1836; see Jones (1974: 211–33).
14. Bowley's figures are cited in Mitchell and Deane (1962: 348–349).
15. Drawing on settlement hearings, Snell (1985) argues that there was a significant decline in women's employment opportunities in the wheat-growing regions from the 1790s onward. However, Horrell and Humphries (1995) use family budget data to show women and children providing an increasing share of family income in the later period.
16. Marx was bitterly critical of Malthus, but he generally treated Ricardo with respect as an intellectually honest defender of the interests of the bourgeoisie. For Marx's writings on Malthus, see Meek (1954). Keynes reversed this ordering and praised Malthus's underconsumptionist views while criticizing Ricardo's confidence that markets would reach equilibrium. See Keynes (1951 [1933]).
17. The actual impact of the New Poor Law is still intensely debated. For recent discussions, see Driver (1993); King (2000).
18. For the precariousness of Ricardian orthodoxy in this period, see Checkland (1949). On the intensity of the anti-Ricardo backlash after the 1825 crash, see Gordon (1976: ch. 4).

References

Allen, R.C. (1992). *Enclosure and the Yeoman.* Clarendon, Oxford, pp. 246–248.

Barnett, D.C. (1967). Allotments and the Problem of Rural Poverty, 1740–1840. In E.L. Jones and G.E. Mingay (eds) *Land, Labour and Population in the Industrial Revolution.* Edward Arnold, London, pp. 162–183.

Baugh, D.A. (1975). The Cost of Poor Relief in South-East England 1790–1834. *Economic History Review*, XXVII (1) (February) 50–68.

Berg, M. (1994). *The Age of Manufacturers 1700–1820: Industry, Innovation and Work in Britain*, 2nd edn. Routledge, London.

Blaug, M. (1963). Myth of the Old Poor Law and the Making of the New. *Journal of Economic History*, XXIII (2) (June), 151–245.

Blaug, M. (1964). The Poor Law Report Reexamined. *Journal of Economic History*, XXIV, (June), 229–245.

Block, F. (2003). Karl Polanyi and the Writing of The Great Transformation. *Theory and Society*, 32 (3), 275–306.

Block, F. and Manza, J.(1997). Could We End Poverty in a Postindustrial Society? The Case for a Progressive Negative Income Tax. *Politics & Society*, 25 (December), 473–511.

Bluestone, B. and Ghilarducci, T. (1996). Rewarding Work. *The American Prospect*, (26) (May-June), 40–46.

Boyer, G.R. (1990). *An Economic History of the Poor Law 1750–1850.* Cambridge University Press, Cambridge.

Brundage, A. (1978). *The Making of the New Poor Law: The Politics of Inquiry, Enactment, and Implementation, 1832–1839.* Rutgers University Press, New Brunswick, NJ.

Checkland, S.G. (1949). The Propagation of Ricardian Economics in England. *Economica, New Series*, 16 (61) (February), 40–52.

Chwialkowska, L. (2000). Subsidies Paid in Loaves of Bread in England in 1700s. *National Post* (Canada), 12 December, A6.

Clark, G. (1991). Labour Productivity in English Agriculture, 1300–1860. In B.M.S. Campbell and M. Overton (eds) *Land, Labour and Livestock: Historical Studies in European Agricultural Productivity.* Manchester University Press, Manchester, pp. 211–235.

Clark, G. (1999). Too Much Revolution: Agriculture and the Industrial Revolution, 1700–1860. In J. Mokyr (ed.) *The British Industrial Revolution: An Economic Assessment*, 2nd edn. Westview, Boulder, pp. 206–240.

Clark, G. (2001). Farm Wages and Living Standards in the Industrial Revolution: England, 1670–1869. *Economic History Review*, LIV (3), 477–505.

Clement, A. (1979). Revenue Minimum: Les Leçons de Speenhamland. *Lien Social et Politique*, 42, 49–60.

Congdon, L. (1990). The Sovereignty of Society: Polanyi in Vienna. In K. Polanyi-Levitt (ed.) *The Life and Work of Karl Polanyi.* Black Rose, Montreal, pp. 78–84.

Cowherd, R.G. (1977). *Political Economists and the English Poor Laws.* University Press, Athens, ch. ix–x.

Driver, F. (1993). *Power and Pauperism: The Workhouse System, 1834–884.* Cambridge University Press, Cambridge, ch. 7.

Dunkley, P. (1982). *The Crisis of the Old Poor Law in England: An Interpretative Essay.* Garland, New York.

Eccleston, B. (1986). Malthus, Wages and the Labour Market in England 1790– 1830. In M. Turner (ed.) *Malthus and His Time.* St. Martin's, New York, pp. 143–156.

Emmison, F.G. (1933). The Relief of the Poor at Eaton Socon, 1706–1834. *Publication of the Bedfordshire Historical Record Society*, 15, 3–98.

Finer, S.E. (1972). The Transmission of Benthamite Ideas 1820–1850. In G. Sutherland (ed.) *Studies in the Growth of Nineteenth-Century Government.* Routledge & Kegan Paul, London, pp. 11–32.

Fox, N.E. (1978). The Spread of the Threshing Machine in Central Southern England. *Agricultural History Review*, 26 (1), 26–28.

Fussell, G.E. and Compton, M. (1939). Agricultural Adjustments after the NapoleonicWars. *Economic History*, III, no. 14 (February), 184–204.

Gash, N. (1935). Rural Unemployment, 1815–1834. *Economic History Review*, VI (1) (October), 90–93.

Gordon, B. (1976). *Political Economy in Parliament 1819–1823.* Macmillan, London.

Hammond, J.L. and Hammond, B. (1966 [1911]). *The Village Labourer.* Longmans, Green, London.

Henriques, U.R.Q. (1979). *Before the Welfare State: Social Administration in Early Industrial Britain.* Longmans, London, ch. 2.

Hilton, B. (1977). *Corn, Cash, Commerce: The Economic Policies of the Tory Governments 1815–1830.* Oxford University Press, Oxford.

Hobsbawm, E.J. and Rude, G. (1968). *Captain Swing.* Pantheon, New York.

Holderness, B.A. (1989). Prices, Productivity and Output. In G.E. Mingay (ed.) *The Agrarian History of England and Wales.* Cambridge University Press, Cambridge, vol. 6, pp. 84–189.

Horrell, S. and Humphries, J. (1995). Women's Labour Force Participation and the Transition to the Male-Breadwinner Family, 1790–1865. *Economic History Review*, XLVII, no. 1 (February).

Howell, D. (1997). Block and Manza on the Negative Income Tax. *Politics & Society*, 24 (4) (December), 533–539.

Hudson, P. (1986). *The Genesis of Industrial Capital: A Study of the West Riding Wool Textile Industry, c. 1750–1850.* Cambridge University Press, Cambridge.

Hudson, P. (ed.) (1989). *Regions and Industries: A Perspective on the Industrial Revolution in Britain.* Cambridge University Press, Cambridge.

Hudson, P. (1992). *The Industrial Revolution.* E. Arnold, London.

Huzel, J. (1989). The Labourer and the Poor Law. In G.E. Mingay (ed.) *The Agrarian History of England and Wales*, vol. 6. Cambridge University Press, Cambridge, pp. 755–809.

John, A.H. (1989). Statistical Appendix. In G.E. Mingay (ed.) *The Agrarian History of England and Wales*, vol. 6, pp. 972–1155.

Jones, E.L. (1974). The Agricultural Labor Market in England, 1793–1872. In E.L. Jones (ed.) *Agriculture and the Industrial Revolution.* Basil Blackwell, Oxford, pp. 211–233.

Keynes, J.M. (1951 [1933]). Robert Malthus: The First of the Cambridge Economists. In J.M. Keynes, *Essays in Biography.* Rupert Hart-Davis, London, pp. 81–124.

Kindleberger, C.P. (1975). The Rise of Free Trade in Western Europe, 1820–1875. *Journal of Economic History*, 35 (1) (March), 20–55.

King, S. (2000). *Poverty and Welfare in England 1700–1850: A Regional Perspective.* Manchester University Press, Manchester.

Kriedte, P., Medick, H., and Schlumbohm, J. (1981). *Industrialization before Industrialization.* Cambridge University Press, Cambridge.

Lees, L.H. (1998). *The Solidarities of Strangers: The English Poor Laws and the People, 1700–1948.* Cambridge University Press, Cambridge.

Lipson, E.E. (1943). *The Economic History of England*, vol. 3. A. & C. Black, London, p. 253.

Mandler, P. (1987). The Making of the New Poor Law Redivivus. *Past and Present*, 117 (November), 131–157.

Mantoux, P. (1962 [1928]). *The Industrial Revolution in the Eighteenth Century.* Harper & Row, pp. 431–439.

Marshall, J.D. (1985). *The Old Poor Law, 1795–>1834*, 2nd edn. Macmillan, London.

McCulloch, J.R. (1938 [1845]). *The Literature of Political Economy.* London School of Economics, London, p. 290.

Meek, P. (ed.) (1954). *Marx and Engels on Malthus.* International Publishers, New York.

Mitchell, B.R. and Deane, P. (1962). *Abstract of British Historical Statistics.* Cambridge University Press, Cambridge, pp. 348–349.

Moynihan, D.P. (1973). *The Politics of a Guaranteed Income: The Nixon Administration and the Family Assistance Plan.* Vintage, New York.

Neuman, M. (1982). *The Speenhamland County: Poverty and the Poor Laws in Berkshire, 1782–1834.* Garland, New York.

Overton, M. (1989). Agricultural Revolution? England 1540–1850. In A. Digby and C. Feinstein (eds) *New Directions in Economic and Social History.* Macmillan, Houndsmill, pp. 9–21.

Overton, M. (1996). Re-establishing the English Agricultural Revolution. *Agricultural History Review*, 44 (1), 1–20.

Polanyi, K. (2001 [1944]). *The Great Transformation.* Beacon Press, Boston.

Polanyi-Levitt, K. and Mendell, M. (1987). Karl Polanyi: His Life and Times. *Studies in Political Economy*, 22 (Spring).

Poynter, J.R. (1969). *Society and Pauperism: English Ideas on Poor Relief, 1795–1834.* Routledge & Kegan Paul, London.

Procacci, G. (1991). Social Economy and the Government of Poverty. In G. Burchell, C. Gordon, and P. Miller (eds) *The Foucault Effect: Studies in Governmentality.* University of Chicago Press, Chicago, pp. 151–168.

Prothero, R. (1912). *English Farming Past and Present.* Longmans, Green and Co., London, pp. 313–315.

Reay, B. (1996). *Microhistories: Demography, Society and Culture in Rural England, 1800–1930.* Cambridge University Press, Cambridge.

Richardson, T.L. (1991). Agricultural Labourers' Wages and the Cost of Living in Essex, 1790–1840: A Contribution to the Standard of Living Debate. In B.A. Holderness and M. Turner (eds) *Land, Labour and Agriculture, 1700–1920: Essays for Gordon Mingay.* Hambledon, London, pp. 70–90.

Royal Commission Report, (1834). published as *Report from His Majesty's Commissioners for Inquiring into the Administration and Practical Operation of the Poor Laws.* B. Fellowes, London.

Semmel, B. (1970). *The Rise of Free Trade Imperialism.* Cambridge University Press, Cambridge.

Sen, A. (1982). *Poverty and Famines: An Essay on Entitlement and Deprivation.* Clarendon, Oxford.

Snell, K.D.M. (1985). *Annals of the Labouring Poor: Social Change and Agrarian England.* Cambridge University Press, Cambridge.

Sokoll, T. (1993). *Household and Family among the Poor.* Universitatsverlag Dr. N. Brockmeyer, Bochum.

Somers, M. (1994a). Citizenship and the Place of the Public Sphere: Law, Community, and Political Culture in the Transition to Democracy. *American Sociological Review*, 58 (5), 587–620.

Somers, M. (1994b). Rights, Relationality and Membership: Rethinking the Making and Meaning of Citizenship. *Law and Social Inquiry*, 19 (1), 1301–1350.

Tawney, R.H. (1972 [1938]). The Assessment of Wages in England by the Justices of the Peace. In W.E. Minchinton (ed.) *Wage Regulation in Pre-industrial England.* Barnes and Noble, New York, pp. 37–92.

Tawney, R.H. and Power, E. (eds) (1924). *Tudor Economic Documents*, vol. 1. Longmans, London, pp. 338–350.

Tilly, C. (1995). *Popular Contention in Great Britain 1758–1834.* Harvard University Press, Cambridge, MA, pp. 228–232.

Valenze, D. (1995). *The First Industrial Woman.* Oxford University Press, New York.

Van Parijs, P. (ed.). (1992) *Arguing for Basic Income: Ethical Foundations for a Radical Reform.* Verso, London.

Van Parijs, P. Cohen, J. and Rogers, J. (eds) (2001). *What's Wrong with a Free Lunch?* Beacon Press, Boston.

Viner, J. (1965 [1937]). *Studies in the Theory of International Trade.* Augustus Kelley, New York.

Webb, S. and Webb, B. (1927). *English Local Government: English Poor Law History. Part 1: The Old Poor Law.* Longmans, Green, London.

Wells, R.A.E. (1988). *Wretched Faces: Famine in Wartime England, 1793–1801.* Sutton, Gloucester, UK.

Wrigley, E.A. (1986). Men on the Land and Men in the Countryside: Employment in Agriculture in Early-Nineteenth Century England. In L. Bonfield, R.M. Smith, and K. Wrightson (eds) *The World We Have Gained: Histories of Population and Social Structure.* Basil Blackwell, London, pp. 295–336.

Chapter 47
The Stability of Basic Income

Jos de Beus

Excerpts from de Beus, J. (unpublished) The Stability of Basic Income.

Institutionalizing Basic Income

I will concentrate myself on the supposed relation between transparency of Basic Income reinforcement of solidarity, and the realization of equal economic freedom.

The first feature of this claim which has to be clarified is its strength. In his historical monograph about the welfare state in Denmark, France, Germany, the United Kingdom and Sweden, Peter Baldwin is demonstrating that complexity within social policy and solidarity do not correlate negatively, but positively (Baldwin, 1990).[1] According to Baldwin, the welfare state is a set of provisions for common risk-sharing in which all members of society are seen as equal potential victims of certain risks: almost everyone can grow old, become sick, have children, and so on. The real distribution of certainty or coverage of losses is eventually only accidently equal, since it depends on three capricious variables. The first variable is the incidence of collective risks, such as the risk of unemployment. The second variable is the self-reliance of groups, a fortune which itself depends on the exchange-economic prospects of a group and its demographic prospects (for example the scanty defensibility of a growing army of unskilled migrants). The third variable is the actuarial logic of the provisions chosen, that is the relation between risk, financial ability, contribution, nominal rights and the exercise of these rights. In theory it is quite possible that the expected risk-group coincides with the factual risk-group, so that graduations of profit and solidarity are to be determined unambiguously. But in the practice of social policy the criteria for membership of an economic class (such as being a farmer, a professional or a civil servant) are not the same as the criteria for membership of risk-groups (such as the elderly, the disabled and the poor).

Thus, there will be permanent lack of clarity about the question who is a material winner in social policy, who is a loser, and how much net equality will be realized precisely. Baldwin argues that a clear dichotomy between a strong class/risk-group and a weak class/risk-group is hardly conducive to social policy, since this policy then stands or falls with the privileges or humanitarianism of the strong or the incidental political power of the weak. What is conducive, though, is the fading away of social stratification or the democratization

From de Beus, J. (unpublished) The Stability of Basic Income.

Basic Income: An Anthology of Contemporary Research, First Edition. Edited by Karl Widerquist, José A. Noguera, Yannick Vanderborght, and Jurgen De Wispelaere.

of risks, so that a middle class (people with average fortune and average risk) becomes at least indifferent between a universal solution (joining public insurance) or a selective solution (being privately insured against all risks except for the publicly insured risk of misery and unrest amongst the most vulnerable citizens). This middle class becomes solidary with the vulnerable: "Solidarity, in those few instances where it has been realized, has been the outcome of a generalized and reciprocal self-interest. Not ethics, but politics explain it." (Baldwin, 1990: 299).

From this angle, Basic Income must really be an innovation, a breakthrough in the historical development of social policy. First, it is not based on a plausible public argument about risk-sharing and insurance, but on arguments about background equality, citizenship and liberal neutrality (Van Parijs, 1992). Some meritorious attempts have been made to apply the models of John Rawls (constitutional consensus via a social contract) and Ronald Dworkin (voluntary exchange via auctions and insurance) and to develop a concept of primary solidarity behind a veil of ignorance. But these exercises give a very abstract and rationalistic picture of the formation of civic nationalism and the spirit of community at the national or the transnational level. Also, they do not penetrate into the image of future society of the new Bismarcks and Beveridges who determine the political agenda for social policy today (Delors, Reich, perhaps Blair). In the debate on the social dimension of Europe, one would expect to find the political argument of Basic Income as converging or centrally standardized risk-sharing in the European market. But it is still insignificant in that disourse.

Second, Basic Income is egalitarian in a simple way, intuitively recognizable for everyone. Everyone receives a start premium in order to survive, as a kind of entry ticket or voting-paper. Some framing (irrational differences in valuation of identical options) will be going on when some get this amount in cash and others see it back as deduction from their taxable income. But I assume that this psychic effect detracts nothing from the egalitarian ethos of Basic Income. However the welfare state, in particular the social-democratic model of the welfare state, is featured by complex or deep equality: there are many circles of holders of social rights, and there is no equal treatment of all residents across all circles (Rae et al. 1981; De Beus, 1993: 57, 80–81).

Third, the relation between winners and losers is clearly visible, at least on the moment of introduction (the short run). The big winner is that part of the so-called inactives that is liberated from all pressing duties – means test, application test, schooling test and so on. According to Bill Jordan this winner is the underclass. Jan-Jaap Heij et al. rightly draw our attention to the various reactions of labor supply to Basic Income and the diffuse pattern of job redistribution following from this (Heij et al., 1993). The Dutch Central Planning Bureau assumes that inactive persons (in particular those without extra entitlements) will want to join the labor process, pushed by the low benefit of Basic Income and pulled by a low marginal tax rate, while the active persons (in particular those with high incomes) will want to retire, pulled by lower opportunity costs of leisure and pushed by a high marginal tax rate (CPB, 1992). But according to Heij et al. everything depends here on the valuation of work: Does it provide status? Is it intrinsically satisfying? Is it unpleasant and dirty? Even these authors establish that people with low or fully lacking earning capacities in a market economy are the big winners when Basic Income is introduced (Heij et al., 1993:138–150).

Finally, there is still the connection between solidary and unsolidary citizens in the long run. Durkheim suggested that solidarity "is not susceptible to exact observation and especially not to measurement." I doubt whether sociologists were ever much worried by this opinion, but I am sure that social planners never took it seriously for obvious reasons. An unsolidary member of a political community with Basic Income is someone who is able to perform paid or unpaid labor, who confines her- or himself to receiving and spending Basic Income and who refuses to do some work or pay some tax when the financial base of Basic Income happens to be under high pressure. It is generally known that, in a free society, it is almost unfeasible for both social inspectors and independent researchers to quantify upaid labor and compare it interpersonally (even in the case of paid labor this is quite difficult, witness the presence of illegals and tax dodgers). Intimate and manipulable data are always at stake here. Therefore, there is always lack of clarity about the connection between what someone is bringing in (the costs of Basic Income) and what someone is receiving (the benefits of Basic Income). But this vagueness is not the ambiguous relation between profit and loss which is the inevitable and legitimizing consequence of a complex welfare state in Baldwin's analysis. Baldwin is pointing at such a dilution of the calculus of profit and loss, that many (especially the members of the middle class) see themselves as winners without knowing exactly how much one wins vis-à-vis other citizens. This is coupled with an expansion of the spirit of solidarity. These dispositions are promoted by rough, yet quite accurate and enrichable knowledge about everyone's financial contributions and takings. In the case of Basic Income situations may occur in which the calculation of profit and loss can only be made by or for the solidary persons in the formal economic sector. If these persons establish that they are losing and also have growing evidence at their disposal about one-sided solidarity on their side, this does not imply, of course. that the relation between the solidary and the unsolidary is objectively getting worse. There may well be prejudice or endemic underrating of voluntary work, domestic labor or contributions to the quality of the public domain on the side of other citizens. But this lack of clarity does block the road to generalization and dilution of both the calculus of profit and loss and the conception of solidarity. the mechanism for legitimization of social policy which Baldwin puts in front.[2]

Two Proposals

For all these reasons (no risk-sharing involved, simple equality, visibility of winners and losers, unclarity about the distribution of solidary acts), the claim of the Basic Income movement is a strong one. With that I do not want to argue that Basic Income is unfeasible in all rich nations. Baldwin's mechanism can work, say when economic growth is stable and the introduction of Basic Income is piecemeal. It is not conceptually impossible that a single social right to Basic Income for the whole population will presently sustain the same or more solidarity than the accumulation of many different entitlements today. But is it likely? To answer this question, I turn to a comparison of certain proposals which focus on both economic incentives and formal rules. I restrict the argument to two blueprints, namely the proposal of the Dutch Scientific Council for Government Policy (WRR) plus a variant of Robert van der Veen, and the British proposal of Hermione Parker. Both proposals dominate the debate in both these countries.[3]

The WRR draws a distinction between the responsibility of government for maintaining a social minimum for all citizens (coerced social protection) and the responsibility of individual citizens for acquiring security above this minimum (voluntary insurance). Social protection needs to be tiered, in order to account for the necessary adaptation of the social minimum to diverse specific circumstances of individual citizens. The first tier of the WRR scheme is a Partial Basic Income (PBI). Everyone who stays legally in the Netherlands and is between 18 and 65 years old, receives PBI. The level of PBI is equal to the difference between the current welfare norm for married couples and this norm for single households (= 30% of the welfare norm for a married couple). This difference amounted to about 450 Dutch guilders in 1985, the year in which the WRR published its proposal. The elderly receive a higher Basic Income up to the level of their current benefit: children receive a lowered Basic Income, equal to the current child allowance. A specially heightened PBI also applies to widows, orphans, the handicapped and the disabled. The second tier is a General Insurance against Income Loss (GIIL). In case of unemployment, sickness, or disability, each active person (employee, civil servant or self-employed) receives a supplement to PBI up to the social minimum of a single household. The generally insured income share is maximally equal to the difference between this "individual" minimum and PBI (= 40% of the welfare norm for a married couple). The GIIL is an insurance for workers. It amounted to about 600 guilders in 1985. The third and final tier is general social assistance, targeted at those who are unable to support themselves, in particular households whose sum of claims owing to PBI and GIIL falls short of the relevant social minimum (e.g., unemployed young graduates and divorced women with young children). Here the means test will be applied. The social minimum is coupled to the growth of national income per capita. The legal minimum wage is abolished.

The WRR does not ignore matters of implementation (WRR, 1985: 49–68). Residents with labor income which is not taxed in the Netherlands, are excluded from PBI. Certain increases of PBI are omitted when and because social rights (in particular those of widows) are meanwhile abolished. Taxation will be simplified, with a view to shifting from the wage sum to other tax bases, to integration of taxes and national insurance, and to a moderate progressive or proportional system of tax rates. Employers pay out PBI. Howerver, other bodies are also involved in the scheme, such as the central government's fiscal service, the local government's welfare service and the corporatist organs that implement social security for employees. The GIIL entails detailed arrangements regarding the self-employed, duration (half of the number of work or child care years till the moment of request, maximally six years) and the distribution of premiums between employers and employees. The assignment of special allowances in the social assistance system disregards wealth and income out of wealth as much as possible. The freedom of contract permits employers' associations and trade unions – engaged in collective bargaining – to supplement social protection. In order to guarantee voluntariness, the lawgiver controls the individual right to entry (a worker is allowed to refuse extra insurance), the indestructability of individual insurance clauses in collective labor contracts, the prohibition of premium differentiation, and an obligation to accept bad risks.

The group van der Veen does not desire so much to consolidate PBI, but aims at a gradual transition of PBI to a full Basic Income within 25 years. Its ultimate goal is a full Basic Income for all Dutch people at the level of 50% of the current welfare norm for unmarried couples, linked to the average wage growth (Heij et al., 1993). This amounted to about 900 guilders in 1993. As to other issues, the approach of the WRR is followed and elaborated. First, the good social-policymaker must differentiate to age. This is done by lowering or heightening Basic Income, that is a lower transfer to childeren till a certain age (16 or 18) and a higher one to the elderly from a certain age (65 or 70). Second, there has to be some differentiation caused by certain needs or deprivations, such as disability. This is done by completing Basic Income in a strictly regulated market for social insurances (including a legal regulation of premium uniformity across all economic sectors) or supplementary assistance for "small, strictly selected" groups, or a combination of these two arrangements in the spirit of the WRR. Third, Basic Income has to be fully included in a coherent and simple system of taxes (tax reform). Finally, there must be "flanking" policy. This is a mix of destructive and constructive measures. The first kind includes the abolishment of legal minimum wage, deregulation of the labor market (in particular compulsory participation to collective labor contracts), "social workshops," student subsidies, and some national insurance, such as old-age pensions and widow allowances. Constructive measures concern active labor market policy: education policy (company training based on cooperation between local firms, governments and trade unions; a regulated capital market for students), child care and general policies for economic growth (infrastructure).

In Parker's scheme Guaranteed Income is a mix of age-related partial Basic Income, selective supplements, a disability cost allowance, an income-tested housing benefit, and an emergency provision (Parker, 1989). This income replaces the current benefits in the British welfare state, among which all tax exemptions. Old criteria for taxation, allowance, disability, housing and financial need are to be reconsidered. Two new public agencies are established, namely the national Transfer Income Account (TIA), responsible for Basic Incomes and a new income tax or Basic Income contribution, and the local Cash and Care Departments (C&C), responsible for housing benefit, emergency cash provision and certification of claims for disability. Both earnings restrictions and the cohabitation rule in welfare are abolished. Opposite to that is a general obligation to work or train, coupled to a guaranteed job at the local level.

The new ministry TIA will unburden some other ministries. It is engaged in Partial Basic Income, selective allowances and allowances for the disabled and handicapped. Basic Income is differentiated to age: more to adults than to children and more for old children than young ones. The allowances are earmarked for special categories of citizens, such as the elderly, the disabled, widows, widowers, pregnant women, and single mothers. Ideally, Partial Basic Income and allowance are constituting full Basic Income. The old-age allowance takes discouragement of immigration and the demand of minimal stay into account. Total absence of opportunities for work are indicating disability in the disability costs allowance. There is no allowance for the unemployed.

The new local agencies C&C are engaged in assigning disability benefits, housing subsidies, welfare in emergency cases, welfare work and residual TIA assistance. These agencies assess individual claims and apply the criteria of the central administration. When someone's claim is valid and hers or his original income is zero, the costs of renting, gas, water, maintenance and special local utility rates will be fully covered.

It will be immediately clear that both proposed schemes are complex. They demand far ranging articulation of procedures, prescriptions and criteria. Furthermore, these criteria are connected to some status quo in social policy (it matters, then, whether the introduction of Basic Income has been preceeded by a rigourous policy of retrenchment or not). Parker's proposal is more complex and maintains the obligation to work, although it implies a shift of policy costs from employers and maintains the obligation to work, although it implies a shift of policy costs from employers and trade unions to the central administration (compare Roche, 1992: 178–195). Both proposals are driven by a multiple of restrictive rules of the game. These rules are both formal rules with a constitutional, legal, administrative or organizational standing and informal rules: social norms, conventions, or ethical principles. Their stake is solidarity. This conclusion is important to my argument. It can be corroborated by solely looking at the obligations for different groups of affected actors.

Citizens play different roles. They are coproducer, receiver, party in the insurance market and client. As coproducer, you are supposed to have a reasonable share in the economic basis of Basic Income. You ought to report your fiscal income honestly, and you actually ought to pay the tax you owe, earmarked to partially finance Basic Income. According to Parker, this implies a legal obligation to work and to train. A voluntary decision to confine yourself to consuming Basic Income, can be followed by negative sanctions (fines, imprisonment, withdrawal of Basic Income.) There is also a soft response, of course. van der Veen points at a special obligation of employees. They ought to accept a special increase of their taxes but also a linkage of their wages to Basic Income. This forces them to mitigate their wage demands. As receiver, you are supposed to respect everyone's claim to Basic Income. You are to welcome the other's freedom to use Basic Income to hers or his taste. This puts pressure on families where the father's will is law, or on communities where one is held responsible for getting or using leisure, or where certain modes of recreation (drinking beer or hanging about streetcorners) are seen as unmeritorious. Furthermore, you are supposed to set apart some Basic Income for the wellbeing of your children and to transfer it to them as soon as they are competent enough to spend the money rationally. As party in the insurance market in a broad sense, you have to insure yourself via your employer, your union, your collective labor contract or some private insurance company. As a client, you are supposed not to fake, that is not to do as if you enter a state which entitles you to additional allowances (when this is not really the case) and not to create this state consciously with an eye for these allowances.

Policymakers are supposed to develop "flanking" measures in behalf of general economic development (public investment, labor market policy, education policy and so on). Organized employers and employees are supposed not to shift off the public burden to prices and wages, partly to preempt inflation. They also have to provide some additional collective security. They are not permitted to block Basic Income (in a campaign for maintaining some social rights which are established in industrial relations), when Basic Income is supported by a majority in parliament. In short, Basic Income forces the organizations of capital and labor to function as "state bearing forces" (Crouch, 1993). Civil servants, in particular the ones who implement the new regime for social assistance, are supposed to implement law in the spirit of the will of politicians and of meta-legal principles, such as the principle of legal equality.

Robert van der Veen has included the right to maximally sustainable Basic Income in an "ethical constitution" (van der Veen, 1991: 75). If the argument so far is correct, this constitution has to be amplified with a number of moral obligations.

The Compromise between Simple Rules and Balanced Solidarity

The supporters of Basic Income are appealing to the social science critique of the Byzantine heaviness of the regulating and steering apparatus of the welfare state, and to the preference of legal philosophy for simple and general rules (van der Veen, 1990; Schauer, 1991). They see deregulation of welfare and of insurance against (long-term) unemployment as the first step in the journey to a simple organization of solidarity. This is based on an optimistic expectation about the decrease of illegality and crime and about the increase of the quality of inner cities, work and family life.

I endorse the necessity and desirability of simple universalism in social policy. Yet my argument about the transformation of solidarity *before* into solidarity *after* indicates that the Basic Income movement is facing a dilemma. Either there will emerge a simple Basic Income scheme, which will turn out to be a short-lived experiment because it undermines solidarity. Or there will emerge a stable Basic Income which reproduces solidarity, but is complex and entails many moral rules of the game and moral obligations. There seems to be no escape from a compromise between the longing for simple rules and the longing for balanced solidarity. The rules will become both formal and informal: the most essential of them will be part of the unwritten section of an "ethical constitution." This solidarity will preserve the happy mean between on the one hand parametric, primary, slack and coldly practiced solidarity, and on the other hand strategic, secondary, tight and hotly practiced solidarity.

The most important implications of this analysis for the philosophic and political-economic debate on Basic Income is twofold. In the first place, the liberal-egalitarian justification of abolishing the obligation to work and to train is irrelevant. However plausible the new thinking about unpaid labor, state neutrality and equality of resources, it will not undo that respect for economic freedom of the other means certain economic obligations for yourself.

In the second place. an arrangement of Basic Income in the constitution or in a basic law is a necesssary but not a sufficient condition for promoting solidarity. The crux of the matter is nonorganizable and nonenforceable rule-following. Therefore, there is a role to be played by credible social leaders who are engaged in generating trust in the state (in particular its publicness and its minimal distributive function), in clarifying the justice and multi-functionality of Basic Income, in opening communication between workaholics and spongers and everyone between these two categories, and by appealing to certain symbols of communitarian commitment and togetherness (compare Miller, 1992).

Notes

1. In this section I leave out Baldwin's interesting results about the international variety of motives and arrangements, about failing explanations (such as the game-theoretical one about a coalition of the middle class and the poor), and about successful explanations (the worries of certain economic groups, path-dependency, and political mobilization of the most vulnerable).
2. Baldwin's point is that clear rights and fair shares should not add up to the possibility to calculate one's own net profit out of social policy "to the second decimal."
3. This is a bit unfair to the CPB (1992) and creative minds like De Beer, Boerlage, Duindam, Hamminga, Nooteboom, Roebroek, Stroeken en Van Wijngaarden (in the Netherlands) and Atkinson, Brittan and Meade (in the United Kingdom). A wide comparison would make this chapter too long. I think my conclusions also apply to the excluded proposals.

References

Baldwin, P. (1990). *The Politics of Social Solidarity.* Cambridge University Press, Cambridge.

Centraal Planbureau (CPB) (1992). *Nederland in Drievoud.* Staatsuitgeverij, Den Haag.

Crouch, C. (1993). *Industrial Relations and European State Traditions.* Clarendon Press, Oxford.

De Beus, J. (1993). *Economische gelijkheid en het goede leven.* Contact, Amsterdam.

Heij, J.-J. et al. (1993). *Basisinkomen in drievoud.* Het Spinhuis, Amsterdam.

Miller, G.J. (1992). *Managerial Dilemmas.* Cambridge University Press, Cambridge.

Parker, H. (1989). *Instead of the Dole.* Routledge, Landen.

Rae, D. et al. (1981). *Equalities.* Harvard University Press, Cambridge, MA.

Roche, M. (1992). *Rethinking Citizenship.* Polity Press, Cambridge.

Schauer, F. (1991). *Playing by the Rules.* Clarendon Press, Oxford.

van der Veen, R.J. (1900). *De sociale erenzen van beleid.* Stenfert Kroese, Leiden.

van der Veen, R.J. (1991). *Between Exploitation and Communism.* Wolters-Noordhoff, Groningen.

Van Parijs, P. (1992). Assurance, solidarité, equité. *Cahiers de l'Ecole des Sciences Philosophiques et Religieuses,* 12.

Wetenschappelijke Raad voor het Regeringsbeleid (WRR) (1985). *Waarborgen voor zekerheid.* Staatsuitgeverij, Den Haag.

Chapter 48

Basic Income and the Welfare State

Samuel Brittan

Excerpts from Brittan, S. (1995). Basic Income and the Welfare State. In *Capitalism with a Human Face*. Edward Elgar, Aldershot.

The Torn Net and Shaky Ladder

It would be wrong just to throw in the towel in the face of current pressures on the welfare state without making a few suggestions about remedying the obvious weaknesses at tolerable cost. It is still worth undertaking a summary of the key features of Basic Income (BI), both because they highlight present weaknesses and because it might be possible to achieve some features of BI incrementally without committing oneself to going the whole hog. It should not be seen as a messianic movement whose aims have to be achieved in total or not at all.

What, however, needs to be reformed? No system of state-provided financial rights can cover all the varying personal problems which drive people into degradation and despair. But, despite the high sums expended, the welfare state has not succeeded even in providing the standard safety net for which its founders, such as Beveridge, hoped.

Very nearly a half of all British benefits are accounted for by National Insurance payments, such as retirement pensions, invalidity and sickness benefit (and, for a minority of eligible cases, unemployment benefit). These are paid irrespective of means and are financed by employer and employee National Insurance contributions. They are essentially tax payments. The system is called pay-as-you-go to distinguish it from the funded schemes normal in the private sector where contributions are paid into a fund, the investment of which finances all the benefits. Thus, contrary to popular belief, recipients of National Insurance contributory benefits, such as state pensions, have not paid for them in any actuarial sense.

Next in importance are non-contributory income-related benefits designed to support those not eligible for contributory benefit, or whose benefit is inadequate to standard needs. By far the most important example of these is now called Income Support, on which many pensioners and most unemployed rely. The name is one of a succession of labels that have been invented to take the sting out of what was once known as National Assistance, and which ultimately goes back to the medieval Poor Law. A much more recent benefit is

From Brittan, S. (1995). Basic Income and the Welfare State. *Capitalism with a Human Face*. Edward Elgar, Aldershot. Reprinted with permission of Edward Elgar.

Basic Income: An Anthology of Contemporary Research, First Edition. Edited by Karl Widerquist, José A. Noguera, Yannick Vanderborght, and Jurgen De Wispelaere.

known as Family Credit, designed to supplement the incomes of low-paid working families with children. Housing Benefit, which accounts for much larger sums, is designed to provide help in paying rents and some local authority taxes. All these top-up benefits are subject to a test of means and are withdrawn as income from other sources rises.

Finally, there is a group of miscellaneous benefits where entitlement neither relates to contributions nor varies with income. Of these, overwhelmingly the most important is Child Benefit, which is paid to all parents, rich or poor, and is not taxed. Additional benefit is provided where children are cared for by a single parent.

Yet, despite this great array, there are still loopholes which prevent people from claiming the conventional minimum. First, there is incomplete coverage. Family Credit, for instance, is not available to childless working families. Then again, unemployed claimants can be disqualified if their condition is regarded as voluntary or if they are involved in an industrial dispute. A benefit may also be withheld or reduced if claimants have capital in excess of certain moderate limits (£8,000, apart from the value of a residence, for Family Credit and Income Support in 1994); and Income Support is lower for adults under 25.

A particular problem with means-tested benefits is that of inadequate take-up. Some of the estimates of non-take-up give an exaggerated impression, as it is quite rational for households to avoid detailed scrutiny of their affairs if their net entitlement is likely to be very small. But even in terms of the *value* of unclaimed benefit, the take-up percentages are disappointing, particularly in the case of Family Credit.

It is not only the safety net, but the ladder of opportunity that is in a shaky condition. This is because the high rates of benefit withdrawal, when the unemployed obtain work, or people with low incomes move up the earnings ladder, produce serious disincentives to work, effort and savings, known as the unemployment and poverty traps, respectively. By these traps I do not mean that income is literally lower or the same if an unemployed person takes a job or an employed person obtains a better one. The trap exists if the withdrawal rate for benefit is so high that the gains from the better job are negligible. The very high implicit marginal tax rates of 90 to 100% which used to affect some lower-income households have been nearly eliminated, but at the price of increasing the number of households paying marginal rates of 70% and over – amounting to more than 500,000 in 1993.

The Systems Compared

How does Basic Income differ from existing social security benefits? Nearly all existing social security payments are contingent. Even the contributory benefits depend on certain conditions prevailing – such as unemployment, sickness or age. One idea behind Basic Income is to move away from this kind of conditionality and to make a payment to everyone. Basic Incomes have many other names, such as Citizens' Income, Social Dividend or Minimum Income Guarantees. They are all inherently the same; and so is a Negative or Reverse Income Tax.

Basic Incomes could be paid across the counter like state pensions – this is called the Post Office Principle. Alternatively, they could take the form of a tax credit, which would be set off against income tax for those with sufficient tax liabilities, but received as a positive payment from the state by those with insufficient liabilities.

For all the sound and fury, the distinctions between the two methods of payment are essentially administrative. The important differences relate to the size of basic payment and the rate or rates at which it is withdrawn or taxed away as income comes in from other sources.

Deconstructing Basic Income

In our original paper Steven Webb (Brittan and Webb, 1990) outlined a modest scheme for integrating two types of income-related benefit: Family Credit and Income Support with income tax. The idea was to provide a Guaranteed Income for all households at the conventional subsistence minimum governing these schemes. It would have amounted in 1994 terms to about £44 for a single adult over 25 and around £115 for a typical family with two children. Webb also stuck to the existing practice in income-related benefits in tying the new benefits to households rather than individuals, which is rank heresy to many Basic Income campaigners.

Nevertheless, even the limited proposal that we did consider would have cost in 1994 some £34 billion per annum on a no-losers basis. More realistically, if financed from personal direct taxation, the basic rate of income tax plus employee National Insurance contribution would have to rise by 15 percentage points: to 50 pence in the pound starting from 1994 levels. The personal allowance would go except for a small disregard, and be replaced by a tax credit.

If we are to rescue anything from the idea it is essential to consider how the cost of it could be reduced. By far the most logically extensive economic study of alternatives (which is yet free of social security technicalities) has been made by James Meade (Meade, 1993). Here I can only offer a few pointers for those who want to start with a less exhaustive approach.

The best chance of advance is to unpack the Basic Income idea into its components to see how it can be introduced by stages, starting from the present. In so doing people of all views should be able to discover why the latter fails to provide even a conventional subsistence minimum for all.

I list first the most controversial aspects which are either prohibitively costly or towards which some people would object on principle, and then go on to the more modest components where action could be taken much sooner:

- *Unconditionality.* The Basic Income would be made available to all with no conditions about incapacity, availability for work and so on. Nor would there be questions about capital ownership.
- *Uniform withdrawal rate.* There would be a uniform withdrawal rate at no more than the normal tax rate, including employee National Insurance contributions.
- *Payment to individuals.* Many proponents of Basic Income regard a shift from a household to an individual basis payment as essential, despite its absence from the Webb scheme (Brittan and Webb, 1990) which was drafted in terms of households.
- *Post Office Principle.* Under BI, people would have the option of receiving BI across the counter, as Child Benefit is now received. This would help with the problem of incomplete take-up which arises from the reluctance of potential recipients to come forward at social security offices.
- *Integration.* Alternatively, recipients could offset their Basic Income receipts against income tax, thus making or receiving a single payment without "churning."
- *Generality.* Working adult families on low incomes without children would for the first time have their incomes topped up (UK Family Credit at the time of writing only

supplements the incomes of families with children.) The 100% withdrawal rate for Income Support for working-age adults would thus be trimmed back.

- *Non-discrimination.* There would be no discrimination in size of payment to working-age adults – in the UK the under-25s now receive less as a deliberate act of policy.
- *Adequacy.* This is inevitably subjective and controversial. But some existing benefits – for example, for adults under 25 and for households with low earnings but without children – do not even aim to provide a conventional minimum.

The lower items in the list demonstrate some of the improvements that could be achieved by building on the present system without waiting for the full merging of the tax and social security systems. The latter is an administrative move often wrongly seen as the heart of all BI and Negative Income Tax ideas.

Any government could quite inexpensively take a first step and extend family credit to single people and childless families, individuals and households. This move would have cost only about £350 million per annum in 1994 – trivial by the standards of modern public finance.

In principle, the extension of Family Credit to all adult workers would eliminate the extreme forms of the unemployment trap. For anyone deemed to have a full-time job will have his or her income topped-up to minimum levels and will always gain from taking employment. But whatever reforms are made, it is difficult to imagine a swift and easy transition from Income Support to Family Credit for some of the people on the fringes of the labor market.

It would thus also help if the withdrawal rate for Income Support for adults of working age could be reduced below 100% and preferably brought in line with the 70% taper used for other income-related benefits. Specifically, it would encourage people to take spasmodic, casual or part-time jobs that do not qualify them for Family Credit and to take them on a legal basis.

The removal of discrimination against younger adults will arouse strong passions. The discrimination was put in by the Thatcher government to encourage the work habit and to discourage young people from moving away from their families to other parts of the country where they did not have assured jobs or accommodation. As young people did nevertheless move – and often with good reason – this discrimination has increased the number of homeless and the size of the underclass in general. A middle-of-the-road approach might be to eliminate the discrimination but make young people's benefits conditional on genuine attempts to find work or to train – as they are supposed to be for the over-25s.

Of the more radical ideas higher up the list, it is the uniform withdrawal rate that I would most readily put on the back burner. The very high cost of Webb's simulation, as of other schemes, arises from reducing the withdrawal rate for benefit so that it is no higher than the income tax rate. High marginal rates for all taxpayers are then necessary to eliminate completely the high "poverty" marginal rates at the bottom.

If there are any doubts about priorities for people of working age, there can be none about pensions, where the subtleties of work incentives do not apply. The majority of pensioners are not on or below the poverty line. But a minority do need Income Support to keep them above it. Modest funds spent in increasing Income Support for the elderly and providing it in a more user-friendly way would do far more good than much larger sums spent in increasing the basic pension.

Yet the centrepiece of the British Labour Party's policy in several elections has been a substantial rise in the basic pension, to be followed by annual re-rating at the faster of prices or earnings growth. The Labour governments of the 1960s and 1970s both started off with an across-the-board pensions increase which they spent the remainder of the Parliament paying for. This exhausted their redistributionary zeal, or at least means; and they were extremely strapped for cash for other kinds of redistribution, both towards low-income families and towards the poorest minorities among the old. Across-the-board increases in state pensions – and for that matter Child Benefit which John Major unfroze and then relinked to prices – are a wasteful and inefficient means of helping the poor; and while politicians may need to buy votes, the rest of us should resist emotional blackmail.

I am more reluctant to abandon unconditionality: the "modest competence" available to all. It is difficult to say in advance how many people would want to take advantage of an Unconditional Income Guarantee at Income Support levels to drop out of the official labor force or cut their hours of work, and how their numbers would compare with those taking jobs for the first time, because it paid them to do so. In any case, voters do not feel either rich enough or sufficiently laid back to tolerate intentional subsidies to those opting out of paid work.

But I would still like to avoid postponing the whole project indefinitely. One suggestion is a partial Basic Income. This has been suggested by the person who has done more than anyone else to promote the cause in the UK , namely Hermione Parker. It was also the approach chosen by the Liberal Democrats in the run-up to the 1992 election. Such a partial Basic Income would have the advantage of introducing the principle of non-work incomes for all. To start with, it would have to be little more than a token payment, but it would be something on which to build.

When we come to the argument between the administrative integration of tax and benefit and the Post Office Principle, it is an argument about means among reformers. The advantage of the Post Office Principle is that the "caring parent" (usually modern jargon for the mother) of a family could be made the recipient of benefits intended for herself and her children without being dependent on her partner to hand over the cash. The advantage of integration is that the mass of two-way payments between the citizen and the state could be netted out so that the principal breadwinner would either receive or make a single payment.

It is said that assessment for tax benefit must always be separate because benefit needs fluctuate week to week according to family circumstances and need. Tax, on the other hand, is adjusted for under- or overpayment once a year. I have myself suggested a good liberal compromise whereby the "caring parent" could opt whether to receive benefit across the counter or allow it to be netted off against her own or her partner's tax bill.

In any case, changes could be made to make benefit assessment more like the tax variety and less like a medieval inquisition. While capital holdings can never be completely irrelevant – or we would have eccentric millionaires with houses full of Picassos drawing benefit – the typical benefit drawer is not full of clever financial tricks for transforming income into capital and is more concerned with meeting the household readies. Much higher levels of capital disregard would probably make little difference to the cost of social security. At least this is a conjecture worth investigating.

Too much of the discussion about making benefits more like the tax system and less like the Poor Law has been of a Great Leap Forward kind. We are extremely unlikely to wake up one morning to find either a completely integrated tax – benefit scheme or benefits available to all at the Post Office with minimal scrutiny. But a great deal can be done incrementally.

Toward Conclusions

Social security is often treated as an instrument of redistribution. Yet between two-thirds and three-quarters of gross welfare benefits (including education and health as well as social security) are effectively paid for by the same person at another time in his or her own lifetime. (See, for instance, the Economic and Social Research Council Report by Hills (1993).) It is therefore tempting for non-pater-nalists to say that only the one-third of genuine redistribution should be retained, leaving people free to make their own decisions about smoothing expenditure over time. But before coming to any such conclusion we should hold on to our safety belt – here a very apt metaphor.

For the estimate of two-thirds lifetime recycling is an average over millions of people. It is impossible for the individual to know beforehand how the vagaries of life in terms of illness, unemployment and so on are going to affect him. Some people will receive back from the state far more than two-thirds, others much less. Moreover, if a person has been improvident in providing for adversity his fellow citizens will not be happy to see him starve or live in the gutter. Knowledge of this fact creates a moral hazard which will make it rational to underinsure and undersave.

On the other hand, it is also common knowledge that state benefits are never likely to provide more than some conventional minimum. People wanting to maintain as much as possible of their living standards in adversity will be well advised to take out their own insurance.

Drawing the threads together, one is led to envisage a three-deck structure. First, there will be a partial Basic Income for all, unconditional and not means-tested. Second, there will be income-related benefits intended to bring people up to a conventional minimum which will rise with inflation, but only partially with income. Third, over and above these supports, people will make their own arrangements.

This is a neat, but not entirely satisfactory, picture. Many of the risks of life are not in practice or even in theory insurable. Cover might be obtained for a few months of unemployment or illness, but not for many years of impaired earnings capacity. This represents a problem for people above the poverty line who have nevertheless been victims of change in the demand for their skills or whose activities have been displaced through changes in the pattern of international specialization. There is a limit to what the social security system or even private insurance can achieve here. Indeed, if everyone were compensated against all change, there would be no pressure ever to shift employment, occupation or activity.

The task of cushioning people against specific economic industrial shocks is better carried out by the kind of special payment that has been developed in the United States under the name of Adjustment Assistance for those hit by imports. Another model is the social payments that will gradually replace farm price support in the Enropean Common Agricultural Policy – but without the wasteful component of compulsory withdrawal of land from cultivation. Something too may be gained from studying past British schemes to compensate workers in specific industries, such as the mines and textiles.

A careful trawl through these and many other projects should provide some lessons for the future. The problem with them is that taxpayers' aid is channelled to those who are geographically and industrially concentrated and therefore highly visible on the political scene. Yet no extra help is provided for even greater numbers of affected people who are less politically visible because they are thinly spread over many industries, occupations and areas.

References

Brittan, S. and Webb, S. (1990). *Beyond the Welfare State: An Examination of Basic Incomes in a Market Economy.* Aberdeen University Press, for the David Hume Institute, Aberdeen.

Hills, J. et al. (1993). *Investigating Welfare: Final Report of the ESRC Welfare Research Programme.* Suntory-Toyota International Centre, London School of Economics, London.

Meade, J.E. (1993). *Liberty, Equality and Efficiency.* Macmillan, London.

Chapter 49

Basic Income and Contributory Pensions

José A. Noguera

Excerpts from Noguera, J.A. (2001). La Renta Básica y el principio contributivo. In D. Raventós (ed.) *La Renta Básica*. Editorial Ariel, Barcelona.

Basic Income and the Problem of Contributory Schemes

At present, social insurance in the form of pay-as-you-go (PAYG) and earnings-related contributory pension systems is the most important type of cash benefit in European countries, at least if we have to judge upon the volume of resources involved and the number of recipients. In these systems, paying contributions during a number of years generates eligibility for the benefit when individuals reach retirement age (and the same contributory logic often applies to other important social insurance programs such as unemployment benefits, sick-leaves, or survival pensions). It is easy to notice that there is some tension between the principles of equality and unconditionality that inspire Basic Income (BI) proposals and the contributory nature of many cash benefits in present welfare states. However, this tension has been rarely studied as a possible obstacle for the feasibility of a BI.

Note that commodification and a market-orientation is somehow inherent to the contributory principle in the following sense: since eligibility is based on previous contributions, benefits are not paid out of necessity or citizenship, but only to those who "have earned" or "deserve" them, judging upon their employment and contribution records. This logic entails the meritocratic mechanism of "individual deservingness," and has nothing to do, as such, with the fight against poverty and necessity, nor with redistributive purposes (Lawlor, 1998). The earnings-related character of most contributory schemes implies that the capacity to pay is the most valued property when generating rights: the more you earn, the more you contribute, and, therefore, the more generous the benefit you will receive.

However, the undeniable historical success of social insurance in the form of PAYG contributory systems, and the strong support they continue to receive from most workers and unions, are based mainly on a specific feature of those systems that BI lacks: their

From Noguera, J.A. (2001). La Renta Básica y el principio contributivo. In D. Raventós (ed.) *La Renta Básica*. Editorial Ariel, Barcelona. Translated by J.A. Noguera (ed.) Reprinted with permission of Editorial Ariel.

Basic Income: An Anthology of Contemporary Research, First Edition. Edited by Karl Widerquist, José A. Noguera, Yannick Vanderborght, and Jurgen De Wispelaere.

capacity to maintain workers' usual income levels (though in a variable proportion) when their wage income vanishes for whatever reason (retirement, unemployment, or sickness). Certainly, the perception of this capacity by workers is partly due to a kind of "contributory delusion," since wages' replacement rates are often far from 100%, minimum contributions and work records are quite demanding, and coverage of the working population is far from being universal (Agulnik, 2000; Clasen, 1997; Johnson, 1999; Noguera, 2001). But, be that as it may, PAYG earnings-related contributory systems still ensure, first, a certain level of income maintenance which is quite a lot higher than the one provided by social assistance benefits (and than the one universal flat-rate benefits such as BI could possibly ever reach); and, second, they apply some degree of "risk redistribution" among contributors, which allow the payment of benefits in a more generous way than would be possible under a strict private actuarial logic. Otherwise, they would have lost their popularity among European working populations very long ago.

Additionally, contributory public systems allow high coverage of the middle classes precisely because of their income-maintenance effect; in this way, they help to avoid the spread of private insurance plans, and give incentives to middle class workers and professionals in order to press politically to keep and improve the quality of the public social protection system (Goodin and LeGrand, 1987).

Irrespectively of how contributory systems may fare in normative terms (that is, of whether their inspiring principles respect some compelling theories of distributive justice), the truth is there are strong pragmatic, psychological, and political reasons to keep them as central pillars of the welfare state. The widespread perception of "acquired rights" because of previous contributions is very strong among working and middle classes in most European countries. It is necessary to insist on the reasons behind this social and political support (Goodin, 1990): contributory systems are not, as such, efficient instruments to fight poverty nor to achieve equality and redistribution; they are seen as justified because they ensure a certain degree of income maintenance at the individuals' accustomed level.

It seems clear, then, that there is a latent conflict between the egalitarian and unconditional logic of BI and the principles that inspire and justify the support for contributory systems. This conflict is not unsolvable, since BI would not necessarily replace contributory benefits (or not entirely). However, if BI supporters' commitment to tax-benefit integration is really serious, sooner or later they will have to face the problem of a total or partial transition from contributory systems to a BI system, or, alternatively, of a radical reform of contributory schemes (Parker, 1989).

It seems obvious that the difficulty would not only have to do with how to design and execute those reforms, but also, and primarily, with how to legitimate them politically. At least in countries with well-functioning and consolidated contributory schemes, a sudden transformation which channelled all the contributions into the payment of a BI would of course be widely seen as unfair by most past and present contributors, whose opposition would likely defeat the proposal. As suggested above, the widespread concept of "acquired rights" because of previous contribution records would collide strongly with BI's egalitarian assumptions and with its flat-rate nature. Therefore, if BI is conceived as a replacement of all cash benefits (including contributory ones), it may not be politically feasible, because of the claims of past contributors who would see the link between their rights and previous contributions disappear. Of course, a transitory period could be established, during which citizens might chose either of the two systems which was most favorable to them; but this might just neutralize the opposition of current *recipients* of contributory benefits, leaving untouched that of millions of current *contributors* (and, therefore, future recipients). In the same way, more moderate strategies based on gradual or partial replacement (Sevilla, 1999; Offe, 1992, 1997) seem not very promising, since they would raise the same initial opposition for the very same motives, and they might be stopped and reversed by the outcome of socio-political struggles at any point of the process.

The conclusion is that the prospects for BI in most European countries (and especially in continental ones) are strongly dependent on how it is articulated with the contributory principle, as well as on respecting the political perceptions this principle promotes among millions of present contributors to social insurance. Acknowledging this can only lead us to think of new imaginative architectures for the welfare state, in which BI may play a central part, but probably not in isolation from other public principles of income allocation.

A Feasible Alternative: Basic Income Plus a Public Funded Scheme

An entirely different model could be inspired somehow in some proposals by Robin Blackburn (1999): once a decent minimum income floor is granted by a BI, public social insurance systems could be kept as supplementary benefits, but it would not make a lot of sense to keep them as PAYG systems; instead, they could be transformed into pension funds controlled by the state or by unions and non-profit organizations, who would have to decide in a democratic way how to invest the resources according to social and ecological concerns. This would allow a voluntary element to be introduced in social insurance, eliminate all tax exemptions for private pension plans, successfully compete with them, and generate in the long term a volume of capital so huge that it led Milton Friedman to see the proposal as a direct path to "doctrinaire socialism" (Friedman, 1962: 187).

It should be noted that a public funded scheme of social insurance, as a complement to a BI scheme, would open the possibility for BI supporters of solving three important political problems:

1) The problem of the transition from present welfare state, which is based mainly in the contributory principle, to a BI system: under the public funded scheme, citizens would continue to receive their expected earnings-related contributory benefits, since past contributions under the PAYG system could be recognized by the public fund, or even compensated somehow (for example, with tax exemptions).
2) The problem of maintaining the usual income level and avoiding sudden income loss. As said above, this is the main rationale of present earnings-related contributory systems. Under a public funded scheme the benefits would still be earnings-related, and, moreover, the proportionality between individuals' contributions and benefits would be higher than in PAYG systems, since the redistributive function of social policy would be already covered by the BI scheme.
3) The public fund would also prevent the spread of private pension funds, since the state would guarantee the public benefits against any economic crisis and would ensure stable profitability rates, something that private funds are not always able to grant. It would be difficult for private funds to compete successfully with the public fund in the long term. Besides, the resources of the public fund could be devoted to social and ecological investments, and this would in turn increase the appeal and competitiveness of the fund in the eyes of many citizens.

In order to achieve all these aims, such a public fund would have to be:

1) Voluntary, not compulsory. Under a BI system which grants a minimum income floor for everyone, there is no reason to keep the compulsory character of present social insurance any more (though some tax incentives could be established for the contributors to the fund). Every citizen would have the free option to contribute to the fund, and to do it in different amounts and periods of time.
2) Funded, not PAYG. With a universal and unconditional BI funded out of general taxation, there would be no reason to keep the redistributive elements of present PAYG contributory systems (whether they are progressive or regressive). The redistributive function of the welfare state would be satisfied by BI in combination with personal taxation. The voluntary public fund would have as its sole function and rationale to allow citizens to top up their BI during specific periods of their life cycle (unemployment, sickness, old age), preventing sudden falls of their usual income levels and offering an attractive alternative to private insurance. Each contributor to the public fund would have a personal contribution account, and would receive, when necessary, a benefit strictly related with the value of his/her past contributions plus the corresponding interest rate.
3) Guaranteed by the state. The state should back the fund in order to ensure it is competitive with private plans, and should eliminate any tax exemption or reduction for the latter. The state would have to grant the financial stability and profitability of the fund.
4) Devoted to ear-marked investments. Eventual tax reductions applied to the amounts contributed to the public fund would be justified by the fact that these contributions would be ear-marked, and would only be invested in a politically approved list of goods, services or activities with some degree of social and/or ecological utility.

There is no doubt that the proposed combination of BI and a public funded scheme is no more than a hypothetical institutional design option, which lacks any empirical implementation at this moment. However, it seems an interesting way of joining the attractiveness of BI with some of the pragmatic rationales of present earnings-related contributory systems.

References

Agulnik, P. (2000). Maintaining Incomes After Work: Do Compulsory Earnings-Related Pensions Make Sense? *Oxford Review of Economic Policy*, 16 (1).

Blackburn, R. (1999). The New Collectivism: Pension Reform, Grey Capitalism and Complex Socialism. *New Left Review*, 233.

Clasen, J. (ed.) (1997). *Social Insurance in Europe*. Policy Press, Bristol.

Friedman, M. (1962). *Capitalism and Freedom*. Chicago University Press, Chicago.

Goodin, R.E. (1990). Stabilizing Expectations: The Role of Earnings-related Benefits in Social Welfare Policy. *Ethics*, 100 (3).

Goodin, R.E. and Le Grand, J. (eds) (1987). *Not Only the Poor: The Middle Classes and the Welfare State*. Allen & Unwin, London.

Johnson, P. (1999). The Measurement of Social Security Convergence: The Case of European Public Pension Systems from 1950. *Journal of Social Policy*, 28 (4).

Lawlor, S. (1998). *Beveridge or Brown? Contribution and Redistribution: The Real Social Security Debate.* Politeia, London.

Noguera, J.A. (2001). Some Prospects for a Basic Income Scheme in Spain. *South European Society & Politics*, 6 (3), 86–102.

Offe, C. (1992). A Non-Productivist Design for Social Policies. In P. Van Parijs (ed.) *Arguing for Basic Income.* Verso, London, pp. 61–78

Offe, C. (1997). Precariedad y mercado laboral. Un análisis a medio plazo de las respuestas políticas disponibles. In C. Offe, *¿Qué crisis? Retos y transformaciones de la sociedad del trabajo.* Tercera Prensa-Hirugarren Prentsa, Donostia.

Parker, H. (1989). *Instead of the Dole: An Enquiry into Integration of the Tax and Benefit Systems.* Routledge, London.

Sevilla, J. (1999). Sobre pobres y ricos. Una propuesta de renta fiscal universal para España. In J.A. Garde (ed.) *Políticas sociales y Estado de Bienestar en España. Informe 1999.* Fundación Hogar del Empleado-Trotta, Madrid.

Chapter 50

Basic Income as a Minimally Presumptuous Social Welfare Policy

Robert E. Goodin

Excerpts from Goodin, B. (1992). Towards a Minimally Presumptuous Social Welfare Policy. In P. Van Parijs (ed.), *Arguing for Basic Income*. Verso, London.

Instead of arguing that the Basic Income strategy is somehow more accurate in its underlying assumptions about social reality than other approaches are, I shall be arguing that it is simply more noncommittal. It simply makes fewer assumptions. And by so doing, it manages to be less prone to sociological error and less vulnerable to social change than alternative modes of social security provision. That, in itself, counts very much in its favor in a world in which sociological facts are uncertain, highly variable and, in any case, constantly changing.

The Particular Presumptions of Current Policies

Let us start, then, by reflecting upon the various substantive presumptions built into current social security policies. For the more normative purposes of the present exercise, I shall eschew the grand sweep of empirical sociology. I shall focus more tightly upon particular programs, their administrative arrangements and their benefit structures in search of the substantive sociological presumptions that are embedded in them.

First, notice that across the world – in both Bismarck and Beveridge countries alike[1] – administrative arrangements for vesting social security pensions presuppose something very much like "full employment." The old-age pension is, in virtually all those countries, a contributory scheme, and the predominant mode of vesting one's old-age pension entitlement is through employment-based contributions (typically, matching contributions from both employer and employee) to the social security fund on the employee's behalf (United States Social Security Administration, 1978; Palme, 1990). True, those contributions typically serve to vest pension rights not only for employees but also for their dependants (typically, spouses and dependent children of tender years), so it is not quite true to say

From Goodin, B. (1992). Towards a Minimally Presumptuous Social Welfare Policy. In P. Van Parijs (ed.), *Arguing for Basic Income*. Verso, London. Reprinted with permission of Verso.

Basic Income: An Anthology of Contemporary Research, First Edition. Edited by Karl Widerquist, José A. Noguera, Yannick Vanderborght, and Jurgen De Wispelaere.

that this arrangement for vesting pension rights presupposes full employment, in the sense of literally everyone of working age being in paid employment. But it does presuppose, in effect, that society is organized into household units such that all heads of households are in paid employment. It presupposes, that is to say, that everyone is either in work or in a stable, long-term liaison with someone who is.

Now, in a way this presumption constitutes little more than an administrative convenience. Like "pay as you earn" arrangements for withholding taxes from wages (and for withholding taxes at source more generally), withholding social security contributions from wages is undeniably convenient. The state is more certain of getting its money that way; and individuals are thereby relieved of the burden of having to find large sums of money all at once, quarterly or at the end of every year. But if that is all there is to the matter – if employment-based contributions to a pension fund are no more than an administrative convenience – then such contributions are not in any way a necessary part of such pensions. There is no reason to believe that they constitute the only logically possible way of vesting one's old-age pension entitlements.

Given the administrative convenience of such an arrangement, that is of course how pension entitlements will accrue for those actually in employment. But for those who are not, or whose employment is somehow radically non-standard, other sorts of arrangements could in principle perfectly well be made. The self-employed could contribute – or even be required to contribute – to the pension fund to vest their own pension rights. For those who are persistently unemployed or literally unemployable, the contribution requirement could be waived altogether; they could be allowed to draw a pension without having made any contributions. Or, if we insisted upon retaining the fiction that contributions are needed to vest one's pension rights, the state agency responsible for the relief of the unemployed and unemployable might be required to make periodic payments into the pension fund on each client's behalf.

Such possibilities are not always taken up, of course. In the United States, social security pensions are simply unavailable to those without the requisite employment-based contribution history. The permanently unemployed and unattached may well be able to claim other means-tested social benefits, but they cannot claim old-age (social security) pensions. And even where those who have made no contributions are none the less allowed to draw the old-age pension, such arrangements are inevitably awkward for all concerned. Insofar as social insurance schemes are run principally on the basis of workplace contributions, it seems that the unemployed will always be second-class participants in such schemes.

A second central presupposition of current social security policy is that people, for the most part, live in stable family units where income is shared equitably, if not necessarily equally.[2] Some such presupposition about family life is revealed in the way – mentioned above – in which dependants can claim social security on the strength of workplace contributions made by the head of the household, but it also figures centrally in other aspects of social security policy.

Consider, for example, the way in which means tests characteristically work to assess the family's need for social assistance. The test is not on the means of each individual member but, rather, on the means of the household as a whole. The presumption, obviously, is that households pool all their available resources, at least in times of crisis. Or consider, again, the way in which American authorities used to calculate Aid to Families with Dependent Children (AFDC). For many years, in calculating the amount of aid due to a woman, they would simply assume that any child-support payments which courts have ordered would actually be paid by the absent father, even though defaulting fathers had typically moved outside the jurisdiction of the court in question. Or consider, yet again, the way in which British authorities operate the means-tested grant to students in higher education. They calculate how much each student's parents should be able to afford to pay, and then award the student a grant representing the difference between that amount and the full grant, on the assumption (which is merely an assumption) that the student's parents will actually contribute whatever they have been putatively assessed.

Again, these presumptions are not strictly necessary to the policies in question. If we doubted that husbands shared income equitably with wives (and the evidence suggests that they do not (Edwards, 1981; Piachaud, 1982; Pahl, 1983)), we could assess each on an individual basis rather than all on a family basis for all sorts of purposes – taxes, means-testing of social benefits, and so on. If we doubted that child-support payments are necessarily forthcoming, whatever the courts may order, we could pay the single parent the whole AFDC stipend on condition that she transfer child-support claims to the state, which would then in turn press the claim against the delinquent father.[3] If we doubted that parents would voluntarily pay as much towards their child's education as we think they should, we could pay the child the full grant and collect the putative "parental contribution" through a special tax levied against that child's parents. None of this is impossible, and much of it has already happened to some extent in one place or another. But while no particular presumption is necessary, some presumption or another is again apparently necessary in all such schemes.

Note, finally, a third set of presumptions of a related sort that is built into recent social security reforms instigated by the New Right. Those reforms are couched in terms of catch phrases like "self-reliance," "community care" and "mediating structures." At root, all involve transferring large portions of the state's welfare functions to families, friends and voluntary community charities.[4] And, more often than not, they involve transferring those responsibilities to female care-givers within those groups (Land, 1978). Of course, even the New Right envisages a system of residual, safety-net programs of social assistance to cater for those who excite little sympathy among family, friends or charitable institutions. But these, being residual programs, will – like all safety-nets – be deliberately spare and underfunded. The expectation is that most cases – and, by unspoken implication, almost all "really deserving cases" – will be adequately catered for elsewhere.

Much might be said against such schemes. The questionable morality of imposing upon already overworked and underpaid female care-givers in this way makes such schemes anathema to feminists – and rightly so. But quite apart from all that, there is also the simple empirical question of whether such schemes could possibly hope to work as envisaged, given a society such as ours now is.

Underlying all such schemes for devolving the state's welfare function on to private parties – and for dramatically running down public provision in consequence – is the basic assumption that most people in need actually have someone to whom they can turn In the sociological literature, though, there is much to suggest that social support networks are considerably less dense than they once were. There is a strong suggestion that this trend will continue, with the increasing shift of females (the traditional care-givers) out of the home and into the labor market. In short, recent New Right social welfare reforms presuppose a sociological reality that is rapidly waning and is unlikely to be re-created (d'Abbs, 1982; Blumer, 1987).

My problem, though, is not so much with the particular assumptions currently embodied in these or any other particular social security policies. It is not as if those assumptions were somehow inherent in the very fabric of current social security policy: alterations of various sorts could be – and in many places have been – incorporated into such policies without any undue strain to their fundamental fabric. The point is just that where social policy does incorporate any specific assumptions, we must face the fact that they will inevitably need to be altered in the light of changing social knowledge and changing social circumstances. And those alterations will inevitably lag somewhat behind (and possibly a very long way behind) the changes occasioning them. Hence, policies will inevitably fail to fit social reality for some (possibly considerable) time, insofar as they are predicated in this way on any particular sociological assumptions.

Basic Income as a Minimally Presumptuous Strategy

For all these reasons, it is desirable that our social policies should rely as little as possible upon presumptions. The Basic Income strategy can be commended, against that background, as the minimally presumptuous form of social security policy. It achieves that honour, of course, by also being the least discriminating form of social security policy. Whereas other forms of social security policy attempt to distinguish between more and less deserving categories of claimants, the Basic Income strategy attempts no such distinctions. It simply gives everyone in the society the same Basic Income.

There are, of course, obvious costs and disadvantages to being so indiscriminate in our policy, but there are also advantages. By attempting fewer discriminations, the Basic Income strategy also manages to get by with fewer presumptions. In other more discriminating two-tier social security strategies, it is crucial to specify our categories correctly, and to set the treatment differentials between them correctly. Sociological presumptions which may or may not (now) be empirically warranted enter as we try to establish any such distinctions. An advantage of a policy that attempts no such distinctions – whatever its other disadvantages – is that at least no such precarious presumptions are smuggled into social policy.

Thus, for example, programs of categorical assistance attempting to aid only those who are genuinely unable to work need to draw sharp lines between one sort of disability and another, or one cause of impairment and another. In so doing, those programs make various sociological assumptions – assumptions about the nature of paid work and about what is and is not compatible with performing it in our society. Those assumptions are naturally prone to sociological error and to social change, in the ways described above.

A Basic Income approach runs no such risks. The reason is, quite simply, that it takes no notice of why a person's income is low – or, indeed, of how high or low their income is. Whether a person is unable to work or merely unwilling to do so is of no consequence, in terms of a Basic Income approach to social security. Such an approach merely arranges, without further question, to bring everyone's income at least up to some stipulated social minimum. That example was chosen deliberately. It shows the Basic Income strategy in what would seem to be its worst light – or at least I presume that most people would intuitively scorn a policy that proposed to pay identical social benefits to the severely disabled and to the merely idle. Contrary to our immediate intuitive reactions, however, I now want to argue that this is the right thing to do.

No doubt, if we could get benefits to the deserving and only the deserving, we should do so, but those categories are not themselves clear-cut. The "undeserving" might look a lot more deserving if we took into account alternative forms of socially useful activity (caring for young children or aged relatives, for example) performed outside the labor market. Or, again, we might count as "deserving" all those who would work if they were provided with good jobs at decent wages – thus shifting the onus from unemployed individuals to the society that fails to provide them with decent employment opportunities.[5] And all this, in a way, merely betokens what are truly massive conceptual problems with notions of moral desert – problems which prove particularly vexing in these realm (Goodin, 1988: ch. 10).

Even assuming that the concepts of "deserving" and "undeserving" are clearer than they actually are in these realms, we would face the problem of applying them to particular cases. As discussed above, there is always a serious prospect of sociological error and social change in these matters. Those risks vitiate, in turn, any categorical distinctions with which we might try to capture those two concepts in our policies. The risk of error is always with us, and the question is simply on which side we should prefer to err. Is it more important to deny benefits to the undeserving, even if that means denying them to some of the deserving, too? Or is it more important to make sure that all the deserving get the benefits, even if that means giving them to some of the undeserving, too?

The answer is, of course, sensitive to actual numbers. If getting the benefits to the last dozen deserving cases means giving them to thousands of undeserving cases, we might decide that on balance it is better to deny them to those last few deserving cases. And, conversely, if weeding out the last dozen spongers means denying the benefits to thousands of deserving cases, we might decide that it is on balance better to accept that a few people will get undeserved rewards.[6]

The calculation upon which the case for an indiscriminate Basic Income approach to social security policy rests is just this: the harm done by deserving cases being denied benefits by errors that accompany a more discriminating policy is, it is judged, worse than the harm done by undeserving cases being granted benefits by a less discriminating policy. [. . .] It is judged on balance to be worse to take the chance that errors in categorical social security policies will deny benefits to those who are genuinely unable to work than it is simply to swallow the fact that some idle louts will get a Basic Income they do not deserve. If we put it that way, the repugnant conclusion is surely more appealing.

Notes

1. That is, in at least two out of Esping-Andersen's (1990) "three worlds of welfare capitalism."
2. The American case is well discussed by tenBroek (1954).
3. As is now done under the US Social Security Amendments of 1974. For a discussion, see Mondale, Bentsen and Ribicoff (1974).
4. These proposals from New Right writers like Berger and Neuhaus (1977), Murray (1984) and Novack (1987) won the qualified support even from the OECD (1981). For analyses of how such schemes work in practice, see Johnson (1987, 1990); for an ethical critique, see Goodin (1988: ch. 12).
5. As Claus Offe has usefully reminded me.
6. Goodin (1985). Atkinson (1990) has powerfully extended this analysis, with particular reference to unemployment benefits in the UK.

References

Berger, P.L. and Neuhaus, R.J. (1977). *To Empower People.* American Enterprise Institute, Washington, DC.

Blumer, M. (1987). *The Social Basis of Community Care.* Unwin Hyman, London.

d'Abbs, P. (1982). *Social Support Networks: A Critical Review of Models and Findings.* Institute of Family Studies, Melbourne.

Edwards, M. (1981). *Financial Arrangements within Families.* National Women's Advisory Council, Canberra.

Esping-Anderson, G. (1990). *The Three Worlds of Welfare Capitalism.* Princeton University Press, Princeton, NJ.

Goodin, R.E. (1985). Erring on the Side of Kindness in Social Welfare Policy. *Policy Sciences*, 18, 141–156.

Goodin, R.E. (1988). *Reasons for Welfare.* Princeton University Press, Princeton, NJ.

Johnson, N. (1987). *The Welfare State in Transition: The Theory and Practice of Welfare Pluralism.* Wheatsheaf, Brighton.

Johnson, N. (1990). Problems for the Mixed Economy of Welfare. In A. Ware and R.E. Goodin (eds) *Needs and Welfare.* Sage, London, pp. 145–164

Land, H. (1978). Who Cares for the Family?' *Journal of Social Policy*, 7, 257–284.

Mondale, W.F., Bentsen, L., and Ribicoff, A. (1974). Senate Report Number 93-1356: Social Security Amendments of 1974. *United States Code: Congressional and Administrative News* (93rd Congress, 2nd Session) 4, 8133–8160.

Murray, C.A. (1984). *Losing Ground: American Social Policy, 1950–1980.* Basic Books, New York.

Novack, M. et al. (1987). *The New Consensus on Family and Welfare.* American Enterprise Institute, Washington, DC.

Offe, C. (1992). A Non-productivist Design for Social Policies. In P. Van Parijs (ed.) *Arguing for Basic Income.* Verso, London, pp. 61–78.

Organization for Economic Co-operation and Development (OECD) (1981). *The Welfare State in Crisis.* OECD, Paris.

Pahl, J. (1983). The Allocation of Money and the Structuring of Inequality within Marriage. *Sociological Review*, 31, 237–262.

Palme, J. (1990). Models of Old-Age Pensions. In A. Ware and R.E. Goodin (eds) *Needs and Welfare.* SAGE, London, pp. 104–125.

Piachaud, D. (1982). Patterns of Income and Expenditure Within Families. *Journal of Social Policy*, 11, 469–482.

tenBroek, J. (1954). The Impact of Welfare Law upon Family Law. *California Law Review*, 42, 458–485.

United States Social Security Administration (1978). *Social Security Programs Throughout the World 1977* (Social Security Administration, Office of Research and Statistics, Research Report no, 50). Government Printing Office, Washington, DC.

Chapter 51

The Basic Income Guarantee as an Exit Option

Joel Handler and Amanda Sheely Babcock

Excerpts from Handler, J. and Sheely Babcock, A. (2006). The Failure of Workfare: Another Reason for a Basic Income Guarantee. *Basic Income Studies*, 1 (1).

Faced with sluggish labor markets and growing "compassion fatigue," especially with increasing number of social assistance recipients – unemployed youth, the long-term unemployed, single parents, and, increasingly, immigrants – the "socially excluded," Western Europe has opted for the American model of activation – decentralization, monetary incentives for local governments to reduce rolls, and privatization (called "marketization"). They have not done this with the welfare state for the "insiders". These programs remain national (Van Berkel, 2006).

Both in the US and Western Europe, activation programs pose substantial risks for the most vulnerable. In both the US and Western Europe there are strong tendencies for the bureaucracies, both public and private, to concentrate on those who are most likely to succeed in the paid labor market. The tasks required to help recipients find jobs require professional and individualized service decisions that are not easily monitored. The compliance requirements of offices dominate the professional structure needed to administer work programs. Monitoring focuses on process rather than the quality of the interactions. Those who are excluded run the risk of additional stigmatization. In the Netherlands, Heather Trickey concludes that compulsion has led to an increase in marginalization and exclusion (Trickey, 2001). In an article titled, "Miracle or Nightmare? A Critical Review of Dutch Activation Policies," van Oorschot states, "Clearly, the activation policies of the 1980s and 1990s have not been able to alter existing patterns of exclusion" (van Oorschot, 2002: 416; see also Becker, 2002).

Theoretically, this could be changed. Substantial resources could be directed to local offices. There could be professional training, small caseloads and, most importantly, rewards for helping the most vulnerable. But how likely is this? This almost always never happens. The basic thrust, in both the US and Western Europe, is to move social assistance recipients as quickly as possible into the paid labor market ("work first") and to reduce welfare costs (for social assistance). In both the US and the Netherlands, local governments are rewarded

From Handler, J. and Sheely Babcock, A. (2006). The Basic Income Guarantee as an Exit Option. In The Failure of Workfare: Another Reason for a Basic Income Guarantee. *Basic Income Studies*, 1 (1). Reprinted with kind permission of the authors.

Basic Income: An Anthology of Contemporary Research, First Edition. Edited by Karl Widerquist, José A. Noguera, Yannick Vanderborght, and Jurgen De Wispelaere.

for reducing caseloads. The sad truth is that most commentators on welfare policy, with few notable exceptions, *assume* that complex, difficult, individually based programs can be administered efficiently and fairly. The most absurd idea is the idea of contract. Contract implies at least a rough equality of bargaining, negotiation and taking into account the needs of the recipient. How likely is this with dependent recipients, often with multiple barriers to employment, and caseworkers, both public and private, who are, for the most part undertrained, overworked, and under pressure to get through the caseloads? At the same time, in most countries, the low-wage labor market is quite problematic, While not as bad as in the US, there is unemployment and discrimination in most countries (*Economist*, 2006: 45). In France, Germany, and the Netherlands, the unemployment rates of immigrants are significantly higher than those of the indigenous population.

So, what should be done? The first thing to recognize is that if social assistance and welfare recipients are to successfully enter the labor market, instead of activation, there have to be significant improvements in the labor market. In the US, as stated, it is assumed that if a family is off welfare, everything is fine. Western Europe is much better in addressing poverty, especially child poverty. But activation, except in the most unusual circumstances, will not be successful unless there are decent jobs. At least in the US, it has been demonstrated in the late 1990s, the vast majority of welfare recipients would opt for employment rather than welfare, even low-wage jobs and even though most remained in poverty.

Improving the labor markets is a long, difficult, complex, and expensive process. Many countries in Western Europe have been struggling unsuccessfully to expand employment. In the meantime, there are the poor and the socially excluded. While activation is not going to be of much help, a Basic Income Guarantee would be of considerable help. As many have argued, a Basic Income Guarantee would reduce poverty and improve well-being (Van Parijs, 1992). It will also give clients *an exit option* (Standing, 2002). It would redistribute power in the client-caseworker relationship. Under present arrangements in both the US and Western Europe, caseworkers control the terms of individualized work plans. If clients disagree with the activities they are given, they may lose all benefits. The caseworker is not under any obligation to create a contract that meets the need of clients. As stated by Brodkin (1997: 110), "welfare clients have little capacity to hold the state accountable for providing any specific quality or content of services. Consequently, for welfare recipients, the so-called 'welfare contract' between client and state is virtually unenforceable." If caseworkers no longer had to administer benefits, they could focus on truly creating contracts that met client needs. More importantly, clients would no longer be obligated to take whatever assignments they were given. In this way, a Basic Income Guarantee would redistribute the power in the client-caseworker relationship. Recipients would no longer be subject to the whims of an overtaxed welfare system trying to decide whether recipients have fulfilled the conditions for benefits. Social services, education, training, and employment would still be offered by the state; but now, the caseworkers would have to listen to the clients, assess their individual needs, and make offers attractive enough to encourage clients who have the "real freedom" to decide whether to participate. In other words, caseworkers could concentrate on the functions needed to successfully run a work program, and client could hold them accountable for fulfilling these functions. The US welfare reform is one of decentralization and denial. Western Europe should not be seduced by the US "success." A Basic Income Guarantee would go a long way to reducing poverty, restoring dignity to the poor, and avoiding the false promises of "activation." Implementation issues cannot be ignored.

References

Becker, U. (2000). Welfare State Development and Employment in the Netherlands in Comparative Perspective. *Journal of European and Social Policy*, 10 (3), 219–239.

Brodkin, E. (1997). Inside the Welfare Contract: Discretion and Accountability in State Welfare Administration. *Social Service Review*, 71 (1) 1–33.

The Economist (2006) Squaring the Circle. A Survey of Germany. February 11, 8.

Standing, G. (2002). *Beyond the New Paternalism: Basic Security as Equality*. Verso, London.

Trickey, H. (2001). Comparing Welfare Programmes – Features and Implications. In I. Lødemel and H. Trickey (eds) *An Offer You Can't Refuse: Workfare in International Perspective*. The Policy Press, Bristol.

Van Berkel, R. (2006). The Decentralization of Social Assistance in The Netherlands. *International Journal of Sociology and Social Policy*, 26 (1/2), 20–31.

Van Oorschot, W. (2002). Miracle or Nightmare? A Critical Review of Dutch Activation Policies. *International Social Policy*, 31 (3), 399–420.

Van Parijs, P. (1992). *Arguing for Basic Income. Ethical Foundations for a Radical Reform*. Verso, London.

Chapter 52

Practical Bottlenecks in the Implementation of a Universal Basic Income

Jurgen De Wispelaere and Lindsay Stirton

Excerpts from De Wispelaere, J. and Stirton, L. (2012). A Disarmingly Simple Idea? Practical Bottlenecks in Implementing a Universal Basic Income. *International Social Security Review*, 65 (2), 103–121.

Discussion of Basic Income has concentrated largely on the ethics, economics and, more recently, the politics of universal and unconditional income maintenance schemes. By contrast, little effort has gone into considering implementation issues; an unfortunate state of affairs that we have previously challenged (De Wispelaere and Stirton, 2007; 2011a; 2011b). The reasons for this neglect of implementation issues can, in our view, be attributed to a combination of three factors: an overly restrictive conception of the nature and role of public administration as a "controlling bureaucracy" (Standing, 2002); a comparative focus in which Basic Income easily emerges as the natural winner in comparison with selective social assistance policies; and a conviction that Basic Income is administratively efficient because it does not suffer from the many deficiencies found in selective social assistance programs.

What Basic Income advocates fail to see, however, is that a universal and unconditional scheme leads to a novel set of implementation challenges, or else presents familiar problems in new guises, precisely because of important differences compared to the selective policies commonly associated with the welfare state.[1] More specifically, this chapter argues that Universal Basic Income schemes give rise to three practical "bottlenecks":

- maintaining a population-wide list, or "cadaster," of eligible claimants ensuring full takeup
- instituting robust modalities of payment that reach all intended beneficiaries
- designing an effective oversight mechanism in a policy context that explicitly opposes client monitoring.

From De Wispelaere, J. and Stirton, L. (2012). A Disarmingly Simple Idea? Practical Bottlenecks in Implementing a Universal Basic Income. *International Social Security Review*, 65 (2), 103–121. Blackwell Publishing Ltd, Oxford.

Basic Income: An Anthology of Contemporary Research, First Edition. Edited by Karl Widerquist, José A. Noguera, Yannick Vanderborght, and Jurgen De Wispelaere.

Bottlenecks amount to serious hurdles on the path to the effective implementation of a Basic Income scheme, but this does not mean that such difficulties are beyond resolution. Quite on the contrary, each bottleneck may well give rise to several practical solutions, but these are neither obvious nor without cost, and require careful examination before committing to any one of them (De Wispelaere and Stirton, 2011b). Moreover, the way we dispose of any one of these bottlenecks has implications in terms of the feasibility and desirability of potential solutions to the others. In short, we view the three bottlenecks examined in this chapter as implementation challenges that must be jointly fulfilled for Basic Income to become policy reality: they are necessary conditions, not to be dismissed lightly by Basic Income advocates.

Many welfare policies suffer from the problem of under-consumption, or non-takeup as it is often referred to in the literature (Craig, 1991). While easily dismissed as a matter of (rational) personal choice, from a policy perspective the widespread non-takeup of entitlements to social assistance in fact amounts to a serious case of policy failure, reflecting ineffectiveness as well as injustice (van Oorschot, 1991; 1998; 2002). Poor takeup rates are typically associated with selective social assistance policies because of the complex interactions between clients and bureaucracies attempting to negotiate a labyrinthine set of rules. Key factors affecting takeup rates include knowledge, stigma, and perceptions of eligibility or need on the client side, but equally a number of crucial factors associated with a scheme's structure and its administration (van Oorschot, 1991; 1998). Reviewing the state of affairs, van Oorschot (1991: 20) concludes that non-takeup is more likely to occur when schemes

- have a "density" of rules and guidelines
- contain complex rules
- contain vague criteria of entitlement
- contain a means test
- are aimed at groups in society which are associated with negative prejudices
- supplement other sources of income
- leave the initiative to start the claiming process fully to the claimants themselves.

Selective social assistance schemes typically fit this description, with means-testing in particular having been identified as a dysfunctional policy mechanism (van Oorschot, 2002; Atkinson, 1996). But a certain threshold of non-takeup may be inherent to selective schemes for yet another reason: there are limits to how far (and how fast) bureaucratic processes and routines can accommodate constantly and rapidly changing personal and social circumstances (Goodin, 1992). For some commentators, the traditional pillars of the selective welfare state – market, state and community or family – are quite literally crumbling (Goodin, 2002; also Goodin and Rein, 2001; Offe, 2008).

Basic Income claims to offer a "universal antidote" to the difficulties of selective income support, and thereby potentially offer governments a means of delivering on the evident yet hard-to-fulfill commitment to reducing the complexity of the benefits system (see Harris, 2008). There is no denying that Basic Income schemes, by virtue of being unconditional as well as universal, bypass many of the concerns raised above, and are able to outperform selective schemes in this regard. According to Robert Goodin (1992), this is largely so because Basic Income operates with fewer policy presumptions than selective social assistance schemes. Basic Income proposals are "less presumptuous" in two relevant senses:

> They are less presumptuous . . . [because they are] . . . less prying and intrusive, and in consequence less demeaning and debasing. They are also less presumptuous in the sense that they make fewer presumptions: they assume less about the people to whom they are aiding. (Goodin, 1992: 195).

Basic Income is said to be more universal, not merely in the sense of embracing a larger share of the total population (i.e. almost all citizens), but also in terms of effectively capturing a larger share of the target population. Proponents thus proclaim the superior "target efficiency" of a Universal Basic Income. The question remains, however, whether a Basic Income scheme indeed leads to full takeup, or whether there might be other obstacles impeding its target efficiency? Our view, in brief, is that Basic Income indeed faces a number of difficulties (the "bottlenecks" we refer to in the introduction) that may prevent it from achieving the universal reach both desired and proclaimed by its advocates. The purpose of this chapter is to survey a selective few and outline their role in Basic Income implementation.

At this point we should stress the importance of target efficiency for the Basic Income ideal.[2] Non-universal takeup constitutes a genuine problem for Basic Income, much more so than for selective schemes. We can illustrate this point by considering briefly how Basic Income is committed to safeguarding "substantive" (or "effective") and not merely "nominal" universalism (De Wispelaere and Stirton, 2011a). Basic Income is nominally universal when it does not impose any overt restrictions on eligibility, such that each citizen is in principle entitled to a grant. But this does not in itself ensure that every citizen ends up receiving a Basic Income, and in many cases those most at risk of falling through the proverbial cracks are the poor, the destitute and the socially excluded – precisely those who merit special attention in a progressive Basic Income (Van Parijs, 1992; 1995; 2004; Standing, 1999; 2002; Wright, 2004; 2006; Raventós, 2007; Offe, 2008). Ensuring that all citizens – particularly all the vulnerable and disadvantaged – effectively receive their entitlement to a Basic Income is what makes a scheme substantively universal. The philosophical justification of a progressive Basic Income scheme implies that takeup must be genuinely universal; from this perspective, nominal universalism risks becoming a mere "token policy." Practically, substantive universalism constitutes a much more demanding requirement, since, as we have previously argued, "providing a Universal Basic Income that robustly includes vulnerable and hard-to-reach social groups such as the homeless, disabled people, immigrants and many others requires positive administrative effort, not just the removal of barriers to eligibility" (De Wispelaere and Stirton, 2011a: 118).[3]

Two broad concerns now arise when contemplating the practical implementation of a substantively Universal Basic Income. First, precisely because Basic Income is universal, it comprises a target population that in sheer size easily surpasses familiar large-scale selective policies. Compared to most social assistance programs, this places Basic Income in a unique position: even a very small relative non-takeup rate may affect a sizeable absolute number of entitled individuals. This size or scale effect implies that we should not stare ourselves blind at the relative takeup rates of universal programs (in comparison with their selective counterparts), but instead appreciate the human cost involved in terms of sheer numbers of individuals affected by non-universal takeup. Second, being universal as well as unconditional means Basic Income, at best, partially overlaps with existing administrative systems or operational mechanisms that make up the traditional, selective welfare state. This may make it particularly difficult to piggyback on existing systems, the way selective policies are often able to. In each case the universal nature of Basic Income requires careful consideration of its "administrability" (its ability to be implemented congruent with stated or implied objectives), which in turn is highly dependent on the administrative capabilities of the policy environment. In our view, such an analysis requires close examination of several practical bottlenecks.

The first bottleneck facing the implementation of a Basic Income relates to one of the central tasks of welfare administration: to identify those within the population who meet eligibility criteria for a grant, and to distinguish them from those not so entitled. This administrative task consists of two components that are often wrongly assumed to produce identical outcomes. Looked at from one side, identifying beneficiaries is largely a matter of preventing those who are not eligible from entering a program, often at great cost to those included as well as to those excluded (Danz, 2000; Herd, Mitchell and Lightman, 2005). In other words, so-called programs of inclusion necessarily also exclude (Handler, 2003; 2004). Basic Income advocates maintain that the establishment of a universal and unconditional scheme eliminates the task of excluding non-beneficiaries, and consequently Basic Income happily does away with the bureaucratic control apparatus geared at monitoring the compliance of beneficiaries. However, eliminating restrictions does not itself solve the problem of identifying all those eligible.

Second, much of the discussion surrounding the inclusive nature of a Universal Basic Income is devoted to the "claiming stage," in particular the absence of any personal or bureaucratic barriers to claiming one's entitlement. However, when looked at from the practical perspective of rolling out a policy, this covers only part of the implementation process. At least as important is to ensure that each eligible person effectively receives the grant to which she or he is entitled. Here, again, the implementation of a Basic Income faces an important bottleneck that merits explicit examination: the specific modalities through which Basic Income will be disbursed (see De Wispelaere and Stirton, 2011b).

A radically universal scheme such as a Basic Income imposes increased pressure on existing implementation channels or systems. The concerns with building a robust cadaster of all eligible individuals and offering effective universal payment modalities both point at the operational difficulties of offering income security at the vast scale of a truly universal policy. The size or scale effect of Basic Income implies we need to rethink the operational or practical dimension of providing income support to the population at large. Equally, these bottlenecks offer a critical perspective on the argument that Basic Income easily bypasses situational specifics of diverse groups of claimants; *pace* Goodin's (1992) claims about the "less presumptuous" nature of Basic Income. Reflection about practicalities suggests that complexity returns at the level of implementation, a reality that Basic Income advocates must deal with head-on to retain their strong commitment to substantive universalism.

Let us now address a different type of bottleneck, one which arises from the common observation that the implementation of large-scale social programs – including a Basic Income – is typically less-than-perfect. In both cases discussed above, imperfect implementation results in some level of non-takeup, particularly amongst the most vulnerable or disadvantaged in society.[4] This suggests the need for a robust oversight mechanism, an administrative process by which those who fail to receive their Basic Income are identified, the error is swiftly rectified, and a feedback mechanism prevents the same error from occurring again. However, as we show in this section, oversight constitutes a third bottleneck, one that is little appreciated by Basic Income advocates predominantly concerned with avoiding client monitoring (see Standing, 2002; also Handler, 2004; Handler and Hasenfeld, 2006).

As before, we believe the inclination of Basic Income advocates to rely on the mere removal of barriers as the main pathway to achieving substantive universalism is flawed: it fails to appreciate the extent of error that is part and parcel of implementation systems. There are two reasons to think Basic Income faces considerable difficulties regarding oversight. On the one hand, we again have the problem of scale: monitoring the effective disbursement of a grant scheme that encompasses the whole population requires considerable administrative capacity and effort. Paradoxically, in this respect universal schemes may require more administrative effort than selective ones (De Wispelaere and Stirton, 2011a). On the other hand, because Basic Income does not imply repeated monitoring of eligibility conditions – the much-reviled client monitoring – it has lost an important instrument to cross-check whether payments are effectively received by beneficiaries (Hood, 1986: 78–79; 1985: 24–25).

Consider for a moment, by way of contrast, the oversight capability of a workfare program (see De Wispelaere and Stirton, 2007). First, workfare approaches, far from dispensing with oversight, rely on extensive intervention from caseworkers. This face-to-face oversight through a variety of "bureaucratic encounters" (see Hasenfeld, Rafferty and Zald, 1987) offers an immediate channel for cross-checking actual receipt of benefits, provided the caseworkers' role is not restricted to that of a budgetary gatekeeper. Since Basic Income schemes purposefully restrict client interaction with caseworkers, they cannot avail themselves of this mechanism. A second potential advantage of workfare is that the focus on training and formal employment provides a host of institutionally embedded oversight mechanisms, such as payroll systems, that allow for effective cross-checking in so far as the necessary administrative resources are kept in place. Such mechanisms enable workfare administrators to monitor the delivery of payment systems; again, an option not readily available to Basic Income administration. The points above are not meant to argue the case for workfare, but merely to illustrate the particular oversight bottleneck that Basic Income implementation faces.

The public administration literature distinguishes usefully between "police patrol" and "fire alarm" oversight mechanisms (McCubbins and Schwartz, 1984; Lupia and McCubbins, 1994). Where police patrol oversight is centralized and offers a direct approach to obtaining relevant information (e.g. through audits), fire alarm oversight establishes "a system of rules, procedures, and informal practices that enable [third parties] to examine administrative decisions [and] to seek remedies" (McCubbins and Schwartz, 1984: 166). The lack of institutionally-embedded mechanisms discussed in the previous paragraph affects a police patrol type of oversight, making it more difficult for Basic Income administrators to identify false negatives (in either cadasters or payment conduits), and possibly even responding less efficiently in rectifying the situation once such failure is identified.

This of course leaves Basic Income implementation with the possibility of a fire alarm type of oversight. At first sight this seems a promising avenue. The fact that Basic Income does not require clients to submit to any intrusive type of bureaucratic evaluation, but merely to lodge a complaint that they have not received their entitlement, certainly bodes well for increased self-regulation on behalf of clients. Nevertheless, here too we should perhaps give some thought to several considerations.

First, clients will only respond "efficiently" if they fully trust administrators not to use information for other purposes. However, it may be tempting for bureaucracies to use available client information to complement information deficits across separate policy areas, with little consideration of what clients want in this regard. Here we must appreciate the variability in experience and sensitivity of populations in different countries. Belgian citizens, accustomed to featuring in all sorts of official registers are likely to respond quite pragmatically to requests to self-register, while United Kingdom citizens' more sceptical attitudes towards official information-gathering may lead them to respond differently, even where failure to register is penalized. The efficiency of a fire alarm oversight mechanism depends critically on background conditions – such as the level of public trust in politics or bureaucracy – which vary from one case to another, making it difficult to generalize its usefulness across countries.

Second, fire alarm oversight still requires claimants to obtain relevant information and to go through the process of lodging a complaint. Even supposedly user-friendly approaches may prove too much for many recipients who may be already socially disadvantaged, such as the homeless. The solution of using technology to facilitate administrative complaints, in which many Basic Income proponents place their faith, may again exclude precisely this target group. Hood and Margetts (2007) caution against the belief that modern information technology offers a "technological fix" to the perennial challenges of administration. "Such a change [to the digital era] does not mean that new policy problems have appeared or old ones disappeared. Rather, they present themselves in new ways" (Hood and Margetts, 2007: 14). Failure to appreciate novel forms of information exclusion easily leads to a variant of the "restrictions fallacy" according to which getting rid of explicit barriers in itself ensures full access.

Third, assessing and addressing complaints requires significant administrative processing that inevitably results in time lags and backlogs, triggering difficulties similar to those discussed in relation to payment modalities. To reiterate a point made earlier, to signal that one is not on a particular list or has not received one's entitlement is only the start of a "processing chain" resulting in rectifying an error (and, ideally, preventing its future occurrence). Signalling by fire alarm is a necessary condition for efficient oversight, but it is not sufficient. Of course, similar processing problems occur in police patrol types of oversight, but the longer the chain the more points at which the process can break down. Where police patrol oversight proceeds internally, fire alarm oversight instead "externalizes" part of the process by requiring individual clients to interface effectively with administrators.

Finally, moving away from a police patrol to a fire alarm oversight mechanism means shifting part of the administration of a Basic Income scheme onto the recipient. In contrast with police patrol monitoring, recipients end up bearing all the relevant inconveniences – investments in time and effort, experience of fustration, and even delay of payment – as well as some burdens of intrusion in so far as complaints require bureaucratic checking to confirm their veracity. Where police patrol oversight implicitly entails monitoring, a fire alarm type of oversight consists of two different processes: the signalling procedure initiated by the recipient and the explicit monitoring of the veracity of the complaint by administrators. The second step reintroduces the much vilified "controlling bureaucracy." Furthermore, effective oversight depends in large part on the solutions adopted to remedy previous bottlenecks. For instance, the administrative burden of oversight will correlate with the existence of robust cadasters or limited numbers of payment modalities, as the latter affect both the expected size of error (i.e. number of complaints) and the available instruments to monitor and correct error. Somewhat paradoxically, this means fire alarm oversight functions most effectively in cases of low or moderate error, while the situations where oversight is most valuable (because error is more common) defy the easy administration of fire alarm monitoring and require the more costly and burdensome police patrol type of monitoring.

Solutions to this third bottleneck may well exist, but again a commitment to substantive universalism requires Basic Income advocates to carefully think through this aspect of its implementation.

Conclusion

The existence of such bottlenecks does not invalidate the general case for Basic Income, but they give Basic Income advocates reasons to consider issues of implementation and administration more carefully. Insofar as Basic Income is committed to granting all citizens a Basic Income entitlement by right, it is also committed to ensuring all effectively receive their entitlement. This philosophical commitment to substantive universalism has obvious practical connotations that require taking the bottlenecks outlined above seriously.

Notes

1. The bottlenecks we examine below are concerns that arise particularly for the most radical form of a Basic Income as advocated by Philippe Van Parijs (1992; 1995; 1996; 2004). Elsewhere, we argue that the basic income ideal constitutes a family of cognate proposals (De Wispelaere and Stirton, 2004), and that less radical cognates face their own set of problems (De Wispelaere and Stirton, 2007; 2011a).
2. Strictly speaking, this is only true for a progressive Basic Income. Conservative variants (see Murray, 2006) could relax this condition, but in this article we restrict ourselves to the more familiar progressive proposals.
3. De Wispelaere and Stirton (2011a; 2011b) argue that devoting considerable administrative resources to ensuring the worst-off obtain their Basic Income affects the administrative efficiency of Basic Income, at least when understood as saving on the use of bureaucratic resources (budget, time, effort, operational capabilities, etc.) typically in short supply.
4. It might also result in "false positives," by paying a Basic Income to some who are not entitled or some entitled claimants more than once. We abstract from this concern here, although advocates should not underestimate the importance of avoiding false positives for the political resilience of Basic Income.

References

Atkinson, A.B. (1996). *Incomes and the Welfare State.* Cambridge University Press, Cambridge.

Craig, P. (1991). Costs and benefits: A review of research on take-up of income-related benefits. *Journal of Social Policy*, 20 (4).

Danz, S.M. (2000). A nonpublic forum or a brutal bureaucracy? Advocates' claims of access to welfare center waiting rooms. *New York University Law Review*, 75 (4).

De Wispelaere, J. and Stirton, L. (2004). The many faces of universal basic income. *The Political Quarterly*, 75 (3).

De Wispelaere, J. and Stirton, L. (2007). The public administration case against participation income. *Social Services Review*, 81 (3).

De Wispelaere, J. and Stirton, L. (2011a). The administrative efficiency of basic income. *Policy and Politics*, 39 (1).

De Wispelaere, J. and Stirton, L. (2011b). The basic income guarantee: Reconsidering the administrative factor. Conference paper, 61st PSA Congress, London, 19–21 April. Political Studies Association, Newcastle-upon-Tyne.

Goodin R.E. (1992). Towards a minimally presumptuous social welfare policy. In P. Van Parijs (ed.) *Arguing for Basic Income: Ethical Foundations for a Radical Reform*. Verso, London.

Goodin, R.E. (2002). Crumbling pillars: Social security futures. *The Political Quarterly*, 71 (2).

Goodin, R.E. and Rein, M. (2001). Regimes on pillars: Alternative welfare state logics and dynamics. *Public Administration*, 79 (4).

Handler, J.F. (2003). Social citizenship and workfare in the US and Western Europe: From status to contract. *Journal of European Social Policy*, 13 (3).

Handler, J.F. (2004). *Social Citizenship and Workfare in the United States and Western Europe: The Paradox of Inclusion*. Cambridge University Press, Cambridge.

Handler, J.F. and Hasenfeld, Y. (2006). *Blame Welfare, Ignore Poverty and Inequality*. Cambridge University Press, Cambridge.

Harris, N. (2008). Simplification of social security: The international experience. *Journal of Social Security Law*, 15 (1).

Hasenfeld, Y., Rafferty, J.A., and Zald, M.N. (1987). The welfare state, citizenship, and bureaucratic encounters. *Annual Review of Sociology*, 13.

Herd, D., Mitchell, A., and Lightman, E. (2005). Rituals of degradation: Administration as policy in the Ontario works programme. *Social Policy and Administration*, 39 (1).

Hood, C. (1985). British tax structure development as administrative adaptation. *Policy Sciences*, 18 (1).

Hood, C. (1986). *Administrative Analysis: An Introduction to Rules, Enforcement, and Organizations*. Wheatsheaf, Brighton.

Hood, C. and Margetts, H. (2007). *The Tools of Government in the Digital Age*. Palgrave Macmillan, London.

Lupia, A. and McCubbins, M. (1994). Learning from oversights: Fire alarms and police patrols reconstructed. *Journal of Law, Economics and Organization*, 10 (1).

McCubbins, M. and Schwartz, T. (1984). Congressional oversight overlooked: Police patrols versus fire alarms. *American Journal of Political Science*, 28 (1).

Murray, C. (2006). *In Our Hands: A Plan to Replace the Welfare State*. AEI Press, Washington, DC.

Offe, C. (2008). Basic income and the labor contract. *Basic Income Studies*, 3 (1).

Oorschot, W. van. (1991). Non-take-up of social security benefits in Europe. *Journal of European Social Policy*, 1 (1).

Oorschot, W. van. (1998). Failing selectivity: On the extent and causes of non-take-up of social security benefits. In H.-J. Andreß (ed.) *Empirical Poverty Research in a Comparative Perspective*. Ashgate, Aldershot.

Oorschot, W. van. (2002). Targeting welfare: On the functions and dysfunctions of meanstesting in social policy. In P. Townsend and D. Gordon (eds) *World Poverty: New Policies to Defeat an Old Enemy*. The Policy Press, Bristol.

Raventós, D. (2007). *Basic Income: The Material Conditions of Freedom*. Pluto Press, London.

Standing, G. (1999). *Global Labour Flexibility: Seeking Distributive Justice*. Palgrave, Basingstoke.

Standing, G. (2002). *Beyond the New Paternalism: Basic Security as Equality*. Verso, London.

Van Parijs, P. (1992). Competing justification for unconditional basic income. In P. Van Parijs (ed.) *Arguing for Basic Income: Ethical Foundations for a Radical Reform*. Verso, London.

Van Parijs, P. (1995). *Real Freedom for All: What (If Anything) Can Justify Capitalism?* Clarendon, Oxford.

Van Parijs, P. (1996). Basic income and the two dilemmas of the welfare state. *The Political Quarterly*, 67 (1).
Van Parijs, P. (2004). Basic income: A simple and powerful idea for the twenty-first century. *Politics and Society*, 32 (1).
Wright, E.O. (2004). Basic income, stakeholder grants, and class analysis. *Politics and Society*, 32 (1).
Wright, E.O. (2006). Basic income as a socialist project. *Basic Income Studies*, 1 (1).

Part VIII
Institutions

Introduction

Institutional Versions and Cognates of Basic Income

José A. Noguera

There is a relatively wide consensus on the "standard" definition of Basic Income: an income paid to every individual in a given political community, without means-test or work requirement. However, it is also true that most Basic Income advocates adopt a more flexible stance when discussing the concrete institutional design that a Basic Income scheme should have, and the different shapes this scheme may take in specific social and political contexts and circumstances. In fact, the literature on Basic Income is full of nuances and pragmatic proposals in order to get the ideal closer to reality. As De Wispelaere and Stirton (2004) have suggested, there are "many faces" that a non-ideal Basic Income program may show. What are these different "faces?" What are their pros and cons when compared with an "ideal" model of Basic Income? Do they all really qualify as versions or "cognates" of the "standard" proposal? Do they really foster the socio-political and economic feasibility of a Basic Income? Should one focus on the differences between them or on their common features?

The texts included in this section give an overview of different policy proposals that are often presented as "friendly" alternatives to (or "realistic" versions of) Basic Income in its "pure" form. Some of them are conceived as steps in the direction of the final goal. Some others are meant to avoid some feasibility problems that Basic Income supposedly faces. Still others try to make the idea of Basic Income acceptable for some sensibilities or to avoid some widespread normative objections. Finally, some proposals are just context-sensitive versions of Basic Income that aim to adapt it to different circumstances.

For instance, Thomas Pogge's (2001) proposal for a Global Resources Dividend (GRD) is a likely basis on which to build, both normatively and institutionally, a worldwide Global Basic Income. In a similar fashion, Philippe Van Parijs and Yannick Vanderborght (2001) strongly argue in favor of a Euro-Dividend, that is, a Basic Income at the level of the European Union. This proposal, according to the authors, would enhance supra-national citizenship in the European Union while avoiding the main shortcomings of conditional transfers and fragmented social benefit schemes at the level of the member-states (the chapter is a response to a previous proposal for a means-tested Euro-Stipendium by P.C. Schmitter and M. W. Bauer, 2001).

Basic Income: An Anthology of Contemporary Research, First Edition. Edited by Karl Widerquist, José A. Noguera, Yannick Vanderborght, and Jurgen De Wispelaere.

The most well-known income guarantee policy which is often presented as a version of Basic Income is the Negative Income Tax (NIT). In his seminal contribution, Milton Friedman (1962) introduced the idea in a very simple fashion, as an efficient means to tackle poverty while avoiding what he considered to be the shortcomings of traditional welfare policies. A most recent and developed NIT proposal for the United States is defended by Fred Block and Jeff Manza (1997), who quantify the proposal in detail and explain how it would solve the main dilemmas faced by anti-poverty policy.

Another version of a Basic Income is Basic Capital (also known as a Capital Grant or a Stakeholder Grant): it consists in paying a considerable amount of capital to every citizen once he reaches adulthood. In "Stakeholding versus Basic Income" (2004), Bruce Ackerman and Anne Alstott make a compelling defence of capital grants vs. a Basic Income. They do it from a liberal point of view which focuses on values such as individual autonomy and anti-paternalism.

An important group of universal or almost-universal income guarantee proposals aims to be reciprocity-sensitive, so they endorse some "soft" or very flexible work conditionality, even taking into account unpaid work or training as a possible basis to qualify for benefits. Stuart White (2003) gives a good account of two of these proposals: what he calls "Development Grant" (a moderate Capital Grant to be spent only in a list of previously approved activities) and the "time-limited Basic Income" (a Basic Income restricted to some years in an individual's lifetime). White argues that the reasons to support such policies instead of a pure Basic Income are based on political feasibility as much as normative grounds.

A.B. Atkinson's (1996) original idea of a Participation Income was presented for the first time in the text included in this section. He contends that Participation Income would avoid reciprocity-based objections, since the benefit would be conditional to the performance of some previously defined socially useful activity (be it paid or unpaid). However, in one of the few detailed critiques of the proposal, Jurgen De Wispelaere and Lindsay Stirton (2007) show how this advantage may be more than counterbalanced by the "administrative nightmare" that a Participation Income program would have to face in order to determine who is eligible for the benefit without becoming a *de facto* Basic Income or a more stringent workfare scheme.

The case for a Sabbatical Grant scheme is consistently made by Claus Offe and Johan de Deken (1999). Departing from the analysis of already existing (and generous) parental leave programs in some European countries, the authors discuss the political and economic implications of extending those programs towards a generalized Sabbatical Grant, by which all citizens could spend some part of their lifetime out of the labor market while receiving a benefit.

A special case of reciprocity-sensitive cash benefits are tax credits schemes, such as those already existing in the United States, the United Kingdom, or France. Those programs are designed in order to top up the wages of low paid workers, thus "making work pay." Under some versions, they can get very close to a Negative Income Tax. In "A Uniform Refundable Tax Credit," Lily Batchelder, Fred T. Goldberg Jr. and Peter R. Orszag (2007), defend the transformation of all present tax incentives into a universal uniform tax credit, and consider some of the possible objections to that reform.

An essential difference between Basic Income and conventional social benefits is that it would be paid on a strictly individual basis. However, in "A Household Basic Income," Rafael Pinilla and Luis Sanzo (2004) show the advantages of a combined household-individual Basic Income: each individual ***and*** each household would receive a Basic Income, such that an individual living alone would globally get a "full" Basic Income. This proposal, the authors argue, would take into account income equivalence scales among different households' sizes, would not discriminate against those who live alone, and would lower considerably the cost of a Basic Income program.

Finally, in "A COAG vs. a COG" (2004), Guy Standing introduces another different form of capital grant: Community Capital Grant, understood as a democratic and egalitarian form of capital-sharing similar to workers' funds. Contrary to individualized payments such as Basic Income or individual Capital Grants, a Community Capital Grant would, according to Standing, promote social values such as sharing, redistribution, democracy and participation.

In sum, there are many institutional ways of approaching the idea of a Basic Income, and many policy options once the decision has been made of implementing a Basic Income Guarantee. It is an open question whether this diversity of proposals is useful to enhance the political and economic feasibility of Basic Income, or, on the contrary, may lead to casting a shadow on the potential of the idea.

References

De Wispelaere, J. and Stirton, L. (2004). The Many Faces of Universal Basic Income. *The Political Quarterly*, 75 (3), 266–274.

Schmitter, P. and Bauer, M.W. (2001). A (modest) proposal for expanding social citizenship in the European Union. *Journal of European Social Policy*, 11 (1), 55–65.

Further Reading

Bergmann, B. (2006). A Swedish-style welfare state or a basic income: which should have priority? In E.O. Wright (ed.) *Redesigning Distribution: Basic Income and Stakeholder Grants as Cornerstones for an Egalitarian Capitalism*. Verso, London, pp. 130–142.

Carter, I. (2011). Distributing freedom over whole lives. In A. Gosseries and Y. Vanderborght (eds) *Arguing about Justice. Essays for Philippe Van Parijs*. Presses universitaires de Louvain, Louvain-la-Neuve, pp. 135–143.

De Wispelaere, J. and Stirton, L. (2004). The many faces of universal basic income. *The Political Quarterly*, 75 (3), 266–274.

Dowding, K., De Wispelaere, J., and White, S. (eds) (2003). *The Ethics of Stakeholding*. Palgrave Macmillan, Basingstoke.

Eyal, N. (2010). Near-universal basic income. *Basic Income Studies* 5 (1), Article 5. http://www.degruyter.com/view/j/bis

Goldsmith, S. (2005). The Alaska Permanent Fund: An experiment in wealth distribution. In G. Standing (ed.) *Promoting Income Security as a Right: Europe and North America*. Anthem, London, pp. 553–566.

Goodin, R.E. (2000). Crumbling pillars: Social security futures. *The Political Quarterly*, 71 (2), 144–150.

Goodin, R.E. (2003). Sneaking Up on Stakeholding. In K. Dowding, J. De Wispelaere, and S. White (eds) *The Ethics of Stakeholding*. Palgrave Macmillan, Basingstoke, pp. 65–78.

Griffin Jr., C.L. (2012). Stakeholding through the Permanent Fund Dividend: Fitting Practice to Theory. In K. Widerquist and M.W. Howard (eds) *Alaska's Permanent Fund Dividend: Examining its Suitability as a Model*. Palgrave Macmillan, New York.

Groot, L. and van der Veen, R. (2000). How attractive is a basic income for European welfare states? In R. van der Veen and L. Groot (eds) *Basic Income on the Agenda. Policy Objectives and Political Chances.* Amsterdam University Press, Amsterdam, pp. 13–38.

Haagh, L. (2011). Basic income, social democracy and control over time. *Policy and Politics*, 39 (1), 43–66.

Harvey, P.L. (2006). The relative cost of a universal basic income and a negative income tax. *Basic Income Studies*, 1 (2), Article 6. http://www.degruyter.com/view/j/bis

Haveman, R. (1996). Reducing poverty while increasing employment: A primer on alternative strategies, and a blueprint. *OECD Economic Studies*, 26, 7–42.

Howard, M.W. (2012). A Cap on Carbon and a Basic Income: A Defensible Combination in the United States? In K. Widerquist and M.W. Howard (eds) *Alaska's Permanent Fund Dividend: Examining its Suitability as a Model.* Palgrave Macmillan, New York.

Howard, M.W. and Widerquist, K. (2012). Why Link Basic Income to Resource Taxation? In K. Widerquist and M.W. Howard (eds) *Alaska's Permanent Fund Dividend: Examining its Suitability as a Model.* Palgrave Macmillan, New York.

Le Grand, J. and Nissan, D. (2003). A capital idea: Helping the young to help themselves. In K. Dowding, J. De Wispelaere, and S. White (eds) *The Ethics of Stakeholding.* Palgrave Macmillan, Basingstoke, pp. 29–41.

Moffitt, R.A. (2003). The Negative Income Tax and the evolution of U.S. welfare policy. *Journal of Economic Perspectives*, 17 (3), 119–140.

Offe, C. (1997). Towards a new equilibrium of citizens' rights and economic resources. In OECD (ed.) *Societal Cohesion and the Globalising Economy: What Does the Future Hold?* OECD, Paris.

Petersen, H.-G. (1997). Pros and Cons of a Negative Income Tax. In H. Giersch (ed.) *Reforming the Welfare State.* Springer, Berlin, pp. 53–82.

Segal, P. (2012). Alaska's Permanent Fund Dividend as a Model for Reducing Global Poverty. In K. Widerquist and M.W. Howard (eds) *Exporting the Alaska Model: Adapting the Permanent Fund Dividend.* Palgrave Macmillan, New York.

Tobin, J., Pechman, J.A., and Mieszkowski, P.M. (1967). Is a Negative Income Tax Practical? *The Yale Law Journal*, 77 (1), 1–27.

van der Veen, R. (2003). Assessing the Unconditional Stake. In K. Dowding, J. De Wispelaere, and S. White (eds) *The Ethics of Stakeholding.* Palgrave Macmillan, Basingstoke.

Van Parijs, P., Jacquet, L., and Salinas, C.C. (2000). Basic income and its cognates. In L. Groot and R. van der Veen (eds) *Basic Income on the Agenda. Policy Objectives and Political Chances.* Amsterdam University Press, Amsterdam, pp. 53–84.

White, S. (2003). *The Civic Minimum: On the Rights and Obligations of Economic Citizenship.* Oxford University Press, Oxford.

White, S. (2011). Basic income versus basic capital: can we resolve the disagreement? *Policy and Politics*, 39 (1), 67–81.

Widerquist, K. (2012). Citizens' Capital Accounts: A Proposal. In K. Widerquist and M.W. Howard (eds) *Exporting the Alaska Model: Adapting the Permanent Fund Dividend.* Palgrave Macmillan, New York.

Widerquist, K. and Howard, M.W. (eds) (2012a). *Alaska's Permanent Fund Dividend: Examining its Suitability as a Model.* Palgrave Macmillan, New York.

Widerquist, K. and Howard, M.W. (eds) (2012b). *Exporting the Alaska Model: Adapting the Permanent Fund Dividend.* Palgrave Macmillan, New York.

Wright, E.O. (2000). Reducing income and wealth inequality: Real utopian proposals. *Contemporary Sociology*, 29 (1), 143–156.

Wright, E.O. (ed.) (2006). *Redesigning Distribution: Basic Income and Stakeholder Grants as Cornerstones for an Egalitarian Capitalism.* Verso, London.

Chapter 53
A Global Resources Dividend

Thomas W. Pogge

Originally published as Pogge, T.W. (2001). Eradicating Systemic Poverty: brief for a global resources dividend. *Journal of Human Development and Capabilities*, 2 (1), 59–77.

> Article 25: Everyone has the right to a standard of living adequate for the health and well-being of himself and of his family, including food, clothing, housing and medical care.
> Article 28: Everyone is entitled to a social and international order in which the rights and freedoms set forth in this Declaration can be fully realized.
>
> (Universal Declaration of Human Rights)

In two earlier essays (Pogge, 1994, 1998a), I have sketched and defended the proposal of a global resources dividend. This proposal was meant to show that there are feasible alternative ways of organizing our global economic order, that the choice among these alternatives makes a substantial difference to how much severe poverty there is worldwide, and that there are weighty moral reasons to make this choice so as to minimize such poverty. My proposal has evoked some critical responses (Kesselring, 1997; Reichel, 1997; Crisp and Jamieson, 2000) and spirited defenses (Kreide, 1998; Mandle, 2000) in the academy. But if it is to help reduce severe poverty, the proposal must be convincing not only to academics, but also to the people in governments and international organizations who are practically involved in poverty eradication efforts. I am most grateful therefore for the opportunity to present a concise and improved version of the argument in this journal.

Introduction: Radical Inequality and Our Responsibility

One great challenge to any morally sensitive person today is the extent and severity of global poverty. Among six billion human beings, 790 million lack adequate nutrition, one billion lack access to safe water, 2.4 billion lack basic sanitation (United Nations Development Programme, 2000: 30), more than 880 million lack access to basic health services (United

Pogge, T.W. (2001). Eradicating Systemic Poverty: brief for a global resources dividend. *Journal of Human Development and Capabilities*, 2 (1), 59–77. Reprinted with permission of Taylor & Francis.

Basic Income: An Anthology of Contemporary Research, First Edition. Edited by Karl Widerquist, José A. Noguera, Yannick Vanderborght, and Jurgen De Wispelaere.

Nations Development Programme, 1999: 22), one billion are without adequate shelter, and two billion without electricity (United Nations Development Programme, 1998: 49). Two hundred and fifty million children aged between 5 and 14 do wage work outside their household – often under harsh or cruel conditions: as soldiers, prostitutes, or domestic servants, or in agriculture, construction, textile or carpet production (World Bank, 2000: 62). About one billion adults are illiterate (United Nations Development Programme, 2000: 30). Roughly one-third of all human deaths, some 50,000 daily, are due to poverty-related causes and thus avoidable insofar as poverty is avoidable (UNICEF, 1999; World Health Organization, 2000). If the US had its proportional share of these deaths, poverty would kill some 820,000 of its citizens per year – more each month than were killed during the entire Vietnam War.

There are two ways of conceiving global poverty as a moral challenge to us. We may be failing to fulfill our *positive* duty to help persons in acute distress. And we may be failing to fulfill our more stringent *negative* duty not to uphold injustice, not to contribute to or profit from the unjust impoverishment of others.

These two views differ in important ways. The positive formulation is easier to substantiate. It need be shown only that they are very badly off, that we are very much better off and that we could relieve some of their suffering without becoming badly off ourselves. But this ease comes at a price: some who accept the positive formulation think of the moral reasons it provides as weak and discretionary, and thus do not feel obligated to promote worthy causes, especially costly ones. Many feel entitled, at least, to support good causes of their choice – their church or *alma mater*, cancer research or the environment – rather than putting themselves out for total strangers half a world away, with whom they share no bond of community or culture. It is of some importance, therefore, to investigate whether existing global poverty involves our violating a *negative* duty. This is important for us, if we want to lead a moral life, and important also for the poor because it will make a great difference to them whether we affluent do or do not see global poverty as an injustice we help maintain.

Some believe that the mere fact of *radical inequality* shows a violation of negative duty. Radical inequality may be defined as involving five elements (extending Nagel, 1977).

(1) The worse-off are very badly off in absolute terms.
(2) They are also very badly off in relative terms – very much worse off than many others.
(3) The inequality is impervious: it is difficult or impossible for the worse-off substantially to improve their lot; and most of the better-off never experience life at the bottom for even a few months and have no vivid idea of what it is like to live in that way.
(4) The inequality is pervasive: it concerns not merely some aspects of life, such as the climate or access to natural beauty or high culture, but most aspects or all.
(5) The inequality is avoidable: the better-off can improve the circumstances of the worse-off without becoming badly off themselves.

The phenomenon of global poverty clearly exemplifies radical inequality as defined. But I doubt that these five conditions suffice to invoke more than a merely positive duty. And I suspect most citizens of the developed West would also find them insufficient. They might appeal to the following parallel: suppose we discovered people on Venus who are very badly off, and suppose we could help them at little cost to ourselves. If we did nothing, we would surely violate a positive duty of beneficence. But we would not be violating a negative duty of justice, because we would not be *contributing* to the perpetuation of their misery.

This point could be further disputed. But let me here accept the Venus argument and examine what *further* conditions must be satisfied for radical inequality to manifest an injustice that involves violation of a negative duty by the better-off. I see three plausible approaches to this question, invoking three different grounds of injustice: the effects of shared institutions, the uncompensated exclusion from the use of natural resources and the effects of a common and violent history. These approaches exemplify distinct and competing political philosophies. We need nevertheless not decide among them here if, as I will argue, the following two theses are true. First, all three approaches classify the existing radical inequality as unjust and its coercive maintenance as a violation of negative duty. Second, all three approaches can agree on the same feasible reform of the *status quo* as a major step toward justice. If these two theses can be supported, then it may be possible to gather adherents of the dominant strands of Western normative political thought into a coalition focused on eradicating global poverty through the introduction of a Global Resources Dividend (GRD).

Three Grounds of Injustice

The effects of shared institutions

The first approach (suggested in Nagel, 1977; O'Neill, 1985; Pogge, 1989: Section 24) puts forward three additional conditions.

(6) There is a shared institutional order that is shaped by the better-off and imposed on the worse-off.
(7) This institutional order is implicated in the reproduction of radical inequality in that there is a feasible institutional alternative under which so severe and extensive poverty would not persist.
(8) The radical inequality cannot be traced to extra-social factors (such as genetic handicaps or natural disasters) that, as such, affect different human beings differentially.

Present radical global inequality meets Condition 6, in that the global poor live within a worldwide states system based on internationally recognized territorial domains, interconnected through a global network of market trade and diplomacy. The presence and relevance of shared institutions is shown by how dramatically we affect the circumstances of the global poor through investments, loans, trade, bribes, military aid, sex tourism, culture exports and much else. Their very survival often crucially depends on our consumption choices, which may determine the price of their foodstuffs and their opportunities to find work. In sharp contrast to the Venus case, we are causally deeply involved in their misery. This does not mean that we should hold ourselves responsible for the remoter effects of our economic decisions. These effects reverberate around the world and interact with the effects of countless other such decisions and thus cannot be traced, let alone predicted. Nor need we draw the dubious and Utopian conclusion that global interdependence must be undone by isolating states or groups of states from one another. But we must be concerned with how the rules structuring international interactions foreseeably affect the incidence of extreme poverty. The developed countries, thanks to their vastly superior military and economic strength, control these rules and therefore share responsibility for their foreseeable effects.

Condition 7 involves tracing the poverty of individuals in an explanatory way to the structure of social institutions. This exercise is familiar in regard to national institutions, whose explanatory importance has been powerfully illustrated by domestic regime changes in China, Eastern Europe and elsewhere. In regard to the global economic order, the exercise is unfamiliar and shunned even by economists. This is due in part, no doubt, to powerful resistance against seeing oneself as connected to the unimaginable deprivations suffered by the global poor. This resistance biases us against data, arguments and researchers liable to upset our preferred world view and thus biases the competition for professional success against anyone exploring the wider causal context of global poverty. This bias is reinforced by our cognitive tendency to overlook the causal significance of stable background factors (e.g. the role of atmospheric oxygen in the outbreak of are), as our attention is naturally drawn to geographically or temporally variable factors. Looking at the incidence of poverty worldwide, we are struck by dramatic local changes and international variations, which point to local explanatory factors. The heavy focus on such local factors then encourages the illusion, succumbed to by Rawls (1999: 108) for example, that they completely explain global poverty.

This illusion conceals how profoundly local factors and their effects are influenced by the existing global order. Yes, a culture of corruption pervades the political system and the economy of many developing countries. But is this culture unrelated to the fact that most affluent countries have, until quite recently, allowed their firms to bribe foreign officials and even made such bribes tax-deductible?[1] – Yes, developing countries have shown themselves prone to oppressive government and to horrific wars and civil wars. But is the frequency of such brutality unrelated to the international arms trade, and unrelated to international rules that entitle anyone holding effective power in such a country to borrow in its name and to sell ownership rights in its natural resources (Wantchekon, 1999)? – Yes, the world is diverse, and poverty is declining in some countries and worsening in others. But the larger pattern is quite stable, reaching far back into the colonial era: "The income gap between the fifth of the world's people living in the richest countries and the fifth in the poorest was 74 to 1 in 1997, up from 60 to 1 in 1990 and 30 to 1 in 1960. [Earlier] the income gap between the top and bottom countries increased from 3 to 1 in 1820 to 7 to 1 in 1870 to 11 to 1 in 1913" (United Nations Development Programme, 1999: 3). The affluent countries have been using their power to shape the rules of the world economy according to their own interests and thereby have deprived the poorest populations of a fair share of global economic growth (Pogge, 2001) – quite avoidably so, as the GRD proposal shows.

Global poverty meets Condition 8 insofar as the global poor, if only they had been born into different social circumstances, would be just as able and likely to lead healthy, happy and productive lives as the rest of us. The root cause of their suffering is their abysmal social starting position, which does not give them much of a chance to become anything but poor, vulnerable and dependent – unable to give their children a better start than they had had themselves.

It is because the three additional conditions are met that existing global poverty has, according to the first approach, the special moral urgency we associate with negative duties, why we should take it much more seriously than otherwise similar suffering on Venus. The reason is that the citizens and governments of the affluent countries – whether intentionally or not – are imposing a global institutional order that foreseeably and avoidably reproduces severe and widespread poverty. The worse-off are not merely poor and often starving, but are *being* impoverished and starved under our shared institutional arrangements, which inescapably shape their lives.

The first approach can be presented in a consequentialist guise, as in Bentham, or in a contractualist guise, as in Rawls or Habermas. In both cases, the central thought is that social institutions are to be assessed in a forward-looking way, by reference to their effects. In the present international order, billions are born into social starting positions that give them extremely low prospects for a fulfilling life. Their misery could be justified only if there were no institutional alternative under which such massive misery would be avoided. If, as the GRD proposal shows, there is such an alternative, then we must ascribe this misery to the existing global order and therefore ultimately to ourselves. As, remarkably, Charles Darwin wrote in reference to his native Britain: "If the misery of our poor be caused not by laws of nature, but by our own institutions, great is our sin" (quoted in Gould, 1991: 19).

Uncompensated exclusion from the use of natural resources

The second approach adds (in place of Conditions 6–8) only one condition to the five of radical inequality.

(9) The better-off enjoy significant advantages in the use of a single natural resource base from whose benefits the worse-off are largely, and without compensation, excluded.

Currently, appropriation of wealth from our planet is highly uneven. Affluent people use vastly more of the world's resources, and they do so unilaterally, without giving any compensation to the global poor for their disproportionate consumption. Yes, the affluent often pay for the resources they use, such as imported crude oil. But these payments go to other affluent people, such as the Saudi family or the Nigerian kleptocracy, with very little, if anything, trickling down to the global poor. So the question remains: What entitles a global elite to use up the world's natural resources on mutually agreeable terms while leaving the global poor empty-handed?

Defenders of capitalist institutions have developed conceptions of justice that support rights to unilateral appropriation of disproportionate shares of resources while accepting that all inhabitants of the earth ultimately have equal claims to its resources. These conceptions are based on the thought that such rights are justified if all are better off with them than anyone would be if appropriation were limited to proportional shares.

This pattern of justification is exemplified with particular clarity in John Locke (cf. also Nozick, 1974: ch. 4). Locke is assuming that, in a state of nature without money, persons are subject to the moral constraint that their unilateral appropriations must always leave "enough, and as good" for others, that is, must be confined to a proportional share (Locke, 1689: sections 27 and 33). This so-called Lockean Proviso may, however, be lifted with universal consent (Locke, 1689: section 36). Locke subjects such a lifting to a second-order proviso, which requires that the rules of human coexistence may be changed only if all can *rationally* consent to the alteration, that is, only if everyone will be better off under the new rules than anyone would be under the old. And he claims that the lifting of the enough-and-asgood constraint through the general acceptance of money does satisfy this second-order proviso: a day laborer in England feeds, lodges and is clad better than a king of a large fruitful territory in the Americas (Locke, 1689: sections 41 and 37).

It is hard to believe that Locke's claim was true in his time. In any case, it is surely false on the global plane today. Billions are born into poverty in a world where all accessible resources are already owned by others. It is true that they can rent out their labor and then buy natural resources on the same terms as the affluent can. But their educational and employment opportunities are almost always so restricted that, no matter how hard they work, they can barely earn enough for their survival and certainly cannot secure anything like a proportionate share of the world's natural resources. The global poor get to share the burdens resulting from the degradation of our natural environment while having to watch helplessly as the affluent distribute the planet's abundant natural wealth among themselves. With average annual *per capita* income of about \$82, corresponding to the purchasing power of \$326 in the US, the poorest fifth of humankind are today just about as badly off, economically, as human beings could be while still alive.[2] It is then not true, what according to Locke and Nozick would need to be true, that all are better off under the existing appropriation and pollution rules than anyone would be with the Lockean Proviso. According to the second approach, the citizens and governments of the affluent states are therefore violating a negative duty of justice when they, in collaboration with the ruling elites of the poor countries, coercively exclude the poor from a proportional resource share.

The effects of a common and violent history

The third approach adds one condition to the five of radical inequality.

(10) The social starting positions of the worse-off and the better-off have emerged from a single historical process that was pervaded by massive grievous wrongs.

The present circumstances of the global poor are significantly shaped by a dramatic period of conquest and colonization, with severe oppression, enslavement, even genocide, through which the native institutions and cultures of four continents were destroyed or severely traumatized. This is not to say (or to deny) that affluent descendants of those who took part in these crimes bear some special restitutive responsibility toward impoverished descendants of those who were victims of these crimes. The thought is rather that we must not uphold extreme inequality in social starting positions when the allocation of these positions depends upon historical processes in which moral principles and legal rules were massively violated. A morally deeply tarnished history should not be allowed to result in *radical* inequality.

This third approach is independent of the others. For, suppose we reject the other two approaches and affirm that radical inequality is morally acceptable when it comes about pursuant to rules of the game that are morally at least somewhat plausible and observed at least for the most part. The existing radical inequality is then still condemned by the third approach on the ground that the rules were in fact massively violated through countless horrible crimes whose momentous effects cannot be surgically neutralized decades and centuries later (cf. Nozick, 1974: 231).

Friends of the present distribution sometimes claim that standards of living, in Africa and Europe for instance, would be approximately the same if Africa had never been colonized. Even if this claim were both clear and true, it would still be ineffective because the argument I have sketched applies to persons, not to societies or continents. If world history had transpired without colonization and enslavement, then there would perhaps now be affluent people in Europe and poor ones in Africa, much like in the Venus scenario. But these would be persons and populations quite different from those who are now actually living there. So we cannot tell starving Africans that *they* would be starving and *we* would be affluent even if the crimes of colonialism had never occurred. Without these crimes, there would not be the actually existing radical inequality that consists in *these* persons being affluent and *those* being extremely poor.

So the third approach, too, leads to the conclusion that the existing radical inequality is unjust, that coercively upholding it violates a negative duty, and that we have urgent moral reason to eradicate global poverty.

A Moderate Proposal

The reform proposal now to be sketched is meant to support my second thesis: that the *status quo* can be reformed in a way that all three approaches would recognize as a major step toward justice. But it is also needed to close gaps in my argument for the first thesis: the proposal should show that the existing radical inequality can be traced to the structure of our global economic order (Condition 7). And it should also show that Condition 5 is met; for, according to all three approaches, the *status quo* is unjust only if we can improve the circumstances of the global poor without thereby becoming badly-off ourselves.

I am formulating my reform proposal in line with the second approach, because the other two would support almost any reform that would improve the circumstances of the global poor. The second approach narrows the field by suggesting a more specific idea: those who make more extensive use of our planet's resources should compensate those who, involuntarily, use very little. This idea does not require that we conceive of global resources as the common property of humankind, to be shared equally. My proposal is far more modest by leaving each government in control of the natural resources in its territory. Modesty is important if the proposed institutional alternative is to gain the support necessary to implement it and is to be able to sustain itself in the world as we know it. I hope that the GRD satisfies these two desiderata by staying reasonably close to the global order now in place and by being evidently responsive to each of the three approaches.

The GRD proposal envisions that states and their governments shall not have full libertarian property rights with respect to the natural resources in their territory, but can be required to share a small part of the value of any resources they decide to use or sell. This payment they must make is called a dividend because it is based on the idea that the global poor own an inalienable stake in all limited natural resources. As in the case of preferred stock, this stake confers no right to participate in decisions about whether or how natural resources are to be used and so does not interfere with national control over resources, or eminent domain. But it does entitle its holders to a share of the economic value of the resource in question, if indeed the decision is to use it. This idea could be extended to limited resources that are not destroyed through use but merely eroded, worn down, or occupied, such as air and water used for discharging pollutants or land used for farming, ranching, or buildings.

In light of the vast extent of global poverty today, one may think that a massive GRD would be necessary to solve the problem. But I doubt this is so. Present radical inequality is the cumulative result of decades and centuries in which the more affluent societies and groups have used their advantages in capital and knowledge to expand these advantages ever further. This inequality demonstrates the power of long-term compounding more than powerful centrifugal tendencies of our global market system. It is then quite possible that, if radical inequality has once been eradicated, quite a small GRD may, in the context of a fair and open global market system, be sufficient continuously to balance those ordinary centrifugal tendencies of markets enough to forestall its re-emergence. The great magnitude of the problem does suggest, however, that initially more, perhaps as much as 1% of the global product, may be needed so that it does not take all too long until severe poverty is erased and an acceptable distributional profile is reached.[3] To get a concrete sense of the magnitudes involved, let us then consider this higher figure. While affluent countries now provide $52 billion annually in of.cial development assistance (United Nations Development Programme, 2000: 218), a 1% GRD would currently raise about $300 billion annually.[4] This is $250 per year for each person below the international poverty line, over three times their present average annual income. More broadly spread, $300 billion is $107 per year for each person below the doubled poverty line, 82% of their present average annual income. Such an amount, if well targeted and effectively spent, would make a phenomenal difference to the poor even within a few years. On the other hand, the amount is rather small for the rest of us: close to the annual defense budget of just the US alone, significantly less than the annual "peace dividend", and less than half the market value of the current annual crude oil production.[5]

Let us stay with the case of crude oil for a moment and examine the likely effects of a $2 per barrel GRD on crude oil extraction. This dividend would be owed by the countries in which oil is extracted, although most of this cost would be passed along, through higher world market prices, to the end-users of petroleum products. At $2 per barrel, over 18% of the high initial revenue target could be raised from crude oil alone – and comfortably so: at the expense of raising the price of petroleum products by about a nickel per gallon. It is thus clearly possible – without major changes to our global economic order – to eradicate world hunger within a few years by raising a sufficient revenue stream from a limited number of resources and pollutants. These should be selected carefully, with an eye to all collateral effects. This suggests the following desiderata: the GRD should be easy to understand and to apply. It should, for instance, be based on resources and pollutants whose extraction or discharge is easy to monitor or estimate, in order to ensure that every society is paying its fair share and to assure everyone that this is so. Such transparency also helps fulfill a second desideratum of keeping overall collection costs low. The GRD should, thirdly, have only a small impact on the price of goods consumed to satisfy basic needs. And it should, fourth, be focused on resource uses whose discouragement is especially important for conservation and environmental protection. In this last respect, the GRD reform can produce great ecological benefits that are hard to secure in a less concerted way because of familiar collective-action problems: each society has little incentive to restrain its consumption and pollution, because the opportunity cost of such restraint falls on it alone while the costs of depletion and pollution are spread worldwide and into the future.

Proceeds from the GRD are to be used toward ensuring that all human beings will be able to meet their own basic needs with dignity. The goal is not merely to improve the nutrition, medical care and sanitary conditions of the poor, but also to make it possible that they can themselves effectively defend and realize their basic interests. This capacity presupposes that they are freed from bondage and other relations of personal dependence, that they are able to read and write and to learn a profession, that they can participate as equals in politics and in the labor market, and that their status is protected by appropriate legal rights that they can understand and effectively enforce through an open and fair legal system.

The scheme for disbursing GRD funds is to be designed so as to make these funds maximally effective toward those ends. Such design must draw upon the expertise of economists and international lawyers. Let me nonetheless make some provisional suggestions to give more concreteness to the proposed reform. Disbursement should be made pursuant to clear and straightforward general rules whose administration is cheap and transparent. Transparency is important to exclude political favoritism and the appearance thereof. It is important also for giving the government of any developing country clear and strong incentives toward eradicating domestic poverty. To optimize such incentive effects, the disbursement rules should reward progress: by allocating more funds to this country and/or by assigning more of its allocation directly to its government.

This incentive may not always prevail. In some poor countries, the rulers care more about keeping their subjects destitute, uneducated, docile, dependent and hence exploitable. In such cases, it may still be possible to find other ways of improving the circumstances and opportunities of the domestic poor: by making cash payments directly to them or to their organizations or by funding development programs administered through United Nations agencies or effective non-governmental organizations. When, in extreme cases, GRD funds cannot be used effectively in a particular country, then there is no reason to spend them there rather than in those many other places where these funds can make a real difference in reducing poverty and disadvantage.

Even if the incentives provided by the GRD disbursement rules do not always prevail, they will shift the political balance of forces in the right direction: a good government brings enhanced prosperity through GRD support and thereby generates more popular support, which in turn will tend to make it safer from coup attempts. A bad government will find the poor harder to oppress when they receive GRD funds through other channels and when all strata of the population have an interest in realizing GRD-accelerated economic improvement under a different government more committed to poverty eradication. With the GRD in place, reforms will be pursued more vigorously and in more countries, and will succeed more often and sooner, than would otherwise be the case. Combined with suitable disbursement rules, the GRD can stimulate a peaceful international competition in effective poverty eradication.

This rough and revisable sketch has shown, I hope, that the GRD proposal deserves serious examination as an alternative to conventional development aid. While the latter has an aura of hand-outs and dependence, the GRD avoids any appearance of arrogant generosity: it merely incorporates into our global institutional order the moral claim of the poor to partake in the benefits from the use of planetary resources. It implements a moral right – and one that can be justified in multiple ways: namely also forward-looking, by reference to its effects, and backward-looking, by reference to the evolution of the present economic distribution. Moreover, the GRD would also be vastly more efficient. The disbursement of conventional development aid is heavily influenced by political considerations as is shown by the fact that only 21% of these $52 billion go to the least developed countries (United Nations Development Programme, 2000: 218). A mere 8.3%, $4.3 billion, are spent on meeting basic needs (United Nations Development Programme, 2000: 79), less than 1 cent per day for each person in the poorest quintile. The GRD, by contrast, would initially raise 70 times as much exclusively toward meeting the basic needs of the global poor.

Since the GRD would cost more and return less in direct political benefits, many of the wealthier and more powerful states might be tempted to refuse compliance. Would the

GRD scheme not then require a global enforcement agency, something like a world government? In response, I agree that the GRD would have to be backed by sanctions. But sanctions could be decentralized: once the agency facilitating the flow of GRD payments reports that a country has not met its obligations under the scheme, all other countries are required to impose duties on imports from, and perhaps also similar levies on exports to, this country to raise funds equivalent to its GRD obligations plus the cost of these enforcement measures. Such decentralized sanctions stand a very good chance of discouraging small-scale defections. Our world is now, and is likely to remain, highly interdependent economically. Most countries export and import between 10 and 50% of their gross domestic product. No country would profit from shutting down foreign trade for the sake of avoiding its GRD obligation. And each would have reasons to fulfill its GRD obligation voluntarily: to retain control over how the funds are raised, to avoid paying extra for enforcement measures and to avoid the adverse publicity associated with noncompliance.

To be sure, such a scheme of decentralized sanctions could work only so long as both the US and the European Union (EU) continue to comply and continue to participate in the sanction mechanism. I assume that both will do this, provided they can be brought to commit themselves to the GRD scheme in the first place. This prerequisite, which is decisive for the success of the proposal, is addressed in the penultimate section. It should be clear, however, that a refusal by the US or the EU to participate in the eradication of global poverty would not affect the implications of the present section. The feasibility of the GRD suffices to show that massive and severe poverty is avoidable at moderate cost (Condition 5), that the existing global order plays an important role in its persistence (Condition 7), and that we can take what all three approaches would recognize as a major step toward justice (second thesis).

The Moral Argument for the Proposed Reform

By showing that Conditions 1–10 are met, I hope to have demonstrated that present global poverty manifests a grievous injustice that can and should be abolished through institutional reform – involving the GRD scheme, perhaps, or some superior alternative. To make this train of thought as transparent and criticizable as possible, I restate it now as an argument in six steps. The first two steps involve new formulations, so I comment on them briefly at the end.

(1) If a society or comparable social system, connected and regulated by a shared institutional order (Condition 6), displays radical inequality (Conditions 1–5), then this institutional order is *prima facie* unjust and requires justification. Here the burden of proof is on those who wish to defend this order and its coercive imposition as compatible with justice.

(2) Such a justification of an institutional order under which radical inequality persists would need to show either:

- (2a) that Condition 10 is not met, perhaps because the existing radical inequality came about fairly: through an historical process that transpired in accordance with morally plausible rules that were generally observed; or
- (2b) that Condition 9 is not met, because the worse-off can adequately benefit from the use of the common natural resource base through access to a proportional share or through some at least equivalent substitute; or

(2c) that Condition 8 is not met, because the existing radical inequality can be traced to extra-social factors (such as genetic handicaps or natural disasters) which, as such, affect different persons differentially; or

(2d) that Condition 7 is not met, because any proposed alternative to the existing institutional order either:

- is impracticable, i.e. cannot be stably maintained in the long run; or
- cannot be instituted in a morally acceptable way even with good will by all concerned; or
- would not substantially improve the circumstances of the worse-off; or
- would have other morally serious disadvantages that offset any improvement in the circumstances of the worse-off.

(3) Humankind is connected and regulated by a shared global institutional order under which radical inequality persists.

(4) This global institutional order therefore requires justification (from 1 and 3).

(5) This global institutional order can be given no justification of forms 2a, 2b, or 2c. A justification of form 2d fails as well, because a reform involving introduction of a GRD provides an alternative that is practicable, can (with some good will by all concerned) be instituted in a morally acceptable way, would substantially improve the circumstances of the worse-off and would not have disadvantages of comparable moral significance.

(6) The existing global order cannot be justified (from 4, 2 and 5) and hence is unjust (from 1).

In presenting this argument, I have not attempted to satisfy the strictest demands of logical form, which would have required various qualifications and repetitions. I have merely tried to clarify the structure of the argument so as to make clear how it can be attacked.

One might attack the first step. But this moral premise is quite weak, applying only if the existing inequality occurs within a shared institutional order (Condition 6) *and* is radical, that is, involves truly extreme poverty and extreme differentials in standards of living (Conditions 1–5). Moreover, the first premise does not flatly exclude any institutional order under which radical inequality persists, but merely demands that it be justified. Since social institutions are created and upheld, perpetuated or reformed by human beings, this demand cannot plausibly be refused.

One might attack the second step. But this moral premise, too, is weak, in that it demands of the defender of the *status quo* only one of the four possible showings (2a–2d), leaving him free to try each of the conceptions of economic justice outlined in the second section, even though he can hardly endorse all of them at once. Still, it remains open to argue that an institutional order reproducing radical inequality can be justified in a way that differs from the four (2a–2d) I have described.

One might try to show that the existing global order does not meet one of the 10 conditions. Depending on which condition is targeted, one would thereby deny the third premise or give a justification of forms 2a or 2b or 2c, or show that my reform proposal runs into one of the four problems listed under 2d.

The conclusion of the argument is reached only if all 10 conditions are met. Existing global poverty then manifests a *core injustice*: a phenomenon that the dominant strands of Western normative political thought jointly – albeit for diverse reasons – classify as unjust and can jointly seek to eradicate. Insofar as advantaged and influential participants in the present international order grant the argument, we acknowledge our shared responsibility for its injustice: we are violating a negative duty of justice insofar as we contribute to (and fail to mitigate) the harms it reproduces and insofar as we resist suitable reforms.

Is the Reform Proposal Realistic?

Even if the GRD proposal is practicable, and even if it could be implemented with the good will of all concerned, there remains the problem of generating this good will, especially on the part of the rich and mighty. Without the support of the US and the EU, massive global poverty and starvation will certainly not be eradicated in our lifetimes. How realistic is the hope of mobilizing such support? I have two answers to this question.

First, even if this hope is not realistic, it is still important to insist that present global poverty manifests a grievous injustice according to Western normative political thought. We are not merely distant witnesses of a problem unrelated to ourselves, with a weak, positive duty to help. Rather, we are, both causally and morally, intimately involved in the fate of the poor by imposing upon them a global institutional order that regularly produces severe poverty, and/or by effectively excluding them from a fair share of the value of exploited natural resources, and/or by upholding a radical inequality that evolved through an historical process pervaded by horrendous crimes. We can realistically end our involvement in their severe poverty not by extricating ourselves from this involvement, but only by ending such poverty through economic reform. If feasible reforms are blocked by others, then we may in the end be unable to do more than mitigate some of the harms we also help produce. But even then a difference would remain, because our effort would fulfill not a duty to help the needy, but a duty to protect victims of any injustice to which we contribute. The latter duty is, other things equal, much more stringent than the former, especially when we can fulfill it out of the benefits we derive from this injustice.

My second answer is that the hope may not be so unrealistic after all. My provisional optimism is based on two considerations. The first is that moral convictions can have real effects even in international politics – as even some political realists admit, albeit with regret. Sometimes these are the moral convictions of politicians. But, more commonly, politics is influenced by the moral convictions of citizens. One dramatic example of this is the abolitionist movement that, in the nineteenth century, pressured the British government into suppressing the slave trade (Drescher, 1986). A similar moral mobilization may be possible also for the sake of eradicating global poverty – provided the citizens of the more powerful states can be convinced of a moral conclusion that really can be soundly supported and a path can be shown that makes only modest demands on each of us.

The GRD proposal is morally compelling. It can be broadly anchored in the dominant strands of Western normative political thought outlined in the second section. And it also has the morally significant advantage of shifting consumption in ways that restrain global pollution and resource depletion for the benefit of future generations in particular. Because it can be backed by these four important and mutually independent moral rationales, the GRD proposal is well-positioned to benefit from the fact that moral reasons can have effects in the world. If some help can be secured from economists, political scientists and lawyers, then moral acceptance of the GRD may gradually emerge and become widespread in the developed West.

Eradicating global poverty through a scheme like the GRD also involves more realistic demands than a solution through private initiatives and conventional development aid.

Continual mitigation of poverty leads to fatigue, aversion, and even contempt. It requires the more affluent citizens and governments to rally to the cause again and again, while knowing full well that most others similarly situated contribute nothing or very little, that their own contributions are legally optional and that, no matter how much they give, they could for just a little more always save yet further children from sickness or starvation.

The inefficiency of conventional development aid is also sustained by the competitive situation among the governments of the donor countries, who feel morally entitled to decline to do more by pointing to their even less generous competitors. This explanation supports the optimistic assumption that the affluent societies would be prepared, in joint reciprocity, to commit themselves to more than what they tend to do each on its own. Analogous considerations apply to environmental protection and conservation, with respect to which the GRD also contributes to a collective solution: when many parties decide separately in this matter, then the best solution for all is not achieved, because each gets almost the full benefit of its pollution and wastefulness while the resulting harms are shared by all ("tragedy of the commons"). An additional point is that national measures of development aid and environmental protection must be politically fought for or defended year after year, while acceptance of the GRD regime would require only one – albeit rather more far-reaching – political decision.

The other optimistic consideration concerns prudence. The times when we could afford to ignore what goes on in the developing countries are over for good. Their economic growth will have a great impact on our environment, and their military and technological gains are accompanied by serious dangers, among which those associated with nuclear, biological and chemical weapons and technologies are only the most obvious. The transnational imposition of externalities and risks will ever more become a two-way street because no state or group of states, however rich and mighty, will be able effectively to insulate itself from external influences: from military and terrorist attacks, illegal immigrants, epidemics and the drug trade, pollution and climate change, price fluctuations and scientific-technological and cultural innovations. It is then increasingly in our interest, too, that stable democratic institutions shall emerge in the developing countries – institutions under which governmental power is effectively constrained through procedural rules and basic rights. So long as large segments of these peoples lack elementary education and have no assurance that they will be able to meet even their most basic needs, such democratic institutions are much less likely than explosive mixtures of religious and ideological fanaticism, violent opposition movements, death squads and corrupt and politicized militaries. To expose ourselves to the occasional explosions of these mixtures would be increasingly dangerous and also more costly in the long run than the proposed GRD.

This prudential consideration has a moral side as well. A future that is pervaded by radical inequality and hence unstable would endanger not only the security of ourselves and our progeny, but also the long-term survival of our society, values and culture. Not only that: such a future would, quite generally, endanger the security of all other human beings and their descendants as well as the survival of their societies, values and cultures. And so the interest in peace – in a future world in which different societies, values and cultures can coexist and interact peacefully – is obviously also, and importantly, a moral interest.

Realizing our prudential and moral interest in a peaceful and ecologically sound future will – and here I go beyond my earlier modesty – require supranational institutions and organizations that limit the sovereignty rights of states more severely than is the current practice. The most powerful states could try to impose such limitations upon all the rest while exempting themselves. It is doubtful, however, that today's great powers will summon the political will to make this attempt before it is too late. And it is doubtful also whether they could succeed. For, such an attempt would provoke the bitter resistance of many other states, which would simultaneously try very hard, through military build-up, to gain access to the club of great powers. For such a project, the "elites" in many developing countries could probably mobilize their populations quite easily, as the recent examples of India and Pakistan illustrate.

It might then make more sense for all to work toward supranational institutions and organizations that limit the sovereignty rights of all states equally. But this solution can work only if at least a large majority of the states participating in these institutions and organizations are stable democracies, which presupposes, in turn, that their citizens are assured that they can meet their basic needs and can attain a decent level of education and social position.

The current geopolitical development drifts toward a world in which militarily and technologically highly advanced states and groups, growing in number, pose an ever greater danger for an ever larger subset of humankind. Deflecting this development in a more reasonable direction realistically requires considerable support from those other 85% of humankind who want to reduce our economic advantage and achieve our high standard of living. Through the introduction of the GRD or some similar reform, we can gain such support by showing concretely that our relations to the rest of the world are not solely devoted to cementing our economic hegemony and that the global poor will be able peacefully to achieve a considerable improvement in their circumstances. In this way, and only in this way, can we refute the conviction, understandably widespread in the poor countries, that we will not give a damn about their misery until they will have the economic and military power to do us serious harm. And only in this way can we undermine the popular support that aggressive political movements of all kinds can derive from this conviction.

Conclusion

We are familiar, through charity appeals, with the assertion that it lies in our hands to save the lives of many or, by doing nothing, to let these people die. We are less familiar with the herein examined assertion of a weightier responsibility: that most of us do not merely let people starve, but also participate in starving them. It is not surprising that our initial reaction to this more unpleasant assertion is indignation, even hostility – that, rather than think it through or discuss it, we want to forget it or put it aside as plainly absurd.

I have tried to respond constructively to the assertion and to show its plausibility. I do not pretend to have proved it conclusively, but my argument should at least raise grave doubts about our commonsense prejudices, which we must in any case treat with suspicion on account of how strongly our self-interest is engaged in this matter. The great moral importance of reaching the correct judgment on this issue also counsels against lightly dismissing the assertion here defended. The essential data about the lives and deaths of the global poor are, after all, indisputable. In view of very considerable global interdependence, it is extremely unlikely that their poverty is due exclusively to local factors and that no feasible reform of the present global order could thus affect either that poverty or these local factors. No less incredible is the view that ours is the best of all possible global orders, that any modification of it could only aggravate poverty. So, we should work together across disciplines to conceive a comprehensive solution to the problem of global poverty, and across borders for the political implementation of this solution.

Notes

1. A *Convention on Combating Bribery of Foreign Of.cials in International Business Transactions*, which requires signatory states to criminalize the bribery of foreign officials, was finally drafted within the OECD under public pressure generated by the new nongovernmental organization Transparency International (www.transparency.de). The Convention went into effect in February 1999. Thirty-one states have rati.ed it at the last count (http://www.business-anti-corruption.com/about-corruption/oecd/).
2. The World Bank estimates that 1.2 billion out of six billion human beings live below the international poverty line, which it currently defines in terms of $32.74 PPP 1993 per month or $1.08 PPP 1993 per day (World Bank, 2001: 17, 23). "PPP" stands for "purchasing power parity," so people count as poor by this standard when their income per person per year has less purchasing power than $393 had in the US in 1993 or less purchasing power than $466 have in the US in the year 2000. Those living below this poverty line, on average, fall 30% below it (Chen and Ravallion, 2000, Tables 2 and 4, dividing the poverty gap index by the headcount index). So they live on $326 PPP 2000 per person per year on average. Now the $PPP incomes the World Bank ascribes to people in poor developing countries are, on average, about four times higher than their actual incomes at market exchange rates. Thus, the World Bank equates China's *per capita* GNP of $780 to $3291 PPP, India's $450 to $2149 PPP, Indonesia's $580 to $2439 PPP, Nigeria's $310 to $744 PPP, and so on (World Bank, 2001: 274–275). Since virtually all the global poor live in such poor developing countries, we can then estimate that their average annual *per capita* income of $326 PPP 2000 corresponds to about $82 at market exchange rates. The aggregate annual income of the poorest fifth of humankind is then about $100 billion at market exchange rates or about one-third of 1% of the global product.
3. In the face of 18 million poverty-related deaths per year, the go-slow approach governments have non-bindingly endorsed at the 1996 World Food Summit in Rome – halving world hunger within 19 years – is morally unacceptable. I also think that the World Bank's poverty line is far too low to define an acceptable goal. The World Bank provides statistics also for a more adequate poverty line that is twice as high: $786 PPP 1993 ($932 PPP or roughly $233 in the year 2000) per person per year. 2.8 billion people – nearly half of humankind – are said to live below this higher poverty line, falling 44% below it on average (Chen and Ravallion, 2000, Tables 3 and 4, again dividing the poverty gap index by the headcount index). The aggregate annual income of these people is then about $365 billion at market exchange rates or about 1.25% of the global product.
4. The global product (sum of all gross national products) is currently about $30 trillion per year: 78.4% thereof belongs to the "high-income economies," including 33 countries plus Hongkong, which contain 14.9% of world population (World Bank, 2001: 275). The US, with 4.6% of world population, accounts for 28.6% of global product (World Bank, 2001: 275) – and has just managed to renegotiate its share of the UN budget from 25% down to 22%.
5. The end of the Cold War enabled the high-income countries to cut their aggregate military expenditure from 4.1% of their gross domestic product in 1985 to 2.2% in 1998 (United Nations Development Programme, 1998: 197, 2000: 217). The peace dividend these countries reap can then be estimated at $420 billion annually (1.9% of their current aggregate GDP of over $22 trillion; United Nations Development Programme, 2000: 209). Crude oil production is currently about 77 million barrels daily or about 28 billion barrels annually. At $25 per barrel, this comes to $700 billion annually.

References

Chen, S. and Ravallion, M. (2000). *How Did the World's Poorest Fare in the 1990s?* http://elibrary.worldbank.org/content/workingpaper/10.1596/1813-9450-2409

Crisp, R. and Jamieson, D. (2000). Egalitarianism and a global resources tax: Pogge on Rawls. In V. Davion and C. Wolf (eds) *The Idea of a Political Liberalism: essays on Rawls.* Rowman and Littlefield, Lanham, MD.

Drescher, S. (1986). *Capitalism and Antislavery: British mobilization in comparative perspective.* Oxford University Press, Oxford.

Gould, S.J. (1991). The moral state of Tahiti – and of Darwin. *Natural History*, 10, 12–19.

Kesselring, T. (1997). Weltarmut und Ressourcen-Zugang. *Analyse und Kritik*, 19 (3), 242–254.

Kreide, R. (1998). Armut, Gerechtigkeit und Demokratie. *Analyse und Kritik*, 20 (3), 245–262.

Locke, J. (1689). An essay concerning the true original, extent, and end of civil government. In P. Laslett (ed.) *John Locke: Two Treatises of Government.* Cambridge University Press, Cambridge.

Mandle, J. (2000). Globalization and justice. *Annals of the American Academy*, 570, 126–139.

Nagel, T. (1977). Poverty and food: why charity is not enough. In P. Brown and H. Shue (eds) *Food Policy: the responsibility of the United States in life and death choices.* Free Press, New York.

Nozick, R. (1974). *Anarchy, State, and Utopia*, Basic Books, New York.

O'Neill, O. (1985 [1974]). Lifeboat earth. Reprinted in C. Beitz, M. Cohen, T. Scanlon, and A.J. Simmons (eds) *International Ethics.* Princeton University Press, Princeton, NJ.

Pogge, T. (1989). *Realizing Rawls.* Cornell University Press, Ithaca, NY.

Pogge, T. (1994). An egalitarian law of peoples. *Philosophy and Public Affairs*, 23 (3), 195–224.

Pogge, T. (1998a). A global resources dividend. In D.A. Crocker and T. Linden (eds) *Ethics of Consumption: the good life, justice, and global stewardship.* Rowman & Littlefield, Lanham, MD.

Pogge, T. (2001). Priorities of global justice. *Metaphilosophy*, 32, 6–24.

Rawls, J. (1999). *The Law of Peoples.* Harvard University Press, Cambridge, MA.

Reichel, R. (1997). Internationaler Handel, Tauschgerechtigkeit und die globale Rohstoffdividende. *Analyse und Kritik*, 19 (3), 229–241.

UNICEF (United Nations Children's Fund) (1999). *The State of the World's Children 1999.* Oxford University Press, New York.

United Nations Development Programme (1998). *Human Development Report 1998.* Oxford University Press, New York.

United Nations Development Programme (1999). *Human Development Report 1999.* Oxford University Press, New York.

United Nations Development Programme (2000). *Human Development Report 2000.* Oxford University Press, New York.

Wantchekon, L. (1999). Why do resource dependent countries have authoritarian governments?' Working Paper. Yale University. www.yale.edu/leitner/resources/docs/1999-11.pdf

World Bank (2000). *World Development Report 1999/2000.* Oxford University Press, New York. www.worldbank.org/wdr/2000/fullreport.html

World Bank (2001). *World Development Report 2000/2001.* Oxford University Press, New York. www.worldbank.org/poverty/wdrpoverty/report/index.htm

World Health Organization (2000). *The World Health Report 2000. Health Systems: improving performance.* WHO Publications, Geneva. www.who.int/whr/2000

Further Reading

Aiken, W. and LaFolette, H. (eds) (1996). *World Hunger and Morality.* Prentice Hall, Upper Saddle River, NJ.

Beitz, C. (1979). *Political Theory and International Relations.* Princeton University Press, Princeton, NJ.

Dasgupta, P. (1993). *An Inquiry into Well-Being and Destitution.* Oxford University Press, Oxford.

Eichengreen, B., Tobin, J., and Wyplosz, C. (1995). Two cases for sand in the wheels of international finance. *Economic Journal*, 105 (428), 162–172.

Murphy, L. (2000). *Moral Demands in Non-Ideal Theory.* Oxford University Press, Oxford.

Pogge, T. (1998b). The bounds of nationalism. In J. Couture, K. Nielsen, and M. Seymour (eds) *Rethinking Nationalism, Canadian Journal of Philosophy*, Supplementary Volume 22. University of Calgary Press, Calgary.

Sen, A. (1981). *Poverty and Famines.* Oxford University Press, Oxford.

Shue, H. (1980). *Basic Rights.* Princeton University Press, Princeton, NJ.

Singer, P. (1972). Famine, affluence and morality. *Philosophy and Public Affairs*, 1 (3), 229–243.

Tobin, J. (1978). A proposal for international monetary reform. *Eastern Economic Journal*, 4, 153–159.

Unger, P. (1996). *Living High and Letting Die: our illusion of innocence.* Oxford University Press, Oxford.

United States Department of Agriculture (1999). *US Action Plan on Food Security.* http://www.fas.usda.gov/icd/summit/usactplan.pdf

Chapter 54

From Euro-Stipendium to Euro-Dividend

Philippe Van Parijs and Yannick Vanderborght[1]

Originally published as Van Parijs, P. and Vanderborght, Y. (2001). From Euro-Stipendium to Euro-Dividend. *Journal of European Social Policy*, 11 (4), 342–346.

Do we need to rethink fundamentally the way in which trans-national solidarity is organized within the European Union? Yes we do, and Schmitter and Bauer's essay (Schmitter and Bauer, 2001), is therefore most welcome to get this rethinking going, not with grand or vague wishes, but with a modest and precise proposal. Is their Euro-Stipendium (ES) the best way forward? We believe not, partly because of some design defects that can be corrected at the cost of some complications, but also partly because of a more fundamental defect whose correction requires jumping straight away to what Schmitter and Bauer view only as the possible end point of a gradual development.

Havoc in The Incentive Structure

According to Schmitter and Bauer, the ES should be introduced as a lump sum of €1,000 a year paid to every European citizen classified as "extremely poor." In the first phase, restricted to EU15, this category should include all individuals whose (household adjusted) disposable incomes amount to less than a third of the EU's (annual) average income, that is, €5,295. Falling below this threshold entitles one to the full ES. Getting above it entails its total withdrawal.

One unavoidable consequence of this scheme is that low-income households would face effective marginal tax rates of over 100% once they reach the poverty threshold, in an income range that grows proportionally with household size. To illustrate, take the case of Artemis, who lives on her own and whose total pre-ES disposable income consists in a social assistance benefit of €5,200. She is entitled to an ES of €1,000, which boosts her income up to €6,200. Suppose she finds a part-time job, which allows her to increase her pre-ES disposable income to €6,000: she then gets above the threshold and sees her ES removed. Although she earns €1,000 more than she did before, her post-ES disposable income falls by €200, which amounts to an effective tax rate of 120%, even on the assumption that her national income

Van Parijs, P. and Vanderborght, Y. (2001). From Euro-Stipendium to Euro-Dividend. *Journal of European Social Policy*, 11 (4), 342–346. Reprinted with permission of SAGE.

Basic Income: An Anthology of Contemporary Research, First Edition. Edited by Karl Widerquist, José A. Noguera, Yannick Vanderborght, and Jurgen De Wispelaere.

tax and social security systems are such that the €1,000 she earns are free of taxes and contributions. The impact is likely to be even worse if Artemis is, say, the single mother of one child, as her exceeding the threshold would then entail the loss of two ESs.[2]

Given the structure of the scheme, there is bound to be a range of incomes – which will be the broader, the higher the level of the ES and the larger the household – within which all financial incentives to work or save more are destroyed. How crowded this poverty trap is likely to be depends on the distribution of disposable incomes. In Schmitter and Bauer's proposal, as one moves from EU15 to EU22 or EU27, the level of the ES and hence the depth of the trap remain unchanged, but the threshold of eligibility sinks (from €5,295 to €4,506). As a result, the proportion of people likely to be affected by the trap will shrink in the richer countries, but the figures cited in the appendix suggest that in the poorer newcomer member states a huge proportion of the population will be stuck in it.

How can we prevent Schmitter and Bauer's scheme from wreaking havoc in the incentive structures at the bottom of the income distribution, which some national governments have painstakingly started to design so as to make them less dissuasive? The answer is evident: by fashioning the ES so that it is gradually phased out as the household's pre-ES disposable income increases, instead of being abruptly cut off at a certain threshold. Unavoidably, this would involve a more differentiated and thinner spreading of whatever resources are allocated to the scheme, and would come at the expense of the initial proposal's attractive simplicity.

A Shaky Floor

Schmitter and Bauer propose to establish a common threshold for eligibility throughout the EU, defined by reference to the EU's average income. This cutoff point would change annually to track per capita income in the previous year, whether due to fluctuations within the existing limits of the EU or due to the entry of new EU members. The fact that per capita EU income may go down as a result of either of these factors implies that, despite an unchanged pre-ES income, some poor households may suddenly fail to satisfy the eligibility condition and see themselves deprived of their entitlement to the ES. The creation of such insecurity towards the bottom of the income distribution is a most unwelcome feature of Schmitter and Bauer's proposal.

As far as dependency on internal fluctuations is concerned, a solution is not hard to come by. It consists of relating the ES cutoff point to the average EU per capita income in, say, the previous five or 10 years. As long as one can bank on a long-term upward productivity trend, the annual substitution of the latest per capita income figure for one that is five or 10 years older should guarantee a slow but secure increase of the level of real income below which one qualifies for the ES.

Obviously, the insecurity that results from new entries cannot be handled in the same way. But it is pretty clear that something should be done about this as well. For it is, to say the least, rather bizarre that much of the economic cost of admitting a comparatively poor country as a new member state should be borne by a section of the poorest households in the older member states, namely those who suddenly find themselves stripped of their entitlement to the ES as a result of their unchanged pre-ES disposable income now exceeding a third of the EU's new per capita income. The resulting insecurity for ES claimants in the old member states could easily feed a xenophobic anti-enlargement populist rhetoric. If only to avoid this additional obstacle to the admission of new members, it would therefore be wise to connect the cutoff point to an index of European prosperity that would not be affected by enlargement in this direct way, for example by choosing straight away a fixed percentage (which could be more than a third) of GDP per capita in EU27, without waiting for all, or indeed for any, of the candidate countries to acquire member status.

Country Gaming

Schmitter and Bauer's proposal also suffers from a more fundamental defect which cannot be mended by tinkering at the margin. A transnational transfer scheme which is, like the ES, targeted at households with a level of postnational-tax-and-transfer disposable income below some threshold unavoidably penalizes those countries which – with a given GDP per capita – have more effective antipoverty policies. This is both *unfair* – it rewards those member states with the least inclusive welfare states – and *counterproductive* – it provides national governments (which are still in control of the main instruments of income distribution) with an incentive to neglect the poor. This is a serious objection, whose incentive side Schmitter and Bauer did anticipate. To counter it, they offer two suggestions.

One simply consists in forbidding what they call "gaming" by member states, that is, opportunistic changes in national or local policies, designed to take advantage of the new scheme by increasing the number of individuals satisfying the eligibility condition. But how could the relevant European authority identify the policies which it should sanction? These cannot be the policies *motivated* by the objective of taking advantage of the new scheme, for social and fiscal policies are bound to be chosen in the light of many considerations, and the desire to cheat is most unlikely to be explicit. Nor can culpable policies be identified by analysing their *effects* on poverty levels, since the latter will always reflect the complex interaction of many factors, only some of which are under the government's control. The proposed solution therefore appears to have to rely on presumptions which are likely to trigger endless controversies, especially as it does nothing to alleviate the unfairness side of the objection: why should a member state be sanctioned if all it does is bring its institutions in line with those of other member states, which happened to be such that they could take greater advantage of the ES scheme from the start?

The second suggestion consists of neutralizing the member states' incentive to game by stipulating that the total level of gross transfers to any particular country (ES + agricultural and structural/regional funds) should remain unchanged. This provides no longterm solution either, as it would generate unsustainable distortions. Depending on the poverty figures, the farmers and disadvantaged regions of some countries will be lavishly or stingily treated, since the part of the funds allocated within each member state for agricultural or regional purposes will vary according to the budget that needs to be mobilized by the ES. A central reason why Schmitter and Bauer's proposal is attractive is that it channels net transfers automatically to the least favored areas. The second antigaming device they suggest would destroy this central feature of their proposal.

Two Real Solutions

Yet it is not unusual to have two levels of power involved in anti-poverty policy, and there are ways of articulating them so that gaming by lower-level units is kept within bounds.

The conventional way consists of copayment by the two levels. For example, the EU could conceivably introduce a right to the ES for anyone under the threshold, but require the relevant member state to pay half of the €1,000. Individual governments would then retain a strong incentive to shape employment and social insurance in such a way that few end up "extremely poor."

An alternative way of achieving a sensible incentive structure is suggested by Schmitter and Bauer when they indicate that the ES could be extended to a growing proportion of the European population through a gradual increase of the relative level of the eligibility threshold, until it is converted, ultimately, into a Basic Income paid to all. At the end of this process, gaming of the sort feared by Schmitter and Bauer would obviously be eradicated. Whatever each member state, region or local authority does for its poor would then come on top of the floor provided by the ES and would run no risk of reducing the number of its beneficiaries. If this is Schmitter and Bauer's long-term goal, we have no deep disagreement with them. But because of the perverse incentives and distortions that would plague their scheme, as explained above, over the long, possibly endless transition period during which only part of the population would be entitled to the ES, we believe there is a more promising alternative path.

A Euro-Dividend

Schmitter and Bauer propose introducing a uniform ES of €1,000 throughout the EU and gradually increasing the threshold up to which it is paid until all citizens are covered. What about paying a Euro-Dividend (ED) to *all* EU citizens *from the start*, though at a lower average level and at levels that are differentiated according to the cost of living in the various member states? The ED would be, say, €1,000 in those countries in which the cost of living is highest, lower elsewhere, with an upward convergence as immersion in a single market makes general price levels converge.

Despite this differentiation, the gross cost of a universal ED would necessarily be substantially higher than that of a means-tested ES. This additional cost would need to be picked up through a higher GDP-based contribution by member states or, more imaginatively, through a common energy tax.[3] National authorities could be given some scope in determining the best way to administer the benefit. Some countries may for example choose to deliver it in the form of a refundable tax credit, or to subject it to some participation condition. Needless to say, the increased gross cost would not be reflected in a correspondingly higher net cost to each country's taxpayers, as the latter would all receive the (henceforth universal) benefit.

Differentiation of the level of the ED according to the cost of living in each country will smooth the shock of both the substitution of individual transfers for regional and agricultural funds and of the entry of comparatively poorer new member states. Compared to what would happen if the ED were uniform, a larger share of the net transfers will go to those areas that will suffer most from the scrapping of existing subsidies. The immediate net cost of expanded membership to the taxpayers of current EU members will also be less, and hence less of an obstacle to the admission of new members, without this being unfair to the latter, and in particular to their poorest citizens, since the (average) purchasing power conferred by the ED would be the same everywhere.

Providing such differentiation is allowed, a modest universal ED provides a sound and feasible alternative to Schmitter and Bauer's ES in the service of the same fundamental objectives. A persuasive case for it would no doubt require the tightening of a number of bolts, and greater effort to clear the common confusion between the net cost and the gross cost of a redistributive scheme. But some of its key advantages should be clear enough. As the ED scheme works without an eligibility threshold (every citizen is entitled to the benefit), it avoids the havoc in the incentive structure that was depicted above. For the same reason, it does not require a common operational definition of income in all member states – a highly sensitive question which the various national tax and transfer systems solve in quite different ways. Last but not least, it offers the best tangible expression of the material benefit – the dividend of durable peace and unhindered economic exchange – which the EU is supposed to bring to *all* its citizens.

The EU's cross-border transfer machinery is about to face unprecedented challenges. Bold, innovative yet realistic thinking is urgently needed if one is to make positive use of the opportunities which impending crises will create. Schmitter and Bauer's modest proposal is an exploratory step in the right direction. Our modest suggestion for improving it is another one – we hope.

Acknowledgements

This paper was prepared within the framework of the inter-university research project PAI P4/32 "The New Social Question," funded by the Belgian federal government's Prime Minister's Office (Scientific, Technical and Cultural Services).

Notes

1. Editor's note: This text was written as a reply to Schmitter and Bauer (2001), who proposed a guaranteed means-tested stipendium to eradicate extreme poverty in the European Union.
2. We are here assuming, on the basis of Schmitter and Bauer's paper (in particular, Note 5 and the Appendix), that the Euro-Stipendium (ES) is paid at a uniform level to all individuals entitled to it, but that entitlement derives from membership in a household whose total pre-ES disposable income, divided by a coefficient that appropriately reflects household composition, falls short of a third of per capita disposable income. Hence, we interpret for example the statement that "there were an estimated 9,929,524 persons in EU-15 who earned less than one third of average income for the unit as a whole" as referring to the number of people living in households whose household-size-adjusted disposable income after national taxes and transfers is less than this amount.
3. About 10 years ago, Genet and Van Parijs estimated that a Euro-Dividend (ED) of €100 per month for every EU resident aged 18 or more would require, keeping the volume of energy consumption unchanged, a tax of €425 per ton-oil equivalent (toe) on all energy uses of oil, gas, coal and electricity. This amount was far above the EU's average level of taxation on these uses of energy at the time (about €100 per toe), but close to estimates of the environmental cost of such uses by various groups of European experts. Abstracting again from any effect on consumption among EU member states, net losers and net gainers from the scheme would be about the same as (then) with the existing social funds, but the net transfer to the net gainers would be about 14 times as much as under the social funds. See Genet (1991); Genet and Van Parijs (1992). Obviously, this sort of estimate would need updating and refining, but it gives an idea of the magnitudes involved.

References

Genet, M. (1991). *Calcul d'un mode de financement d'une allocation universelle européenne.* Master's thesis. Université Catholique de Louvain: Département des Sciences Economiques.

Genet, M. and Van Parijs, P. (1992). Eurogrant. *BIRG Bulletin*, 15, 4–7.

Schmitter, P.C. and Bauer, M.W. (2001). A (Modest) Proposal for Expanding Social Citizenship in the European Union. *Journal of European Social Policy*, 11 (1), 55–65.

Chapter 55

Negative Income Tax: The Original Idea

Milton Friedman

Originally published as Friedman, M. (1962). The Alleviation of Poverty. In *Capitalism and Freedom*. University of Chicago Press, Chicago.

The extraordinary economic growth experienced by Western countries during the past two centuries and the wide distribution of the benefits of free enterprise have enormously reduced the extent of poverty in any absolute sense in the capitalistic countries of the West. But poverty is in part a relative matter, and even in these countries, there are clearly many people living under conditions that the rest of us label as poverty.

One recourse, and in many ways the most desirable, is private charity. It is noteworthy that the heyday of laissez-faire, the middle and late nineteenth century in Britain and the United States, saw an extraordinary proliferation of private eleemosynary organizations and institutions. One of the major costs of the extension of governmental welfare activities has been the corresponding decline in private charitable activities.

It can be argued that private charity is insufficient because the benefits from it accrue to people other than those who make the gifts. I am distressed by the sight of poverty; I am benefited by its alleviation; but I am benefited equally whether I or someone else pays for its alleviation; the benefits of other people's charity therefore partly accrue to me. To put it differently, we might all of us be willing to contribute to the relief of poverty, provided everyone else did. We might not be willing to contribute the same amount without such assurance. In small communities, public pressure can suffice to realize the proviso even with private charity. In the large impersonal communities that are increasingly coming to dominate our society, it is much more difficult for it to do so.

Suppose one accepts, as I do, this line of reasoning as justifying governmental action to alleviate poverty; to set, as it were, a floor under the standard of life of every person in the community. There remain the questions, how much and how. I see no way of deciding "how much" except in terms of the amount of taxes we – by which I mean the great bulk of us – are willing to impose on ourselves for the purpose. The question, "how," affords more room for speculation.

From Friedman, M. (1962). The Alleviation of Poverty. In *Capitalism and Freedom*. University of Chicago Press, Chicago. Reprinted with permission of University of Chicago Press.

Basic Income: An Anthology of Contemporary Research, First Edition. Edited by Karl Widerquist, José A. Noguera, Yannick Vanderborght, and Jurgen De Wispelaere.

Two things seem clear. First, if the objective is to alleviate poverty, we should have a program directed at helping the poor. There is every reason to help the poor man who happens to be a farmer, not because he is a farmer but because he is poor. The program, that is, should be designed to help people as people not as members of particular occupational groups or age groups or wage-rate groups or labor organizations or industries. This is a defect of farm programs, general old-age benefits, minimum-wage laws, pro-union legislation, tariffs, licensing provisions of crafts or professions, and so on in seemingly endless profusion. Second, so far as possible the program should, while operating through the market, not distort the market or impede its functioning. This is a defect of price supports, minimum-wage laws, tariffs and the like.

The arrangement that recommends itself on purely mechanical grounds is a Negative Income Tax. We now have an exemption of $600 per person under the federal income tax (plus a minimum 10% flat deduction). If an individual receives $100 taxable income, that is, an income of $100 in excess of the exemption and deductions, he pays a tax. Under the proposal, if his taxable income minus $100, that is, $100 less than the exemption plus deductions, he would pay a negative tax, that is, receive a subsidy. If the rate of subsidy were, say, 50%, he would receive $50. If he had no income at all, and, for simplicity, no deductions, and the rate were constant, he would receive $300. He might receive more than this if he had deductions, for example, for medical expenses, so that his income less deductions was negative even before subtracting the exemption. The rates of subsidy could, of course, be graduated just as the rates of tax above the exemption are. In this way, it would be possible to set a floor below which no man's net income (defined now to include the subsidy) could fall – in the simple example $300 per person. The precise floor set would depend on what the community could afford.

The advantages of this arrangement are clear. It is directed specifically at the problem of poverty. It gives help in the form most useful to the individual, namely, cash. It is general and could be substituted for the host of special measures now in effect. It makes explicit the cost borne by society. It operates outside the market. Like any other measures to alleviate poverty, it reduces the incentives of those helped to help themselves, but it does not eliminate that incentive entirely, as a system of supplementing incomes up to some fixed minimum would. An extra dollar earned always means more money available for expenditure.

No doubt there would be problems of administration, but these seem to me a minor disadvantage, if they be a disadvantage at all. The system would fit directly into our current income tax system and could be administered along with it. The present tax system covers the bulk of income recipients and the necessity of covering all would have the by-product of improving the operation of the present income tax. More important, if enacted as a substitute for the present rag bag of measures directed at the same end, the total administrative burden would surely be reduced.

A few brief calculations suggest also that this proposal could be far less costly in money, let alone in the degree of governmental intervention involved, than our present collection of welfare measures. Alternatively, these calculations can be regarded as showing how wasteful our present measures are, judged as measures for helping the poor.

In 1961, government amounted to something like $33 billion (federal, state, and local) on direct welfare payments and programs of all kinds: old-age assistance, social security benefit payments, aid to dependent children, general assistance, farm price support programs, public housing, and so on.[1] I have excluded veterans' benefits in making this calculation. I have also made no allowance for the direct and indirect costs of such measures as minimum-wage laws, tariffs, licensing provisions, and so on, or for the costs of public health activities, state and local expenditures on hospitals, mental institutions, and the like.

There are approximately 57 million consumer units (unattached individuals and families) in the United States. The 1961 expenditures of $33 billion would have financed outright cash grants of nearly $6,000 per consumer unit to the 10% with the lowest incomes. Such grants would have raised their incomes above the average for all units in the United States. Alternatively, these expenditures would have financed grants of nearly $3,000 per consumer unit to the 20% with the lowest incomes. Even if one went so far as that one-third whom New Dealers were fond of calling ill-fed, ill-housed, and ill-clothed, 1961 expenditures would have financed grants of nearly $2,000 per consumer unit, roughly the sum which, after allowing for the change in the level of prices, was the income which separated the lower one-third in the middle 1930s from the upper two-thirds. Today, fewer than one-eighth of consumer units have an income, adjusted for the change in the level of prices, as low as that of the lowest third in the middle 1930s.

Clearly, these are all far more extravagant programs than can be justified to "alleviate poverty" even by a rather generous interpretation of that term. A program which supplemented the incomes of the 20% of the consumer units with the lowest incomes so as to raise them to the lowest income of the rest would cost less than half of what we are now spending.

The major disadvantage of the proposed Negative Income Tax is its political implications. It establishes a system under which taxes are imposed on some to pay subsidies to others. And presumably, these others have a vote. There is always the danger that instead of being an arrangement under which the great majority tax themselves willingly to help an unfortunate minority, it will be converted into one under which a majority imposes taxes for its own benefit on an unwilling minority. Because this proposal makes the process so explicit, the danger is perhaps greater than with other measures. I see no solution to this problem except to rely on the self-restraint and good will of the electorate.

Writing about a corresponding problem – British old-age pensions – in 1914, Dicey said, "Surely a sensible and a benevolent man may well ask himself whether England as a whole will gain by enacting that the receipt of poor relief, in the shape of a pension, shall be consistent with the pensioner's retaining the right to join in the election of a Member of Parliament" (Dicey, 1914).

The verdict of experience in Britain on Dicey's question must as yet be regarded as mixed. England did move to universal suffrage without the disfranchisement of either pensioners or other recipients of state aid. And there has been an enormous expansion of taxation of some for the benefit of others, which must surely be regarded as having retarded Britain's growth, and so may not even have benefited most of those who regard themselves as on the receiving end. But these measures have not destroyed, at least as yet, Britain's liberties or its predominantly capitalistic system. And, more important, there have been some signs of a turning of the tide and of the exercise of self-restraint on the part of the electorate.

Note

1. This figure is equal to government transfer payments ($31.1 billion) less veterans' benefits ($4.8 billion), both from the Department of Commerce national income accounts, plus federal expenditures on the agricultural program ($5.5 billion) plus federal expenditures on public housing

and other aids to housing ($0.5 billion), both for year ending June 30, 1961 from Treasury accounts, plus a rough allowance of $0.7 billion to raise it to even billions and to allow for administrative costs of federal programs, omitted state and local programs, and miscellaneous items. My guess is that this figure is a substantial underestimate.

Reference

Dicey, A.V. (1914). *Law and Public Opinion in England*, 2nd edn. Macmillan, London, p. xxxv.

Chapter 56

The Case for a Progressive Negative Income Tax

Fred Block and Jeff Manza

Excerpts from Block, F. and Manza, J. (1997). Could We End Poverty in a Postindustrial Society? The Case for a Progressive Negative Income Tax. *Politics & Society*, 25 (4), 473–511.

This diversity in the employment situation of the poor means that any concerted effort to reduce poverty must do three things simultaneously. First, income levels of the poorest workers have to be raised. Families with a full-time wage earner must be able to live above the poverty line. But many poor families dependent upon a part-time or part-year wage earner must also see their income rise. This group will benefit from the second necessary step – expanding the availability of employment. This means more working time for many of those working part-time or part-year and job opportunities for at least some of those in the group who have no earned income. Third, transfers have to be increased for the substantial group of poor households that cannot take advantage of expanded opportunities to earn income.

There is room for considerable disagreement about priorities among these tasks. For example, many analyses suggest that the first two objectives – increasing the compensation for work and expanding the availability of work – are far more urgent than taking care of households with no employment income. But any antipoverty strategy that completely ignores the latter group has two obvious flaws. First, even if it were entirely successful on the other two fronts, it would leave a significant number of people, including children, in poverty. Second, even when jobs are available, numerous contingencies – disabilities, mental problems, addiction, illness of other family members, and unanticipated family breakup – can leave households without earned income. As a matter of fairness, people need to be protected from these contingencies.

Once it is recognized that a morally defensible antipoverty strategy needs to move forward on all three of these fronts, it becomes apparent that there is a serious policy trilemma.[1] There are three distinct goals of antipoverty policy – to increase employment, to increase the incentives to work, and to treat those without employment income humanely. Yet it appears impossible to progress toward all three goals simultaneously.

From Block, F. and Manza, J. (1997). Could We End Poverty in a Postindustrial Society? The Case for a Progressive Negative Income Tax. *Politics & Society*, 25 (4), 473–511. Reprinted with permission of SAGE.

Basic Income: An Anthology of Contemporary Research, First Edition. Edited by Karl Widerquist, José A. Noguera, Yannick Vanderborght, and Jurgen De Wispelaere.

The first horn of the trilemma results from efforts to increase the incentives to work by raising the wages of low-wage workers. When this is done either through higher minimum wages or some system of collective bargaining, it is likely that the creation of new employment opportunities will be slowed. Conservatives take this argument further and insist that any increase in the minimum wage will lead to a net contraction of available employment. While this extreme formulation is theoretically and empirically dubious,[2] there can be little doubt that with sharp increases in the price of unskilled labor, employers will attempt to save on labor costs by hiring fewer employees. If the minimum wage in the United States suddenly rose from $5.15 an hour to $7.15 an hour – a level comparable to some European labor markets – many employers would reconsider their need for certain employees and try to substitute machinery for newly expensive labor.[3] Some of the sharp divergence between Western European and U.S. labor market experience over the past 15 years can be traced to such a cost difference. Labor market regulations in Western Europe assure that most employees at the bottom of the labor market make high enough wages to escape poverty. In response to the cost of labor, the creation of new jobs has been relatively slow, leading to very high rates of unemployment. In the United States, with far weaker labor market regulation, compensation for low-wage employees has fallen relative to average wages and to the poverty line. The result has been much more dynamic employment creation in the United States, while many workers at the low end of the labor market remain in poverty.[4]

Governments can circumvent this policy conflict, but their actions produce a second conflict. It is possible to keep minimum wage levels and other labor market regulation low in order to maximize job creation and use transfer payments to bring low-wage workers out of poverty. This is the idea behind the Earned Income Tax Credit. This policy choice makes it easier to raise income levels of the working poor and expand employment opportunities simultaneously. But if such a program succeeds in expanding the supply of low-wage jobs, the aggregate cost of the tax credit is likely to be quite high.[5] The second horn of the trilemma is that such expensive transfers to the working poor will generally come at the expense of transfers to the nonworking poor. Since politics limits the total amount of funds available at any particular time for antipoverty efforts, more generous income subsidies for the working poor mean less generous transfers to those who are outside the labor force. Thus those who are entirely dependent on transfers are likely to remain well below the poverty line.

This second horn of the trilemma is also evident when government seeks to expand employment opportunities by deliberately creating more public sector jobs (whether temporary or permanent). The problem is that public sector job creation tends to be even more expensive than the policy of tax credits for the working poor. There are two reasons for this. First, there are usually strong pressures on government to compensate such public service jobs at least at the minimum wage in order to protect existing public sector workers from being replaced by cheaper labor. Second, to protect such programs from patronage and corruption, the people employed need to be carefully monitored. But the hiring of many supervisorial employees substantially escalates the cost of the program. The consequence is that public sector job creation also tends to come at the expense of generosity to those who depend on transfers.

The third horn is the one that has dominated the welfare debate. If transfer payments are generous enough to allow those without earned income to escape poverty, this weakens the incentive to work. This drives up the budgetary costs of transfer payments and reduces the resources that might otherwise be available for public sector job creation or for subsidies to low-wage employees. Moreover, when reliance on transfers becomes widespread, subcultures can develop in which neither employment nor the preparation for employment are important factors in people's lives.

In recent U.S. politics, discussion of the work disincentive effects of transfers has centered on Aid to Families with Dependent Children (AFDC), but the issues are just as serious with programs that assist the disabled. While the "disabled" are generally seen as deserving of government support, there is considerable ambiguity in deciding who is disabled and whether particular disabilities prevent people from working. When eligibility for such programs depends on proving that one is incapable of holding down a job, recipients are unlikely to experiment with employment for fear that their eligibility will be withdrawn.

While this trilemma exists in any developed market society, its severity depends critically on two factors. The first is the strength of "postindustrial trends" such as the expansion of women's participation in the paid labor force, the growth of part-time work, the rise in female-headed households, and the more rapid turnover of skills and jobs in the labor market.[6] These trends increase the number of households at any point in time that do not include a full-time earner. Many of these households will be in danger of slipping into poverty without transfer payments.

The second factor is the level of public support for redistributive spending. In a number of other countries, public support for such spending has been strong enough that the percentage of the population living in poverty is much lower than in the United States. In the United States, 20% of children grew up in poverty in the 1980s, compared to 9% of Canadian children, 7% of children in the United Kingdom, and even lower rates in most of Western Europe.[7] The successes elsewhere can be traced to a combination of higher minimum wages and more generous transfer programs. The intense opposition in the United States to higher antipoverty spending means that any set of policy choices will be quickly caught on one or another horn of this trilemma.

A major contribution to the national conversation about transfer strategies came from Milton Friedman's advocacy of a Negative Income Tax (NIT) in his 1962 book, *Capitalism and Freedom* (Friedman, 1962). The core idea was that households below a certain income level would receive a cash transfer from the government. Unlike means-tested programs that effectively taxed income above a certain level at 100% rate, the Negative Income Tax would establish positive work incentives for all of the poor. Friedman linked this proposal with the elimination of policies that he saw as interfering with the working of the market, such as minimum wage laws and other transfer programs.

Support for the idea of income guarantees from both the political left and the political right succeeded in putting the issue on the national political agenda. A Guaranteed Income was endorsed by several hundred economists in a full-page and in *The New York Times* in 1969, and it was an important ingredient in Richard Nixon's ill-fated Family Assistance Plan in 1971.[8] Interest in the idea was sufficiently strong that the federal government carried out a series of major social experiments (lasting from 1968 to 1982) to determine how well a system of income guarantees would work.[9]

Despite the ongoing experiments, the idea of a Guaranteed Income largely disappeared from U.S. political debates by the mid-1970s. However, a similar idea emerged in Western Europe in the 1980s in apparent response to dramatic increases in unemployment rates that made historic demands for "full employment" policies appear wildly unrealistic. Under the names "Basic" or "Citizen's Income," the idea of a universal and unconditional income grant has received increasing attention in a number of European countries, and a group of Basic Income supporters – the Basic Income European Network (BIEN) – has been remarkably successful in getting the idea heard within European policy circles (Van Parijs, 1992a).

Each of these main versions of the Transfer Paradigm[10] has serious weaknesses. The income guarantee proposals that came out of the political left in the 1960s were generally insensitive to the problem of work incentives because support for the Guaranteed Income was so closely tied to arguments about automation and fear that jobs were quickly disappearing from the U.S. economy. The income guarantee was seen as parallel to pensions for old people; it was supposed to provide a life of economic dignity to people even when work was not available. In the same way that the question of work disincentives for pension recipients appeared irrelevant, so it appeared irrelevant for those who would receive the income guarantee. In fact, one influential advocate of the Guaranteed Income – Robert Theobald – proposed that those who received the grant would be allowed to work, but they would keep only 10% of their earned income (Theobald, 1963). Proposing a 90% tax rate on even the poorest wage earners shows a striking disinterest in work disincentives.

In retrospect, these analysts misunderstood how automation would reshape the labor force. Rather than a disappearance of all job opportunities, there has been a sharp decline in the full-time, blue-collar manufacturing jobs that had provided an important mobility route for generations of immigrants and minorities. Since the 1960s there has been considerable job growth, but it has been disproportionately in service sector jobs that are part-time or poorly compensated. The issue of work disincentives looms large in determining whether or not poor people will take these part-time or poorly compensated jobs. Furthermore, in thinking about "pensioning off" preretirement adults, these analysts failed to consider the long-term negative consequences of living in communities where few adults can find work.

While Milton Friedman and his followers took the issue of work incentives seriously, their proposal risked deepening rather than alleviating poverty. The combination of rather stingy negative income tax grants with the elimination of minimum wages and other social welfare programs threatened to recreate Speenhamland.[11] In sections of rural England at the end of eighteeth century, a system of income subsidies to low-wage workers combined with strict laws against trade unionism is thought to have dramatically lowered living standards. On one side, employers could lower wages because payments from the parish subsidized living standards. On the other side, employees had no choice but to take this low-wage work, and they had no means to bargain for higher wages. The result was that both labor productivity and wages fell, further impoverishing the rural population. Friedman's Negative Income Tax threatens to create similar conditions because of the subsidy to low-wage employers and the loss of employee bargaining power as the poor have no recourse other than work.

More recent European proposals for a Basic Income Grant (BIG) are vulnerable to an entirely different critique – the difficulty of financing. One of the main attractions of the BIG is that everybody gets it; the government check arrives every month without any system of means-testing at all.[12] Hence, even the richest households could still count on the arrival of the BIG check. But the key to the financing problem is that marginal tax rates for the highest income households are between 35% and 50%, so that high-income households would keep half or more of their grants and middle-income households would keep even higher percentages. Beyond the additional revenues required to increase transfers to households at the bottom of the income distribution, one also has to finance the substantial transfer to millions of middle-income and high-income households that do not need additional income. The attempt to raise all of this additional revenue through the personal income tax would require very large increases in marginal tax rates for middle-income and high-income households. While such increases might be economically justifiable, they are likely to encounter serious political resistance.[13]

Despite these difficulties with various versions of the Transfer Paradigm, it has influenced the major enduring U.S. antipoverty initiative of the post-World War II period – the Earned Income Tax Credit. The EITC is a Negative Income Tax plan that provides cash support – either as tax refunds or monthly checks – to significant numbers of low-income households with earned income.[14] The initial justification for the EITC was the recognition that government payroll taxes represented a significant burden on families of the working poor, so the tax credit was initially designed to offset Social Security payroll taxes. However, Congress has progressively expanded the EITC. The most recent expansion in 1993 provides eligible families with a maximum credit of $3,560. Until the 1993 reform, eligibility for the EITC was limited to families with earned income, but that legislation also provided for a small EITC credit for childless workers between the ages of 24 and 65. The maximum benefit of $306 is designed to exactly offset the Social Security payroll tax. The total dollar value of EITC transfers beginning in 1996 (when the most recent program expansion is fully implemented) is around $25 billion (Danziger and Gottschalk, 1995). But the EITC falls far short of an effective antipoverty strategy because it does nothing for households with low or insignificant amounts of earned income, and it leaves many of the part-time or part-year working poor below the poverty line.

An Alternative Approach

Can elements of the Employment and Transfer paradigms be combined to generate a politically feasible antipoverty strategy that could weave a successful course through the policy trilemma? We think this can be done by structuring a system of income guarantees to achieve the objectives historically favored by advocates of full employment – a tighter labor market in which even low-skilled workers have substantially more bargaining power than they do now. Rather than seeing income guarantees as an alternative to work, we think they can be used to create a less inegalitarian society in which the lives of most adults will continue to revolve around paid work. (While the specific proposal that we advance is based on a Negative Income Tax, other income guarantee designs might produce the same results.)

The key is to distinguish between two techniques for tightening the labor markets – the macrostrategy and the microstrategy. The macrostrategy assumes that people's preferences about work and leisure are relatively stable and that the labor market can be tightened by adding new jobs at decent wages until virtually everyone who wants a job is employed. This is the approach – drawing on the World War II experience – that advocates of full employment have taken. Assuming an employed labor force of 100 million people, it might take 6 to 8 million new full-time jobs to bring about the desired level of labor market tightness given unemployment, involuntary part-time employment, and those who want work but are not actively seeking employment.[15] In contrast, the microstrategy begins from the observation that at any given moment, tens of millions of people – both employed and thinking about employment – are making a complex calculation as to how many hours of paid labor they need to perform. They are weighing family responsibilities education or training, various avocational interests, their budgetary needs, and the rate of compensation of available work. If a Negative Income Tax placed a floor under income, it could influence these calculations by giving many people the economic security to reduce their hours of work. With such reductions, it would be possible to tighten the labor market by reducing the aggregate hours of work supplied by those already in the labor force. With the same example of an employed labor force of 100 million people averaging 1,500 work hours a year. an average reduction in hours of work of just 6% could open year-round, half-time jobs for as many as 9 million people who are currently not working.[16]

What makes the microstrategy potentially viable is the tremendous expansion of part-time employment, so that people no longer face a stark choice between a full-time job or full-time leisure. Rather, they can work anywhere from zero hours per week to as many as 60 or 80 hours a week. To be sure, the choices of many employees are severely constrained. Some employers impose mandatory overtime on their employees and refuse them the opportunity to work less than full-time. Furthermore, part-time employees usually do not receive even a proportionate share of the employee benefits, such us health insurance, available to full-time employees. But these rigidities could be eased through legislation that assured benefits for part-time workers and provided employees with more room to negotiate hours with their employers.[17]

From an economic point of view, the expansion of opportunities to work less than full-time is clearly desirable. Even though the U.S. economy has been very successful in creating jobs, it is far from providing full-time employment for even the two-thirds of adults below 65 who are currently in the labor force. By expanding the number of jobs that were less than full-time, the labor market could absorb a higher percentage of the adult population.[18] Moreover, the growth of part-time employment plays a vital role in allowing individuals and families to combine paid work with the vital tasks of child rearing. In short, using transfers to encourage people to reduce their hours of paid work makes both economic and social policy sense.

When this relatively generous NIT is evaluated in relation to the trilemma, the results are positive. The NIT would provide increased incentives to work for the poor by assuring a substantial improvement in the living standard of those households with a full-time wage earner. It also assures that households with no earned income or part-time earned income will be brought close to the poverty line. And if the work disincentive effects are relatively strong, the NIT will also provide more opportunities for employment for many of those who are currently unable to find additional hours of paid work. But much hinges on how much such a program would cost, since political support and generosity toward those dependent on transfers is likely to diminish as the program becomes more expensive.

The proposal

Our proposal is that the Earned Income Tax Credit be expanded into a full-scale Negative Income Tax. This NIT would provide a level of support for households without earned income that would bring those with children close to or above the federal poverty line. It would also replace a whole series of categorical programs that are designed to protect households from specific contingencies, such as unemployment insurance, disability programs, food stamps, and the successor program to AFDC.

All adult, resident[19] citizens[20] under 65 would be entitled to an income supplement that would guarantee them an income of $6,000 in 1990 dollars.[21] Children who are between 18 and 20 are eligible for a benefit of $2,500, and for children under 18, the custodial parent is entitled to $2,500 for the first child, $2,000 for the second child, and $1,500 for each additional child.[22] These benefit levels are designed to bring all households to 90% of the federal poverty line or higher. For example, the poverty threshold for single adults in 1990 was $6,802, so the grant for a single adult with no income would provide 88.2% of that amount. A family of two adults and two young children with no income would be entitled to transfers of $16,500 – 123% of the poverty line.

Households with earned or other income below the threshold for eligibility would be taxed at a 50% rate.[23] (For illustrations of the benefit levels for different incomes and household types, see Table 56.1) For example, if the four person family mentioned above were to earn $5,000 in income, the grant they would receive would be reduced by $2,500 making their after-tax income $19,000. If they earned $10,000, their after-tax income would be $21,500. Even with $30,000 of earned income, they would still be entitled to a transfer of $1 ,500, bringing their total income to $31,500. It is only at income above $33,000 – double their benefit level – that they would no longer be eligible for any income supplement.

This design assures that the NIT will provide very substantial benefits to those households now just above the federal poverty line. A family of four earning $20,000 a year will receive an annual transfer of $6,500. Thus even as many of the poor are raised up to the federal poverty line, these nonpoor but hard-pressed families will experience a dramatic improvement in their living standards.

Moreover, we also propose to raise the level of the individual income tax exemption to make the NIT work more effectively. Adults who did not receive a NIT transfer would

Table 56.1 NIT Examples.

Recipient #1: Single Individual

If nontransfer income is . . .	Then NIT Grant will be . . .	Total income will be . . .
0	$6,000	$6,000
$2,000	$5,000	$7,000
$5,000	$3,500	$8,500
$9,000	$1,500	$10,500
$12,000 or higher	0	

Recipient #2: Single Parent, One Child Under 18

If nontransfer income is . . .	Then NIT Grant will be . . .	Total income will be . . .
0	$8,500	$8,500
$2,000	$7,500	$9,500
$5,000	$6,000	$11,000
$9.000	$4,000	$13,500
$14,000	$1,500	$15,500
$17,000 or higher	0	

Recipient #3: Two Parent, Two Children Under 18

If nontransfer income is . . .	Then NIT Grant will be . . .	Total income will be . . .
0	$16,500	$16,500
$5,000	$14,000	$19,000
$10,000	$11,500	$21,500
$15,000	$9,000	$24,000
$20,000	$6,500	$26,500
$25,000	$4,000	$29,000
$30,000	$1,500	$31,500
$33,000 and higher	0	

not pay income tax on the first $13,000 of earnings and the exemption for children would be $6,500. Thus a two-adult family of four would not owe any federal income tax until they reached an income of $39,000.[24] This change is designed to protect people who are near the phase-out level for a transfer from both losing the transfer and facing a positive income tax obligation. Even for people near the phase-out level, any increment in the family's earned income will result in higher after-tax income. (This change could be linked to the elimination of many of the complex deductions and exemptions in the current tax code.)

While directly responding to the needs of the poor and the working poor, the proposed NIT would also provide important income insurance for households higher up in the income distribution, Households that can now be plunged into poverty as a consequence of divorce, death, disability, or prolonged unemployment would be protected from impoverishment by the NIT. For example, a nonworking mother whose husband suddenly departed would be immediately eligible for the NIT for herself and her children. To be sure, higher-income households would not be able to sustain their living standnrds for long with only the NIT transfer. It would make sense for them to supplement the NIT protection with private insurance policies against contingencies that interrupt earnings.[25]

Estimating program costs

We have estimated how much this program would cost using the 1990 Census. We followed the following procedures in constructing our population of households: first, we eliminated from consideration all households in which more than 40% of the members were 65 or older. The assumption here is that the Social Security system already works to provide reliable income security for older Americans, and our intention is to estimate the costs of providing comparable income security for the rest of the population. Hence, our cost calculations do not address any continuing problems of poverty among older households.[26]

We have followed special procedures for the population of single people who are between the ages of 18 and 20. Since the census data record many of these individuals as living away from home even if they are students, there is no way of effectively linking people in this age category to their family of origin. Hence, we treat all people in this category as single individuals even though many of them remain dependants for tax purposes. Based upon the information on their earnings, we have provided 80% of these 18-to-20-year-olds with a grant of $2,500. We have assumed that the other 20% of this age category are fully emancipated – living on their own and fully self-supporting. This 20% subgroup is, therefore, eligible for the full $6,000 income supplement. (If we were to assume that 30% of this group were emancipated, the additional cost would be $3.1 billion. It is roughly that amount for each additional 10% of the 18-to-20 population who are given the full $6,000 grant.) Yet the resulting estimate is still too high because dependent 18-to-20-year-olds will only receive the $2,500 income supplement when their family's income is low enough to make them eligible. Hence, we make another relatively conservative adjustment by assuming that one-third of the nonemancipated 18-to-20-year-olds will not receive any grant because of their parents' tax bracket. As a consequence, the final cost of the transfer to the single 18-to-20-year-olds comes to $14.8 billion.

Beyond these adjustments the data analysis is straightforward. All households are arrayed in a grid by family structure and income level.[27] The income measure is quite comprehensive, but we have deliberately excluded income from transfer programs such as AFDC and

Table 56.2 Estimating the Cost of the NIT (in billions of 1990 dollars).

Cost of income transfers	$205.8
Downward adjustment for number of prisoners	–9.6
Adjusted cost	196.2
Upward adjustment for work disincentive effects	+11.8
Gross cost of NIT	208.0
Savings from existing programs	
Income maintenance programs	–127.6
Social security programs	–42.0
Total program savings	–169.6
Adjustment for double counting on cost saving	+16.9
Adjusted programs savings	–152.7
Net cost of NIT	$55.3

Social Security. At the lower end, there are 16 increments of $2,500, then six increments of $10,000 from $40,000 to $90,000, and then all households above $100,000 are grouped together. Households that reported negative income are assumed to have an income of zero. Each household assumed to have an income equal to the midpoint of its category; households with income between zero and $2,500 are assumed to have $1,250 of income.

We calculated the size of the transfer that each household would receive based on household size and its reported amount of nontransfer income. These are aggregated across the grid and yield an overall estimate of the cost of the program (see Table 56.2).[28] An additional adjustment has been made for convicted inmates of state, local, and federal prisons since they would lose their grant for the duration of their imprisonment.[29] There were 1.64 million prisoners in June 1996 (Butterfield, 1997). Consequently, the total cost of the NIT has been adjusted downward by $9.6 billion. We have also made an upward adjustment of $11.8 billion to reflect the increased costs associated with work disincentive effects. If we assume an average 6% reduction in work effort, that would increase the cost of the program by approximately $11.8 billion because of the need to offset the reduction in earned income that follows from reduced hours of work.[30] Hence, we suggest the gross cost of the program would be $208 billion in 1990 dollars.

Estimating savings from existing programs

This income support system would replace or reduce the cost of many existing programs that are currently funded out of federal or state budgets.

We have been quite selective in the government programs that are slated for elimination. In contrast to conservative NIT proposals, we do not propose to do away with welfare state programs altogether. While a NIT of the size we have proposed will make it easier to solve some problems, it cannot substitute for current levels of federal spending on health, education, and housing programs. Many of these programs are targeted toward lower-income households and need to be continued. In the case of housing, for example, there are severe shortages of appropriate housing for low-income people, and increased federal efforts are still necessary to expand the supply of such housing. Yet the NIT would make it possible for some families of the working poor to do without housing subsidies that they currently receive.

Revenue sources

This proposal requires two different changes in revenue flows. First, it is necessary to adjust for the loss of revenues that would result from the upward shift in individual exemption amounts for the income tax. Our estimate is that this change would result in a loss of $30 to $40 billion per year. In 1993, the bottom half of all filers with income paid $24.6 billion in federal income tax, and that constitutes the bulk of the lost revenue (Cruciano and Strudler, 1996). But with the much higher personal exemptions that we are proposing, some households with income only slightly above the exemption level – who are among the top half of filers – would also receive some tax relief. For example, a family of four earning $50,000 would pay at a 33% rate on all income above the exemption level, producing a tax bill of $3,630. This compares to a tax of about $5,000 for such a family in 1993 assuming the stundard deduction.[31]

Our proposal is to offset this $30 to $40 billion loss of revenue by raising taxes on higher-income households. This would not require further increases in marginal tax rates, but it could be done by strengthening the alternative minimum tax and eliminating or capping certain exemptions and deductions. The Clinton Tax Reform in 1993 raised the effective tax rate on the top 10% of filers from 18.05% to 19.14% – resulting in an additional $16.7 billion of revenue. Hence, tax reforms that raised the effective rate on high-income households to 22% should offset the tax relief for lower-income households.

The second revenue problem is to raise the $60 to $70 billion (in current dollars) of additional revenue required to fund the NIT transfers. In comparison to other developed nations, the United States ranks 26th among 28 countries in its tax burden, but the personal income tax does account for a comparatively large share of U.S. taxation? (Congressional Budget Office, 1997. See also Heilbroner, 1991) Hence, it makes sense to explore revenue options that would not involve changes in the personal income tax beyond those suggested already.

One potential source of the revenues would be spending cuts. Military spending in the United States remains far too high for a country that no longer faces any major superpower enemy. U.S. military spending of $262 billion per year represents 37% of global military spending. The Pentagon argues that the United States has to be prepared simultaneously to fight two regional conflicts on the scale of the war against Iraq. If one rejects this premise, it is possible to reduce military spending by $40 to $70 billion per year (Korb, 1995; Hartung, 1995). Since the NIT would provide a safety net for those likely to face unemployment as a result of further military cutbacks, it is logical to combine the implementation of the NIT with further reductions in defense spending.

A second obvious revenue source is the corporate income tax. Over the past 30 years, Congress has repeatedly modified the rules governing the corporate income tax in ways that have dramatically reduced its effective rate. Corporate tax revenues fell from 3.9% of Gross Domestic Product in 1961 to 2.4% in 1994.[32] Had the percentage of GDP remained stable, the corporate tax in 1994 would have generated another $103 billion in revenue. While the strategy of inducing corporations to invest more by paying lower taxes has had only limited success, the reduction in the effective rate of the corporate income tax has been a major contributor to budgetary shortfalls at the federal level.

Implementing the NIT would represent a different strategy for stimulating investment since demand among the bottom half of households would rise. Since many corporations would benefit from this expanding economy, it is logical for them to contribute to this in the form of a higher rate of effective corporate taxation. The standard objection is that such increased taxes would place U.S. firms at a competitive disadvantage, but it is important to recognize that our major trading rivals – Germany and Japan – have higher effective rates of corporate taxation (Kuttner, 1984).

The recent rise in income and wealth inequality has generated two other ideas that could generate a large portion of the needed revenue. In a study of the growing inequality of wealth distribution in the United States, Edward Wolff has suggested that a wealth tax along the lines of what currently exists in Germany would be a means both to increase equity and assure more productive uses of existing wealth. This would be a tax of around 1% on the value of assets – both financial holdings and real property. Germany's tax excludes pension holdings and the first $129,000 of holdings for a family of four. His simulation suggests that a wealth tax following this German model would have raised $67.5 billion in 1989 (Wolff, 1995).

Robert Pollin and Dean Baker have recently argued that a transaction tax on financial exchanges in the United States would both raise very substantial revenues and dampen some of the excess volatility that currently exists in stock, bond, and derivative markets (Pollin and Baker, 1994). The idea is that if traders had to pay a small transaction tax on each trade, it would discourage certain speculative strategies that tend to destabilize the markets. Their estimates are that 0.5% transaction tax would generate between $30 and $60 billion per year in revenue. Recently, there has also been renewed discussion of international agreement to establish a "Tobin Tax" on foreign exchange transactions which is also designed to reduce excess volatility in those markets. One recent study finds that such a tax at the rate of 0.25% would have generated revenues of $46.8 billion for the United States and $300 billion globally based on the 1995 level of foreign cxchange trading (Felix and Sau, 1996).

Some combination of these measures could raise the revenue necessary to finance the NIT without requiring further increases of the personal income tax. Moreover, there is good reason to believe that over the medium term, the NIT would contribute to a faster rate of increase in tax revenues. As that happens, it would be possible to gradually increase the generosity of the income supplement to assure that it was completely effective in eliminating poverty.

Finally, as with any major shift in social policy, it would be desirable to phase in the NIT over a period of several years. Such a phase-in strategy would mean that all of the additional revenue would not have to be raised in one year. One possible strategy would be to implement the NIT initially only for those households with children. This would reduce the total cost of the program by about 45%, but it would provide immediate protection for poor children and their families. Another strategy would be to increase the grant that households receive from the current EITC level to the full NIT level in stages over three years with a corresponding phasing down of grant levels from existing transfer programs.

The NIT and the Dilemmas of Social Policy

One of the major axes in debates over social policy has been the distinction between universal and targeted programs – those that provide benefits to the whole population and those that limit their benefits to certain subgroups of the population.

The NIT is a "universal" program because it can potentially assist any citizen who suffers a dramatic reduction in income and wealth, but its benefits are targeted on those low-income households most in need of help. It is true that the administration of the NIT requires an income test, but this need not entail the degradation of clients historically involved with means-tested programs.[33] Both the EITC and the NIT preserve the anonymity of clients; they need not be subject to the public scrutiny and possible stigmatization involved, for example, in using food stamps. Most important, once a NIT was implemented, it would generate the kind of sustained political support associated with universal programs because its potential availability would be built into the calculations of millions of households.

Notes

1. We have borrowed the idea of a policy trilemma from Peter Swenson who elaborated it in Swenson (1989).
2. The important study by Card and Krueger (1995) has helped reshape the debate about the effects of increases in the minimum wage.
3. One of the often overlooked social gains from minimum wage legislation is the collective good of higher productivity that comes when employers are encouraged to substitute capital for labor.
4. To be sure, the United States has also been far more successful than Western European countries in expanding the number of well-paying employment opportunities. Estimates are that half of the 10 million jobs created between 1992 and 1996 paid above the median (Ilg, 1996: 29–36).
5. By subsidizing low-wage job creation, EITC-type programs also run the danger of shifting incentives so that employers substitute low-wage labor for investments in productivity-enhancing technology. Such a shift would slow overall productivity growth. This problem can be avoided if subsidized job creation coincides with a tightening of the labor market so that employers are under continuous pressure to improve productivity.
6. These are identified as postindustrial trends in Block (1990). See also Stacey (1996).
7. Fischer et al., (1996: 132) 132. Timothy Smeeding has shown that the gap between low- and high-income individuals in the United Stales is far larger than the gap in Western Europe. For example, individuals in the lowest income decile in the United States receive 37% of the median income while in Germany and France, the comparable figures are 57% and 55% (Smeeding, 1996: 45–53).
8. Nixon's ambivalence about his own proposal is suggested by an entry in the diary of Nixon aide, H.R. Haldeman. Haldeman summarizes the president's views: "About Family Assistance Plan, wants to be sure it's killed by Democrats and that we make big play for it, but don't let it pass, can't afford it." (Haldeman, 1994: 181).
9. On the Family Assistance Plan, see Quadagno (1994: ch. 5). On the experiments, see Munnell (1987).
10. Editor's note: In previous parts of the original article, the authors distinguish between two different policy paradigms to tackle poverty: the Employment Paradigm, focused on employment creation, and the Transfer Paradigm, centered on creating a minimum income guarantee for the poor.
11. Polanyi (1957: 77–102). There has been considerable historical debate about the accuracy of Polanyi's account of Speenhamland. For a recent review of the debate and evidence, see Boyer (1990).
12. The theoretical justification for the unconditional nature of the BIG is elaborated in Van Parijs (1995).
13. Van Parijs acknowledges this need for an increase in marginal tax rates to finance the BIG, but he insists that the economic benefits could outweigh the costs. This could be true, but the political obstacles to large increases in marginal rates are formidable (Van Parijs, 1992b: 215–240). A more promising path would be to link the BIG to its own dedicated revenue

source that was independent of the income tax. For example, a BIG might be linked to the initial implementation of a value-added tax. However, given the politics of taxation in the United States, it is difficult to see the feasibility of any revenue source producing the kinds of funds needed to fund an unconditional BIG.

14. The Earned Income Tax Credit is a tax rebate program for the working poor that is administered by the Internal Revenue Service. It was originally enacted in 1975 and expanded several times since. If they make the proper arrangements with employers, individuals in eligible households can receive the credit in their paychecks as "negative withholding." (Alstott, 1995: 533–592).
15. These examples are meant only to be illustrative, since actual labor markets are far more complex than this kind of static analysis can indicate. Moreover, in both of these scenarios, one would expect that some who are currently working part-time would move into full-time positions and some who are currently unemployed would move into part-time positions.
16. In actuality, the reduction in working time would likely be concentrated among the bottom half of earners both because they would be the beneficiaries of the NIT and because salaried employees often have little control over their working hours. Hence, the 6% reduction in hours of work given in the example should be thought of as a 10% average reduction extending over the bottom 60% of employees.
17. For policies to improve the position of part-time workers, see Tilly (1996: 176–188).
18. Reductions in the length of the "standard" full-time workweek below 40 hours would also be a logical part of this effort to draw more of the population into the active labor force.
19. Residency is a requirement to prevent U.S. citizens from collecting their checks abroad where a lower standard of living might allow someone to live in luxury with an amount of money that was not intended to support luxury.
20. The relationship between transfer programs and immigration is difficult and complex and requires much further elaboration. Briefly, our view is that the entitlement of legal immigrants to the NIT transfer could be handled through a vesting process. Adult legal immigrants might become eligible for a certain number of months of a NIT transfer for every two or three years of gainful employment. Those in the United Slates without proper documentation would not be eligible for the NIT, but we also think that improving the bargaining leverage of citizens who are low-wage workers requires stricter enforcement of existing laws against employing undocumented individuals. However, the special character of the U.S.-Mexico border calls for some kind of more imaginative solution because there are tens of thousands of people who have constructed some kind of "binational" existence. These people could be granted some form of quasi-citizenship rights that include legal protections in the U.S. labor market.
21. We use 1990 dollars because our estimates of the cost of such a program are down from 1990 census data, but we would increase grant levels to keep pace with inflation. Since the cost of living as measured by the Consumer Price Index (CPI) has risen approximately 15% from 1990 through 1996, the actual grant level that we are proposing for adults would be $6,900. In order to adjust for differences in the cost of living across states, grant levels could vary from 90% to 110% of this central amount, depending upon where a state ranked in its relative cost of living.
22. Young people between 18 and 20 who are emancipated – living on their own and not claimed as dependants on someone else's income tax return – would receive the adult grant level. Hence, a 19-year-old single mother of one child living on her own would be entitled to $8,500. The parents or custodians of a teen mother under 18 would receive the child's benefit for both the daughter and the grandchild. Single mothers under 18 could receive the adult grant if they were living in a supervised group home. The latter option would help teen mothers to escape from abusive home situations.
23. We have chosen the 50% tax rate primarily because of its simplicity. While a somewhat lower tax rate would make the NIT more expensive, it might be desirable because lower-income workers currently face payroll and other taxes that further erode their gains from additional

earned income. However, our view is that the impact of these differences in tax rates on labor supply tends to be small. See Triest (1994).

24. A similar dramatic increase in the size of the personal exemption was included in a number of Republican tax reform proposals in 1995 and 1996. Such proposals are politically feasible because the aggregate contribution of these lower-income households to income tax revenues is very small.
25. It might be sound social policy to encourage this resort to supplemental private insurance. This could be done by treating this income differently from other types of income when calculating the size of the NIT. For example, if the tax rate on disability income were reduced to 30%, a family of four with a $20,000 per year disability payment would have a total income of $30,500 after the NIT.
26. The 40% exclusion means that a household in which two grandparents, one over 65 and one under 65, are caring for a dependent child will be included in our population. While the number of such families is very small, their presence also means that we have overstated the total costs of the NIT. Since we exclude Social Security income before calculating the size of the transfer for which houses are eligible and we do not calculate any savings from the main Social Security program, we are likely to record such a household as needing an additional transfer when its needs might already have been met by Social Security.
27. The actual census survey was carried out in 1989 before the beginning of the recession. Hence, the reported income levels have not been distorted by abnormal levels of unemployment.
28. For efficiency in data analysis, families with more than six children are coded as though they only have six and are only provided a transfer appropriate for six children. However, the number of households reporting more than six children under eighteen is very small and the resulting underestimation of program cost is very small.
29. Alternatively, they could be required to sign over their check to the prison authorities in partial compensation for the costs of their incarceration.
30. The work disincentive issue is discussed at greater length below.
31. The estimated tax is calculated from *1040 Forms and Instructions*, 1993. It is difficult to make these estimates more precisely with published IRS data because IRS does not report tax paid by income and family size.
32. Calculated from data in White House Council of Economic Advisers (1996).
33. For both our proposed NIT and for the integrity of the current EITC, a broader definition of income is needed than the current IRS definition. For example, tax-exempt interest income must be counted as part of income for purposes of calculating the NIT. See Alstott, "The Earned Income Tax Credit," 570–576. Tax rules should also be modified to discourage the use of investment in income-deferred assets as a means to take advantage of the NIT.

References

Alstott, A.L. (1995). The Earned Income Tax Credit and the Limitations of Tax-Based Welfare Reform. *Harvard Law Review*, 108 (January), 533–592.

Block, F.L. (1990). *Postindustrial Possibilities: A Critique of Economic Discourse*. University of California Press, Berkeley and Los Angeles.

Boyer, G.R. (1990). *An Economic History of the English Poor Law, 1750–1850*. Cambridge University Press, Cambridge.

Butterfield, F. (1997). Slower Growth in the Number of Inmates. *New York Times*, January 20, A1O.

Card, D. and Krueger, A.B. (1995). *Myth and Measurement: The New Economics of the Minimum Wage*. Princeton University Press, Princeton, NJ.

Congressional Budget Office (1997). *Reducing the Deficit: Spending and Revenue Options.* U.S. Government Printing Office, Washington, D.C.

Cruciano, T.M. and Strudler, M. (1996). Individual Income Tax Rates and Taxes Shares. *Statistics of Income Bulletin*, (Summer).

Danziger, S. and Gottschalk, P. (1995). *America Unequal.* Harvard University Press, Cambridge, MA.

Felix, D. and Sau, R. (1996). On the Revenue Potential and Phasing in of the Tobin Tax. In M. ul Haq, I. Kaul, and I. Grunberg (eds) *The Tobin Tax: Coping with Financial Volatility.* Oxford University Press, New York, pp. 223–245.

Fischer, C., Hout, M., Jankowski, M., Lucas, S. et al (1996). *Inequality by Design: Cracking the Bell Curve Myth.* Princeton University Press, Princeton.

Friedman, M. (1962). *Capitalism and Freedom.* University of Chicago Press, Chicago.

Haldeman, H.R. (1994). *The Haldeman Diaries: Inside the Nixon White House.* G.P. Putnam, New York.

Hartung, W.D. (1995). Notes from the Underground: An Outsider's Guide to the Defense Budget Debate. *World Policy Journal*, (Fall), 15–28.

Heilbroner, R. (1991). *Lifting the Silent Depression. New York Review of Books*, October 24.

Ilg, R. (1996). The Nature of Employment Growth, 1989–1995. *Monthly Labour Review* (June), 29–36.

Korb, L.J. (1995). Our Overstuffed Armed Forces. *Foreign Affairs* (Nov.–Dec.) 22–34.

Kuttner, R. (1984). *The Economic Illusion: False Choices between Prosperity and Social Justice.* Houghton Mifflin, Boston.

Lichter, D. and Eggebeen, D. (1994). The Effect of Parental Employment on Child Poverty. *Journal of Marriage and the Family*, 56, 633–645.

Munnell, A.H. (ed.) (1987). *Lessons from the Income Maintenance Experiments.* Federal Reserve Bank, Boston.

Polanyi, K. (1957). *The Great Transformation.* Beacon, Boston.

Pollin, R. and Baker, D. (1994). Taxing the Big Casino. *The Nation*, May 9.

Quadagno, J. (1994). *The Color of Welfare.* Oxford University Press, New York.

Smeeding, T. (1996). America's Income Inequality: Where Do We Stand. *Challenge*, (Sept.–Oct.), 45–53.

Stacey, J. (1996). *In the Name of the Family.* Beacon, Boston.

Swenson, P. (1989). *Fair Shares: Unions, Pay and Politics in Sweden and West Germany.* Cornell University Press, Ithaca, NY.

Theobald, R. (1963). *Free Men and Free* Markets. Clarkson Potter, New York.

Tilly, C. (1996). *Half a Job: Bad and Good Part-Time Jobs in a Changing Job Market.* Temple University Press, Philadelphia.

Triest, R. (1994). The Efficiency Cost of Increased Progressivity. In J. Slemrod (ed.) *Tax Progressivity and Income Inequality.* Cambridge University Press, Cambridge, pp. 137–169.

Van Parijs, P. (ed.) (1992a). *Arguing For Basic Income: Ethical Foundations for a Radical Reform.* Verso, London.

Van Parijs, P. (1992b). The Second Marriage of Justice and Efficiency. In Van Parijs (ed.) *Arguing for Basic Income.* Verso, London and New York, pp. 215–240.

Van Parijs, P. (1995). *Real Freedom for All: What (If Anything) Can Justify Capitalism?* The Clarendon Press, Oxford.

White House Council of Economic Advisers (1996). *Economic Report to the President 1996.* White House, Washington DC.

Wolff, E. (1995). *Top Heavy: A Study of the Increasing Inequality of Wealth in the United States.* Twentieth Century Fund, New York.

Chapter 57
Stakeholding versus Basic Income

Bruce Ackerman and Anne Alstott

Excerpts from Alstott, A. and Ackerman, A. (2004). Why Stakeholding? *Politics & Society*, 32 (1), 41–60.

There are deep injustices in our nation's treatment of the poor, but we reject the idea that poverty relief is the only, or even the best, target for reform. Today, the very rich inherit from their parents the resources they need to shape a life plan. The government directs aid toward the top 25% of the population in the form of college subsidies, and toward the bottom 20% through means-tested social programs. But young adults in the vast middle group embark on their adult lives without the resources they need to make meaningful choices.

The basics of stakeholding reflect our philosophical commitments. At age 21, as each liberal citizen steps forward to begin her adult life, she should receive a stake of $80,000 from the government.[1] The $80,000 is hers to spend, with just a few conditions intended to ensure that she has the capacity to make meaningful choices. First, she must graduate from high school. Without a high school diploma, she receives a variation on Basic Income – interest on her stake each year.[2] Second, she must stay clear of crime.[3] Once a young citizen has met these requirements, she may collect her money in four annual installments of $20,000 each.[4] The money is hers to spend or invest. She may go to college, or not. She may save for a house or a rainy day – or blow her money in Las Vegas.

We will raise the necessary stakeholding fund in different ways as time marches on. During the "short term" – the first 50 years or so – we rely on a flat tax of 2% on each individual's wealth in excess of $230,000. This high exemption level means that 80% of Americans will pay no tax, and that the burden will be borne entirely by the big winners in a market society.[5] As the first generation of stakeholders begins to die out, we propose to shift the burden by means of a "payback requirement." Stakeholders who have done well with their $80,000 must pay back their stake, with interest, upon their death.[6] As the first generation of stakeholders recognizes their responsibility to sustain the institution for their successors, it will be possible to reduce, or perhaps eliminate, the wealth tax.

Although stakeholding and Basic Income share a commitment to progressive redistribution, they challenge the identity politics and watered-down Marxism that have come to

From Alstott, A. and Ackerman, A. (2004). Why Stakeholding? *Politics & Society*, 32 (1), 41–60. Reprinted with permission of SAGE.

Basic Income: An Anthology of Contemporary Research, First Edition. Edited by Karl Widerquist, José A. Noguera, Yannick Vanderborght, and Jurgen De Wispelaere.

dominate conventional "left" thinking. Every citizen may claim her stake – or collect a Basic Income – simply because she is a human being, capable of shaping a life plan. She does not claim more – or less – by virtue of being female, or being a minority, or possessing a disability. Stakeholding and Basic Income take a concrete step toward initial equality, recognizing the individual not the group.

But is there such a thing as too much freedom? Here is where stakeholding and Basic Income begin to part ways. Under Basic Income, citizens are not allowed to go to their neighborhood bank and capitalize their lifetime stream of Basic Income payments into a single stake. While Van Parijs prohibits citizens from switching to our program, we are more tolerant: any stakeholder can switch to Basic Income simply by buying an annuity policy from an insurance company and asking it to send a monthly check.

To fix ideas, suppose that an insurance company would sell a young stakeholder a lifetime annuity of $400 a month in exchange for a stake of $80,000. The Ackerman-Alstott plan permits each citizen to arrange for her own Basic Income of $400 – but only if she wants to! Van Parijs would give her $400 a month but forbids her to capitalize it into a single $80,000 payment.[7] Basic Income, in short, is a fancy name for a *restraint on alienation.*

Anglo-American law contains a wonderfully evocative term to describe this particular restraint. Suppose you wanted to give $80,000 to your nephew when you die, but you didn't trust his judgment. Rather than providing him with a flat $80,000 in your will, the law permits you to create a *spendthrift trust* – which grants your nephew access to the money only with the permission of a trustee, who acts under the explicit instructions provided in your will. Van Parijs would extend this principle to the new liberal form of social inheritance. He would impose a *universal* spendthrift trust on all citizens as they rise to maturity.

We reject this extension as a matter of principle. Some citizens undoubtedly lack the capacity to make reasonable use of their economic freedom – and we do not oppose some broad sifting devices to identify them. This is why we have required all stakeholders to obtain a high school degree and refrain from criminal activity before gaining full access to their $80,000. But treating all young men and women as presumptive spendthrifts demeans their standing as autonomous citizens and radically constrains their real freedom.

A Guaranteed Income of $4,800 a year, every year, may be fine for surfers. But most young adults will find that Basic Income restricts their real freedom to shape their lives, often severely. Most obviously, the restraint sharply cuts into the freedom of people who want to invest their stakes in the development of their own "human capital." Consider a 21-year-old high school graduate aiming to become a first-rate auto mechanic. He needs $20,000 to learn the skills of this increasingly high-tech trade. Under Basic Income, he will have to wait four or five years to accumulate the money. Why?

Or consider newlyweds who want to have kids and share parenting responsibilities. In support of this decision, they would pour most of their joint stake of $160,000 into a small house and use the rest to reduce their work commitments out of the home and share child-rearing responsibilities. Suppose they can't do this on $8,800 a year. Why stop them?[8]

More broadly: Basic Income encourages a short-term consumerist perspective, but stakeholding invites young adults to take the longer view. Most people in their twenties are crushed by the vast gap between adult responsibilities and small financial resources.[9] Although their future is still ahead of them, they live lives of quiet desperation – trying to make ends meet from month to month. Although $400 a month will ease short-term financial crises, it is too small a sum to give them real freedom to look decades ahead and appreciate the life-shaping choices they are making, often by default.

Stakeholding, by contrast, invites them to take charge of their lives. With $80,000 in the bank, young adults may pause and consider how their aims and abilities are likely to unfold over time, and whether a short-term perspective will lead them down paths that they will later bitterly regret.

Stakeholding's distinctive emphasis on the life-shaping perspective is dramatized by the way it treats the problem of premature death. If Jane Citizen dies at 35, she has received her full stake, but her stream of monthly payments has fallen far short of $80,000. On stakeholding's view, this is perfectly appropriate. Each young adult should have the precious opportunity to put meaning on the shape of her life as a whole. The only regret is that Jane probably hasn't had a decent opportunity to live out the commitments and investments she made in her twenties. Basic Income proceeds on a different moral foundation. It presumes that Jane should get fewer payments because she will have fewer months to consume.

We reject this consumerist premise. Each citizen's claim to real freedom is independent of the number of months she will enjoy herself as an adult. It should depend instead on her status as a person capable of impressing a meaning on the shape of her life. If a young person uses her stake to pursue a risky but rewarding life, and this decision increases her chances of an early death, her claim to basic resources is worthy of no less respect than that made by risk-averse types.[10] "One person, one life, one stake" is the fundamental principle of the Stakeholder Society (see Ackerman, 1980: 49–53).

Turn now from liberal ideals to some crucial real-world matters of administration. Suppose that John Citizen is grimly determined to obtain his $20,000 course as an auto mechanic despite efforts to impose a spendthrift trust on his money. Here, some clever lawyering may suffice to convert Basic Income into stakeholding. Depending on how strictly the spendthrift provisions are written, John may be able to walk into a bank and take out a mortgage, pledging his Basic Income as security for the monthly repayments. To prevent this kind of transaction, the government would have to insulate John's Basic Income from creditors' claims. That rule would prevent advance borrowing, but it would also create a distasteful spectacle: bankrupts would walk out of the bankruptcy court with Basic Income rights intact, no matter how high their debts. We propose to insulate young adults' stakes from creditors, but only to prevent advance borrowing before ages 21 to 24. After that, every citizen must take responsibility for his or her actions – and debts. In contrast, Basic Income runs the risk of underwriting adult irresponsibility: how to justify letting the ***40-year-old*** default on her credit card debts while keeping her Basic Income intact?

And then there is the black market. Suppose that John, the would-be auto mechanic, is not deterred when legitimate banks refuse to deal with him on the ground that any loan that capitalizes his $400 monthly payments is illegal. He simply gets his neighborhood loan shark to lend him the $20,000, promising to use his $4,800 a year as collateral. Since this deal is illegal, Mr. Shark won't be able to go to court to enforce it – but he will hire thugs, at his own expense, if John refuses to cough up when the time comes. All this expense and uncertainty will greatly increase the interest that Shark will charge his customer. But John is willing to pay the price to begin executing his life plan.

How does Basic Income propose to respond? Putting the expense of an ongoing campaign of criminal prosecution to one side, do we really want to transform John into a criminal – simply because he wants to make an investment in his future? What kind of crime is that?[11]

Sort of like making consensual sex into a crime. Only less sensible. After all, some people think that consensual sex outside of marriage is a mortal sin. But nobody thinks that it is a sin to become a trained mechanic. Whatever the law may say, it is virtually certain that it won't be enforced by draconian sanctions. The black-market option not only lets the loan sharks appropriate the lion's share of John's economic birthright, but it will also reorient his relationship to the entire program. Under stakeholding, John could proudly come forward and claim his stake as a free citizen; now the state's efforts to restrain his freedom have turned him into a devious thief. When John finally becomes a skilled mechanic, he will not remember the stakeholding experience with pride, and seek to reciprocate by acts of loyal citizenship. Instead, he will more probably reflect on the ways he cheated, and was cheated, in the process of turning his Basic Income into a capital grant.

The resulting demoralization is a matter of the first importance. We have thus far presented only one side of the case for stakeholding – emphasizing its function as a major new vehicle for the exercise of real freedom. But the initiative also discharges a second major function: we expect it to serve as the institutional focus for a dynamic culture of citizenship. From their earliest days, children will learn that stakeholding is part of their birthright as citizens: "When you grow up, you won't be casually left at the mercy of the market or the arbitrary will of wealthy friends and relations (if you have any). You will confront your future under economic conditions worthy of a citizen of a free society." Parents and schools will continually urge their charges to use their freedom in a responsible fashion, and as the stakeholding period draws near, each man and woman will be enmeshed in an ongoing and multilayered conversation about their stakes: "Did you hear how Jane spent her first payment $20,000 – what a fool! If she keeps this up, she'll never make anything of her life!" Stakeholding will provoke millions of such conversations – and they will forge a cultural bond that will make stakeholders' common citizenship into a central reality of social life. As they grow older, citizens will forever be returning to their youthful days, reflecting on their choices and what has become of them.

The dynamics of Basic Income would be different. Even if payments began on the eagerly awaited twenty-first birthday, the stream of small checks would not create a proud culture of free citizenship. Stakeholding creates a focal point at age 21 for young citizens and their elders alike, dramatizing the importance of the rise to maturity. Basic Income makes its impact gradually and incrementally, adding a few thousand to the annual budget. Those sums would make a difference in day-to-day life, especially at the bottom of the income distribution. There is much to be said for replacing grudging handouts with a dignified income entitlement. But the power of stakeholding reaches well up the economic ladder and offers all an opportunity to take their life-shaping decisions seriously.

To be sure, the stakeholding culture will have its dark side. Some stakeholders will curse the day they made such foolish, youthful choices. But all will recognize the fundamental role stakeholding played in their lives. And except for the most bitterly disappointed, these reflections will prompt a patriotic determination to pass on the heritage of stakeholding to the next generation.

This reciprocating sense of membership lies at the heart of liberal understandings of citizenship. The liberal state does not bind its citizens by an appeal to a common race or language or religion or other moral authority. It seeks to engage people in the common project of ensuring equal freedom to all, and to take pride in a polity that guarantees everybody the resources needed to confront the mystery of life with dignity and responsibility. If this noble ideal is ever to become a reality, it must be embodied in social institutions that ordinary people find meaningful. Stakeholding promises to be such an institution, but Basic Income threatens to destroy the integrity of this message as millions predictably undermine its imposition of a universal spendthrift trust by countless deviations and obfuscations.

Van Parijs may respond by calling on us to face some harsh facts. Some young people *will* undoubtedly "blow" their stakes – going on a gambling spree or crashing a fancy sports car. We agree, but is this a good reason for depriving millions of other people of the economic power over their own lives? After all, neither the auto mechanic nor the newlyweds are planning a trip to Las Vegas anytime soon. Why should their claims to real freedom be sacrificed simply to prevent others from "abusing" their freedom?

We reject this utilitarian calculus. Each person is her own person. Each is entitled to real freedom to shape her own life. This precious freedom should not be compromised merely to save others from the consequences of their own choices.

To be sure, this liberal commitment leaves us with an obvious problem: how to respond to somebody who goes directly from the Stakeholding Office to the nearest casino and loses everything?

Van Parijs doesn't have this problem because he has imposed a spendthrift trust on everybody. Ms. Stakeblower is free to lose $400 a month at the casino but can't go for broke. She must wait till next month for her next $400 check before she again spins the wheel of fortune.

But for us, stakeblowing raises a distinctive question: what to do when Ms. Stakeblower returns empty-handed and confronts the political community with her starving self?

We think it is a plus, not a minus, for stakeholding to place this question at the center of discussion surrounding the next reform agenda. The effort to provide answers will invite the polity to confront a question much in need of fundamental reappraisal. Call it the problem of *life-cycle distribution.*

Speaking broadly, welfare states of the twentieth century distributed different benefits during three different phases of life: youth, adulthood, and old age. During youth, the accent is on education; during adulthood, on need; during old age, on cash pensions. The average American, for example, has a fundamental right to a free high school education but is then left to fend for himself in the marketplace unless he demonstrates a dramatic "need" for assistance. Even then, he can expect American government to respond in a miserly fashion until old age arrives, when more generous forms of cash (and medical) assistance are available.

Stakeholding suggests the importance of identifying a fourth moment in this distributional cycle – the moment of transition from youth to maturity. Just as all children receive an unconditional grant of educational resources, regardless of parental ability-to-pay, young adults should receive an unconditional grant of economic resources, regardless of parental ability-to-give. Just as liberal education provides each citizen with vital cultural resources for self-understanding, an economic stake provides them with the material resources for real freedom.

Within this life-cycle framework, stakeblowing is a special case of a much more general problem: how does the grant of a new right at an early stage of life (in this case, $80,000 to young adults) shape the collective response to claims of entitlement at later stages (in this case, Stakeblower's claim to "need" assistance)? Does the enhancement of entitlements early in the life cycle justify a reduction of entitlements at later stages? And if so, which ones, and on what principles?

The particular problem raised by stakeblowing seems pretty easy. *Of course* Ms. Stakeblower should be held responsible for her conduct in Las Vegas when she tries to collect a second time on the basis of her newly acquired financial "need." While a decent society shouldn't allow anybody to starve in the streets, Stakeblower's prior conduct disqualifies her from more than this minimum.[12] If she wants more out of life, let her work for it. (In other words, stakeblowers will be obliged to face a situation similar to that confronted by the overwhelming majority of people in any Western society.)

Other life-cycle issues are much harder: How should the earlier receipt of an $80,000 stake change government policy for the provision of unemployment benefits, or retraining assistance, or health insurance? What is the appropriate relationship between stakes to the young and government pensions to the elderly?

Our book proposes a few principles for confronting these life-cycle tradeoffs (Ackerman and Alstott, 1999: 129–180). Rather than revisiting these controversial matters, we focus on an important question of process. Given the likelihood of serious disagreement on lifecycle trade-offs, how to structure the ongoing process of political decision?

Begin with Basic Income, and consider the chaotic resolution that it will likely generate. If a political party seriously proposed a $400 monthly payment, this would *immediately* provoke a debate on Basic Income's ramifications on every other monthly payment provided by the modern welfare state – ranging from disability to unemployment to health care and beyond. Each affected group will predictably clamor to preserve its entire benefit while fiscal conservatives will be on the rampage for massive cutbacks to make room for the new fiscal requirements imposed by Basic Income.

This doesn't sound like a recipe for deliberate attention to the demands of justice in particular contexts. Perhaps it is Utopian to expect much from any scenario, but stakeholding does permit greater hope. Rather than proposing yet another monthly payment, it frames the key question in a different way: are we making a big mistake ignoring the distinctive predicament of young adults as they start off in life with new responsibilities but without significant assets?

To answer this question responsibly, it isn't necessary to undertake a comprehensive scrutiny of every monthly payment made by the welfare state. Over time, the adoption of stakeholding will lead to reconsideration of other programs as they reach the top of the political agenda. But there is no compelling necessity to resolve all these loose ends at once.

And a good thing too. The effort to do so might readily defeat any serious progress on the Basic Income front. Once beneficiaries of all existing welfare programs are alerted to the danger, they may well join with conservatives to fight for the status quo. This right-left coalition would be tough to beat.

In contrast, the structure of stakeholding will predictably diffuse potential opposition. Consider, for example, the clever way Tony Blair introduced stakeholding as the "big new idea" behind his successful campaign for reelection. Under the Labor Party initiative, each Briton would receive a "baby bond" of $750 or so at birth, which would accumulate compound interest until he received a stake at age eighteen.[13] Supplemental amounts would be added to each child's account on his fifth, eleventh, and sixteenth birthdays – with the aim of providing him with as much as $7,500 when he reaches maturity.

From a dollars-and-cents view, Blair's initiative doesn't cost much in the near future. Surely it doesn't pose a clear and present danger to the monthly checks received by present beneficiaries of the welfare state. Indeed, even when payouts begin 18 years down the line, $7,500 isn't very much at all. Nevertheless, it is substantial enough to raise the question, Doesn't the next generation deserve something better than the indefinite extension of the present welfare state?

In framing his initiative, Blair copied a move out of Franklin Roosevelt's political playbook. When introducing Social Security in 1935, the President also took steps to minimize the short-run cost of his proposal. While he took immediate credit for pensions for the elderly, the first payout occurred five years later in 1940. The same political calculus is evident in the Prime Minister's program: every prospective parent breathes a bit easier today, even though payouts won't occur for a generation.

Similarly, the initial Social Security statute was a transparently inadequate response to the plight of the elderly. For example, Roosevelt secured the support of white southern Congressmen by excluding agricultural and domestic workers from coverage, which immediately deprived most blacks of any benefits. So far as the President was concerned, it was far more important to secure public support for the principle of retirement pensions. Once this was accomplished, Roosevelt was confident that its success would generate pressure to expand coverage over time.

So too with the Prime Minister's "baby bonds." The important point at this stage is to gain public recognition of the imperative need to promote the real freedom of young adults at the threshold of life. It will then be time enough for activists to start campaigning for bigger stakes and quicker transitions.

It will be much harder to generate a similar political dynamic in the case of Basic Income. Within the context of stakeholding, it did not seem arbitrary for Blair to announce that only children born after the statutory date of enactment would qualify for a "baby bond." After all, the entire point of the program is to channel resources to the rising generation, and so it would have seemed bizarre for a 50-year-old, say, to demand that he should be granted a "baby bond" retroactively.

In contrast, Basic Income does not focus on the particular predicament of the young but spreads its concern to all citizens – 50-year-olds no less than 18-year-olds. Nobody would even think of proposing a "transitional scheme" that barred a particular age group as a cost-cutting measure. But this means, of course, that politicians will not find themselves in the delicious situation of granting immediate symbolic benefits to a large constituency while the financial costs only mount up later.

Which immediately leads to a second political problem. Since Basic Income's costs are immediate, and broadly distributed to the adult population, practical politicians won't be in a position to begin Basic Income with very generous monthly payments. Imagine, for example, that Tony Blair had taken the first year's budgetary cost of supplying "baby bonds" and had distributed this money to every adult Briton (of working age)[14] as a Basic Income. This would have amounted to the princely sum of $1.25 a month![15]

This simply doesn't have the same pizzazz as promising the next generation "baby bonds" that, upon maturity, will provide $4,500 to $7,500 to each young adult.[16] While these sums are rather small, they are big enough to suggest a certain seriousness of purpose in aiming for a more just future for the next generation. In contrast, a monthly Basic Income of a dollar and twenty-five cents is just a joke.

Call this the "chump change" problem. To solve it, proponents of Basic Income must insist that, *from the very beginning*, budgetary expenditure be large enough to fund a significant-looking sum for every adult recipient. But this makes a Roosevelt-Blair gambit impossible. There is no prospect for gaining big symbolic gains at low short-term cost. Instead, the protagonist for Basic Income must immediately wrest big budgets away from competing programs, and somehow overcome the resistance of well-organized vested interests who will fight for their familiar share of the pie.

We do not say that victory is impossible. But the political calculus for Basic Income does suggest a certain Utopianism that presently afflicts much liberal theorizing. It is one thing – and a great thing – to propose deep philosophical resolutions of the conflict between liberty and equality. But it is no less great to structure initiatives that have half-a-chance of enactment.

We must rid ourselves, once and for all, of Marxist delusions that history will mysteriously work on behalf of the oppressed. The challenge is to design programs that promote justice and make political sense in real-world democracies.

This is where the taxation side of the equation becomes especially important. By casting itself as a form of *capital* endowment, stakeholding invites the construction of a symbolic tie to underutilized forms of taxation that focus on the present maldistribution of wealth. Just as the promise of $80,000 at age 21 is readily comprehensible to ordinary citizens, so is the funding for the program: an annual wealth tax on everything above $230,000 and a payback from stakeholders at the time of their deaths. In an age of sound-bite journalism, it is no small virtue to convey the essence of a program in a sentence or two. More importantly, the link between stakeholding and its funding taps into the expressive power of taxation. The payback rule underlin esthe importance of intergenerational justice. To ensure a universal social inheritance, decedents must give back something from their estates. The old make way for the new – but in an egalitarian way. Regrettably, Democrats who opposed the 2001 repeal of the estate tax had no such symbolism on which to draw. Faced with Republican attacks on a macabre "death tax" that (ostensibly) forced family businesses into bankruptcy, Democrats managed only a muddled protest at "regressivity." Without any clear platform, their general commitment to progressive taxation met an easy defeat. Stakeholding, in contrast, makes the egalitarian debate vivid. Large inheritances for a few versus a meaningful inheritance for everyone.

The wealth tax weaves in a second symbolic message. By spotlighting the concentration of wealth in America, it both reveals a problem and, linked with stakeholding, suggests a remedy. The revenue potential of a 2% wealth tax is stunning – $406 billion using 1998 data. And it speaks volumes about the vast gap in wealth. With a $230,000 exemption and a 2% rate, only the top 20% would pay any wealth tax at all (Wilhelm, 2001: 10).

Our commitment to the wealth tax over an income or consumption tax reflects several considerations, both principled and pragmatic.[17] From a principled perspective, the extreme concentration of wealth reflects past injustice and perpetuates it. In an ideal setting, with true equal opportunity, differences in individual wealth-holdings would be untroubling – simply an indicator of one's life choices.[18] There would be no reason to penalize savers relative to spenders, or those with great material wealth over those with little, because (by hypothesis) everybody received a fair start. But today, the wealthy cannot plausibly claim that their fortunes were earned on a level playing field. It is impossible to know who would have prevailed in a fair competition, but lacking that information, the annual wealth tax is rough-cut justice.

The wealth tax also targets inequality in the next generation. Wealth buys advantages not merely for oneself but, crucially, for one's children, who go to better schools, get into better colleges, and can rely on the security of the family bank account to get them out of future scrapes. Once again, a truly just state would remedy those inequalities directly, through education and the restriction of inheritance. But in the absence of such measures, it is fair to tax the wealthy to fund better opportunities for every child.

From a practical viewpoint, wealth taxation provides a useful backstop to the payback requirement, ensuring that wealthy market-winners who spend-down their assets before death will still contribute to stakeholding for the next generation. The wealth tax could even enhance the functioning of the income tax. The cumulation of administrative compromises and deliberate tax breaks has reduced the effective rate of income taxation on capital to very low levels (Slemrod and Bakija, 1996: 179). By taxing capital directly, the wealth tax could do what the income tax, now hopelessly riddled with loopholes, cannot:

extract a fair contribution to the polity from capital owners. Although the wealth tax would require new administrative structures for valuing – and locating – assets, that technocratic challenge is also a virtue, because it offers the potential to broaden the capacity of the income tax as well.[19]

Basic Income shares some of these virtues, but less clearly. Like stakeholding, it can be described in a sound bite that conveys its egalitarian character. But the tax side of Van Parijs's proposal is less expressive. In *Real Freedom for All*, Van Parijs proposes funding a Basic Income with an income tax and an inheritance tax (Van Parijs, 1995: 100–102, 113–119). The inheritance tax taps into the same symbolism we employ: the justice of social inheritance (or, more precisely for Van Parijs's plan, a social dividend) for all. The income tax reflects Van Parijs's conclusion that income from good jobs and investments is a scarce resource that should be considered to be owned collectively and shared equally through Basic Income. There is a fine symmetry here: unequal income streams transformed into an egalitarian minimum income. But the real-world income tax muddies that principled symmetry and may create harder political battles for the Basic Income idea. In the United States, as in most Western countries, the income tax is the workhorse of the fiscal system. Here, it accounts for 47% of revenue (compared to 28% in Germany, 34% in Italy, and 37% in Britain, though only 18% in France).[20] The result is a long line of political claimants for income tax revenue. Basic Income is just one more. Given the already dismal record of the income tax in reaching income from capital, a hike in the income tax may amount, in effect, to yet another burden on wages, which are already heavily taxed for various social-insurance programs.

While we would be happy if Van Parijs were persuaded to adopt a wealth tax, the marriage of Basic Income to a wealth tax lacks the same symbolic meaning generated by our proposal. The Ackerman-Alstott combination of universal stake and focused wealth tax speaks a language that everybody immediately understands: the time has come to create a world in which inheritance is not merely a function of family but of *citizenship* – where all members of the commonwealth have a right to inherit a fair share of the material endowment created by previous generations and are not merely forced to rely on the luck of inheriting wealth from a rich family.

Notes

1. Only citizens may claim stakes. The citizenship restriction raises a number of moral quandaries, which we explore in Ackerman and Alstott (1999: 46–44). We permit citizens not yet 21 to receive advance stake payments to fund higher education (Ackerman and Alstott, 1999: 51–52).
2. Interest on a principal amount is not equivalent to the annuitized payment, which includes a partial return of principal, but especially for a long-term annuity, the numbers are close.
3. In many cases, commission of a crime should only lead to a postponement of a stake, not forfeiture. But we do support the selective use of forfeiture if the alternative is a lengthy term in prison. See Ackerman and Alstott (1999: 49–51).
4. College-bound stakeholders may collect $20,000 each year beginning at eighteen. To equalize the present value of payments made to college-bound stakeholders and others, who wait until age twenty-one, we provide for the accrual of interest (Ackerman and Alstott, 1999: 51).
5. Our book proposes a 2% wealth tax with an exemption of $80,000 (Ackerman and Alstott, 1999: 94–112). That proposal was based on 1995 Federal Reserve data, the most recent available at the time. As of 2001, we are able to draw on data from the 1998 Survey of Consumer Finances. Between 1995 and 1998, wealth in the middle and top of the distribution grew

significantly (Wilhelm, 2001: 1). These data show that a 2% tax on net worth in excess of $80,000 would raise $547 billion, far more than the cost of stakeholding, and far more than the $402 billion (in 1998 dollars; $378 billion in 1995 dollars) we originally proposed to raise (Wilhelm, 2001). We estimate that the 1998 cost of stakeholding would be $268 billion. Authors' calculations, updating the calculation in Ackerman and Alstott (1999: 219–220).

We propose to take advantage of the nation's increasing prosperity by retaining the 2% rate but increasing the exemption level to increase the progressivity of the tax. With an exemption of $230,000 per individual, we could raise $406 billion from the top 20% of individual wealth-holders (Wilhelm, 2001: table 3, 10). Alternatively, a tax rate of 1.5% with an exemption of $80,000 would raise $410 billion (in 1998 dollars).

Although 1998 numbers are the most recent available, they are outdated today. Nevertheless, there is no reason to suppose, a priori, that they systematically understate wealth tax revenues compared to 2001. As of June 2001, the S&P500, the broadest major stock index, is higher than or flat relative to 1998; the Dow Jones Industrials are higher than in 1998; and the NASDAQ is flat compared to that year. See "Corporate Snapshot: New Standard & Poors," *Business Week Online* (website stock quote, ten-year time period chart), retrieved May 24, 2003 from http://host.businessweek.com; "Corporate Snapshot: Dow Jones 30 Industrials," *Business Week Online* (website stock quote, ten-year time period chart), retrieved May 24, 2003 from http://host.businessweek.com; "Corporate Snapshot: NASDAQ Composite," *Business Week Online* (website stock quote, ten-year time period chart), retrieved May 24, 2003 from http://host.businessweek.com.

6. Of course, those who have not done well financially will not be able to contribute to the stakeholding fund at death (Ackerman and Alstott, 1999: 77–93).
7. Throughout our discussion of Basic Income, we assume that a Basic Income would be paid to adults from, say, age 21 to retirement age. We do this because we advocate stakeholding in lieu of Basic Income only for this group. We favor children's allowances and other initiatives for children, and a flat-rate pension for old age. See Ackerman and Alstott, 1999: 129–154. It is only for the group rising to maturity that we believe stakeholding is the right idea.
8. Or will Van Parijs allow them, covertly, to capitalize their stake by taking out a mortgage on their home, pledging their Basic Income as security? If so, he is well on the way to the stakeholder society. We will return to this point shortly.
9. In 1998, the median wealth for all U.S. households was $60,700. Thirty percent of U.S. households had net worth of less than $10,000 (Wolff, 2000: table 1, 10). Wolff does not provide data on median wealth by age, but he does show that mean wealth of households headed by adults under age 35 was just 22% of mean wealth (Wolff, 2000: table 10, 18).
10. This point, unfortunately, has great salience for minorities, who live with multiple injustices, including greater poverty rates, poorer health, and greater exposure to violence. African American men, for example, have an average life expectancy of just 66 years at birth, compared to 74 for white men (U.S. Bureau of the Census, 1999: table 127). Black men are far more likely to die from criminal violence than are white men (U.S. Bureau of the Census, 1999: table 145).
11. To respond to these difficulties, some have suggested a more elaborate form of "spendthrift" trust under which young adults receive $80,000 but can only obtain access to their money by convincing a bureaucrat of the merits of their proposed expenditures. See, for example, Nissan and Le Grand (2000: 12–13). But bureaucrats will inevitably import their own value judgments into the process, and claimants will be made to feel like supplicants. A standard list of worthy projects would avoid egregious forms of caseworker paternalism but would encourage legalistic manipulation and downright cheating. In purely practical terms, it would be impossible to design a process that is flexible and fair. Think of the borderline cases, which would quickly discredit the system. Amy may use her stake to open a hair salon because that is entrepreneurship, but Ben may not become a street musician because it is not a "business." Chris can enroll in divinity school and become an ordained minister because that is "education," but Dana may not travel to Asia to live in Buddhist monasteries because that is merely "travel." Extra procedural protections –

like agency adjudication or judicial review – may worsen the situation. See generally Mashaw (1983); Lipsky (1980). More fundamentally, stakeholders are free men and women, not claimants on state charity. They should not be required to bend the knee to some caseworker before moving on with their lives. The entire ritual smacks of a welfare state mentality inconsistent with the liberal spirit of stakeholding.

12. In fact, Stakeblower would be lucky to get a half-decent handout in America today. So much the worse for America.
13. For details, see HM Treasury (2003). Contributions would be based on a sliding scale – $750 to children born to poor families, reduced to a minimum of $450 for children in better-off circumstances. See HM Treasury (2003); see also Broder (2001: 21(A)).
14. As noted above, we focus on a Basic Income for working-age adults; we have endorsed a Basic Income – type scheme of our own for the elderly, in addition to stakeholding (Ackerman and Alstott, 1999: 129–154).
15. Translated into dollars, the baby bond proposal would pay up to $750 to each of the 750,000 infants born in Britain annually, or a total of $563 million. That estimate overstates the first-year cost of the program, because a means-testing rule would limit to $450 the grant to babies born to higher-income parents. But the first-year estimate also understates the steady-state program cost, because in future years the Blair plan would make deposits into each child's account of $75 to $150 at ages five, 11, and 16. For purposes of a rough estimate, we have settled on $750 per newborn. According to Downing Street statisticians, there are 36.1 million Britons between the ages of 16 and retirement age. See Office of National Statistics (2001). Thus, a Basic Income costing $563 million and paid only to working-age adults would yield $15.60 per year, or $1.30 per month.
16. For the particular details of the Blair plan, see HM Treasury (2001: 17–23); for a discussion in U.S. terms, see Broder (2001: 21(A)).
17. For a more detailed discussion of the ideas in this paragraph and the next, see Ackerman and Alstott (1999: 96–101). For additional arguments on behalf of wealth taxation, see Shakow and Shuldiner (2000: 499–584).
18. We emphasize that stakeholding alone will not guarantee anything like true equality of opportunity. Aggressive steps are also required to ensure liberal education for all, to fight racial and other forms of invidious discrimination, and to remedy serious handicaps. See Ackerman (1980: 3–227).
19. For a detailed consideration, see Ackerman and Alstott (1999: 101–109).
20. U.S. Bureau of the Census (1996: table 1373). France collects a larger percentage of its revenue in social security wage taxes and in consumption taxes (U.S. Bureau of the Census, 1996).

References

Ackerman, B. (1980). *Social Justice in the Liberal State.* Yale University Press, New Haven, CT.

Ackerman, B. and Alstott, A. (1999). *The Stakeholder Society.* Yale University Press, New Haven, CT.

Broder, D. (2001). Tony Blair's Eye-Catchers. *Washington Post,* May 2, 21(A).

H.M. Treasury. (2001). Saving and Assets for All: The Modernization of Britain's Tax and Benefits System, Number Eight. Consultative document online. HM Treasury, London. http://archive.treasury.gov.uk/pdf/2001/savings_assets_2604.pdf

Lipsky, M. (1980). *Street-Level Bureaucracy.* Russell Sage Foundation, New York.

Mashaw, J.L. (1983). *Bureaucratic Justice.* Yale University Press, New Haven, CT.

Nissan, D. and Le Grand, J. (2000). *A Capital Idea: Start-up Grants for Young People.* Fabian Society, London.

Office for National Statistics (2001). *Census 2001.* Office for National Statistics, London. http://www.statistics.gov.uk/census2001/default.asp (accessed May 24, 2003).

Shakow, D. and Shuldiner, R. (2000). A Comprehensive Wealth Tax. *Tax Law Review*, 53 (4), 499–584.

Slemrod, J. and Bakija, J. (1996). *Taxing Ourselves: A Citizens' Guide to the Great Debate over Tax Reform*. MIT Press, Cambridge.

U.S. Bureau of the Census (1996). *Statistical Abstract*. U.S. Bureau of the Census, Washington, D.C., table 1373 (1996 data).

U.S. Bureau of the Census (1999). *Statistical Abstract of the United States: 1999*. U.S. Bureau of the Census, Washington, D.C.

Van Parijs, P. (1995). *Real Freedom for All*. Oxford University Press, Oxford.

Wilhelm, M. (2001). A Proposed Wealth Tax: Revenue Estimates and Distributional Analysis Using the 1998 Survey of Consumer Finances. Unpublished paper on file with authors.

Wolff, E.N. (2000). Recent Trends in Wealth Ownership, 1983–1998. Working paper no. 300 (April). Jerome Levy Economics Institute, Annandale-on-Hudson.

Chapter 58

Reciprocity-sensitive Forms of Basic Income

Stuart White

Excerpts from White, S. (2003). Freedom, Reciprocity, and the Citizen's Stake. In K. Dowding, J. de Wispelaere, and S. White (eds) *The Ethics of Stakeholding*. Palgrave Macmillan, New York.

Responding to the Reciprocity Concern 1: The Development Grant

Some proponents of Citizen's Income (CI) do think that a CI, in and of itself, may create a problem of objectionable free-riding or parasitism. However, they reply that while this exploitation objection is a *valid* objection, one which points up a real moral cost of CI, it is nonetheless not a *decisive* objection. It is not decisive because the prospective moral cost from CI is outweighed by the prospective gains, in particular, to freedom. Whereas some proponents of CI, such as Philippe Van Parijs, defend the view that CI is best from the standpoint of social justice, proponents of this second, more concessionary view, such as Brian Barry, hold that CI is the most reasonable second-best from the standpoint of social justice – at least for societies like our own here and now (Barry, 1997; 2001). And they hope that the evident benefits of a CI for personal freedom, and the priority generally accorded to this value in liberal democratic societies, can win people over to the proposal in spite of its apparent weakness from the standpoint of reciprocity. The concessionary response can be strengthened further by showing how, in certain respects, a CI might actually help individuals better to satisfy their reciprocity-based obligations, for example by making it easier to take part-time employment rather than stay unemployed (for more on this argument, see White, 2002; 2003a: ch. 7).

I am quite sympathetic to the concessionary reply to the reciprocity objection, but there are at least two problems with it. The first is a philosophical problem. We can only point to the benefits of a CI to justify or excuse the moral cost it allegedly carries, if it is the case that no other policy instrument will produce these same benefits at this or equivalent moral cost. It is possible, however, that there are some variants of CI, variants which depart from the pure form of CI in specific ways, that will secure the same benefits at less cost.

From White, S. (2003). Freedom, Reciprocity, and the Citizen's Stake. In K. Dowding, J. de Wispelaere, and S. White (eds) *The Ethics of Stakeholding*. Palgrave Macmillan, New York. Reprinted with permission of Palgrave Macmillan.

Basic Income: An Anthology of Contemporary Research, First Edition. Edited by Karl Widerquist, José A. Noguera, Yannick Vanderborght, and Jurgen De Wispelaere.

If so, we should surely prefer these variants over the pure form of CI. Moreover, turning to the second problem with this reply, it is far from clear that the appeal to personal freedom on its own *will* win political support for a radical citizen's stake policy like CI if this policy is seen to flout norms of productive reciprocity. The establishment and maintenance of a generous citizen's stake policy will require considerable social solidarity (Van Parijs, 1995: 226–233). There is, however, a body of evidence which suggests that solidarity is more readily built and maintained in support of social programs that are seen to be respectful of the demands of productive reciprocity.

This point is central, for example, to Theda Skocpol's recent discussion of what makes for successful innovations in American social provision (Skocpol, 1997; see also Bowles and Gintis, 1998; 1999). Reviewing a number of successful social policy initiatives, including public schools, benefits for Civil War veterans, Social Security, and the GI Bill of 1944, Skocpol considers what features these initiatives had in common that explains their success. She argues that one key feature in this regard is their consistency with a norm of reciprocity:

> The most enduring and popularly accepted social benefits in the United States have never been understood as poor relief or as mere individual entitlements. From public schools to Social Security, they have been morally justified as recognitions of or as prospective supports for individual service to the community. The rationale of social support in return for service has been a characteristic way for Americans to combine deep respect for individual freedom and initiative with support for families and due regard for the obligations that all members of the national community owe to one another. (Skocpol, 1997: 111)

According to Skocpol, "liberal Democrats" in the United States have suffered a "political impasse" in enacting new social policy initiatives for many years because since the 1944 GI Bill they have abandoned "the long-standing formula for successful American social provision – giving support to people who are seen as contributors to the community, whatever their social class" (Skocpol, 1997: 118).

So, what are these variants on the pure CI policy that address both the concerns for personal freedom and reciprocity? I shall consider two possibilities here which I think are worth serious attention.

One possibility I think worth exploring is the idea of what we might call the *Development Grant* (also van Donselaar, 2003). The Development Grant is not a periodic, non-mortgageable income, but a lump-sum capital grant akin to that proposed by Ackerman and Alstott (Ackerman and Alstott, 1999). In contrast to their proposal, however, use of the Development Grant is restricted to specific purposes such as education, training, or establishing a new business. One example is the scheme recently proposed in Britain by Julian Le Grand and David Nissan (Le Grand and Nissan, 2003; also Nissan and Le Grand, 2000). This has much in common with Robert Haveman's earlier proposal for a "universal personal capital account for youths," and with a number of other more recent proposals in the United States (Haveman, 1988; Unger and West, 1998; Halstead and Lind, 2001).

Obviously, under the Development Grant, citizens have less immediate choice as to how to employ their capital grants as compared with a proposal like that of Ackerman and Alstott. One might try to defend this on two distinct grounds. Firstly, one might defend the restrictions on paternalistic grounds. Again, we come back to the distinction between manifesting our concern for freedom as a concern to prevent dependency and as a concern to respect freedom of choice. Like a CI, though in a different way, the Development Grant takes a stand in favor of the first of these alternatives. The restrictions on use of the grant can be seen as a way of limiting the risk of "stakeblowing" and resultant dependency – as limitations on freedom of choice intended to preserve freedom as nondependency (for further discussion, see White, 2003b). Secondly, many of the uses which are mentioned in Development Grant proposals, such as education, training, and the establishment of new businesses, are related to productive participation in the community. Citizens are thus encouraged and, to some extent, constrained, under these proposed schemes to use their grants in support of their productive contributions to the community. In this way, as Skocpol recommends, social support is connected with service. The historical, agrarian parallel is the idea of giving people rights to land on condition that they make productive use of this asset endowment, the model adopted in the United States in the 1867 Homestead Act (a model which William Simon calls a social-republican property right: see Simon, 1991). The Development Grant is a contemporary variant on this farmer, yeoman model of the citizen's stake. Thus, on the face of it, the Development Grant might seem a particularly attractive option in that it seems to be good for freedom (as nondependency) ***and*** for reciprocity. The choice apparently forced upon us by CI seems to be wholly avoided, and we get the best of both worlds.

However, the Development Grant has some obvious drawbacks. One drawback is the probable administrative cost of the proposal. It will cost society resources to monitor individuals' compliance with the use-restrictions it places on the grant. Some of these restrictions may be quite easy and cheap to monitor (for example, use of the grant for higher education purposes). Other permitted uses, such as setting up a business, may be much harder and expensive to monitor. This drawback is not necessarily decisive, however. Such costs mean that society has to pay something for having a Development Grant rather than an unconditional lump-sum scheme like that proposed by Ackerman and Alstott. But society may regard this price as worth paying for the benefits it gets from opting for the Development Grant over this alternative: extra security, at the individual level, against the risk of "stakeblowing." A second drawback with the Development Grant is that the restrictions on how such a grant may be used make it less effective than a CI as a possible cushioning device which individuals can use to help them through difficult periods when they might face financial difficulty and, therefore, increased risk of dependency. If we could be confident that the responsible uses to which the grants are put would always result in individuals having good opportunities in the marketplace this might not be something to be too concerned about. But we cannot be sure of this. Citizens could quite conceivably use their grant in responsible ways, for example to acquire specific skills or set up a new business, but then find that these investments fail: the skills become unexpectedly outmoded by a new turn in technological development, or the business which looked a promising bet flounders in the face of an unanticipated change in consumer demand. Once again, I am not sure this is necessarily a decisive argument against having a Development Grant at all, but I think it sufficiently strong to make it worth considering what other forms of citizen's stake policy might offer us a way of bridging the concerns for freedom and reciprocity.

Responding to the Reciprocity Concern 2: Time-Limited Citizen's Income

At this point it may help to take a step back for a moment and remind ourselves of the existing terms of the debate over "welfare reform" in liberal capitalist countries such as Britain and the United States. Putting to one side the libertarians who would like to scrap all forms of welfare, at one extreme in this debate are those who advocate a welfare system in which benefits are both work-tested and time-limited, that is, available only for a limited period over the course of a whole working life. This is the workfare model exemplified in the United States in the 1996 Personal Responsibility and Work Opportunity Reconciliation Act. At the other extreme, are those who advocate welfare benefits that are neither work- or participation-tested nor time-limited. Proponents of a pure CI, as replacement for most other welfare benefits, fall into this second camp. But we certainly do not have to choose between these two extremes. One alternative that we might explore would be to develop an income support system that has two tiers. The first tier, which I will call the conventional tier, is work- or participation-tested, but not time-limited. So long as one continues to meet the relevant work or participation conditions, one continues to receive the relevant benefits. So, for example, those who are out of work will be eligible for unemployment benefits, and will have to satisfy job search requirements as a condition of receiving benefit, but provided that they do meet these requirements there will be no termination of benefit. People who make a good-faith effort to find work will not be penalized by termination of assistance should they have the misfortune to fail to find work within a fixed time period. In addition to benefits for the unemployed, this first conventional tier of income support might include refundable tax credits for the low paid, subsidies for certain categories of care worker, and so on. The second tier of this proposed two-tier system of income support consists of a *Time-Limited Citizen's Income*: an income grant that one can choose to draw on without satisfying a work/participation-test (or means-test) but which can only be enjoyed for a fixed number of years (one, two, three?) over the whole course of one's working life. For example, individuals might have a right to draw up to a maximum of £20,000 in CI over the course of a working life, with, perhaps, a maximum of £8,000 drawable in any given year. This second tier of income support is not work- or participation-tested; but it is, in effect, time-limited. A modest Time-Limited CI is proposed here, then, not as an alternative to conventional welfare, but as a vital supplement to it.[1]

From the standpoint of the public values that have framed our discussion in this chapter, freedom and reciprocity, there is apparently much to be said for this two-tier model of income support relative to the alternative workfare and pure CI models. The concern for reciprocity is obviously addressed by making the benefits available under the first tier work- or participation-tested. In contrast to the contemporary workfare model, however, we also address the concern for freedom as nondependency by refusing to impose a time-limit on support of this kind: as said, potentially vulnerable citizens are not going to be thrown to the mercy of others if, through no fault of their own, they fail to find employment. And, of course, the concern for freedom as nondependency is also addressed by supplementing the first tier of work- or participation-tested support with the Time-Limited CI. Prudently managed, a Time-Limited CI could provide individuals with crucial financial independence in periods of difficulty which might otherwise expose them to dependency. If individuals go through periods of crisis and transition – due to divorce, or changes in jobs or careers – they can look to their Time-Limited CI to provide crucial support, helping them to get through these transitions constructively rather than floundering vulnerably in desperation. Of course, they could also look to the first tier of support. But if the conditionality of the first tier creates problems – perhaps the nature of the crisis or transition is such that the individual in question cannot meet the relevant eligibility conditions for conventional welfare in the short-run – then they can trigger this second tier of support to help them through. At the same time, because this CI entitlement is time-limited, it cannot be used to underwrite a life-style of long-term withdrawal from productive contribution to the community, and this aspect of the proposal addresses the concern for reciprocity.

Of course, a Time-Limited CI also has some drawbacks. In particular, it is essentially an instrument to help people manage crises and transitions. It could be used to facilitate new business ventures, or investments in human capital, but is not really aimed at supporting asset-building activities of this kind which can help in the long run to bolster an individual's material security. For this reason, it may be advisable to regard it as one element (albeit an important one) in a citizen's stake policy, rather than as sufficient in itself.

Conclusion: The Merits of "Hybridity"

Citizen's stake policies ought to address two basic moral concerns, a concern for freedom (understood to include a concern for nondependency), and a concern for productive reciprocity. While the CI proposal has obvious and strong attractions in terms of the concern for freedom, it has drawbacks in terms of the concern for reciprocity. One possibility, of course, is that we simply have to accept these drawbacks for the sake of doing what is effective for personal freedom. But before we jump to this conclusion, we should first consider other forms of citizen's stake policy that potentially go further towards bridging and reconciling these two concerns. One possibility is the Development Grant; another is the Time-Limited Citizens' Income, understood as the second tier of a two-tier system of income support. A further possibility, not considered above, is a hybrid form of citizen's stake which combines a Development Grant and a Time-Limited Citizen's Income (both operating, moreover, against the backdrop of a range of more conventional welfare programs). To be concrete: imagine, for purely illustrative purposes, that on maturity each citizen receives a Citizen's Account with an initial real value of something like £40,000 in today's prices. This account is divided into two parts. The first part, of, say, at least half the total value of the initial Citizen's Account, is a Development Grant, akin to the account proposed by Nissan and Le Grand. Citizens would be free to use the funds in this account to help finance a range of activities that are broadly related to productive participation in the community, such as education, training, and the establishment of a new business. The second part is a Time-Limited CI: a sum, perhaps not interest-bearing but inflation-indexed, that citizens are free to draw down at their discretion to supplement income from other sources, subject perhaps to restrictions on how much they can withdraw within a given time period.[2] Such a hybrid would serve freedom, both in the sense of nondependency, and in terms of making freedom of occupational choice effective; and it would respect the concern for productive reciprocity. I cannot, and do not, claim that a hybrid of this kind is uniquely consistent with the concerns for freedom and reciprocity. Specific policies seldom follow so simply and straightforwardly from basic value commitments. If, however, we are to give due weight to both concerns in the design of a citizen's stake policy (understood largely as a complement to, rather than substitute for, much conventional welfare policy), then a hybrid of this kind has much to recommend it as a long-term aim.

Notes

1. Some ongoing work by Will Paxton and Sue Regan at the Institute for Public Policy Research (London) on "Life Accounts" as a form of "asset-based welfare" points in a similar direction. See Regan (2001); Paxton and Regan (2001).

2. I set out and defend such a hybrid at more length in White (2003a). See also White (2003b) for a detailed discussion of the merits of such a hybrid from a paternalist perspective (as opposed to the justice-based perspective adopted in this chapter).

References

Ackerman, B. and Alstott, A. (1999). *The Stakeholder Society.* Yale University Press, New Haven.

Barry, B. (1997). The Attractions of Basic Income. In J. Franklin (ed.) *Equality.* IPPR, London.

Barry, B. (2001). UBI and the Work Ethic. In P. Van Parijs, J. Cohen and J. Rogers (eds) *What's Wrong with a Free Lunch?* Beacon Press, Boston.

Bowles, S. and Gintis, H. (1998). *Recasting Egalitarianism.* Verso, London.

Bowles, S. and Gintis, H. (1999). Is egalitarianism passé? Homo reciprocans and the future of egalitarian politics. *Boston Review*, 23, 4–10.

Halstead, T. and Lind, M. (2001). *The Radical Center: The Future of American Politics.* Doubleday, New York.

Haveman, R. (1988). *Starting Even. An Equal Opportunity Program to Combat the Nation's New Poverty.* Simon and Schuster, New York.

Le Grand, J. and Nissan, D. (2003). A Capital Idea: Helping the Young to Help Themselves. In K. Dowding, J. De Wispelaere and S. White (eds) *The Ethics of Stakeholding.* Palgrave, London.

Nissan, D. and Le Grand, J. (2000). *A Capital Idea: Start-Up Grants for Young People.* Fabian Society, London.

Paxton, W. and Regan, S. (2001). Progressing asset-based policies in the UK. Paper prepared for International Assets Seminar, Center for Social Development/Institute for Public Policy Research, London, January 2001.

Regan, S. (2001). Asset-based Welfare: Options and Policy Design Questions. In S. Regan (ed.) *Asset-based Welfare – The International Experience.* Institute for Public Policy Research, London.

Simon, W. (1991). Social-republican property. *UCLA Law Review*, 38, 1335–1413.

Skocpol, T. (1997). A Partnership with American Families. In S. Greenberg and T. Skocpol (eds) *The New Majority: Toward a Popular Progressive Politics.* Yale University Press, New Haven.

Unger, R. and West, C. (1998). *The Future of American Progressivism: An Initiative for Political and Economic Reform.* Beacon Press, Boston.

Van Donselaar, G. (2003). The Stake and Exploitation. In K. Dowding, J. De Wispelaere and S. White (eds) *The Ethics of Stakeholding.* Palgrave, London.

Van Parijs, P. (1995). *Real Freedom for All: What (If Anything) Can Justify Capitalism?* Clarendon Press, Oxford.

White, S. (2002). Fair Reciprocity and Basic Income. In A. Reeves and A. Williams (eds) *Real Libertarianism Reassessed.* Macmillan, London.

White, S. (2003a). *The Civic Minimum: On the Rights and Obligations of Economic Citizenship.* Oxford University Press, Oxford.

White, S. (2003b). The Citizen's Stake and Paternalism. In E.O. Wright (ed.) *Redesigning Redistribution.* Verso, London.

Chapter 59
Participation Income

Anthony B. Atkinson

Originally published as Atkinson, A.B. (1996). The Case for a Participation Income. *Political Quarterly*, 27 (1), 67–70.

I have an unconventional view of Citizen's Income and favor departing from the usual proposals in two significant respects.

First, Citizen's Income is usually seen as an alternative to social insurance – as a replacement for the Beveridge principle of social security. In my judgement, this is a mistake: the aim of Citizen's Income should rather be to cut dependence on means-tested benefits. Complementing, rather than replacing, an improved social insurance scheme, it could reduce the number of people who have to rely on income support or family credit, and help low-wage workers without need for a scheme like earnings top-up. Moreover, it could be complementary to a minimum wage.

Secondly, I believe that it will be difficult to secure political support for a Citizen's Income while it remains unconditional on labor market or other activity. One of the legacies of the Thatcher years has been concern about dependency, and this is not limited to Britain. A number of countries are anxious to ensure that social security works with, rather than against, the grain of active labor market measures.

The aim of this chapter is to argue these two points and specifically to make the case for a *Participation Income.*

Against Means-testing

The 1980s saw a big increase in dependence on means-tested benefits in the United Kingdom. As insurance benefits have been cut back, more of the unemployed have become dependent on social assistance. Taking income support and family credit together, there has been a large increase in the proportion of the population dependent on these means-tested benefits.

Why is this increase in means-testing the wrong approach? First, the means-tested approach necessarily penalizes personal effort. Even if the poverty trap no longer involves marginal tax rates in excess of 100%, the marginal rates are still higher than those levied on

Atkinson, A.B. (1996). The Case for a Participation Income. *Political Quarterly*, 27 (1), 67–70. Reprinted with permission of John Wiley & Sons Ltd.

Basic Income: An Anthology of Contemporary Research, First Edition. Edited by Karl Widerquist, José A. Noguera, Yannick Vanderborght, and Jurgen De Wispelaere.

the rest of the population. Perhaps more importantly, it is not just the individual's efforts that are penalized, but those of that person's family. Unlike individualized social insurance, social assistance discourages the partners of those out of work from earning income. I find it strange that a government so concerned with incentives should not see that reliance on means-testing has such a counterproductive effect. In the case of pensioners there is the "savings trap," which applies to pension income and capital income. For a range of such income, there is little or no net gain from saving on account of the withdrawal of means-tested benefits. People with capital in excess of a specified amount are not eligible for income support, and, if they realize this in advance, they may decide that there is little point in saving.

The second major objection to means-tested benefits is that a significant minority of those with incomes below the assistance level do not claim the benefits to which they are entitled. There is a recurrent problem of incomplete take-up. The reasons are doubtless manifold, but the failure of successive take-up advertising campaigns indicates that it is not simply a matter of inadequate information. There are deep-seated objections to claiming means-tested benefits. Unlike non income-tested benefits, where take-up is thought to be close to 100%, in the case of family credit only some two-thirds of the potential benefit is claimed.

Thirdly, the means test can only make sense when applied to the family or the household as a unit. As such, it runs counter to the desire to have a social security system which ensures independence. This is particularly important for women, but it also applies to young people, as has become clear with the problems of young adults and income support.

In short, means-testing is economically inefficient, provides an incomplete safety net, and takes social policy backwards rather than forwards.

Social Insurance and/or Citizen's Income?

One of the great attractions of a Citizen's Income is that it would reduce dependence on means-testing. Its introduction would undoubtedly lower the number of people who have to have recourse to income support. The take-up problem is unlikely to be important. By floating people off means-tested benefits, it would reduce the poverty, unemployment and savings traps.

Citizen's Income has the further merit of meeting the gaps which arise with social insurance. Most importantly, it would provide for those in paid work. Beveridge took it for granted that a man's wages would cover the needs of at least two adults and one child. Today we cannot do this. Not only have the low-paid been left behind, with the widening of earnings inequality in the 1980s; we also have to look at the wages of women, and the extent to which they can provide for one-parent families, or indeed for the needs of a single adult.

At the same time, I do not believe that Citizen's Income should *replace* social insurance, particularly when one takes account of the European dimension of social policy. There remains strong support for social insurance, not least among the social partners who are influential in a European context. Moreover, this support is not without foundation. The differentiation involved in the typical social insurance scheme is not arbitrary, and the Citizen's Income payments would need to retain some categorical elements. The relation of benefits received to contributions paid reduces the risk of fiscal competition between governments in the European Union.

In my view, it is therefore a mistake to see Citizen's Income as an *alternative* to social insurance. It is more productive to see it as complementary. Of course, social insurance needs reform. Unemployment insurance should be paid for an unlimited duration. The basic state pension should once again be indexed to net average earnings. The state earnings-related pension should be restructured to provide a benefit which is close to those available in France and Germany. There should be new benefits for carers and the disabled.

I envisage therefore a two-pronged strategy of modernised social insurance *plus* Citizen's Income.

The Participation Criterion

One has to ask why, despite finding supporters in all political parties, Citizen's Income has not yet come close to being introduced. Consideration of this question has led me to the view that, in order to secure political support, it may be necessary for the proponents of Citizen's Income to compromise: not on the principle that there is no test of means, nor on the principle of independence, but on the unconditional payment.

In my proposal, the Basic Income would be paid conditional on *participation*. I should stress at once that this is not limited to labor market participation. While the qualifying conditions would include people working as an employee or self-employed, absent from work on grounds of sickness or injury, unable to work on grounds of disability and unemployed but available for work, it would also include people engaging in approved forms of education or training, caring for young, elderly or disabled dependants or undertaking approved forms of voluntary work, and so on. The condition involves neither *payment* nor *work*; it is a wider definition of social contribution. (It would also, of course, cover those who have reached the minimum retirement age.)

The determination of these conditions would be different from those involved with income support at present: for example, an unemployed person who undertook part-time work would be qualifying rather than the reverse. But there would undoubtedly be problems which would not arise with the Unconditional Citizen's Income; and these problems would mean that there were people who failed to secure the Citizen's Income. There would undoubtedly also be behavioral responses, as people adjusted their actions in order to qualify. But such a scheme does offer considerable prospects, particularly in what I conceive to be its main role, namely the reduction in dependence on means-tested benefits. Moreover, I believe that such a scheme offers the only realistic way in which governments may be persuaded that Citizen's Income offers a better route forward than the dead end of means-tested assistance. This is particularly true at the European level, where the driving forces are very much concerned with the labor market.

For this reason, I believe that the basic income movement may have made a misjudgement in changing the name to a "Citizen's Income." (I am here leaving on one side the problems which arise if the concept of citizenship is applied to the determination of benefit eligibility.) It could be called an "Active Citizen's Income," but I rather prefer the term – not my own invention – of "Participation Income."

A Concrete Proposal

What would such a scheme look like in more concrete terms? The version of the Participation Income outlined here is based on the proposals set out by Hermione Parker in 1989 for the first phase of a move to a Citizen's Income. She outlines a scheme that would replace income tax allowances, although retaining an earned income disregard, but would keep the existing structure of social insurance benefits. More precisely, my version of the Participation Income involves:

- complete abolition of income tax allowances;
- abolition of the upper earnings limit on national insurance contributions;
- abolition of the 20% income tax band, but retention of the present 24% and 40% bands;
- taxation of all social insurance benefits.

Indeed, all income would be taxed, except for the disregard of the first tranche of earnings (say, £10 a week).

On the benefits side, there would be:

- payment of a Basic Income to all children of £12.50 a week, in place of the current child benefit;
- payment of a Participation Income to all those aged 18 and over who are in work or self-employment, or are away from work on account of sickness or injury, or are unemployed and available for work, or are disabled, or are caring for dependent children, the elderly or the disabled, or are over the minimum retirement age.

This scheme was run through the tax-benefit model POLIMOD (produced by Holly Sutherland, Director of the Microsimulation Unit at the Department of Applied Economics, Cambridge). The calculations suggested that in 1992 the revenue-neutral level of adult Participation Income would have been some £18.25 a week. This would cover the great majority of the population. If all others were to change their behavior in order to qualify, then the amount would be reduced to £17.75 a week.

With such a Citizen's Income, the number dependent on means-tested benefits would be reduced by half a million. A third of families would be worse off in cash terms; 10% would be virtually unaffected; and 57% would gain. Among the latter would be many women.

If the basic income tax rate had been raised from 25% to 35%, and the higher rate to 50%, then the Citizen's Income for adults would have risen to between £37 and £39 a week (in 1992 terms). The number receiving means-tested benefits would have been reduced by more than 2,250,000. This would be a major improvement. However, these figures indicate that the Participation Income would not on its own be enough; there would have to be improvements too in social insurance. The Participation Income would be a complement to modernized social insurance.

Conclusions

The means-tested route followed by the present Government cannot offer an effective solution to the reform of the welfare state. For all the rhetoric about targeting, means-testing has not worked, and a major aim of policy in Britain should be reduced dependence on means-tested benefits. The route to providing an effective national minimum for Britain is a Participation Income, complementing improved social insurance.

Reference

Parker, H. (1989). *Instead of the Dole: An Enquiry into Integration of the Tax and Benefit Systems.* Routledge, London.

Chapter 60

The Trilemma of Participation Income

Jurgen De Wispelaere and Lindsay Stirton

Excerpts from De Wispelaere, J. and Stirton, L. (2007) The Public Administration Case Against Participation Income. *Social Service Review*, 81 (3), 523–549.

Many scholars of the modern welfare state agree with Robert Goodin (2000) that the crumbling of its traditional pillars limits the ability of welfare policies to achieve a range of often contradictory objectives. However, they disagree about which policies might be introduced as alternatives. In particular, a fault line separates those favoring increased emphasis on universal mechanisms such as Unconditional Basic Income (UBI), commonly understood as an income granted by right to each individual, without means test or work requirement, from those who favor increased targeting of benefits through a host of conditional and activating measures that are commonly captured under the label "workfare." This article challenges the idea that the modern welfare state would be improved by the introduction of a Participation Income (PI) in an attempt to accommodate the twin objectives of universal social protection and broad social participation.

Superficially, PI appears to be extraordinarily well suited to bridge the divide between welfare reform's universalists and selectivists, that is, between those favoring UBI (and its cognates) and those favoring workfare. Like UBI, PI grants each adult citizen a right to a secure Basic Income regardless of the individual's living arrangements and whether he or she has alternative sources of income or wealth (Atkinson, 1995; 1996; 1998). However, unlike UBI, PI requires that recipients satisfy a broad participation requirement as a condition of support. Forms of participation include a range of such socially useful activities as caring for an elderly relative, volunteering in a neighborhood project, and engaging in a human capital-enhancing activity (e.g., vocational training or studying for an educational qualification). Participation Income is thus conceptually distinct from workfare because PI expands the notion of social participation well beyond the narrow frame of labor-market participation. Nevertheless, PI retains a strong notion of eligibility conditions; this conditionality seems to allow PI to bridge the gap between, on one side, those who believe universal social protection and inclusion are the key objectives of the modern welfare state and, on the other side, those who think its primary task ought to be the increased activation (i.e., engagement in socially productive behavior) of adult citizens.[1]

From De Wispelaere, J. and Stirton, L. (2007) The Public Administration Case Against Participation Income. *Social Service Review*, 81 (3), 523–549. Reprinted with permission of University of Chicago Press.

Basic Income: An Anthology of Contemporary Research, First Edition. Edited by Karl Widerquist, José A. Noguera, Yannick Vanderborght, and Jurgen De Wispelaere.

In this chapter, we take issue with this view of PI. Unlike those who regard PI as a policy solution that merges the best features of two worlds, a welfare scheme that appears to be genuinely inclusive and activating, we argue that PI has very little to offer either side of this debate. By critically assessing PI from the standpoint of administrative analysis and by drawing on evidence of existing programs, we identify several concerns at the level of implementation and find that these concerns are largely ignored in existing debates. Once these concerns are confronted, we argue, it becomes clear that although PI may seem attractive as a political compromise, this does not translate into a stable administrative solution, given the divergent priorities and agendas of those within the universalist and selectivist camps.

Our first aim is to demonstrate that, in its current underdeveloped state, PI does not constitute a workable proposal.[2] A closer examination reveals significant weaknesses in PI's administrability: the program's capacity to be administered in a practical and efficient manner, in accordance with its primary objectives, and in keeping with existing constraints. These weaknesses make PI's endorsement by UBI supporters, in particular, premature if not altogether gratuitous. Although recognizing these weaknesses primarily affects what we refer to as the first-best justification of PI, it also has important applications for what we will call the second-best case for PI.

This brings us to the second theme of this chapter. The administrative instability of PI, we maintain, confronts would-be supporters of the proposals with what we label the "trilemma of Participation Income." If one assumes that effective enforcement of a broad participation requirement imposes substantial moral and economic costs on welfare bureaucrats and clients alike, the implementation of any PI scheme effectively presents the following alternatives: (i) institute a weak enforcement of any participation requirements, rendering PI barely distinguishable from UBI; (ii) structure a participation requirement around narrowly selective eligibility criteria, effectively resulting in a version of workfare; or (iii) accept the substantial administrative costs of ironclad enforcement. Because selectivists and universalists hold explicit and opposing views on how to resolve this trilemma, it is difficult to see how PI can attract a sufficient coalition in support of it. In short, because administrative instability produces political instability, PI may well represent the worst of all possibilities instead of a perfect compromise between proponents and opponents of universal welfare reform.

The Trilemma of Participation Income

PI proponents face a trilemma of Participation Income. The first horn of the trilemma consists of the requirement that PI must remain substantively inclusive if it is to satisfy the concerns of Basic Income advocates. The second horn is represented by the equally important requirement, insisted upon this time by reciprocity theorists and soft workfare proponents, that recipients must satisfy a genuine participation requirement. Such a requirement in turn demands that any PI scheme must be capable of differentiating between those who fulfill their social obligations, however defined, and those who do not. Finally, the third horn is made up of the previously discussed concerns that pertain to the economic and human costs associated with administrability. The trilemma arises because PI can only avoid two of three horns simultaneously. The scheme inevitably gets pinned on a third. Each of the three routes out of the trilemma will appeal, if at all, only to a small subset of those attracted at a general level to PI, and each therefore has obvious negative consequences for the political feasibility of PI.

The ironclad administration strategy

A first possible resolution of the trilemma would be to reject any compromise on ease-of-administration considerations; if these conflict with a participation requirement, the former should always give way. In this way, PI might hope to retain the support of both UBI and workfare supporters, as well as of those who support PI on first-best grounds. Although this constitutes a coherent position that some PI proponents implicitly seem willing to adopt, there are nevertheless important consequences that adherents to this position may be reluctant to accept.

The ironclad administration strategy sacrifices some of the chief advantages related to providing benefits without a means test – notably, PI's ability to use bureaucracy sparingly. Hood (1983: 142) identifies two senses in which one may seek to use bureaucracy sparingly: first, by economizing on the administrative resources or on the administrative capacity used to execute welfare policy, and, second, by minimizing what Adam Smith (1776/1998: 454) calls the "trouble, vexation, and oppression" visited upon the citizenry by the welfare administrators. Concerns with using bureaucracy sparingly in the first sense are captured by the notion of program efficiency (Goodin et al., 1999). The second sense is captured in concerns that easy and objective measures of compliance are needed to limit welfare administrators' constant interference in recipients' lives. Such interference is an all too familiar issue in welfare policy; freedom from it is often cited as one of the key advantages of universal and unconditional measures (Van Parijs, 1992; 2004; Wolff, 1998; Fitzpatrick, 1999; Standing, 1999; 2002; Offe, 2005).[3]

To the extent that one or both of these two senses of using bureaucracy sparingly is relevant to the feasibility and desirability of any income support scheme, considerations of administrability are obviously material to the choice between rival income support mechanisms. A PI scheme that fails to use bureaucracy sparingly by economizing on administrative resources may achieve its objectives only at considerable administrative cost, satisfying demands for improved target efficiency, if at all, only at the cost of poor program efficiency (Goodin et al., 1999). Poor program efficiency, in turn, is likely to negatively affect PI's capacity to attract a necessary enacting coalition. It would also negatively affect public opinion because one of the core arguments in support of UBI (that the cost of administration is low) no longer holds.

If a proposed scheme also fails to use bureaucracy sparingly in Hood's second sense of limiting administrative interference in beneficiaries' lives, the administrative demands of effectively enforcing a broad participation requirement are borne not only by administrators, but also directly by welfare recipients and by the general population. In the absence of easy and objective verification procedures, intrusive inspections, threats, punitive sanctions, and the like may all prove necessary to discourage cheating. This is an important observation with clear effects on the considerations, such as these for the freedom and respect of recipients, that often inform universal approaches to income support (Wolff, 1998; Eyal, 2006). In short, a considerable cost comes with negotiating the trilemma by embracing ironclad administration; workfare proponents will lament the increased resource cost of welfare administration, and UBI proponents will denounce the interference cost associated with increased monitoring and enforcement.

The soft workfare strategy

A second approach would be to formulate the participation requirement in a deliberately underinclusive fashion. This effectively drafts a participation requirement in such a way as to include only those activities that are easy to specify precisely and to monitor efficiently. It includes (as far as possible) those beneficiaries to whom it is administratively simple to make payments. Such a strategy of creaming suitable welfare applicants is familiar in the workfare literature (Wilson et al., 1999; Handler, 2004).

Although this approach is less attractive in principle than the broad participation requirement envisaged by Atkinson and others, it might be regarded as a viable compromise between the theoretical advantages of PI and the requirements for ease of administration. However, the approach also narrows the gap between PI and selective workfare schemes. In practice, the scheme will necessarily focus participation requirements to include those social categories or activities that already feature prominently in current administrative systems. In other words, such an approach exhibits the conservative tendency to reinforce existing institutionalized practices by excluding alternative social activities, such as voluntary work or care work, that PI in theory embraces. Such a solution would be unacceptable to those UBI proponents, notably feminists and postproductivists, who consider the recognition and valuation of nontraditional forms of work a key objective of welfare reform. Moving away from broad acceptance of nontraditional forms of work is likely to lose the support of political factions that represent these points of view and might even incur active resistance.

In the extreme, there is even a danger that PI would prove less inclusive than workfare because, as mentioned before, it lacks the myriad of support programs (e.g., training, in-work assistance, and placement) that, at least in theory, constitute an integral part of workfare.[4] Advocates of PI may well acknowledge the need to supplement basic security with additional activation support. But what we might call PI-plus programs face two important constraints. First, if activation support is to be designed and implemented on top of a PI scheme, it is unlikely that such support will be instituted at a large scale with appropriate levels of funding. These efforts face a political environment of permanent austerity and the sort of political constraints that are common to workfare programs in the United States and United Kingdom (Pierson, 2001). Second, even if we could resolve such concerns as they pertain to labor-market activation, part of the attraction of PI is that it expands the notion of social participation to include a wide range of activities. It remains unclear whether a PI-plus proposal would offer support for individuals to engage in such activities over and beyond the grant they receive; also unclear is what form such support would take.

The lax enforcement strategy

A third resolution of the trilemma, an alternative compromise between the incorporation of a participation requirement and ease of administration, is to adhere to a broad specification of the participation requirement, accepting that effective monitoring of compliance will be problematic. This resolution is the welfare state equivalent of "rigid rules" and "lax practice" that for de Tocqueville (1856/1962: 73) characterized France's Ancien Régime. If the previous soft workfare approach narrows the gap between PI and workfare, the present strategy all but obliterates any distinction between PI and UBI.

Instituting an overly broad PI implies that a participation requirement represents only a symbolic commitment to eliminating free-riders. This would more than likely be acceptable to those who prefer to adopt a UBI and only supported PI as a politically feasible, second-best option. In addition, it is likely to satisfy political entrepreneurs who oppose UBI on purely strategic grounds and who regard this second route as a unique opportunity to save on administrative resources, opposing big government and the like, while retaining a firm and public stand on the need for social participation in return for state support.[5]

However, this route out of the trilemma would hardly be acceptable to those who favor PI as a first-best policy. Symbolism aside, lax enforcement of a broadly specified social participation requirement does not engender commitment to promoting reciprocity or a stand against free-riding. If PI ceases to meet the needs of a core partner in the fragile compromise, that party will seek suitable alternatives (with robust activation components) elsewhere. In addition to more genuine workfare schemes, research of the past 10 years has opened up some interesting possibilities. Time-limited policies represent one option under consideration. Stuart White (2003), for instance, suggests combining unconditional, time-limited policies with conditional unlimited schemes. The recent surge of interest in (conditional) asset-based welfare schemes in the United States and the United Kingdom represents another possibility (Ackerman and Alstott, 1999; Goodin, 2003; Le Grand and Nissan, 2003; Paxton, White, and Maxwell, 2006).

Implications for the Basic Income Agenda

Our analysis of the difficulties in administering a PI scheme, and of the resulting trilemma, points to several potentially far-reaching implications for the Basic Income debate. First, the analysis calls into question the assumption that a PI can be easily slotted into existing social security and welfare assistance arrangements. The discussion emphasizes the challenges posed in the formulation, application, and fulfillment of standards that institute a broad participation requirement, the defining feature of PI, as part of welfare policy. Because both UBI and workfare attempt to accommodate such difficulties, albeit in very different ways, these alternative visions of welfare may be regarded as better able to meet the challenges faced by all income support mechanisms. Our analysis of the trilemma points to various resolutions; each resolution has important consequences for first- and second-best supporters of PI.

Those who support PI on first-best grounds must squarely confront the issue of whether the advantages they claim for PI are sufficient to justify the high administrative costs, which are borne by both administrators and welfare recipients. If these advantages are not sufficient, the next step is to ascertain whether they might be sufficiently realized by a scheme that resembles workfare or, alternatively, by another that is barely distinguishable from UBI. The trilemma is still more uncomfortable for supporters of PI on second-best grounds. Because support for PI as a second-best option represents a political compromise, the risk arises that such a compromise will evaporate as policymakers face tough choices in the design and implementation of a scheme. Specifically, compromise may falter over the means by which the state will accomplish the tasks discussed in the previous section. Except under the somewhat implausible scenario in which supporters of universal and active welfare give up ironclad administration, these two positions opt for incompatible routes out of the trilemma. At some point in the implementation process, the political compromise is expected to collapse and, as noted earlier, solutions to the trilemma may essentially turn PI into UBI or workfare.

These considerations lead to a second significant implication for Basic Income debates. Implicit in many discussions of universal welfare reform is the assumption that, in key respects, PI closely approximates a UBI. The trilemma suggests, however, that depending on the fine-grained details of any proposed scheme, PI may just as likely come to resemble workfare schemes (though without the benefit of the activation mechanisms that in theory are part of the workfare program). This undermines the dynamic and the static versions of the second-best case for PI. In a recent essay, Brian Barry (2001: 66) writes, "My guess is that something like 'participation income' might be necessary politically to get a basic income introduced, but that the expense and intrusiveness of administering it (as well as its lending itself so easily to fraud) would lead either to abandoning the whole experiment or moving to an unconditional basic income." There is, however, a third plausible alternative; given the problems identified by Barry, criticism of such a scheme could lead to a tightening of both the formulation and enforcement of the participation criterion. The resulting outcome is essentially a workfare scheme. In response to such scholars as Barry, Offe, Yannick Vanderborght, and Van Parijs, we caution against using PI's political and administrative instability as a means to introduce Basic Income by stealth. Such a strategy might lead to the abandonment of experiments with universalism, and it is also plausible that the fine-tuning of such schemes might open the door for workfarist schemes. Furthermore, our analysis shows how this backdoor strategy might plausibly require universalists to sacrifice the two greatest advantages of their preferred policies: ease of administration and nonintrusiveness.

The final lesson of this analysis is that supporters of Basic Income and related policies cannot ignore the administrative realities of welfare reform. Abstract discussion seldom sets the supposed advantages of a broad participation requirement against the costs of administrative complexity in the implementation of such a requirement. This absence of administrative consciousness impoverishes discussion of universal welfare reform more generally. The risk arising from this neglect of the administrative factor is that conditions on which the feasibility and desirability of particular proposals depend may be ignored. The current analysis shows how administrative analysis can generate important insights that go beyond abstract theorizing. Supporters of UBI ignore these insights at their peril. Much progress can be made by applying the insights from welfare studies to anticipate the likely effects of proposed schemes. In this particular case, such analysis clearly suggests that PI proposals suffer from important weaknesses. Although none of our conclusions is necessarily decisive, the findings together present a strong public administration case against Participation Income.

Notes

1. Van Parijs (1996, 2004) proposes a UBI as a means of simultaneously combating exploitation and exclusion, but most policy analysts insist that inclusion in the form of labor-market participation can only be secured through an approach that increases participation.
2. Fairness requires us to mention that Atkinson is well aware of problems with PI that might not arise with UBI. For example, some people may fail to secure a PI but would otherwise have received a UBI (Atkinson 1996: 69).
3. Although UBI is often advocated because of its optimal efficiency in regard to both senses of using bureaucracy sparingly, we urge some caution in this assessment because UBI has an inherent flaw; part of the administrative apparatus is made obsolete, and this may affect administrative

redundancies or even administrative capacity. Lack of administrative capacity may cause problems that UBI proponents have thus far failed to appreciate.

4. In this respect, PI remains crucially underspecified; it is compatible with but does not explicitly require the installment of programs offering support to individuals who face difficulties entering the labor market.
5. Charles Murray's (2006) recent proposal for introducing a "Plan," his version of what essentially amounts to a neoliberal UBI scheme for the United States, would fit this scenario.

References

Ackerman, B.A. and Alstott, A. (1999). *The Stakeholder Society.* Yale University Press, New Haven, CT.

Atkinson, A.B. (1995). *Public Economics in Action: The Basic Income/Flat Tax Proposal.* Oxford University Press, Oxford.

Atkinson, A.B. (1996). The Case for a Participation Income. *Political Quarterly*, 67 (1), 67–70.

Atkinson, A.B. (1998). *Poverty in Europe.* Blackwell, Oxford.

Barry, B. (2001). UBI and the Work Ethic. In Van Parijs, P., Cohen, J., and Rogers, J. (eds) *What's Wrong with a Free Lunch?* Beacon, Boston, pp. 60–69.

De Tocqueville, A. (1962 [1856]). *L'Ancien Regime.* Patterson, M.W. (transl.). Reprint. Blackwell, Oxford.

Eyal, N. (2006). Basic Income Guarantee and the Social Bases of Self-Respect. Paper presented at the Fifth Congress of the U.S. Basic Income Guarantee (USBIG) Network, Philadelphia, February 24.

Fitzpatrick, T. (1999). *Freedom and Security: An Introduction to the Basic Income Debate.* Palgrave, Basingstoke.

Goodin, R.E. (2000). Crumbling Pillars: Social Security Futures. *Political Quarterly*, 71 (2), 144–150.

Goodin, R.E. (2003). Sneaking up on Stakeholding. In Dowding, K.M., De Wispelaere, J., and White, S. (eds) *The Ethics of Stakeholding.* Palgrave, Basingstoke, pp. 65–78.

Goodin, R.E., Headey, B., Muffels, R., and Dirven, H.-J. (1999). *The Real Worlds of Welfare Capitalism.* Cambridge University Press, Cambridge.

Handler, J.F. (2004). *Social Citizenship and Workfare in the United States and Western Europe: The Paradox of Inclusion.* Cambridge University Press, Cambridge.

Hood, C.C. (1983). *The Tools of Government.* Macmillan, Basingstoke.

Le Grand, J. and Nissan, D. (2003). A Capital Idea: Helping the Young to Help Themselves. In Dowding, K.M., De Wispelaere, J., and White, S. (eds) *The Ethics of Stakeholding.* Palgrave, Basingstoke, pp. 29–41.

Murray, C.A. (2006). In *Our Hands: A Plan to Replace the Welfare State.* AEI Press, Washington, DC.

Offe, C. (2005). Wasteful Welfare Transactions: Why Basic Income Security Is Fundamental. In Standing, G. (ed.) *Promoting Income Security as a Right: Europe and North America.* Anthem, London, pp. 69–82.

Paxton, W., White, S., and Maxwell, D. (eds) (2006). *The Citizen's Stake: Exploring the Future of Universal Asset Policies.* Policy Press, Bristol.

Pierson, P. (ed.) (2001). *The New Politics of Welfare.* Oxford University Press, Oxford.

Smith, A. (1998 [1776]). *An Inquiry into the Nature and Causes of the Wealth of Nations.* World Classics Paperback Edition, Sutherland, K. (ed.) Oxford University Press, New York.

Standing, G. (1999). *Global Labour Flexibility: Seeking Distributive Justice.* Palgrave, Basingstoke.

Standing, G. (2002). *Beyond the New Paternalism: Basic Security as Equality.* Verso, London.

Van Parijs, P. (ed.) (1992). *Arguing for Basic Income: Ethical Foundations for a Radical Reform.* Verso, London.

Van Parijs, P. (1996). Basic Income and the Two Dilemmas of the Welfare State. *Political Quarterly*, 67 (1), 63–66.

Van Parijs, P. (2004). Basic Income: A Simple and Powerful Idea for the Twenty-first Century. *Politics and Society*, 32 (1), 7–39.

White, S. (2003). Freedom, Reciprocity, and the Citizen's Stake In Dowding, K.M., De Wispelaere, J., and White, S. (eds) *The Ethics of Stakeholding*. Palgrave, Basingstoke, pp. 79–93.

Wilson, L.A., Stoker, R.P., and McGrath, D. (1999). Welfare Bureaus as Moral Tutors: What Do Clients Learn from Paternalistic Welfare Reforms? *Social Science Quarterly*, 80 (3), 473–86.

Wolff, J. (1998). Fairness, Respect, and the Egalitarian Ethos. *Philosophy and Public Affairs*, 27 (2), 97–122.

Chapter 61
Sabbatical Grants

Claus Offe and Johan de Deken

Excerpts from Offe, C. and de Deken, J. (1999). Work, Time, and Social Participation. Policy Options for Dealing with Labor Market Precariousness. Paper presented at the Workshop "Back to Full Employment? Employment Subsidies vs. Sabbatical Grants" (Brussels, 5 November). Previously unpublished.

One model of reducing the labor supply takes off from the idea of extending the list of excuses whereby people are exempted from the general expectation to perform gainful employment and still are granted some measure of income maintenance other than poor relief. Up to now such exemptions were mostly limited to the lower end or upper end of the third phase of the standard life course: extending the period during which young persons are being trained for gainful employment or promoting an early exit from the period in which older people perform paid work. One could, however, add other reasons for being exempted from the expectation to perform gainful employment. Thus, several countries have added the event of giving birth and of being a parent of infants to the list of exemptions and introduced various forms of parental leave schemes. Some countries, including Belgium, Denmark, the Netherlands and Sweden, have further extended this list to include training, care work for family members, and in the end conceivably any type of nonmarket activities. Let us examine two such schemes providing for paid leave from the labor market in more detail.

During the 1980s, Belgium started to extend its parental leave scheme, first transforming it into a *family* leave scheme that not only granted a sabbatical for educating children, but also for taking care of elderly or other relatives in need of personal care. Later on, the government added "training" and "the preparation of becoming self-employed" to the list of recognized reasons for a paid leave. The Belgian sabbatical scheme allows for a leave of 3–12 months. It is possible to extend this period, though the total duration of leave during a person's occupational career is limited to a total of five years. Eligible for the scheme are all persons in full-time or part-time employment. The scheme includes a so-called "replacement condition": employers have to agree with the employee's taking up a sabbatical period and replace the person on leave with an unemployed person who is eligible for an unemployment insurance benefit. As a result, the person on leave "hands over" his or her job to an unemployed person, who gets a normal job with a standard wage and full social security coverage, limited in duration to the period of the sabbatical.[1]

From Offe, C. and de Deken, J. (1999). Work, Time, and Social Participation. Policy Options for Dealing with Labor Market Precariousness. Paper presented at the Workshop "Back to Full Employment? Employment Subsidies vs. Sabbatical Grants" (Brussels, 5 November). Previously unpublished. Printed with kind permission of the authors.

Basic Income: An Anthology of Contemporary Research, First Edition. Edited by Karl Widerquist, José A. Noguera, Yannick Vanderborght, and Jurgen De Wispelaere.

The main backdrop of the scheme is that the flat-rate benefits are very modest indeed. They range from 20 to 25% of the average wage, with the higher amount being paid in case of a parental leave and the lower benefits applying to all other types of sabbatical.[2] If a person takes a full-time leave, he or she keeps most of the social security rights and entitlements associated with the job from which he temporarily quits.[3] The Belgian scheme is financed out of the unemployment insurance funds and is said to have the potential of important savings because the sabbatical benefit is substantially lower than the average unemployment benefit. But, as the allowances granted under the scheme are both flat-rate and set at a very low level, most beneficiaries tend to be women who use the sabbatical in order to take care of their children. One must therefore conclude that the scheme largely failed to transcend its original purpose of an arrangement for parental leave. Moreover, the scheme can be suspected to have a built-in gender bias: its low flat-rate benefits can only induce female earners of relatively low incomes to give up their job and exit the labor market. In contrast, their better earning husbands will prefer to use early retirement schemes as an exit from employment. This is likely to be so because, in contrast to the sabbatical scheme, early retirement arrangements provide for earnings-related benefits. A final problem with the Belgian scheme is that, even if the job status of the person taking the position of a person on leave is less precarious (concerning income) than those of people enrolling in other types of labor market programs, they too are exposed to limited job security as they may end up being unemployed again once the person on leave returns. In other words, the sabbatical scheme is necessarily accompanied by a further increase of persons with a precarious employment status.

The sabbatical leave schemes that came into operation in Denmark in 1994 offer significantly more attractive conditions than the Belgian system. Similar to the arrangements in Belgium, there are three main reasons for applying for a leave: (i) child raising for a "parental leave," (ii) education or occupational training for a "training leave," and (iii) sabbatical purposes that need not to be specified for a "sabbatical leave." All the schemes are open to persons in both employment and self-employment. Persons in employment must negotiate their leave with their employer, while self-employed persons are required to demonstrate that it is possible to suspend their self-employment activities during the leave by, for instance, recruiting a replacement. For a "parental leave" the only additional qualifying condition is that applicants must be eligible for health insurance benefits. Even unemployed persons can apply, provided they receive an unemployment insurance benefit or a social assistance allowance. The "training leave" and "sabbatical leave" schemes, on the other hand, are restricted to the members of unemployment insurance funds (in Denmark, this includes both employed and self-employed persons).

Applicants here also must be at least 25 years old and they must have been full-time employed for at least three out of the last five years. The benefits are paid out of the unemployment insurance funds – except for "parental leave" of non-insured persons: these are financed by the municipal authorities. Allowances in the "training leave" scheme are set at 100% of the maximum rate of unemployment benefits.[4] Allowances in the "parental leave" and "sabbatical leave" schemes are set at 70%.[5] This means that even the lowest benefits under the Danish scheme are still almost three times as high as the highest benefits the Belgian system has to offer. A "parental leave" can be applied for a period ranging from 13 weeks up to one year. A "training leave" can last between one week and one year, and beneficiaries have to enrol in a formally recognized training program. As a rule, though, the leave can not be obtained for enrolling in higher- or medium-level education programs.

A "sabbatical leave" can be taken for any kind of purpose and requires no specification. In the "parental leave" and the "training leave" schemes there is no obligation for employers to recruit a person to take over the job of the person on leave. The "sabbatical leave" scheme, on the other hand, does require that a long-term unemployed person is recruited to replace the person temporarily "opting out."

Both the Belgian and the Danish schemes took off from the idea of extending the recognized conditional exemption from labor market participation by expanding the list of recognized "excuses" for non-participation that already exist in most OECD societies. These excuses include the conditions of disability, old age, illness, giving birth and being a parent of an infant, doing military or alternative community service, and undergoing preparation for labor market participation. All these conditions are associated with claims to income support granted without the person in question performing market-valued productive services. The income granted is usually limited as to its level and duration, as well as contingent upon further conditions, and most entitlements are actually intimately intertwined with preceding gainful employment. There are important variations depending on the regime type of welfare state in question. If one considers, for instance, the exemption from labor market participation because of old age, the link to preceding gainful employment is far stronger in a "pure" social insurance system, such as the German one, than in a flat-rate citizenship-based pension system such as the Danish one. Both the Danish and Belgian sabbatical schemes sought to weaken this sort of link by granting flat-rate benefits, but in Belgium rates were set at such a low level that the scheme ended up being unattractive for better earning male breadwinners.

A relatively low replacement rate may well be inevitable for political reasons. The major problem involved in policies of rewarding nonmarket activities through state-financed transfer income has to do with the suspicions which can always be mobilized concerning the usefulness and worthiness of particular nonmarket activities (as well as the particular persons performing them). Suspicions can also be raised concerning the question of whether these activities, which as a rule take place outside of formal enterprises, are actually being reliably performed by the recipients of the respective transfers. Furthermore, it has been a routine objection even to second labor market types of administered employment that they tend to take away business and potential employment from the market sector, thus worsening rather than solving the problem of unemployment. Finally, there is the complaint that the possibility cannot be excluded that the recipients of such income will in addition take on a paid job in the informal or illegal economy. All these fears, complaints, and suspicions add up to powerful political obstacles to more generous and encompassing policy initiatives along these lines. Even if it were politically agreed that it would be desirable to reduce the total volume of labor supplied through the provision of nonmarket alternatives of useful activities and claims to income, the actual implementation of such schemes is bound to be contested as to who receives what while doing (or refraining from doing) what. But conversely, if benefits and eligibility stipulations are being fixed at a very restrictive level, the collectively beneficial effect of unburdening the labor market is likely to approach zero. In Denmark, the government sought to tackle some of these sensitive political problems by providing for differentiated conditions depending upon the reason given for applying for a leave: the most favorable conditions exist in the "training leave" scheme where both the "usefulness" and the actual "performance" of the activity can be checked comparatively easily. The least favorable conditions are offered in the case for sabbaticals claimed for personal and unspecified purposes. But in spite of these less attractive conditions, the legitimacy of the sabbatical leave still ended up coming under fire; and this prompted the government to phase out the scheme by the end of March 1999.

The paradox is this: All of us would be better off if some of us were to perform other activities than those stipulated by labor contracts. But doesn't that mean that some of us get "something for nothing"? Accordingly, each of us who is actually prepared to opt out comes under suspicion of free-riding and hence is put under constraints and reservations which, taken together, obviate the desired overall effect. Outright individual punishments are attached to choices that are deemed collectively beneficial. As a way out of this dilemma, one could think of strictly generalizing the right to temporarily opt out of employed labor while still maintaining a tolerable income status through income claims tied to citizenship, not previous employment, present unemployment, availability for employment, or the nature of the nonmarket activities pursued.

This proposal takes off from the arguments advanced in support of a Guaranteed Basic Income, or "citizen wage." It provides entitlements, if only for a limited length of time, for both the employed and the self-employed. Every citizen could be seen as born with a personal "sabbatical account" as a right of citizenship, upon which he or she can draw at any point of time for whatever purpose. This drawing right could be made contingent on certified conclusion of some vocational training (or, alternatively, some previous employment record), on the condition that the claimant opts out for a minimum time of six months at a time, and on the credibly enforced further condition that no paid activity is taken up during the sabbatical period. The minimum time provision is important in order to create more than very short-term job vacancies. (Leaves as short as one week, as are allowed in the Danish "training leave," or 13 weeks in the other schemes in that country, can hardly be expected to result in any significant substitution effects.) The account could cover up to 10 years of a flat rate subsistence income fixed at a level somewhere between unemployment benefits and the median income. Being flat rate implies that the income sacrifice is least for those in the lowest income categories who would presumably (although they are not required to) find it in their interest to use some or all of their account for the upgrading of their skills. Furthermore, as people in lower income brackets are relatively more likely to become unemployed, it would make sense to give them a greater incentive to actually make use of the opting out option. It is important for the allowance to be sufficiently high so as to prevent the claimant becoming dependent upon family support and thus to limit the range of sabbatical-users to those who are in the position to do so.

The costs of such a sabbatical scheme could be partly covered from funds that are earmarked for unemployment insurance (as is the case in the Belgium and Danish leave schemes). In addition, one could redirect some of the funds that are currently being reserved for social assistance (even if social assistance payments would still be needed), as well as part of the resources that are currently being used to finance maternity leaves, family allowances, early retirement schemes, various training programs, and perhaps even transfer payments for long-term sickness. The freedom of choice of time uses that sabbatical rights provide is regulated and disciplined by the awareness that the time funds made available to citizens are strictly limited. In this respect, the time that is "granted" through institutional arrangements is likely to have different motivational effects from, on the one hand, the uncertain, unstructured and indeed unwanted time that comes with redundancy and unemployment and, on the other, the unlimited time made available through an unlimited subsistence level Basic Income. The attractiveness of the limited withdrawal option could further be enhanced by provisions for the preferential rehiring of those who, after having taken a leave, wish to be reemployed. Such a provision, as well as the inclusion of some (weak) replacement condition applying to employers (as it already exists in the Belgian and the Danish schemes), could further promote a desirable revolving door effect which helps to prevent a rigid division of the work force into permanent labor market participants and permanent nonparticipants – a risk that seems likely to be associated with unlimited Basic Income schemes.

The principles guiding this arrangement are citizenship universalism and the liberty ("optionality") of time use. Only if "all of us" (as opposed to particular social categories) can envisage themselves actually becoming users of the options provided, and only if the option is made available for whatever purpose (as opposed to specified kinds of time use and activities), these two generalizations (across people and across purposes) can conceivably invalidate the adverse politics of the "something for nothing" objection. There is also a generalization across time: Benefits could be drawn upon at any time after the age of early adulthood and before retirement age, with the conceivable specification that those who have not used all or part of their account are rewarded through increments of their pension. The number of years contained in the account could be varied in reverse relation to the general employment performance of the economy. In order to minimize the dangers of ill-considered and premature use of the sabbatical option, a provision of positive and negative "time interest rates" could be considered. This would establish a rule that "the earlier you start spending your account (e.g., before the age of 30), the less there will remain to be spent," and vice versa. These incentives, however, would have to be modified through special allowances for the activities of child bearing, care giving and the upgrading of skills. Needless to say, all these parameters serve just illustrative purposes here. The institutional reordering of labor and time proposed here would of course not eliminate "unemployment." To the contrary, in a certain way it would institutionalize and socialize it by providing a legitimate place (however limited in time) for those who wish to pursue activities other than contractual labor or the self-employed production of marketable goods and services. But it would also conceivably be instrumental in restoring full employment (if at a decreased level of total employment) in a labor market that is evidently incapable of operating without generating increasing volumes of either of the two forms of precariousness.

It would be wrong to assume, however, that the "liberation of time use" that the proposal we have outlined is designed to serve is primarily a strategy to allow people to opt out from the overcrowded supply side of the labor market. It should also provide incentives to "opt in" into types of activity the significance of which seem to be eclipsed by the institutional preponderance of the labor contract as the presumed cornerstone of the orderly conduct of life and, in fact, of social order. While it would remain to be seen what people would chose to opt into and actually do under the premises of sabbatical rights, the normative case can be made that two types of activities would be particularly desirable and worthy of encouragement, namely the activities of learning and of caring. For, firstly, there is the need to promote learning, training, and the continuous upgrading of skills, as it seems evident that the socialization and education that people receive during the first two phases of their life course no longer provides them with the stock of skills and abilities that is required, not only for the sake of durable employability, but also for the sake of consumer, parent, and citizen competence. But even if we limit our attention to issues of job-related skills and competencies, it must be observed that jobs differ vastly according to the opportunities they provide for on-the-job learning and training, and thus for the maintenance and adjustment of human capital. Sabbatical rights would serve to distribute these opportunities more evenly and, as a consequence, have favorable effects upon productivity and the aggregate human capital stock of a society.

Secondly, the increased optionality of time use that the sabbatical arrangement is designed to serve would allow people to pursue matters that they "care about," but often do not actually have the time to take care of. The arenas where this time dilemma between nominal and actual caring becomes manifest are well known. They range from family and friendship to networks, associational life and "third sector" voluntarism; they concern activities related to education, health, the environment, performing arts and music, sports, religious and political activities. Sabbatical rights would provide both the time resources and the generalized challenge to perform nonmarket activities in these arenas and substantive areas. They would conceivably allow for spillover effects by making available those skills and experiences people have acquired in their working life to concerns and needs that the market fails to accommodate for in equitable ways, thus fostering the accumulation of what has become known as "social" capital.

Notes

1. Recently, changes have been implemented that have to some extent eroded the social security status of the unemployed replacing a person on sabbatical: contributions paid by and on behalf the replacing person have been reduced, and as a result, so are the claims this person is building up during his "replacing" employment.
2. The benefits provided a non-taxable income of 12,066 to 14,363 Belgian Francs.
3. The only exception here are holiday allowances (which are not paid at all for the period the person is on leave) and pension entitlements. Contributions to the pensions scheme and entitlements for the person on leave only continue to be paid for during the first 12 months of a sabbatical. For all additional months the persons on leave themselves have to pay the employee contributions, that is, 7.5% of wages received during the year the sabbatical started.
4. In 1995, this maximum unemployment benefit amounted 11,000 Danish crowns before taxes (in Denmark, social security transfers are subject to income tax).
5. Though for "parental leave" municipal authorities supplement this allowance with up to 35,000 Danish Crowns per year.

Chapter 62
A Uniform Refundable Tax Credit

Lily L. Batchelder, Fred T. Goldberg Jr., and Peter R. Orszag

Originally published as Batchelder, L.L., Goldberg Jr., F.T., and Orszag, P.R. (2007). Reforming Tax Incentives into Uniform Refundable Tax Credits. *Basic Income Studies*, 2 (2).

Introduction

The US federal tax code provides about $500 billion each year in incentives intended to encourage socially-valued activities, including homeownership, charitable contributions, health insurance, and education (Joint Committee on Taxation, 2006). Structuring these tax incentives most efficiently is therefore an immensely important policy matter. The vast majority of these incentives operate through deductions or other approaches that link the size of the tax break to a household's marginal tax bracket, which means that higher-income taxpayers receive larger incentives than lower-income taxpayers. Such an approach is often appropriate for provisions, such as deductions for business expenses, designed to measure income or ability to pay. But such an approach for incentives intended to promote socially-valued activities excludes more than a third of the US households, and misses an important opportunity to increase efficiency and economic growth.

We propose a dramatic change in how the government provides these tax incentives, which could be done on a revenue-neutral basis. Under our proposal, the default for all tax incentives intended to promote socially-beneficial behavior would be a uniform refundable tax credit, which would be available to qualifying households even if they owe no income tax. These tax credits would provide a much more even and widespread motivation for socially-valued behavior than the current set of tax incentives, and could help smooth out fluctuations in household income and macroeconomic demand.

Refundable Tax Credits Versus Other Forms of Tax Incentives

Policymakers have created tax incentives for homeownership, retirement saving, education, and medical expenses. Other tax incentives seek to promote work, charitable giving, and

Batchelder, L.L., Goldberg Jr., F.T., and Orszag, P.R. (2007). Reforming Tax Incentives into Uniform Refundable Tax Credits. *Basic Income Studies*, 2 (2). Reprinted with permission of DeGruyter.

Basic Income: An Anthology of Contemporary Research, First Edition. Edited by Karl Widerquist, José A. Noguera, Yannick Vanderborght, and Jurgen De Wispelaere.

investment in life insurance, annuities, and state and local bonds. Together, these tax incentives reduce federal tax revenues by about $500 billion a year, or roughly 4% of Gross Domestic Product (Bureau of Economic Analysis, 2006). Approximately $420 billion of these existing tax incentives operate through deductions, exemptions, or exclusions (Joint Committee on Taxation, 2006). Such tax incentives tie the size of the tax break to an individual's marginal tax bracket: a deduction of $1, for example, is worth 35 cents to someone in the 35% marginal bracket but only 15 cents to someone in the 15% marginal bracket. Such incentives thus provide relatively weak incentives to those in low tax rate brackets. Furthermore, these types of tax incentives fail to reach the increasingly significant share of low- and moderate-income individuals and families who do not have any federal income tax liability to offset in any given year. More than 35% of households during any given year have no income tax liability; these households are home to almost half of all US children (Gale, 2004; Hodge, 2005; Orszag and Hall, 2003).

Refundable tax credits represent a different approach. Since they are a credit, rather than a deduction or exclusion, they do not depend on a household's marginal tax bracket. A tax credit of $1, for example, reduces taxes by $1 and is thus worth the same to households in the 35% bracket or the 15% bracket. When such tax credits are refundable, they provide benefits to all tax filers, regardless of whether they owe income taxes on net.

The Growth of Refundable Tax Credits

Currently the tax code contains three main refundable tax credits: the Earned Income Tax Credit (EITC), the Child Tax Credit (CTC), and a small health insurance credit. The EITC, which provides an earnings subsidy to low-income families, is the largest anti-poverty program for the nonelderly in the country (Meyer and Holtz-Eakin, 2001). In inflation-adjusted terms, the budgetary cost of the EITC has risen by a factor of nine since it was enacted in 1975, and it tripled between 1990 and 2000 alone (Carasso and Steuerle, 2003). More recently, the partially refundable CTC and the fully refundable health insurance credit (HIC) were enacted, and the refundability of the CTC was expanded and accelerated (Ellwood and Liebman, 2001). The CTC provides a work-contingent credit for children, while the HIC subsidizes health insurance costs for a very small class of eligible workers who have been displaced by trade.

Several factors likely contributed to the dramatic growth of refundable credits over the past three decades (see Figure 62.1). For example, policymakers have increasingly relied on the tax code rather than direct government expenditures to subsidize households and influence their behavior as a result of perceived or real incentives within the tax legislative process. These and other developments have supported the rise of refundable credits (Sammartino et al., 2002; Steuerle, 2002).

The Case for Uniform Refundable Credits

Despite the growth in refundable credits, most tax incentives intended to promote socially-beneficial behavior take the form of deductions or other approaches linked to marginal tax rates. But if policymakers want to broadly promote socially-valued behavior through the tax code, refundable credits are generally necessary.

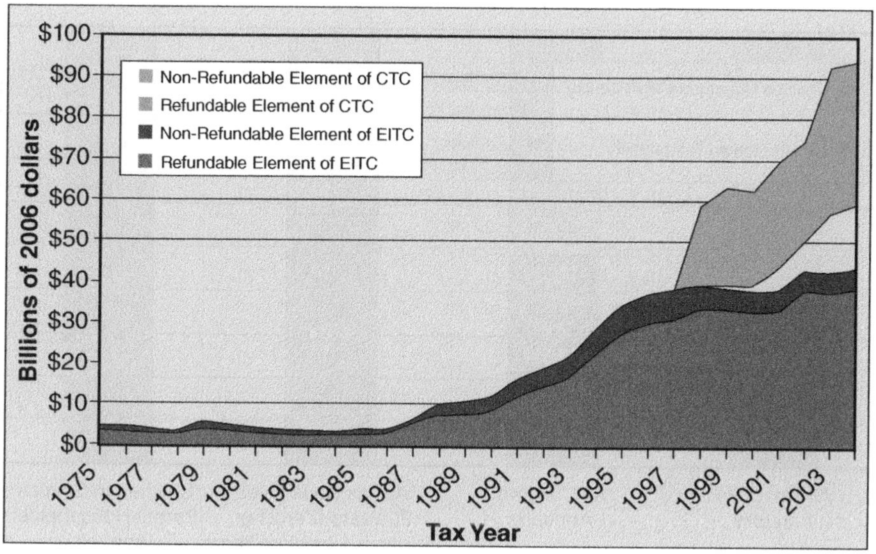

Figure 62.1 Growth in Refundable Credits over Time.
Sources: Authors' calculations based on tax credit data from the Internal Revenue Service, Statistics of Income; Ways and Means 2004 Green Book; and the Joint Committee on Taxation.

As illustrated in Figure 62.2, in any given year more than one-third of households do not have any federal income tax liability. About a quarter of tax units file a tax return but have no income tax liability, and another 13% do not file (Hodge, 2005; Orszag and Hall, 2003). Moreover, almost half of all children, and 80% of children in single parent households, live in tax units with no income tax liability in any given year (Gale, 2004).

As a result, if policymakers want to create incentives through the individual income tax for all or most tax units to engage in certain behavior every year, such as saving or obtaining education for themselves or their children, refundability should not only be considered an acceptable instrument of tax policy – it is imperative. Furthermore, unless there is evidence that certain households are more responsive to the incentive than others or generate larger social benefits from engaging in the activity, tax incentives are most efficient if they provide the same incentive to all households. This can only be accomplished in a straightforward manner through a uniform (and refundable) credit.

The reason that a uniform incentive is the most efficient approach in the absence of evidence regarding differences in responsiveness or social benefits is that a small number of large mistakes in under- or over-subsidizing an activity are more costly in efficiency terms than a large number of small mistakes. Stated technically, since the deadweight loss from an uncorrected (or overcorrected) externality rises with the square of the uncorrected externality, the expected deadweight loss is minimized when the subsidy is uniform.

For example, imagine that certain behavior, perhaps charitable contributions, on average generates 5 cents of social benefits per dollar contributed per year and policymakers have determined to subsidize contributions by, on average, 5 cents per dollar. Imagine further that there is a 50% chance that a dollar of contributions by a high-income household generates 10 cents of social benefits, while a dollar of contributions by a low-income household generates none, and a 50% chance that this pattern is reversed. A uniform subsidy of 5 cents would leave 5 cents of lost social benefits in both cases. Meanwhile, a

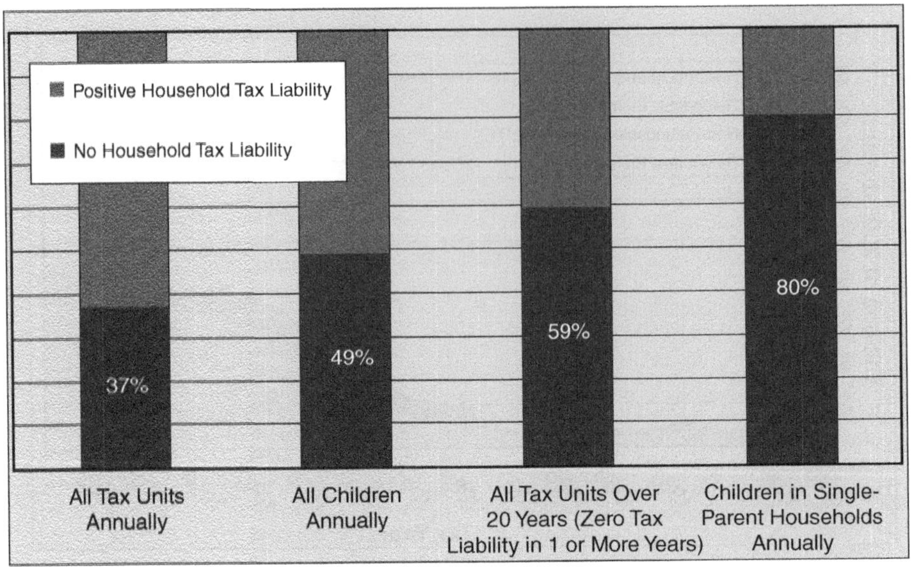

Figure 62.2 Federal Income Tax Liability.
Sources: Orszag and Hall (2003: 723); authors' calculations based on a simple model of 2003 law and longitudinal earnings data from the Panel Survey of Income Dynamics.

subsidy of 10 cents given to one group would result in 10 cents of lost social benefits in one case and none in the other. The uniform subsidy is more efficient because a small number of big errors (one case of a 10 cents error) results in a larger expected deadweight loss (a 50% change of a $1.00 deadweight loss) than a large number of small errors (two cases of 5 cent errors, resulting in 25 cent deadweight loss either way).

We acknowledge that many behavioral tax incentives may be bad policy regardless of whether they take the form of uniform refundable credits. Perhaps the behavior in question does not actually generate social benefits or perhaps such social benefits are best addressed through direct government provision of the good or regulation. However, given that it is highly unlikely politically that many tax incentives will be repealed, our default structure is generally preferable because it minimizes the expected social losses from the tax incentive, regardless of whether the behavior actually is socially beneficial.

We also acknowledge that tax incentives should not provide the same incentive to all households in all circumstances. If there is evidence that the associated social benefits vary systematically by income class, or that different income groups exhibit different levels of responsiveness to the subsidy, the tax incentive should not be identical for all households. Indeed these differences between various income groups surely exist in reality. But when, as is frequently the case, the evidence on these issues is non-existent or inconclusive, the most efficient form for a tax incentive is a uniform refundable credit. The burden of proof should therefore be on those who prefer some other form of tax incentive to demonstrate that such deviations from a uniform refundable credit are justified by empirical evidence rather than arbitrarily excluding more than a third of American individuals and families from their reach.

Moreover, even when there is empirical evidence suggesting that the optimal tax incentive should not be the same for all households, the most efficient incentive is almost certainly still some type of refundable credit. It is extremely unlikely that there is a sharp break in social benefits or responsiveness to an incentive exactly at the point of no income tax liability, and these types of discontinuities are inherent in the application of all other basic forms of tax incentives.

The potential benefits of refundable credits are magnified further by a second feature: their ability to help smooth household income. That is, during hard years, transforming existing tax incentives into uniform refundable credits would boost after-tax income, and thus help to cushion the blow of a drop in earnings, unemployment, or other hardships. Such income smoothing is desirable for several reasons. It can reduce the costs associated with economic instability and offset failures in insurance markets (Rosen, 2005). It also allows families to plan their expenditures more confidently and avoids the additional costs (such as moving costs and credit card debt) of financing constant changes in household living standards. Income smoothing is particularly beneficial for lower-income households because they generally don't have easy access to credit to make it through tough times, because they tend to have more volatile incomes than other families in general, and because income shocks can result in declines in their economic circumstances that persist over a long periods of time and are passed on to their children (Huff Stevens, 1995; Oreopoulos, 2005).

The final element of the case for uniform refundable credits is their ability to smooth the macroeconomy. Like household income smoothing, macroeconomic smoothing can enhance economic efficiency. In particular, macroeconomic demand fluctuations make it difficult for companies to optimize their investment and production functions, resulting in adjustment costs. These difficulties can inhibit domestic and foreign investment, which is correlated with economic growth. As a result, there is broad consensus in support of taxing and spending policies that are automatically countercyclical (Auerbach, 2002; Taylor, 2000). Uniform refundable credits can help stabilize macroeconomic demand fluctuations by raising cash payments to families during recessionary periods, which then helps to boost spending – precisely the desired response during such periods.

A Specific Example: Retirement Contributions to 401(k)s and IRAs

William Gale, Jonathan Gruber and Peter Orszag have recently proposed a specific example that is similar in spirit to our broader policy suggestion. They note that current incentives for contributions to tax-preferred retirement savings accounts, like 401(k) plans and IRAs, deliver their largest immediate benefits to higher-income individuals in the highest tax brackets.

Gale, Gruber, and Orszag would replace the existing tax deductions for contributions to retirement saving accounts with a 30% government matching contribution (Gale et al., 2006). Unlike the current system, workers' contributions to such accounts would no longer be deductible or excluded from income subject to taxation. Furthermore, any employer contributions to such accounts would be treated as taxable income to the employee (just as current wages are). However, all qualified employer and employee contributions would be eligible for the 30% government matching contribution regardless of the employee's income. This proposal would be roughly revenue neutral for the federal government according to estimates from the Tax Policy Center microsimulation model.

This proposal is a specific example of how a tax deduction or exclusion could be transformed, on a revenue neutral basis, into a uniform refundable credit. Our analysis generally supports this transformation as the default structure for retirement savings incentives, assuming such incentives are intended to promote the social benefits generated by retirement savings and that no other aspects of the tax code are intended to play that role.

Opposition to Refundable Credits

Opponents of refundable credits typically raise four main concerns. First, some question the extent to which government should engage in redistribution between different income groups. Second, some argue that the tax system should only be used to raise revenue, not to provide subsidies. Third, some believe that all Americans should pay at least some tax, even if just one dollar, as a duty of citizenship and so that they feel some stake in governmental decisions. Finally, some argue that refundable credits would increase administrative and compliance costs on net and are particularly subject to fraud and abuse.

Concerns about the extent of governmental redistribution do not justify rejecting refundable credits that are enacted to enhance economic efficiency, not redistribution, by subsidizing socially-beneficial behavior. Meanwhile, concerns about delivering subsidies through the tax system instead of the transfer system are generally objections to tax incentives overall, not to structuring tax incentives as refundable credits specifically.

The third objection – that all Americans should pay some tax as a duty of citizenship does not strike us as a compelling principle. But even if it did, it ignores the fact that most households claiming refundable credits pay a variety of federal, state and local taxes other than income taxes. It also ignores the likelihood that, over time, most refundable credit beneficiaries pay a positive amount of federal income tax alone as a result of the income variations that people tend to experience over their lives. Indeed, a simplified model of 2003 federal income tax law using data from the Panel Survey of Income Dynamics suggests that about three-quarters of tax units who are eligible for the refundable element of the EITC or CTC at some point during a 20-year period would nevertheless have positive net federal income tax liability over that period if historic earnings patterns are any guide. Thus, even if one accepts the odd principle that paying some income tax (and only income tax) is necessary for feeling a stake in government decisions, this principle would not necessarily preclude refundable credits once income tax liabilities are examined over longer time periods.

The final objection to refundable credits is that they could increase fraud and related compliance problems. There is no reason in theory, though, and no empirical evidence in practice that there is a "cliff effect" in fraud precisely at the point of positive income tax liability. If anything, fraud may be easier to hide when it comes in the form of a deduction or exclusion, which reduces taxable income. Instead, reducing fraud and related compliance problems for all tax incentives, including refundable credits, requires structuring the incentives simply, relying on third-party reporting, and investing in enforcement staffing.

We recognize that increasing the prevalence of refundable credits may create incentives for tax units who are currently non-filers to begin filing, thereby increasing administrative costs for the government and compliance costs for these households. These costs are real and should be taken into account. Nevertheless, they should not be overstated. Currently only about 13% of tax units are non-filers (Orszag and Hall, 2003). As a result, non-filers represent a relatively small share of the households who stand to gain from structuring tax incentives as uniform refundable credits. Moreover, all tax incentives are elective and, even for non-filers, the administrative and compliance costs associated with claiming them are likely to be swamped in many instances by the dollar value of the credit (Guyton et al., 2005).

Conclusion

Uniform refundable tax credits are generally the most efficient structure for a tax incentive to encourage desired behavior when, as frequently occurs, evidence of how the desired behavior and its associated social benefits vary across the income distribution is unavailable or inconclusive. Indeed, refundable tax credits are generally the only way to ensure a tax incentive reaches the roughly two-fifths of tax units with no positive income tax liability in a given year. These efficiency benefits are magnified by the ability of refundable credits to help smooth income at a household level and by their ability, to a greater or less extent, to bolster the role of the tax system as an automatic stabilizer of macroeconomic demand. The United States spends almost 4% of GDP each year subsidizing socially-valued activities through the tax code. Our proposal would dramatically improve the effectiveness and fairness of this substantial investment.

References

Auerbach, A.J. (2002). Is There a Role for Discretionary Fiscal Policy? NBER Working Paper No. 9306. http://www.nber.org/papers/w9306.

Bureau of Economic Analysis (2006). Current-Dollar and "Real" Gross Domestic Product.

Carasso, A. and Steuerle, E. (2003). Growth in the Earned Income and Child Tax Credits. *Tax Notes*, 98, 401.

Ellwood, D.T. and Liebman, J.B. (2001). The Middle-Class Parent Penalty: Child Benefits in the U.S. Tax Code. In J.M. Poterba (ed.) *Tax Policy and the Economy*. MIT Press, Cambridge, MA.

Gale, W.G. (2004). Tax Bracket and Tax Liabilities for Families with Children. *Tax Notes*, 105, 1145.

Gale, W.G., Gruber, J., and Orszag, P.R. (2006). Improving Opportunities and Incentives for Saving by Middle- and Low-Income Households. The Hamilton Project Discussion Paper 2006–02. http://www.brookings.edu/research/papers/2006/04/saving-gale.

Guyton, J.L., Korobow, A.K., Lee, P.S. et al. (2005). The Effects of Tax Software and Paid Preparers on Compliance Costs. Research Report, Urban Institute. http://www.urban.org/url.cfm?ID=1000802.

Hodge, S.A. (2005). Number of Americans Outside the Income Tax System Continues to Grow. *Fiscal Fact*, 27. Tax Foundation, Washington, D.C. http://www.taxfoundation.org/publications/show/542.html.

Huff Stevens, A. (1995). Long-Term Effects of Job Displacement: Evidence From the Panel Study of Income Dynamics. NBER Working Paper No. 5343. http://www.nber.org/papers/W5343.

Joint Committee on Taxation, 109th Congress (2006). Estimates of Federal Tax Expenditures for Fiscal Years 2006–2010. Committee Print. http://www.house.gov/jct/s-2-06.pdf.

Meyer, B.D. and Holtz-Eakin, D. (eds) (2001). *Making Work Pay: The Earned Income Tax Credit and its Impact on America's Families.* Russell Sage, New York.

Oreopoulos, P., Page, M., and Huff Stevens, A. (2005). The Intergenerational Effects of Worker Displacement. NBER Working Paper No. 11,587. http://www.nber.org/papers/w11587.

Orszag, P.R. and Hall, M.G. (2003). Nonfilers and Filers With Modest Tax Liabilities. *Tax Notes*, 100, 723.

Rosen, H. (2005). *Public Finance*, 7th edn. McGraw Hill/Irwin, Boston, MA.

Sammartino, F., Toder, E., and Maag, E. (2002). Providing Federal Assistance for Low-Income Families Through the Tax System: A Primer. Urban-Brookings Tax Policy Center Discussion Paper No. 4. http://www.urban.org/url.cfm?ID=410526.

Steuerle, E. (2002). Tax Policy from 1990 to 2001. In J.A. Frankel and P.R. Orszag (eds) *American Economic Policy in the 1990s*. MIT Press, Cambridge, MA.

Taylor, J.B. (2000). Reassessing Discretionary Fiscal Policy. *Journal of Economic Perspectives*, 14 (3), 21–36.

Chapter 63
A Household Basic Income

Luis Sanzo and Rafael Pinilla

Excerpts from Sanzo, L. and Pinilla, R. (2004). Necesidades Individuales y por Unidad de Convivencia In *La Renta Básica. Para una Reforma del Sistema Fiscal y de Protección Social*. Fundación Alternativas, Madrid.

In its original formulation, Basic Income (BI) is conceived as a universal right. A way of interpreting this right to a BI is to consider that the benefit to be paid to each citizen should be equal for all. However, the fact that the vast majority of people live together with others in the same households generates economies of scale. In order to enjoy an equivalent potential welfare, a person who lives alone needs more than half of the resources required for two persons living together. Therefore, an equal amount of BI for everyone would not have the same results in terms of real freedom. As a consequence of the existence of different household sizes, the apparent uniformity of the individual real freedom provided by a BI vanishes, so different degrees of individual real freedom would be associated with different household types.

BI is a means to achieve an aim, not the aim in itself. If one wants to guarantee people's freedom and equality through a BI scheme, and if the real freedom to be guaranteed is meant to have equal real value for all, then it would be necessary to neutralize the differential effect of the household size. That is to say, it is essential to take into account the number of members of each household when establishing the income levels guaranteed by a BI scheme. It is advisable for BI supporters to consider strategies that enhance people's real autonomy to decide how to live, and that ensure the compatibility between two principles: on the one hand, the principle of an individual and equal right to BI, and, on the other hand, the principle that the amount paid is effectively equal in its capacity to cover basic needs for any individual in any type of household (for individuals living alone, in family households, and in community households).

There are different solutions for this problem from a technical point of view. We want to present here two possible options: the first one (Sanzo, 2001; 2002) is to reduce the individual BI and supplement it with a BI paid to households; the second one (Pinilla,

From Sanzo, L. and Pinilla, R. (2004). Necesidades Individuales y por Unidad de Convivencia In *La Renta Básica. Para una Reforma del Sistema Fiscal y de Protección Social*. Fundación Alternativas, Madrid. Translated by J.A. Noguera (ed.) with kind permission of authors.

Basic Income: An Anthology of Contemporary Research, First Edition. Edited by Karl Widerquist, José A. Noguera, Yannick Vanderborght, and Jurgen De Wispelaere.

2002a; 2002b) combines a slightly higher individual BI with an individual minimum income supplement to top up the income of those living alone.

The First Strategy

The first solution aims to neutralize the effect of household size by introducing a BI for each household, as a supplement of individual BI. This "household BI" would guarantee the average consumption level which is common to all households, independently of their size. The underlying idea is that, in fact, there are two kinds of needs to be covered: individual needs, and the specific needs linked with the existence of an independent household.

Under this scenario, every resident person would have the right to an individual and unconditional BI. But, in addition, and in order to prevent the inequalities raised by different household sizes, each household would have the right to a benefit we may call "household BI." This benefit might be paid to one of the adult members of the household, who has been authorized by the other members to be the recipient, or alternatively distributed among all of them. Persons who live alone would also receive this supplementary benefit.

The Second Strategy

The second approach is more strictly close to the original idea of BI, and involves all of its essential tenets: in addition to the principles of universality and unconditionality, the individual uniformity of BI is also endorsed. Under this strategy, BI would not be split into two different payments (for the individual and for the household), but there would be a uniform individual benefit for the entire adult population.

In this case, the level of individual BI would be higher than under the first approach, so that it would cover the basic needs for persons living in households with two or more members. But, in order to prevent the lack of sufficiency of BI for those who live alone, they would receive a supplementary benefit in a traditional targeted way.

We calculated the effects of the two approaches for the levels of income to be guaranteed by a BI scheme in Spain in 2003. The reference individual amount for an adult's standard BI is taken from noncontributory pensions, and the household equivalence factor, according to Eurostat, should be 0.5 for each additional adult in the household, and 0.3 for each additional child (0.5 in the case of single parenthood: that is to say that the first and second members of a household are always considered as adults).

The monthly amounts guaranteed by BI under the first approach would be then:

Amount of an individual adult's BI: €177.69
Amount of an individual child's BI: €106.61
Amount of a household BI: €177.69

And the amounts guaranteed under the second approach would be:

Amount of an individual adult's BI: €266.53
Amount of the supplementary benefit for those living alone: €88.84
Amount of an individual child's BI: €106.61

Table 63.1 Examples of Basic Income for different types of households (in euros).

Household type	*Total payment under strategy 1*	*Total payment under strategy 2*
One person alone	355.38	355.37
Two adults	533.07	533.06
One adult with one child	533.07	533.06
Adult couple with one child	639.68	639.67
One adult with two children	639.68	639.67
Adult couple with two children	746.29	746.28
Three adults with one child	817.37	906.20
Adult couple with three children	852.90	852.89
Three adults with two children	923.98	1012.81

Table 63.1 presents the results of applying each of the two approaches to different household types. It may be seen that both strategies give the same income guarantee for any combination of one or two adults with or without children. The differences between them start when there are more than two adults in the household: in this case, the second strategy guarantees a higher global BI for the household. However, these types of households are uncommon, so that the total costings of the second approach should not be much higher than those of the first one.

References

Pinilla, R. (2002a). A diversified basic income scheme for federal states and multinational communities. Paper presented at the BIEN 9th International Congress, Geneva, September 12–14. Available at www.basicincome.org.

Pinilla, R. (2002b). Un propuesta de renta básica diversificada para el Estado español. Paper presented at the 2nd Spanish Symposium on Basic Income, Vitoria, December 14. Available at www.redrentabasica.org.

Sanzo, L. (2001). Líneas de actuación para el impulso de una política de garantía de ingresos. Paper presented at the 1st Spanish Symposium on Basic Income, Barcelona, June 8. Available at www.redrentabasica.org.

Sanzo, L. (2002). Allocation universelle et garantie de resources en Espagne et au Pays Basque. Paper presented at the BIEN 9th International Congress, Geneva, September 12–14. Available at www.basicincome.org.

Chapter 64

A Coming-of-Age Grant versus a Community Capital Grant

Guy Standing

Excerpts from Standing, G. (2006). CIG, COAG and COG: A comment on a debate. In B. Ackerman, A. Alstott, and P. Van Parijs, *Redesigning Distribution: Basic Income and Stakeholder Grants as Cornerstones for an Egalitarian Capitalism.* Verso, London and New York, pp. 175–195.

COAG, CIG, and COG

Consider the so-called "stakeholding grant" or "capital grant" idea, which should be called a Coming-of-Age Grant (COAG). In this chapter, I want to bring out differences between it and the Citizenship Income Guarantee (CIG), but in doing so also highlight why a more generalized *social dividend* approach should give a place both to a CIG *and* to some form of Capital Grant. The variant of the latter that seems desirable is closer to what might be called a *Community Capital Grant (COG).*[1]

Before considering each proposal, note that the COAG and the CIG have a common heritage and set of objectives, which might be summarized as a desire to enhance real freedom and a desire to promote a more egalitarian form of capitalism.

A danger of the debate between advocates of the CIG and the COAG is that both can be depicted as contrasting panaceas, when neither side believes in that. A CIG advocate would argue that a CIG is a necessary but not sufficient component of a package of policies to create the Good Society, whereas she might contend that a COAG is neither necessary nor sufficient. A COAG advocate might argue that while neither would be sufficient, a COAG would be helpful in enhancing economic freedom, whereas a CIG would not be politically feasible.

In considering the merits of a COAG and a CIG, one must reflect on the nature of modern capitalism. We are in the midst of a great transformation, in which the economy has been disembedded from society, such that there are no adequate systems of regulation, redistribution or social protection to moderate the inequalities and insecurities being thrown up.[2] Globalization and the spread of flexible, informal labor markets are associated with capital and labor *fragmentation*, in which *controls* (unfreedom) over workers and citizens are becoming more complex and indirect, and in which income flows are also becoming more complex. In brief, a small minority are receiving income mainly from capital, with

From Standing, G. (2006). CIG, COAG and COG: A comment on a debate. In B. Ackerman, A. Alstott, and P. Van Parijs, *Redesigning Distribution: Basic Income and Stakeholder Grants as Cornerstones for an Egalitarian Capitalism.* Verso, London and New York, pp. 175–195. Reprinted with permission of Verso.

Basic Income: An Anthology of Contemporary Research, First Edition. Edited by Karl Widerquist, José A. Noguera, Yannick Vanderborght, and Jurgen De Wispelaere.

a minority share coming from the performance of highly-paid labor (inter alia). At the top is an elite, blessed by absurdly high incomes and windfall gains that are a spreading dark stain on global capitalism. It is common to read of some executive receiving $10 million in bonuses, or *much* more. The stain is spreading, nor just because more executives are joining that way of remuneration but because these incomes convert into huge wealth that is passed from generation to generation, producing the concentration of financial wealth that is the starting point for the COAG proponents.

Alongside the wealthy elite, a diminishing *core* group of workers are receiving income from a variable mix of wages, state benefits, enterprise benefits and capital (shares). Below both groups in terms of income, a heterogeneous group has mushroomed, which for present purposes may be called *outsiders* (flexiworkers, unemployed, and a lumpenized detached group of homeless or socially ill people scraping by). The outsiders put the fear of insecurity up the stomachs of the insiders, who in turn retreat into implicit or explicit "concession bargaining" with their firms.

One can complicate this basic labor market model, and for many purposes should do so. But for our purposes it is sufficient to depict the fragmentation in this way, to think of the implications of a COAG, CIG and COG.

The Dilemmas with COAG

A COAG would be a one-off grant given to 21-year-olds, or spread over several years in certain circumstances, and given to all those who had graduated from secondary school, excluding drop-outs and those who have foolishly criminalized themselves before they reached that age. The UK "baby bond" scheme would not apply such conditions, apparently.

By contrast, a CIG would provide *basic* economic security, in which to avoid the worst excesses of labor commodification, and it would do so in an essentially non-moralistic way. It would not make a judgment on *when* a person deserves a blast of security, and would not make any moralistic judgment about who should receive it and who should be excluded. A COAG seems to fail on both these scores. Giving a 21-year-old a huge lump sum offends the idea of *basic* security. It is also arbitrary because the age of 21 is not necessarily ideal or optimal; people mature at widely different ages, and their capabilities develop differently. The development of a capacity to make rational choices will vary across individuals and groups and communities. And excluding those 21-year-olds who have been *criminalized* or who have dropped out from, or failed to complete, high school seems both moralistic and arbitrary, as well as inegalitarian.[3] A COAG offers enhanced security, wealth and future income for the more secure (the middle class) relative to the least-secure groups in society. It thereby offends the Security Difference Principle.

A COAG is also not neutral in terms of what type of behavior it encourages and rewards. It offers to benefit the commercially astute over those who have no commercial acumen. In what way is that fair? A COAG would give to those with relatively good talents (high-school graduates without criminal records) the opportunity to become Winners in a winners-take-all, losers-lose-all market society.

Both a COAC and a CIG would be given to individuals. A danger is that schemes for *individuals* can be depicted as *individualistic*, that is, encouraging and facilitating selfish and opportunistic behavior and attitudes. Surely a Good Society could not come about if policies and institutions were to promote individualistic behavior in the absence of policies to facilitate *social solidarity* (of some sort). One of the concerns about a block grant such as a COAG is that it would indeed foster the ethos of competitive individualism, while further eroding the already weak sense of social solidarity in most industrialized societies. It is definitely not neutral in that respect.

In the last quarter of the twentieth century, as globalization gathered strength, governments all over the world moved to cut back on policies that were mechanisms of social solidarity and to create more individualistic systems, limiting protective regulations, putting controls on unions, and cutting back on redistributive direct taxation. These trends accelerated the growth of more fragmented labor markets and social structures. How would a COAG affect this? It might give more meaning to *equality of opportunity*. But it would be equalizing the opportunity to become more unequal. It would not affect the societal fragmentation or resultant inequalities in a direct way. By contrast, a CIG would strengthen the income security (albeit modestly) of what we have called *outsiders*, and would increase the bargaining position of flexiworkers, simply because increasing basic security usually strengthens backbones. Presuming that increased bargaining capacity would result in their obtaining higher incomes, which would thereby help to reduce intra-class income differentiation.

What about the impact of a COAG and a CIG on the so-called "self-employed," a poorly named group that includes a lot of people working on contract or on a piece-work basis? On the face of it, both a COAG and a CIG would boost the *supply* of self-employed, including the number of petty capitalists (all those small-is-beautiful enterprises), for which a grant would help in dealing with set-up costs whereas a CIG would make risk-taking less daunting. But one cannot be so confident about the positive impact on *demand* for the self-employed goods and services, which might be such that average net incomes would fall among the "self-employed," even widening the *income* differential between those involved and those in (core) wage labor. This is an empirical issue.

The COAG seems more dearly problematical in that, by targeting on young labor force entrants, it is in effect a subsidy to the young that gives them an advantage over older workers.[4] As such, it suffers from the defects of any selective subsidy. It would enable the young to accept a lower wage and thus help them displace older, more experienced workers. This could, on certain assumptions, actually lower the overall productivity, and even output, of the self-employed as a group. It might also have negative effects on the skill reproduction propensities of older workers, discouraging them from trying to update or broaden their skills because they would face a double competitive disadvantage (being older *per se*, and facing a subsidised competitor group in the labor market).

By contrast, a CIG does not give one group an inbuilt advantage, and if anything would help to reduce segregation. This is an advantage of a universal income scheme.

Finally, in thinking of a COAG on its own terms, one must allow that such a concentrated influx of money targeted on one narrowly defined age group is almost certain to raise the price of goods and services consumed by that age group – good news for surfboard makers, bad news for 30-year-old new surfers. And interest rates for loans to this age group will tend to rise. The outcome could be that much of the transfer would go to other groups, leaving youth little better off.

A COAG versus a COG

A more general concern with COAG is that it offers to fill the space where another variant of a capital grant could fulfill both the objectives of its proponents and the dictates of a

Good Society, without its behavioral and distributional drawbacks. What are the *ideal* properties of a Utopian capital grant scheme? This big question is not asked or answered here. Before considering that, consider the semantics.

What attracts us to the underlying idea of a Capital or Stakeholding Grant is that it suggests a capital *sharing* device, coupled with a *participatory* component and a *redistributive* capacity. The principal proponents of the COAG use the term Stakeholding Grant, which has these connotations. However, in fact they are liberals and are primarily concerned with what they believe are the scheme's *freedom-enhancing* characteristics, rather than its redistributive egalitarian properties (which are not too hot). One does not doubt the laudable motives, but the term is misleading. And in using the term "stakeholding" they tend to block consideration of genuinely more Utopian capital-sharing or stakeholding ideas.

Now let us consider the big question. If what is attractive about the idea of stakeholding and capital grant is a complex image of sharing, redistribution, participation and freedom-enhancement, then we could say that the *optimum* design of a (Real Utopian) scheme is that it should (i) encourage, or at least not discourage, investment, (ii) encourage investment that is more ecologically and socially responsible, (iii) redistribute income to the most insecure and disadvantaged groups in society, (iv) promote participation in economic and social activities, (v) strengthen (or at least not weaken) a sense of *social solidarity*, (vi) strengthen real democracy, (vii) promote good "corporate governance," and (viii) limit economic opportunism.

No scheme could do well on all these counts. And, of course, neither the CIG nor the COAG addresses most of these issues and are not intended to do so. However, unlike a CIG, a COAG might be seen as occupying the space for a more progressive stakeholding grant.

In this respect, there is surely more to be gained by promoting moves towards *economic democracy through collective forms of profit-sharing*. This brings to mind something like the early version of the Swedish *wage-earner funds*, as proposed by Rudolf Meidner, and even the Alaska Permanent Fund. We may call the ideal a COG (Community Capital Grant). It should contain three elements that reflect the emerging character of the productive system and the distributive system emanating from it.

A COG is close to what seemed to be at the heart of the "stakeholder capitalism" debates that emerged in the late 1980s and early 1990s, when stakeholding was primarily seen as a quasi-Keynesian method of promoting growth and employment. The emphasis was on *profit-related pay*, but many economists also touted collective profit sharing for incentive and capital-sharing reasons. Most crucially, any desirable COG scheme must be at least partly *collective*, must go beyond the firm as a unit, and must allow for workers and their representatives to have a Voice in decisions over the use of the resultant funds. The democratic governance is crucial. The main difficulties with a purely company-oriented approach to stakeholding is that it would exclude the "flexiworkers" (casual workers, contract workers, agency workers, etc.) on the edge of companies and it would be a scheme that would widen inequalities between workers in high-tech, high-profit, tradable firms relative to those working in or for low-tech, non-profit-oriented and non-tradable firms and organizations, including those working in public social services.

This is why an ideal model of capital sharing or stakeholding should have a broader *community* element, which might take the form of a *social investment fund*, by which a percentage share of profits would go into a fund that would be governed democratically, as a means of social infrastructural and skill development. Such a fund could be broken into one component for re-investment inside the firm and another that would be for the community outside the firm, which would facilitate redistribution to people other than outside the privileged insiders.[5]

If properly designed, a COG could limit the leakage of capital from the national and local economy, because a key point of the system should be a restructuring of corporate governance, with the social investment funds having voting rights on the firm's investment strategies as stakeholders in their own right.[6] This contrasts with the classic so-called Anglo-American model of shareholder capitalism, because in the latter the *principals* (shareholding elites, including nominal salaried employees) are only interested in their income, which comes mainly from shares.[7]

As such, there are good reasons for thinking that a COG could combat the biggest threat to the emergence of a moderately egalitarian capitalism, by providing a capital-sharing scheme with inbuilt mechanisms to limit leakage in capital flight. Whether or not companies *report* that tax rates on corporate profits and capital are influential in determining their location and marginal investment decisions, the fact is that, over the past 20 years, country after country has reduced or abolished taxes on capital. A sensibly constructed COG could check capital flight and encourage high and socially responsible investment in the local economy. It would also make for a greater degree of participation in corporate and communal decision-making and so encourage *economic democracy*. This is what *stakeholding should be all about.*

The proponents of COAG have sold it as a *stakeholder grant*, and have claimed that it would be "democratic." Yet it is neither an extension of democracy nor a reflection of stakeholding in the production process. By contrast, a COG would be an extension of real democracy – economic democracy – and would be real capital sharing.

Almost incidentally, a COG would also have the potential to improve the way people live and work (unlike the commercialized individualistic frenzy that would be opened up by a generous COAG). By giving workers and working communities a greater Voice inside firms *and* inside the surrounding communities, a COG would tend to give workers a means of altering labor relations and workplace organization, so taking the place of the weakening Voice of old-style trade unionism.

Concluding Remarks

What is remarkable is the timidity of those talking about Stakeholding Grants. A COAG is fundamentally a populist measure, in the proper sense of that emotive term. It is likely to appeal most to those who do not have a stake in the system, but it does not touch the basic *structure* of capitalism. In that sense, it is profoundly un-Utopian. One could imagine TV chat shows and tabloids having endless items on "how Jane splurged her $80,000," and another patting Jim on his broadening shoulders for having been an exemplary young adult.[8] There would be a splurge of sentimentality. If anything it would help legitimize the unequal society by encouraging people to adopt a casino-type set of attitudes.[9]

By contrast, a CIG is a low-key measure that could reduce the extent of frenzied commercialism, facilitating and encouraging a more gentle pace of life, and facilitating the sort of workstyle that is the essence of all Utopias painted throughout the ages: A mix of labor force work, care work, voluntary community work and constructive leisure.[10] It would not discourage work per se, and of course would actually encourage labor compared with the current means-tested social assistance, through weakening poverty traps and unemployment traps.

This brings me to a last point. Freedom and complex egalitarianism – the pillars of the Good Society – require basic security (the prerequisite for real freedom), capital sharing (high inequality being freedom-constraining) and basic Voice representation security (equally strong for all representative interests in society). This is why it is instructive to think of Karl Polanyi, and recognize that for any economic system to be sustainable and stable it must have a main functioning system or scheme of *social protection*, a main system of redistribution and a main system of labor regulation, as well as a public structure for providing those services (merit goods), where the drawbacks of paternalistic provision are outweighed by the drawbacks of private deprivation or market failure. Basic income security, capital sharing and Voice regulation should be the mainstays of a Real Utopia. Without those three elements, the Utopia on offer would not be worth visiting.

Notes

1. Note the neutral use of euphemisms and acronyms. Who would want a COAG if you could have a COG? Regrettably, the terms one uses are significant aspects of legitimizing reform proposals. In South Africa, we have used the term Solidarity Grant for a CIG. Note also that a "baby bond," the term used in the UK by the government, is merely a COAG with a COA defined as registered date-of-birth. An advantage of the baby bond over the Ackerman-Alstott proposal is that, presumably, no recipient would have a criminal record, so it would be more universal. [Editor's note: Standing refers here to a proposal discussed in the following two books: Ackerman and Alstott (1999) and Ackerman, Alstott, and Van Parijs (2006).]
2. This theme, drawing on Karl Polanyi's *The Great Transformation*, is developed at length in my recent book (Standing, 2002). [Editor's note: See Polanyi (1944).]
3. It would also seem to offend a basic principle of justice, that a person should not be punished twice for the same offence. One senses that the proposal to exclude those who have fallen foul of the justice system is merely a sop gain middle-class political support for the COAG.
4. Also, of course, it would worsen the relative and absolute position of the youth who have been criminalized or who have dropped out of school. This is an inegalitarian feature of the COAG. Another distorting aspect is that it would alter inter-generational relations, notably inside families. A COAG would give teenagers or 21-year-olds financial freedom from their parents, compromising parental guidance and potentially severing inter-generational ties. One may or may not like that prospect; one should not ignore it.
5. Of course, deciding what is "the community" is a political and administrative matter. Although it had earlier antecedents, the modern thrust to this way of thinking was Rudolf Meidner's original version of "wage-earner funds" in Sweden in the mid-1970s. This was partly stimulated by the strains in the Swedish *solidaristic wage policy*, and in particular by the way Volvo was bypassing the wage policy by introducing individual profit-sharing pay, thereby increasing wage inequality.
6. The *agents* would become *part-principals*, just as many managers and chief executives have become largely *principals* (receiving most of their income from capital).
7. The Enron implosion is indicative of the danger of having elite *principals* divorced from the *agents*, which management is expected to be in shareholder capitalism. If corporate executives receive most of their income from share options rather than from their salary, they will not have the interest of their workforce very high on their priority list.
8. Hissing and loud clapping in the studio would be amplified, with appropriate music.
9. I recall visiting lower "middle-class" families in small-town Pennsylvania who were living from state lottery to state lottery, all their hopes crystallized in the monthly set of numbers. Is this freedom?

10. A CIG would also reduce the widespread tendency, induced by flexible labor markers and the international drift to conditionality and means-tested state benefits, for much labor to drift into the grey or illegal economy, evading taxes and contributions, and thereby contributing to pervasive disentitlement. For instance, a CIG would do away with the arbitrary conditionality of unemployment insurance benefits, which have long been a misnomer.

References

Ackerman, B. and Alstott, A. (1999). *The Stakeholder's Society.* Yale University Press, New Haven.

Ackerman, B., Alstott, A., and Van Parijs, P. (2006). *Redesigning Distribution: Basic Income and Stakeholder Grants as Cornerstones for an Egalitarian Capitalism.* Verso, London and New York.

Polanyi, K. (1944). *The Great Transformation.* Rinehart & Company, Inc., New York.

Part IX
Politics

Introduction
Politics

Yannick Vanderborght, José A. Noguera, and Karl Widerquist

The issue of political feasibility stands out among politics issues in the Basic Income debate. Basic Income proponents like to present it as an idea whose time has come. Many of them strongly believe that, given the state of the discussion and the impressive amount of sophisticated arguments in its favor, Basic Income shall gradually but inevitably move onto the top of the political agenda. Some political developments in OECD countries, and even beyond, support their optimism. Basic Income advocates can be found in most political parties, from extreme-left movements to right-conservative parties. Prominent political actors openly express favorable views, and in some cases governmental authorities have studied it and officially presented it as an alternative deserving careful consideration. In January 2004, the President of Brazil, Luiz Inácio Lula da Silva, signed a law authorizing the gradual introduction of a universal Basic Income for all Brazilians – admittedly as a long-term prospect. The state of Alaska has given a yearly resource dividend (a sort of small, variable Basic Income) to all citizen-residents since 1982. Since 2010, Iran is phasing-in a similar dividend given on a bimonthly basis, and since 2008, Mongolia is considering the introduction of a similar program.

And yet, despite these developments, there are good reasons to remain cautious – if not skeptical – about the political future of Basic Income. As it clearly appears in the following selection of chapters, the implementation of Basic Income comes up against huge political obstacles that cannot be neglected. Among them, the fact that its proponents are scattered across the political spectrum, far from being an advantage, might in fact be considered as a potential drawback. To put it briefly, it could perhaps turn Basic Income into a weak proposal in terms of political marketing. More generally, all authors seem to agree that no country in the world appears likely to introduce a full Basic Income in the immediate future.

David Purdy has dealt directly with such issues for decades (see also Further Reading). In a previously unpublished chapter, Purdy's (1988) starting point is that Basic Income needs to be backed by a "broad, popular alliance of social and political forces" in order to be politically feasible. Hence, his focus is on the three following questions. First, is there a potential majority support? Second, can this potential majority turn into an effective political movement? Third, can this movement overcome adverse reactions and strategic

Basic Income: An Anthology of Contemporary Research, First Edition. Edited by Karl Widerquist, José A. Noguera, Yannick Vanderborght, and Jurgen De Wispelaere.

resistance? In bringing a tentative reply to these three questions, Purdy argues that welfare states will not move quickly into the direction of implementing a Basic Income.

Aaron Wildavsky, was a prominent figure in public policy analysis. "The Lack of Political Support for an Income by Right," co-authored with Bill Cavala (1971), was written in the context of intense discussions of the issue in the United States. Referring to various proposals such as Milton Friedman's *Negative Income Tax* and James Tobin's *Demogrant* (see the "Economics" and "Institutions" sections in this anthology), Cavala and Wildavsky argued that Basic Income was by no means politically feasible "in the near future" at the time. They were proven right indeed. They insisted, in particular, on the lack of support in the U.S. Congress. In the light of some 50 interviews, they maintained that Basic Income was seen by many Congressmen as irreparably undermining the work ethic. The only hope for Basic Income supporters, they concluded, must lie in some sort of back door strategy, carefully designed in order to avoid heated debates that are detrimental to the political chances of the idea.

Yannick Vanderborght (2006) focuses on the role played by trade unions, which remain central players in discussions about tax-and-transfer systems in most industrialized countries. The chapter offers a review of several key arguments that could be used by trade unions to oppose or, alternatively, support a Basic Income. In the light of empirical information collected in Belgium, Canada, and the Netherlands, Vanderborght shows that most trade unions decidedly oppose it, and are thus far from being natural allies of Basic Income advocates.

In a dialogue on the future of social Europe, Fritz Scharpf (2000) and Philippe Van Parijs (2000) express divergent views on this feasibility issue. Scharpf is quite skeptical about the political prospects of Basic Income in the European context, essentially because the normative arguments developed by Basic Income supporters run against the views of the average taxpayer. Furthermore, European welfare states and EU institutions tend to actively promote welfare-to-work programs in order to reduce social expenditures. This political climate, Scharpf argues, is all but favorable to a shift towards Basic Income. In his reply, Philippe Van Parijs insists on some of the specific difficulties of Basic Income in the European context. National Basic Income schemes will be undermined by fiscal competition between EU-member states and, possibly, by welfare migration. Hence, one of the most promising ways to think about a politically feasible version of Basic Income would be to consider the implementation of some sort of EU-wide dividend.

While the dialogue between Scharpf and Van Parijs is restricted to European countries, Philippe Van Parijs, in "Basic Income in the South" (2002), compares the prospects of Basic Income between northern and southern nations. He exemplifies his analysis with such cases as South Africa and Brazil. The specificities of those countries, Van Parijs argues, call for a strategy of soft selectivity plus universal grants for children and/or the elderly, as an intermediate, but affordable and politically acceptable, step towards a full fledged Basic Income.

In "How Cash Transfers Promote the Case for Basic Income," Guy Standing (2011) discusses the growing reliance on conditional cash transfers in developing nations as a solution to poverty. Often the conditions are minimum, such as ensuring that children are immunized or attend school. Standing argues that although it was the conditions that first attracted many policymakers to the idea, evidence indicates that it is the cash that is really making a different in the lives of the poor. Standing believes that this experience makes a strong case for Basic Income.

In "Basic Income and the New Class Struggle" (1987), Philippe Van Parijs makes the innovative case for considering the distribution of job assets in an imperfect labor market equilibrium as the basis of a new class division in welfare capitalism, which has a growing explanatory relevance for social conflicts and dynamics. As a result of the analysis of this new class structure, Van Parijs concludes that only a Basic Income would be a politically feasible way of redistributing those assets, thus deactivating the potential class conflict involved.

A complementary strategy to enhance the political chances of Basic Income is presented by Claus Offe, Ulrich Mückenberger and Ilona Ostner in "A 'Package Solution' for Basic Income" (1996): it consists in introducing Basic Income as a building block of a social policy package, including the reduction in working hours, the development of the "informal sector" or social economy, the flexibilization of labor time, and the recognition of socially useful activities outside the labor market. Implementing Basic Income as a part of that package, the authors argue, will improve their normative acceptability as well as avoid some of its possible undesired consequences.

Claus Offe (2001) argues that even if Basic Income supporters – including himself – seem to have an impressive stock of good arguments, they must accept the fact that the implementation of an income by right is not just around the corner. One of the reasons, he writes, lies in the fact that "the anticipation of freedom causes fear," and reluctance to move in that direction. Hence, in order to be viable every political strategy in favor of Basic Income should be characterized by "the principles of gradualism and reversibility." Once again, policy by stealth seems to be considered as the key condition for feasibility.

Further Reading

Bertram, C. (1997). The need for basic income: An interview with Philippe Van Parijs. *Imprints*, 1 (3), 5–22.

Caputo, R. (ed.) (2013). *Basic Income Guarantee and Politics: International Experiences and Perspectives on the Viability of Income Guarantees.* Palgrave, New York.

Cummine, A. (2012). Overcoming Dividend Skepticism: Why the World's Sovereign Wealth Funds are Not Paying Dividends. In K. Widerquist and M.W. Howard (eds) *Exporting the Alaska Model: Adapting the Permanent Fund Dividend.* Palgrave Macmillan, New York.

De Wispelaere, J. and Noguera, J.A. (2013). On the political feasibility of universal basic income. In R. Caputo (ed.) *Basic Income Guarantee and Politics: International Experiences and Perspectives on the Viability of Income Guarantees.* Palgrave, New York.

Elster, J. (1986). Comment on Van der Veen and Van Parijs. *Theory and Society*, 15 (5), 709–721.

Goodhart, M. (2007). "None so poor that he is compelled to sell himself": Democracy, subsistence, and basic income. In S. Hertel, and L. Minkler (eds) *Economic Rights: Conceptual, Measurement and Policy Issues.* Cambridge University Press, Cambridge, pp. 94–114.

Groh, C. and Erickson, G. (2012). The Improbable but True Story of How the Alaska Permanent Fund and the Alaska Permanent Fund Dividend Came to Be. In K. Widerquist and M.W. Howard (eds) *Alaska's Permanent Fund Dividend: Examining its Suitability as a Model.* Palgrave Macmillan, New York.

Haagh, L. (2011). Basic income, social democracy and control over time. *Policy and Politics*, 39 (1), 43–66.

Hartzok, A. (2008). *The Earth Belongs to Everyone.* Institute for Economic Democracy, Sun City, Arizona.

Hemerijck, A. (2000). Prospects for basic income in an age of inactivity? In L. Groot and R. van der Veen (eds), *Basic Income on the Agenda.* Amsterdam University Press, Amsterdam, pp. 137–154.

Jordan, B. (1988). The Prospects for Basic Income. *Social Policy and Administration*, 22 (2), 115–123.

Jordan, B. (2011a). Prospects for basic income: a British perspective. In A. Gosseries and Y. Vanderborght (eds) *Arguing about Justice. Essays for Philippe Van Parijs*. Presses universitaires de Louvain, Louvain-la-Neuve, pp. 253–259.

Jordan, B. (2011b). The perils of basic income: ambiguous opportunities for the implementation of a utopian proposal. *Policy and Politics*, 39 (1), 101–114.

Jordan, B., Agulnik, P., Burbidge, D. et al. (2000). *Stumbling Towards Basic Income. The Prospects for Tax-Benefit Integration*. Citizens Income Study Centre, London.

Liebig, S. and Mau, S. (2005). A legitimate guaranteed minimum income? In G. Standing (ed.) *Promoting Income Security as a Right: Europe and North America*. Anthem, London.

Moynihan, D.P. (1973). *The Politics of a Guaranteed Income*. Random House, New York.

Mulvale, J.P. (2008). Basic income and the Canadian welfare state: Exploring the realms of possibility. *Basic Income Studies* 3 (1), Article 6. http://www.degruyter.com/view/j/bis

Murphy, J.B. (2010). Baby steps: Basic income and the need for incremental organizational development. *Basic Income Studies* 5 (1), Article 7. http://www.degruyter.com/view/j/bis

Nattrass, Nicoli and Seekings, J. (2005). The Political Economy of Basic Income in South Africa. In K. Widerquist, M.A. Lewis, and S. Pressman (eds) *The Ethics and Economics of the Basic Income Guarantee*. Ashgate, Aldershot, pp. 13–54.

Offe, C. (2000). The German welfare state: Principles, performance and prospects after unification. *Thesis Eleven*, 63, 11–57.

Offe, C. (2008) Basic Income and the Labor Contract. *Basic Income Studies*, 3 (1). http://www.degruyter.com/view/j/bis

Pasma, C. (2010). Working through the work disincentive. *Basic Income Studies*, 5 (2), Article 4. http://www.degruyter.com/view/j/bis

Pateman, C. and Murray, M. (eds) (2012). *Horizons of Reform: Basic Income Around the World*. Palgrave Macmillan, New York.

Purdy, D. (1994). Citizenship, basic income and the state. *New Left Review*, 208 (Nov.-Dec.), 30–48.

Standing, G. (2004). Income security: Why unions should campaign for a basic income. *Transfer: European Review of Labour and Research*, 10 (4), 606–619.

Standing, G. (2011). Responding to the crisis: Economic Stabilisation Grants. *Policy and Politics*, 39 (1), 9–25.

Steensland, B. (2008). *The Failed Welfare Revolution: America's Struggle over Guaranteed Income Policy*. Princeton University Press, Princeton.

Suplicy, E. (2011). Towards an unconditional basic income in Brazil? In A. Gosseries and Y. Vanderborght (eds) *Arguing about Justice. Essays for Philippe Van Parijs*. Presses universitaires de Louvain, Louvain-la-Neuve, pp. 337–346.

Tabatabai, H. (forthcoming). From Price Subsidies to Basic Income: The Iran Model and its Lessons. In K. Widerquist and M.W. Howard (eds) *Exporting the Alaska Model: Adapting the Permanent Fund Dividend*. Palgrave Macmillan, New York.

van der Veen, R. and Groot, L. (eds) (2000). *Basic Income on the Agenda*. Amsterdam University Press, Amsterdam.

Vanderborght, Y. (2005). The Basic Income Guarantee in Europe: Backdoor Strategies. In K. Widerquist, M.A. Lewis, and S. Pressman (eds) *The Ethics and Economics of the Basic Income Guarantee*. Ashgate, Aldershot, pp. 13–54.

Vobruba, G. (1990). Redistribution of work and income in crisis: actors problems of working time reduction and a guaranteed Basic Income. *Contemporary Crises*, 14 (2), 57–67.

Widerquist, K. and Howard, M.W. (2012). Conclusion: Lessons from the Alaska Model. In K. Widerquist and M.W. Howard (eds) *Alaska's Permanent Fund Dividend: Examining its Suitability as a Model*. Palgrave Macmillan, New York.

Wright, E.O. (1986). Why something like socialism is necessary for the transition to something like communism. *Theory and Society*, 15 (5), 657–672.

Chapter 65

Political Strategies for Basic Income

David Purdy

Excerpts from Purdy, D. (1988). The Political Feasibility of the Transition to a Basic Income Society. In W. Van Trier (ed.) *Basic Income and Problems of Implementation: Proceedings of the Second International Conference on Basic Income.* BIEN, Antwerp, pp. 45–64.

Proponents of Basic Income (BI) must offer more than a critique of the present order of society and a vision of an alternative future: they must also show how to get from the one to the other. This chapter considers what agencies and strategies are needed and may be expected to bring about the transition to a BI society.

Society is unlikely to take the radical step of phasing out the existing system of personal taxes and transfers and replacing it by BI unless the move is backed by a broad, popular alliance of social and political forces. If it is to attract support on the scale required, BI must be represented as the centerpiece of a new social settlement which offers the best way forward for everyone – both each individual and society as a whole. This conception is better suited to the political conditions which have come to prevail in the advanced capitalist states since the collapse of the post-war consensus: it also makes the most of the ethic of universality and social citizenship which the principle of BI proclaims.

What is Meant by "Political Feasibility"

It is useful to distinguish four broad areas of argument about the pros and cons of BI: (i) ethical desirability; (ii) historical preconditions; (iii) economic viability; and (iv) political feasibility. The boundaries between these areas are not watertight: and the first three cannot be explored in any detail here. But it is worth briefly reviewing the issues at stake in each one in order to clarify precisely what is meant by asking whether BI is politically feasible.

The ethical case for BI rests on a specific conception and combination of social ideals: social justice as a tenacious and thoroughgoing egalitarianism; personal freedom as positive self-determination; participatory democracy as a community of self-activating and

Basic Income: An Anthology of Contemporary Research, First Edition. Edited by Karl Widerquist, José A. Noguera, Yannick Vanderborght, and Jurgen De Wispelaere.

self-managing citizens; and ecological harmony as a balanced and sustainable relationship between human society and its natural base. What has to be shown is that this conception is coherent and cogent; and that it could be incarnated in a BI society without unacceptability jeopardising other cherished values. A subsidiary, but ideologically important task is to rebut standard objections against making transfer payments universal and unconditional - in particular, the argument that it is wrong and unjust to award benefits to people who can lay no claim to them on grounds of either desert or need.

However desirable BI may be on ethical grounds, it could still turn out to be Utopian: certain economic and cultural preconditions for its successful implementation may be lacking. To refer to these viability conditions as "historical" is by no means to invoke some alleged "iron laws" of history. It simply means that at any given time relatively slowly changing features of any society's economic structure and way of life set tolerance limits on its range of evolutionary options. To ask whether BI is "historically available" is to ask whether it lies inside these limits, or, if not, whether and over what timespace structural change is likely to bring it within the horizon of possibility. There is, of course, nothing to rule out the possibility that an option may lie within reach without ever being taken up. Thus although today's advanced capitalist societies long ago broke free from the grip of gross material scarcity, their economic dynamics and cultural dispositions may prove too hostile for BI to take root.

Strictly speaking, the economic viability issue is simply one aspect of this wider debate about whether advanced capitalist societies can accommodate BI without intolerable stress. It is singled out for separate treatment because it is particularly problematic and looms large in public discussion. There is little doubt that in a purely static, accounting sense the advanced capitalist states could afford to introduce BI. The level and proportions of GDP now prevailing in these states could in principle permit all their citizens to receive an adequate BI without encroaching on investment and public consumption, and still leave a positive residue to meet the "non-fundamental" components of private consumption.

The key question is whether BI is sustainable once the predicable responses of economic agents are taken into account. What has to be shown is that the introduction of an adequate level of BI would not cause either total economic collapse, or, less drastically, an unacceptable, though finite, fall in measured GDP, as a result of any tendency for labor and/or capital to withdraw from activity in the monetized economy. A BI regime might also have to contend with other induced, but unwanted economic tribulations - notably, a resurgence of inflation driven by distributive conflict.

These problems reflect a deeper tension. The tendency of a BI regime is egalitarian, democratic, life-enhancing and eco-friendly. But these impulses are radically incongruent with the hierarchical, dominative, accumulative and boundlessly expansionist regime of capital, which not only rules the economic realm of the social formations identified by its presence, but also permeates their politics and culture. Capitalism may have matured to the point where it can be made to host a new civilization struggling to be born. But the powerful priorities and interests which give the old civilization its historical center of gravity, are likely to resist and retard the birth and early development of its "unnatural" offspring.

This cursory survey enables us to distinguish between broad and narrow interpretations of political feasibility. To ask about political feasibility in the broad sense is to ask: "Is the transition to a BI society an attainable objective?" without being specific about the timescale of transition. An adequate answer to this question must deal explicitly with the first three areas of debate as well as with issues peculiar to the art/science of politics. An affirmative answer depends on the soundness of the case advanced in each area. Alternatively, one can focus on political feasibility in the narrow sense by posing the more restrictive question: "How probable is it the transition can be accomplished over the kind of timescale normally contemplated by political actors (e.g. some electoral timetable or the political lifetime of one generation)?"

Political feasibility in the narrow, time-specific sense does not really arise unless there is a plausible case for arguing that BI is ethically desirable, historically opportune and economically viable. On the other hand, even if there are serious doubts about BI's strictly political prospects, it does not follow that there is no point in discussing its other qualities. The old adage that politics is the art of the possible is double-edged: it has both a realist and a transformatory significance. Reasoned speculation about possible, but, for the time being probable, futures is one way of widening the boundaries of political argument and action: in Oscar Wilde's immortal [quote] "Every map of the world should contain utopia."[1] Moreover, the tempo of political change is not always uniform: at moments of political crises, discontinuity and fluidity, prospects which once looked unpromising can sometimes improve very quickly.

Nevertheless, if the political outlook for BI is gloomy, it would be a mistake to rest content with waging the battle of ideas in the hope that a more propitious conjuncture will eventually turn up. This is to fall into the voluntarist and idealist delusion that sooner or later a sound case is bound to be crowned with success. A serious transformatory politics must be interventionist, constantly searching out allies and scanning the scene for opportunities to shift the balance of forces in its favor.

Political argument is not decided by the force of reason alone: the persuasiveness of a case is amplified or muffled by who is making it and how many others believe it. Visionaries who neglect the entrepreneurial skills of the political trade, lack credibility and are easily marginalised, just as shrewd opportunists and demagogues may come to command huge popularity and resonance. Politics offers plenty of scope for "unappreciated genius" as well as successful mediocrity.

Assessing Political Feasibility in the Narrow Sense

Narrow political feasibility turns on three issues:

1. Is there a potential majority support for BI?
2. If so, can this potential majority realize itself, that is, achieve coherence and effectiveness as a political movement?
3. If so, and if political support for BI advances to the point at which a government plans and implements a BI system, could the government and movement overcome or neutralize (i) predictable adverse reactions by economic agents acting in their self-interest as they see it; and (ii) concerted strategic resistance by political opponents?

Only the first two of these questions are dealt with in any detail here. A full treatment of the economic frictions mentioned in question (3) is beyond the scope of this chapter; the prospect of organized political resistance is either too contingent and remote from our present vantage point to allow for more than abstract generalizations or flights of fancy, or else already covered by comments on questions (1) and (2).

It is, however, worth pointing out that the risks of economic or political destabilization are not just problems which would become important at the point when a BI program is implemented. Spontaneous acts of self-defense undertaken by sectional interests – flights of financial capital across the foreign exchanges, adverse movements in stock market confidence, investment strikes, attempts by organized labor to offload the perceived burden of higher taxes by pressing for higher gross money wages – as well as more self-consciously political acts of defiance, are all contingencies which could be anticipated in advance,· not least by BI's opponents. It follows that discussing how best to insure against such challenges forms part of the antecedent struggle to push BI up the political agenda until the point of implementation is reached.

1. Is there potential majority support for BI?

The answer to this question is more complex than is commonly supposed. Likewise, head-counts which purport to demonstrate that BI will benefit a numerical majority of the population are less critical to its political prospects than is commonly supposed. Three considerable problems bedevil any simple political calculus.

The first is that the distributive effects of BI are complex, especially when account is taken of the longer run economic adjustments it is likely to induce. Moreover, any given individual may be affected favorably in some respects and unfavorably in others both before and after the process of adjustment. It follows immediately that there is no unique or self-evident basis for judging the probable distribution of political support.

Suppose for the sake of argument that people's attitudes to BI rest entirely on self-regarding (and accurate) assessments of its effects in raising or lowering their personal disposable income or otherwise altering their available range of economic options. Even on this dubious assumption several alternative balance sheets of "gainers" and "losers" can be devised. The initial impact pattern of gain and loss will differ from the post-adjustment pattern; and there could be several variants of the latter depending on what assumptions are made about the behavioral responses of economic agents. Nor is there any good reason to set aside the various longer run scenarios in favor of a strictly myopic approach: it is unsafe to assume that even self-interested individuals are short-sighted.

Second, even if we confine attention to narrowly defined distributive issues, it is unrealistic to suppose that people will base their stance on purely self-regarding, individualistic criteria. The balance of gain and loss among families or households will differ from that among persons. And attitudes may be set within in other, wider frames of social identity – class, gender, race and so on up to and including society as a whole.

Third, even if we were sure whose gains and losses to count, with respect to which issues, over what timescale and on what assumptions about induced responses, we should still be unable to predict the distribution of political opinion. People's views about where either their own or society's best interests lie are not passively predetermined by their social circumstances, but depend on the dynamics of political and ideological contestation. The full import of this point will emerge when we turn to consider the prospects for promoting BI as an organized political cause.

There may be no harm in cutting through these complexities in order to play the numbers game. Roughly speaking, BI redistributes income and life-chances away from those who currently hold varying degrees of privilege within the system of employment, to those who stand at the bottom of the employment hierarchy, and to those who are outside paid employment altogether. On certain simplifying assumptions, it can be shown that "gainers" will outnumber "losers."

This kind or exercise may reassure supporters or provide useful ammunition for rhetoric and propaganda. But it is not a substitute for the creative task of political mobilization. It seems unwise to use the results to "forecast" the outcome of an imaginary referendum over the introduction of BI. Appeals to some hypothetical majority of self-interested voters sit uneasily beside the principled case for BI as the keystone of a new civilization. They also risk becoming sidetracked on to diversionary points of order about whether a referendum would be an appropriate decision-making procedure. More fundamentally, political majorities do not simply inhere in the social structure: they always have to be synthesized if they are to become effective.

2. Political coherence and effectiveness

Suppose for the sake of argument that in some sense a majority of the population stands to benefit materially from the introduction of BI. It by no means follows that the cause of BI is best furthered by seeking to build a political movement which draws its main support and driving force from the ranks of these potential beneficiaries. Indeed, there is every reason to expect that any movement built on this basis would suffer from crippling weaknesses.

Consider first the sociological implausibility of the enterprise. Some of the groups which have most to gain from BI are unstable in composition. Most unemployed or intermittently employed workers, for example, together with many part-time employees, either do not expect or do not wish to retain their current status, which therefore provides them with no strong source of identification or interest affiliation. The presumed beneficiary majority is also internally fragmented. Prior to the advent of a BI system, it would be a Herculean task to knit these fragments together into a unified political force, though once the system was in place it would become easier to assemble coalitions around common objectives. Finally, even if the losers are a minority, they are nevertheless a numerous and substantial minority. They encompass not only the wealthiest social strata with the greatest direct or indirect influence over public policy, but also large numbers of workers in the privileged core of the labor market, including the majority of trade union members.

These structural difficulties are compounded by the bleak terrain of contemporary politics. The collapse of the Keynesian-social democratic consensus and the neo-liberal revolution have dramatically reshaped the political landscape. The labor movement as the organized political presence of the working class is almost universally in decline: trade union membership has fallen and socialism as a political ideology is severely debilitated.

Admittedly, socialism is a broad church and there are some exceptions to this general judgment. It is the mainstream currents of the socialist tradition – Labourism, "revisionist" social democracy, Eurocommunism and the various parties and sects which stand for fundamentalist, revolutionary, class struggle – which have languished. Those minority tendencies which cleave to a communitarian, decentralist, participatory vision of the socialist project have been less overwhelmed by adversity and are better adapted to survival in the new era. But they have yet to prove their capacity either to regenerate the ailing labor movement or to evolve into a new historic agency for social transformation.

The labor movement's travails seriously handicap the cause of BI. Historically the labor movement has acted as a democratic resistance to capitalist power and a motor, or at least umbrella, for the achievement of welfare reforms. Its demise deprives the struggle for citizenship rights of any serviceable political cutting edge. It also clears the way for the process of class dealignment. As traditional class values and allegiances decay, workers become more receptive, or at least less resistant, to definitions of interest emphasizing market freedom, property ownership, enterprise, competition and selectivity.

This process of political and ideological realignment hastens the coalescence of a new dominant social bloc which would be profoundly hostile to BI. The new formation is by no means solid or complete. But the design and foundations are already in place for the construction of a real or imaginary community of interest centered on the privileged core of the labor market and uniting the workplace rank and file with the highest powerholders in economy and state. Even if the disparate groups which stand to gain from BI somehow managed to overcome the obstacles to effective political action, there is an evident risk that this very achievement would polarize political conflict and consolidate the emergent bloc in opposition to their demands. For whatever else divides its various factions, they all stand to lose, or so they believe, from a policy which strikes at the pre-eminence of the employment system, whether as a source of income, power and social distinction, or as a source of personal meaning and purpose.

A strategy which ranges the poor and disinherited against an alliance of organized workers, big business and the state, is clearly doomed to failure. Some way has to be found of avoiding this unequal contest. The most obvious strategic imperative is to detach trade unions and their members from the nascent power bloc. They have to be weaned away from their conservative adherence to the priorities and norms of the present system of employment; persuaded to regard BI as a liberating potency rather than a mortal threat; and convinced that their best interests lie in striving to overhaul and redesign society's arrangements for organizing work and distributing income.

This is a formidably arduous task, the requirements of which cannot be explored here. Suppose, however, that it is tackled and that the labor movement – revitalized, though still relatively impoverished in membership and votes compared with its historical peaks – champions the cause of BI and supplies the armature of an effective political movement. This disposition of forces certainly offers the cause a fighting chance. It still, however, falls short of a winning combination.

For one thing, even if trade unions and socialist parties lend their blessing and weight to BI, they still have to carry members and voters with them. But, more importantly, a strategy which casts the labor movement as the exclusive or leading agency of transition is probably misconceived. The discussion so far has proceeded from the assumption that BI is in some sense the natural political property of a more or less clearly defined constituency of the dispossessed. This constituency is unlikely to be capable of organizing itself into an effective force; and even if it could, its prospects of political success are slim. It needs, therefore, to hitch its star to an already organized political savior. Despite the evidence that its best years lie behind it, the Labour Party still looks like the most promising candidate for this role.

The strategy consists of assembling a single or primary political formation – whether movement or party – dedicated to promoting the presumed material interests of certain sectional social groups. An alternative approach is to conduct BI politics in terms of general principles of social organization and to project BI as a universalistic program embodying the higher interests of society as a whole. On this conception there is no predetermined organizing focus and architect of transition. Rather, what is required is to draw together from across the political spectrum a broad coalition of forces which share BI as their common sense. The final section of this chapter explains why this strategy is better suited both to the scale of the undertaking and to the novel political environment in which it must perforce be attempted.

A Broad Alliance Strategy for BI

The past two decades have witnessed fundamental changes in the coordinates of politics. As David Marquand (1988) argues, it no longer makes any sense to think in terms of a single dimension in which the Left is for change, the Right against it and the Center undecided. The political map now has two, quite distinct axes: one running from left to right, the other making out points on a radical-conservative scale.

Hitherto this distinction has been overlooked since the two dimensions were thought to coincide. The "Left" stood for reform/revolution; progress/emancipation; modernity and the future; the interests of the exploited and oppressed. The "Right" stood for conservatism/reaction; order/stability; tradition and the past; the interests of the exploiters and dominators. The "Center" stood somewhere in between.

Nowadays the distinction is indispensable to finding one's political bearings. In Britain, for example, over the past decade the New Right has been easily the most dynamic, forward-looking, change-promoting political force. The old reformist or revolutionary left, together with the "One Nation" Tories, have been the most conservative and backward-looking. And no two-class model can possibly do justice to the variegated, cross-cutting class divisions of "actually existing pluralism."

These shifts in the patterns of contemporary politics make it both necessary and possible to envisage BI as a central, unifying element in a radical political project which transcends any narrowly sectional or partisan affiliation. The transition to a BI society could not be negotiated and secured without positive support, or at least benevolent neutrality, amongst all the main political parties and currents of opinion. It would have to be part of what everyone, including its opponents, perceived as a new socio-political settlement, representing a decisive break with the past.

At the same time BI is eminently qualified to act as a focal point for a broadly based, radical alliance capable of contesting the ground now occupied by the New Right and bidding for ideological and political hegemony. This is precisely because it is not inherently tied to any corporate class or sectional interests, but offers a wider, societal frame of reference.

The universal discourse of BI challenges conventional sectional conceptions of individual and collective interests: but it also provides a higher-order court of appeal to moderate sectional claims without in any way denying their right to exist. BI inevitably throws into sharp relief the multitude of overlapping class divisions which run like fault lines through the social formation between employed and unemployed, propertied and propertyless, high paid and low paid, men and women, mental labor and manual labor. By the same token it furnishes the political task of strategic integration with a common language and design.

In these respects certain parallels can be drawn with the emergence of the Keynesian social democratic state. In its own day and its own terms this regime also offered a new, strategic direction for the advance of social citizenship and a new framework for the organization of employment and income-entitlement. To cite this historical precedent is not to reinstate the social values, intellectual paradigm programmatic themes or methods of governance associated with the Keynesian social democratic era. This old order is dead and could not be resurrected even if it were desirable.

Rather, the analogy is intended to make two points. The first is that the robust popular alliance and cross-party consensus which made it possible to reconstruct the state in the 1940s provides a model – probably our old model – for the kind of political strategy which is needed to inaugurate and sustain a BI regime. The second is to call attention to the antecedents of Keynesian social democracy in the 1930s.

The most significant political division of the inter-war years was not the traditional contest between political parties, but the argument over unemployment policy between economic radicals and economic conservatives. Representative of both sides, in this argument were to be found in all the main parties. The radical camp, for example, included figures as diverse as Keynes, Lloyd-George, Bevin, Macmillan and Mosley. The radicals differed over detailed programs for tackling the Depression, and differed in their views on other issues. But at a deeper level they shared a common discourse and vision of the future: they all wanted to institute a state which systematically used its power to remedy the evils of unregulated capitalism.

The inter-war experience also reminds us that even if a radical consensus began to crystallize around the principle of BI in opposition to the conservative values and assumptions of the present system of work and income-entitlement, this would not in itself assure political success. In the 1930s it was economic conservation which prevailed: the radicals' moment had to await the arrival of the war emergency.

Their modern counterparts can hardly expect to rely on the recurrence of such a favorable, but devastating opportunity. Neither the threat of military defeat nor the threat of working class revolution – the two main factors which have prompted conservative governments to make welfare concessions in the past – looks like a remotely probable catalyst of reform today. It is conceivable that a succession of ecological catastrophes or urban disorders might serve as functional substitutes, but it seems improbable. The most realistic prospect for the BI project is a slow, patient, positional struggle rather than a fast-moving war of maneuver. Its strongest asset in this long haul is the optimistic and expansive view of the future which it brings to bear on the dismal and pressing problems of the present.

Note

1. Editor's note: This is a paraphrase of the following quotation: "A map of the world that does not include Utopia is not worth even glancing at, for it leaves out the one country at which Humanity is always landing. And when Humanity lands there, it looks out, and, seeing a better country, sets sail. Progress is the realisation of Utopias" in Oscar Wilde, *The Soul of Man under Socialism*, 1891, reprinted in Wilde (1969).

References

Marquand, D. (1988). *The Unprincipled Society. New Demands and Old Politics.* Jonathan Cape, London.

Wilde, O. (1969). *The Artist as Critic: Critical Writings of Oscar Wilde.* R. Ellmann (ed.). Random House, New York.

Chapter 66

The Lack of Political Support for an Income by Right

Bill Cavala and Aaron Wildavsky

Excerpts from Wildavsky, A. with Cavala, B. (1970). The Political Feasibility of Income by Right. Reprinted in A. Wildavsky (2003). *The Revolt Against the Masses and Other Essays on Politics and Public Policy.* Transaction Publishers, New Brunswick, NJ, pp. 71–102.

Our task is to determine the political feasibility of those public policies which would give poor people income as a right. Such a task involves little more than outlining the steps (or, in our case, the major step) through which any policy must necessarily pass, while providing an assessment of the chances of passage. This type of analysis provides information about the nature and strengths of obstacles that stand in the way of a new proposal. It offers counsel to the proponents of a policy, providing them with a set of its predicted strengths and weaknesses to emphasize or modify. The utility of this approach is, of course, founded on several assumptions, the most basic of which is the belief that the political process will continue to function much the same as it has in the past.

If this perspective is accepted, then our task becomes all too simple. Income policies are not politically feasible because few people want them. Why? Policies that provide people with unearned income run counter to widely held and deeply felt American values such as achievement, work, and equality of opportunity. The large tax increase or drastic reallocation of public funds required to guarantee income has few supporters. Labor unions fear that a Guaranteed Income would render them superfluous. Militant black leaders take the same position for a similar reason. Income policies are not serious subjects for discussion in Congress. Those who do care about them are trying to find ways to put them on the agenda of those issues safe to discuss.

In view of the high cost of failure, proponents of income maintenance have an obligation to take a hard look at the argument that it will both improve the lot of the poor *and* increase support for existing political institutions. For while advertising income maintenance as the panacea for violence[1] may well make it a more "feasible" policy, if the

From Cavala, B. and Wildavsky, A. (2003 [1970]). The Political Feasibility of Income by Right. In A. Wildavsky, *The Revolt Against the Masses and Other Essays on Politics and Public Policy.* Transaction Publishers, New Brunswick, NJ, pp. 71–102. Reprinted with permission of Transaction Publishers.

Basic Income: An Anthology of Contemporary Research, First Edition. Edited by Karl Widerquist, José A. Noguera, Yannick Vanderborght, and Jurgen De Wispelaere.

advertisement proves false the ultimate price of that feasibility may be paid in the coin of more expectations crushed, more hostility, and less opportunity for future success.

Lack of Support in Congress[2]

If the strongest arguments for income plans are the arguments against our present system of public assistance, an initial optimism is justified. There is high awareness of the failures of the present system among members of the 91st Congress.[3] Almost every member has a personal atrocity story dealing with the failure of the poverty program and welfare system in his state or district. All were aware of the disincentives now built into our public assistance programs. With only a single exception, they agreed that the present approaches to the problems of poverty are not working now and would probably not work in the future. Fertile soil, it would appear, for the income-maintenance arguments. But rejection of present welfare policies has not yet been transformed into acceptance of income by right.

Most of the members of Congress we interviewed[4] did not understand what was meant by any of the terms commonly used to describe income by right. After a short explication by the interviewer, however, they did not lack for opinions. Congressmen typically would say, "No, absolutely not, you just can't give people money, you have to leave them some sense of self-respect." Others would speak of "something for nothing" or the "work ethic" to explain why they or their constituents were opposed. As soon as the idea became clear, they immediately made a connection with socialism planning, and other disagreeable things. "Whatever the plan," one Congressman noted, "if it can be labeled Guaranteed Income with any kind of correctness, then it would be defeated."

Although we thought the Congressmen would be concerned about work incentives, we did not realize how persistent and deeply felt these feelings would be. A respected and hard-driving Congressman insisted that poverty gives people its own incentive to overcome adversity. "I myself," he said, "would have been a lush if people had paid me not to work."[5] It was not enough to remind the legislators about the disincentives in the present welfare system, for they knew and objected already; their answer, however, was to suggest that the welfare system be made more unpleasant. When we pointed out the resultant human degradation, they would acknowledge it but then claim that a Guaranteed Income would only worsen the problem: giving away money undermines the pride, responsibility, and motivation of the recipient. These representatives would seriously argue that they were protecting the poor from their own weaknesses by refusing to give them money. They said this, apparently, not out of malice but out of a conviction that men are weak and will take the easy path – to their own ruin. Three of the most powerful and respected members of the House noted that if they in their poor youth had been given a Guaranteed Income they would be "bums" today.

As in society at large, Congressmen who grew up in hard times do not have much sympathy for income policies. They believe that people have to work for their own salvation. "If you cut your own wood," the philosophy of the conservative legislators went, "it warms you twice." That might be true of [working] adults, we said for the sake of argument, but what about [dependent] women and kids? The typical answer was consistent with the philosophy of earning one's way: "It's a fine object lesson for kids, having free money in the family. They're not going to learn responsibility *that* way."

High on the list of congressional objections to income proposals (though never mentioned before the moral difficulties) was the necessity for a large increase in income taxes.

Everyone had the same arguments: we are facing a taxpayers' revolt; people are unhappy with the present system's cost; redistribution would hurt middle-class incentives; the money isn't available, and so on. The last theme was naturally prevalent among members of the House Appropriations Committee. One of them explained, "We really just don't have enough money to fill our needs, let alone our wants," and he gave the example of a family sitting around after dinner, planning what they'd do if they had the money. They'd build boats, sail around the world, things of this sort. "But," he said, "you eventually have to get up and wash the dishes and leave those plans among the after-dinner smoke."

A return to reality meant that a huge tax increase was required. "To get that kind of money," we were told, "you have to have an increase in taxes, and to get the kind of plan you want through Congress, it would have to be Presidential initiative. Something that big simply couldn't come from the Congress. There is no Congressman big enough. The leadership itself won't move without a Presidential initiative." No one we interviewed was willing to say that he would ask his constituents to support a substantial tax increase at the present time.

Even the most liberal proponents of the plans agreed that the money for income maintenance just would not be there (given other needs and demands) unless defense spending could be cut. Whether true or not, this is the conviction of the Congress; it means that the fight for authorization, and especially for appropriations, will be perceived as an adjunct of the fight against military spending. Alternatives (raising taxes, cutting spending in other areas) are not considered viable by many members. The argument that income plans could be financed out of revenue gained by growth in GNP is not taken seriously: conservatives want to have the money before they spend it; liberals feel that most of this money is already earmarked for increased defense expenditures.

The Congressmen we interviewed did not believe that their middle- and working-class constituents and their union leaders would support income maintenance. Raising the minimum wage is a major goal of labor unions, and that would be weakened by any income plan. Even if some labor union leaders could be persuaded to support income maintenance, the rank and file probably would not, on grounds of equity. Most unions and their members will have to change their views on income maintenance before it is a feasible policy, and most Congressmen will not take this gamble. "In my state," one reported, "it would be political suicide. My supporters are primarily working-class people; they oppose the notion of something for nothing. They tell me they bust their butts over their jobs, and they're not about to have somebody living off the fruits of their energies." Another expressed similar sentiments and ended, "In short, I am extremely pessimistic on almost every ground you can imagine, and I myself am not anywhere near convinced that such a program is morally defensible, let alone politically feasible." Rather than asking why most Congressmen oppose income maintenance, it might be more instructive to ask why a few actually support it.

Support for income maintenance came from Congressmen perceived by their more hesitant colleagues as "safe-seat liberals," that is, from members of the Democratic Study Group (DSG)[6] in the House and from a handful of crusaders in the Senate. Characteristically, they knew only that income maintenance was a liberal issue and that they were liberals; ergo, their support was automatic. When queried as to what would be required for passage of such a plan, all cited a need for more liberals and fewer conservatives in Congress (about 205 more by our count).

Among the members of the Democratic Study Group we interviewed, there was little concern with the moral or even the knotty technical issues involved in income maintenance.

They would merely repeat what became a familiar litany: the more Democrats the more progressives, the more progressives the more support for progressive issues, the more progressive issues the better the chance of a Guaranteed Income. There was not even much talk about income proposals among DSG members because "everyone knows where each other stands."[7] When asked about the chances of passing an income maintenance proposal, however, they all give the same answer: "None, zero, absolutely no chance."

The strategy adopted by these liberals was to introduce vast comprehensive bills covering everything from Guaranteed Income to higher education for all to total employment and so on. They do not mean to push these measures, however, but merely to introduce them. If they were really serious, several members told us, important blocs of voters they need for re-election would be mad at them. In addition, party leaders and their fellow Congressmen would be angry at them for exposing the party to danger without any hope of accomplishment. A *pro forma* introduction of a comprehensive bill, however, had certain virtues summed up by a Senator: "It at least presents the issue to the other Senators and gets them thinking about it. It tends to be true that when an idea is written up in bill form it takes on some kind of legitimacy.[8]·Also, people looking for a liberal record will probably stand up for it, which gives them a stake in defending it in the future when they run for re-election." Yet even Congressmen with the most liberal constituencies would observe that income maintenance was not popular with the voters in their districts nor with various groups such as labor unions that had provided support for them in the past. Hence their support was "nominal and not really very serious."

Our preinterview guess had been that liberals would favor income plans, that conservatives would oppose them, and that a large body of Congressmen in the middle would have no opinion one way or the other. We wanted to determine whether this group could be reached by a combination of better information and a proposal modified to take their most serious objections into account. What we found, however, was that this "middle group" was virtually nonexistent. The moderates were either opposed on moral grounds or frightened by the political consequences of the issue. In order for them to consider supporting income maintenance, they felt that three things would be needed: (i) modifications to take care of their concern about incentives, equity, and cost; (ii) sufficient support in their own constituencies to make the risk worth taking; (iii) strong public support from the President. "I'd hate to stand for that issue in 1970," a legislator insists. "I could do it if it were a matter of supporting a Presidential program, but it's tough to stand alone – they'd crucify me." New York liberals might go around introducing "silly" bills but not the man in the middle. "Those boys," a Congressman said, referring to liberals from safe districts, "they don't have to worry about a thing back home in talking to voters, but for people like me – and there are quite a few of us here in the Congress – it's just too big an issue to stand up on alone. If the President was for it, then we could stand up with him."

Many members of Congress felt that income by right would be a survival issue. It would be highly visible in a campaign and would result in the defeat of Congressmen from shaky districts. The issue would combine higher taxes, increasing numbers of allegedly lazy bums on welfare rolls, and riots and rising crime rates as part of undesirable tendencies in American life. In order to make the income plans sound reasonable, moderate Congressmen would need to supply information of a complex sort to the voter. All felt that conservative opponents could effectively simplify the issue and provide objections which would immediately be understood and favorably received by the voter. Between those Congressmen who shared the views of their constituents that Guaranteed Income was "a payoff for laziness" and others who considered the political risks too high, the question of political feasibility was uniformly regarded as hopeless for the present. "Right now, it's not even an issue which could be viably discussed."

So they don't like income maintenance, they don't like the present system, and they don't have the money available to do better. Would they do anything about welfare policy? Responses to this question did not vary from liberal to conservative: "An honest day's dollar for an honest day's work." All favor increased job opportunity but they were vague as to what that meant, as to who could work at what level of wages and so on. Some of the southern members talked in sentimental terms about the value and discipline of the old Works Progress Administration (WPA) and Civilian Conservation Corps (CCC) camps, which is how they perceive the notion of the government as the employer of last resort. Despite the lack of clarity, job programs were as strongly preferred by members of Congress as they are in the general population.

Virtually all Congressmen agreed that "hunger is a problem" and were sympathetic to Senator McGovern's efforts to eliminate hunger. To them this meant that people should be given food for survival. Poverty meant real hunger, not inability to have what others had. The basic idea, as several Congressmen put it, was that "no one should starve – but to be at a better-off level than starvation one should put some element of oneself into one's work." These Congressmen "[. . .] don't mind giving away food, but it shouldn't be steak. People should not be satisfied with living on a food stamp program. I'm sure the Agriculture Department could come up with some nutritious food that isn't too tasty so that you'd want to get off it as soon as possible, but that as long as you had to be on it then it would keep you alive." So far as these Congressmen are concerned, all carrot and no stick is not going to work.

Specific Political Difficulties

Dignity and bureaucracy

One of the great selling points of income maintenance is its purported superiority over the present welfare system. Conservatives are expected to support it because they believe it provides the opportunity of dismantling the great welfare bureaucracy. Poor people are expected to support it because it substitutes the dignity of "income by right" for the degradation of welfare investigations and the "means test." We must now ask whether the proposals that are feasible do in fact provide more dignity and less bureaucracy than the welfare system.

The answer appears to be a flat "no." For one thing, even if new programs were instituted with a level of appropriations that would make feasible a cutback of present welfare, a bureaucracy would still be required. None of the plans, with the exception of Friedman's proposal (Friedman, 1962; 1968), could be administered directly through the existing apparatus of the Internal Revenue Service.[9] All the plans would involve the elimination of state and county welfare machinery; hence a new or expanded national bureaucracy would be necessary. The result would be more centralization, not decentralization. Given the difficulty of forms, the literacy levels of the recipients, and necessity of quarterly payments and estimations of income, the need for bureaucratic assistance is not likely to diminish appreciably. If we assume that the elimination of categories and their concomitant stigma will make more people eligible for aid and more eligible people willing to apply for it, bureaucracy may well increase.

Let us also ponder the problem of coordination of bureaucracies. Will county social workers be administering the federal program? Will the complexities of the new forms require as much of their time as the old investigations? Will not the increased numbers of recipients also increase the need for casework and counseling? Will we then need more social workers, paid by the local government to administer a federal program?

If administrative costs increase or remain the same after adoption of income maintenance, the main argument with political appeal to congressional conservatives is lost. Support from these men would be improbable at best: prior to authorization it must be demonstrated in a clear and convincing way that the size of the bureaucracy will decrease both in cost and in numbers. Unfortunately, the only situation in which such a demonstration could be made is likely to be one in which the present system of aid is eliminated in favor of an income maintenance with low levels of support. This, of course, has the undesirable consequence of making large numbers of poor people economically worse off than they are now.

From the perspective of the poor, some of the arguments which stress the human advantages of income by right over the present system do make sense. Much of the harassment (such as midnight raids) associated with enforcement of degrading rules would be eliminated. There would be no need to spy around for "the man in the house." But these problems could also be eliminated through a simple modification of the present system. The real argument for income maintenance as a source of dignity is stronger: it purports not simply to decrease the indignities of welfare, but promises also to remove the stigma associated with poverty. We seriously question whether income maintenance would achieve this crucial goal.[10] In America the stigma of poverty, after all, lies less in the fact of being poor than in the implication that one is lacking in those abilities which are rewarded. The idea of an income floor is a step toward modifying this implication. It suggests that the poor are not completely responsible for their fate, that they may have lacked a real (as against formal) opportunity to participate in our race for gain. But it is a far different thing to say that the losers in that race will not starve than it is to say that the race itself is not a worthy one.

Income by right would remove the stigma of being poor only to the extent that it succeeded in removing the opposite status from being rich, that is, only to the extent that it signaled acceptance of the principle of equal result rather than equal opportunity. The recognition that equality of result is involved quite naturally leads conservatives to oppose income maintenance in principle. But where, in principle, income by right would lead to a demand for income leveling that truly would remove the stigma (as well as the fact) of poverty, the proposals we are dealing with do not. They do not (at least initially) propose an equalization of the distribution of income in the United States. They do not, as a consequence, eliminate the stigma of being a loser in the competitive race which is American life. What they offer is, in effect, a consolation prize. The amount of dignity which such a prize would salvage is problematical at best.[11]

But if income-maintenance plans are unable to eliminate the stigma of being poor per se, at least they can spare the poor from the indignity and embarrassment of having their condition publicly proclaimed. There are moral advantages to a silent check received in the privacy of one's own home with no strings attached as to how you spend it and no need to justify to someone how you got it. That is the real strength of the income-maintenance proposals: it is private and impersonal, not public, personal, and degrading.

The power of this argument, however, is based on the contrast between the theory of the proposals and the present practices of the welfare system. We have argued that in practice the new proposals would have many of the disabilities of the old. In short, while the benefits of the plans would be invisible and private to the community, the means of obtaining those benefits would be visible and public. (Note that if the stigma of poverty were really removed by such plans the need for privacy would not be there.) The degradation of being publicly identified as poor would remain for numbers of recipients. If the most onerous features of the present system were eliminated, it might be difficult indeed to determine whether categorical assistance or Guaranteed Income served the value of dignity the best.

Equity

The political strength of the present system of categorical aid lies in its strict coverage: no nonneedy are supposed to be given support. The abhorrence that some people feel at giving "something for nothing" may be mitigated by their acceptance of aid to the needy. Unfortunately, several of the new plans for Guaranteed Income are unable to maintain this political credit. Attempts to fill the "poverty gap" completely while at the same time moving toward the idea of income by right tend to produce loose coverage as a necessary byproduct.

An income plan with loose coverage would pay money to substantial numbers of middle- and low-income wage earners as well as to the defined "poor," unless an offsetting tax of high rate is placed against income earned in addition to the subsidy. While there is still widespread sentiment against any form of government aid to the poor, federal policies over the past 30 years have accustomed people to the concept (Mueller, 1965: 215). Income plans with loose coverage, however, do not involve simply redistributing income from the nonpoor to the poor; they demand a redistribution from the "wealthy" nonpoor to the less wealthy nonpoor. Plans which include such leakages could not be defended as aid to the needy. Rather, defenders of such plans would have to justify them in terms of arguments for equality of income.

Thus the first liability which "loose" proposals tend to accrue is a conflict with some of the widely shared values of Americans. While the concept of equality is an important value to mobilize in support of any proposal, it is the notion of equal opportunity rather than equality of result which is basic to the American tradition.[12] Equality may be used to justify removing some of the handicaps which make the opportunity to compete meaningless, but equality of result would negate the idea of competition itself and render equality of opportunity meaningless. Opponents of income plans, we suggest, would be in a much better position to use the persuasive value of the tradition of equality. In more concrete terms, we must ask whether families of about median income can be expected to sit back while poorer families are raised by government subsidy to income levels as high as their own.

The main difficulty with any plan that involves loose coverage, however, lies in the fact that it tends to pyramid liabilities. Where ordinarily the opposition of upper-income groups who are concerned with their economic interests can be countervailed to some extent by an appeal to their moral values, in this case the two would reinforce rather than conflict with one another. It is not wise to allow those groups who would oppose income proposals on strict economic grounds the additional weapon of ideological purity. From this perspective, then, the political recommendation would have to be against opting for one of the proposals with loose coverage. The vital point is the necessity of separating the concept of income maintenance for the *poor* (which could be rationalized in terms of equal opportunity arguments) from the idea of income redistribution per se (which could not be so justified).

Incentives

The problem of incentives involves deeply felt moral values as well as important economic considerations. In form the problem is simple to state: if we are to avoid payments to the nonpoor, then as the earned income of the poor rises the amount of the subsidy should decline. The question is: at what rate should the subsidy decline? Or, put differently, what portion of his nontransfer income will the poor person be allowed to retain? As this "offset rate" (the tax imposed on earned income) rises, economic theory tells us that the incentive to work will drop. Under our present welfare system (Assistance to Families with Dependent Children-Unemployed Parent (AFDC-UP) and Old-Age, Survivors, and Disability Insurance (OASDI) up to age 72), the offset rate is 100% or more.[13] A built-in disincentive to working, this problem has been the source of much of the political criticism of our public assistance programs.

In fact, the high offset rate associated with our present welfare system has served the proponents of income-maintenance proposals as one of their strong arguments. The fact that all of the proposed income plans[14] feature less than 100% offset rates on earned income is taken as a major plus factor. Usually this is spoken of as a "bonus," or incentive factor, accompanied by an argument contrasting it favorably with our present "disincentives."[15]

But, at least in theory, any offset of earned income will tend to act as a disincentive. While this is recognized as a disability of our present welfare system, the categorical nature of that assistance has helped to make it at least politically palatable. Among the critics of income assistance there is a widespread conviction that poor people can and should be separated into classes of those who either *can* or *will* work and those who "can't" or "won't." The present system of aid is intended to reach only those who cannot work for some reason or another; thus disincentives are not really a problem. However, income-by-right proposals make no such distinctions between "deserving" and "nondeserving" poor. With every poor person eligible for payment, with no category to eliminate those who could work, the incentive problem will appear much more relevant to critics of the proposals than is now the case.

There are two dilemmas: the economic problem, involving questions of whether productivity will be affected, and the problem of equity. As succinctly stated by a person interviewed in the Gallup Poll, "I don't want my tax money going to someone who is sitting around with his feet up in the air." The answer to both of these objections, of course, could be found if we had empirical evidence which demonstrated that subsidies would not materially impair the incentive to work among recipients. Unfortunately, what evidence we do have on this problem is scanty and contradictory. G.F. Break found little evidence of disincentives among upper- and upper-middle income earners who face a high tax rate (Break, 1951). But the political value of this study is dubious; most critics of income maintenance would argue that individuals in this bracket are qualitatively different from those less fortunate: they are committed to the "work ethic"; the poor are not. The problem of generalizability is common to most of the studies on incentives: can they be applied to the situation of those directly affected by the income plans?[16] That is why the Trenton experiment[17] has been undertaken. By actually giving income supplements to people in need one can try to determine what this does to their incentives. Even when results are in, however, we fear that they cannot possibly be conclusive. If the results are mixed, no one will know what to make of them. If they appear to show that incentive is not lost but actually grows, opponents of income maintenance will talk about how the people selected are not quite representative or about an alleged "Hawthorne effect." If the experiment shows a decline in incentive, proponents will argue away the results but they will have a harder time. A positive finding will by no means end the dispute.

These considerations are important because any new income proposal must be sold on the basis that (i) it is more congenial to the work ethic than our present welfare system; (ii) it would be less permanent than that system; and (iii) it would eventually cost less. The public and their representatives must be convinced that those poor people who are able, when presented with the new opportunities that income maintenance would give them, would seek work and income levels high enough to remove them from the reach of the subsidy. This question does not involve in any substantial number those presently on the welfare rolls: the Kerner Report[18] estimates that only about 60,000 of the 7.5 million now receiving assistance would be aided by new job opportunities; the others are either children, mothers with children, the aged, the blind, or the otherwise handicapped.[19] The real problem concerns the working poor, those who are now employed but receiving low wages: will they find it advantageous to continue to work when the remuneration for their services is cut by some set percentage? We do not know.

The problem of incentives is complicated by the need to maintain some type of offset if only to keep costs down and strict coverage up. With no offset, the high cost of the plan (when combined with present tax rates) would make for high marginal rates on taxable income for upper-middle and upper-income families (Green and Lampman, 1967). And high taxes mean near-fatal political risks.

Taxes

This threat of increases in federal taxation is, quite naturally, a great obstacle to any income proposal. The problem is political feasibility. While the present federal tax rate, even with the surcharge, is lower than the pre-1964 rate, state and local taxes have increased. Since, with few exceptions, municipal taxes are collected in lump sums rather than by means of a withholding system, their political visibility has risen considerably to property owners, who must bear the full burden of property taxation. Any new tax burden would fall primarily on this middle and upper-middle income group. Over two-thirds of them oppose Guaranteed Income.[20] Yet they are politically articulate and well organized, thus able to resist the imposition of new taxes or to take political retribution upon the imposers.

Even if new money is made available, there will be competing demands for the funds. Most cities have no money, poor revenue sources, and are faced with problems beyond welfare assistance. These city problems – education, sanitation, housing, police and fire protection – are only connected indirectly and in the long run with the problem of poverty. While some of them may be mitigated after decades of increased income for the poor, none will disappear with the adoption of the income proposals, for none of the proposals provides any base from which the city could obtain new revenue in the near future. Income plans will thus be in direct competition with the proposal of bloc grants to the cities.

The adoption of an income proposal which would allow for the virtual elimination of present assistance programs might mean that more state money could be funneled into the cities – but not necessarily. For one thing, safeguards would have to be erected to insure that state administration would not simply use their savings for tax relief. For another, only the social dividend proposals would allow for much reduction of public assistance. Yet we have seen that they result in loose coverage. They cost so much – \$30 to \$50 billion a year – that there would be no way to argue that they represented a net saving to the taxpayer. The savings for the states amount to approximately \$3 billion a year; considerably less than they could expect to gain in the long run from most of the bloc grant proposals. Finally, while the income proposals have the desirable quality of dealing with rural as well as urban poverty, this also involves dealing, to a certain extent, with rural problems at the expense of the politically more visible cities.[21]

These bleak facts rule out, we think, any possibility of enacting one of the large proposals in the next few years. Any proposal that is adopted would have to be substantially compatible with the two politically more important priorities: the demands of the cities and lower taxes. Analyzed in terms of cost,[22] the only viable proposals would be Friedman's ($10 billion), Lampman's ($8–11 billion), and Tobin's ($10–14 billion) (Friedman, 1962; Green and Lampman, 1967; Tobin, Pechman, and Mieszkowski, 1967). Even with these lower-cost plans, however, most of these political difficulties would remain and new ones would be added because of their lesser effectiveness in reducing poverty.

Notes

1. Editor's note: Originally published in 1970, this paper was written within the context of civil disorder and violent urban riots in U.S. cities, especially the Watts riots in Los Angeles in 1965.
2. To a large extent our argument in this chapter ignores the problems associated with the political aspects of bureaucratic behavior. There may be, for example, bureaucrats whose careers are or could be tied to income maintenance, men or groups whose aid could be critical in the construction of a winning coalition. Our primary explanation for this failure on our part is simple lack of time. A second reason, and perhaps a more justifiable one, is that in the case of income maintenance the issue is much more likely to become an important public question than is usually the case in welfare-related matters. As interest groups and constituents become more concerned with an issue, the influence of bureaucracies on congressional decisions decreases. Income by right is not an issue that will slide by unnoticed.
3. Editor's note: 91st Congress: 1969–1971. The Democratic Party had a majority of seats in the House and the Senate. At the time, the U.S. President was Richard Nixon.
4. We undertook approximately 50 interviews lasting from 15 minutes to over two hours. House interviews were clustered around three major committees: Appropriations, Ways and Means, and Education and Labor. Our Senate interviews, while containing several representatives of the corresponding relevant committees, were much more broadly scattered. We attempted, both in the case of relevant committee members and of others to cover a broad spectrum of views which we assumed would be distributed according to a number of measures (for example, party, ideological position within party, type of district, region of country). Although the consistency of responses is persuasive to us, no claims of "representativeness" can be made. The interviews themselves were unstructured and open-ended. So few of the Congressmen interviewed knew anything of the various proposals by any name (Negative Income Tax, income supplements, income maintenance, etc.) that a short description was usually necessary. This tended to be followed by the eventual realization on the part of the interviewee that some sort of "Guaranteed Income" was involved.
5. There was no end of anecdotes on this subject. One Congressman told of being on a football team. One day he was replaced on the varsity by another player. "All week long I worked my ass off," he reported, but still he was kept with the scrubs. On the day of the big game he was named to start, and then played the best game of his life. Summing up, this Congressman said that "the point lay in incentive." "You take that away and people won't play as hard. They lose the satisfaction of winning while the country loses the benefit of their contribution." Another Congressman made a homely observation to the effect that if you take 50 gallons of pure, clean water and one gallon of bad water and mix them up, you get 51 gallons of bad water. "In the same way," he said, "the Guaranteed Income, with its destructive quality in terms of incentives,

would infect the entire country. Some people would want that because that would leave us in a position where we'd have to move toward socialism and the elimination of freedom." As a final example among many choice statements, a Congressman told the story of a man stranded in the desert with not a tree in sight. A bear approached. What do you do? "Why, up that tree!" he exclaimed. But there was no tree, we reminded him. "There damn well had to be a tree" he said. His moral was that if the pressure is there, people will find a way to alleviate it.

6. Editor's note: The Democratic Study Group is an intra-party organization of the Democratic Party within the U.S. House of Representatives. It was founded in 1959.
7. See Wildavsky (1962: 117–732), for a discussion of the structure of similar polarizing issues.
8. See Polsby (1969) for an analytical discussion of this process.
9. Editor's note: The IRS is the U.S. government agency responsible for tax collection and tax law enforcement.
10. It should be clear that we are speaking here of the indignity of being poor per se in a nation where many consider poverty a sign of failure. These arguments do not touch upon the indignities visited upon the poor because their lack of resources closes off so many alternatives to them. Any money from any means helps to alleviate petty victimization by landlords, markets, and so on. The syndrome of relative deprivation usually associated with arguments about poverty must refer more to the psychological problems than to the physical facts of being poor.
11. The analogy is suggested by Schaar (1964).
12. Schaar, (1964). Few Congressmen interviewed felt that equality in the distribution of goods was required by any moral consideration. Their primary fear was that income maintenance, ostensibly designed to end poverty, would end up as a proposal for total equality of income, indistinguishable from "socialistic" planning.
13. In several states, an earned income of $1 not only disqualified potential payment recipients but also made them ineligible for health care and other nonincome benefits.
14. Editor's note: The expression "proposed income plans" refers to proposals by (respectively) M. Friedman; J. Tobin, J.A. Pechman and P.M. Mieszkowski; and C. Green and R.J. Lampman.
15. For example, Theobald's proposal for a 10% "premium" (90% offset) in Theobald (1963).
16. *Cf.* the controversy between Gallaway (1966) and Taussig (1967).
17. Editor's note: The expression "Trenton experiment" refers to a Negative Income Tax experiment conducted in Trenton, New Jersey, between 1968 and 1972. For further details, see Part V of this anthology.
18. Editor's note: United States. Kerner Commission. (1968).
19. United States: Kerner Commission (1968).
20. Gallup Poll, June 16, 1969. Sixty-four percent of those with an annual family income of $7,000 to $10,000 oppose such plans; 68% of those in the $10,000-and-over category are in opposition.
21. The objection might be overcome if it could be demonstrated that these proposals would dampen rural migration to urban areas. National welfare standards would have a similar effect.
22. Estimates taken from Vadakin (1964).

References

Break, G.F. (1951). Income Taxes and Incentives to Work: An Empirical Study. *American Economic Review* (September).

Friedman, M. (1962). *Capitalism and Freedom*. University of Chicago Press, Chicago.

Friedman, M. (1968). The Case for a Negative Income Tax: A View from the Right. In J.H. Bunzel (ed.) *Issues in American Public Policy*. Prentice-Hall, Englewood Cliffs, NJ, pp. 111–120.

Gallaway, L.E. (1966). Negative Income Taxes and the Elimination of Poverty. *National Tax Journal* (September).

Green, C. and Lampman, R.J. (1967). Schemes for transferring income to the poor. *Industrial Relations*, 6 (2), 121–137.

Mueller, E. (1965). Public Attitudes Toward Fiscal Programs. *Quarterly Journal of Economics*, (May), 215.

Polsby, N.W. (1969) Policy Analysis and Congress. In *The Analysis and Evaluation of Public Expenditures.* Joint Economic Committee, U.S. Congress, 3: 493.

Schaar, J. (1964). Some Ways of Thinking about Equality. *Journal of Politics*, 26.

Taussig, M. (1967). Negative Income Taxes and the Elimination of Poverty: Comment. *National Tax Journal* (September).

Theobald, R. (1963). *Free Men and Free Markets.* C.N. Potter, New York.

Tobin, J., Pechman, J.A., and Mieszkowski, P.M. (1967). Is a Negative Income Tax Practical? *The Yale Law Journal*, 77 (1), 1–27.

United States: Kerner Commission (1968). *Report of the National Advisory Commission on Civil Disorders.* Government Printing Office, Washington DC.

Vadakin, J.C. (1964). A Critique of the Guaranteed Annual Income. *The Public Interest* (Spring).

Wildavsky, A. (1962). The Analysis of Issue Contexts in the Study of Decision-Making, *Journal of Politics*, 24, 717–732.

Chapter 67

The Ambiguities of Basic Income from a Trade Union Perspective

Yannick Vanderborght

Excerpts from Vanderborght, Y. (2005). Why Trade Unions Oppose Basic Income. *Basic Income Studies. An International Journal of Basic Income Research*, 1 (1), 1–20.

The introduction of such an unconditional income is to be viewed not as the dismantling but as the culmination of the welfare state.

(Van Parijs, 1992)

Introduction

In most OECD countries trade unions remain key players in the field of welfare state reform. In Belgium and Scandinavia, where they still represent a large majority of the workforce, they are traditional and pivotal partners in the policymaking process. In other countries, even those with low union density (such as France) they are often able to mobilize mass support in favor of the status quo, sometimes through huge demonstrations and paralyzing strikes. But surprisingly little attention has been paid by universal Basic Income (BI) proponents to the very position of workers' unions on the radical reform that they are advocating.

The Ambiguities of Basic Income From a Trade Union Perspective

Let us assume that a BI scheme would replace existing means-tested minimum income schemes, the bulk of tax credits and exemptions, and be integrated with family allowances and, possibly, basic pension schemes. In the field of social insurance, BI would replace the bottom part of the earnings-related unemployment, pension, health and sickness benefits. The income floor it provides would remain supplemented by earnings-related benefits,

From Vanderborght, Y. (2005). Why Trade Unions Oppose Basic Income. *Basic Income Studies. An International Journal of Basic Income Research*, 1 (1), 1–20.

Basic Income: An Anthology of Contemporary Research, First Edition. Edited by Karl Widerquist, José A. Noguera, Yannick Vanderborght, and Jurgen De Wispelaere.

designed to make up the difference between BI and current benefit levels. Its level would be close to €500 per month. Why should unions support, or oppose, such a reform?

Collective and individual bargaining power

If the level of the BI is sufficient, it could easily be used (as part of or in total) as a source of funding for strike purposes. First, members' BI could be "taxed" by the union on a regular basis in order to raise the level of its strike fund, thereby increasing workers' relative power within the firm or branch. Second, even in the absence of such a mechanism, a BI would make each single strike less harmful financially, since workers would keep their entitlement to a Guaranteed Income floor outside the labor market. With a BI, strikers would be able to face long-lasting resistance from employers, and the collective power of unions would therefore be enhanced.

But BI would not only foster workers' independence in the case of strikes or crises. At a more micro-level, it also provides individual workers with a true, reliable, and unconditional *exit option*, hence fostering their own individual bargaining power. Even if their jobs remain the primary source of income, the existence of an income floor outside the labor market, without means-testing or work requirements, could lead them to negotiate for higher wages – even in the absence of a collective threat, such as a strike.

The first and second reasons to support a BI are thus both related to the power resources it would confer on workers, both collectively and individually.[1] The existence of an individual exit option and the prospect of long-lasting conflicts with unions would force employers to preventively increase wages and improve working conditions and make jobs as attractive as possible. This would, in particular, be true for most undesirable or stigmatizing jobs.

Prima facie, there are thus good reasons to believe that, in a BI scenario, employers would be gradually obliged to make jobs more attractive in the poorly paid end of the income distribution spectrum. But one should not too quickly conclude that a general increase of salaries is necessarily to be expected in the aftermath of the introduction of such a scheme. On the contrary, one could even assume that its implementation might well engage a downward spiral: employers could start lowering all wages, considering that a BI is providing the complement needed to reach the level of legal minimum wages. Under such a wage-deflationary scenario the latter would, inescapably, come under discussion.[2]

The end of wage labor?

Other reasons, still related to the exit option provided by the introduction of a BI, might justify trade union suspicion towards a BI. It is sometimes argued that this exit option would offer new opportunities to those wanting to launch their own small business (Nooteboom, 1986). It would, in other words, facilitate self-employment. As a consequence, its implementation could foster a gradual decline of wage labor as the core of capitalist economies. If this were true, a BI would, for this very reason, erode the traditional basis of trade union influence and action.

More generally, the exit option provided by the unconditional income floor would negatively affect the cultural centrality of paid work (and the work ethic). If current employment remains the main source of social recognition, with a (sufficiently high), BI, not only self-employment but all kinds of informal and care activities would become financially viable options (see, e.g., Jordan, 1989). Hence, they would receive proper social consideration, and wage labor would lose its central role in society. Presumably, unions might see this development as a threat to their own position, even if in recent years the labor movement has been much less reluctant to recognize the importance of informal activities in general, and care work in particular.

Job sharing and flexibility

Having heard the previous counterarguments, BI proponents could reply that the exit option is not likely to provoke a mass desertion of the traditional labor market. A BI policy would, rather, help lower the unemployment rate, partly because it is consistent with voluntary job sharing – an objective that has been endorsed by major trade unions in Europe. BI has sometimes been described as the "soft strategy" to achieve this goal (Van Parijs, 1996: 65), in contrast with compulsory work-time reduction programs – as they were implemented in some European countries (notably France). BI makes it, indeed, easier for workers to take part-time jobs, or even to quit their job temporarily and go on sabbatical leave, since the revenue loss is partly offset by the guaranteed payment of an unconditional grant outside the labor market. Hence, a BI would help create jobs without worsening insiders' positions, and without threatening the centrality of wage labor.

This is no doubt a plausible interpretation. But if a BI would facilitate part-time work, does it really follow that it constitutes a desirable path of reform from a trade-union perspective? BI advocates generally focus on opportunities: individual workers could choose to work for less, provided the Guaranteed Income floor is high enough. But in most cases, it might well happen that part-time work and flexible timetables will be imposed by employers, rather than being the result of workers' increased individual autonomy. BI would then serve as a costly state-subsidized shock absorber, softening the harmful effects of an increasingly flexible labor market for the most vulnerable part of the working class through a higher taxation of gross wages of the middle class.

The end of exploitation?

At a more general level, Philippe Van Parijs and Robert van der Veen argue that the implementation of a BI would open a "capitalist road to communism" (Van Parijs and van der Veen, 1986; see also van der Veen and Van Parijs, 2006). In their view (at tie time), capitalist societies have already reached the stage of "weak abundance," and the gradual introduction of a BI could allow workers to skip the stage of socialism (public ownership of the means of production) and go directly to the establishment of a communist society. Within this framework, raising the level of the Guaranteed Income to a maximal level would meet the Marxian criterion "from each according to his abilities to each according to his needs." In such a scenario, of course, exploitation would not only be ***diminished*** through the increase of workers' collective and individual bargaining power, it would simply be ***abolished***. It would be difficult for unions to sweep this perspective aside.

But perhaps the most decisive reason to oppose a BI from a trade union perspective is that such a scheme would not, contrary to what has been asserted by Van Parijs and van der Veen, ***abolish*** exploitation; it would more probably change its very nature. The argument would then go as follows: in the case of a society with a BI, "the idle exploit the industrious by receiving an income generated (inter alia) by the activity of those who choose to work" (Reeve, 2003: 11). Seen from this perspective, the introduction of a BI widens the scope of exploitation: whereas in "classic capitalism" true exploitation remains the vice of a small minority, in "BI capitalism" exploiters would constitute a substantial fraction of the population. Incidentally, this has been the most controversial issue in philosophical debates about the proposal (Couillard, 2002).

What Do We Learn From the Empirical Investigations?

In order to further enlighten the issues raised by the shortlist of theoretical arguments, it is useful to go into the field and compare national debates. Keeping the theoretical discussion in mind, what do we learn from the empirical evidence?

Drawing upon a larger research on OECD countries, this second section focuses on three relevant national debates: Belgium, Canada, and the Netherlands. Note that BI has never been a hot item on union agendas in OECD countries.[3] The explanation is quite obvious: in most countries BI has never been high on the *political* agenda. Why bother then, with the pet idea of eccentric academics? In may countries labor has often seen the proposal as "too remote a possibility to be worth considering seriously" (Ziegler and Jordan, 2001: 3). In a few cases, however, BI has been thoroughly discussed by workers' representatives and, sometimes, even officially endorsed.

Belgium: "no basic income"!

With a unionization rate of approximately 60%, Belgium has, no doubt, some of the most representative trade unions in Western Europe.[4] The two main confederations, CSC-ACV (Christian Unions Confederation) and FGTB-ABVV (Socialist Unions Federation), remain powerful in most sectors of the economy, and they are – directly or indirectly – involved in each substantial reform of the welfare state. They are not only able to mobilize workers on a large scale, they also benefit from privileged links with political actors, including MPs and ministers. Furthermore, they take part in formal institutions such as the National Labor Council (CNT-NAR), as well as in the administrative management of social insurance programs, especially unemployment insurance.[5]

Belgium has played a crucial role in the BI debate. The Basic Income European Network's (BIEN) founding congress (1986) and second international conference (1988) were held in Belgium, under the aegis of philosopher Philippe Van Parijs, author of *Real Freedom for All* (1995). BIEN's archives are located at Louvain University. With social scientist Walter Van Trier and others, Van Parijs has advocated BI on many occasions in French- and Flemish-speaking parts of Belgium. One should also keep in mind that Belgium has the only European single-issue partly focused on BI: Vivant, founded in 1997 by businessman Roland Duchâtelet, has participated in several elections and attracted public attention to the proposal. Belgium, no doubt, might thus represent an interesting test case regarding the political prospects of BI.

To put it crudely, it's impossible to be recognized as a prophet in one's own country. Belgiums' main trade unions have not shown much interest in BI, and on the rare occasions when they did they expressed very hostile opinions. From the very start of the discussion in the mid-1980s, the main confederation (CSC-ACV) attacked what it called a "silly and worrying utopia" (CSC, 1985). After almost 20 years of debate, some union officials are still among the most uncompromising opponents of Basic Income. In January, 2002, CSC published a preparatory report in anticipation of its national congress. It includes a section titled "No basic income" (CSC, 2002: 42).

What do Belgian unionists hold against the proposal? At least four grievances are worth mentioning.[6] First, unions – in particular officials of Socialist Unions Federation – fear that the introduction of a BI would make it more difficult for them to negotiate wage increases with employers (Bodson, 2003: 2). Since a BI could be seen as an indirect wage subsidy, employers would urge union representatives to negotiate with public authorities and lobby their political allies in order to get a general increase of the BI level. A BI would, in sum, negatively affect the relative power of workers at the firm, branch, or federal level, especially if it were to be accompanied by the abolition of the minimum wage legislation. In saying that a BI would increase individual workers' bargaining power, BI proponents seem to believe that the class struggle is passé, which is – Belgian unionists argue – obviously false.

Second, Belgian union officials also believe that the existence of a Guaranteed Income floor would justify further developments along the lines of increasing flexibility of the labor market. According to a FGTB-ABVV representative, BI advocates seem to accept that contracts for unlimited periods should be abolished, and that in coming decades "all work contracts would have to be short-term and precarious" (Wernerus, 2004: 47).

Third, in most writings and interviews, union representatives also express their commitment to selective and targeted schemes. They see these schemes as a better and more efficient way of using public resources that are massively sustained by the taxation of wages, be it through social contributions or the income tax. To provide a Basic Income equivalent to the level of the conditional minimum income, they say, one should substantially raise the tax rates, an unacceptable perspective for most workers. And if it were not the case, the system would be absurdly inefficient: some would have to work hard in order to pay for a miserable grant. Obviously, Belgian unions do not believe that a BI would abolish exploitation.

Fourth, Belgian unions are quite ambiguous on the question of work requirements. If both CSC-ACV and FGTB-ABVV have repeatedly opposed the strengthening of these requirements and the tightening of eligibility rules in unemployment insurance, they are not ready to argue in favor of a fully unconditional benefit, even if it were targeted at the poor along the lines of a Negative Income Tax schedule. It seems that the question of the optimal equilibrium between rights and duties of beneficiaries remains open. It is perfectly legitimate, CSC-ACV officials argue, to require that the able-bodied contribute to the production of collective wealth.[7]

It would be unfair, though, to assert that Belgian unions are therefore only defending the interests of insiders. Most officials emphasize that the least advantaged should be helped, but stress that the poor need much more than the automatic payment of a Basic Income floor. They see the introduction of a BI as a crucial step that leads to a "slippery slope" – a massive disinvestment in social work. They fear that public authorities would progressively stop all programs aimed at socio-professional integration, which would further widen the gap between insiders and outsiders (compare, for instance, Bodson, 2003). And yet, union officials insist, paid work remains the crucial precondition for social recognition and self-esteem. Belgian unions thus remain unconvinced by the arguments of BI advocates. It does not mean, of course, that their reasons for adopting such a position are logically and universally valid. But it certainly means that in a country with such a high union density, the political feasibility of BI might well be very low, to say the least.

Canada: the mixed feelings of Québecois unions

In 2004 Canadian union density amounted to a small 25.1% average, with a peak of more than 40% in the French-speaking province of Québec – a very respectable rate by North American standards (Human Resources Development Canada, 2005; Labrosse, 2005: 2).

At the federal level, unions benefit from the fact that the Canadian electoral system, contrary to the US system, allows for the existence of a true labor party somewhere between liberal and conservative.[8] However, the New Democratic Party (NDP) remains a small player on the political scene. Furthermore, the liberal character of the welfare system has always kept Canadian unions at the margins of the social policy debates (Banting, 1987).

BI has been widely debated in Canada. It had already been briefly on the agenda in the 1930s, thanks to the rise of the Social Credit Party, which came to power in Alberta in 1935. But the real discussion strated in the 1960s, with a few social scientists inspired by the American debates on "Demogrants" and the Negative Income Tax (NIT). For the late 1960s until the early 1990s, the idea came up quite regularly in official publications at federal and provincial levels (especially in Québec), and in the 1970s NIT experiments were launched in Manitoba. At the end of 2000, Prime Minister Jean Chrétien even launched a BI trial balloon via newspapers such as the much respected *Ottawa Citizen*. Under catchy headlines, the press reported that the Federal PM had decided to set up an expert group to study the feasibility of a guaranteed annual income (GAI) in the Canadian context.[9] But faced with harsh criticisms from the Conservatives, Chrétien quickly denied his part in suggesting the idea.[10]

What about trade unions? According to political scientist Rodney S. Haddow, "the [Canadian] union movement has always treated the GAI with considerable caution and viewed it as potentially antithetical to its social policy goals" (1994: 350). But it did not always take coherent positions on the topic, Haddow argues: "Organized labor's early response to the GAI was *muted and confused* [. . .] it was *slow to form a coherent assessment* of the implications of a negative income tax for its program" (1994: 353). However, the publication in 1985 of a bulky and influential report by the Royal Commission on the Economic Union and Development Prospects for Canada (the so-called "Macdonald Commission"), which included a scenario for the introduction of partial Basic Income, triggered harsh reactions. In 1986, the convention of the Canadian Labour Congress (CLC), Canada's largest union confederation, expressed serious doubts about the desirability of such a reform and denounced its "neo-liberal character". A BI, the CLC argued, was going to undermine the minimum wage legislation (Haddow, 1993). At the same time, Belgian unions were using the same sort of arguments to dismiss the idea.

The story is quite different, though, in the province of Québec. Michel Chartrand, a colorful – and tremendously popular – retired figure of the trade union movement, has been advocating BI for many years (Bernard and Chartrand, 1999).[11] In 1999, the CSN (National Unions Confederation) – Québec's main union in terms of membership – published a detailed and balanced study on BI in order to foster a peaceful discussion of the proposal. Even if other unions (FTQ and CSQ) did not undertake similar initiatives, they never expressed any hostility towards the idea of an unconditional minimum income. It does not mean, however, that they would support any move in that direction. Recent interviews with Québecois union officials have shown that they have mixed feelings about the possible introduction of a BI in Canada or Québec (Wernerus, 2004: 36–39). Most of them do actually endorse the proposal on ethical grounds, but reject it for pragmatic reasons.

In Québec, union officials recognize that providing everyone with an Unconditional Income floor is a matter of fundamental rights. Contrary to their Belgian counterparts they do not put the very idea of an income by right into question. They also admit that – in theory, at least – such a scheme could help solve (part of) the problem of unemployment traps without worsening poverty, through a significant reduction of marginal tax rates at the bottom of the income distribution. In this perspective, they do not even see BI as antithetical to the cultural values of a society in which paid work remains, as is the case in Belgium, a crucial precondition for social recognition.

And yet in spite of these positions very few union officials openly argue for a BI. For, representatives say, they lack the power resources needed to impose a truly *progressive* package of reform. Hence, in the context of an increasingly competitive economy, and at a time when provincial and federal governments are pleading for a more "active welfare state", the defense of such a radical reform would amount to political suicide. At present, a discussion of the introduction of a BI would necessarily degenerate into a Friedman-like scenario: a dismantling of the welfare state, not a culmination. For a few years these fears have been vigorously sustained by the electoral rhetoric of a powerful right-wing liberal party, the Action démocratique du Québec (ADQ), which campaigns in favor of an NIT.[12] Unions are on the defensive: "we should defend what we already have," a FTQ official says (Wernerus, 2004: 113). "We should keep fighting for higher wages" and "progressively improve the current welfare system," a CSN representative argues (Wernerus, 2004: 114). In other words, for Québecois unions BI is ethically appealing but too much a risky social policy reform.

The Netherlands: a trade union in favor of Basic Income

Dutch trade unions have never been as powerful as their Belgian counterparts in the field of social policy and industrial relations. In the early 2000s, net union density had dropped to a low level of 22%.[13] But Dutch unions remain directly involved in various councils and committees at a national level, and through these institutions they still have an important say in the matter of welfare reform. Throughout the 1980s and 1990s, unions even became central players in the mechanisms of "competitive corporatism" (Rhodes, 1998), which lies at the basis of the much discussed "Dutch miracle" (Visser and Hemerijck, 1997). Through innovative types of negotiations, the unions, employers and the state were able to conclude agreements that resulted in the combined introduction of new rights for workers and more flexible arrangements for the labor market, along with wage moderation. Wim Kok, the former head of the biggest union confederation, FNV, was leading the country as a prime minister from 1994 to 2002.

In the 1980s and early 1990s, BI was relativley high on the public agenda in the Netherlands. From 1980 onwards, it was debated in several political parties across the political spectrum. In 1994, it was openly advocated in the press by two ruling ministers. Even if their initiative was short-lived, the prime minister at the time, Wim Kok, declared that a BI should not be dismissed as a long-term perspective for the reform of the Dutch welfare state.[14] Interestingly, during the second half of the 1980s, the Voedingsbond FNV (Union of Food Workers) – an important group of affiliated workers within the FNV union confederation – was one of the most prominent proponents of a "basisinkomen" (Basic Income). In many ways, this was a unique position within Western democracies. The Union of Food Workers published plenty of leaflets and documents arguing in favor of the proposal, and organized regular workshops in order to enlighten its own members.[15]

As was stressed by Rik van Berkel, who made an in-depth analysis of this episode of the Voedingsbond's history, when reading the pamphlets "one is struck by the utopian nature of BI alleged effects. [. . .] In short, the Voedingsbond presented its BI as a panacea for the problems of contemporary society" (van Berkel, 1994: 19). Since the very start of the discussion in the late 1970s, Voedingsbond leaders had been questioning the work ethic and the cultural centrality of wage labor, calling for a radical reform that would confer social recognition to "those who do unpaid work, have no income and no social status" (Lubbi, 1991: 15). Unfortunately, as van Berkel and his colleagues discovered, the perspective of a BI did not really appeal to the union's members. It was more a "top-down" debate: the influence of well-educated staff members was decisive in the choice of the BI strategy. As the leaders themselves conceded afterwards, "it proved difficult to mobilise members on such an abstract and long-term objective as BI." This abstract perspective, mainly supported by the executive, contradicted "the more concrete members' interests that they were experiencing in the daily life" (van Berkel et al., 1993: 24–24). Furthermore, the FNV confederation, to which the Voedingsbond belonged, did not support the initiative. As a result, the debate ran out of steam and stopped altogether in the early 1990s.

As the unemployment rate dropped to 2.4% in 2002, traditional supporters of Basic Income – who had always advocated the idea as an alternative to full employment and the work ethic – were pushed off to the margins of political discussions. Claimants' organizations, which had been associated with the Voedingsbond on the BI issue, gradually disappeared from the political landscape as the unemployed were finding jobs. But in the real world of welfare capitalism, miracles never last. In 2003 and 2004, the Dutch growth was almost negative, and the unemployment rate was rising again. This is, undoubtedly, part of the reason why Agnes Jongerius, (leader of the union confederation, FNV) who was elected in May 2005, now argues that workers' representatives should think again about the idea of a BI for all. Jongerius maintains that all Dutch citizens should receive a monthly check of €350 or 400: "With such a plan, we could get rid of a lot of administrative difficulties," she declared in an interview.[16] Even if she still believes that people should make their best endeavor to find a paid job, controls should become softer and be incentive based. Most importantly, Jongerius stated that a well-designed BI proposal would allow the labor movement to stop being too conservative and defensive about welfare state reforms.

In sum, throughout its recent history the Dutch trade union movement has been less cautious about BI than Canadian unions, and much less reluctant than Belgian labor organizations. As mentioned before, one should certainly not underestimate the role played by the peculiar character of the Voedingsbond leadership in the 1980s. But one should nevertheless keep in mind that, during the same period, BI was also debated within mainstream political parties, including the Labor Party (PvdA) itself. In other words, it would be misleading to maintain that discussions about BI were the privilege of a tiny minority, whether within the labor movement or across other political streams. Furthermore, it should be stressed that specific features of the Dutch welfare state – and of its transformations – might also provide some keys to the understanding of the Dutch exception. The existence of a basic pension scheme, as well as the existence of non-means-tested student grants, has certainly constituted a favorable background for the discussion of a basic cash guarantee for all. The fact that a greater proportion of the Dutch unemployed are social assistance beneficiaries, hence receiving non-earnings-related benefits, may also have eroded trade union opposition to BI. Above all, since 1982 and the so-called "Wassenaar agreement," Dutch trade unions have been directly involved in a process of wage moderation and work-time reduction. In return for a gradual strengthening of the social rights of part-time workers, they have accepted the perspective of a massive creation of flexible and temporary jobs. One could thus cautiously conclude that, today, Dutch unions have more reasons to support the introduction of BI than to oppose it.

Conclusion

Theoretical and empirical investigations demonstrate that trade unions are far from being natural allies of BI advocates within developed welfare states. As evidenced by the Belgian case, they can even constitute a significant obstacle to the political progression of the idea. At the same time, the Dutch case shows that the labor movement is not bound to be a perpetual opponent to such a scheme.

At least two general conclusions can be drawn from this comparative inquiry. First, it provides a manifest confirmation of the idea that "institutions matter." Briefly, in countries where the financing of the welfare system is massively based on social contributions, and not on the income tax, each step towards a BI is seen as a radical reform. Through worker contributions, unions are involved in the financing and management of social security. What would happen, they legitimately ask, if the minister of finance were to become the key player in social policy?[17] In Belgium, furthermore, trade unions are pivotal actors in a "Ghent system." In such systems, "unions run voluntary (though heavily subsidized by the state) unemployment insurance programs, generally through the operation of local labor exchanges" (Scruggs, 2002: 286). Thus Belgian unions, contrary to the Dutch and Canadian workers' organizations, are handling individual cases of unemployed workers. It might partly explain why they have always looked more suspiciously at the implementation of an automatic payment system that would replace earnings-related payments.

The second conclusion is closely connected to the first one. It seems that the introduction of a BI has not much to offer to the vast majority of union members. In times of retrenchment in core sectors of the welfare system (pension and health insurance), it is a difficult task to convince insiders of paying for an unconditional grant that will mainly benefit outsiders. It is not a surprise that, as van Berkel pointed out, within the Dutch union Voedingsbond, BI was mainly supported by unemployed members. BI, van Berkel writes, "comes across as predominantly a claimants' issue. Most of its supporters (almost 75 percent) are claimants, whereas most of its opponents (again almost 75 percent) are paid workers" (van Berkel, 1994: 20). Investigations in France have also shown that BI had been almost exclusively advocated by independent claimants' organizations, which had been created in the 1980s as a result of workers' unions incapacity to take the specific needs of unemployed people into account. Even if they were able to launch a public discussion on BI in the winter of 1997–1998, they did not manage to get the proposal on the political agenda. In Belgium, due to the Ghent system, claimant's organizations have always been very weak, and most unemployed are members of a trade union.

Claus Offe (1992: 72) argues that gains for the well-off middle class represent the "necessary precondition for making social security for the underclass (including the less privileged segments of the working class) politically feasible." Without the support of well-established trade unions, it might prove very difficult for BI advocates to get their proposal on the agenda in OECD countries. Hence, they should certainly start working more systematically towards converting union representatives on ethical and pragmatic grounds. They should no doubt try to boost any emerging discussion of the issue within workers unions, since empirical research shows that good arguments in favor of a BI from a trade union perspective are unknown to most union representatives. For even if the latter are not natural allies of BI supporters, they remain inescapable players as well as irreplaceable partners.

Acknowledgement

This paper is partly based on a presentation made at the Xth Congress of the Basic Income Earth Network (Barcelona, 2004). I am grateful for comments and suggestions from participants at this Congress, Philippe Van Parijs, Jurgen De Wispelaere, Karl Widerquist and two anonymous referees.

Notes

1. One the "power resources approach" in comparative social policy, see, for instance, O'Connor et al. (1998).
2. This scenario comes close to what James Meade advocated in his Agathotopia (Meade, 1989). The threat to the minimum wage legislation is precisely why French trade unions opposed any move towards the introduction of a tax credit targeted at low-paid workers in late 1990 (see, for instance, the position of Marc Blondel, a leader of Force Ouvrière, expressed in Nathan (2001)).
3. Compare Vanderborght and Van Parijs (2005: 79–82) for a short overview of the discussions within unions in the OECD and in developing countries.
4. According to Ebbinghaus (2004: 580), net union density in Belgium was 62% in 2002.
5. Compare Kuipers (2004: 79–86) for a good overview of the role played by unions and employers in Belgian policy-making.
6. This account is based on two main sources: sociologist Sabine Wernerus's master's thesis (Wernerus, 2004), which was based on fieldwork and interviews with union representatives, and part of my own PhD research (Vanderborght, 2004). I also benefited from discussions with union officials during a seminar on "Trade Unions Against Basic Income?" organized by the Hoover Chair (Université Catholique de Louvain, Belgium) on May 13, 2004.
7. Compare Palsterman (2005) for a balanced evaluation by a CSC-ACV official, of "active social policies" in the field of Belgian unemployment insurance.
8. The description often made of the Canadian system as a "third party" system is not entirely accurate. In fact, with the passing of years, a fourth party, the nationalist Bloc Québecois, became a significant political force at the federal level.
9. See "Chrétien Wants to Leave Mark With Cradle-to-Grave Program of Guaranteed Annual Income" (*Ottawa Citizen*, December 9, 2000). In Canada, the expression "Guaranteed Annual Income" has mainly been used to refer to a Negative Income Tax and, on some occasions, to a Basic Income.
10. For further details on the Canadian debate, see Vanderborght (2004: 166–176).
11. Editor's note: Chartrand was a leader of the CSN. He died in 2010.
12. In Québec a much more progressive version of BI was defended, 2000–2001, by a marginal left-wing party, the Rassemblement Pour L'alternative Progressiste (RAP). In 2002 it was merged into the Union des Forces Progressistes (UFP), which also advocated a "universal citizen's income". UFP became Québec Solidaire in February 2006. Note that in October 2005, 12 academics and politicians, including the former prime minister of Québec, Lucien Bouchard, published a manifesto calling for the introduction of a "guaranteed minimum income" in the Province.
13. According to Ebbinghaus (2004: 580), net union density in the Netherlands was 22% in 2002.
14. For further details on the Dutch debate, see Vanderborght (2005).
15. Compare, for instance, Voedingsbond (1981) and, in English, Voedingsbond (1989).
16. *Het Financiële Dagblad*, May 25, 2005.

17. Compare the critique of FGTB leader Thierry Bodson (2003: 3) on the end of "social citizenship."

References

Banting, K. (1987). *The Welfare State and Canadian Federalism.* McGill-Queen's University Press, Montreal.

Bernard, M. and Chartrand, M. (1999). *Manifeste pour un revenu de citoyenneté.* Editions du renouveau québécois, Montreal.

Bodson, T. (2003). L'allocation universelle face à la liaison au bien-être des allocations sociales. Paper presented at the *Forum Social de Belgique* (Belgian Social Forum), May 10, 2003.

Couillard, P. (2002). Justice as Reciprocity and the Universal Basic Income: A Possible Reconciliation of Two Enemies? *Document de travail de la Chaire Hoover,* Working Paper 78. Université Catholique do Louvain.

CSC (Confédération des Syndicats Chrétiens) (1985). L'allocation universelle: les effets immédiats d'une utopie. *Info-CSC,* April 19.

CSC (Confédération des Syndicats Chrétiens) (2002). Dans quelle mesure mon revenu est-il juste? Special Issue of *Syndicaliste CSC* 560, January 25.

Ebbinghaus, B. (2004). The Changing Union and Bargaining Landscape: Union Concentration and Collective Bargaining Trends. *Industrial Relations Journal,* 35 (6), 574–587.

Haddow, R.S. (1993). *Poverty Reform in Canada, 1958–1978: State and Class Influences on Policy Making.* McGill-Queen's University Press, Montréal and Kingston.

Haddow, R.S. (1994). Canadian Organized Labour and the Guaranteed Annual Income. In A.F. Johnson, S. McBride, and P.J. Smith (eds) *Continuities and Discontinuities: The Political Economy of Social Welfare and Labour Market Policy in Canada.* University of Toronto Press, Toronto.

Human Resource Development Canada (2003). Union Membership in Canada – 2002. *Workplace Gazette,* 5 (3), 38–45.

Human Resources Development Canada (2005). *Union membership as a percentage of civilian labour force.* http://www.hrsdc.gc.ca (accessed March 30, 2006).

Jordan B. (1989). *The Common Good: Citizenship, Morality and Self-interest.* Blackwell, Oxford.

Kuipers, S.L. (2004). *Cast in Concrete? The Institutional Dynamics of Belgian and Dutch Social Policy Reform.* Eburon Academic Publishers, Delft.

Labrosse, A. (2005). *La présence syndicale au Québec en 2004.* Ministère du Travail, Québec.

Lubbi, G. (1991). Towards a full BI. *Basic Income Research Group Bulletin (London),* February 12, 15–16.

Meade, J. (1989). *Agathotopia: The Economics of Partnership.* Aberdeen University Press, Aberdeen.

Nathan, H. (2001). Opposants et partisans: les arguments. *Libération,* January 12.

Nooteboom B. (1986). Basic Income as a Basis for Small Business. *International Small-Business Journal,* 5 (3), 10–18.

O'Connor, J., Olsen, G.M., and Korpi, W. (1998). *Power Resource Theory and the Welfare State: A Critical-Approach.* University of Toronto Press, Toronto.

Offe, C. (1992). A Non-Productivist Design for Social Policies. In P. Van Parijs (ed.) *Arguing for Basic Income: Ethical Foundations for a Radical Reform.* Verso, London.

Palsterman, P. (2005). Evolution de la notion de chômage involontaire dans l'assurance-chômage belge (1945–2004). In P. Vielle, P. Pochet, and I. Cassiers (eds) *L'Etat social actif. Vers un changement de paradigme?* Presses Interuniversitaires européennes – Peter Lang, Brussels.

Quadagno, J. (1990). Race, Class, and Gender in the U.S. Welfare State: Nixon's Failed Family Assistance Plan. *American Sociological Review,* 55 (1), 11–28.

Reeve, A. (2003). Introduction. In A. Reeve and A. Williams (eds) *Real Libertarianism Assessed: Political Theory After Van Parijs*. Palgrave Macmillan, Basingstoke.

Rhodes, M. (1998). Globalization, Labour Markets and Welfare States: A Future of "Competitive Corporatism"? In M. Rhodes and Y. Mény (eds) *The Future of European Welfare: A New Social Contract?* Palgrave Macmillan, Basingstoke.

Scruggs, L. (2002). The Ghent System and Union Membership in Europe, 1970–1996. *Political Research Quarterly*, 55 (2), 275–297.

Van Berkel, R., Van Heereveld, E., Van Klaveren, I.-M. et al. (1993). *Met z'n allen zwijgen in de woestijn. Een onderzoek naar het basisinkomen binnen de Voedingsbond FNV*. Vakgroep Algemene Sociale Wetenschappen, Universiteit Utrecht.

Van Berkel, R. (1994). Basic Income as Trade Union Policy. *Citizen's Income Bulletin (London)*, January 17, 18–21.

van der Veen, R.J. and Van Parijs, P. (2006). Retrospective: A Capitalist Road to Communism – Twenty Years After. *Basic Income Studies. An International Journal of Basic Income Research*, 1 (1).

Van Parijs, P. (1992). Basic Income Capitalism. *Ethics*, 102 (3), 465–484.

Van Parijs, P. (1995). *Real Freedom for All: What (If Anything) Can Justify Capitalism?* Oxford University Press, Oxford.

Van Parijs, P. (1996). Basic Income and the Two Dilemmas of the Welfare State. *The Political Quarterly*, 47 (1), 63–66.

Van Parijs, P. and van der Veen, R. (1993). A Capitalist Road to Communism. In P. Van Parijs, *Marxism Recycled*. Cambridge University Press, Cambridge.

Vanderborght, Y. (2004). La faisabilité politique d'un revenu inconditionnel. Analyse comparative des débats politiques sur l'allocation universelle, l'impôt négatif et le revenu de participation dans cinq pays de l'OCDE (1970–2003). PhD thesis, Université Catholique de Louvain.

Vanderborght, Y. (2005). The Basic Income Guarantee in Europe: The Belgian and Dutch Back Door Strategies. In K. Widerquist, M.A. Lewis, and S. Pressman (eds) *The Ethics and Economics of the Basic Income Guarantee*. Ashgate, Aldershot.

Vanderborght, Y. and Van Parijs, P. (2005). *L'allocation universelle*. La Découverte, Paris.

Visser, J. and Hemerijck, A. (1997). *"A Dutch Miracle": Job Growth, Welfare Reform and Corporatism in the Netherlands*. Amsterdam University Press, Amsterdam.

Voedingsbond F.N.V. (1981). *Met z'n allen roepen in de woestijn. Een tussenrapport over het losser maken van de band tussen arbeid en inkomen*. Voedingsbond FNV, Utrecht.

Voedingsbond F.N.V. (1989). *No Frontiers to a Basic Income. Contribution to a European Discussion of the Introduction of a Basic Income*. Voedingsbond FNV, Utrecht.

Wernerus, S. (2004). Les syndicats contre l'allocation universelle? Mise en perspective des points de vue belges et québécois. Masters thesis. Faculté ouverte de politique économique et sociale, Louvain-la-Neuve.

Ziegler, R. and Jordan, B. (2001). The Trade Unions, Tax-Benefit Reform and Basic Income: Stumbling towards a Policy? *Citizen's Income Newsletter (London)*, 3, 2–4.

Chapter 68
Basic Income and Social Europe

Fritz Scharpf

Excerpts from Scharpf, F. (2000). Basic Income and Social Europe. In R. van der Veen and L. Groot (eds) *Basic Income on the Agenda. Policy Objectives and Political Chances.* Amsterdam University Press, Amsterdam, pp. 155–160.

I am doubtful of the political viability of the proposed right to a Basic Income without means-testing and without a concomitant obligation to do work that is useful to, and appreciated by, other members of one's society. In political discourses, it will not be enough to persuade potential recipients of the desirability of "a right to be lazy," but it will also be necessary to make others believe that they have a moral duty to work harder or longer in order to pay for this program. Personally, moreover, I consider mass unemployment, forced inactivity, and the exclusion from the processes of social production, a much greater challenge to the moral integrity of Western European societies than the frustration of leisure preferences.

For these reasons, I would accord normative priority to variants of Basic Income schemes that have the explicit purpose of increasing the incentives and the opportunities for gainful employment, rather than for financially secured inactivity. This implies that quite apart from any questions of financial feasibility, I would prefer the Negative Income Tax over proposals for an Unconditional Basic Income,[1] and I would prefer both over presently existing forms of means-tested social assistance with their strong work disincentiveness. Moreover, if for political, institutional, or financial reasons the Negative Income Tax should not be a feasible option, I would much rather see social insurance contributions for low-wage jobs being reduced than an attempt to increase the generosity of social assistance in its present forms (Scharpf 1990).

Economic Integration Constrains National Welfare States

The connection between European integration and Basic Income proposals is not obvious. So far, at any rate, there appears to be wide agreement that social policy choices should

From Scharpf, F. (2000). Basic Income and Social Europe. In R. van der Veen and L. Groot (eds) *Basic Income on the Agenda. Policy Objectives and Political Chances.* Amsterdam University Press, Amsterdam, pp. 155–160. Reprinted with permission.

Basic Income: An Anthology of Contemporary Research, First Edition. Edited by Karl Widerquist, José A. Noguera, Yannick Vanderborght, and Jurgen De Wispelaere.

remain a national prerogative under the "principle of subsidiarity." National welfare states are too diverse, economically and institutionally, to make policy harmonization a realistic goal; moreover, if harmonization were attempted, Basic Income schemes – which are not realized at the national level, or even on the political agenda in any of the Member States – would be among the least likely candidates for European-wide policy coordination. Nevertheless, there are good reasons for advocates of Basic Income proposals to reflect on the implications of European integration for their chances of success at the national level. Unfortunately, however, these implications are largely negative.

Regulatory competition undermines economic viability

Even though social policy choices must remain at the national level, they are affected by the consequences of European *economic* integration. National social policy is severely constrained if consumers are able to buy goods and services produced anywhere within the Union; if capital owners can invest, and firms produce, anywhere in the Union; and if labor moves freely throughout the Union.

For one, the competition in product markets severely restricts all national solutions that would add to the cost of production. This affects most directly those countries that are financing their welfare state through social security contributions defined as a sur-charge on wages. But it also constrains current proposals to shift from payroll taxes to "green" taxes on energy input or on pollution – unless care is taken to exempt enterprises from such taxes which, however, will defeat or at least weaken the environmental-protection purposes of such shifts.[2]

At the same time, the mobility of capital investments and of firms constrains national policy choices, which would have the effect of reducing after-tax profits and the net return on invested capital, even if these did not affect the cost of production and hence the competitiveness of national products. Hence, countries that are financing their welfare state through taxes on personal and corporate income are under pressure to reduce taxes on business profits and capital incomes, or otherwise risk the out-migration of corporate headquarters and of job-creating investments.

Welfare migration undermines political viability

Regardless of the mode of financing, however, countries that provide generous minimum income support have become vulnerable to welfare migration under the EU's freedom-of-mobility rules which do not allow a country to discriminate against the nationals of another EU Member State. These rules, it is true, are so far applicable only to workers seeking employment. But they continue to apply after workers become unemployed, and they apply to their dependent family members. To illustrate, in a case that is presently much discussed in Germany, social assistance is being claimed by the large family of a recently immigrated and now unemployed manual worker from Sicily.

By implication, the fear of welfare migration is weakening the potential political support for Basic Income programs which – if they are tax financed, rather than insurance financed – could no longer be restricted to citizens or long-term residents under EU rules. As I said before, from the point of view of taxpayers, all redistributive programs depend on normative arguments that could justify a duty to transfer parts of their own income to others. I have learned to my surprise that the Basic Income Movement tends to rely on negative, rather than positive, justifications based explicitly (Schutz, 1998: 2) or implicitly on the logic of Proudhon's dictum that "Property is theft." The argument, in other words, is that much of the current income of the better off is "unearned," depending on accidents of birth, of genetic endowment, of inheritance, or of "brute luck" in obtaining valuable and scarce "external assets" (Van Parijs, 1995; Widerquist, 1998), including attractive jobs (Gamel, 1998; De Wispelaere, 1998).[3] The normative implication is that since these incomes are undeserved nobody could rightly object if they are being taxed away.

At the level of practical politics, however, it may be difficult to persuade most tax payers of the sinfulness of their possessions. Instead, the justification of real-world welfare states seems to depend on positive arguments implying a duty of mutual help among the members of a solidaristic community.[4] And while universalist moral philosophy may find it logical to extend solidarity to all of mankind,[5] real-world solidaristic communities depend on historically grounded, and emotionally salient collective identities that are defined more narrowly.[6] The largest unit that so far has been able to achieve this status is the nation state – and even national solidarity is currently being challenged by the assertion of sub-national identities: Padanian in Italy, Flemish in Belgium, Bavarian in Germany. The European Union, at any rate, has not yet achieved the status of a solidaristic community in the eyes of the citizens of individual Member States. Hence, one cannot presume broad political support for the postulate of a moral duty to include citizens of other Member States in national programs of Basic Income support. As a consequence, not only proposals for new welfare programs, but also existing programs are now increasingly scrutinized with a view to their likely incentive effects on welfare migration, especially under the perspective of the Eastern enlargement of the European Union.

National Solutions?

National welfare states are everywhere under fiscal stress because of exceptionally high levels of unemployment and because of demographic changes that increase the size of the inactive population that must be supported by the active population. Quite apart from that, however, European economic integration has created additional constraints which also tend to reduce the capacity for generous welfare policies. If economic competition discriminates against taxes that will either add to the cost of production or that will reduce the post-tax return on capital investments, welfare finance will increasingly be raised from taxes on the possession of immobile and non-business property, from taxes on income from labor from taxes on consumption, and from user charges. Since property taxes play only a minor, and generally declining, role in most advanced welfare states, the main burden has generally fallen on the incomes from work and on the consumption expenditures of the less mobile majority of the population. The welfare state, in other words, has come to depend mainly on what one might describe as "solidarity within one class" (Scharpf, 1991).

But while such shifts may be economically plausible, they are also quite unattractive politically. Thus, if tax payer resistance is compounded by fears of welfare migration, it is not unreasonable to conclude that European economic integration and the guarantees of free mobility throughout the Union have greatly increased the political and fiscal difficulties that must be overcome by Basic Income proposals. The question is whether there are solutions that could avoid these difficulties. If they exist, they must require a major restructuring of both welfare financing and spending patterns with a view to making them more robust against international economic competition as well as against tax payer opposition. In other words, international economic competition forces national welfare states to transform themselves into "competitive welfare states" if they wish to remain true to their solidaristic commitments.

One consequence is the apparently general shift "from welfare to workfare" and toward stricter means-testing. In my view, this has probably less to do with an ideological shift back to the "work ethic" than with an attempt to reduce expenditures either by deterring "welfare chiselers" through more stringent controls or by getting welfare recipients back into regular employment, preferably in the private sector of the economy.

Another direction that restructuring may take is toward a separation of "individualistic" and "solidaristic" programs – the former providing protection against insurable risks over the life course of the individual, and the latter providing for interpersonal redistribution. Examples of individualistic programs are health insurance and funded pension insurance schemes in which the equivalence between individual contributions and expected individual benefits is emphasized. Even if contributions are made compulsory in order to compensate for presumed lack of individual foresight, they can be plausibly justified as being in the interest of the contributing individuals. Hence, they should be relatively immune to taxpayer resistance. Economically, they should be considered as individual savings or consumption expenditures that do not create competitive disadvantages for the national economy; and obviously there are also no problem of welfare migration.

It is my impression that countries like Switzerland or the Netherlands that have traditionally tended to separate the individualistic and the redistributive components of their welfare states – for instance by establishing different "pillars" of their pension systems – are presently less under pressure than countries like Germany that have integrated individualistic and redistributive elements in single, contributions-based systems of health insurance, pension insurance and unemployment insurance. Another indication are recent reforms in Sweden that have strengthened the individualistic insurance elements of the pension system, and I would expect that other countries will be moving in the same direction.

The main advantage of the separation strategy is, of course, that it reduces the apparent size of the redistributive welfare state that is considered a disadvantage in international competition, and that must be legitimated by appeals to solidaristtic motivations. Moves in the same direction can be seen in the introduction of means-tested user charges – such as student fees in Dutch and British universities or co-payments in the German health care system – which emphasize the value-for-money element of public services while at the same time targeting tax-financed expenditures on lower income clients that could not afford to pay the full cost of these services. An even simpler model is provided by the Swiss system of compulsory health insurance which requires cost-covering individual premia from all inhabitants, and which achieves redistribution by public subsidies to reduce contributions of low-income individuals and large families.

To the extent that such strategies succeed, they will reduce the quantitative dimension of the problems created for the welfare state by European economic integration. At the same time, however, they have the disadvantage of making redistribution much more visible and thus increasing the need for explicit political justification, and the vulnerability to political criticism and opposition. In a democracy, this is as it should be. I would expect, however, that under such conditions proposals for Unconditional Basic Income support would have a hard time in mobilizing political support, and that even means-tested social-assistance programs would remain at relatively low levels of support for recipients who are able to work. By contrast, proposals for subsidizing low incomes form work – in the form of a Negative Income Tax of the American "Earned Income Tax Credit," – or of subsidies that directly reduce the cost of certain types of work to the employer – are likely to fare better in public debates. The question is whether the Basic Income movement should therefore concentrate its efforts on such proposals.

European Support for National Solutions?

European integration, I have argued, forces national welfare states to become competitive. The danger is, of course, that this competition could turn into a ruinous "race to the bottom" in which the British deregulation of the labor market induces France to cut employers' social contributions, which in turn provides justification for cutting sick pay in Germany and Sweden, and so on. In the end, all countries could end up with lower levels of social security than would be preferred domestically, without having improved their relative competitiveness at all.

If this scenario is considered undesirable, the obvious solution would seem to be harmonization. However, as I suggested at the outset, uniform European rules are out of the question because of existing differences in the economic capacity of EU Member States. Among the present Member States, per capita incomes differ at the ratio of 1:2 or 1:3, and with the Eastern enlargement the difference between the richest and the poorest Member States would increase further by a factor of two or three. As a consequence, welfare expenditures at a level that is acceptable in the rich states would simply destroy the less advanced economies. But even if the economic obstacles were less steep, present differences in the spending patterns of European welfare states, and even more so, differences in the institutional structures of welfare financing and welfare provision, would surely prevent the adoption of uniform European rules (Scharpf, 1997).

What might be possible, however, are agreements and rules that would avert the dangers of ruinous competition among the European welfare states (Scharpf, 1999). One such possibility arises from the fact that in spite of their structural and institutional diversity, EU Member States are remarkably similar in their overall commitment to social welfare. More specifically, since the share of *total social spending* in GDP increases in direct proportion to the wealth of Member States, it might be possible to translate this latent consensus into an explicit agreement among EU Member States to avoid welfare cutbacks that would significantly reduce their overall spending position. This would leave all countries free to pursue structural and institutional reforms, but it would eliminate welfare cutbacks from the tool set of economic competition.

Beyond that, there is now some hope that some forms of tax competition will be constrained by political agreement on common ground rules for the taxation of foreign firms, whereas similar agreements on the taxation of capital interest seem to remain more difficult. By contrast, there seems to be no progress at all on the more important issue of establishing a Europe-wide social minimum. For the countries that already have relatively generous schemes of minimum income support and social assistance, harmonization would again run into difficulty because of structural and institutional differences – which could be overcome through agreement on purely quantitative standards of minimum support, defined again in relation to a country's average-income position. For the Southern countries, however, that do not yet have such programs, and even more so for the future Member States in Central and Eastern Europe, the implementation of Europe-wide minimum-income standards would require major additional expenditures, that would not be feasible without financial support from the Union. However, if such support were forthcoming – perhaps through a redirection of the cohesion funds[7] – it might be necessary and possible to avoid the work disincentives inherent in the present social assistance programs of the richer Member States. In that case, Basic Income programs, most likely in the form of the Negative Income Tax, might indeed provide the most effective and efficient solution to the twin problems of poverty and unemployment, and European policymakers might well be persuaded to promote this strategy.

Notes

1. I realize that *Basic Income and Its Cognates* can be made to generate similar incentive structures through the appropriate manipulation of parameters (Van Parijs et al., 2000). But the different versions emphasize different justifications and are designed to optimize the achievement of different purposes.
2. The most plausible solution would be to raise the value-added tax on energy or material inputs into production which would shift the entire cost to the ultimate consumers of energy-intensive products, and which would not affect export competitiveness as long as the EU regime still operates under the "country-of-destination" principle. But in view of the regressive distributional consequences of VAT increases, this solution would have high political costs.
3. In addition, there seems to be a second line of argument that attempts to avoid the need to justify redistribution by proposing sources of revenue that seemingly belong to no one – such as a "Land Trust" collected from commercial uses of the national territory (Lehmann, 1998), a "European Eco-dividend" created by taxing the use of the environment (Quilley, 2000), or a "Tobin tax" on speculative transactions (Standing, 1998). It is clear that none of these ideas could produce the "free lunch" that they seem to promise. At best, they would direct redistributive efforts at particularly unpopular target populations.
4. Civil and criminal law seem to rely on the same assumption when they impose a *universal* duty to refrain from positive action that would injure another's life, liberty or property, whereas the duty to engage in positive action in order to prevent, or compensate for, damages caused by external forces arises only from *specific* (familial, contractual or situational) relationships between the parties.
5. Interestingly, Basic Income articles that begin by asserting "that the income from the resources of the planet and the universe should be divided equally among us because that is the only way that is fair, that is moral, that is right" (Schutz, 1998: 1) continue by calculating Basic Income payments to inhabitants of the United States on the basis of unearned American wealth (Schutz, 1998: 7). In fact, I did not come across one contribution at the 1998 BIEN Congress that advocated Basic Income payments based on an equal distribution of unearned incomes among the population of the planet. In practical terms, therefore, Basic Income advocates also seem to assume that entitlements will be nationally circumscribed.
6. Moreover, since solidarity is based on assumptions of reciprocity, it creates, not only a duty to assist other members in case of need, but also a duty of recipients to make use of opportunities to help themselves. This would morally justify means-testing as well as a duty to accept available and suitable work opportunities.
7. Editor's note: As it is used by the author here, the expression "cohesion funds" refers to the various financial funds within the framework of the European Regional Policy.

References

De Wispelaere, J. (1998). Job Rights, Reciprocity, and the Constitutional Approach to Basic Income. Paper presented at the 7th International Conference on Basic Income, Amsterdam.

Gamel, C. (1998). The Use of "Employment Rents" for the Financing of Basic Income. Paper presented at the 7th International Conference on Basic Income, Amsterdam.

Lehmann, M. (1998). Opposing Globalization Could Justify Resource-Based Basic Income. Paper presented at the 7th International Conference on Basic Income, Amsterdam.

Quilley, S., Tickell, A., and Coates, D. (2000). European Basic Income or the Race to the Bottom: Why European Politicians Might Come to Think the Unthinkable. In R. van der Veen and L. Groot (eds) *Basic Income on the Agenda. Policy Objectives and Political Chances.* Amsterdam University Press, Amsterdam, pp.170–185.

Scharpf, F.W. (1991). *Crisis and Choice within European Social Democracy.* Cornell University Press, Ithaca.

Scharpf, F.W. (1997). Economic Integration, Democracy, and the Welfare State. *Journal of European Public Policy*, 4 (1), 18–36.

Scharpf, F.W. (1999). *Governing in Europe: Effective and Democratic?* Oxford University Press, Oxford.

Schutz, R. (1998). More Basic Income. Paper presented at the 7th International Conference on Basic Income, Amsterdam.

Standing, G. (1998). Seeking Equality of Security in the Era of Globalization. Paper presented at the 7th International Conference on Basic Income, Amsterdam.

Van Parijs, P. (1995). *Real Freedom for All. What (If Anything) Can Justify Capitalism?* Oxford University Press, Oxford.

Van Parijs, P., Jacquet, L., and Salinas, C.C. (2000). Basic Income and its Cognates. In R. van der Veen and L. Groot (eds) *Basic Income on the Agenda. Policy Objectives and Political Chances.* Amsterdam University Press, Amsterdam, pp. 53–84.

Widerquist, K. (1998). Reciprocity and the Guaranteed Income. Paper presented at the 7th International Conference on Basic Income, Amsterdam.

Chapter 69

Is Basic Income Politically Feasible in a Social Europe?

Philippe Van Parijs[1]

Excerpts from Van Parijs, P. (2000). Basic Income at the Heart of Social Europe? Reply to Fritz Scharpf. In R. van der Veen and L. Groot (eds) *Basic Income on the Agenda. Policy Objectives and Political Chances.* Amsterdam University Press, Amsterdam, pp. 161–169.

No nonsense. This is the tone of Fritz Scharpf's contribution (see Chapter 68). This is the language which Basic Income supporters must be able to grasp – and willing to hear – at least if they are not to degenerate into a motley assembly of soft-minded do-gooders; if they are not to be ruthlessly driven into the margins by a harsh, uncompromising reality, but instead to help shape the future in accordance with their visions of freedom and equality. Not through relentless, repetitive preaching, but by means of the resolute and astute action which they must aim to inspire and guide, but will never successfully steer unless they adopt the no-nonsense attitude advocated and practiced by Fritz Scharpf.

Political Feasibility: National Solutions

A no-nonsense approach does not only need to think hard about goals and instruments, but also about what conditions need to be fulfilled for the best instruments to be politically feasible, or indeed what the best remaining instrument might be once the politically unfeasible ones have been filtered out. Here we enter the specifically European dimension of the social policy debate, regarding which I have found Fritz Scharpf's earlier writings particularly illuminating and congenial.[2] The no-nonsense news, in this area, is not good. Here it is.

All proposals in the set which Scharpf (rightly) favors over the *status quo* have one important feature in common: they all imply an increase in the progressiveness of the overall transfer system in such a way that low earners end up with a higher income than before.[3] But what if one of the Member States of the EU introduces such a policy in the context of a single market with a growing mobility of capital, consumer demand and skilled

From Van Parijs, P. (2000). Basic Income at the Heart of Social Europe? Reply to Fritz Scharpf. In R. van der Veen and L. Groot (eds) *Basic Income on the Agenda. Policy Objectives and Political Chances.* Amsterdam University Press, Amsterdam, pp. 161–169. Reprinted with permission.

Basic Income: An Anthology of Contemporary Research, First Edition. Edited by Karl Widerquist, José A. Noguera, Yannick Vanderborght, and Jurgen De Wispelaere.

workers? True, for the time being, mobility is still low enough for the economic feasibility of such national moves not to be in doubt. A sufficiently resolute government should be able to take advantage of this slack, and to credibly dismiss as part of a dishonest scare campaign, the claim that any major increase in net transfers towards low earners would dangerously rock the boat. A no-nonsense view of political feasibility, therefore, should not preclude advocating a vigorous use of one or more of the instruments mentioned above. But it does require one to look ahead, to anticipate in time, without exaggerating its immediate relevance, a growing tension, whose irresistible political exploitation could soon become a painfully binding constraint.

For a higher net taxation of high earners (or their employers) will tend to put off the carriers of increasingly crucial human capital.[4] The lower net taxation of low earners, on the other hand, will not only make double sure the country keeps its least productive workers, but will also make the country more attractive for low-skilled immigrants, whether from other EU countries or from the outside world, in search of a better place to settle. The very success of the various policies considered in fostering the expansion of permanent low paid jobs (many of which may well enjoy a net subsidy, taking all aspects of collective consumption into account) will thus create a sucking effect on poorly productive workers.[5] Combined with the deterrent effect on net contributors, this pressure, if sizeable enough, will make it unwise for any member state to try it alone.[6] Or at the very least, it will make it irresistibly easy for people opposed to it for any reason to brandish so effectively the risk of unsustainability that those advocating significant steps in this direction, indeed even those who will want to do no worse than now in this respect, will be in for a tough political ride.[7]

How can the rise of these predictable constraints be halted? I cannot see how this could be, as elliptically suggested by Fritz Scharpf, through the introduction – arguably desirable for other reasons – of a clearer institutional separation between redistributive and social insurance schemes (on the Dutch, as opposed to German, pattern). Nor can I see how this could be through the reduction of the visible tax burden that would result from introducing, on the Swiss pattern, means-tested user charges (for education, for example) or means-tested public contributions to a compulsory health insurance package. For either the phasing out of the benefit operates steeply at the bottom of the wage scale, in which case the unemployment trap of standard means-tested assistance is deepened, and the objective of fighting unemployment is sacrificed. Or the phasing out operates more smoothly and reaches higher earners, in which case it amounts again (compared to a more universalistic *status quo*) to an increase in the effective net taxation of the high-earners, through the withdrawal of benefits they previously enjoyed, and the constraint of "tolerable" taxation is presumably not better met.[8]

Political Feasibility: Harmonization

Any serious hope of loosening the constraints that stem from fiscal and social competition in a single market must lie in a coordinated action on a higher scale, that is, in "social Europe." Harmonization in a strong sense is not very promising, if only because, as Scharpf emphasizes here and elsewhere, the structures and levels of social protection are too different in the various Member States. One could, however, envisage something very general and supple, but nonetheless firm enough, such as Scharpf's interesting suggestion of a requirement that no country should be allowed to deviate (by too much) from a ratio of social spending to GDP which would increase as GDP per capita increases. But apart from technical difficulties, there are two fundamental stumbling blocks that undermine the political chances of such a proposal.

First of all, think of two countries with family support schemes which affect identically the disposable incomes of identically situated families, one through cash benefits and the other through (refundable) tax credits. This plainly illustrates how arbitrary it would be to only take explicit expenditures into account. Some tax reductions and exemptions will also have to count. But clearly not all: not a tax reduction conceded, for example, to expatriates or to innovating businessmen. But if such discrimination is made among tax expenditures, why not also among explicit public expenditures? Can family allowances to affluent households count, for example, or expenditure on higher education, which more than proportionally benefit people who are likely to come from, and are even more likely to move into, comparatively affluent income categories? Though convenient, because of the relative ease with which it can be measured, the ratio of social spending to GDP is therefore far too crude an indicator of a country's redistributive performance for it to perform the job assigned to it.

Something more sophisticated – and complicated – could conceivably be designed to provide a better proxy for this redistributive performance. One might think, for example, of some measure of the gap between pre-tax-and-transfer and post-tax-and-transfer lifetime income inequality. But both the cruder indicator and the more sophisticated one meet a second obstacle. Both the level of social spending of one country and its redistributive performance, as measured by such an index, may be higher than those of another, despite the fact that, for any given distribution of income, its tax-and-transfer institutions would redistribute less than those of the other country. This can easily happen simply because the pre-tax-and-transfer income distribution can be more equal in the former country than in the latter. And since the level of pre-tax-and-transfer inequality is at least partly under the control of a country's institutions – its educational system, industrial relations, inheritance laws, and so on – it would seem wrong to castigate a country whose redistributive performance is comparatively poor because its primary incomes are comparatively equal. Something more sophisticated still could be thought up, but we would then have moved a very long way from the simple, easily intelligible, readily verifiable, uncontroversial index which would have had some chance of being accepted by Member States as the basis for a binding, firmly enforceable rule.

Political Feasibility: The Euro-Dividend

If this path is no good, then perhaps it is not too early to start thinking about something that sounds more radical, but may in the end prove more realistic. Instead of trying to harmonize the various national systems, be it only in order to block a race to the bottom, should one not start building an EU-wide interpersonal transfer system? The ambition cannot and must not be to erect an EU welfare state that would replicate the structure of national welfare states. There are good reasons, not only for regarding this as unfeasible, but also as undesirable.[9] Being far less under pressure, the insurance component of the national welfare states does not require urgent protective action. The focus should rather be on "the more important issue of establishing a Europe-wide social minimum" (Scharpf, 2000). Especially if the EU expands into Central and Eastern Europe, this will require "major additional expenditures, that would not be feasible without financial support from the Union" (Scharpf, 2000).

What form should this Income Guarantee take? According to Fritz Scharpf (Scharpf, 2000), "it might be necessary and possible to avoid the work disincentives inherent in the present social-assistance programs of the richer Member States." A.B. Atkinson (1998: 146) emphatically agrees. A means-tested minimum Income Guarantee, he argues, is definitely not the way forward for social Europe. Not only for the general reason that it unfairly penalizes the work of poor households more than anyone else's, but also for the specific reason that a European-wide minimum "has to be based on a benefit that is simpler than means-tested social assistance."[10] The alternative, which Atkinson favors is a Universal Basic Income that would replace all income tax allowances, but not social insurance benefits. After conceding that, "despite finding supporters in all political parties, the scheme has not got close to being introduced," he expresses his conviction "that, in order to secure political support, it may be necessary for the proponents of Basic Income to compromise – not on the principle of no test of means, nor on the principle of independence, but on the unconditional payment" (Atkinson, 1998: 148). He therefore proposes, also at the European level, a "Participation Income," a Universal Basic Income for all those who satisfy some minimal participation condition (not just full- or part-time paid work, but also education, care and voluntary work). He is aware that the question of how to interpret this broad participation condition may prove even trickier at the European than at the national level.[11] Nonetheless, he believes "that such a Participation Income offers a realistic way in which European governments may be persuaded that a Basic Income offers a better route forward than the dead end of means-tested assistance." (Atkinson, 1998: 149).

I have no problem with such a strategy. Nor should, I believe, Fritz Scharpf, given his concern to work out a compromise around which like-minded people could gather. As argued above, once goals are suitably clarified, I doubt much disagreement will remain at that level. Once instruments are evaluated in terms of their actual or likely consequences for the achievement of these goals, the universal floor favored by Atkinson and others (including myself) dominates Negative Income Tax schemes, or the combination of earned income tax credit (or *a fortiori* other forms of employment subsidy) and existing means-tested assistance.[12] Finally, once the new European context is taken into account, Fritz Scharpf's insightful analysis of political constraints itself leads, step by step, to the radical idea of an EU-wide Universal Basic Income. There is no reason to expect this path, to which the exploration of dead ends has led us, to be easy to tread. And there will need to be compromises at every stage. One of them is on the so-called "counterpart," on the idea of subjecting the right to Basic Income to the fulfillment of some socially useful activity. For reasons stated by both Atkinson and Scharpf, there is no doubt that subjecting a Universal Basic Income to such a condition would increase its immediate political chances.

Hence, without neglecting the potential that still exists and must keep existing at national levels, let us pay serious attention to this Euro-dividend for all "active" European citizens. Let us work out a precise scheme that credibly offers, at the same time, a strong brake on fiscal and social competition between Member States and a decisive contribution to solving Europe's unemployment problem. Let us find ways of persuasively presenting it for what it is: not a mega-welfare state, not a substitute for national welfare policies, but rather a floor under them all that will enable them to survive more easily and to do a better job. Let us map in detail the transition path, how the adjustments will most smoothly be done in the EU budget and in national tax and benefit structures. Let us get ready for when the strains created by the co-existence of a single currency and separate governments will make themselves felt; for when the seed to stabilize populations will become more acute; for when European decision-makers will be looking for a realistic way of preserving and developing, under unprecedented conditions, something they claim to be a central component of the European project: "social solidarity."

Wishful thinking? Perhaps not, if goals are lucidly stated, if instruments are appropriately assessed, and if political constrainsts are properly understood. Not, in other words, if Fritz Scharpf's welcome invitation is taken seriously, if his no-nonsense approach is consistently, tirelessly practiced.

Notes

1. This paper was written within the framework of the PAI project "The New Social Question" (Belgian Federal Government, Prime Minister's Office, Federal Office for Scientific, Technical and Cultural Affairs).
2. See for example Scharpf (1994; 1996a; 1996b; 1996c).
3. This fits in with Scharpf's (1999: section 3.2) most striking conclusion from a systematic comparative analysis between a country's employment performance and the structure of its transfer system: there appears to be a significantly negative impact of proportional forms of taxation (consumption tax and social contributions) on employment levels, while there is little effect of progressive taxation (in particular the income tax).
4. This is not a matter of increasing compulsory contributions yielding corresponding insurance-based benefits, in the form of pensions, sick leave or unemployment benefits. Growing mobility may put somewhat greater pressure on such transfers (because of enhanced adverse selection), but there is no comparison, as Atkinson (1998: 143–144), for example, emphasizes and as Scharpf is well aware, with the increased pressure on the non-insurance-based, *ex ante* redistributive aspects of Europe's welfare states.
5. See, for example, what Krause-Junk (1996) regards as the most crucial objection to Negative Income Tax proposals of the type advocated by Joachim Mitschke (1985; 1995). As wages would no longer need to cover subsistence, neither employers nor Unions will be under the same pressure to keep jobs productive, and Germany will become a low-productivity country, with a combination of low wages and Bürgergeld that will be particularly attractive for poorly skilled immigrants from Southern (and soon Eastern) Europe.
6. For those who dread this inflow of poorly productive labor power, the threat should be worse if the attraction is the prospect of (henceforth profitable) low-productivity jobs, rather than that of benefits. For claimants can, more easily than workers, be kept away by *ad hoc* rules or by the social assistance administration's unwelcoming attitude.
7. There may perhaps be some hope of hiding the net subsidies to low-paid work, probably greater in the case of NIT, EITC or reduced social security contributions than in the case of a Universal Basic Income. Hence, presumably, one source of Scharpf's lower assessment of the latter's feasibility.
8. Two provisos are in order. Firstly, if the phasing out for higher earners affects selectively those provisions which disproportionately benefit households with children (family allowances, child care, education), sustainability may be hardly affected. For households with children arguably tend to be less mobile than childless households (and the less mobile, the greater the loss from the phasing out of these benefits) and hence less able to issue credible threats of leaving, in the emerging globalized context. Secondly, political feasibility may not only be affected by the political use of the risk of economic unsustainability caused by excessive net taxation, but also by the political use of the perception of gross taxation. In this respect, the phasing out of a benefit may be less damaging than a higher explicit marginal rate, just as a funding of the Basic Income by the value added tax (e.g. Duchatelet, 1994; 1998), by energy taxation (e.g. Genet, 1991; Robertson, 1998), or indeed by (non-inflationary and de-privatized) money creation

(e.g Huber, 1998; 1999) would have an advantage, in this respect, over the income tax, even though it also essentially amounts to reducing the purchasing power of relatively high income earners.

9. I develop the reasons behind this normative undesirability in Van Parijs (1999).
10. See Schmitter (1999) for a radical proposal of a means-tested European minimal income. See Van Parijs (1996) for an argument against it along lines similar to the one taken by Atkinson (1998).
11. Note, however, that, even if the implementation of the condition is pretty much left to the discretion of national governments, there would be no perverse incentives of the sort generated by a centrally funded but locally administered means test. With a means-tested Guaranteed Income funded at the European level, national or local governments would systematically find it in their political interest to disregard some potential recipients' means (and hence to compete with each other in terms of how lax an interpretation they give to an insufficient-means condition). But with a counterpart-tested Guaranteed Income, they would not have a similar incentive to disregard the failure to perform some socially useful activity (nor therefore to compete with each other in terms of how lax an interpretation they give to a participation condition).
12. Even if, as in all reasonable short-term variants, the Universal Basic Income or Negative Income Tax is not a full substitute for social assistance, it always implies a significant reduction in its level, whereas EITC does not, since by itself (unlike Universal Basic Income and Negative Income Tax) it grants no benefit whatever to nonworkers.

References

Atkinson, A.B. (1998). *Poverty in Europe.* Blackwell, Oxford.

Duchatelet, R. (1994). An Economic Model for Europe Based on Consumption Financing on the Tax Side and the Basic Income Principle on The Redistribution Side. Paper presented at the 5th Conference of the Basic Income European Network, London.

Duchatelet, R. (1998). *N.V. België. Verslag aan de aandeelhouders.* Globe, Gent.

Genet, M. (1991). *Calcul d'un mode de financement d'une allocation universelle européenne, mémoire de maîtrise.* Département des sciences économiques, Université catholique de Louvain.

Huber, J. (1998). *Vollgeld. Beschäftigung, Grundsicherung und weniger Staatsquote durch eine modernisierte Geldordnung.* Duncker & Humblot, Berlin.

Huber, J. (1999). Plain Money. A Proposal for Supplying the Nations with the Necessary Means in a Modern Monetary System, *Forschungsberichte des Instituts für Soziologie.* Martin-Luther-Universität, Halle-Wittenberg.

Krause-Junk, G. (1996). Probleme einer Integration von Einkommensbesteuerung und steuerfinanzierten Sozialleistungen. Anmerkungen zum Gutachten der Experten-Kommission, *Wirtschaftsdienst*, 7, 345–349.

Mitschke, J. (1985). *Steuer- und Transferordnung aus einem Guss. Entwurf einer Neugestaltung der direkten Steuern und Sozialtransfers in der Bundesrepublik Deutschland*, Schriften zur Ordnunspolitik 2. Baden-Baden, Nomos.

Mitschke, J. (1995). Jenseits der Armenfürsorge. *Die Zeit*, 50 (December 8), 30–31.

Robertson, J. (ed.) (1998). Sharing our Common Heritage: Resource Taxes and Green Dividends. Proceedings of a One Day International Conference. Oxford Centre for the Environment, Ethics and Society, Oxford University.

Scharpf, F.W. (1994). *Optionen des Föderalismus in Deutschland und Europa.* Campus Verlag, Frankfurt.

Scharpf, F.W. (1996a). Negative and Positive Integration in the Political Economy of European Welfare States. In G. Marks, F.W. Scharpf, P.C. Schmitter, and W. Streeck (eds) *Governance in the European Union.* Sage, London, pp. 15–39.

Scharpf, F.W. (1996b). Föderalismus und Demokratie in der transnationalen Ökonomie. In K. von Beyme and C. Offe (eds) *Politische Theorie in der Ära der Transformation.* Westdeutscher Verlag, Opladen, pp. 211–235.

Scharpf, F.W. (1996c). Demokratische Politik in Europa, *Staatswissenschaften und Staatspraxis*, 6 (4), 565–591.

Scharpf, F.W. (1999). The Viability of Advanced Welfare Slates in the International Economy: Vulnerabilities and Options. Working paper. Max Planck Institute for the Study of Societies, Cologne.

Scharpf, F.W. (2000). Basic Income and Social Europe? In R. van der Veen and L. Groot (eds.) *Basic Income on the Agenda. Policy Objectives and Political Chances.* Amsterdam University Press, Amsterdam, pp. 155–160.

Schmitter, P. (1999). *The Scope of Citizenship in a Democratized European Union: From Economic to Political to Social and Cultural?* European University Institute: Department of political and social sciences, Florence.

Van Parijs, P. (1996). Basic Income and the Two Dilemmas of the Welfare State. *The Political Quarterly*, 67 (1), 63–66.

Van Parijs, P. (1999). *Just Health Care and the Two Solidarities.* Harvard Center for Population and Development Studies, Working Paper 99.03.

Chapter 70

Basic Income in the South

Philippe Van Parijs

Excerpts from Van Parijs, P. (2003). La Renta Básica: ¿Por qué, cómo y cuándo en el Norte y en el Sur? In J. Giraldo (ed.) *La Renta Básica, más allá de la sociedad salarial.* Escuela Nacional Sindical, Medellín.

There are some developing countries which are making significant steps towards Basic Income, both in terms of public debate and institutional reality. More specifically, there are two countries where the present political discussion is focused on the Basic Income proposal and where we can find particularly interesting experiments.

The first of these countries is South Africa. Since the final period of *apartheid*, before the African National Congress came to office, there has been a minimum pension paid to every women over 60 and to every man over 65 if they do not receive a pension from other sources. The case of South Africa is very interesting because the benefit was established in the last years of *apartheid*, and is the most redistributive social policy scheme in the South African welfare system. Moreover, it is the most redistributive cash benefit in all sub-Saharan Africa. This benefit is particularly interesting because it does not create dependency relations, contrary to other schemes in the welfare state. In this case, more than 90% of the black population in South Africa keep this right even when the youngest members of their family start to work: the grandparents do not lose the benefit, nor is the income from work in the household deducted from it. But there are also some disadvantages: for many households, the death of a grandmother is a financial disaster; it is not surprising, then, that many grandmothers "die" administratively several years after their physical death.

At present, there is an important social movement in South Africa, which includes the union confederation COSATU (Congress of South African Trade Unions) and the Catholic Church, that demands the introduction of a Basic Income in the radical sense of an unconditional income at the level of US$10 per month. The contrast with the amounts of US$250 and US$600 I mentioned earlier is evident,[1] but one should understand this in a context where half of the 40 million South Africans live with a monetary income of less than US$2 per month. I think that for the inmediate future this proposal is Utopian

From Van Parijs, P. (2003). La Renta Básica: ¿Por qué, cómo y cuándo en el Norte y en el Sur? In J. Giraldo (ed.) *La Renta Básica, más allá de la sociedad salarial.* Escuela Nacional Sindical, Medellín. Translated by J.A. Noguera (ed.). Reprinted with permission of the publishers and the author.

Basic Income: An Anthology of Contemporary Research, First Edition. Edited by Karl Widerquist, José A. Noguera, Yannick Vanderborght, and Jurgen De Wispelaere.

in South Africa, but it is interesting that this social movement, partially inspired by BIEN (Basic Income European Network), exists.

The second country I find particularly interesting is Brazil. There is a very strong debate since the introduction in the Federal Senate of an ambitious proposal: a guaranteed minimum income for all Brazilians in the form of a Negative Income Tax, presented by senator Eduardo Suplicy, who was elected in São Paulo as a candidate of the Workers' Party. Incidentally, one of the senators who voted in 1991 in favor of the introduction of this minimum income scheme was Fernando Henrique Cardoso.[2]

During the 1990s there were a lot of local experiments of *Bolsa Escola*, which is a form of minimum income for families with children who do not reach a certain income level, but conditioned to school attendance of children between 7 and 14 years of age; if this condition is not satisfied, the family is not eligible for the benefit. This is an important aspect in a country where school attendance is far from 100%, especially among the poorest families. But there are a lot of experiments of this kind. The most extensive ones take place in Brazilia's Federal District, in the city of Campinas, and now in São Paulo thanks to the mayor Martha Suplicy.

Obviously, we are far from a universal citizen's income like the one proposed by senator Suplicy in his book *Renda de Cidadania* (2004). According to him, the implementation of a universal and unconditional income which avoids dependency traps is an aim to be achieved in a quite distant future; but, though I am pessimistic about an early realization of the idea, I think it works as an horizon for short-term proposals. This is very important in countries such as Brazil for two reasons.

In the first place, in the light of other countries' experiences, the problems of dependency traps, which are inherent to the selective mechanisms of the welfare state, should be anticipated. A solution should be ready when the moment arrives for those problems to threaten the legitimacy of the steps already made towards Basic Income. Secondly, we should be able to propose a societal model that is an alternative to traditional socialism, understood as collective ownership of the means of production, as well as to neo-liberalism and to the conventional welfare state associated with social democracy.

This point of view is important in order to guide and motivate action, but probably it is even more important in order to elaborate feasible proposals in the short term. In a country like the Netherlands a modest Unconditional and Universal Basic Income is a realistic proposal for the inmediate future: its net cost would be quite low, since a guaranteed minimum income already exists. But in countries like Brazil, where no general targeted minimum income program exists, and where an important part of aggregated income is not detected by the tax system, it is obvious that the immediate introduction of a Universal Basic Income would be irresponsible. It would also be irresponsible to argue that it is possible to fund this program without trouble simply through money creation. It would be unsound to argue that one can count on the self-financing of the program through a positive macroeconomic effect on economic activity. Therefore, it is unavoidable that progress be made in the short term through selective schemes.

I want to define this idea a little bit more. It is clear for me that in countries like Brazil it is not possible to progress in the short term by applying completely universal programs, with benefits paid to the rich as well as to the poor, which is one of the central tenets of the idea of a Basic Income; on the contrary, I think progress should be made through selective schemes. However, the big problem of selective schemes is that they necessarily tend to create dependency and unemployment traps, which partly threaten their own economic feasibility and political credibility.

There are different ways of reducing this risk. In what follows I will make three brief remarks on the chances to do that.

1. One may think in a design which gradually reduces the level of the benefit for the poor as a function of the income they get from other sources, so that the benefit is not suddenly withdrawn. Suplicy's original proposals for Brazil, for instance, are of this kind. The administrative feasibility of this strategy should be explored, because it would be necessary to establish means tests for a number of persons much higher than the number of excluded persons, and for a huge number of households; some households with many children would be eligible for quite high levels of the benefit, and in these cases it should be possible to test in a reliable way their family income, with all the administrative costs associated with that. This type of scheme obviously has a higher coverage than a strictly targeted one, because a larger proportion of the population would be eligible, but it also has a higher risk of creating dependency traps.
2. Secondly, I will mention family benefit schemes in countries that have completed their demographical transition. In countries such as Brazil it is sound to link the payment of a Basic Income with the duty to attend school, but the danger exists for families with children of creating a dependency trap for the parents, because when an adult member's income increases they may lose the benefit. But in Brazil there is a small tax credit for working class families. An intelligent measure would be to gradually integrate tax credits for families with formal income within a universal family benefit; at present, there are, on the one hand, the formal workers who receive a family benefit in the form of a tax credit, and, on the other hand, the poorer informal workers who are only eligible for *Bolsa Escola*. But, in addition, there is a third part of the population that is eligible for nothing, and this possibility of having nothing is what creates a dependency trap for people in the lower levels of income distribution. Therefore, a gradual integration of all family benefits in the form of a Basic Income for children paid to the mothers is an intelligent step in the right direction which is in no way Utopian in some developing countries, but always on the condition that they have completed the demographical transition. I think this is an intelligent move for Brazil, but not for sub-Saharan Africa, where a basic pension would be much more effective.
3. My third remark is that a basic pension for all those who do not receive a formal pension is a mechanism that should be explored not only in sub-Saharan Africa but also in other developing countries; one difficulty is that it would create a kind of "formal employment trap," because it would lower the incentives to work in the formal economy, where the right for a formal pension is generated: if you do not have a formal pension you will always have the right to the basic pension. But it is also important to make steps in the direction of basic unconditional pensions and basic unconditional family benefits.

It is clear that these type of measures may be defended on such grounds as solidarity and social justice, but, especially in developing countries, they should also have a positive effect on economic efficiency and a visible impact on development. For instance, there are very accurate studies on the effect of basic pensions on health standards in South Africa; there are also empirical studies that show that the Brazilian type of minimum income has an important impact on school attendance for many young people. It seems evident that minimum income mechanisms of this or other types have a remarkable effect on the stabilization of rural population, because they entail a net transfer to the most rural local areas, and that avoids overpopulation and concentration of large unemployed masses in urban areas, with all the typical consequences in terms of crime rates, and so on.

Notes

1. Editor's note: Earlier in the original text, the author gave these amounts as corresponding to possible partial and full Basic Income schemes in developed countries.
2. Editor's note: Fernando Henrique Cardoso was president of Brazil when Philippe Van Parijs was giving this lecture, and he opposed the proposal during all his mandate.

Reference

Suplicy, E.M. (2004). *Renda de Cidadania: A saída é pela porta.* Cortez, São Paulo.

Chapter 71

How Cash Transfers Promote the Case for Basic Income

Guy Standing

Originally published as Standing, G. (2008). How Cash Transfers Promote the Case for Basic Income. *Basic Income Studies*, 3 (1), 1–30.

This chapter first presents some principles for assessing the effectiveness of various forms of income-support scheme in combating economic insecurity. In the light of those principles it goes on to review experience with food aid and vouchers, seen as the main alternatives to cash transfers, before discussing the growing use in developing countries of both conditional and unconditional cash transfers. Separate sections deal with cash transfers in emergency and development aid, incomes for school attendance, social pensions and disability grants. In concluding remarks, it is argued that experience with cash transfer schemes to date gives empirical support to arguments in favor of a universal Unconditional Basic Income.

Economic Insecurity and Social Justice Principles

In assessing the potential of cash transfers, it may be useful to identify the nature of economic insecurity, clarify types of income-support scheme, and set out some principles or criteria by which to judge alternative ways of assisting the economically insecure and disadvantaged.

Economic insecurity

Briefly, economic insecurity reflects exposure to several forms of risk and uncertainty and a limited capacity to cope with adverse outcomes and recover from them. To a greater or lesser extent, any individual could be said to be exposed to idiosyncratic risk that reflects life-cycle contingencies, such as a spell of unemployment, an illness or a disabling accident. This is the sphere of classic social security schemes. But there is also co-variant risk, where one adverse event has a high probability of triggering others, and systemic risk, where whole communities are exposed.

From Standing, G. (2008). How Cash Transfers Promote the Case for Basic Income. *Basic Income Studies*, 3 (1), 1–30.

Basic Income: An Anthology of Contemporary Research, First Edition. Edited by Karl Widerquist, José A. Noguera, Yannick Vanderborght, and Jurgen De Wispelaere.

This leads to the distinction between shocks and hazards. Shocks have become more numerous as a result of globalization and global warming. Included are sharp economic downturns that sweep entire communities, economies or regions. More generally, there are circumstances that one can characterize as socio-economic disasters, whether they be quick-onset disasters, as in the case of earthquakes, floods, tsunamis or a sudden economic collapse, or slow-onset disasters, as in the case of droughts, famines, or and epidemic such as HIV/AIDS.

These situations of shock should be distinguished from the notion of hazards, which are important sources of economic insecurity in many developing countries. Hazards may be defined as predictable (and often desired) life events that have a high probability of an adverse effect, or a sequence of adverse effects, for an individual or family. They include a death of a relative, weddings, births, a migration event, and retirement.

Whether shock or hazard, the resultant costs can erode a household's capacity to sustain its normal livelihood base, perhaps by pushing it into debt or into mortgaging land, or by preventing it from buying seeds or fertilizers.

Economic insecurity also arises from uncertainty. With uncertainty, one is unsure about one's actual interests or unsure how to realize them. The outcome of decisions cannot be predicted with any confidence, and often this is combined with a perceived inability to know what to do if an adverse outcome materializes. A high degree of uncertainty pushes people into more risk-averse behavior, especially if the consequences of an adverse outcome could be catastrophic. Those producing in agrarian economies or where economic activity is dependent on climate conditions are likely to face chronic uncertainty. Anything that lessened that uncertainty could be expected to have a beneficial effect on higher-yielding investment, innovation and purposive decision-making.

So, security arises from being able to deal with shocks, hazards and uncertainty. Although it will not be argued here, it is a premise of this chapter that basic economic security is essential for freedom and development. Basic economic security is in turn defined as a threefold set of circumstances. First, it requires *limited exposure* to idiosyncratic, co-variant and systemic risks, uncertainty, hazards and shocks. Second, it requires an *ability to cope* if they materialize. And third, it requires an *ability to recover* from adverse outcomes.

Types of income support scheme

With those points in mind, to assess possible policies a further set of distinctions should be made. We may say that a scheme is universalistic if it is intended as a right for all the population, although perhaps based on citizenship or long-term residence. A scheme is targeted if it is intended for a specific group, defined by some test of eligibility, be it poverty, age, employment capacity or whatever. A scheme is selective if it uses some specified criteria to determine eligibility, such as a means test. A scheme is conditional if it requires some specified behavior, usually work-related, on the part of the recipient, or in some cases family members of the recipient.

In practice, there are instances of targeted universalistic schemes for which all those belonging to a particular group are eligible regardless of their means. An example is the universalistic social pension introduced in several countries, such as Namibia and Mauritius. More common at the moment are targeted selective schemes, which define intended beneficiaries by their social group (e.g., women with young children) and by their poverty (having an income or assets below some threshold value).

Means-testing has been criticized as inequitable and a deterrent to work, especially for low-skilled worker, through what are known as poverty traps or unemployment traps. In developing countries, the problems are compounded by the difficulty of applying meaningful tests to undocumented income that may fluctuate erratically and substantially. This has prompted many countries to resort to proxy means-testing, where visible indicators of income (such as quality of housing) are used to determine eligibility for a particular benefit, since it was first tried in Chile in 1980 (Clert and Woden, 2001; Raczynski, 1991).

Proxy means-testing requires selection of relevant proxy indicators of social deprivation, such as location of residence, quality of dwelling or type of economic activity the household is engaged in. None of these is a very reliable indicator of poverty per se. Accordingly, some authorities have been drawn to rely on relatively sophisticated statistical models using a few variables to estimate the profile of somebody who should be regarded as in need. However, the technique is prone to all three types of failure that should be used to assess any social protection scheme.

Schemes can have a high or low exclusion error – that is, they may exclude a large or small number of those for whom the benefit is supposedly intended. This is particularly likely with area-based targeting. Schemes may also have a high or low inclusion error – that is, they may include people for whom the benefit is not intended. Third, schemes may have a high administrative cost relative to the cost of the overall scheme. Many schemes are vitiated by excessive administrative costs that mean that far fewer people can be beneficiaries, given limited resources.

In the case of proxy means tests, collecting and analyzing data to be used in a formula to identify the targeted group will involve hefty administrative cost. There will also be substantial exclusion errors, since even the best econometric equations estimate only about 50% of the variability of income, implying a very imperfect means of identification of potential recipients (Coady, Grosh, and Hoddinnott, 2004). Such schemes also involve obvious immoral hazards if the proxy indicator is known to the possible recipients.

Policy evaluation principles

Following earlier work,[1] this chapter is based on a belief that policies should be judged, or evaluated, by whether or not they satisfy the following five policy principles:

The Security Difference Principle – A policy or institutional change is socially just only if it improves the security of the least secure groups in society. The Security Difference Principle stems from Rawls, who from a liberal philosophical perspective essentially argued that social and economic inequalities are only just if they allow for the betterment of the worst-off groups in society (Rawls, 1971).

The Paternalism Test Principle – A policy or institutional change is socially just only if it does not impose controls on some groups that are not imposed on the most free groups in society. Underlying this principle is the Millian liberal view that there is a prima facie case against paternalism (except in the case of young children and those who are medically frail), particularly against those forms that constrain the freedoms of the disadvantaged.

The Rights-Not-Charity Principle – A policy or institutional change is socially just if it enhances the rights of the recipient of benefits or services and limits the discretionary power of the providers. This third priciple is also crucial for assessing alternative benefit schemes. A right is possessed by virtue of a person's humanity or citizenship, and cannot be made dependent on some behavioral conditionality. Social and economic entitlements should be rights, not matters for the discretionary decisions of bureaucrats or philanthropists or aid donors.

The Ecological Constraint Principle – A policy or instititional change is socially just only if it does not involve an ecological cost borne by the community or by those directly affected. Benefit schemes should be subject to the constraint that they should not deliberately or carelessly jeopardize the environment.

The Dignified Work Principle – A policy or institutional change is just only if it does not impede people from pursuing work in a dignified way and if it does not disadvantage the most insecure groups in that respect. The two-part test in this principle involves two implicit value judgements – that work that is dignifying is worth promoting (whereas any deterioration in working conditions or in opportunities would not be), and that the policy should enhance the range and quality of work options of the most insecure groups relative to others, or more than for others. The main point is to determine whether or not a scheme favors the development of more freely chosen work opportunities and work capabilities.

Before proceeding, it is also worth recalling Tony Atkinson's two measures of poverty-reduction efficiency – vertical and horizontal, the former measuring the extent to which there is leakage of money intended for the poor going to the non-poor, the latter measuring the extent to which the poor are actually helped (Atkinson, 1995).

The difficulty with this dualism is that, for example, a scheme may reach 70% of a target group, but they may be the least severely affected, leaving the worst-off 30% no better off or even worse off. Using the horizontal-vertical efficiency approach could produce other difficulties. For example, if another program reached 70% who were the worst-off and did so at the cost of some leakage to the non-poor, that might be judged less efficient. It is thus advisable to be cautious about evaluating policies using the language of efficiency.

The following discussion looks first at the main alternatives to direct cash transfers and then turns to a more detailed discussion of conditional and universal forms of transfer. It leaves out of consideration cash-for-work and emergency public works schemes, which the author has written about elsewhere (United Nations, 2007, ch. VI).

Food Aid

The primary claim in favor of food aid, including subsidized food, is that it responds to the priority needs of the poor. It is an anti-poverty device. It is also perceived as horizontally efficient in that it is self-selecting. The poor will want the food aid; the wealthier will not. Food aid, it is reasoned, will also be relatively appreciated by recipients, as well as easy to legitimize with donors and the median voter.

The main criticism of food aid is that the vulnerable may not lack food per se, or may not see their future as made secure by access to more food. Such commodity-based aid is also paternalistic, in that it presumes that what people want is more food, and/or that they would not spend money on food if given the freedom to make choices for themselves.

Food aid is also potentially market distorting, eroding incentives for local farmers, especially if the food is coming from outside the community. It can thus disrupt local livelihoods and employment. Even the prospect of an influx of food aid can act as a deterrent to local farmers or producers or market traders. It may thus fail the Dignified Work Principle.

Food aid and subsidies also engender a sense of charity rather than economic rights. As with all subsidies, the food will be less appreciated than if the actual monetary value was paid. Food aid will therefore tend to result in waste, due to undervaluation, and/or excessive consumption just because it is "free" (Tabor, 2002). Distributing food aid also has high transaction and administrative costs. For instance, in India, the widely used meals-for-school scheme is notorious – each rupee of food costs a rupee to distribute.

Finally, food aid often leads to perverse targeting, reaching those without much need for food while not reaching those who do need it, who may be more inaccessible.[2] Thus it may, perversely, fail to satisfy the Security Difference Principle as well.

Though food aid has been the classic form of aid in times of emergency, there is growing recognition that to be effective it must be combined with cash grants if the intervention is to prevent the collapse of livelihood capacity in the affected communities. There is now considerable evidence from food-aid schemes that, without monetary assistance, many recipients are obliged to sell their food aid or cannot retain their land or raw materials because of accumulating debt. This was found to be the case, for instance, in and evaluation of food aid given to refugees in Chad (LeJeune, 2004) and in a review of emergency food interventions in the Great Lakes region of Africa (Levine and Chastre, 2004).

In Afghanistan, beneficiaries of food aid were found to be selling the food they had received for less than a third of the cost of its delivery (Development Researchers Network, 2003). And an evaluation of food aid in Ethiopia concluded that households would have taken much less in cash than the market value of their food aid and been equally satisfied (Barrett and Clay, 2003; see also Barnett, Holden and Clay, 2002). Cash would have been less expensive, and would have been freedom-enhancing. Yet paternalism has typically prevailed, at the cost of limiting the revival capacities in local communities.

Vouchers and Food Stamps

The most common voucher schemes in developing countries have been for seeds and other agricultural inputs, the intention being to boost agricultural output and employment while curbing food poverty. Vouchers have also been used in foreign aid to communities hit by economic or natural disasters, for instance, in the aftermath of the tsunami, in Indonesia, Sri Lanka and elsewhere, in the occupied Palestinian territories, and by the UK Government in its response to the Montserrat volcanic eruption. Significantly, in the last case, the authorities eventually switched to cash grants after recipients complained that the vouchers were too restrictive.

Among the claims in favor of vouchers is that they are, or could be made, self-selecting of those in need, if the items that can be obtained with the vouchers are what the wealthy have in abundance or simply do not want. Some have even argued that there should be a stigma attached to receipt of vouchers precisely to increase the self-selectivity of the poor.

One criticism of vouchers is that they require considerable planning and preparation, including the agreement of local traders to accept the vouchers. There have been reports that shops do not like dealing with vouchers because they involve extra administrative costs and uncertainty about reimbursement.

Another criticism is that – contrary to the claim that they promote self-selection – the stigmatization entailed by vouchers leads to lower take-up, not higher. Applying for and using a voucher are visible transactions that signal poverty or dependency, and there is no reason to presume that this will result in self-selection by the poorest and most insecure. In the UK, to take an extreme case, the Government had to abandon a special voucher scheme for asylum seekers because recipients were being identified and harassed.

Almost by definition, vouchers are paternalistic, in that they involve a decision by the state (or donor) on what people should be spending money on. However benevolent and well-meaning, that is undeniably a restriction of individual liberty. This is perhaps why the best form seems to have been "seed vouchers" combined with "seed fairs," in which the paternalistic element has been moderated by enabling recipients to choose from among a large range of seeds. There have been reports that such seed fairs have worked quite well in various parts of Africa.

Any subsidy tends to distort spending patterns. Extensive research has shown that the US food stamps program has resulted in people buying more food than they would have done had they received the equivalent in cash. Given the high incidence of obesity among the US poor, that in itself would be a reason to convert the voucher scheme into a cash transfer. Giving cash would not ensure that it was spent on healthier food, but there would be a lower probability that it would be spent on excessive food. How it would be spent would be a matter of individual freedom.

Conditional Cash Transfers

As noted at the outset, until recently there was little interest in the idea of using cash transfers as a means of reducing poverty in developing countries, even as part of international aid in times of emergency. Thus a review of all UN consolidated aid appeals in 2004 found almost no use of cash or vouchers; the appeals were dominated by traditional humanitarian responses, such as food aid, materials for shelter, clothing, seeds and so on.

However, there is a growing movement in favor of introducing cash transfers and even universal income grants in developing countries where it is commonly claimed that no universal system of social protection is financially feasible. As a senior World Band economist, in surveying the empirical literature, put it:

> The conventional wisdom in mainstream development policy circles is that income transfers to the poor, and safety net policies more generally, are at best a short term palliative and at worst a waste of money. These views are starting to be questioned at two levels. Firstly, evidence from careful evaluations has pointed to a number of success stories. [. . .] Secondly, the presumption of an overall trade-off between redistribution or insurance (on the one hand) and growth (on the other) has come to be questioned. (Ravallion, 2003)

Claims in favor of unconditional cash transfers overlap to a certain extent with claims for so-called conditional cash transfers. Currently, the latter are the type in vogue, though the distinction is not as sharp as is sometimes depicted. One reason is that in some cases policymakers and their advisers use conditionality as a political device to legitimize the transfer with middle-class voters and financial agencies.[3] In practice too, the difficulty and costs of implementing the criteria used for identifying beneficiaries can lead to merely token or discretionay application of the formal conditions. This has been the case of the state old-age pension in South Africa, which has been a celebrated success in redistributing income and boosting local small-scale economic activities.

Nevertheless, when commentators talk about conditional cash transfers they usually, at present, mean a selectivity device that goes beyond conventional means-testing. The most well-known is the requirement that recipients should send their children to school. This is a form of paternalism, but it is a modest one given that society usually has a constitutional commitment to ensure that children are enrolled in and attend school. Other forms of conditionality are harder to rationalize on ethical or freedom-enhancement grounds.

It is a contention guiding this chapter that the growing interest in conditional cash transfers as an aid and development tool will lead to a realization that most forms of selectivity and conditionality are conveniences at best while being costly, inequitable, inefficient and offensive to basic egalitarian principle. Nevertheless, the current phase of policy development is promising because experimentation with conditional cash transfers is proving that they can and do have a beneficial development role. We will returen to unconditional, universal income transfers later.

Cash Transfers in Emergency and Development Aid

Whatever the claims and counter-claims, support for providing the poor and disadvantaged with straightforward cash grants has taken off. Examples of experimental schemes are multiplying. Their advantages include speed, transparency and the ability to allow those in need to make choices about how they spend the aid, thereby enabling them to retain a greater sense of dignity in times of crisis (Creti and Jaspars, 2006).

Based on experience in Africa, Asia and Latin America, Oxfam has issued guidelines for such schemes, recognizing that they are particularly appropriate for socio-economic crises where local purchasing power has been wiped out while food and other basic goods are potentially available.

They also have low administrative costs. As a World Bank study on Colombia's experience with cash transfers concluded:

> The cost of SISBEN design and application has been modest in absolute terms (about US$0.21 per person in the registry, US$0.52 per beneficiary), and relative to the total amount of resources that have been targeted with SISBEN. It has been estimated that to target US$100 dollars to a beneficiary costs less than US$70 cents. For some programs, such as the Conditional Cash Transfer (CCT-Familias en Acción), the cost of SISBEN is about 0.5 percent of the total cost of the program (assuming this is the only program using SISBEN). (Castañeda, 2003).

A cash transfer scheme that has been carefully evaluated is the Cash for Relief Programme (CfR) in Ethiopia. One of its primary objectives was to enable households hit by crop failure to rebuild their assets. The evaluation for the primary funders of the scheme, the US Agency for International Development (USAID), found that the cash grants had been very successful in regenerating livelihoods (Brandsetter, 2004). Rather than merely consume (which would have been likely with food aid alone), the recipients had controlled debts and invested in restoring land productivity. The donors found that cash grants "allowed individuals and communities to begin making a series of decisions, giving them the power to prioritize needs for their families and presenting them with a creative way to receive relief assistance with dignity" (USAID, 2004).

An evaluation carried out for Save the Children, a UK-based NGO, of the Meket Livelihood Development Pilot Project, involving cash transfers provided in two areas of Ethiopia in 2001–2004, found that the cost of implementing the scheme was much less than the equivalent for food-aid schemes (Kebede, 2005). The latter also had substantial transaction costs for beneficiaries (which are rarely taken into account in monitoring and evaluation analyses), including time spent waiting for deliveries and sharing out food as well as the work involved in loading and transporting the aid.

By contrast, cash transfers allowed the beneficiaries to make strategic choices for themselves. The evaluation observed that not only did the cash transfers allow households to build up assets, notably through the acquisition of livestock, but they also enabled many households to reduce distress renting out of land. Indeed, among the benefits were that they enabled recipients to obtain higher crop prices, partly because they were able to sell when prices were more favorable, rather than when they were desperate for cash. This is a classic advantage of basic economic security. They also helped some recipients to pay off debts, other to pool savings in an *equb* (group saving scheme) and others to buy seeds, sheep or goats, thereby enabling them to work.

Evaluations of several other cash relief projects in Ethiopia implemented by Save the Children in response to food crises have concluded that they too have functioned efficiently, proved more cost-effective than food aid and had no inflationary effect (Gebre-Selassie and Beshah, 2003; Save the Children UK, 2004; Knox-Peebles, 2001). Successful cash relief programs have also been implemented in north-eastern Somalia (the Emergency Cash Relief Program), and in two districts of Zambia (the polot Kalomo Social Cash Transfer Scheme) initiated by the Zambian Government with financial support from the German development agency GTZ.

Those operating the Zambian scheme, which focused on very poor households with little access to paid work, have claimed that the money was spent on basic consumption goods and education and healthcare for family members (Schubert, 2005). In other words, people were able to spend such cash transfers rationally and for their own longer-term welfare. A majority of the beneficiary households were headed by elderly persons or women, about half of the households were AIDS-affected, and nearly half contained orphans. As with other schemes of this sort, it was evident that when women, rather than men, controlled the transfers they were more likely to spend a large part of them on their children and their family.

The Zambian scheme had a more general message. It has been estimated that if it were scaled up to reach the poorest 10% of all Zambian households the cost would amount to merely 5% of the total overseas aid to the country, or about 0.5% of its Gross National Income. In other words, a national scheme is financially feasible. It would be much cheaper than the country's food aid, and would have the advantage of going directly to the poor and vulnerable, without the high administative costs and various forms of corruption associated with commodity-based schemes. And whereas food aid damages local food markets by deterring local producers, cash transfers would do the opposite by helping to stimulate local markets. In Zambia, no less that 70% of all social transfers are spent on locally produced goods and services, thus generating local employment or livelihoods (DFID, 2005; Samson et al., 2006).

The Zambian, Ethiopian and Somalian cash transfer experiences offer encouraging evidence that they are affordable and are conducive to livelihood revival in chronically poor areas. Of course, in times of emergency, cash grants should not be seen as pure alternatives to other forms of commodity-based aid. Such transfers might be inflationary if local food supplies were not available. In the initial aftermath of a disaster, particularly a quick-onset disaster, food aid may need to complement cash transfers, to restrain inflationary pressures. Direct commodity aid can then be gradually phased out as local producers respond to the increased demand for staple goods and services. However, cash transfers may need complementary programs designed to boost local supply, as was found to be the case following the Mozambique floods in 2000.

Under this scheme, which was implemented by the private sector, USAID funded cash grants of about US$92 for 106,280 flood-local goods and services, which stimulated the local economy, regenerating livelihoods in a sustainable way (Abt Associates, 2002; Christie and Hanlon, 2001; Hanlon, 2004).

Among the growing number of schemes launched outside Africa as part of emergency and rehabilitation programs funded by foreign donors is the Cash for Herder scheme in Mongolia, implemented by the Swiss Agency for Development and Cooperation (SDC) and the Red Cross in 2002–2003. The evalution two years later found that while another in-kind project that they had operated was "appreciated" by recipients, it had not helped regenerate the local economy, whereas the cash transfer had led to investment in assets that regenerated livelihoods. The evaluation concluded,

> The cash approach made use of the creativity and experience of beneficiary families to develop strategies out of their crisis . . . [It] showed that poor people and people under severe economic stress are very well capable to handle cash responsibly and develop and take strategic decisions on what to spend the money in order to improve the livelihood and their families in the medium and long term . . . most important, beneficiaries do become economic and social actors in their own community again, taking their dicisions on how to spend the money. (SDC-IFRC, 2005).

The evaluation found additional advantages, in that "the response and preparation time" was short, and administrative overheads were low. By 2005, the SDC had implemented 13 cash grant projects of this type in eight countries.

Tellingly, the growing legitimacy of simple cash transfers was reflected in the Group of Eight Statement of 2004, which, when referring to the internatinoal response to famines, made the commitment, "we will unleash the power of markets through cash-for-work and cash-for-relief programs" (G8 Statement, 2004). The scope for cash transfers in Africa and Asia is thus recognized as part of the armoury of aid and humanitarian responses to poverty and insecurity. Meanwhile, in Latin America, cash transfers have become a central part of social and development policy.

Incomes for School Attendance and Child Benefits

One form of conditional cash transfer that has become enormously popular in the past decade or so is a monthly sum of money paid to families, or more usually to mothers, on condition that their children attend school. The main claim is that incomes for school attendance lower the poverty and economic insecurity of women and lower child poverty. It is hard to dispute this. By the same token, it is claimed that they reduce child malnutrition, as well as promote child school enrolment and school attendance. Such schemes are obviously less paternalistic than food parcels and food aid, or other commodity-based forms of transfer to the poor. They are also a means of redistributing income that is relatively easily legitimized among the middle class and "median voters."

Critics argue that, by focusing only on school-age children these schemes neglect families with children under the age of seven, the group most at risk of ill-health due to malnutrition and impoverishment. There are also claims that they discourage female labor force participation, and that they involve high administrative costs, particularly as they are means-tested.

These criticisms have been swept aside for the moment. Country after country has opted for this policy. The main examples are in Central and South America, starting in Mexico, where the original Progresa (literally "progressing") scheme, introduced in 1992, has evolved into the Oportunidades scheme.[4] Progresa was supposed to support school-age children in poor households in marginalized rural communities, but in 2002 Oportunidades extended that aid to other rural and urban areas.

The Mexican scheme has evolved into a complex mechanism of social engineering. The cash transfer consists of three components – a household nutrition allowance, a schooling subsidy for each school-age child that rises in amount by grade and that is higher for girls of secondary-school age, and an annual payment to cover the cost of books and uniforms. To complete the social engineering function, the amount of cash transfer that any household can receive is capped, one intention being to avoid giving families an incentive to have more children, another being to reduce what the policymakers think might be benefit dependence. To receive the transfers, children must maintain a school attendance record of 85%, while mothers and children must have regular medical checks and parents must attend parenting classes.

The targeting takes place via a two-stage process. First, poor geographical areas are identified and then poorer households in those areas are identified on the basis of a proxy index of poverty (using indicators of housing, health, and schooling). As a result of this procedure, about three million Mexican households are reached at any one time.

Although awkward questions remain about the efficiency and equity of the selectivity process, Progresa has been legitimized. It is been shown to be less expensive to distribute than food aid (Gertler, 2005). Above all, it has been shown to have reduced poverty in recipient households and to have resulted in increased school enrolment and attendance, as well as improved health in beneficiary households (Skoufias, 2001). Oportunidades can be expected to do much the same. In short, the Mexican scheme has become a central part of the country's social protection system.

The other major example is Brazil's Bolsa Família ("family stipend"), the flagship of the country's cash transfer schemes, which undoubtedly contributed to President Lula's re-election in October 2006. It evolved from a series of localized schemes introduced in urban areas during the 1990s. Among the precursors were the PETI (Programme for the Eradication of Child Labour), introduced in 1996 in coalmining areas, then sugar cane and sisal production areas, and subsequently extended to all areas in 1999. Various forms of Bolsa Escola ("school stipend") and Renda Minima ("minimum income") schemes spread in the late 1990s; these became a federal program in 2001, which reached over 8 million children in 5 million households by 2003. In 2004, four income transfer schemes, including the Bolsa Escola, were consolidated into the Bolsa Família.

This became a central part of the Lula Government's Zero Fome ("Zero Hunger") campaign, and has been seen as a way of reducing the country's enormous income inequality. It has also unified a variety of more paternalistic and selective schemes, such as the gas allowance and school stipends. An intention has been to break the inter-generational transfer of poverty by conditioning access to the transfers on key human development objectives (schooling, nutrition and health). It is also seen as a means of "empowering" women, giving them more bargaining power in their households and enabling them to make decisions on their children's education and on their own work.

By 2006, the Bolsa Família was reaching over 11 million households living below the official poverty line, or over 44 million people. The scheme is nominally means-tested, with the transfer amount being determined by number of children in the household. Autonomy is granted in the sense that recipients can choose how to spend the money, but the conditionalities ("incentives") are restraining, and include school attendance by children aged 5–15, anti-natal classes for pregnant women, and vaccination for children under the age of seven.

The Bolsa Família has generated enormous global interest. Although a comprehensive evaluation by the Ministry of Social Development had yet to be completed at the time of writing, the scheme has been particularly beneficial for those lacking access to income-earning employment. Already there have been a series of evaluations and monitoring research projects. Some have been critical, but most have been favorable (see Britto, 2005; Fonseca, 2006, inter alia). The consensus is that the cash transfers have reduced female poverty, increased school attendance and learning performance in school, and apparently led to increased rather than decreased femal labor force participation. Indeed, one study of the earlier scheme concluded, "instead of the expected negative correlation between Bolsa Escola and work, we find the opposite: those receiving the stipend are the ones that work more" (Schwartzman, 2005).

The effect on child labor is more nuanced, since cash transfers seem to have resulted in children doing fewer hours of labor but not necessarily stopping altogether (Cardoso and Souza, 2003; Rocha, 2000). This is partly because prohibiting child labor is not a formal part of the program. Child labor has continued to play a significant role in the subsistence survival of poor households in rural areas and urban slums, accounting for over 20% if family income in about a third of all families. The stipend is too modest to displace that contribution.

The Brazilian scheme is well-established, in spite of criticisms of its design. In Latin America, at least, it seems the way to move cash transfers up the policy ladder. Other schemes similar in type to Progresa and Bolsa Família are Colombia's Familias en Acción, Honduras's Programa de Asignación Familiar (PRAF), Jamaica's Program of Advancement through Health and Education (PATH) and Nicaragua's Red de Protección Social (RPS), which predated the Brazilian model by becoming operational in 2000. There is also growing interest outside Latin America and the Caribbean, the beacon being Bangladesh's Cash for Education scheme. In early 2008, the Indian Government was considering the Bolsa Família as an alternative to its wasteful food subsidies.

To what extent does this type of scheme satisfy the Policy Decision Principles enunciated earlier? As operated in Mexico and Brazil, one cannot pretend that the policy is not paternalistic. Probably most observers would accept that it is desirable to impose conditions that benefit children, and would be satisfied with that as long as the scheme did not put families into some kind of poverty trop. However, the Mexican scheme does seem to go much further, and raises questions about the possibility of excessive bureaucratic intervention in family life of an intrusive kind that could lead to stigma and even non-application for the cash transfer. To the extent that there is a political commitment to weaken the conditionality rather than to increase it, Brazil's less intrusive Bolsa Família scores rather better on the Paternalism Test.

As far as the Security Difference Principle is concerned, the very complexity of Mexico's targeting procedure must raise questions about horizontal efficiency and the omission of many of the poorest households. There could also be a poverty trap if households lose entitlement to the benefit if they move out of poverty, thus discouraging work and modest social mobility. More evidence is needed on this.

As far as targeting is concerned, research has suggested that the Progresa in Mexico was quite effective in reaching very poor households in very poor areas, but was less effective in reaching the "moderately poor" (Skoufias, 2001: 43). To that extent, it could be said to have satisfied the Security Difference Principle in being horizontally efficient. But in all schemes of this type, conspicuously excluded from coverage are households with only pre-school age children and all impoverished households without any children, as well as orphans and others living outside family households altogether. It cannot be claimed that the targeting reaches the most impoverished in society.

Moreover, in both Nicaragua and Mexico, about 20% of the cash transfer beneficiaries were non-poor (Coady, Grosh and Hoddinnott, 2004). In Bangladesh, where targeting has been much weaker, about 40% of beneficiaries have been found to be non-poor. Given that targeting is supposed to exclude the non-poor, this suggests that none of the schemes has been very successful on its own criterion. Whether or not they should be concerned to achieve such "efficiency" is another matter.

Cash transfer schemes of this type also depend on a sophisticated and up-to-date registration system. Unregistered households cannot obtain benefits, which is likely to result in the denial of benefits to a great many families that are poor and economically insecure. In addition, the economically insecure tend to have incomes that fluctuate above and below any imaginable poverty line, making it a bit of a lottery whether or not they manage to qualify.

To succeed in its broader social aims, this type of conditional income scheme depends on there being adequate local schooling and health and transport infrastructure. In urban areas of Latin America and the Caribbean, these may exist to a sufficient degree. In rural areas of those countries, and in large parts of Africa and Asia, the imposition of school-attendance and clinic-attendance conditions may impose onerous burdens on poor households, and actually hit the very poor more than anybody else.

Even in Latin America, the desirability of the extensive conditionality imposed by these schemes has been called into question, which may prompt policymakers to conclude that a move towards less conditionality would be a more efficient and equitable way to go. The complexity of requiring potential beneficiaries to prove they are poor and vulnerable, and to demonstrate regular attendance at schools and clinics (or to prove that they had a valid reason for not doing so) is surely off-putting for people cowed by poverty and chronic insecurity. It is also expensive in administrative time and paperwork (Ayala Consulting, 2003).

The biggest question is one at the heart of all debates on social protection in the twenty-first century. Are all the conditions necessary if the objective is to promote human development and if those conditions simply require people to do what is in their best interest? Obliging a mother to send a child to school might seem obviously beneficial, but the pressure to do so – and the fear of income loss if she does not – may lead to the perverse outcome of a mother sending a sick child to school, to the longer-term detriment of the child and the family. One can think of many other personal circumstances that should cause disquiet.

The fact is that the imposition of conditions for entitlement presumes that a poor person is irrational or incapable of learning, does not know his or her long-term interests, lacks information or cannot or would not act in the child's longer-term interest because of some impediment. Dealing with those issues directly would surely be more effective than imposing behavioral conditions that eat up public resources in administering them, while perhaps ignoring the structural factors that impede seemingly rational behavior. Even in the case of children, one cannot accept state paternalism uncritically.

This concern is one that may come to preoccupy the second-generation reformers as assessments of income-for-school-attendance schemes unfold. What is clear is that they are perfectly compatible with more independent economic activity. The Dignified Work Principle seems to be supported by the fact that women's labor force participation has been boosted by such schemes, contrary to claims that cash transfers foster dependency.

Social Pensions

If Latin America has been the continent leading the way with cash transfers for the young, Africa has been the region where non-contributory cash transfers at the other end of the age spectrum have been gaining most ground.

With global ageing and the social dislocation of families that is pushing more elderly people out of family-based support networks, support for social pensions has grown. Many developing countries have some sort of means-tested state pension, but more interesting is the non-means-tested variety, that is, a basic universal state pension provided to all citizens above a certain age without prior conditions, such as a record of contributions, being required to gain entitlement.[5] It is sometimes depicted as a primary pillar of a multi-pillar pension sysytem. The interest arises not just because it offers the prospect of cutting old-age poverty quite dramatically but because it may be a producitve investment as well, directly and indirectly boosting dignified work and livelihoods.

It seems ironic that social pensions have been pioneered in a few developing countries where poverty and inequality are rife and where many economists would say there are not the resources available to pay for such schemes. Variants exist in South Africa, Namibia, Nepal and Mauritius, where the amount paid rises with the age of the pensioner, and Botswana, Bolivia, Samoa, rural areas of Brazil and Lesotho, which introduced it in 2004 for those over the age of 70. The NOAPS in India (National Old Age Pension Scheme) is tending towards being a social pension as well, albeit giving a very small amount and with notorious inefficiency. Chile has also recently introduced such a scheme. In addition, by 2007, over 30 developing countries and transition countries were operating means-tested, non-contributory pensions (Johnson and Williamson, 2006).

Besides enhancing old-age income security, social pensions are potentially significant instruments for influencing the patterns of work and labor in society. The primary claim in favor of the non-means-tested variant is that it is universal and rights-based – all citizens above a certain age are entitled to receive a monthly cash transfer. Advocates point out that social pensions reduce old-age poverty better than any alternative, are redistributive, affordable and transparent, while having very low administrative costs. They typically account for a very small percentage of GDP; in Costa Rica, for example, they took only 0.3% in 1999, and in Zimbabwe only 0.1% (Coady, Grosh and Hoddinott, 2004; Munro, 2003). Another strong empirical finding is that the South African pension has been the only successful redistributive social policy in the post-apartheid era (Case and Deaton, 1998).

It is still often claimed that social pensions are costly precisely because they are universal. The main response to that is that by being universal they reach nearly all the elderly, and do so remarkably cheaply. It falls to Namibia to have the simplest and most efficient social pension, operated via an electronic card and biometric identification of claimants. Each month, vans go to the numerous villages and urban payment spots, each van containing cash-dispensing machines and computers. The pensioners (or designated surrogates if the pensioner is too ill or frail to go) present their cards at the van and are paid the equivalent of US$30 (as of 2006). The take-up rate is close to 90%, which is remarkably high by comparison with all other pension schemes in developing countries, and is higher than any means-tested scheme operating anywhere.

The scheme in Namibia is administered by a private company on contract to the Government. The costs are equivalent to about 30 US cents per person per month, also remarkably low by comparison with other systems. To counter the possibility of fraudulent claims made on behalf of dead people, the authorities ingeniously introduced a burial insurance scheme within the pension; the pensioner, on registering to receive the pension, takes out a mandatory life insurance, whereby funeral costs are covered when he or she dies; application for the burial funds enables the authorities to cancel the card at the same time. Given the symbolic significance of decent burials and their cost, the insurance scheme has been found to be very successful in all respects.

Also remarkable is the effect on work and livelihoods. Social pensions have helped preserve family structures, enabled grandparents to pay for the schooling of grandchildren, paid for the case of family memebers suffering from HIV/AIDS, made the elderly creditworthy and promoted sustainable livelihoods, particularly in rural areas.

Too many economists have failed to appreciate that social pensions are productive. They have forgotten a lesson from European history, which is that old-age security acted as a powerful force in modernizing agriculture, precisely because it led to more risk-taking innovation. It is also been shown to do so in rural areas of Brazil. As one study concluded, "the regularity, certainty and liquidity of pension benefits meant that they played a key role in shifting households from subsistence to surplus agriculture" (Barrientos and Lloyd-Sherlock, 2002: 17).[6]

Besides its consistency with the Dignified Work Principle, the social pension is likely to satisfy the Security Difference Principle if it takes the non-means-tested form. Being universalistic, it should reach all the poor in the relevant age group. It is also paid to individuals rather than households, thus satisfying a universalistic concern. It is non-paternalistic, in that it allows the beneficiary to spend on what he or she chooses; and it is granted as a right rather than a discretionary matter of charity. In brief, it is a feasible first step in the direction of a universal right to income security.

The debate on whether a basic state pension should be universalistic or means-tested is rumbling on, but the signs are that the universalistic variant is gaining ground. In 2007, South Africa was just one country in which the pressure was growing to end the residual use of means-testing in its social pension. There and elsewhere in Africa, the IMF and other financial agencies have been trying to move governments in the other direction – including Namibia. But the evidence that this would be sensible from and equity or efficiency point of view is simply not there.

Disability Grants

Disability grants are another form of targeted, selective income transfer. Here we will deal with a particular variant, as introduced in southern Africa, in Mauritius, Mozambique, Namibia and South Africa. This is an income transfer that is both means-tested and work-tested. As operated in the region, it is proving disastrous.

Under the South African scheme, a permanent grant is supposed to be available to anyone with a disability that is expected to last for more than a year; a temporary grant is supposed to be given to anyone with a recognized disability expected to last between six and twelve months. If a person deemed disabled is below the age of 18, they can obtain a care dependency grant instead. Access to the grant is based on a complex means test, based on an assets value test and an earned income test; there is also a joint assets test, since for married couples the joint assets must be less than a designated amount. But the conditionality does not stop there, because the scheme also requires applicants to demonstrate a medical condition and an incapacity ot work. It is this cocktail of tests that is a recipe for social disaster.

In Namibia, although the social pension (a Basic Income for the elderly) has been the pillar propping up many small communities, a disability grant modelled on the South African scheme has been growing in significance in the context of the HIV/AIDS pandemic. The disability grant has already become Namibia's second most prevalent income support mechanism, part of an evolving system of selective, targeted cash transfers that also includes three family benefits – the foster parent grant, the child maintenance grant and the orphan's grant. So far, only a few households are receiving any of these family benefits, which are means-tested, and thus involve poverty traps and the conventional moral hazards that come with all means-tested schemes.

It is thus not surprising that the means-tested disability grant reaches no more than about 20% of all those who should be reached, according to Namibian census figures for the number of people suffering from a chronic physical or mental impairment.[7] It is moot whether it reaches many AIDS victims who become disabled as the sickness intensifies. If it does not reach them, the danger is that anti-retroviral (ARV) treatment will fail since unless a person can eat reasonably well the medication will not work. However, if the grant were to reach a large proportion of AIDS victims the fiscal cost would be large.

The immediate problem, however, is the conditionality attached to the disability grant. To be entitled, a person must obtain a doctor's certificate stating that he or she is not only disabled but is also unable to work in income-earning activity. The rule has been that those with a CD4 count – a measurement of the body's immunity – below a value of 200 are entitled to a temporary disability grant, if they pass those means tests. They are supposed to de-register if their CD4 count improves to above 200 due to anti-retrovirals. Because of this, coupled with the nature of the ARV rollout, in Namibia as in South Africa, a bizarre *sickness poverty trap* has been created.

In those areas where the rollout of ARVs is operating thus far, if an AIDS victim is sufficiently sick, he or she qualifies for treatment. Most of the recipients are wretchedly poor. So, it should not be surprising that two tendencies have emerged. Some of those receiving ARVs have been sharing their pills with relatives and friends who are not quite sick enough to qualify. Taking half the dose does not slow down the rate of recovery from the disease; it makes the treatment ineffectual and may build up drug resistance. Other ARV recipients have been prone to go one stage further – they have been selling the pills. In Namibia, some have been selling them over the border in Angola. The need for food to survive in the short term overrides the need for health to survive in the longer term. Thus, the ARV rollout is likely to fail because it is not linked to income security.

Second, the work capacity test for eligibility for the disability grant is creating a unique moral hazard. If the ARV treatment begins to improve the physical and social condition of the patient, so the capacity to work improves. And if it does, the patient will lose entitlement to the benefit. Already, in Namibia and in South Africa, there are credible anecdotal reports that people are stopping ARV treatment in order to push themselves back below the physical capacity-for-work level, for fear of losing the grant.[8] According to the Treatment Action Campaign in South Africa, which has been advocating a Universal Basic Income instead, there have been many instances in which patients have simply refused treatment for fear of losing their disability grant.

Furthermore, there are fears that the yo-yo effect, in which sick individuals take treatment for a while, see their health improve slightly, stop treatment until it worsens, start again, stop again, and so on, is contributing to the development of treatment-resistant strains of the disease.

Thus the disability grant as it has operated in South Africa and Namibia must rank as one of the worst designed cash transfer schemes in the world. It is unlikely to satisfy any of the policy principles outlined earlier. It is a classic case of how a combination of means-testing and behavior testing can achieve precisely the opposite of what policymakers intend. Surely, enough is known to scrap the work test and the means test in disability grants.

By contrast, in the early 1990s following Mozambique's civil war, the Government introduced a simple unconditional cash transfer scheme for those disabled or displaced known as GAPVU, or "cash payments to war-displaced urban destitute households program." This reached about 16% of urban households, and raised average household incomes by as much as 40%, significantly reducing poverty (Devereux et al., 2005; DFID, 2005; Samson et al., 2006). It also helped boost small-scale employment and the livelihoods of the urban poor, having a notable effect on food production and trading activity. The scheme had a means test, but the authorities largely ignored it, which contributed to the program's success.

Concluding Remarks

Industrialized affluent countries have responded to the challenge posed by globalization to the traditional social insurance model – fragmentation of family structures, decline of full-time stable jobs, the changing nature of risk exposure and so on – with a mix of means-testing and behavior testing, coupled with a drift towards social therapy. Yet there is a counter-movement led by what is happening in developing countries, where the baggage of twentieth-century social security is light. The industrial labor model clearly does not apply; most people, as workers, are outside the "formal" wage labor system; and, most importantly, the range of risks to which most people are exposed does not correspond to the simple contingency risks that underpinned welfare state development.

In particular, communities and individuals are exposed much more to systemic or co-variant risk. It is absurdly arbitrary to make sharp distinctions between the deserving and undeserving in contexts where brute ill-luck and chronic uncertainty are the undeniable realities. Emergencies, shock, crises – all force those involved in shaping policy and reacting to events to abandon old prejudices and look to what works.

What does that mean? Ultimately, it means not just having food at the end of some dusty road, but being able to develop sustainable livelihoods in viable communities based on functioning systems of social solidarity. That lesson is being re-learned, posing awkward questions to those wedded to selectivity, targeting and conditionality.

A principal claim in favor of unconditional cash transfers is that, being universal, they are socially just. They are non-laborist, in that they do not presume that some forms of work are deserving of income support and others are not. By making all forms of work equally deserving, they help to promote work, and allow individuals to make choices between types of work more easily. For that reason, among others, universal cash transfers favor women relative to many other forms of social security because each individual receives an individual transfer and because those doing nonwage work, such as child care or care for the elderly, are not penalized.

Because a universal, unconditional cash transfer is granted as a citizensip right, it would enhance full freedom. It would also strengthen the bargaining position of disadvantaged groups, whose members usually have to accept degrading working conditons and low wages because they are desperate. From an economic point of view, it would shift money into the hands of those most likely to spend on locally produced goods and services, thus helping to boost local demand and employment.

Compared with means-tested social assistance and social insurance schemes, a universal cash transfer would remove the infamous poverty trap, whereby someone who raises their earned income just above the threshold used to determine eligibility for the cash transfer loses all benefit, and the related unemployment trap. As such, it would immeasurably reduce the incidence of moral hazards and immoral hazards.

There is another reason for thinking that sooner or later Universal Basic Income security will emerge as the sensible and equitable objective from experience with targeted, conditional cash transfers. Surveys in many countries have found that strong majorities of people believe that everybody should have Basic Income security as right (ILO, 2004: ch. 13).

Apart from the moral and political arguments, there are good economic and social reasons for moving towards a situation of basic economic security. Universal schemes of security are fundamentally market neutral, that is, they do not introduce market distortions and, therefore, have relatively little effect on competitiveness. Unlike means-tested social assistance, universalistic schemes do not introduce negative incentives to dissave (which would merely store up economic vulnerability), and there is no tendency to reward "labor" relative to other forms of work.

At the same time, experience of cash transfer schemes has shown that far from breeding dependency and passivity, they foster independence and activity. Thus, one study, drawing on data from various surveys conducted by Statistics South Africa (the official agency for national statistics), showed that the country's old-age pension, the Child Support Grant and the Disability Grant, all helped to raise labor force participation and employment (Samson et al., 2004).

Moreover, universal security schemes are administratively simple and low-cost. There is relatively little scope for bureaucratic abuse, discretion or petty corruption. The benefits are non-stigmatizing and, being universal, they help strengthen social solidarity, reinforcing community and social cohesion.

The cost of cash transfers is not the primary issue, since even poor countries could afford modest schemes, and most could do so if more aid were diverted to that end. In a simulation study, the UN Development Program found that cash transfers targeting all rural children rather than all identifiably poor children would have a greater poverty reduction effect for an allocation of just 0.5% of GDP (Kakwani, Soares and Son, 2005). The study reckoned that cash transfers to achieve an income of 40% of the poverty line would cost 5% of GDP for the Ivory Coast and more for some other African countries. But even small cash transfers would have a big effect in reducing poverty in all the 15 countries studied.

Other simulation studies have found that in countries such as Namibia and South Africa a modest Basic Income as a monthly grant would be affordable, and at least one government committee in South Africa has recommended its introduction.[9] Cash grants were also proposed as a response to the Indian Ocean tsunami and for the aftermath of the invasion and occupation of Iraq. In the case of the post-tsunami recovery phase, the Swiss Agency for Development and Cooperation actually implemented such a scheme, with apparent success.

For many years, critics held sway in debates on cash transfers. Now conditional cash transfers are legitimized. But the flaws of all forms of targeting selectivity and conditionality, as well as their unnecessary cost, are making more people question the need for them. What we can say is that only universalistic transfers would satisfy all the Policy Decision Principles enunciated earlier and that where they have been tried, including in some of the world's poorest countries, such transfers have proved an effective means to combat poverty and income insecurity while promoting livilihoods and work.

At the time of writing, a small pilot scheme had just been launched in a rural area of Namibia that will give all residents aged 0 to 60 a Guaranteed Basic Income transfer each month for two years, along the lines of the social pension already received by those over 60.[10] It is being carefully monitored and the outcomes will be carefully evaluated. The evidence should speak.

Notes

1. See, for example, ILO (2004). The writer was principal author of that report, which drew on extensive empirical work cited in it. See also, Standing (2002).
2. A series of People's Security Surveys in Africa and Asia found that it was the near-poor who were more likely to be aware of such schemes and more likely to benefit from them compared with the poor or destitute (ILO, 2004).
3. This was a common theme among early advocates of the Bolsa Escola and Renda Minima schemes in Brazil.
4. The original scheme was called the program for education, health and nutrition, symbolizing its multiple objectives.
5. For one review of these, see Palacios and Sluchynsky (2006).
6. See also Barrientos et al. (2003).
7. For a review of the evidence, see Standing (2006).
8. On the situation in South Africa, see Nattrass (2006a; 2006b).
9. See, for example, the papers in Standing and Samson (2004) and Taylor Committee (2002).
10. For details, see http://www.bignam.org/BIG_pilot.html.

References

Abt Associates Inc. (2002). Mozambique 1999–2000 Floods Impact Evalution: Resettlement Grant Activity; Emergency Recovery: Agriculture and Commercial Trade (ER: ACT). *Agricultural Policy Development Project (APD)*. US Agency for International Development (USAID), Washington, DC.

Atkinson, A.B. (1995). On Targeting and Family Benefits. In A.B. Atkinson (ed.) *Incomes and the Welfare State: Essays on Britain and Europe*. Cambridge University Press, Cambridge.

Ayala Consulting (2003). Workshop on Conditional Cash Transfer Programmes (CCTs): Operational Experiences. Ayala Consulting, Quito.

Barrett, C. and Clay, D. (2003). How Accurate is Food-for-Work Self-Targeting Accuracy in the Presence of Imperfect Factor Markets? Evidence From Ethiopia. *Journal of Development Studies*, 39 (5), 152–180.

Barrett, C., Holden, S., and Clay, D. (2002). Can Food-for-Work Programmes Reduce Vulnerability? WIDER Discussion Paper 2002/24. UNU-WIDER, Helsinki.

Barrientos, A. and Lloyd-Sherlock, P. (2002). Non-Contributory Pensions and Social Protection, Discussion paper no. 12, Issues in Social Protection. ILO, Geneva.

Barrientos, A. et al. (2003). Non-Contributory Pensions and Poverty Prevention: A Comparative Study of Brazil and South Africa. Final Report of DFID Project R787. Pensions and Poverty Prevention. Institute of Development and Policy Management (IDPM) and HelpAge International, Manchester.

Brandsetter, R.H. (2004). Evaluation of OFDA Cash for Relief Intervention in Ethiopia. Report prepared for USAID/OFDA. USAID/OFDA, Washington, DC.

Britto, T. (2005). *Recent Trends in the Development Agenda of Latin America: An Analysis of Conditional Cash Transfers.* Institute for Development Policy and Management (IDPM), Manchester.

Cardoso, E. and Portela Souza, A. (1998). The Impact of Cash Transfers on Child Labour and School Attendance in Brazil, University of Sao Paulo Working Paper, Sao Paulo.

Case, A. and Deaton, A. (1998). Large Cash Transfers to the Elderly in South Africa. *The Economic Journal*, 108 (450), 1330–1361.

Castañeda, T. (2003). *Targeting Social Spending to the Poor With Proxy-Means Testing: Colombia's SISBEN System.* World Bank, Washington, DC.

Christie, F. and Hanlon, J. (2001). *Mozambique and the Great Flood of 2000.* The International African Institute in association with James Currey. Oxford and Indiana University Press, Bloomington and Indianapolis.

Clert, C. and Woden, Q. (2001). The Targeting of Government Programs in Chile. In E. Gacitua-Mario and Q. Woden (eds) *Measurement and Meaning: Combining Quantitative and Qualitative Methods for the Analysis of Poverty and Social Exclusion in Latin America.* World Band Technical Paper 518. World Bank, Washington, DC.

Coady, D., Grosh, M., and Hoddinnott, J. (2004). *Targeting of Transfers in Developing Countries: Review of Lessons and Experience.* World Bank, Washington, DC.

Creti, P. and Jaspars, S. (eds) (2006). *Cash-Transfer Programming in Emergencies.* Oxfam, London.

Department for International Development (DFID) (2005). *Social Transfers and Chronic Poverty: Emerging Evidence and the Challenge Ahead.* Department for International Development, London.

Department Researchers Network (2003). *Assistance to the Transitional Authority of the Islamic State of Afghanistan to Elaborate Policy Guidance Regarding Food Aid Utilisation in Afghanistan.* Development Researchers Network, London.

Devereux, S., Marshall, J., MacAskill, J. et al. (2005). Making Cash Count: Lessons From Cash Transfer Schemes in East and Southern Africa for Supporting the Most Vulnerable Children and Households. Save the Children UK. HelpAge International and Institute of Development Studies, Brighton and Sussex.

Fonseca, A. (2006). *Programas de Transferencia de Ingresos en una Perspectiva Internacional: Características y Desafíos.* UNDP, New York.

Gebre-Selassie, S. and Beshah, T. (2003). Evaluation of Cash for Relief Project in South and North Wollo Zones of the Amhara National Regional State, Ethiopia. Ethiopian Economic Research Institute and Ethiopian Economic Policy Research Institute, Addis Ababa.

Gertler, P. (2005). The Impact of Conditional Cash Transfers on Human Development Outcomes: A Review of Evidence From PROGRESA in Mexico and Some Implications for Policy Debates in South and Southern Africa. Paper presented to Southern African Regional Policy Network, January 27, 2005, Pretoria.

Group of Eight (G-8) (2004). Statement on Ending Famine in Horn of Africa. http://www.g8.utoronto.ca/summit/2004seaisland/famine.html.

Hanlon, J. (2004). It is Possible to Just Give Money to the Poor. *Development and Change*, 35 (2), 375–383.

ILO (2004). *Economic Security for a Better World.* Socio-Economic Security Programme, ILO, Geneva.

Johnson, K.M. and Williamson, J.B. (2006). Do Universal Non-Contributory Old-Age Pensions Make Sense for Rural Areas in Low Income Countries? *International Social Security Review*, 59 (5), 47–65.

Kakwani, N., Soares, F.V., and Son, H. (2005). Conditional Cash Transfers in African Countries, Working Paper 9. UNDP International Poverty Centre, Brasilia.

Kebede, E. (2005). Breading the Poverty Cycle? Cash Dstribution and Safety Nets in Ethiopia. Paper presented at meeting organized by Overseas Development Institute and the Great Lakes and East Africa Inter-Agency Emergency and Preparedness Working Group, May 11, 2005, Nairobi.

Knox-Peebles, C. (2001). *Impact Assessment of Save the Children's Cash for Relief Project in Legambo and Meket (Wollo), Ethiopia.* Save the Children, London.

LeJeune, S. (2004). *Rapid Household Economy Assessment: Farchana Refugee Camp, Eastern Chad.* Save the Children, London.

Levine, S. and Chastre, C. (2004). Missing the Point: An Analysis of Food Security Interventions in the Great Lakes. Network Paper 47. Humanitarian Practice Network, London.

Munro, L. (2003). A Social Safety Net for the Chronically Poor? Zimbabwe's Public Assistance in the 1990's. Chronic Poverty Research Centre, University of Manchester, Manchester.

Nattrass, N. (2006a). Trading Off Income and Health: AIDS and the Disability Grant in South Africa. *Journal of Social Policy*, 35 (1), 3–19.

Nattrass, N. (2006b). Disability and Welfare in South Africa's Era of Unemployment and AIDS. Working Paper 147. Centre for Social Science Research, University of Cape Town, Cape Town.

Palacios, R. and Sluchynsky, O. (2006). Social Pensions Part I: Their Role in the Overall Pension System. SP Discussion Paper 601. World Bank, Washington, DC.

Raczynski, D. (1991). La Ficha CAS y la Focalización de los Programas Sociales. *Estudios Cierplan*, 141. La Corporación de Investigaciones Económicas para Latinoamérica, Santiago de Chile.

Ravallion, M. (2003). Targeted Transfers in Poor Countries: Revisiting the Trade-Offs and Policy Options. World Bank Social Protection Discussion Paper Series. World Bank, Washington, DC.

Rawls, J. (1971). *A Theory of Justice.* Harvard University Press, Cambridge, Mass.

Rocha, S. (2000). Applying Minimum Income Programmes in Brazil: Two Case Studies: Belem and Belo Horizonte. Discussion Paper 76. Instituto de Pesquisa Econômica Aplicada (IPEA), Rio de Janeiro.

Samson, M. et al. (2004). *The Social and Economic Impact of South Social Security System.* Report commissioned by the Finance and Economics Directorate. Department of Social Development, Pretoria.

Samson, M., van Niekerk, I., and MacQuene, K. (2006). *Designing and Implementing Social Transfer Programmes.* Economic Policy Research Institute, Cape Town.

Save the Children UK (2004). Cash for Relief 2004: Ethiopia Project Proposal. Unpublished, London.

Schubert, B. (2005). The Pilot Social Cash Transfer Scheme, Kalomo District, Zambia. Chronic Poverty Research Centre Working Paper 52, IDPM/CPRC. Chronic Poverty Research Centre, Manchester.

Schwartzman, S. (2005). Education-Oriented Social Programs in Brazil: The Impact of Bolsa Escola. Paper presented at Global Conference on Education Research in Developing Countries, Global Development Network, March 30–April 2, 2005, Prague.

SDC-IFRC (2005). Joint SDC-IFRC External Review on In-Kind and Cash Distribution Projects in 2003 in Zavkhan Aimag, Mongolia. Swiss Agency for Development and Cooperation and International Federation of the Red Cross and Red Crescent Societies, Bern and Geneva.

Skoufias, E. (2001). *Progresa and its Impact on the Human Capital and Welfare of Households in Rural Mexico: A Synthesis of the Results of an Evaluation by IFPRI.* International Food Policy Research Institute, Washington, DC.

Standing, G. (2002). *Beyond the New Paternalism: Basic Security as Equality.* Verso, London.

Standing, G. (2006). Two Paths to Basic Income Security in Developing Countries: Responding to the Tsunami and to HIV/AIDS. Socio-Economic Security Programme, ILO, Geneva.

Standing, G. (2007). Labour Recommodification in the Global Transformation. In A. Buğra and K. Ağartan (eds) *Re-Reading Polanyi for the 21st Century*. Palgrave Macmillan, New York.

Standing, G. and Samson, M. (eds) (2004). *A Basic Income Grant for South Africa*. University of Cape Town Press, Cape Town.

Tabor, S. (2002). Assisting the Poor With Cash: Design and Implementation of Social Transfer Programs, Social Protection Discussion Paper Series 223. World Bank, Washington, DC.

Taylor Committee (2002). *Transforming the Present, Protecting the Future: Report of the Committeed of Inquiry Into a Comprehensive System of Social Security for South Africa*. Government Printer, Cape Town.

UN (2007). *The Employment Imperative*. Report on the World Social Situation 2007. United Nations, New York.

US Agency for International Development (USAID) (2004). *USAID/OFDA Uses Cash Grants to Alleviate Chronic Food Insecurity in Ethiopia*. USAID, Washington, DC. http://www.usaid.gov/out_work/humanitarian_assistance/disaster_assistance/publications/focus_articles/6_2004_Ethiopia.html.

Chapter 72

Basic Income and the New Class Struggle

Philippe Van Parijs

Originally published as Van Parijs, P. (1987). A Revolution in Class Theory. *Politics & Society*, 15, 453–482. Reprinted with permission of SAGE.

Many Europeans in my generation – among them some of my closest friends – have never had a "real" job. They have spent their adult life alternating between the dole and precarious, often government-sponsored jobs. And as they grow older, they have less and less hope that their situation will ever improve. The stark contrast between their position and, say, my own or that of most of my readers – a safe job with a decent wage, career prospects, pension rights, sizable perks and so on – has made me increasingly uneasy, not least because the dark side of this contrast has been growing with the arrival of each new cohort on European labor markets. If this deep split has, as I have come to believe, become a permanent feature of welfare-state capitalism, there is at least some intuitive appeal in looking at it as a cleavage between two classes.

The Class Structure of Welfare-State Capitalism

Just how significant is this job class division under advanced welfare-state capitalism? Does the unequal distribution of job assets generate inequalities in material welfare to anything like the same extent that the unequal distribution of capital does? Is there any sign that it affects consciousness and behavior, in particular collective action aimed at changing the corresponding property relations? Should a class struggle between those endowed with a job and the jobless be expected to play an increasingly prominent role under welfare-state capitalism?[1]

To tackle these questions, let us first ask in which counterfactual situation the material welfare of the millions of West Europeans who are currently receiving unemployment or

From Van Parijs, P. (1987). A Revolution in Class Theory. *Politics & Society*, 15, 453–482. Reprinted with permission of SAGE.

Basic Income: An Anthology of Contemporary Research, First Edition. Edited by Karl Widerquist, José A. Noguera, Yannick Vanderborght, and Jurgen De Wispelaere.

welfare benefits would be most enhanced: in a situation in which capital income were equally divided among all adults or in a situation in which labor income were equally shared among all those wanting to work? There is no doubt as to the answer: the unemployed would gain much more from a redistribution of jobs than from a redistribution of wealth.[2] Admittedly, this is only a very rough estimate of the significance of job assets. On the one hand, it overestimates that significance quite considerably by assuming skills to be evenly distributed between the employed and the unemployed. Although the gap between the educational level of the average worker and that of the average unemployed person has narrowed strikingly in the past 10 years of massive unemployment,[3] it is still far from having closed completely. Consequently, the simple test described above captures the effect of some redistribution of skills as well as of job assets. On the other hand, there are also a number of reasons why this test greatly underestimates the real impact of job assets. First, it completely ignores the indirect incomes associated with having a job, mainly pension rights, to which the unemployed fail to gain entitlement. Second, it reduces the material welfare derived from having a job to the wage attached to it. But being unemployed does not just mean a cut in one's standard of living. It also means a loss of social integration and self-respect, which badly affects the material welfare of the people affected – most notoriously their health.[4]

Most important, however, this test completely ignores the unequal distribution of job assets *among the employed*. There is, of course, a world of difference between a part-time, casual, poorly paid job and a full-time, well-protected, and well-paid one. Some of the differences simply reflect the fact that people are at different stages in their careers. Others directly reflect inequalities in skills or inequalities in the control over organizational assets. But many, possibly most, of the differences are irreducibly rooted in what happens to be the distribution of "ownership" over jobs. Both the insiders-outsiders approach and efficiency wage theories predict wage differences among workers with identical skills; for example, as a function of intersectoral differences in hiring and firing costs or in the cost of monitoring performance.[5] Whether the underlying mechanism involves the unequal bargaining power attached to different jobs (insiders-outsiders approach) or the unequal interest the employer has in paying more than the reservation wage (efficiency wage theories), it is the holding of the job itself that is the source of the relevant material advantages.

One implication of this remark is that it is not just the unemployed who would gain from an equalization of job assets. Another is that even the purely static impact of such equalization becomes difficult to assess with any precision. Such an overall assessment is required, however, if one is to be able to compare the current significance of class divisions based on different types of assets. To establish that the job divide has now become more significant than the class divide, it is not enough to show that the jobless would gain more from a redistribution of jobs than from a redistribution of wealth – just as showing that the propertyless would gain more from the latter than from the former would not suffice to establish that capital ownership remains the central determinant of the class structure. What needs to be shown is that a greater share of the interindividual variation in material welfare can be (causally) explained by the distribution of job assets than by the distribution of capital assets. Needless to say, these remarks do not pretend even to start seriously investigating the empirical validity of this conjecture. But they suffice to show, I hope, that at least in some of the most developed welfare-state capitalist countries, the claim that the job class division has become the central component of the class structure makes enough sense for such an investigation to be worth undertaking.

The New Class Struggle

Suppose that, for some countries at least, such a claim can be established. Should one then expect the central class struggle under welfare-state capitalism to be one between those with a stable, decently paid job and those deprived access to such a job, rather than, say, between capitalists or manager-entrepreneurs and workers? For this to happen, a movement of the *job poor* – the unemployed and the casually employed – needs to get off the ground and formulate a coherent social project that would remove the property relations from which they suffer. But however deep the job class divide, is there not ample ground for skepticism about the possibility of mobilizing the job poor into collective action and of giving such action a coherent positive objective?

Even if the job poor are a class in the objective sense considered here, many argue that they will never become a class in a subjective sense; that is, that they will never acquire class consciousness or organize class action.[6] The unemployed and casual workers form a heterogeneous group, which they are unaware of belonging to, let alone proud to belong to. Dole queues, unlike factories, do not lend themselves to the sort of interaction that can lead to collective demands and actions. Unlike workers, who can strike, the unemployed have no weapon they can use in support of their claims. Those among them who are able to organize and mobilize the others are "good" enough to get a real job and leave the class.[7] All these arguments point to genuine practical obstacles in the way of the rise of a movement of the job poor. The most serious obstacle, however, may be of an ideological nature. What is the social model, the change in property rights, that the job poor should be fighting for in order to abolish or reduce inequalities stemming from the unequal distribution of job assets?

In a way, centralized socialism provides the most straightforward answer to this question. Only a system in which the means of production are centrally controlled could in principle ensure that job assets are equally shared by all those wanting to work. However, even leaving aside the possible cost in terms of other values (such as freedom), the risk that even the asset poor may end up worse off as a result of the implementation of such a system (taking all dynamic effects into account, not just the static effects considered when applying the criterion for exploitation) is now broadly perceived in our societies as an overwhelming one. Indeed, the notion that centralized socialism has a seriously adverse effect on efficiency gains further credibility if a legal right to a (decent) job is made an intrinsic component of it – as it needs to be in the present context.[8]

Instead of dwelling on this controversial, but academic, issue, let us ask whether there is an alternative; that is, whether there is any way of drastically reducing job asset-based inequalities within the framework of a decentralized economy, either capitalist or market socialist. A general and significant cut in maximum working hours (with matching cuts in gross wages), as advocated in Europe by some of the unions and parties that claim to have the interests of both employed and unemployed workers at heart, may seem to fit the bill. However, both theoretical considerations and empirical data on the history of work-sharing policies raise doubt about their ability to do much to solve the problem of mass unemployment without such a heavy loss in efficiency that even their "beneficiaries" would end up worse off.[9]

Instead of trying to equalize job assets, one may then (reluctantly) tum to neutralizing the effects of their unequal distribution – just as the working-class movement has turned away from the objective of socializing capital to that of raising the share of wages. In the case of job assets, however, this sort of strategy seems to contain an internal contradiction. By increasing the incomes of the jobless – unemployment benefits and welfare payments – is one not bound, by virtue of the mechanism sketched above in connection with efficiency wage theories, to increase their numbers? When trying to improve their current, disadvantaged station, the jobless would then be forced to worsen their chances of leaving it. Given that this strategy does nothing about the nonpecuniary advantages of having a job – or about inequalities among the employed – the net result of any effort in this direction will soon become an increase in job-related inequalities in material welfare.

This quick run through three possible objectives for a movement of the job poor may suggest that such a movement is doomed for lack of any coherent positive project. But what about the following, fourth possibility, which is now coming to the fore in those European countries in which an organized unemployed movement has more or less managed to get off the ground?[10] The proposal is to give every permanent inhabitant, whether waged, self-employed, or jobless, a completely unconditional "Universal Grant" or "Basic Income" sufficient to cover at least fundamental needs.[11] At first sight, this is no more than a slight variant of the previous strategy for attenuating the pecuniary inequalities generated by the unequal distribution of jobs. However, there are a number of crucial differences, one of which is particularly relevant in the present context. An adequate Universal Grant does not mean just a reduction in the cost of not having a job. It also means that everyone is now given the real possibility of creating, alone or with others, her/his own job. Why? Because the very notion of what constitutes a (paid) job is substantially altered since fundamental needs are unconditionally covered. A job no longer needs to be an activity yielding an income sufficient to cover at least these needs; creating one's own job, therefore, no longer requires an amount of capital out of proportion to what the vast majority can afford.[12] Even with a substantial Universal Grant, however, job assets could still be very unequally distributed among the employed (including the self-employed). Nevertheless, whether under capitalism or, *mutatis mutandis*, under market socialism, the Universal-Grant strategy offers the unemployed (and "poorly employed") movement a way of attempting to systematically reduce the privilege conferred by job assets while expanding (unlike the previous strategy) the circle of those with access to a job. Moreover, through a general increase in every individual's bargaining power on the labor market, it also means a gradual erosion of the inegalitarian impact of job assets among the employed.

If the argument sketched in the preceding paragraph is correct, the ideological obstacle to class struggle along the job-asset dimension is now removed. What about the practical obstacles mentioned earlier? There are good grounds for believing that something like the introduction of a Universal-Grant first at a modest level and without total replacement of current social transfers – is itself the key condition for the building of a strong movement in the service of the strategy described above. Such an institution would provide those wishing to set up an organization along these lines with the minimum amount of financial security and undisturbed leisure they need for this purpose. More important, it would homogenize a large number of people currently split into numerous categories with no perceived common interest (the registered unemployed, welfare claimants, low-paid workers, housewives, students, pensioners on a low pension). And it would dramatically curtail the current vulnerability of the unemployed movement to upward mobility (getting a job would no longer amount to leaving the group) and to stigmatization (no need to be ashamed of receiving what everyone receives).[13] In stating that the existence of something like a Universal Grant is the key condition for the building of a strong movement pursuing the Universal-Grant strategy, I am not implying that the latter is stuck in a vicious circle. The degree of universality of the grant system that is here claimed to be a prerequisite for the building of a strong job-poor movement and – even more so – the grant levels involved can fall far short of those such a movement should aim for.

Is there any chance that this prerequisite will be met anywhere on earth in the foreseeable future? One favorable factor is the current crisis of the welfare state. On both the left and the right, there is widespread frustration and discontent with its complexity, intrusiveness, administrative cost, and frequent counterproductivity. This provides a background on which a plan for radical reform has a fighting chance. But who is going to fight, given that it cannot be the movement that the success of this fight would make possible? It is hard to believe that the basic impulse will come from mainstream parties on the right or on the left, whose interests are too closely linked to those of big business and the established trade union movement. My guess is that the only serious hope in the near future lies in the emerging Green parties' ability both to survive and to bring this demand to the forefront of their platforms. The importance these parties attach to solving the unemployment problem without counting on the resumption of rapid growth and the relative value their typical members ascribe to "leisure" (including unpaid work) as against "consumption" (of purchased goods) combine to make it likely that most of their members will find the idea of a Universal Grant most congenial and well worth fighting for.[14]

Whether this fight will prove successful, I do not know. Nothing in the extended framework for class analysis developed in this chapter enables us to say whether it will. What this framework has made possible is the identification of a new class divide that has – I conjecture – become even more important than the standard division between capitalists and workers in those capitalist societies in which the welfare state is most developed. This identification has prompted questions about the conditions under which class struggle along these lines could take shape. Tackling these questions has, in turn, led to a novel interpretation of the historical significance of the European Green movement. If this line of thinking is, even approximately, on the right track, the revolution set in motion by the Roemer/Wright approach amounts to much more than academic hairsplitting. It is of central importance for a proper understanding of the fate of Western societies.

Notes

1. For interesting analyses of the specific nature of class relations under welfare-state capitalism quite different from the one proposed here, see Krätke (1985); and de Beus (1986).
2. In a typical welfare-state capitalist society such as Belgium, the officially unemployed have an average monthly income of about $390 (1982 figures). If (declared and undeclared) post-tax capital income were distributed equally among all adults, each of them would receive an estimated additional $120 every month, bringing their income up to $510. The average monthly income of employed people is $740. If all jobs (and their incomes) were divided equally among all those wanting to work, each would get $690 (total income from work or benefits divided by the number of people currently employed or claiming benefits). For the officially unemployed, this amounts to an average increase of $300 per month, that is, more than double the increase they can expect (statically speaking, of course) from an egalitarian redistribution of wealth. The difference would be even larger if the unofficially (but involuntarily) unemployed had also been taken into account: most of them get far less than the average $390 of the officially unemployed, and many of them (mostly housewives) receive nothing at all. For them, of course, the income gains from the redistribution of paid work would be even greater. (I

thank Paul-Marie Boulanger for helping me work out these estimates on the basis of Belgium's national accounts figures.)

3. See, for example, Vanheerswynghels (1987) for the case of Belgium.
4. Such effects are well documented by numerous sociological studies; see, for example, Jahoda, Lazarsfeld, and Zeisel (1975 [1933]); Sinfield (1981); and Schnapper (1981).
5. See, for example, Malcolmson (1981); and Shapiro and Stiglitz (1984).
6. See, for example, Dahrendorf's (1986) unambiguous statement: "The unemployed are not a class"; or Gorz's (1983) description of this category as a "non-class of non-workers."
7. For a beautiful firsthand report and an illuminating analysis of many of these difficulties, see Jordan (1973; 1986).
8. This is one implication of the efficiency wage theories presented above, as pointed out, for example, by Elster (1988).
9. For a well-documented, sympathetic, but sobering assessment of the chances of work-sharing politics in a broad sense, see Dreze (1986). To indicate briefly the nature of the difficulties I believe lie at the core of the working time-reduction strategy, let me ask four questions: How can you significantly reduce the working time of the low paid without either pushing them below the poverty line or pricing them out of their jobs by raising their (relative) hourly wages? How can you absorb most of the jobless in those trades in which unemployment is high without creating unmanageable bottlenecks – as well as sizable rents – in many other trades? How can you be fair to wage workers without imposing costly controls on the working time of the self-employed? And how can you impose compensatory new hirings without inducing useless (and possibly fatal) hiring and training costs in many firms that are currently hoarding labor?
10. See, for example, Hogenboom and Janssen (1988); Rosemeyer (1986); and Albert (1986).
11. This proposal is not new, of course. What is new is the broader perspective in which it has been put (see van der Veen and Van Parijs, 1986, including six comments and the authors' reply) and, above all, the intense interest and broad support it is beginning to attract throughout Europe (see Van Parijs, 1987).
12. See the various arguments in favor of Basic Income from the viewpoint of small firms and the self-employed, well summarized in Nooteboom (1986).
13. This conjecture gets some empirical support from the fact that countries – most typically the Netherlands – where support for the Basic Income strategy is comparatively widespread, especially among the unemployed organizations, are also those countries in which welfare-state benefits are most universal (child benefits, basic state pensions, minimum Guaranteed Income, etc.). See the country-by-country survey presented at the First International Conference on Basic Income, to be published in *The Economics and Politics of Basic Income*, ed. A. Miller (1988).
14. This is no political fiction since most European Green parties now include the proposal of a Universal Grant in their platforms, as has the Green-Alternative Faction in the European Parliament. For more details, see Van Parijs (1986).

References

Albert, P. (1986). Un système pour redonner la dignité aux chômeurs: l'allocation universelle. *Partage* (journal of the French Unemployed Union), 31, 19–21.

Dahrendorf, R. (1986). Für jeden Bürger ein garanteirtes Mindesteinkommen. *Die Zeit*, (January 17), 32.

de Beus, J.W. (1986). Schept sociale zekerheid een nieuwe klasse? [Does social security generate a new class?]. In J.W. de Beus and G.A. van Doorn (eds) *De reconstrueerde samenleving*. Meppel, Boom, Netherlands.

Dreze, J.H. (1986). Work Sharing: Some Theory and Recent European Experience. *Economic Policy*, 3, 546–619.

Elster, J. (1988). Is There (or Should There Be) a Right to Work? In A. Guttman (ed.) *Democracy and the Welfare State*. Princeton University Press, Princeton, pp. 53–78.

Gorz, A. (1983). *Farewell to the Working Class*, part 3. Pluto Press, London.

Hogenboom, E. and Janssen, R. (1988). Basic Income and the Claimants' Movement in the Netherlands. In A.G. Miller (ed.) *Proceedings of the First International Conference on Basic Income*. Basic Income Research Group, London – Basic Income European Network, Antwerp, pp. 237–256.

Jahoda, M., Lazarsfeld, P.F., and Zeisel, H. (1975 [1933]). *Die Arbeitslosen von Marienthal*. Suhrkamp, Frankfurt.

Jordan, B. (1973). *Paupers: The Making of the New Claiming Class*. Routledge and Kegan Paul, London.

Jordan, B. (1986). Basic Incomes and the Claimants' Movement. Paper delivered at the First International Conference on Basic Income, Louvain-la-Neuve, Belgium (September).

Krätke, M. (1985). Klassen im Sozialstaat [Classes in the welfare state]. *Prokla*, 58, 89–108.

Malcolmson, J.M. (1981). Unemployment and the efficiency wage hypothesis. *Economic Journal*, 91 (364), 848–866.

Miller, A.G. (ed.) (1988). *Proceedings of the First International Conference on Basic Income*. Basic Income Research Group, London – Basic Income European Network, Antwerp.

Nooteboom, B. (1986). Basic Income: A Basis for Small Business. Paper delivered at the First International Conference on Basic Income, Louvain-la-Neuve, Belgium (September).

Rosemeyer, P. (1986). Basic Income and the Unemployed Movement in Western Germany. Paper delivered at the First International Conference on Basic Income, Louvain-la-Neuve, Belgium (September).

Schnapper, D. (1981). *L'Epreuve du chômage*. Gallimard, Paris.

Shapiro, C. and Stiglitz, J.E. (1984). Equilibrium employment as a worker discipline device. *American Economic Review*, 74 (3), 433–444.

Sinfield, A. (1981). *What Unemployment Means*. Martin Robertson, Oxford.

van der Veen, R.J. and Van Parijs, P. (1986). A Capitalist Road to Communism. *Theory and Society*, 15 (5), 635–655.

Vanheerswynghels, A. (1987). Les jeunes, leurs chômages, leurs employs. *La Revue Nouvelle*, 85, 403–410.

Van Parijs, P. (1986). L'Avenir des écologistes: Deux interpretations. *La Revue Nouvelle*, 83, 37–48.

Van Parijs, P. (1987). Quel destin pur l'allocation universelle? *Futuribles*, 106, 17–31.

Chapter 73

A "Package Solution" for Basic Income

Claus Offe, Ulrich Mückenberger, and Ilona Ostner

Excerpts from Offe, C., Mückenberger, U., and Ostner, I. (1996). A Basic Income Guaranteed by the State: A Need of the Moment in Social Policy. In C. Offe (ed.) *Modernity and the State: East, West.* Polity Press, Cambridge, pp. 214–218.

Objections to a decoupling of income from income-earning activity and to the resulting demand for a Basic Income are justified up to a point. But they do not compel us to drop this demand and to acquiesce in the foreseeable financial crises of the social insurance system or in the "new poverty" which is institutionalized through social assistance. Behind the facade of everyday political rhetoric there is widespread agreement that the crisis of the welfare state and of traditional institutions of social policy cannot be resolved along conservative lines. A basic guarantee is a building block of a progressive and socially just solution – but only if it is *one* building block placed together with two others. Only such a "package solution" can counter objections raised against the allegedly "universal solution" of a Basic Income.

The two supplementary elements ot a comprehensive solution are, first, a comprehensive *reduction in working hours*, promoted in all its variants; and, second, the *political stimulation* and development of the "informal sector," of organized independent labor, *and all other forms of socially useful work which are not mediated by the labor market.*

With respect to the first, further drastic reductions in daily, weekly, annual, and lifetime (Offe, Hinrichs, and Wiesenthal, 1982) working hours would mean that shrinking opportunities for wage labor and therewith for earned income could be distributed equally among all those seeking work. This solution is based on the priciple of equality and avoids current trends toward a social division between those in work and a marginal labor force. But it cannot be put into practice by means of quotas alone. This is because individual employees and trade unions have long been caught in an unresolvable dilemma between individual and collective interests. This is exemplified by reductions in working hours, whose intention is primarily to improve the income-earning opportunities of the *un*-employed, but which must be paid for by *those in employment* with considerable losses of real earnings (or of the increases in income which would otherwise be possible). As a result, an acceptable

From Offe, C., Mückenberger, U., and Ostner, I. (1996). A Basic Income Guaranteed by the State: A Need of the Moment in Social Policy. In C. Offe (ed.) *Modernity and the State: East, West.* Polity Press, Cambridge, pp. 214–218. Reprinted with permission of Polity Press and The MIT Press.

Basic Income: An Anthology of Contemporary Research, First Edition. Edited by Karl Widerquist, José A. Noguera, Yannick Vanderborght, and Jurgen De Wispelaere.

framework for these sacrifices of income has to be maintained through partial compensation in the form of subsidiary state benefits. These could be organized in such a way that the total income of those in work is no longer paid as wages. Rather, the income entitlement resulting from the labor contract increasingly takes on the character of income which is "additional" to Basic Income. For example, were employees to draw only a third of their income as net income based on a contract, but the other two-thirds as guaranteed Basic Income, it is likely that even with a linear reduction in earned income proportional to a reduction in working hours, this "sacrifice" would be more acceptable, and the reduction in working hours easier to carry through, than under present circumstances. In this sense a Basic Income (or a partial, preliminary version of it) is a necessary condition for the realization of interventionary reductions in working hours.

But, conversely, an interventionary reduction in working hours is a necessary condition for a Basic Income's proving to be a solution which does not bring with it unintended and undesirable side-effects. As has been said, social democratic critics fear that with Basic Income the mere appearance of a solution is being promoted, and that in practice it will only produce a division of society into relatively well-placed full-time employees and necessarily marginalized unemployed or part-time workers. But this fear is ungrounded if access to paid work is more evenly distributed as a result of reductions in working hours, if the difference between full and part-time work is leveled off, and if a new type of "full employment" is created for all those who seek paid employment, even if this means that – as Gorz first proposed (Gorz, 1984; see also 1989) – the proportion of a lifetime spent by each individual in formal wage labor is decisively reduced. In this way, not only would social division be prevented, but partial account would be taken of the feminist critique of the gender codification of the labor market. In addition to reductions in working hours, a particularly effective way of avoiding social division and disintegration would be to encourage processes of socialization, qualification (Mückenberger, 1986), and in some cases rights of access to waged work (quotas, entitlement to be taken on or to be reemployed after a break, etc.), which would make *all* workers aware of the labor market and of the income-earning opportunities open to them. Just as reductions in working hours would create a universal *demand* for labor power, so the educational measures developed alongside them would ensure that the *suppliers* of labor power were actually able to fill the places offered. As long as we recall this functional connection between Basic Income, a reduction in working hours, and education policy, there can be no talk of "opting out" from work or of the marginalization of certain categories of worker.

As well as the compensations for loss of income which a Basic Income provides, a further stimulus to reductions in working hours would be the possibility that individual employees, in accordance with their own needs and obligations outside work, could themselves choose the *particular* hours, days, weeks, or years in which their working hours would be reduced. This right to choose to do "less work," and to determine how this would be organized, could be legislated for, and would markedly increase the attraction of reduced working hours for individual employees. For in this way entire blocks of time would be at their disposal, blocks whose individual utility would be much greater than a uniform reduction in working hours of, say, 30 minutes per day. Such "labor time flexibility" *on the part of the employee* would merely be a justified and easily legitimated counterweight to those forms of labor time reduction already in existence which are aimed solely at the needs of the *enterprise* (for productivity, orders, etc.).

The second key component of the "package" proposed here is the encouragement, development, and formal recognition of "informal" independent labor and activity in associations, cooperatives, neighborhoods, and self-help organizations, and under voluntary arrangements. Given falling labor market demand, the explicit purpose of a Basic Income is to rid employees of the need to tie themselves to the labor market and to seek employment through it. For this carries with it a high risk of pauperization. But the option of voluntarily forgoing waged work over a shorter or longer period would be a realistic one for most employees only if, instead of being ignored, their demand for useful activity and for the social worth and recognition associated with it were directed into channels which lay outside the labor market but which were freed of the stigma of work which was devalued or held to be a deviation from a "normal" way of leading one's life. There is no doubt that in the course of capitalist industrialization and modernization the spheres of such activity, external to the labor market and to the field of economic "autonomy," have shrunk, and that today they have congealed into a small residue. For these structural reasons, and also for cultural ones, the prospect of a return to "original" forms of cooperation in extended family, neighborhood, local community, and voluntary association is hardly a good one.

But since interventionary reductions in working hours have created a demand for such forms of activity, and for the concrete services and forms of production associated with them, the only realistic course is to establish and maintain such forms of activity through encouragement from the state, legal guarantees, and political recognition. A Basic Income is a vital presupposition of this. It guarantees an "income without work," in the short or long term, as the sole basis of the existence of those who "work without income." Conversely, the development of independent work and production, and of local and cooperative self-provision, is necessary if a Basic Income, which can be precisely calculated in the short run, is to be an acceptable form of social security. For Basic Income can only be that form of social security – that is, one which does not discriminate through poverty – if, within the framework of these forms of activity and the networks of mutual assistance and exchange associated with them, those services can be maintained which would otherwise have to be created through the market and through the use of monetary income.

There is a relationship of mutual presupposition not only between Basic Income and reductions in working hours and between Basic Income and new forms of independent labor, but also between new forms of independent labor and reductions in working hours. Clearly, the prospects for such new forms of independent labor are good only if these activities are not restricted to the "free time" of full-time employees. Rather, supplementary periods of time will have to be deducted from that devoted to wage labor. Conversely, it will be possible to stimulate the interest of individual employees in reductions in working hours only if they are made aware that such activities are possible.

Basic Income in the Field of Political Conflict

Those who advocate a strategy of social reform in which a Basic Income plays a central role are not pursuing new, let alone revolutionary, goals. Its main purpose is to secure those ethical standards which are already recognized as binding – prevention of poverty, equality of opportunity, solidarity – against losses and regressions which, *without* the introduction of a Basic Income, would inevitably accompany certain current and future socio-economic developments (such as falling growth rates, absence of full employment, demographic "overdemand," the existing social security system's "dependence on employment," the increasing ineffectiveness of laws on maintenance).

Because Basic Income has this "conservative" purpose, the burden of proof falls to its opponents. Either they wish to put an end to the postwar social ethical consensus, or they must show that their demands can be met in the long term by means *other* than that of a Basic Income – something which, for reasons already given, seems to us highly doubtful.

Aside from this social policy front, where the opponents of a Basic Income are challenged either to provide a better alternative or become the champions of regression, there is the question of the *group interests* from which support for a Basic Income can be expected. The following is a review of such socio-economic categories and their associations and representatives.

The recipients of social assistance and unemployment benefit, but also all those with legitimate claims on the social security system, are disposed toward support for the Basic Income model. They have an interest in an adequate income which is secured against fluctuations in the state of the economy and of unemployment. This holds for those with social insurance, especially those in pension schemes, because this model would allow them to rely on a basic "pillar" of monetary income, without preventing them from achieving a standard of living which goes beyond it. They might do so through the accumulation of private means and/or through additional paid work. Those receiving social assistance are likely to give their support for the additional reason that they would be spared having to prove their "availability" for work or to accept a means-test for family supplement.

Under circumstances in which the long-term future of employment is difficult to estimate, the *trade unions*, as bargaining organizations for employees, have a rational interest in a BI model. This is because the chronic "oversupply" of those seeking work inevitably leads to price competition among employees, and threatens a disintegration of trade unions and a restriction of their room for maneuver. For trade unions, a Basic Income would solve this problem by restricting the labor supply. All employees would be given the chance of opting out of their role as employees, either in the short or the long term, and contenting themselves with the subsistence which a Basic Income secures. This would be particularly tempting for those in badly paid or unattractive jobs. Its result, which trade unions would welcome, would be that employers would have to provide their employees with better paid positions, to phase out routine or unskilled tasks, or at least to take steps which significantly increased their attraction.

A social security system financed by taxes gives *employers* in labor-intensive and medium-sized firms the advantage of a relief from supplementary labor costs. It also equalizes competition with large industrial and/or capital-intensive branches of the economy. For these reasons one can expect a weakening of the ideological and political resistance of these groups, and under certain circumstances their unequivocal support.

A Basic Income is also of considerable interest from the point of view of *policy toward women*. A guarantee of such an entitlement would make it easier for women to avoid having to choose between a form of life secured only by the law on maintenance, and participation in work which may be marginal, undervalued, or discontinuous. Instead, they would be able either to reject both, or to make *fully valued* employment the condition of their engagement in paid work.

Finally, where local authorities are responsible for social benefits, they will have a clear interest in the introduction of a Basic Income. Not only would they no longer have to shoulder the responsibility for social benefit, but the resources released could be used, directly or indirectly, to stimulate employment. Following the introduction of the entitlement to a Basic Income, they could thus help to reduce the number of occasions on which the insufficient absorptive capacity of the labor market meant that it was actually claimed.

This apparent paradox, that fewer people *will* claim a Basic Income the greater is the circle of those who, as citizens, *can* do so, is also produced by some of its other socio-economic effects. Far from being an excuse for "laziness," inactivity, and the egotistical exploitation of public resources, it is precisely suited to putting a stop to the widespread squandering of the productive potential of human labor power. It may do so through the stimulation of "informal" modes of work organized outside the rigid forms of a labor contract, or through the generation of employment arising out of fiscal relief granted to businesses and local authorities. It does not seem too far-fetched to assume that in wealthy industrial societies, employees who are accorded the right to withdraw from paid work without penalty and at the cost only of loss of income (but not poverty!) will as a result be better motivated, better qualified, and in a better physical and psychic condition to engage in it (for then they would be choosing it "voluntarily") than those from whom this choice is withheld, and who must consequently work knowing that nonengagement in paid work (or the failure of an attempted engagement in it) carries the threat of material need and social stigma.

References

Gorz, A. (1984). *Paths to Paradise.* Pluto, London.

Gorz, A. (1989). *Kritik der ökonomischen Vernunft*, part 3. Rotbuch, Berlin.

Mückenberger, U. (1986). *Die Ausbildungspflicht der Unternehmen nach dem Grundgesetz.* Nomos Verlagsgesellschaft, Baden-Baden.

Offe, C., Hinrichs, K., and Wiesenthal, H. (eds) (1982). *Arbeitszeit Politik.* Campus, Frankfurt and New York.

Chapter 74
Pathways from Here

Claus Offe

Excerpts from Offe, C. (2001). Pathways from Here. In P. Van Parijs (ed.) *What's Wrong with a Free Lunch?* Beacon Press, Boston, pp. 111–118.

I believe that it is a mark of a good theory to be able to offer a theory about itself. In this second-order component, the theorist must answer, among others, the question: why do so many people oppose my theory? Why isn't it universally shared, given its overwhelmingly evident plausibility? Shared, that is, by a sufficient number of people, both elites and nonelites, to implement its prescriptions.

One answer to this question might be provided by an ad hoc list of propositions: people need to get used to the idea; they have to overcome their moral prejudices and intuitions; they are misled by interested parties into believing that the social costs of a Universal Basic Income (UBI) will be unbearable and that the benefits are dubious. These observations are obviously well taken. They suggest some strategies for improving the chances for a UBI to be successful: try to convince people, talk to political elites, demonstrate that the idea has fallen on fertile ground already in some countries, do more realistic econometric analysis on all kinds of second-order consequences, design and conduct large-scale experiments, and the like. All of this is actually being done, and with considerable success, most prominently by Van Parijs and by other people involved in the Basic Income European Network (BIEN), various national research institutes, advocacy groups, and some left-libertarian political parties.

But while interest in and openness toward UBI schemes are generally on the rise, and not only so in the advanced economies, nobody would seriously claim that the reality of Basic Income is just around the corner anywhere. Why not? I want to suggest an answer and derive a few (second-order) policy implications for proponents of the UBI idea.

The ultimate justification for UBI is freedom: the freedom of individuals to say "no" to employers and state agencies (to say nothing about spouses) without being punished through material deprivation. As a general rule, the anticipation of freedom causes fear. As is the case with other instances of achieving freedom, this fear, although it can be passionate and exaggerated, need not be outright paranoiac. It can be based upon reasons. So,

From Offe, C. (2001). Pathways from Here. In P. Van Parijs (ed.) *What's Wrong with a Free Lunch?* Beacon Press, Boston, pp. 111–118.

Basic Income: An Anthology of Contemporary Research, First Edition. Edited by Karl Widerquist, José A. Noguera, Yannick Vanderborght, and Jurgen De Wispelaere.

who has which reasons to fear what from the freedom that would follow on UBI? In numerous debates and confrontations I have had on the desirability and feasibility of Basic Income, I have encountered various kinds of fear.

1. Employers fear that their control over workers will be weakened, as workers would have a livable withdrawal option. A UBI makes it more difficult for employers to recruit workers for "bad" jobs, and requires employers to increase wages if they still want to fill these jobs.
2. Employees fear that a UBI will require a rate of (direct or indirect) taxation that in turn will involve a downward compression of the scale of net income; similarly the UBI, they fear, will serve as a pretext to replace the wage-graduated "social wage" that employees receive as pensioners, or, in the case of unemployment, with a flat-rate transfer. Wage differences will thus no longer, or not to the extent they are used to, translate into differences in income transfers, and the relative loss of income will have to be made up for through savings.
3. Prospective UBI recipients fear that the level of their income, including the rate of increase of their income, will be contingent upon political decisions and fiscal constraints, and thus be determined in the future by majorities who may or may not endorse and remain faithful to the idea of economic citizenship rights.
4. A great variety of individual and corporate actors fear for the moral underpinnings of a social order that is no longer shaped by the "productivist" assumptions that (employed or self-employed, at any rate market-rewarded) work is "normal," free lunches "anomalous," and the demand of "something for nothing" deviant.

It seems to me that proponents of UBI must take these fears seriously. To suggest otherwise would be to ignore the deep traces that more than 100 years of the hegemony of industrial capitalism have imprinted upon ideas, intuitions, and expectations. In fact, these hegemonic forces have forged an inter-class alliance founded on a work centered normative belief system that appears to be largely immune to revision, even under the impact of the manifest changes of social and economic realities. Numerous and prominent policy intellectuals advocating "welfare-to-work" schemes believe – or at any rate espouse the belief and encourage people to adopt it – that the *only* device by which modern societies can both integrate individuals *and* at the same time grant them a measure of autonomy is the labor contract. Although we can no longer ensure every adult a permanent job that pays a decent wage, this empirically obsolete vision of "normality" is more firmly entrenched than ever at the normative level. Proponents of a UBI have been rightly disgusted by this perversity, but they have yet to find a way of coping with it in politically productive ways.

So what might be done? I suggest that efforts to implement a UBI should be governed by principles of *gradualism* and *reversibility.* The idea is to provide a context in which people can change their preferences through learning, as in the saying that the appetite comes with the eating (rather than with coercive feeding). Instead of thinking about the UBI in terms of "before" and "after," we need to conceptualize and promote it in the dynamic terms of less and more. This intellectual and political mode of experimental approximation could move along the following pathways.

As is well known, in an eventual steady state of a fully implemented UBI even the "surfer" or the "bohemian" would be entitled to a subsistence level citizen (or even resident) income – a scandalous anomaly by today's prevailing standards that proponents of

UBI are usually quick to mitigate by speculating that nobody is likely to adopt the idle life of a surfer for any length of time. But another strategy of response is possible. Note that in most advanced economies and their social policy systems, numerous types of people in various situations and activities are effectively entitled to tax-financed income transfers, at a subsistence level or even higher. Single parents of infants belong in this category, as do people performing mandatory military service. The same applies to families, university students, and – within the European Union and as long as the Common Agricultural Policy lasts – farmers. Institutionalized exemptions from market labor (or the exclusive reliance of market rewards for labor) are numerous and perfectly legitimate.

One gradualist strategy then, would be to expand the list of groups, conditions, and activities that are legally eligible for such exemption. Political initiatives to promote such expansion are all the more promising as the "third" or "voluntary" or "self-help" sector of private foundations, cooperatives, and neighborhood organizations begins to play an increasingly visible role both as a social phenomenon and as a policy device to unburden, as well as increase the effectiveness of, state-provided services. To be sure, such "Participation Income" (as Tony Atkinson has influentially termed it) is still not "unconditional," but rather contingent on nonmarket services performed. But the more popular, normal, and widespread the sector of such voluntary activities becomes, the more effectively can the authoritarianism of external bureaucratic control be fought.

As is equally well known, a fully implemented UBI would eventually reach subsistence level (and preferably also both legislative irreversibility and continuous adjustment to current market income); it would also be free of any means-testing; and it would be effectively paid to all citizens and residents. But these three features constitute as many axes of gradual approximation. More specifically, one could think of starting with an income supplement that does not cover the subsistence level but would still open up a withdrawal option in terms of hours of work. One could make meanstesting less stringent and also invert the means test from one measuring lack of means to one measuring the presence of (significant) assets, with the implication being that all citizens *except* those with assets above a specified level receive a Basic Income.

The UBI is not just universal, unconditional, and subsistence-covering, but also permanent. It is individually paid from adolescence to the end of life. The temporal extension is a further dimension of gradual approximation, and indeed an especially promising one. Elsewhere I have argued for a "sabbatical account" (of, say, 10 years) to which every adult person is entitled and upon which she can draw at any time (after the age of, say, 25) in the form of chunks of time of at least six months, and use the free time, which is covered by a flat-rate income, for whatever purpose she chooses. This scheme can be understood as a temporary Basic Income. The freedom of choice as to when, as well as how much of it, to withdraw will help to reduce the labor supply at any given point in time. It will also allow employees to (threaten to) withdraw from particularly undesirable jobs and working conditions, and it will provide opportunities and incentives to restore skills and other aspects of human capital. Instead of "banning" people from the labor market, they are provided with the economically tolerable option of opting out voluntarily and temporarily, thus contributing to the restoration of "full" employment, if at a lower absolute level. Those making use of the option would also indirectly contribute to what I consider to be one of the most attractive features of UBI (and most of its half-way approximation): the powerful indirect effect it would have upon what we used to call "work humanization" and the gradual elimination of particularly "bad" jobs.

In conclusion, and having in mind the context of the European Union and its integration, let me highlight one dimension in which gradualism is *not* feasible. A UBI (or whichever of its incomplete approximations) cannot be introduced in one country alone. For such unilateralism is likely to trigger migration effects that are bound to undermine the political and economic viability of any even less-than-complete solution. (Such migration, or emigration-prevention effects are, of course, intended in the very special case of Alaska, as they were intended, before 1989, in the comparable case of West Berlin, with its residence premium paid to citizens as tax credit.) In Europe, however, what is possible in one country is constrained by what is possible in all other countries as well and at the same time. This rule may well be interpreted "Euro-skeptically," as proof that the European Union stands in the way of national policy innovation. But it may also be read, more optimistically, as a design for the implementation of a "social" Europe that might be capable of providing some much-needed meaning and broad popular appeal to the project of European integration.

Index

Basic Income: An Anthology of Contemporary Research, First Edition. Edited by Karl Widerquist, José A. Noguera, Yannick Vanderborght, and Jurgen De Wispelaere.

Printed and bound by CPI Group (UK) Ltd, Croydon, CR0 4YY
15/09/2026
14962393-0007